THE BACKGROUND OF THE NEW TESTAMENT AND ITS ESCHATOLOGY

CHARLES HAROLD DODD

THE BACKGROUND OF THE NEW TESTAMENT AND ITS ESCHATOLOGY

EDITED BY

W. D. DAVIES

Professor of New Testament at Princeton University

AND

D. DAUBE

Regius Professor of Civil Law in the University of Oxford

IN HONOUR OF

CHARLES HAROLD DODD

M.A., HON. D.D., F.B.A.

Professor Emeritus of the University of Cambridge

CAMBRIDGE

AT THE UNIVERSITY PRESS

1964

PUBLISHED BY
THE SYNDICS OF THE CAMBRIDGE UNIVERSITY PRESS

Bentley House, 200 Euston Road, London, N.W.1
American Branch: 32 East 57th Street, New York 22, N.Y.
West African Office: P.O. Box 33, Ibadan, Nigeria

First Edition *1954*
Reprinted *1964*

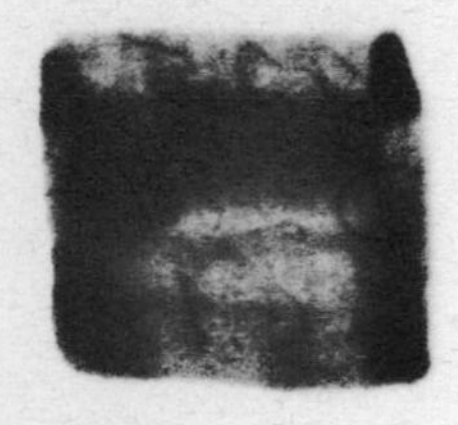

First printed in Great Britain at the University Press, Cambridge
Reprinted by photolitho by Bradford & Dickens, Ltd, London, W.C.1

OPEN LETTER BY THE EDITORS TO CHARLES HAROLD DODD

Dear Professor Dodd,

This book is a tribute of admiration and gratitude. For more than a quarter of a century you have been making a unique contribution to Biblical studies and we represent multitudes in the English-speaking world and beyond in acknowledging our debt to you. It is not for us to try to assess the value of your work here; indeed, it would be premature since you are continually adding to it. But we may fittingly mention the deeper understanding of the background of the New Testament which your works on the Septuagint and *Hermetica* have given us, and the new awareness, which we owe to you, of that eschatological faith linking together the various documents of the New Testament. Your scholarship was nurtured by the exacting discipline of classical studies, and your imaginative insight was born of Celtic tradition; the clarity of your thought and its expression have united with these to make you a prince among exegetes.

Your work as author and teacher has never been merely academic. You have spoken to our times and brought the message of the Bible home to us. And who can doubt that the new translation of the Scriptures on which you are now working with your distinguished colleagues will make the Bible speak with power to modern men?

This book, Dr Dodd, has been a labour of love on the part of its contributors from many different nations and communities; of the two editors one, of the Jewish faith, was long your colleague, and the other was your pupil. Each of us has the deepest respect for your scholarship, and each of us has the warmest feelings for you as a man.

In offering this volume to you we cannot forget her to whom you have dedicated your great study of the Fourth Gospel, and we ask to join her name with yours.

With gratitude and affection,

WILLIAM DAVID DAVIES
DAVID DAUBE

CONTENTS

PART II

TOWARDS AN UNDERSTANDING OF THE ESCHATOLOGY OF THE NEW TESTAMENT

CHARLES HAROLD DODD

CURRICULUM VITAE

Born: 7 April 1884, at Wrexham, N. Wales.

Classical scholar, University College, Oxford, 1902 (Honours Classical Moderations, first class, 1904; Final School of Literae Humaniores, first class, 1906), B.A., 1906; M.A., 1910.

University of Berlin (Research in Roman Imperial Numismatics), 1907.

Senior Demy, Magdalen College, Oxford (Research in Early Christian Epigraphy), 1907–11.

Theological training, Mansfield College, Oxford, 1908–11. Ordained, 1912.

Minister of Congregational or Independent Church, Warwick, 1912–15, 1918–19.

Yates Lecturer (subsequently Professor), in New Testament Greek and Exegesis, Mansfield College, Oxford, 1915–30.

University Lecturer in New Testament Studies, Oxford, 1927–30.

Grinfield Lecturer in the Septuagint, Oxford, 1927–31.

Rylands Professor of Biblical Criticism and Exegesis, University of Manchester, 1930–5.

Speaker's Lecturer in Biblical Studies, Oxford, 1933–7.

Shaffer Lecturer, Yale University, 1935.

Ingersoll Lecturer, Harvard University, 1935, 1950.

Norris-Hulse Professor of Divinity, Cambridge, 1935–49.

Fellow of Jesus College, Cambridge, 1936–49.

Hewett Lecturer, Episcopal Theological Seminary, Cambridge, Mass.; Union Theological Seminary, New York; and Andover-Newton Seminary, 1938.

Fellow of the British Academy, 1946.

Olaus Petri Lecturer, University of Uppsala, 1949.

Visiting Professor of Biblical Theology, Union Theological Seminary, New York, 1950.

Bampton Lecturer in America, Columbia University, New York, 1950.

Stone Lecturer, Princeton Theological Seminary, 1950.

General Director of the New Translation of the Bible, 1950– .

Syr D. Owen Evans Lecturer, University College of Wales, Aberystwyth, 1954.

Sarum Lecturer, Oxford, 1954–5.

Honorary Degrees, etc.: Hon. D.D., Oxford, Cambridge, London, Manchester, Aberdeen, Glasgow, Wales; Hon. S.T.D., Harvard; Docteur, hon. caus., Strasbourg; Hon. D.Theol., Oslo; Hon. Fellow Jesus College, Cambridge and University College, Oxford.

BIBLIOGRAPHY OF THE WORKS OF CHARLES HAROLD DODD

ABBREVIATIONS

J.H.S.	*Journal of Hellenic Studies*
J.T.S.	*Journal of Theological Studies*
J.R.S.	*Journal of Roman Studies*
B.J.R.L.	*Bulletin of the John Rylands Library*
N.C.	*Numismatic Chronicle*
E.T.	*Expository Times*
C.U.P.	Cambridge University Press
O.U.P.	Oxford University Press

1908

The Samians at Zancle-Messana. *J.H.S.* vol. XXVIII.

1911

The Cognomen of the Emperor Antoninus Pius. *N.C.* 4th ser. vol. XI.

Chronology of the Eastern Campaigns of the Emperor Lucius Verus. *N.C.* 4th ser. vol. XI.

Eucharistic Symbolism in the Fourth Gospel. *The Expositor*, 8th ser. vol. II.

1913

Chronology of the Danubian Campaigns of the Emperor Marcus Antoninus. *N.C.* 4th ser. vol. XIII.

1914

On the Coinage of Commodus during the Reign of Marcus. *N.C.* 4th ser. vol. XIV.

1916

'Conscience' in the New Testament. *Mansfield College Magazine*, no. 66.

C. H. Dodd: Bibliography

1918

The Gospel of the Cross (with J. R. Coates and others). Macmillan.

Pauline Illustrations from recently published Papyri. *The Expositor*, 8th ser. vol. xv.

1920

The Meaning of Paul for Today. The Swarthmore Press.

1921

Communism in the New Testament. *The Interpreter*, vol. XVIII.

The Close of the Galilean Ministry. *The Expositor*, 8th ser. vol. XXII.

Notes from Papyri. *J.T.S.* vol. XXIII.

1923

The Eschatological Element in the New Testament and its Permanent Significance. *Interpreter*, vol. xx.

1924

Notes from Papyri. *J.T.S.* vol. XXVI.

1925

The Present Position of the Synoptic Problem. *Congregational Quarterly*, vol. III.

1926

The Gospel in the New Testament. Sunday School Union.

'Amser' and 'Arian'. *Y Geiriadur Beiblaidd*. Hughes, Wrexham.

1927

The This-worldly Kingdom of God in our Lord's Teaching. (A paper communicated to a conference of German and English Theologians.) *Theology*, vol. XIV, no. 83.

The Meaning of the Resurrection to Paul. *The Modern Churchman*, vol. XVII, no. 9–10.

The Ethics of the Pauline Epistles. *The Evolution of Ethics*, ed. E. H. Sneath. Yale and O.U. Presses.

1928

The Authority of the Bible. Nisbet.

Ἰησοῦς ὁ Διδάσκαλος καὶ Προφήτης. (A paper communicated to a second conference of German and English Theologians.) *Theology*, vol. XVII, no. 100.

C. H. Dodd: Bibliography

1929

Ephesians, Colossians and Philemon. *The Abingdon Commentary*. Abingdon and Epworth Presses.

The History of Christianity from the death of St Paul to the reign of Constantine. *Christianity in the Light of Modern Knowledge*. Blackie.

1930

Jesus as Teacher and Prophet. *Mysterium Christi*, ed. Bell and Deissmann. Longmans.

1931

The Bible and its Background. Unwin.

The Church in the New Testament. *Essays Congregational and Catholic*, ed. N. Micklem. The Congregational Union of England and Wales.

The Eucharist in relation to the Fellowship of the Church. (A paper communicated to a third conference of German and English Theologians.) *Theology*, vol. XXII, no. 132.

ΙΛΑΣΚΕΣΘΑΙ, its Cognates, Derivatives, and Synonyms, in the Septuagint. *J.T.S.* vol. XXXII.

1932

The Epistle to the Romans. *Moffatt Commentary*. Hodder and Stoughton.

There and Back Again. Hodder and Stoughton.

The Gospel Parables. *B.J.R.L.* vol. XVI, no. 2.

The Framework of the Gospel Narrative. *E.T.* vol. XLIII, no. 9.

Present Tendencies in the Criticism of the Gospels. *E.T.* vol. XLIII.

1933

Miracles in the Gospels. *E.T.* vol. XLIV, no. 11.

Review of Kittel, *Theologisches Wörterbuch zum Neuen Testament*, Lieferungen 1–7. *J.T.S.* vol. XXXIV.

The Message of the Epistles: Ephesians. *E.T.* vol. XLV, no. 2.

1934

God in Christ. *E.T.* vol. XLVI, no. 3.

1935

The Bible and the Greeks. Hodder and Stoughton.

Parables of the Kingdom. Nisbet.

The Background of the Fourth Gospel. *B.J.R.L.* vol. XIX, no. 2.

1936

The Present Task in New Testament Studies: Inaugural Lecture. C.U.P.

The Apostolic Preaching and its Developments. Hodder and Stoughton.

The Communion of Saints. Ingersoll Lecture on the Immortality of Man. Harvard University Press.

The Sacrament of the Lord's Supper in the New Testament. *Christian Worship*, ed. N. Micklem. O.U.P.

A New Gospel. *B.J.R.L.* vol. xx, no. 1.

La Conception de l'Église dans le Nouveau Testament. *Oecumenica*, 3° année, vol. iii, no. 2.

'The Kingdom of God has come.' *E.T.* vol. xlviii, no. 3.

1937

The First Epistle of John and The Fourth Gospel. *B.J.R.L.* vol. xxi, no. 1.

Hellenism and Christianity. *Factors Determining Human Behaviour*. Harvard Tercentenary Publications.

1938

The Gospels as History, a Reconsideration. *B.J.R.L.* vol. xxii, no. 1.

History and the Gospel. Nisbet.

The Kingdom of God and History (with H. G. Wood and others). Allen and Unwin.

Review of Kittel, *Theologisches Wörterbuch zum Neuen Testament*, Bd. ii, Bd. iii. *J.T.S.* vol. xxxix.

Are the Gospels Authentic? *Spectator*, 18 March 1938.

The Bases of Christian Pacifism (with C. E. Raven and G. H. C. Macgregor). Council of Christian Pacifist Groups.

1939

The New Testament. *The Study of Theology*, ed. K. E. Kirk. Hodder and Stoughton.

The Life and Teaching of Jesus Christ. *A Companion to the Bible*, ed. T. W. Manson. T. and T. Clark.

1940

Review of Hoskyns and Davey, *The Fourth Gospel*. *Theology*, vol. xli, no. 245.

Revelation. *E.T.* vol. li, no. 10.

1943

Review of R. H. Strachan, *The Fourth Gospel*, and W. F. Howard, *Christianity according to St John*. *J.T.S.* vol. xliv, no. 175/6.

C. H. Dodd: Bibliography

1946

The Johannine Epistles. *The Moffatt Commentary*. Hodder and Stoughton.

The Bible Today. C.U.P.

1947

Benefits of His Passion. Lutterworth Press.

The Gospel and the Law of Christ. The Ainslie Memorial Lecture. Longmans.

The Fall of Jerusalem and the 'Abomination of Desolation'. *J.R.S.* vol. xxxvii.

Christian Beginnings: A Reply to Dr Barnes' *The Rise of Christianity*. *London and Holborn Quarterly Review*.

Matthew and Paul. *E.T.* vol. lviii, no. 11.

1948

The Biblical Basis for Christian Unity: An Address to the first assembly of the World Council of Churches, Amsterdam. *World Christian Education* (New York), vol. iii, no. 4.

1950

About the Gospels. C.U.P.

Eternal Life. The Ingersoll Lecture on the Immortality of Man. *Official Record*. Harvard University.

Thirty Years of New Testament Study. *Religion in Life*, vol. xix, no. 3.

1951

The Coming of Christ. C.U.P.

Le Kérygme Apostolique dans le Quatrième Évangile. *Revue d'Histoire et de Philosophie Religieuses*, 31° annee, no. 3.

Gospel and Law. Columbia and C.U. Presses.

1952

According to the Scriptures. Nisbet.

The Old Testament in the New. The Ethel M. Wood Lecture. University of London Athlone Press.

Christianity and the Reconciliation of the Nations. The Burge Memorial Lecture. S.C.M. Press.

A Problem of Interpretation. *Studiorum Novi Testamenti Societas, Bulletin* ii. The Oxonian Press, Oxford.

Man in God's Design according to the New Testament (with P. I. Bratsiotis, R. Bultmann, H. Clavier). Imprimeries Réunies, 3 rue Pasteur, Valence (Drôme).

The Ethics of the New Testament. *Moral Principles of Action*, ed. Ruth Nanda Anshen. Harper.

New Testament Studies. Manchester University Press.

Social and Cultural Factors in Church Divisions (with G. R. Cragg, Jacques Ellul) with the report of a conference held at the Oecumenical Institute at Bossey in November 1951. S.C.M. Press.

1953

The Interpretation of the Fourth Gospel. C.U.P.

Ἔννομος Χριστοῦ. *Studia Paulina in honorem Jonannis de Zwaan*. E. F. Bohn, Haarlem.

Note on John xxi. 24. *J.T.S.* n.s. vol. IV.

1954

The Jews and the Beginnings of the Christian Church. *The European Inheritance*, ed. E. Barker. O.U.P.

The Dialogue Form in the Gospels. *B.J.R.L.* vol. XXXVII.

Three Sermons. S.C.M. Press.

Review of Kittel, *Theologisches Wörterbuch zum Neuen Testament*, Bd. V, Lieferungen 1–7. *J.T.S.* n.s. vol. V.

NOTE BY THE EDITORS

Our intention was to provide this volume with a certain unity which would, nevertheless, include the two areas where Dr Dodd's work has been most discussed, namely, in the background of the New Testament and in its eschatology. Owing to many factors, including the death of one scholar who had already undertaken to contribute, it has not been possible to cover the ground as fully as was planned. We are thankful to Professor T. W. Manson, to the Rev. J. S. Whale, D.D., to the Right Rev. A. M. Ramsey, Bishop of Durham, for help at various stages, to Dr C. H. Dodd for supplying the Bibliography (which contains only what he regards as noteworthy), and to the Syndics of the University Press, Cambridge, for undertaking to publish the work.

W. D. D.
D. D.

May 1954

PART I

*

TOWARDS AN UNDERSTANDING OF THE BACKGROUND OF THE NEW TESTAMENT

THE TASK OF EXEGESIS

E. C. BLACKMAN

HERMENEUTICS is an ungainly word, and the scholarly practice it stands for is, in the judgment of many, an unlovely thing. Critical study of the Bible has managed very well without it, it may be said, since the last book was written upon this subject (about 1890?); and what has died a natural death need not be exhumed. The process of exhumation—or, to speak without caricature, the revival of the study of hermeneutics—has been taken in hand recently by some conservative scholars,[1] and it may be useful to consider the reasons for this, and indeed its justification. If we speak plainly of the rules of Biblical interpretation our discussion will be less fogged by prejudice, and we shall be dealing with all that matters in the subject.

It is a fair question whether critical methods in Bible study have really enabled people to understand its meaning and message better than was possible a century ago, before the Bible was submitted to that process of historical and literary analysis familiarly known as Higher Criticism. Luther affirmed that Scripture was *allgemeinverständlich*. Tyndale's object in translating the Scriptures was to make them intelligible to 'the boy that drives a plough'; and no less has been the aim of modern criticism. It is proper to inquire how far criticism has succeeded in this. The beginning of modern criticism seemed to many to be sacrilegious, for was not the Bible the Word of God, and was not the attempt to judge it by ordinary literary standards an implicit denial of its uniqueness and authority? There were in those days many who trembled for the ark of God and

[1] A. G. Hebert's *Throne of David* (1941) may be taken as an indication of this revival among English scholars. More recently he has been supported by L. S. Thornton and A. M. Farrer. Among Continental scholars we note the work of J. Bonsirven, J. Daniélou, W. Vischer, G. Ebeling.

devised arguments in its defence against the incipient science of Biblical criticism, as if the 'impregnable rock of Holy Scripture' were not, in actual fact, impregnable. The like of Strauss and Renan and Ewald and Colenso were daring with impious hands to treat Holy Scripture as mere scripture, implicitly denying its inspiration by their definition of that inspiration in terms applicable to any literary masterpiece of ancient or modern times. The pioneers of the critical approach were, so to speak, taking the Bible out of the glass case which Christian piety from the very beginning had regarded as appropriate for it. The Reformation had attempted to ensure that no other acknowledged authority in the Church was deposited in the same glass case; but now, behold, a more radical criticism was at work which considered glass cases out of fashion! What guarantee was there that the Book's unique position of authority would be reserved?

It is not enough to ridicule the apprehension of those early champions of Biblical inspiration. It is true that the doctrines of *verbal* inspiration which they elaborated in defence of the authority of Scripture were a most unfortunate manœuvre, for it meant the taking up of a false position which cannot be defended except by those impervious to reason. Nevertheless, their anxiety had some justification, and it is still not superfluous to raise the question whether the critic has any further use for the glass case; or is he satisfied that the proper place for the Bible is by the side of the *Sacred Books of the East*, or on the same shelf as Plutarch's *Lives* or the *Hermetica* or the *Bhagavadgita*? In plainer language, has criticism considered sufficiently the meaning of canonicity, that is, the question of the Bible's essential authority? Has its uniqueness as a religious classic risen clear above the dust of debate? How much more does it appear to be than ancient history and literature? In terms of the traditional phraseology, can the critic still honestly speak of the Bible as the 'Word of God'? These questions must be pressed. The revival of an uncritical attitude is due to the suspicion that criticism is not sure enough about the answers to them, as if there turns out after all to be no Promised Land for the ordinary believer to enter after his long sojourn in the wilderness; the scholarly leaders have tried in vain to ford the Jordan, and the rank and file find themselves still in the plains of Moab.

Modern Biblical study has directed attention almost exclusively to the literal sense of Scripture, in reaction from the medieval doctrine of its multiple sense. It is held, following the Reformation emphasis,[1] that there is only one sense. This is taken to be what the writer meant when he originally wrote, and the sole business of the expositor thus appears to be to use his linguistic and other knowledge to lay bare that meaning. This is unobjectionable and indeed obvious. It may be a real illumination for a modern congregation to have the original reference of a passage made plain, even though it means an excursus into ancient history. Modern criticism has performed an immeasurable service in this insistence on the original historical sense to the exclusion of allegorical fancies. It has maintained the liberating force of the theological insight of the Reformers. But there is something more to be done than relate a passage to its original environment. For Biblical truth is more than ancient history. The interpretation of the Bible must show proper appreciation of its nature and content;[2] that is to say, must handle it as the Word of God to past generations and also as the potential Word of God to *all* generations. To deal with it on any other principle is surely to give up the attempt to be scientific. The implication of this for theological training is that lectures on Biblical Introduction are to be used quite precisely as the title says, as introduction to Biblical theology and exposition, as a preliminary study rather than an end in themselves. It has been too long assumed that one who has had the discipline of historical study of the Bible is *eo ipso* equipped to expound it. It is time to awake out of sleep and to put the tools forged by criticism to their proper use. Hermeneutics has lain too long neglected. To those who are still suspicious of it we should say: Doest thou well to be angry?

[1] 'simplicissimae Scripturae simplicissimus sensus.' Luther says: 'In Scripturis nulla videlicet allegoria, tropologia, anagoge, nisi alibi hystorice idem expresse dicatur. Alioquin ludibrium fieret Scriptura' (quoted in Ebeling, *Evangelische Evangelienauslegung*, p. 280 n. 22). Aquinas had already said as much: 'Nihil sub spirituali sensu continetur fidei necessarium quod Scriptura per litteralem sensum alicubi manifeste non tradat' (*Summa Theol.* Q. 1, 10, quoted in Ebeling, *op. cit.* p. 130).

For the Westminster Confession, see Paragraphs VII and IX of the section on Scripture. The Anglican Articles are not so precise on the subject of Scripture, but Article XX (Of the Authority of the Church) prescribes 'neither may it (the Church) so expound one place of Scripture, that it be repugnant to another'.

[2] '(scriptura) per sese certissima...sui ipsius interpres. scripturas non nisi eo spiritu intelligendas esse quo scriptae sunt' (Luther, quoted in Ebeling, *op. cit.* p. 297 n. 87).

Hermeneutics is not to be regarded as an evil thing once expelled but now trying to make entry again into the house of Biblical understanding swept and garnished by three generations of modern scholarship. It is not to be equated with allegory and its irresponsibility of interpretation. The concern for the literal sense and no other is conditioned by reaction from the allegorical treatment of Scripture. This is mainly known in the abuse, but it is time the question was raised whether in this case the fact that the method has so often been misused means that there is no proper use to which we can safely resort. The allegorist admittedly tends to use a text to stimulate fantasy or confirm prejudice; but this is not listening to the Word of God so much as telling God what he ought to say! But does our condemnation of the method have no regard to the fact that great minds like Origen relied upon it? Could it have attracted such great scholars at all if exegesis was really complete with the establishment of the literal sense? Was Newman completely wrong to insist that 'mystical interpretation and orthodoxy stand or fall together'? Is not allegorism in spite of its extravagances a reminder that literalism, however learned and painstaking, is not a key that opens the door to Biblical truth?[1]

We seem to be embarking on an argument that the literal sense is insufficient and that allegory must in some way be reinstated. Our own opinion, however, must be made clear that the literal meaning of a passage is the indispensable preliminary. Luther's term *sensus grammaticalis* is perhaps to be preferred: the plain meaning of the words as their author intended them with reference to his contemporary situation. Whatever development or application of meaning

[1] Allegory can be regarded as an endeavour to salvage a rational, non-literal sense and to rise above crudities of interpretation that alienated many (Celsus, for example), and turned some potential converts into 'cultured despisers'. Daniélou in his recent book on Origen distinguishes allegory from typology. The latter he regards as the distinctively Christian method of exegesis, while allegory is a pagan importation ('tradition exégètique non-chrétienne'), which incidentally forwarded Origen along the path to beyond orthodoxy. This is illuminating, though it imposes a precision of terminology which Origen might not have accepted. We should not give up the other way of distinction which sees allegory as exegesis of *texts*, and typology as interpretation of *events* (so Florovsky in *Biblical Authority for Today*, p. 175). In support of Daniélou's view that allegory is a pagan method, mediated from the Greeks by Philo, is the fact that the Rabbis on the whole do not use it (see J. Bonsirven, *Exégèse Rabbinique et Exégèse Paulinienne*, especially pp. 246–51).

is attempted by the exegete must be anchored in this meaning. But he must go on to elucidate the perennial meaning of the text, that is, the significance of it which makes it contemporary for the reader today. This has been called the spiritual sense, even by Luther who rejected the multiple sense of the Schoolmen. But Luther is quite emphatic that it is not an addition to the literal sense, but contained within it, and only discerned after thorough study of the literal sense. This emphasis was a very considerable step forward in Biblical interpretation.

The expositor then has to inquire whether the original meaning of a passage is all that it holds for a modern reader. That may indeed be the case, and the original meaning may be of little consequence: in Gen. xxxviii, for example, and most of Leviticus. But a careful explanation of the situation implied in Isa. vii. 1–9, where the prophet is trying to purify the people's longing for political security by relating it to their faith in God, may well be in itself, without laboured application to modern political upheavals, a sufficient elucidation of the meaning of faith. This is a passage where with the establishment of the original reference the task of the expositor is almost completed. In most cases, however, it will be necessary to build some kind of bridge, as it were, between 701 B.C. or A.D. 60 and the present day. The word of Yahweh to King Ahaz by the mouth of the prophet Isaiah needs to be divested of what refers only to the circumstances of Jerusalem and its water supply in 701 B.C. so that its continuing relevance to the circumstances of today stands clear. All this may fairly be regarded as within the scope of exegesis. The distinction is sometimes drawn, particularly by Continental scholars watchful lest the ideas of man become unconsciously intermingled with the truth of God, between exegesis and application. There is of course a sense in which the application of the truth in a passage of Scripture to his own person and circumstances must be left to the conscience of the hearer; he alone, and not the preacher, must make the application under the leading of the Holy Spirit. We prefer to do without the distinction, and to say simply of the risk of the preacher subtly interspersing his own nostrums into his statement of Biblical truth that it is a risk which must be taken. In the providence of God and by the ministration of the Spirit *praedicatio Verbi Dei* does become *Verbum Dei*, and it is not necessary to be content with mere *lectio Verbi*. We use the term exegesis in the comprehensive sense which includes application, and understand its function as dealing with a Biblical incident so that it becomes contemporary; not merely with the literary skill of a Robert Graves, or the actor's genius in presenting Shakespeare successfully in modern dress, but in such a way that what was a veritable word of God to Palestine twenty centuries ago may challenge men in Europe today with the same authority. The shekels and denarii of the ancient world in the pages of Scripture have to be changed into current coin if the modern world is to turn to those pages and heed their message at all.

Our argument at this point may be strengthened by reference to an article by J. N. Sanders,[1] arguing that historical criticism, though performing a necessary task in replacing the centuries-old allegorical interpretation by a true understanding of what Biblical writers really said and meant, is nevertheless often unconscious how much still remains to be done if the message of the Bible is to be transposed into a key of meaning which will claim the attention of the modern reader; for there is the problem of the difference between the ideology of the eighth century B.C. or the first century A.D. and the ideology of today. 'So far the result of the application of historical criticism has generally only been to reveal the existence of the intellectual chasm between men of the first and twentieth centuries, and practically nothing has been done to enable us to cross it and make the thoughts of the man of the first century our own.... The discovery of some scientific method of bridging the chasm is the present problem of exegesis.' And this, as Sanders goes on to point out, involves more than reconstructing New Testament theology ('the purely academic task').

As interpreters of the Bible we are concerned for much more than its aspect as literature or history. It is indeed great literature, though it should not be forgotten that this is more true of certain modern translations than of the Hebrew and Greek originals! The Old Testament appears in the four volumes of the Everyman edition under the title, *Literature of the Hebrew People*, and so indeed it is. And yet that description leaves something to be desired if we are trying to bring out its full religious significance. Again, the Bible

[1] 'The Problem of Exegesis', *Theology* (1941), pp. 324ff.

contains much history, of which the secular historian will naturally take note as he compiles his history of the Near East. The Biblical expositor too is not free to despise the discipline of historical study. But we must contend for the distinctive nature of the Bible as contrasted with, say, the Assyrian chroniclers or the Greek historian Herodotus. The Bible *contains* historical narrative, but it is not simply history. For the events to which its narrative refers are events in which the divine purpose was being worked out. No doubt the Biblical writers compare unfavourably as historians with some of the ancients—the author of Acts with Thucydides for example. No doubt the full understanding of the situation and its relation to sociological and other factors calls for more accurate research than Old Testament or New Testament writers were able or willing to give. But let their own characteristic concern be appreciated, namely to bear witness to revelation and to the events recorded as events in which there is divine intervention for the salvation of man. It is the business of criticism to keep this to the fore; to evaluate the historical situation as the medium of revelation, not the revelation itself. There is some substance in the charge that the liberal critics of the earlier years of this century lacked precision on this point. 'The significance of the narrative reveals itself to the interpreter not through the picture of the happenings which he constructs from his examination of the evidence, but only in so far as he listens to the biblical testimony about this narrative.'[1] Among Luther's *obiter dicta* is the remark that the Devil was the original exegete of Scripture. His well-known depreciation of reason as the Devil's bride (*diaboli sponsa*) is perhaps connected with that. It is provoking enough, and inclines one to show his judgment little respect. But it ought to remind us that a rational explanation of a passage with historical references and so on is not necessarily an exposition of the real Word of God in that passage.[2]

The way in which 'liberal' presuppositions may obscure the characteristic of the Bible as revelation has been exposed by T. W. Manson in a notable chapter from which we quote: 'The focus of

[1] Ebeling, *op. cit.* p. 426.

[2] There is something worth pondering in the remark of Ehrenberg (quoted by Jenkins, *Tradition and the Spirit*, p. 43) that if you wish to find the Holy Spirit in the Bible you look first in passages marked R (Redactor) by the critics.

interest was moved from theology to Religionsgeschichte; from a body of divine truth making claims on believers to successive generations of aspirants seeking for something to believe.... Evolution abhors finality; so the most that can be claimed is that Christianity is the best that has been achieved up to date....' God ceases to be thought of as the living active One who intervenes in history. There is no revelation, only human convictions and ideas. Religion is reduced to 'an element in human civilization, the sum of man's deepest and gradually achieved convictions about ultimate reality'.[1] R. M. Grant makes the same point: 'For most historical interpreters the rationalist attitude towards miracles was taken for granted. Later in the century the Hegelian distinction between external ideas and temporary forms was employed. And in the course of the century the differences between Biblical writing and other writings came to be ignored.'[2] To quote an Old Testament scholar of note: 'Most of our histories of Israel attempt to marshal the facts, and the theories based upon them, in a secularized manner, without any serious attempt to deal with that which was the chief concern of the Biblical writers themselves. The Church cannot afford the luxury of such a seemingly "objective" approach. Its primary aim must be to view Biblical history through the eyes of its interpreters, grappling with those vital questions of faith and meaning with which the Biblical authors themselves were concerned.'[3]

Having made these criticisms of the critical method itself in order to ensure that it starts with a proper evaluation of the nature of its subject-matter, the Bible, we go on to affirm the indispensability of the critical approach. There can be no other. Criticism may not be by-passed. The excesses of rationalism are not cured by flight into irrationalism, but only by a truer use of reason. In the same way, if Biblical research has wandered from the path of advance, or been too much influenced by the prevailing *Zeitgeist* (here twentieth-century existentialism can be as great a seducer as nineteenth-century liberalism), only the same processes of scientific reasoning can provide

[1] *The Interpretation of the Bible* (1944), ed. by C. W. Dugmore, p. 94. Troeltsch's article 'Offenbarung' in the first edition of *Religion in Geschichte und Gegenwart* is a good example of the relativism which beclouded the great liberal critics.

[2] *The Bible in the Church* (1948), p. 132.

[3] G. E. Wright in *Biblical Authority for To-day* (1951), ed. by A. Richardson and W. Schweitzer, p. 222.

correction. To quote an *ipse dixit* of the master whom this volume is intended to honour: 'It is a testimony to the scientific integrity of the critical school that by applying its own methods more strictly it was led to discard many of the presuppositions upon which it formerly relied, and to arrive at what I believe to be a juster estimate of the material with which it deals. Be suspicious of any suggestion that we can afford to by-pass criticism. The way of advance lies through and not round the critical problem.'[1]

The non-critical method is to be rejected not only because of its impossible intellectual demands (assumption of verbal accuracy and the like), but mainly because it obscures the essential truths of Scripture. The supposed denial of Biblical affirmations in the middle of the last century manœuvred that ultra-conservative attitude and method into the false position of contending for the *verbal* inspiration, rather than simply for the inspiration, of the Bible. Fundamentalism[2] obscures the centre, by insisting that the circumference is equally important. It fails to notice that big things become recognizable when other things are admitted to be details and pushed into the background. In their anxiety not to empty out the baby with the bath water Fundamentalists seem to pretend that the water itself is significant! More plainly: they will not admit that there is a problem of interpretation, the problem of the hidden Christ, of the Word not fully revealed: hidden in the practices of ancient Hebrew religion, in the customs and geography of ancient Palestine, in the personal and stylistic idiosyncracies of Biblical writers, in the linguistic difficulties of Hebrew and Greek. Such trembling for the ark of God, instead of wise handling of it, is increasingly noticeable in recent years. Because some positions formerly held by critical scholars have proved untenable there appears to be a danger of reaction into a timid obscurantism or authoritarianism which is really a flight from reason and an abdication from the responsibility of commending basic Biblical doctrines to the contemporary mind.

Our contention is then that exegesis must labour for, and never despise, the literal sense. It may proceed beyond it, but without that

[1] C. H. Dodd, *The Bible To-day*, p. 27.

[2] How regrettable that so expressive a word has become the monopoly of those who believe in verbal inspiration! 'Mere mechanical infallibility is but a poor substitute for a plenary Inspiration' (Westcott, *Introduction to the Study of the Gospels*, p. 41).

as its moorings exegesis becomes as dangerous and deceptive as a drifting balloon. Let us indicate what we mean by some examples.

LAM. I. 12. The applicability of this much-quoted verse to the Crucifixion or to individual sufferers is not to be made without some consideration of the calamity of 586 B.C. in Jerusalem, which is the original reference of the passage.

ISA. LIII. Here there needs to be very serious wrestling with historical possibilities, and in this case textual problems as well, before a safe interpretation can be attempted and the realization in Christ considered.

HOS. II. The reference is not really to Gomer, in spite of the terminology of marriage, but to the land and people, as is clear from *vv.* 8 and 11. But the full meaning only becomes clear when the circumstances of Hosea's unhappy marriage are patiently reconstructed, and this requires a measure of imaginative insight in addition to the industry which has filled the pages of the commentaries. Harper in the *International Critical Commentary* gives a conspectus of views that have been formed of the relationship between Hosea and Gomer. Was Gomer a harlot before Hosea married her; and if so, did Hosea know it? Harper thinks not, pointing to the fact that he calls her not זֹנָה but אֵשֶׁת זְנוּנִים. Did Hosea marry simply by command of Yahweh, without personal feeling, but with the intention of bringing home to the people their apostasy by this piece of prophetic symbolism? This is outrageous to modern sentiment, but there are parallels in the experience of the Hebrew prophets: Jeremiah for example was *forbidden* to marry; we may compare also Isa. vii. 3, viii. 1–4; Ezek. xii. 1–11. Incidentally the very strangeness of all this according to modern ideas needs frank treatment if the passage is to be expounded to a modern congregation. G. A. Smith finds it impossible to suppose that Hosea deliberately took a harlot into his home, but is perhaps too much in the grip of Christian sentiment and forgetful in this instance of the strength of Hebrew determinism. Hosea's bitter private experience, whether he was conscious of it at the time or not, was divinely controlled so as to become a σημεῖον of the divine forbearance. The first verse of ch. iii could conceivably mean that Hosea took a second harlot into his house! All these possibilities of interpreting the bare historical sense have to be sifted before we can reckon to have a sure grasp of any deeper or more permanent meaning concerning the people of God generally. The literal meaning even for Hosea was not his own sad domestic affairs, but the faithlessness of the Israel of his day. The spiritual meaning which arises out of it for subsequent generations of God's people may be taken to be twofold: (*a*) the terrible possibility of apostasy for the Church; and (*b*) the overriding claim of God upon his people, sweeping ruthlessly aside all considerations of personal comfort, careerism and the like.

The writer remembers a moving sermon on the incident of Christ healing the leper. The text was Mark i. 41, and it was developed under the heading: God touched the world in Christ. The theme was the divine compassion, and such might have been announced as the title of the sermon. But this was true Biblical preaching, and the treatment of the text was legitimate because it did start from an exposition of the actual incident.

We take one other example from the Gospels, and that of a different kind: Mark iii. 6. This is generally understood as a historical statement indicating that there was a political move against Jesus, the remarkable thing about it being not that it came at an early stage of his ministry (for the order of Mark's chapters is not necessarily chronological), but that it brought into collaboration two parties, the Pharisees and the Herodians, who normally had no more in common than Plymouth Brethren and Communists today. That might seem to be all that need be inferred. But no, says A. M. Farrer in a recent work on Mark's Gospel, and in the very chapter where he deals with the question of historicity: 'Why did St Mark record the plotting of the Pharisees with the Herodians and place it in a position of emphasis? The prefigurative scheme gives us a sufficient answer. The event is important, not because of its political consequences, but because it foreshadows what would happen at Jerusalem. The Pharisees consulting with the Herodians prefigure the priests compassing Christ's death by bringing the secular power into the case.'[1] This must be pronounced a reading into the case of what is not there, an importing of a spiritual sense without regard to the plain literal sense. In the name of sober exegesis we protest. The justification for it is the theory of the method of the evangelist, his 'prefigurative scheme' which Dr Farrer outlines in the rest of his study. We are

[1] A. M. Farrer, *A Study of St Mark*, p. 188.

not convinced, though we recognize that Dr Farrer starts from the right presuppositions concerning the Bible's uniqueness and authority. We feel that in principle he rejects rather than criticizes the critical method. And his ideas of prefiguration open the door too wide to fantasy, and cause too many images to be reborn.

These instances must here suffice to illustrate the need for thorough examination of the original reference. If that is not honestly tackled, exegesis degenerates into mere guesswork, indistinguishable from allegorizing. The real objection to allegory is not that it goes beyond the literal sense, but that it ignores it. St Thomas Aquinas and the best of the medieval exegetes themselves realized this, and entered the caveat: The spiritual sense contains nothing necessary to faith which is not elsewhere in Scripture presented openly through the literal sense.[1] Exegesis certainly has to include something more than exposition of the original circumstances of history or language; but it depends upon those circumstances for its starting-point.[2]

But a well-meaning person may ask: Cannot there be a plain statement of all that matters in the Bible, such as modern man can appreciate? Cannot the mystery be made plain, and what is old-fashioned, out of date, pre-Christian or merely Jewish subtracted? Much critical work on the Bible has been governed by desire to meet this demand—and the demand is understandable enough. Harnack's *What is Christianity?* may be regarded as the outstanding answer to it; and Schweitzer's *Quest of the Historical Jesus* may be regarded as the most effective exposure of the shallowness of the demand. The demand has taken form recently in the attempt of R. Bultmann to de-mythologize the New Testament, and many well-meaning believers stand by in the hope that he will have more success than his predecessors two generations ago. They hold, to quote G. E. Wright again, that 'the Church's interpretative effort

[1] See p. 5 n. 1 above. The title of this subdivision of Quaestio 9 of the *Summa* is 'Utrum sacra Scriptura sub una littera habeat plures sensus', and the answer given is No. On the relation of the literal to the spiritual sense we have the mature judgment of Westcott: 'When the interpreter of Scripture has availed himself of every help which historical criticism can furnish for the elucidation of the text... his work is as yet only half done. The literal sense is but the source from which the spiritual sense is to be derived' (*Introduction to the Study of the Gospels*, p. 40).

[2] 'Interpretation of ancient texts must always begin in philology. But it cannot end there' (R. M. Grant, *The Bible in the Church*, p. 170).

should be to extricate the essence of the Gospel from its mythical and metaphorical happenings'. But note Wright's conclusion: 'Liberal idealism of the nineteenth century was perhaps the most successful in this effort. Yet the result was an emphasis on emergent value and on the use of metaphors drawn from organic evolution which separate us sharply from those central claims which the Bible makes for itself.'[1]

Has criticism then brought to light with sufficient clarity and authority for the ordinary believer the central truths of Scripture? Does the critical approach enable people to find the divine Word embedded in the mass of human words? The weapons criticism has forged are digging instruments, wherewith to dig down below the crust of primitive folklore, pre-Copernican cosmogony, Judaistic demonology and eschatology, Hellenistic sacramentalism, until the hidden treasure is laid bare. Our business is not to enjoy the digging, but to find the treasure. 'Schlecht und geringe Windeln sind es; aber teuer ist der Schatz der darinnen liegt.' This famous dictum of Luther's with reference to the birth of Christ may indeed be taken to indicate the true function of criticism, namely that of distinguishing between the outer wrappings, i.e. details of history, Semitic idiom, literary style, etc., and their precious contents, God's Word made flesh.

As a general principle that might stand. An opinion of Cullmann's may be adduced in support: 'Historical and philological exegesis should define and describe the human and accidental *setting* within which the Biblical revelation has had to show itself at a given moment of history and in the world situation where the writers found themselves.'[2] But great caution needs to be shown in the application of this principle. It may be argued, for example, that Christ cannot be separated from the swaddling clothes, and divine revelation cannot be separated from its environment, that is, from the concrete situation in which it is first made known to men. We do well to note the concern that is behind that. There can be no slacking in the effort to attain the most accurate acquaintance with the historical setting of Biblical events; no minimizing of their importance; no attempt to by-pass the discipline of patient critical study. If we are to attain

[1] *Op. cit.* p. 223.

[2] *The Student World* (1949), p. 127 (in an article on 'The Necessity and Function of Higher Criticism').

to any spiritual sense of Scripture it must be by the proper use of the historical sense; there is no other inlet or short cut to it. Luther and even St Thomas are already clear about that. Let the fundamentalist and allegorist please take note that scientific methods applied to Bible study have come to stay. But when all that is said, the result of our critical efforts on a passage remains the setting or framework only, and we must not mistake it for the picture itself, but in a manner get through it to the central figure, the Christ in the swaddling clothes, the Word in the flesh.

The preliminary work of historical interpretation is to be the basis of the theological interpretation which is the real goal. It is a kind of anchor, and without it the latter floats in the air. Moreover, historical and philological examination is the objective safeguard against subjective fancy in application: a safety device against *ex*egesis degenerating into *eis*egesis. Sanders in the article referred to above describes it as *ascesis*.

But can the revelation be lifted out of the setting; and then treated like a general truth, a scientific law or a proposition in logic? Truths of revelation are of a different order. They are truths of personal encounter and are made known in life, in history, as recent thought has emphasized, under the stimulus of Buber. Our knowledge of Christ—call him Logos, incarnate Word, Second Person of the Trinity or what you will—must always be squared with what we know of Jesus of Nazareth. The endeavours of criticism to get at the Jesus of history are not to be regarded as the great failure of liberalism in theology. It was magnificent sustained research, worthy to be compared with any series of scientific researches which have reached epoch-making results; and for a Christian believer to profess to regard it as wasted labour is tantamount to stating that Christianity is not Christ-centred. For Christianity takes history more seriously than any other religion. It lays very great stress on the fact that Jesus was a real historical figure, and should therefore treasure every fact about his earthly life that research brings to light. Those facts are indispensable for us. For the Christ of faith is the same as the Jesus of history, each implying the other. And the knowledge of Jesus which historical research has made available—including Strauss and Renan as well as the more orthodox Glover and Fosdick and most recently A. M. Hunter—is to be conserved in spite of the tendency, started by Weiss and Schweitzer, and strengthened by Form Criticism in one way and by Karl Barth in another, to dispense with it. We must rather hold on to it, refusing to be attracted by the preference of the Form Critics for theology over history, or by the docetism of the Barthian Christology. It must be used as the touchstone on which all Christologies are tested.

Thornton in his recent book[1] criticizes the quest of the historical Jesus as the search for an absolute core of Christian faith which was doomed to failure from the start and which exposes the great liberal scholars who engaged in it as misunderstanding the essential nature of the faith. For revelation cannot be separated from its outward form: it is like an onion, which has no core and must be taken as it is; no amount of patient peeling will get to a core which is the genuine thing, so that the rest can be thrown away. Thornton makes this point often: 'It is not enough to say the Word of God is contained in Scripture; we must insist that Scripture *is* the Word of God' (p. 130). 'God came down to the level of our trivialities in order that those same trivialities might be taken up into a context of surpassing significance. Such is the general character of revelation; and it carries this corollary, that nothing in Scripture is too trivial to be relevant. For all the crudeness and strangeness of its varied detail are in some sense organic to the new world which Christ has made in Himself' (p. 6). Thornton argues (p. 16) that it is impossible to separate the inward essence of Israel's religion from its external forms: that would be another case of the onion-peeling referred to above. We may quote here from an early book of Dodd's in which he is discussing this problem of the relation of the permanent to the temporary in the case of the teaching of Jesus in the Gospels, and warning against the assumption that the temporary elements can easily be stripped away: 'The mythological forms in which Jesus' proclamation of it (the Kingdom) is handed down . . . preserve something essential to the idea, which we were in danger of losing altogether in our haste to modernize what He is reported to have said.' Again, 'Who will venture to say: Here He speaks as a Jew of the first century; there as the Eternal Word; as theologians once presumed to distinguish what He did as man from what He did as God?'[2]

[1] *Revelation and the Modern World*, p. 130.
[2] *The Authority of the Bible*, pp. 238 and 237.

We must be patient with this. Thornton's argument has weight and there is a sense in which form is indispensable to content. We are critical of Thornton in so far as he over-emphasizes the form, even to the extent of inferring much from trivialities; but it is not to be denied that to dispense with the outward form or swaddling clothes in an attempt to lay bare the inward truth is a risky piece of surgery. In the older terminology, it is dangerous, when seeking for the spiritual sense, to lose sight of the literal sense.

In becoming man the Son of God became a *particular* man; Christ became Joshua ben Joseph of Nazareth. That was incidental to incarnation, and incarnation is inconceivable apart from this particularity. The truth for universal application is made known in particular sets of circumstances; the divine is mediated through the human, and is never unmediated. If that is what Thornton contends for, we can agree. But the other metaphor has its applicability too. There is a sense in which the Bible is more like a nut than an onion, and the problem—that is, the function of criticism—is to extract the kernel. The Word of God is in the words of the Bible, but is not to be identified with them, as Thornton, with the Fundamentalists, tends to do, but interpreted *out of* them.

This is the problem envisaged by Bultmann, though *Entmythologisierung* is not the most appropriate term to describe the method of its solution. In one sense the mythical form must remain. The mythology is not translatable, and modern Christians must school themselves to understand it. But in another sense that which is simply the form in a Biblical passage—that is, ancient custom or concept—must be made clear as such, so that the discerning person can enucleate the content and express it in contemporary words. This is as necessary and legitimate as translation from the ancient languages into modern; and who dares to assert that the truth of the Bible is withheld from those who cannot read the original Hebrew and Greek? More generally, in response to the impatient inquirer who asks scholars to provide a sort of compendium of Biblical teaching, we must make full use of the general pattern of the Bible which critical study has laid bare.

The term progressive Revelation has become rather hackneyed. It must be used with full realization of its import, and that means with emphasis not on the adjective, as is perhaps too common, but on the noun. For in the Bible we are dealing with the literary deposit of the action of God. The Bible is not itself revelation but is the record of revelation, that revelation being understood as a series of divine interventions for man's benefit, the 'saving acts' of God. The Bible is not properly handled unless there is full appreciation of this causative, divine element. In this sense it may be affirmed that God is the Author of Scripture, and this of course is no contradiction of the multiplicity of human authorship, a thesis upon which critical study has very properly busied itself.

Now this series of divine acts may be discerned as a general pattern within the Bible. This is not a dogmatic scheme imposed upon the Bible, but a central core of the Biblical testimony itself. This should be made familiar to all Bible readers. It is a philosophy of life, an understanding of human existence, as coherent and as worthy of modern man's attention as any more recent *Weltanschauung*. It explains man and his history and his place in the universe in the light of the purpose of a supra-historical Creator who is almighty and merciful.

Among the leading ideas in which this is expressed the most significant are those of Covenant and Kingdom. These are related conceptions, and roughly speaking we may say that the former dominates the Old Testament, and the latter the New. As an example of the comprehensive way in which these terms are used we may refer to the description at the end of Acts of Paul's exposition of the essential Gospel to members of the church at Rome: 'he expounded the matter, testifying the kingdom of God, and persuading them concerning Jesus, both from the Law of Moses and from the prophets' (Acts xxviii. 23).

In terms of the former conception, man's destiny, his sole possibility of self-realization and happiness, is to be 'in covenant' with God. Man's sin, however (call it by other terms if you like, misuse of free will, unwillingness to accept the divine authority—all are taken account of in the classic third chapter of Genesis), puts him out of covenant with God. God's purpose to have man in covenant with himself is not defeated; it does not accept the broken covenant as final, but proceeds to woo man back into covenant. But God's reaction to man's defiance is stern—witness the Deluge story, or the Book of Amos. This is the divine wrath or judgment, but it is to be understood always in relation to the divine mercy and will to redeem. The stern aspect of God's dealing with man is never the whole of it. It is judgment and mercy, mercy and judgment, neither to be understood apart from reference to the other, and both combined in the untranslatable *tsedaqah*, which means essentially an activity of God by which he 'justifies the ungodly', and which is, in Biblical witness, the characteristic activity of God, the differentia of Hebrew religion in contrast with all legalistic and rationalist conceptions. The difficulties partly arise from an inadequate rendering of the root *tsadaq*. Greek *dikaios* goes as far astray as English *just* and German *gerecht*. These words suggest an antithetical forgiveness or leniency, but the antithesis is not implied in the Hebrew word. Modern scholarship has made this clear, and the researches of Dodd have notably contributed.[1] This central teaching of the Bible waits to be emphasized in preaching and teaching, with the confident affirmation born of faith that this is not simply a *conception* of God, but that he is in fact of such a nature, and that history rightly interpreted, and the experience of the Church, confirms it. This is the Gospel and the core of the Bible, both Old Testament and New Testament. This is the developing idea which runs through both Testaments and makes them a unity. Not all passages equally witness to it—some not at all—and it is the function of criticism to indicate these clearly and bring them out in bold relief in the interest of the essential teaching.

The parallel conception which witnesses to the central Gospel affirmation is that of the divine sovereignty (*malkuth*, *basileia*). The word is more prominent in the New Testament as covenant is more prominent in the Old Testament, but the underlying thought in both cases is integral to the whole Bible. Man alternately acknowledges and denies God as King; at best man is a rebellious citizen of God's kingdom. But the Biblical assurance is that the King, while condemning this rebelliousness, does not resign himself to it but is constantly trying to educate the refractory citizens to conformity with his rule, in fact to glad acceptance of it—(revealing his Kingship, establishing his Kingdom). The Kingdom of God is thus in the historic experience of men both obscured and revealed, denied and accepted. Most fully was it revealed in Jesus Christ. The Christian

[1] *The Bible and the Greeks*, pp. 42ff.

hope is that ultimately it will be fully revealed, and everything in human conduct that opposes it will cease. This teaching which both allows the fact of human recalcitrance and proclaims a worthy goal is of the very *esse* of the Bible; and modern critical study has brought it to clear prominence. It needs only to be taken to heart and broadcast upon housetops.

For the New Testament Dodd has taught us to think of a primitive *kerygma* which all New Testament writers presuppose and develop in various ways and with various emphases according to their own insight and the needs of their addressees. Recently Dodd has called this *kerygma* the 'ground-plan of New Testament Theology'.[1] The basic datum of faith and theology is the conviction that, following the series of providential interventions to which the Old Testament bears witness, God operated decisively for man's salvation in the ministry of Jesus and continues to operate in the Church until a final intervention yet to be expected which will terminate history and assess it ('judge the world'). The *eschaton*, a final revelatory act of God expected at the end of history, has become an event in history. The action of God which finally and fully makes known his saving purpose has taken place, and is no longer an object of faith and hope. His character is supremely declared in the ministry, death and exaltation of Jesus. God has shown his hand to such effect that no further revelation is needed for human faith. The ace has been played. Human experience has been made aware of new possibilities; this world's darkness has been bathed in light. In this earthly sphere of the relative the absolute has taken real shape. It is not now an ideal to be visualized and striven for in the hope of an ultimate realization, for it has been actualized in Jesus Christ and an ultimate perfect order can do no more than demonstrate afresh that same actuality on a corporate scale, in a society of redeemed persons. This new apprehension of God's power in action (his ἐνέργεια) created the early Church and was at the heart of that Church's message, was in fact the most primitive element in its *kerygma*. It may be taken as the central point or fulcrum of the Bible. The dominant ideas of covenant-making, and Kingdom-bringing, of creation and providence, of sin forgiven and humanity redeemed, with which both Testaments are everywhere occupied, are here brought to perfect focus.

[1] *According to the Scriptures* (1952), p. 12.

Along this line of interpretation we may speak of the Bible as *Christuszeugnis*. Luther's saying, quoted above, about the centrality of Christ in Scripture may be taken as a summary of Biblical doctrine. 'Precious is the treasure that lies therein.' The whole Bible, Old Testament as well as New Testament, is witness to Christ; more accurately, it is the witness to Christ which constitutes its main message. The Word of God in the primary sense is Christ; the Bible is Word of God in a secondary sense, in so far as it testifies to him and mediates him. It might be stated in this way, that Christ is the spiritual sense of Scripture. This provides us with both a canon of interpretation and a principle of unity.

We must here indicate our attitude to the work of W. Vischer, *Das Christuszeugnis des Alten Testaments*, which on a grand scale in four large volumes demonstrates how the deeper meaning of the Old Testament is its reference to Christ. This is a disappointing work, but if we have to pronounce it a mighty failure we do so recalling Hermann von Soden's three volumes on the text of the New Testament; that was a failure too from several points of view, but it can hardly be said that textual criticism derived no benefit from von Soden's researches. Vischer's study is welcome as a sustained attempt to handle the Old Testament with proper regard for its nature and subject-matter.[1] The attempt itself is significant, even though the result is not a success. In our judgment Hebert's *The Bible from Within* achieves much more along this line. In his detailed execution Vischer is too uncritical. He makes arbitrary links between Old Testament incidents and characters and the New Testament, and on this subject of the reference forward to the New Testament for its fulfilment we feel that Eichrodt's *Theology of the Old Testament* is of far more permanent value. Again, Vischer is too often insensitive to historical problems which must be honestly faced, or is content to elude them with the remark[2] that they arise from 'a type of thinking alien to the Biblical tradition'. He will not pause to consider doubts whether a thing actually happened as narrated, or is only what later tradition supposed to have happened. The historicity of Jacob's wrestling at

[1] 'Sachgemäß' is the convenient German word. To quote from a review of Vischer's book: 'Here the Bible is understood according to its own intention (*als das, was sie sein will*). It is not judged from various external viewpoints, but an earnest attempt is made to understand it *sachgemäß, d.h. aus ihr selbst heraus*.'

[2] Vol. I, p. 240.

the ford Jabbok is assumed, and the identification of the angel with Jesus Christ is asserted (following Luther). More at length, the episode of Solomon's decision between the two mothers (I Kings iii) is given quite disproportionate attention and made the basis of remarkable inferences. Vischer refuses to admit the legendary aspect of the story, and denies the relevance of the non-Hebrew parallels which have been adduced. He insists on the historic uniqueness of Solomon and the actual occurrence of this case, and goes on to affirm that his judgment was a divine judgment deliberately so made by him as God's spokesman. Vischer holds to this with uncritical tenacity. It does not occur to him that we are dealing in this chapter with the theological assessment of Solomon's reign by the later Deuteronomists or Priests who were responsible for the selection and present arrangement of the Old Testament. What Vischer does is to introduce a conception of symbolism by which he can make I Kings iii mean many things which would have astonished both Solomon and the fourth-century scribes: the child concerning whom the judgment was given is connected with the Messianic hope and the presentation of Christ in the Temple and even the Crucifixion, and the mother who overlay her child stands for Israel crucifying her Messiah.[1] This is far from satisfactory, and we murmur: *non tali auxilio!*

But though the book is a failure in its total result, it does define rightly the problem of Biblical exposition. 'Either the Old Testament speaks of Christ or it remains a tragic guess.'[2] Vischer's treatment of the Book of Judges is suggestive and helpful here. The theme is taken to be: Yahweh is King of Israel, and the questions of moment are: Does Israel acknowledge this fully? and, Does it involve Israel in having a human king as well, a Gideon or a David, or only temporary deliverers? Vischer's interpretation of Judges treats it as definitely pointing forward to David as king by divine intention, the history developing providentially to this high point. David is Messiah and as such a forerunner of Christ. This is both the logic of history and the intention of the Biblical author. There may be some strained application and inadmissible cross-referencing here; but it is nevertheless an endeavour to lay bare the inner core of the Old Testament, the line of development which makes it a unity with the New Testament. We value also Vischer's characterization of Biblical

[1] Vol. II, pp. 292–6. [2] Principal John Marsh in a paper privately circulated.

thinking as *ganzheitlich*,[1] that is, concerned to understand a thing in relation to the whole of which it is a part, rather than isolatedly, in and for itself. The tendency of modern thought, influenced by natural science, is analytical and atomistic. This brings great results when applied to objects, but may lead far astray if applied to human experience and the records of it in literature. We murder to dissect. The Bible has been treated analytically, but it claims to be a whole, and as a whole it is distinct from its parts, and it is the appraisal of it in its wholeness which is our present need. Vischer rightly stresses the need for this. A particular passage does not yield its full meaning except in the context of a whole book, and the larger context of the whole Bible.

Part of what Vischer is insisting on is that the Bible is *sui generis*. And with regard to interpretation, *Sacra scriptura sui ipsius interpres*, as Luther laid down. The truly critical method of exposition is that which has due regard to what is distinctive of the Bible, that is to say, not only to its content, but to the intention and basic presuppositions of its writers; and, let us add, of its compilers too. For there is significance not only in the original composition, but in the order and arrangement of the books, particularly when it is remembered that a principle of selection has been at work. All this ministers to the uniqueness of the contribution the Bible makes, of truth concerning human life and its redemption (not simply a contribution to knowledge), which it claimed as divine truth. When this is not realized there may be an excess of explanatory detail which is of relevance for professional scholars only and properly belongs to the field of *Altertumswissenschaft*. Too much, as well as too little, may be made of the literal sense. In dealing with the Epistle to the Hebrews, for example, the references to the Old Testament sacrificial system call for much elucidation. But the Christian expositor is not interested in them for their own sake; his business is to explain the superlative efficacy of Christ's sacrifice in the light of them. The desideratum is to get from a passage its religious meaning for all sorts and conditions of men. There may be much of human or academic interest as well, but that must be pronounced secondary. And if there should appear to be no permanent religious value that must be frankly stated.

[1] Vol. I, pp. 146–8.

The Bible has to be interpreted from its own centre. It is not concentric with Aristotle, as Roman theology posits, nor with modern rationalism, as theological liberalism has assumed. It must be allowed to provide its own canons of interpretation. *Nullius addictus iurare in verba magistri*, it waits upon no external authorization, but authenticates itself and opens its treasures to the man who comes in faith and prays for the inward witness of the Holy Spirit. 'In and through the Bible the God who seeks man and the man who seeks God meet in unmistakable recognition and response.'[1]

Before we close we must define our opinion of Thornton's second volume in his projected trilogy called *The Form of the Servant*, which is in some respects similar to Vischer's work. The title of this second part is *The Dominion of Christ*, and we welcome the Christocentric treatment of Scripture which is implied. 'The whole design of creation was Christ-centred from the first' (p. 4).[2] Christ's sovereignty is understood as the divine activity restoring the original plan of creation. There is a cosmic drama of creation, conflict and rebirth discernible in Israel's history and recapitulated in Christ (pp. 156ff.). We have no quarrel with that; but in detail we are critical. Fertility of imagination and mystical temperament weave a strange pattern on this loom of Biblical learning, and the result is a carpet to be gazed upon rather than trodden upon. Again we are constrained to murmur, *non tali auxilio!* There is too much cross-referencing and reading between the lines and using one passage as a key to another. More than enough is conceived as mystery requiring a 'clue'. There is no conception of revelation as progressive, and the historical is often ignored. One is left wondering whether history counts for nothing in this interpretative method, whether no place is allowed to the literal sense, and whether there is a clear principle on which the exegesis is controlled. As in our criticism of Vischer,

[1] P. L. Lehmann in an article on 'The Reformers' Use of the Bible' in *Theology To-day* (October 1946), p. 341. He says also (p. 328): 'What was new about the Reformers' use of the Bible was the way in which they derived the authority of the Bible from its content.'

[2] Again, 'The New Testament writers reassemble Old Testament images according to a new pattern given in Christ. The shape of revelation is now Christological' (p. 17). Further, in vol. 1, apropos of the identification of Christ with Wisdom Thornton wrote, 'Jesus is not simply the principal actor; He is the whole action in which each of the actors in turn plays his part.'

we feel that the main emphasis is right, but the detailed argument often makes too great demands on our credulity.

When the original sense of a passage is made clear the expositor's task is twofold. He must relate it (*a*) to Christ and the central Biblical doctrine of salvation, (*b*) to the situation of today, for the world of the seventh century B.C. and of the first century A.D. is an alien one to the modern man, and what was then a remedy or a new disclosure may have no help or meaning now. On each of these points the expositor may have to pronounce negatively. The book of Ecclesiastes, for example, has little relation to the general Biblical message, and its inclusion in the canon has perplexed many. On the other hand, when a passage is directly related to the kernel of Biblical proclamation (e.g. Isa. liii), or has clear contemporary relevance (e.g. Amos vi, I Cor. xiii) the expositor need add but few words of his own. For an example from the Gospels we are content to quote Professor Dodd.[1] 'The very elements in His teaching therefore which are most particularly related to His time are relevant to every age... the eternal in it is but thinly disguised, and meets us still with inescapable challenge.' We emphasize that the literal sense does need supplementation in the two directions indicated. We might call (*a*) the literal sense of the Bible as a whole, and (*b*) application.

A passage attains significance in proportion to the clarity with which it sets forth the mighty acts of God, the *Magnalia Christi*. Not all passages are equally significant, just as not all seams in a mine are equally rich in the precious ore. Frank recognition of this does not derogate from the richness of the main testimony to God's redemptive action.

Finally, we submit two controlling considerations which critical work should keep before it in all its detailed and sometimes apparently irrelevant research. First, the Bible is the Word of God, not simply history or literature or philosophy. Its distinction from other writings must be kept clear. It is not secular literature. This affirmation is made with full critical awareness, and not in the interest of an uncritical orthodoxy. As Augustine says, 'In Scripturis per hominem, more hominum, loquitur Deus.' Secondly, the Bible has to be made available as God's Word to the modern man; the Biblical writers becoming in some sense contemporary with their modern readers.

[1] *The Authority of the Bible*, p. 239.

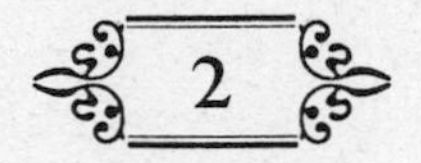

THE EFFECT OF RECENT TEXTUAL CRITICISM UPON NEW TESTAMENT STUDIES

K. W. CLARK

As one looked upon the state of New Testament textual studies in the early 'thirties it must have appeared that an unusual number of important events were transpiring. One read in 1930 about the sensational recovery from Egyptian sands of textual witnesses from the third century, earlier by a century than the oldest and best witness previously available. Here were three papyrus manuscripts attesting the Greek text in substantial portions of the Gospels, Acts, Pauline Epistles and the Apocalypse, as that text was employed by Christians in middle Egypt about A.D. 250.[1] Such discoveries come but rarely even in the amazing modern era, and this discovery, 'the greatest since the Sinaiticus' (Kenyon), offered to scholarship an important new basis for its researches on the primitive text.

There soon followed other papyrus acquisitions, each fragmentary but presenting its own element of importance. There was discovered in Dura (Syria) in 1933 the first known Greek witness of Tatian's Diatessaron.[2] The John Rylands Library reported in 1935 the identification of the earliest extant witness to any part of the Greek New Testament, a small fragment of the Gospel of John written before A.D. 150.[3] Other early papyrus fragments were acquired about the same time, notably by Princeton, Yale, and the University of

[1] Frederic G. Kenyon, *The Chester Beatty Biblical Papyri*, Fasc. I–III (London, 1933–7); Henry A. Sanders, *A Third-Century Papyrus Codex of the Epistles of Paul* (Ann Arbor, 1935).

[2] Carl H. Kraeling, 'A Greek Fragment of Tatian's Diatessaron from Dura', *Studies and Documents*, vol. III (London, 1935).

[3] C. H. Roberts, *An Unpublished Fragment of the Fourth Gospel* (Manchester, 1935).

Michigan.[1] Kenyon reflected the expectant mood of that day when he wrote that 'these recent discoveries of exceptionally early MSS.... justify the hope of other discoveries which may clear up the many obscurities that still beset the early history of the Bible text'.[2]

In the last quarter-century scores of medieval copies of the Greek New Testament have been found and, for the first time, have offered their testimony. Although such manuscripts rarely contribute early readings, they are essential to the investigation of later stages in textual transmission. Notable among them was the Rockefeller-McCormick New Testament (Gregory 2400) which was found in Paris and acquired by the University of Chicago in 1928.[3] With a wealth of miniatures to illustrate the text, this manuscript represents two related areas of research especially prominent in recent years: Christian art, and the Byzantine text. Its appearance in America gave an impetus to manuscript discovery and textual research unprecedented in scope and vigour. About the same time, Streeter and Lake were reporting their studies on a newly discovered early recension, the 'Caesarean text', which must henceforth be considered along with the 'Neutral' and 'Western' forms.[4]

Not least in these matters was the transfer to the British Museum, in December 1933, of the famous Codex Sinaiticus from Leningrad, where it had lain since 1862.[5] Although this Greek Bible from fourth-century Egypt had long been available in photographic facsimile and had been thoroughly examined by Tischendorf and by Westcott and Hort, it was an important step of progress to establish

[1] See Kenneth W. Clark, *A Descriptive Catalogue of Greek New Testament Manuscripts in America* (Chicago, 1937). Also H. I. Bell, *Recent Discoveries of Biblical Papyri* (Oxford, 1937).

[2] Frederic G. Kenyon, *The Text of the Greek Bible* (London, 1937), p. 195.

[3] Goodspeed, Riddle and Willoughby, *The Rockefeller-McCormick New Testament*, 3 vols. (Chicago, 1932).

[4] B. H. Streeter, *The Four Gospels, a Study of Origins*, 4th ed. revised (London, 1930); Lake, Blake and New, 'The Caesarean Text of the Gospel of Mark', *Harvard Theological Review*, vol. XXI, 4 (October, 1928). Hereafter, the terms Neutral, Western, and Caesarean, will be used without quotation marks although the reader will understand that these terms are always thought of as 'so-called'.

[5] See the pamphlets issued by the British Museum, *The Mount Sinai Manuscript of the Bible* (1934) and *The Codex Sinaiticus and the Codex Alexandrinus* (1938).

the manuscript in London where definitive studies might be freely made.[1] Such were the stirring discoveries and researches that marked the early 'thirties. Scholar and layman alike felt an exciting spirit of progress and many anticipated an imminent *dénouement.*

I. THE CRITICAL TEXT

The ultimate task in textual criticism is to reconstruct the lost original documents of the New Testament. A climax was attained in 1881, 350 years after the work of Erasmus and Stephanus. Three successive stages of progress are discernible in review. The first continued until the days of John Mill and Richard Bentley (early eighteenth century) and was marked by the collecting and collating of many new manuscripts. Their contemporary, J. J. Wettstein, collator and cataloguer, listed about 300 manuscripts which had become known in the West by that time. The second period began with Bengel who first classified manuscript witnesses according to a textual history, and sought to establish textual criteria. The Textus Receptus remained dominant throughout that period. It was Lachmann who, in 1830, opened a new era when he created a critical text *de novo*, planting the seed that flowered with Westcott and Hort.

It has been necessary to recall even so briefly the successive periods in textual history in order that we may understand the work of our own age. The course that began with Erasmus reached its full fruition with Westcott and Hort. It is not given to us today merely to perfect the Neutral New Testament by a process of itemized repairs. In textual criticism we have reached the end of an era and entered upon a new cycle of investigation. For some time it has been evident that textual research since Westcott and Hort is similar to that of the sixteenth and seventeenth centuries, for our time again is marked as an age of collecting and collating. As the early critics sought to perfect the Textus Receptus so critics since Westcott and Hort have sought to perfect their 1881 text. The eclectics, of that day and of this, 'improved' the text here and there though without a fundamental principle to guide them. Years ago, F. C. Grant observed

[1] This was early demonstrated by the study published by Milne and Skeat, *Scribes and Correctors of the Codex Sinaiticus* (London, 1938).

that we must return 'to the point where older scholars such as Griesbach and Lachmann left off'.[1] Really, our day is comparable to that of Bentley in that materials have been gathered in great quantity, while we still await the first proposal for a more adequate history of the primitive text.

But the age of Bentley was succeeded by that of Bengel, finally to produce fruit in the age of Lachmann. So our age, we believe, must lead us to a new era of reclassification according to a new historical insight which is as yet obscure to us. To that new insight the researches of our day will contribute, and in future a better text will be found based upon a superior historical understanding.[2] In the meantime, the text of Westcott and Hort (or another quite similar) continues to serve well the needs of this generation and the next. For today, therefore, our work must be undertaken and understood with the objective of laying a new foundation. There is in it this larger meaning, to transcend the laborious researches of the moment. The responsibility of the present generation reflects its opportunity to lay the new foundation. The discoveries that mark our time may be expected to reveal ultimately a new meaning; and each new product of research to assume its place in a new pattern. It is in this faith that we inquire particularly concerning the effectiveness of textual criticism in the present generation.

With reference to the recovery of the original New Testament text, we may expect to find the informed critic more sober and patient than others. Although many thoughtful Christians have come to believe that this objective has been virtually won, awaiting only a finishing touch, the critic is sobered by the realization that the best critical text so far achieved now holds little assurance of being the original text and that to work back from the one to the other has become increasingly difficult. He is the more patient because of his knowledge that textual research has proceeded in a long cycle—discovery, analysis, reconstruction. The former cycle required 350

[1] F. C. Grant, 'Studies in the Text of St Mark', *Anglican Theological Review*, vol. xx (1938), p. 106.

[2] See the discussion of Norman Huffman, 'Suggestions from the Gospel of Mark for a New Textual Theory', *Journal of Biblical Literature*, vol. LVI (1937), pp. 347–59.

years and concluded but recently, with the critical text of Westcott and Hort. The present generation stands at the *beginning* of a new cycle, in the search for the original Greek New Testament. The recent discovery of earlier papyrus manuscripts and the recognition of the Caesarean recension have not settled problems but created new ones. They have not completed the pattern but rather have complicated the solution.

The appearance of numerous critical texts has tended to give the impression that much progress has been made beyond Westcott-Hort, and that great discoveries have largely displaced its twin authorities, Sinaiticus and Vaticanus. A mere roll call of the critical texts produced since Westcott-Hort is impressive: Weymouth (1886), Brandscheid (1893), Hetzenauer (1893), B. Weiss (1894–1900), Blass (1895–1902), Nestle (1898), Saliveros (1902), Antoniades (1904), Souter (1910), Bodin (1911), von Soden (1913), Vogels (1920), Colombo (1932), Merk (1933), Bover (1943); besides numerous revisions of some of these.[1] Translators have made their choices from among these, reflecting a judgment which they may announce but not explain. For example, Weymouth (1903) translated from his own 'resultant' Greek text; Bell (1922), Ballantine (1923) and the R.S.V. (1946) rest upon the Nestle text; Ballentine (1922), Montgomery (1924), C. K. Williams (1952), to say nothing of the popular E.R.V. and A.S.V., reflect the text printed by Souter; Moffatt (1913) used von Soden; Kleist (1932) translated Vogels; while the Twentieth Century (1904) and Goodspeed (1923) rested upon Westcott-Hort. In the midst of such variety it is well to assess the progress made toward recovering the original Greek base, bearing in mind that we are here concerned not with the growing edge of knowledge but with the effects already operative in New Testament studies.

For New Testament studies in the past twenty years, the most used critical editions of the Greek New Testament number six. Protestant editions include Westcott-Hort, Souter, and Nestle; while Roman Catholic editions include Vogels, Merk, and Bover. They fall into two groups: Souter and Vogels on the side of the Textus Receptus;

[1] The Nestle text has appeared in eight editions between 1930 (14th) and 1952 (21st); the text of Merk, in seven editions between 1933 (1st) and 1951 (7th). Other recent editions are those of Brandscheid, 1932 (3rd); Bover, 1950 (2nd) and 1952 (3rd); Souter, 1947 (2nd); and Vogels, 1949–50 (3rd).

and Nestle, Merk, and Bover on the side of Westcott-Hort.[1] The oldest of these texts is Souter[2] for although a posthumous edition was published in 1947 his canonical text remained unchanged, still reproducing the 1881 text of Palmer.[3] Palmer's text was essentially the Textus Receptus eclectically altered to include many 'readings adopted by the revisers of the authorized version'.[4] The Palmer-Souter text was an improvement seventy-five years ago but today we must recognize that it actually antedates the Westcott-Hort text and disregards much substantial progress achieved since its origin. Souter's text differs from the Textus Receptus far less than any of the other texts named above. A collation with Westcott-Hort through an extensive section (Mark i–v) reveals 191 differences, of which 168 are T.R. readings. This reveals the extent to which the posthumous Souter edition even now fails to avail itself of critical improvement. It is a concession of doubtful wisdom that is still found in the guide prepared for both the American Bible Society and the British and Foreign Bible Society, stating that 'translators and revisers...are at liberty to follow that [text] underlying the English Authorized Version (edited by Dr F. H. A. Scrivener, for the Cambridge University Press), or that underlying the English Revised Version (edited by Archdeacon Edwin Palmer, for the Oxford University Press)'.[5] Nestle recently described the Souter text as 'very similar to that of Westcott and Hort',[6] but our detailed examination of its text clearly reveals that its kinship with the Textus Receptus sharply contrasts it with Westcott-Hort. Today the use of the Souter text places unnecessary obstacles in the path of the interpreter or translator, whether or not he be a textual specialist.

[1] In comparing these printed texts we refer to the editor's first choice of each reading, without regard to a possible alternative indicated in the margin or apparatus. Nor are we concerned with proposing or judging possible improvements to be made, but rather with reporting and comparing what the current editions have set before us.

[2] Alexander Souter, *Novum Testamentum Graece, editio altera* (Oxford, 1947). Only the apparatus differs from the first edition of 1910.

[3] E. Palmer, Ἡ Καινὴ Διαθήκη (Oxford, 1881).

[4] Scrivener counted 5788 changes in the entire New Testament (see Philip Schaff, *Companion*, p. 419 n.).

[5] Eugene A. Nida, *Bible Translating* (New York, 1947), pp. 50–1.

[6] Erwin Nestle, 'How to Use a Greek New Testament', *The Bible Translator*, vol. II (1951), p. 55.

The Vogels text, last revised in 1949–50 after a long interval,[1] is only somewhat less influenced by the antiquated Textus Receptus. A similar collation of Mark i–v shows 103 differences from Westcott-Hort, of which seventy-five are T.R. readings. Nestle has remarked of the Vogels text that it 'does not differ much from Souter or Nestle'.[2] But it cannot resemble them both because they differ widely from one another (187 times in Mark i–v, of which only seven of Souter's readings depart from the T.R.). The text of Vogels falls between Nestle and Souter. Actually, Vogels and Souter differ from one another 189 times in these five chapters, with Souter adhering to the T.R. reading 146 times and Vogels following the T.R. forty-three times. But Vogels also differs considerably from Nestle (eighty-seven times, of which seventy-eight are T.R. readings). Indeed a detailed examination of the text of Mark i–v shows Vogels akin to Souter and the Textus Receptus.

In contrast, Westcott-Hort, Nestle, Bover, and Merk form a tight critical group with comparatively little difference among them. Up until 1933 the printed texts of Westcott-Hort and Nestle[3] supplied in the West the basic critical Greek New Testament. Within the next decade there were published the critical texts of two Catholic scholars—the first edition of Merk,[4] followed ten years later by that of Bover.[5] These four critical texts today exert the greatest influence upon the interpretation of the New Testament in Western scholarship. Writing in 1949 (*J.T.S.*), G. D. Kilpatrick referred to Nestle, Souter, and Merk, as 'the three most useful'. But the present trend is away from the 1881 text reflected in Souter, which therefore might well be replaced by Bover. We propose, therefore, a comparison between Westcott-Hort and each of the other three, to set in relief the changes which the years have produced.[6]

[1] Henry Joseph Vogels, *Novum Testamentum Graece et Latine, editio tertia* (Freiburg, 1949–50). The earlier editions appeared in 1920 and 1922.

[2] *Loc. cit.*

[3] Eberhard Nestle, *Novum Testamentum Graece* (Stuttgart, 1898); recent announcement has come of the 21st edition (1952).

[4] Augustinus Merk, S.J., *Novum Testamentum Graece et Latine* (Rome, 1933); the sixth edition appeared posthumously in 1948, edited by S. Lyonnet, S.J.

[5] Joseph M. Bover, S.J., *Novi Testamenti, Biblia Graeca et Latina* (Madrid, 1943), revised in 1950 and 1952.

[6] For this comparison, we employ Nestle 1952[21], Bover 1950[2], and Merk 1948[6], which are the latest editions in hand. Bover published a new edition in 1952, and

Probably the most influential critical New Testament text in use today is that of Nestle. The American Bible Society and the British and Foreign Bible Society especially recommend its use for translation.[1] The fourth edition of 1903 was adopted by the B.F.B.S., which now has in preparation a new edition based upon Nestle's latest printing. Among current critical texts Nestle stands the closest to Westcott-Hort. In the entire Gospel of Mark (one-twelfth of the New Testament), the 1952 Nestle edition shows only eighty-nine changes from Westcott-Hort. A large majority of these are insignificant elements of orthography. Not more than thirty-two instances may be considered substantial; only twelve involve a difference in meaning. All twelve were introduced early into the Nestle text, between 1898 and 1903, and thus do not illustrate improvement in recent years but they still stand in the 1952 edition:

Mark i. 34 χριστον ειναι. Nestle (with Merk and Bover) omits this phrase which Westcott-Hort included in brackets. This was originally omitted by Nestle in 1898.

ii. 23 παραπορευεσθαι (for διαπ.). Adopted by Nestle since 1898 (with Merk and Bover); Westcott-Hort chose διαπ., in half-brackets.

iii. 14 ους και αποστολους ωνομασεν. Nestle since 1898 (with Merk and Bover) has omitted this clause which Westcott-Hort accepted.

iii. 32 και αι αδελφαι σου. Nestle since 1898 (with Bover but not Merk) has added this phrase which Westcott-Hort rejected.

vii. 24 και Σιδωνος. Nestle omitted as early as 1903; Westcott-Hort included in brackets.

vii. 35 ευθυς before ελυθη. Nestle since 1898 has added; Westcott-Hort omitted.

ix. 38 ος ουκ ακολουθει ημιν. Nestle since 1898 has added; Westcott-Hort omitted.

x. 26 εαυτους. Nestle since 1898 (for αυτον in Westcott-Hort).

xii. 23 οταν αναστωσιν. Added by Nestle as early as 1903; Westcott-Hort rejected.

xv. 1 ετοιμασαντες. Nestle, as early as 1903 (for ποιησαντες in half-brackets in Westcott-Hort).

Lyonnet reissued Merk in 1951. The text of Mark in Nestle's 1952 edition shows no change from the 1950 edition.

[1] Nida, *Bible Translating*, pp. 50–1.

xv. 44 παλαι. Nestle, since 1898 (for ηδη in half-brackets in Westcott-Hort).

xvi. 17 καιναις. Nestle, since 1898 (for και εν ταις χερσιν in brackets in Westcott-Hort).

The Nestle text of Mark shows only seventy-five changes through the twenty-one editions between 1898 and 1952 and thirty-five of these are restorations of Westcott-Hort readings. Only thirty-one have entered the Nestle text since 1903 (fourth edition), of which twenty-four are merely orthographic. The other seven involve no difference in meaning, and six of these represent a return to Westcott-Hort:

Mark i. 25 ιησους] + λεγων (so Westcott-Hort).
ii. 17 αυτοις] + οτι (so Westcott-Hort).
ix. 8 αλλα] ει μη (so Westcott-Hort).
x. 35 + δυο [υιοι (so Westcott-Hort).
xiv. 20 + ἓν [τρυβλιον (so Westcott-Hort).
xv. 22 μεθερμηνευομενον.
xvi. 1 + η [μαρια (1) (so Westcott-Hort).

The result of our examination is again to confirm that Nestle's critical text, described by Erwin Nestle himself as 'based on the investigation of the nineteenth century',[1] as late as 1952 still rests heavily upon Westcott-Hort; that few changes have been made from Westcott-Hort; and that the trend of most recent revision has been a return toward Westcott-Hort.

The texts of Merk and Bover are somewhat less conservative though they present few additional substantial changes, of which only the following (in Mark i–v) involve a difference in meaning:

i. 1 υιου του Θεου. Added by both Merk and Bover, rejected by Westcott-Hort.

ii. 16 και πινει. Added by Merk, rejected by Westcott-Hort.

A full composite list for Mark i–v of all variants from Westcott-Hort as found in Nestle, Merk, or Bover totals only seventy-seven (Nestle 31, Bover 52, Merk 56). Twenty-one times all three agree against Westcott-Hort; in thirteen readings Bover and Merk stand together against Nestle and Westcott-Hort. Among these four

[1] Erwin Nestle, 'How to Use a Greek New Testament', *The Bible Translator*, vol. II (1951), p. 54.

critical texts, Bover stands alone fifteen times; and Merk eighteen times. The conclusion is inescapable that these most used critical texts at mid-century show little change from Westcott-Hort and only rarely present a significant variant.

It remains to ask whether the changes made represent progress toward the original text. It is obvious that this limited revision is not the result of the new manuscript discoveries. The Beatty text of Mark is fragmentary and exhibits few of the Marcan variants under discussion, and in these few instances the editors have more often rejected the 𝔓[45] reading. Nor does it appear that the Freer Gospels[1] have played any direct part in recent revision, for all the variants in Nestle were previously known and debated and all have been tried in some good critical text within the last century. Indeed, one notices that many variants slip in and out of the critical texts subject only, it seems, to a shift in judgment. Especially frequent are readings adopted for the first Nestle edition which have in later editions been rejected. This phenomenon of vacillation can be illustrated with a few citations from the early chapters of Mark:

i. 1	υιου Θεου not in N^1, in N^4, but not in N^{20}.
i. 4	ιωαννης in N^1, not in N^4, but in N^{20}.
	ερημω] + και in N^1, but not N^4, in N^{17} but not N^{20}.
i. 8	+ εν [πνευματι in N^1, but not N^4 nor N^{20}.
iii. 4	αγαθοποιησαι in N^1, but not N^4 nor N^{20}.
iii. 8	εποιει in N^1, but not N^4 nor N^{20}.
iii. 17	ονοματα in N^1, but not N^4 nor N^{20}.
iii. 22	βεελζεβουλ in N^1, but not N^4 nor N^{20}.
iv. 5	αυξανομενον in N^1, but not N^4 nor N^{20}.
iv. 32	κατασκηνουν in N^1, not in N^4, but in N^{20}.

It is also apparent that such critics as Nestle, Merk, and Bover often differ in judgment. Bover often stands alone and there is some evidence that he—more than Merk—is influenced especially by the Vulgate, as in the following examples:

Mark i. 41	Add αυτου after ηψατο. Supported by D vg.
iii. 26	μεμερισται και for και εμερισθη. Supported only by vg (*dispertitus est et*).
iv. 8	ἓν . . . ἓν . . . ἓν. Supported only by vg (*unum . . . unum . . . unum*).

[1] Henry A. Sanders, *The New Testament Manuscripts in the Freer Collection*, Part I: *The Washington Manuscript of the Four Gospels* (New York, 1912).

There are, however, many Vulgate readings not favoured by Bover and Merk; but Bover especially is influenced by his theory that it is the Western text that attests a pre-recensional form of the second century (*Proleg.* p. xxxi). None of the editors has made his changes because of his own reconstruction of the history of the text; none attempts any such reconstruction. The chief influence that has altered the Westcott-Hort readings is simply a lower status for its 1881 text. The most influential factor in recent criticism is the general view that the Neutral text is itself a derived text which has passed through a process of revision. Along with a demotion of B and ℵ there goes a somewhat enhanced status for D and Θ and their groups.[1] For an editor, this often is enough to swing the scales to the opposite side. The few readings changed in the texts all show an evenly balanced attestation and many were originally placed in brackets in Westcott-Hort. One concludes that a subjective element plays a considerable part in the eclectic procedure of recent textual revision.

The eclectic method is openly embraced in our day.[2] Indeed, it is the only procedure available to us at this stage, but it is very important to recognize that it is a secondary and tentative method. It is not a new method nor a permanent one; it does not supplant the more thorough procedure of Westcott and Hort but only supplements it temporarily. The eclectic method cannot by itself create a text to displace Westcott-Hort and its offspring. It is suitable only for exploration and experimentation. From it may one day come the insight about which a multitude of itemized researches may gather and find unity and meaning. The eclectic method, by its very nature, belongs to a day like ours in which we know only that the traditional

[1] For recent major studies on the Western text consult especially A. C. Clark, *The Acts of the Apostles* (Oxford, 1933); W. H. P. Hatch, *The Western Text of the Gospels* (Evanston, 1937); Frederic G. Kenyon, *The Western Text in the Gospels and Acts* (London, 1938); G. D. Kilpatrick, 'Western Text and Original Text in the Gospels and Acts...in the Epistles', *Journal of Theological Studies*, vol. XLIV (1943) and vol. XLV (1944); and A. J. K. Klijn, *Survey of the Researches on the Western Text of the Gospels and Acts* (Utrecht, 1949). On the Caesarean text consult especially Lake, Blake and New, 'The Caesarean Text of the Gospel of Mark', *Harvard Theological Review*, vol. XXI (1928), pp. 207–404; B. H. Streeter, *The Four Gospels*, revised (London, 1930), pp. 77–107; and the thorough critique by Bruce M. Metzger, 'The Caesarean Text of the Gospels', *Journal of Biblical Literature*, vol. LXIV (1945), pp. 457–89.

[2] An excellent procedure in eclectic criticism is observed in the 1946 Schweich Lectures by G. N. Zuntz, *The Text of the Epistles* (London, 1953).

theory of the text is faulty but cannot yet see clearly to correct the fault. While, therefore, we are indebted to 'the eclectics' for their scholarly judgments, we should not expect thus to be provided with an improved critical text. Paradoxically, the eclectic method as applied today presupposes the *general* correctness of our traditional textual theory. Yet the eclectic method treats each variant independently, with rare exception. By it even the same editor may lead us in several directions, and certainly different editors will do so even though their basic text is the same. For, let us remember, the basic text of such able editors as Nestle, Merk, and Bover is still the structure established by Westcott-Hort. It is clearly not true that for New Testament studies the 'reign of the "Neutral" text has come to an end', as F. C. Grant declared fifteen years ago.[1] Grant actually referred to 'the long undisputed reign'. Certainly there has arisen dispute about the status of the Neutral text; indeed, it is generally agreed that the Neutral text must be replaced by a better. But we do not have that better text and do not yet know how to reconstruct it; meanwhile the Neutral text continues to reign and, I think, must for some generations to come. It has been demonstrated above how little change from Westcott-Hort appears in any of the current critical texts now in general use for Biblical studies.

Furthermore, such tentative changes as have appeared do not represent an integrated theory of the text and therefore can have no such basic theory to validate them as improvements. Objective textual scholarship must still depend upon manuscript testimony, and it is still true that the most ancient manuscripts are the most valuable. We are often reminded today that there is no infallible manuscript or recension. This is not new information, but what was once a concession has now become an insistence. Yet despite the acknowledged fallibility of all manuscripts, there is still a trustworthy quality of good character in certain manuscripts and even in the Neutral text. For the eclectic critic to declare these false at any point calls for persuasive evidence. A judgment is not validated merely because we like the resultant theology or even because it preserves consistency for the author, for these are elusive and subjective factors. Where variants appear, ultimate judgment must rest upon a basic

[1] F. C. Grant, 'Studies in the Text of St Mark', *Anglican Theological Review*, vol. XX (1938), p. 103.

theory of the primitive text. It is true that the critic has many aids besides manuscript witnesses; a choice between variant readings may be influenced by synoptic research, language, style, vocabulary, orthography, harmonization, theology, or history. But these aids represent knowledge to be gained *from* the true text and their influence must be kept under proper restraint if they would guide us *to* the true text. Furthermore, our purpose has been to learn what was originally written—even if the author or editor should be found inconsistent, or illogical, or faulty in theology or history. Yet we do face a difficult problem in those closely balanced variants which have long been the despair of editors. At least, we are still prone to describe them as *balanced*, in terms of the traditional categories and the traditional theory that one of the ancient texts must be more primitive than the others (if only we might know which!). But the principle of competing witnesses has been giving way to a principle of co-operating witnesses. The Neutral, Western, and Caesarean texts have all been found in use in all sections of early Christianity, and though all of our earliest manuscripts (up to A.D. 400) have come from Egypt alone they attest the use even there of all major textual types. The problematic readings in Mark, such as those referred to above, show in each case the combined support of Neutral, Western, and Caesarean witnesses for each alternate reading. The textual critic has not yet developed an objective criterion to decide these cases. Despite the latest discoveries and the newest researches, New Testament studies today reflect the continued dominance of the Neutral text.

Although technical New Testament studies must ultimately be based upon the critical Greek text, it is relevant here to note the effect of recent textual criticism upon the English version. Since 1930 there have appeared at least forty-five independent translations of the New Testament, or its parts (most frequently, the Gospel of Mark). Clearly the most influential of them is the Revised Standard Version, produced by an American committee in 1946. However much change may be noted in this official translation, little of it may be traced to specific readings in manuscripts or in critical editions, and here again it is proper to ask whether this little represents further recovery of the original documents. Of course, most of the eighty-nine changes from Westcott-Hort in Nestle's text of Mark have no reflection in the English idiom. One of the translators, Frederick C. Grant, has written that 'the readings we have adopted will, as a rule, be found either in the text or the margin of the new (17th) edition of Nestle' (1941).[1] Therefore it will be expeditious to review first the R.S.V. treatment of Nestle's changes from Westcott-Hort. In Mark there are twenty-six such changes which are reflected in the English idiom, and of these the R.S.V. has rejected sixteen (nine of which would alter the meaning):

*ii. 23	διαπ.] παραπορευεσθαι.
*iii. 32	add και αι αδελφαι σου (omission noted in margin).
iv. 40	ουπω] ουτως; πως ουκ.
vi. 9	ενδυσασθαι] ενδυσησθαι.
vi. 51	λιαν] + εκπερισσου.
*vii. 24	omit και Σιδωνος (addition noted in margin).
*vii. 35	add ευθυς before ελυθη.
viii. 20	λεγουσιν] omit αυτω.
*ix. 38	add ος και ακολουθει ημιν (omission noted in margin).
*x. 26	αυτον] εαυτους.
*xii. 23	add οταν αναστωσιν.
xii. 32	add και before ειπεν.
xiii. 2	omit ωδε.
xiii. 22	δωσουσιν] ποιησουσιν.
*xv. 1	ποιησαντες] ετοιμασαντες.
*xv. 44	ηδη] παλαι.

The other ten changes, of which only three involve a difference in meaning, have been adopted in the R.S.V.:

*i. 34	omit χριστον ειναι.
*iii. 14	omit ους και αποστολους ωνομασεν (addition noted in margin).
vi. 22	αυτου] αυτης της.
viii. 12	λεγω] + υμιν.
xi. 17	ελεγεν] + αυτοις.
xii. 17	ειπεν] + αυτοις.
xiv. 7	omit παντοτε (2).
xvi. 14	omit εκ νεκρων.
xvi. 17	ακολ.] παρακολουθησει.
*xvi. 17–18	και εν ταις χερσιν] καιναις.

[1] Luther A. Weigle (ed.), *An Introduction to the Revised Standard Version of the New Testament* (New York, 1946), p. 41.

In addition, there are a few readings adopted by the R.S.V., departing from both Westcott-Hort and Nestle, e.g.:

i. 1	add υιου του Θεου, with Bover and Merk and Westcott-Hort^mg.
i. 29	εξελθοντες ηλθαν] εξελθων ηλθεν, with Merk and Westcott-Hort^mg.
ii. 22	omit αλλα οινον νεον εις ασκους καινους, differing with all these editors and supported only by D and Old Latin.
x. 7	add και προσκολληθησεται προς την γυναικα αυτου, with Merk and many manuscripts (vs. ℵ B Ψ *et al.*).

In all, there appear to be very few cases in which the R.S.V. departs from Westcott-Hort;[1] these are traditionally doubtful cases and, in a few instances, even highly questionable as to authenticity. Sometimes 𝔓45 is deliberately rejected (vii. 4 βαπτισωνται and viii. 15 ηρωδιανων) in favour of Westcott-Hort. Indeed, Grant exclaims that 'it is really extraordinary how often, with fuller apparatus of variant readings at our disposal, and with the eclectic principle now more widely accepted, we have concurred in following Westcott and Hort...still the great classical tradition of modern times'.[2] This is a tribute eminently deserved but often obscured in these days of notable discoveries and theories. Once again, our review of the R.S.V. in Mark has demonstrated how little, and how tentatively, textual criticism since 1930—and much earlier—has altered the New Testament text we study.[3] The effect of textual criticism upon New Testament studies is always a delayed force, and the chief impact upon present studies is the result of the earlier reconstruction of the

[1] Apparently the same observation will hold true for the new British translation now in preparation. Professor C. H. Dodd, who is general director of the British group, has reported that the New Testament panel finds 'no existing published text which could be implicitly followed: we should in effect have to construct our own text, which would necessarily be eclectic. We adopt as a starting-point the Oxford text (Souter), but diverge from it where it seems desirable—[our text] will in the end approximate more closely to the forthcoming edition of Nestle, which is being prepared for the British and Foreign Bible Society, than to any other.' If so, then the changes from Westcott-Hort are not likely to be numerous.

[2] Weigle (ed.), *Introduction to the Revised Standard Version of the New Testament*, p. 41.

[3] E. A. Nida, in *The Bible Translator* (III, 2, 81–94) in 1951 discusses 'Spiritual Values in Better Manuscript Readings of the New Testament'. All seven passages there noted are based on Westcott-Hort readings and illustrate improvements of seventy years ago.

Neutral text. The limited and tentative alterations in this text thus far are peripheral and unstable. Any substantial effort to improve the basic critical text must 'mark time' until the whole complex of textual studies reveals a new integrating pattern.

2. THE BYZANTINE TEXT

It is not to be thought that recent textual criticism has been fruitless simply because the Westcott-Hort text has not yet been superseded. Even in the quest for the original text fundamental studies have indicated the need to reconsider the history of the text. The Western and Caesarean forms have grown in stature to stand beside the Neutral, and the Neutral no longer holds a monopoly on the true text. There is less confidence than ever that we have a true understanding of the origins and relations of the early recensions. The newly recognized Caesarean form has created intricate problems. Third-century papyrus texts have not yet been successfully placed in the historical scheme. But although studies in textual history are in a tentative state they have produced important results in making us aware that a new reconstruction is demanded by the evidence, and to perceive the need is to secure initial insight into the answer. Furthermore, while the history of the early text is essential to the reconstruction of that text, it is true also that that history as derived *from* the manuscripts throws light upon the development of the early Church in the different sections of the Roman Empire.

Neither can it be said that textual research has recently been inactive; on the contrary, no time in history has seen such varied and far-flung textual studies as has this generation.[1] The greatest attention has been directed to the Byzantine manuscripts, in a wide range of studies: the Byzantine text and its various types, textual families, the lectionary text, and related studies in Byzantine theology, palaeography, iconography, and church music. Such studies relate, not directly to the beginnings of the New Testament text but to its transmission, interpretation and use in worship. These are the aspects

[1] This is impressively demonstrated in the forthcoming *Annotated Bibliography of the Textual Criticism of the New Testament* (126 pages) covering the period 1914–39, prepared by Bruce M. Metzger, to be published by Christophers in London as vol. XVI in *Studies and Documents*.

of New Testament studies which today are immediately affected by textual researches, for these researches seek to learn how the New Testament fared in the expanding Christian community. They may ultimately throw light upon the origin of the text, but for the time being they concentrate upon later developments.

The Byzantine text has recently attained importance in its own right. Even in the days of Tischendorf and Westcott and Hort it was defended by Scrivener, Miller, and Burgon for its excellence and validity. Burgon even contended for its superiority over the Alexandrian text, and pronounced ℵ and B 'the most corrupt' and D 'the most depraved text'. But this was the final effort to retain a primary position for the Textus Receptus, 'now universally admitted to be a secondary form of the text'.[1] So complete was its downfall that the mass of Byzantine manuscripts were virtually disregarded until our own generation, but recent criticism is particularly noted for its fresh attention to them. They have again become of high importance, not because Westcott and Hort were wrong about their secondary status but because it is recognized today that they may bear additional witness to the early text and also to later forms employed in the Church. Their usefulness does not lie in the exclusive preservation of an original reading here and there (which would in itself be difficult to judge) but rather in the retracing of main paths back to the major texts, early or late, from which they once departed.

It is well known that distinctive groups of Byzantine manuscripts have long been recognized, such as Family 1, Family 13, the 'purple manuscripts', and Group 1424. These were at first seen as isolated groups whose broader relationships were unknown, distinctively local texts which reflected the peculiar interpretation of the New Testament at some centre. But this was a beginning in textual classification of the increasing mass of later manuscript witnesses. The most extensive effort at classification was made by Hermann von Soden, in whose *Die Schriften des Neuen Testaments* (1902–13) the late manuscripts (excepting the lowly lectionaries) received the fullest attention. His scheme constitutes the background for much textual criticism in the last quarter-century. Great numbers of these

[1] Ernest C. Colwell, 'The Complex Character of the Late Byzantine Text of the Gospels', *Journal of Biblical Literature*, vol. LIV (1935), pp. 211–21.

late manuscripts have in our time been collated and classified. Each investigation may appear unrelated to others and it is not often that a manuscript attaches itself to one of the notable groups. But this extensive and continuing search is accumulating a great reserve of information, until larger patterns appear in which each part will find its place. For example, it is within this generation that the Family Groups 1 and 13 have at last fallen into the larger pattern of the Caesarean form, and since the first small groups were discovered additional members have been recognized so that the families are now much enlarged with sisters and cousins and in-laws. It is perceived that even these late copies of the text, revised though they may be, may like Ariadne's thread assist us in retracing our steps to the source. This is the meaning of such patient labours in textual criticism today.

But there is also an immediate effect upon New Testament studies, for the Byzantine manuscripts have been found useful in teaching us how the Church interpreted the New Testament in the Byzantine era. Textual variation is a living thing. The forms of text have resulted from the shape of thought. Next to knowing how the New Testament originally read, it is important to learn how later generations of believers made it read. The libraries of the world contain thousands of manuscript copies of the New Testament which give full evidence that interpreters differed and sometimes wrote their theological differences into the text. These interpreters have greatly complicated the task of recovering the original text, but their textual variations fill the canvas of the Church's later life and thought. It should be clear that textual criticism is not merely a preliminary exercise in establishing a useful text but is rather a constant associate of church history and historical theology. The textual critic is called upon today to establish not *the* critical text but many critical texts. We now seek to recover, in addition to the original New Testament text, the text used by each of the writing Fathers—the critical text of Clement, of Origen, of Eusebius, of Irenaeus, of Tertullian, of Cyprian, as well as of many a later commentator. Current studies particularly would recover the critical original of local texts and family texts (such as Family 13), and each should be studied in relation to local history and interpretation. Such an association has been pointed out by Kirsopp Lake, who observed that 'the mental attitude of an age is apt to be reflected in its texts....The third and fourth centuries used the Neutral and Caesarean texts; both are marked by clearness of choice and decision between alternatives. It is not an accident that these centuries were those which formulated the great doctrines of Catholic Christianity, and that the fifth century, which used the Antiochian and Ecclesiastical texts, was in the East chiefly characterized by compromise in doctrine and conflation in text.'[1] Nor did theological motivation cease so early to have its effect upon the text. Specifically, an instance in the Byzantine era is set forth by E. W. Saunders, drawn from his study of an early thirteenth-century manuscript influenced by the eleventh-century commentator, Theophylact.[2] Certain variants in the manuscript find *exclusive* support from Theophylact's commentary on the Gospels in the terms in which he explains the true meaning of each passage. That variants in the New Testament text are often laden with theological significance, and may well have theological motivation, is further emphasized by the present writer in an article exhibiting choices of variant readings in the Pauline text.[3] The task, in such cases, is not merely to determine which was the original reading, but to learn as well how each reading played its part in the life of the Church. This interest, in which the textual critic turns historian and theologian, has been increasing in recent criticism and may fruitfully be extended in future textual studies. It presents a direct challenge especially to the historical theologian to collaborate with the textual specialist to produce the most trustworthy conclusions.

The study of manuscript lectionaries is a special department of textual criticism. It has, however, been greatly neglected and although much knowledge about continuous-text witnesses has been garnered through three centuries we still have very little understanding of lectionary witnesses. Until recently a lectionary has mistakenly been used, if at all, in the same manner as a continuous-text manuscript. For example, Tischendorf cited readings from a few lectionaries in eclectic fashion and merely recorded the lectionary side by side with

[1] Kirsopp Lake, 'Excursus on "The Ecclesiastical Text"', *Harvard Theological Review*, vol. XXI (1928), p. 345 n.

[2] Ernest W. Saunders, 'Studies in Doctrinal Influences on the Byzantine Text of the Gospels', *Journal of Biblical Literature*, vol. LXXI (1952), pp. 85–92.

[3] Kenneth W. Clark, 'Textual Criticism and Doctrine', in *Studia Paulina*, honouring Johannis de Zwaan (Haarlem, 1953).

the continuous-text witness, as just another witness to the reading. But the study of the lectionary text has now become a distinctive feature of recent textual criticism, and serious and methodical study of the lectionaries has at last been well established.[1]

Lectionary research has special importance for New Testament studies. In the first place, the reading of the Scripture in corporate worship assumed the lectionary pattern early in the life of the Church. It is generally held, furthermore, that public reading of the lectionary text tended to stereotype it and remove it from the centrifugal forces that shattered the unity of other witnesses.[2] Therefore the lectionary text would be a conservative text and, once understood, should bear valuable witness to the text in the early period of the Church. But textual criticism of the lectionaries can contribute other important knowledge about the early Church. Besides helping to clarify the problem of textual transmission, lectionary studies may throw light upon the early practice of Christian worship. Yet for all the importance of the lectionaries, they have come into their own only in this present generation.

The lectionaries (Gospels and Epistles) do not contain all of the New Testament text (especially notable is the complete absence of the Apocalypse), although some selections appear more than once and often show variant readings. It is because of the lectionary structure that its study is more intricate and difficult and requires a special technique to secure scientific results. For example, it is fairly clear that the lectionary text is composite with a separate development of the week-day system from that of Saturday–Sunday, the latter probably representing the earlier system. If this be so, it is obvious that the two systems must be separately studied and reported. Or again, when the same lectionary in duplicate readings (perhaps within the same system) shows a difference in the text we have a puzzling phenomenon that does not occur in continuous-text witness. Nevertheless, for all its difficulty the lectionary has become a special subject of textual research in this generation. The results of such a study are immediately applicable to certain historical problems

[1] See especially Riddle and Colwell, *Prolegomena to the Study of the Lectionary Text of the Gospels* (Chicago, 1933).

[2] Ernest C. Colwell, 'Is There a Lectionary Text of the Gospels?', *Harvard Theological Review*, vol. xxv (1932), pp. 73–84.

of the early Church, and will ultimately provide essential information on the early history of the text.[1]

There are several subsidiary fields of manuscript research especially active in recent years, which contribute to textual criticism: archaeology, bibliology, palaeography, Byzantine liturgy and music, and iconography. An expedition in 1949–50 to the great but neglected libraries of Jerusalem and Sinai has now made available a great mass of new textual material, especially valuable for patristic and Byzantine studies.[2] Again, the recently discovered Beatty papyri are valuable not only for their witness to an early text but as illustrations of the papyrus codices used by Christians in the second and third centuries. They have better informed us about the primitive format of Scriptural writings, a factor which influences conclusions about the text as well as the canon. To know how Christians made their books contributes to a clearer analysis of the fortunes of a text in transmission.[3] Palaeographical studies were greatly advanced in this generation when Kirsopp and Silva Lake published their massive corpus of dated Greek manuscripts.[4] A new technique for dating Byzantine Greek manuscripts has recently been proposed by Colwell, based upon the proportions of uncial and cursive letter-forms.[5] Especially in the field of Christian iconography, studies relating to the New Testament have demonstrated their value for Biblical criticism. 'Pictures and text in manuscripts often travel together over long stretches of time, so that obviously the process of copying

[1] Allen P. Wikgren observes that 'many lections preserve a text which is that of the best and most ancient codices, a fact which should make lectionaries of great value not only in the history of the transmission of the text, but also in any attempt to reconstruct its most ancient form' (*Journal of Biblical Literature*, vol. LIII (1934), p. 198).

[2] Kenneth W. Clark, *Checklist of Manuscripts in St Catherine's Monastery, Mt. Sinai* (1952); *Checklist of Manuscripts in the Libraries of the Greek and Armenian Patriarchates in Jerusalem* (1953), Washington.

[3] See especially C. C. McCown, 'Codex and Roll in the New Testament', *Harvard Theological Review*, vol. XXXIV (1941), pp. 219–50.

[4] Kirsopp and Silva Lake, *Dated Greek Minuscule Manuscripts to the Year 1200*, 10 vols. and index (Boston, 1934–9 and 1945).

[5] Ernest C. Colwell, *The Four Gospels of Karahissar*, vol. I (Chicago, 1936), pp. 225–41: 'Some Criteria for Dating Byzantine New Testament Manuscripts.' His proposal has been more fully developed in a doctoral dissertation at Yale University, by Howard C. Kee, 'The Paleography of Dated Greek New Testament Manuscripts before 1300' (n.p. 1951).

of the one must have a bearing on that of the other.'[1] Art and text together reveal the mind of the scribal community. All of this paragraph refers to disciplines that support textual studies and, indeed, most of the works cited are by New Testament specialists, several of them being textual critics. The effect of these researches has not yet been fully felt in New Testament studies but they stand upon the threshold of attention.

3. THE INTERNATIONAL GREEK NEW TESTAMENT

The largest single research project in textual criticism of the present, or of any time in history, is the preparation of a basic critical apparatus. Although the effects of this will be fully felt in the future, it is relevant to describe it here because its substantial effect upon New Testament studies is immediate even while it is in progress. It is a broad international effort, turning chiefly upon an axis of British and American collaboration with the main centres at Oxford and Chicago, and including at present a few representative scholars in European countries. Because so many New Testament scholars are active in it—about 150—it is inevitable that current labours exercise an effect upon testamental studies at once.

The international character of the project is the result of independent initiative in England and the United States, yet the movement in England was the earlier. Some years before the Second World War erupted a group of scholars organized such a project under the leadership of the late Bishop Headlam. It was first reported that their objective was to publish a new critical text along with an improved citation of textual variation. But the effort to replace the Westcott-Hort text was abandoned, a development which further demonstrates the thesis that it is untimely to expect a new critical text in our generation. Under the editorship of S. C. E. Legg, two volumes of the projected series were published in 1935 (Mark) and 1940 (Matthew),[2] and a third volume prepared on Luke but not

[1] Kurt Weitzmann, 'Narrative and Liturgical Gospel Illustrations', in Parvis and Wikgren (edd.), *New Testament Manuscript Studies* (Chicago, 1950), p. 152. Cf. Harold R. Willoughby, *The Rockefeller-McCormick New Testament*, vol. III (Chicago, 1932); *The Four Gospels of Karahissar*, vol. I (Chicago, 1936); *The Elizabeth Day McCormick Apocalypse*, vol. I (Chicago, 1940).

[2] S. C. E. Legg (ed.), *Novum Testamentum Graece* (Oxford, 1935–40).

published. The text of Westcott-Hort was printed as a base and the critical apparatus cited manuscripts in support of this text as well as those supporting variant readings. In the apparatus of Mark, about forty uncial manuscripts are cited besides about thirty uncial fragments. The Beatty manuscript (𝔓⁴⁵) is the only papyrus cited. From the mass of minuscules, only twenty of special significance are regularly cited (representing Family 1, Family 13, and the Alexandrian and Caesarean types). In Mark, about 200 additional continuous-text minuscules are occasionally reported. In the succeeding volume on Matthew, about half of all these minuscules is omitted while about fifty additional witnesses appear occasionally. In the unpublished Lucan apparatus about fifty minuscules in the printed volumes are dropped and well over a hundred additional minuscules appear for the first time. In all three Gospels, about 350 minuscules appear at least once in the apparatus but only a small, choice group is reported consistently. This procedure is traditional, for no previous editor has attempted to cite all of his witnesses throughout, but the Legg volumes do report from a much larger number of manuscripts than heretofore.

The above description of the first stage in the project provides a background necessary for the understanding of the succeeding stage. The American initiative arose in 1942 and resulted in a definite plan drawn up in 1948.[1] Happily, the American and British groups joined hands, and at this point a new set of principles was agreed upon in international conference. The original plan, therefore, was substantially revised and the objective differently defined.[2] Therefore the volume on the Gospel of Luke, next to be published, will be reworked to conform to the new principles. In it the Textus Receptus will be printed as the base with (as before) evidence cited both for and against this text.[3] The new agreement calls for the citation of all known uncial witnesses and indeed all manuscripts up to A.D. 900.

[1] M. M. Parvis and A. P. Wikgren, editors, *New Testament Manuscript Studies* (Chicago, 1950).

[2] Merrill M. Parvis, 'The International Project to Establish a New Critical Apparatus of the Greek New Testament', *Crozer Quarterly*, vol. XXVII (1950), pp. 301–8.

[3] Parvis (*ibid.* p. 307) states: 'As far as we know, this is the first time that there has been an attempt to compile an extensive apparatus based upon the *textus receptus*.'

It will include *all* of the extant papyri.[1] An important revision of plan is the basic insistence that every Greek manuscript cited in the apparatus must be *completely* reported so that the apparatus will give full information on each manuscript. The number of minuscule witnesses to be included will be determined by the capacity of the apparatus but sporadic citation has been ruled out. Furthermore, if it were found possible to report the variants of some 300 minuscule manuscripts, they would represent a selection from possibly 900 Byzantine manuscripts to be studied, the criterion of selection being textual distinction.

Another important principle decided is that citation will not be arranged by textual types or groups. Whatever textual relationships may have been recognized in past studies, for the purpose of this reference work all will be levelled and every witness will stand by its own merit. Uncial and minuscule manuscripts will be cited simply in alphabetical and numerical sequence, according to the official designation of each. Nevertheless, in selecting from the great number of Byzantine manuscripts it is purposed to include adequate representation of the various textual types with which present-day critics are accustomed to deal. But the apparatus will reflect the effort to be neutral in all such previous findings and seek to avoid the obstruction of new insights or novel paths of textual investigation. Inasmuch as textual theory appears to have reached an impasse in our time, the fullest scope should be allowed for the discovery of gateways to new progress.

The revised plan further provides that the lectionary witness will be emphasized. A considerable block of lectionaries, whose importance is newly recognized in these days, will be carefully selected for *complete* citation (a recognition never before accorded this type of textual witness). Further, it is proposed to cite all versions into which the Greek text was translated before the year A.D. 1000. To set these translations more clearly against the Greek original, versional variants cited will appear in Greek. Patristic quotations are to be cited with special emphasis upon those Fathers whose text relates to the text-types emerging as dominant in the early cen-

[1] Georg Maldfeld and Bruce M. Metzger, 'Detailed List of the Greek Papyri of the New Testament', *Journal of Biblical Literature*, vol. LXVIII (1949), pp. 359–70. The editors here describe sixty-two extant papyri.

turies.[1] The results of this extensive research to be fulfilled through international co-operation will take the form of eight volumes for the complete New Testament. This type of basic reference work has not been successfully produced since the work of Tischendorf eighty years ago, and never has one utilized the technical principles now to be applied. The present project is necessary for two reasons: first, numerous discoveries of important manuscripts and theories have been made in the interval and, secondly, an improved technique for the *apparatus criticus* of the New Testament text is required in order to support that most difficult and complex problem of all textual criticism—the analysis of the New Testament text in its origins and transmission. If it be granted, in the providence of God, that this pretentious project should find completion, it will mark the end of the first stage of a renewed cycle of textual investigation. The modern period of collecting and collating sources, similar to the period 1516–1734, will have drawn to a close. A new phase may well open then when an adequate *apparatus criticus*, summarizing and ordering the vast data compiled, may provide the source from which new perception and inspiration may arise.

Ultimately, there is only one motivation for textual criticism, and that is the need for a trustworthy text to interpret. Biblical studies may go astray if based upon a corrupted text and, in turn, textual fidelity falls short of virtue if it represents only a mechanical restoration. While the search for the 'true text' does not in itself imply a theory of verbal inspiration, the living word contains a message of life and the importance of that message is one with the importance of the literal word. The textual critic has always been a theologian, but it is equally essential that the theologian shall be a textual critic. Certainly the two functions are indivisible and whether carried on in one mind or in two they must find close partnership. Therefore, the effect of textual criticism upon Biblical studies must be continuous, and the textual critic is called upon at all times to persist in the preparation of a better textual foundation upon which the structure of Christian faith may stand firm.

[1] M. M. Parvis observes that 'this will be the first time that the lectionary text or texts have been adequately cited in any apparatus' (*Crozer Quarterly*, vol. XXVII (1950), p. 307).

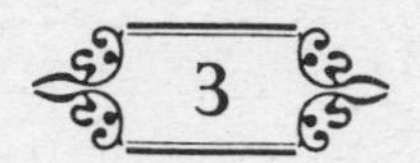

GNOSIS, GNOSTICISM AND THE NEW TESTAMENT

R. P. CASEY

THE terms 'Gnosis' and 'Gnosticism' have been much used in New Testament criticism in the last fifty years but there has been little unanimity about their precise meaning.[1] Harnack in his *Dogmengeschichte* described Gnosticism as an attempt to inject into Christianity more Greek thought than it was able to assimilate; hence his description of Gnosticism as *die akute Hellenisierung des Christentums*.[2] A different tack was, however, soon taken by Bousset in his *Hauptprobleme der Gnosis*,[3] in which he maintained that the Gnostic theologies represented rationalized survivals of Oriental myths. These were unrecorded in their original forms but had been transmitted in Hellenistic versions in which philosophy had blurred the primitive imagery. Their origins were various but all incorporated certain leading ideas: a dualistic view of the universe, a depreciation of matter and the material world, the degrading descent of the soul into the material world and its redemption through a dramatic release from material ties and affections.

Both Harnack's and Bousset's points of view attracted supporters. Anz[4] pressed further Bousset's mythological hypothesis and de Faye,[5] whose study of Gnostic sources marked a new era in their understanding, arrived at conclusions similar to Harnack's. These scholars were theologians, but classical philologists like Wilamovitz-Moellendorf, Norden, E. Schwarz and Reitzenstein[6] who repeatedly ventured

[1] *J.T.S.* vol. XXXVI (1935), p. 45.

[2] *Lehrbuch der Dogmengeschichte* I[4], p. 250.

[3] W. Bousset, *Hauptprobleme der Gnosis* (Göttingen, 1907).

[4] W. Anz, *Ursprung des Gnostizismus* (T.U. 15. 4) (Leipzig, 1897).

[5] E. de Faye, *Gnostiques et Gnosticisme*[2] (Paris, 1925); *Introduction à l'étude du Gnosticisme* (Paris, 1903).

[6] R. Reitzenstein, *Die hellenistischen Mysterienreligionen*[3] (Leipzig, 1927), pp. 66, 285; *Poimandres* (Leipzig, 1904), p. 157.

across the frontiers of classical scholarship to study the religious literature of the Hellenistic and early Christian periods, were all subject to this attraction. Franz Cumont was the greatest master of them all in the study of pagan religions. Of this generation the one most interested in Gnosticism and its relationship to early Christianity was Reitzenstein.

In his early work *Die hellenistischen Mysterienreligionen*, Reitzenstein first showed the peculiar significance attached to *gnosis* in Hellenistic religion and its inheritors. He emphasized its close affinity with current ideas of revelation, dogma, initiation and unity with the supernatural world through the possession and mastery of its secrets. He pointed out that in early Christian literature knowledge involved not only an apprehension of Christian doctrine but also a mystical contact with the Godhead and a consequent increase of spiritual competence and power.

The evolution of Reitzenstein's thought parallels in many respects that of the Viennese historian of art, Strzygowski. Both flitted over the Oriental landscape, pausing now in one country, now in another, contemplating the cultural scene of each and attempting to detect its contribution to Hellenistic civilization. Reitzenstein's field of investigation was Egypt: Philo, the *Corpus Hermeticum*, the magical papyri, and Egyptian Gnosticism, but he soon turned his attention thence to Syria, Babylonia and Persia. In matters of chronology he was singularly cavalier and raised the subjective criticism of documents to a high imaginative art. He saw in the actual *Corpus Hermeticum* the end phase of a long development which had begun and reached its maturity before the beginning of the Christian era.[1] He maintained that its leading ideas were current in the centuries just preceding and following the beginnings of Christianity, so that Hermetic texts could with safety be used to clarify allusions and set the perspectives of early Christian theology. He audaciously rewrote the fragment of a Naassene source embedded in Hippolytus, *Refutatio* v, deleting its Christian references and expounding it in its hypothetical original form as a non-Christian and pre-Christian production.[2] He fastened with zeal upon Lidzbarski's investigation of

[1] *Poimandres*, pp. 35, 248.

[2] *Poimandres*, pp. 83–98; R. Reitzenstein and H. H. Schaeder, *Studien zum antiken Synkretismus* (Leipzig, 1926), p. 161; *J.T.S.* vol. XXVII (1926), p. 374.

Mandean documents and drew Mandeans and all their works and ways into his newly discovered orbit of a pre-Christian *gnosis*, on the periphery of which early Christianity arose,[1] and ideas could be seen as the late offspring of this remote and glittering galaxy. The rewriting of the Naassene document was only the beginning of a series of similar reconstructions. He saw behind the survivals of Mandean literature the outlines of its pre-Christian antecedents. He interpreted the importance attached to John the Baptist in some of the Mandean pieces and the frequency of Mandean baptisms as an indication that Christianity emerged from a sacramental religion with Gnostic theology represented before Jesus by John the Baptist and his disciples.[2] The early history of Mandaeism and the chronology of its literature are in fact obscure, but Reitzenstein found this no obstacle since actual documents could always be explained by their hypothetical archetypes and ancestors. His *chef d'œuvre* was undoubtedly his theory of the literary dependence of the Fourth Gospel on Mandean sources re-edited and reissued as a life of Jesus.[3] In his period of maximum enthusiasm for Persian affinities with Greek, Hellenistic, Jewish and early Christian thought he maintained that Adam and the Gnostic deity Anthropos were Hellenistic reflections of the Avestan Gayomard and regarded the Son of Man in the Gospels as the divine offspring of this remote Oriental deity.[4]

The importance of this development for early Christian scholarship and more particularly for New Testament scholarship was not any one point or series of points made during its course. No one, I fancy, would nowadays take seriously the notion that the Fourth Gospel arose as a Christian adaptation of a Mandean account of John the Baptist. Greater attention is paid to what is actually known of the chronology of the literature at our disposal and of the ideas contained in them, but, in spite of the decisive arguments of Burkitt,[5]

[1] *Das mandäische Buch des Herrn der Größe* (*Heidelberg Sitzungsberichte*, 1919); *Das iranische Erlösungsmysterium* (Bonn, 1921).

[2] C. H. Dodd, *The Interpretation of the Fourth Gospel* (Cambridge, 1953), p. 121; *Das iranische Erlösungsmysterium*, p. 124; R. Bultmann, *Z.N.T.W.* vol. XXIV (1925), p. 100.

[3] *Studien zum antiken Synkretismus*, p. 307; Bultmann, *Z.N.T.W.* vol. XXIV, p. 143; *Eucharisterion* (Gunkel Festschrift), vol. II, p. 1.

[4] *Poimandres*, pp. 81, 108.

[5] *J.T.S.* vol. XXIX (1928), p. 228.

Petermann,[1] Lietzmann,[2] Lagrange[3] and Wilfred Knox,[4] Mandean ghosts haunt the pages of Walter Bauer[5] and Bultmann[6] and even so cautious a scholar as the one to whom this volume is dedicated is loth to abandon the *Hermetica* as a key to Hellenistic religious thought.[7] A general and generalized impression that *gnosis* and Gnosticism were significant factors in the origins of Christianity still widely prevails.

I venture to doubt this thesis and propose to raise questions, the discussion of which may help to clarify the problem and point to its solution. On what particular point was knowledge considered in the New Testament an indispensable asset to a follower of Jesus and in what contexts does it play an important role? What is the evidence for literary and historical connections between the New Testament and Gnosticism?

All religions assert a claim to special knowledge and all religions based on revelation depend on the acceptance of revealed truth as necessary for salvation.[8] Early Christianity derived its notion of revelation from Judaism and accepted the Old Testament as a sacred book, limiting the application of some of its prescriptions to the period before the Incarnation and gradually supplementing it by a sacred literature of its own. This combination of Jewish and Christian Scriptures was the primary source of Christian *gnosis* in the first three centuries of the Christian era. The consequences of this are so familiar to us that we do not always appreciate what it signified to the early Christian convert. To the Jew it meant the abrogation of a part of the Torah, the whole of which he had been taught to believe contained a final statement of God's dispositions and requirements. It meant also the acceptance of new teaching and a new perspective of history which the bulk of his nation had violently repudiated. This was not made easier by the intrusion of

[1] *Z.N.T.W.* vol. XXV (1926), p. 236.

[2] *Berlin Sitzungsberichte* (1930), p. 596.

[3] *Revue Biblique*, vol. XXXVI (1927), p. 194; vol. XXXVII (1928), p. 9.

[4] W. L. Knox, *St Paul and the Church of the Gentiles* (Cambridge, 1939), p. 212.

[5] W. Bauer, *Das Johannesevangelium*² (Tübingen, 1925), *passim.*

[6] *Das Evangelium des Johannes* (Göttingen, 1952), *passim.*

[7] *The Bible and the Greeks* (London, 1935), pp. 201, 248; *Fourth Gospel*, p. 10.

[8] F. C. Burkitt, *Church and Gnosis* (Cambridge, 1932), p. 4; H. H. Schaeder, *Urform und Fortbildungen des manichäischen Systems*, Warburg Vorträge IV (Berlin, 1927), p. 99; Reitzenstein, *Vorgeschichte der christlichen Taufe* (Berlin, 1929), p. 96.

Gentile elements in Christian theology. Any Jew could follow with ease and understanding the arguments of Romans and Galatians, though he might not agree with their conclusions. The cosmology of Colossians and Ephesians, the christocentric universe described in Philippians and the peculiar outlook and terminology of the Johannine writings were a different matter.[1] Even a Jew who had gone far down the road marked out by Philo would have had his difficulties there and might have felt that becoming a Christian meant to an uncomfortable degree becoming a Gentile.

The Gentile on the other hand must have been impressed by the extent to which becoming a Christian meant thinking and feeling like a Jew. However much philosophy may have softened the blow, conversion to Christianity involved submission to the Jewish way of conceiving the origins of the universe and much of the history of mankind. The triumph of Christianity meant, among other things, the victory of Jewish over Egyptian, Persian, Thracian and even Greek speculative imagination. To the Jew therefore Christianity must have appeared as an eccentrically Gentile *gnosis*, to the Gentile it must have seemed an eccentrically Jewish one.

The Hellenizing of the earliest forms of Christianity which emerged from apocalyptic Judaism ran, in large measure, a course parallel to the Hellenizing of Pharisaic Judaism. To what extent the one was dependent on the other in the first century A.D. is still a debated and debatable point. Hellenistic Jews like the Pharisees brought the meaning of the Old Testament up to date and into line with their own thinking but by exegetical devices: the Pharisees by casuistry, the Hellenizers by the allegorical method borrowed from the Stoics. The early Christians employed both means but evinced a marked preference for allegory. Jews and Christians were, however, at one in recognizing the divine origin and redemptive importance of the truth contained in the Old Testament and the necessity of being familiar at least with its rudiments.

Apart from this Jewish heritage, early Christians insisted on other kinds of knowledge important in varying degrees for the understanding and practice of their religion. In following the evolution of these novel ideas it is, however, of the first importance to distinguish between the thoughts which passed between Jesus and his

[1] W. L. Knox, *St Paul and the Church of the Gentiles*, pp. 125ff.

disciples before the crucifixion and early Christian speculation after the resurrection. The latter is reflected in varying degrees in the view of all the authors of the New Testament, the former must be cautiously reconstructed from materials which they provide but did not always understand or accurately interpret.[1]

In the earliest strata of the Synoptic Gospels there is no evidence that Jesus required any more or any different kind of knowledge than was easily available to his Jewish contemporaries. His own views were a combination of Pharisaic theology and apocalyptic. With the Pharisees he held the doctrines of the resurrection of the body and the final judgment and the belief in angels, but differed from them in rejecting the traditions of the Elders, the nucleus of the Unwritten Law which was later to be codified in the Mishnah, and the casuistic treatment of Torah. He pressed the doctrine of particular providence to unusual extremes, at least in relation to his own and his disciples' mission and held independent views on marriage and divorce, Roman taxation, resistance to the government of occupation and the Davidic lineage of the coming Messiah. These, however, constituted no new and compact system of doctrine and did not exceed the amount of originality generally expected of Jewish religious teachers.[2] An opening for a revelation of this kind is recorded in Mark xiii. 3–4 but Jesus took no advantage of it. Instead, he cited a number of conventional disasters and catastrophes as signs of the approaching end, but stated categorically that only God knew the actual time when the Day of the Lord would break.[3] The acceptance of God's sovereignty, however imminent, was in Jesus' view not to be confused with a nice calculation of the margin of safety left for repentance.

It is often maintained that Jesus had a special theory of his own importance and in Caesarea Philippi, before taking the road to Jerusalem, admitted it to his disciples who already had an inkling of it. This is the popular theory of the 'Messianic secret'.[4] In the

[1] F. J. Foakes Jackson and K. Lake, *The Beginnings of Christianity*, vol. I (London, 1920), pp. 300, 322.

[2] L. Zunz, *Die gottesdienstlichen Vorträge der Juden* (Frankfurt a.M., 1892), p. 334 and the material in W. Bacher, *Die Agada der Tannaiten*, 2 Bde. (1884, 1890).

[3] This ignorance is stressed three times (Mark xiii. 32, 33, 35).

[4] The literature is too copious to be listed here. Cf. W. Wrede, *Das Messiasgeheimnis in den Evangelien* (Göttingen, 1901); P. Wendland, *Die hellenistische-römische Kultur*[3] (Tübingen, 1912), p. 269.

Marcan story the incident took place after a period of mounting tension between Jesus and the Jewish authorities, heightened, it appears, by his increasing popularity as a religious teacher among the common folk.[1] In Mark viii. 28 Jesus asks his disciples, 'Whom do men say that I am?' They reply that he was considered by some outside their group as one of the prophets of the Old Testament who had returned, as was expected, in the period just preceding the Day of the Lord. Jesus then asks them what they themselves thought and Peter replies confidently, 'You are the Messiah.' Jesus enjoins them not to discuss him further with others (ἵνα μηδενὶ λέγωσιν περὶ αὐτοῦ) and goes on to explain to them the trials through which he and they must inevitably pass. Peter, reverting to his original theme, reproaches Jesus but is again rebuked, this time more severely: 'Get thee behind me, Satan, for you have no regard for God's concerns but for men's.'

Modern criticism has distorted the Marcan account in two ways. It has been maintained that Jesus covertly acknowledged the Messiahship attributed to him but indicated to the Apostles that its disclosure was for the moment inopportune. It has also assumed that Jesus and the Apostles on this occasion employed the title 'Messiah' in a sense intelligible to Christians of a later generation but unintelligible to Jesus or to most of Jesus' followers at that stage. Peter's avowal brought into the open the 'Messianic secret' which consisted in the knowledge that Jesus was Messiah and that he was Messiah in a sense known only to himself and the Apostles.

'Messiah' means merely the 'Anointed One'[2] and connoted royalty in the same way as the English expression, 'the crowned heads of Europe'. In Western Europe the telling symbol of royalty is the crown, not the anointing which is also a part of the coronation ceremony. In ancient Israel the anointing was the crux of the ceremony of king-making. In Israel a king was expected to rule legitimately and under Yahweh's protection, but when the Jews lost their independence, they were forced to rely on the hope that a prospective ruler would recapture it for them. When the mission of Israel became

[1] F. C. Burkitt, *The Gospel History and its Transmission* (Edinburgh, 1920), pp. 91, 98.

[2] G. F. Moore in *Beginnings*, vol. I, pp. 346ff.; P. Volz, *Jüdische Eschatologie*² (Tübingen, 1934), p. 173.

universalized the sovereignty of the coming ruler was also by implication conceived as universal and supra-national.[1] God's rule and that of his earthly representative, the king of the Jews, would extend over all the peoples of the earth. In apocalyptic Judaism the restoration of Israel was envisaged as the outcome of dramatic divine intervention, even of cosmic catastrophe and the functions of the king were brought into line with the new conception of the future kingdom. Not all systems of apocalyptic Judaism allowed for an earthly ruler but those which did pictured him and his functions in terms appropriate to the realm over which he was to preside.

The notion of a Jewish king who would come and restore Israel's fortunes had implications which could scarcely appeal to the Roman government of occupation, the representatives not of Yahweh's sovereignty but of the *imperium Romanum.* However congenial the thought of an independent Israelite kingdom might be to the minds of the Pharisees and Sadducees, they were political realists. Neither group suffered unduly from the strained economy imposed by the invaders, and the Sadducees were the complacent agents of Rome in maintaining the political *status quo.* Any open display of national aspirations had been severely dealt with by the foreigners, and more than once the zeal of pretenders had worsened the situation and occasioned prompt and severe reprisals. Claims to the kingship of Israel were therefore generally regarded by the middle and upper classes as a danger signal never to be taken lightly and always to be met in a manner which would convince the Roman governors that their authority was not being challenged or their position imperilled.

It is in this context that the incident of Caesarea Philippi, as recounted by Mark, must be understood. Jesus' questions, 'Whom do men say that I am?' and 'Who do you say that I am?' were not designed to evoke an act of faith in his Messiahship, but were grounded in his apprehension lest his real mission be misconceived as a political and nationalistic one. How well justified that apprehension was, was demonstrated by the swiftly moving tragedy at Jerusalem. The failure of the Apostles to heed Jesus' warning, the plaudits of the crowd, perhaps the confirmation of their suspicions by Judas Iscariot decided the issue in the minds of the Pharisees and Sadducees and when the occasion of a public disturbance in the Temple was given

[1] Volz, pp. 66, 78, 380.

by Jesus himself, they seized the opportunity to arrest him, prove their submissive co-operation with Roman rule and secure his condemnation by the Roman authorities as a revolutionary pretender. It is a strange anomaly that an incident so constitutive to the thread and logic of the Marcan narrative should have been misinterpreted as the revelation by Jesus of a 'Messianic secret'. The 'revelation' came not from Jesus but from Peter, and Jesus' reply[1] is scarcely an encouraging confirmation of Peter's declaration. The only *gnosis* to which Jesus attached importance at this point was that hard times lay ahead.

There is, however, one passage in Mark in which Jesus professed to add something new and vital to the accepted content of religious knowledge. This occurs in connection with the healing of the paralytic and the forgiveness of sins.[2] Here Jesus speaks quite categorically, but what he says is neither based on Jewish premises nor in line with Jewish conclusions. When the Jewish theologians objected to his statement to the paralytic, 'Child, your sins are forgiven', he replied, 'Why do you thus reason in your hearts? Which is easier to say to the paralytic, "Child, your sins are forgiven" or "Take up your bed and walk"? But in order that you may know that the Son of Man has power to forgive sins on earth, he said to the paralytic, "Take up your bed and be off to your house".'[3] The use of the expression 'Son of Man' creates a difficulty here, for Mark appears sometimes to substitute the honorific title when it appears more probable that Jesus merely said 'I'[4] and this may well be an instance of Mark's interpretative rendering of Jesus' words. As the passage now stands a claim to be the Son of Man would scarcely have been illuminating to his hearers but would have been highly provocative and would certainly have occasioned protests which Mark confines to the act of forgiveness. Jesus may have absolved the paralytic not on his own authority but on that of the Son of Man's, just as later his disciples were to do so not on their own authority but on his. To the Jews the stumbling-block lay in the claim that anyone could mediate between God and the sinner.

It is significant that in departing so radically from Jewish teaching, Jesus turned, as John the Baptist had turned, in a sacramental direction. The words pronounced by Jesus constituted the matter; the

[1] Mark viii. 30.
[2] Mark ii. 1–12.
[3] Mark ii. 8–11.
[4] *Beginnings*, vol. 1, p. 376.

absolution, the efficacy of which was attested by the cure, was the form. The objection of the Jews to this approach was identical with that implicit in Josephus' forced misrepresentation of John's baptism as unconnected with the forgiveness of sins.[1]

If Mark provides no evidence for a Messianic secret, he has nevertheless a theory about esoteric Christian doctrine which he applies to Jesus' use of parables. After expounding the parable of the Sower to the multitude Mark relates that Jesus retired with his immediate followers (οἱ περὶ αὐτὸν σὺν τοῖς δώδεκα) who ask him its meaning. Before disclosing it he observes, 'You have been permitted to know the secret (μυστήριον) of God's sovereignty but to outsiders all is transmitted in parables in order that seeing they may see yet not perceive and hearing, they may hear yet not understand, lest they change their ways and be forgiven. And he said to them, "You do not understand this parable! How then will you comprehend all the parables?"'

There is more than one arresting feature in this passage. The word μυστήριον occurs nowhere else in Mark and the idea that Jesus' parables served to veil the mystery of God's sovereignty is not suggested elsewhere. It is therefore possible that Mark did not invent it but took it over from one of his sources. The μυστήριον is conceived in purely Jewish terms and an exact parallel is drawn between the delivery of Jesus' apocalyptic message and that of Isaiah's prophetic announcement.[2] In both cases only the few who were pre-ordained to salvation would grasp the essential meaning of what was said. The pagan mysteries were wrapped in hidden formulae but here, as in Isaiah, plain words were to be proclaimed from the housetops; their sense would be clear only to the elect.

Throughout the Synoptic Gospels it is clear that Jesus used parables to illuminate, not to obscure, his meaning, but in this one passage Mark would have it otherwise, and unhappily illustrates his theory of esoteric teaching by a parable transparent without its belaboured explanation and involving no intricate theological or eschatological

[1] *Beginnings*, vol. I, p. 105. 'Εφ' ἁγνείᾳ τοῦ σώματος does not, however, mean merely to get clean. Josephus presents John's baptism as a ceremonial lustration like those practised by the Essenes (*B.J.* II. 8. 7 καθαρωτέρων τῶν πρὸς ἁγνείαν ὑδάτων μεταλάμβανει) and Bannus, a figure similar to John the Baptist (*Vita*, 11), who bathed frequently in cold water day and night πρὸς ἁγνείαν.

[2] Isa. vi. 9–10.

point.[1] The ensuing conversation with the disciples is the only instance in Mark of a highly artificial and implausible exchange between Jesus and his friends. The parable states the obvious fact that when God's sovereignty is proclaimed and the Day of the Lord has been announced as imminent, a few will welcome the news but the majority, for one reason or another, will not profit by it. No one of the classes distinguished in the parable contains those who see but do not perceive and hear but do not understand. The seed sown on bad ground represents those who see and perceive, hear and understand. Their defects are not of the mind but of the will. They lack not vision but concentrated effort and perseverance. It is obvious that the parable and the parabolic theory in which it has been imbedded are of quite different origin. The parable is Jesus' own, the theory reflects the disillusionment which the falling away of the multitudes who at first thronged about Jesus occasioned either in Mark's mind or in that of his source. It is tempting to see in it Peter's reaction to the ups and downs of early missionary preaching.

In reporting Jesus' teaching Mark for the most part assumes Jewish premises and arrives at conclusions intelligible only in terms of Jewish theology. Two passages—one peculiar to Matthew, the other belonging to Q, mark the transition from a Jewish conception of religious knowledge to a specifically Christian one.

In reporting the incident at Caesarea Philippi Matthew departs from the Marcan text before him and substitutes another version of Jesus' reply to Peter in which a Messianic secret is disclosed. Instead of rebuking Peter for claiming him to be Messiah Jesus responds, 'Blessed art thou, Simon Bar Jonah. Flesh and blood has not revealed this to you but my Father in Heaven.' Here indeed *gnosis* is revealed; a truth which had until that point been hidden was proclaimed under inspiration. This *gnosis*, however, required a change in the meaning of the word 'Messiah'. In Mark the usage is Jewish, in Matthew it is Christian, for Matthew had in mind a public which was already thinking, at least on this point, in Christian not in Jewish terms. A corner has been turned and, as is the case more than once in Matthew, the expectation of a restored Israel appears fulfilled by the reality of the nascent Church.

[1] C. H. Dodd, *Parables of the Kingdom*[3] (1936), p. 13; A. Jülicher, *Die Gleichnisreden Jesu*, vol. II (1910), p. 514.

The second passage which marks the transition from a Jewish to a Christian view of religious knowledge is found in Q. It is the much debated logion on the Father's knowledge of the Son and the Son's knowledge of the Father (Matt. xi. 27 = Luke x. 22). The most valiant critical attempt to regard this as a genuine saying of Jesus has been made by Harnack,[1] but has not met with general acceptance. The Matthean text appears to represent the more advanced theology; the Lucan might be interpreted as in some sense 'adoptionist'. The crux of the matter lies in the meaning of 'knowledge'. One possibility, favoured by the Lucan text, is that only the Father knew who the Son really was, i.e. whom he had chosen for this role: and only the Son, Jesus, was in a position to affirm that the only true God was Yahweh. The other possibility, favoured by the Matthean text, is that the Father's and the Son's knowledge of each other involved a mystical union between the two. Such is the relationship envisaged by the Fourth Gospel which also depends on knowledge. The Matthean text of the logion in Q seems to hold this doctrine in embryo.[2] If the question is raised which text, Matthew's or Luke's, is the original, preference should probably be given to the latter. In it the individualities of the Father and the Son are more distinct and therefore more in agreement with Jewish thinking. The knowledge is also no more than acquaintance with the facts, and would imply no mystical or metaphysical relationship. The Matthean text is a kind of spark in the development of a christology which leads through the later Pauline Epistles to the Johannine literature.

There is little reliable information about what the earliest Christians hoped or were required to 'know' about the objects of their faith. The main thing they must know was that Jesus was other than had been supposed either by his own followers during his lifetime or by the Jews who had been hostile to him. The trial and crucifixion had sealed the latter's conviction that Jesus was a dangerous revolutionary whose subversive activities had been nipped in the bud. The former no doubt held differing views but the majority of them had believed

[1] *The Sayings of Jesus* (Eng. trans. London, 1908), p. 272; E. Norden, *Agnostos Theos*, pp. 290, 395.

[2] M.-J. Lagrange, *St. Matthieu*[2] (Paris, 1923), p. 228, insists that 'ἐπιγινώσκει employé deux fois par Mt. ne dit plus que γινώσκει τίς ἐστιν qui paraît même plus réfléchi', but there is a difference between the ability to identify and real acquaintance.

either that he was an aspirant to kingship whose revolutionary plans had failed or that he was one of the Prophets returned before the End, as had been foretold. Few Gentiles had held any views about him at all. Pilate seems to have been sceptical of the charges brought against him, but no doubt dismissed him from his mind as a fanatical teacher whose political significance had been exaggerated by the Jewish authorities but who, as a controversial figure with a large following among the masses, was better out of the way. The centurion at the foot of the cross is reported by Mark to have been impressed by Jesus' heroism and serenity and to have declared, 'Truly this is God's Son' (Mark xv. 39), a statement the meaning of which in the mouth of a Roman officer is difficult to fathom.[1] Not many Jews or Gentiles knew the details of the Passion and both were either ignorant of the claim that Jesus had risen from the dead or were unimpressed by it.

The resurrection appearances and the reassembling of the Apostles and their sympathizers in Jerusalem, followed by similar movements in other localities and the rise of the Gentile mission, created a new situation which required new explanations to justify it. Paul threw down the gauntlet to Jews and Gentiles alike when he wrote defiantly, 'We proclaim a crucified King, a bewilderment to the Jews and an idiocy to the Gentiles but to the elect, both Jews and Gentiles, a King who is God's power and God's wisdom.'[2] All Christians would have subscribed to this statement but differed among themselves when this central conviction came to be developed in detail. The earliest stages of thought are extremely obscure because of the scarcity and tendentiousness of our sources. The apocalyptic title 'Son of Man', was generally ascribed to Jesus but we are imperfectly informed of its exact shades of meaning.[3] Jesus was also called 'Messiah' (in Greek Χριστός) but the original significance of the

[1] The difficulty disappears if the remark be regarded as Mark's invention, in which case Jesus' divine Sonship must be related to the descent of the Spirit at the Baptism and his appointment to the tasks divinely set him. To a Jew the phrase would naturally mean, 'Truly this was an angel'; to a Gentile it might mean a hero of semi-divine origin.

[2] I Cor. i. 23–4.

[3] Volz, *Jüdische Eschatologie*², p. 186; W. Bousset, *Kyrios Christos*² (Göttingen, 1921), pp. 5, 14, 103; *Beginnings*, vol. 1, p. 368; G. Dalman, *The Words of Jesus* (Eng. trans. Edinburgh, 1909), p. 234.

term was either forgotten or ignored, and it is used in Acts and the Epistles as little more than a synonym for 'the Son of Man'.[1] The last of the resurrection appearances was dramatized in Acts by the ascension which preceded the Spirit's descent on the Apostles, the nucleus of the Church, but Matthew, Paul and John appear to have known nothing of this. In Matthew the Church was founded not on the Spirit but on Peter and the disciples were directed by the risen Jesus to go out and baptize all nations forthwith.[2] For Paul, the Lord after the resurrection was the Spirit[3] and the Spirit was conveyed by baptism to Christians who constituted the Church.[4] In the Fourth Gospel Jesus foretells the Spirit's descent on Christians[5] but does not localize it in one single dramatic action, as Luke does. In one of the Johannine resurrection appearances Jesus breathes Spirit on the Apostles and gives them power to remit or retain sins.[6] In the two following appearances Jesus is recognized for what he is but Peter is left not with the assurance that he is the rock on which the Church will be built but with an injunction to exercise the pastoral office. 'Feed my sheep.' 'Feed my lambs.' All these theories belonged in the first instance to different theologies and did not represent complementary aspects of one. The common feature was that the foundation of Jesus' life, death and resurrection was supernatural. This was the central fact which a Christian must know and accept, if he was to be saved but it was not the only one.

The total content of saving knowledge in early Christianity has been described in recent years as apostolic *kerygma* or teaching. Both terms appear in the sources but they have been used by some critics in such a way as to imply that the presentation of Christian doctrine both to those inside the Church and to prospective converts was uniform. This is a view which cannot be substantiated from the evidence. Within the New Testament there are specimens of early Christian preaching only in Acts and of dogmatic instruction in portions of the Epistles and in the Fourth Gospel. In Acts the addresses are attributed variously to Peter, Stephen and Paul but are in fact Lucan compositions. Their content may represent more or less what Peter, Stephen and Paul might have said under the given

[1] Bousset, *Kyrios Christos*[2], pp. 17, 33 ff.
[2] Matt. xxviii. 19. [3] II Cor. iii. 17. [4] *Beginnings*, vol. I, p. 337.
[5] John xvi. 7, 13. [6] John xx. 22–3.

circumstances, but they are not stenographic reports and opinion differs considerably on their relationship to speeches actually made.[1] They are improvisations like the speeches of Jesus in the Fourth Gospel and serve as the vehicle of a Lucan Christian *gnosis*, just as the speeches in John expound a Johannine *gnosis*.

The first bit of instruction in Acts is given not by one of the Apostles but to them by an angel, who announces at the Ascension that Jesus will return from heaven in the same manner as he has been seen to enter it. In the first speech attributed to Peter[2] his hearers are admonished to see in the betrayal and in the necessity for appointing a successor to Judas Iscariot the fulfilment of Old Testament prophecy. In the longer address at Pentecost the descent of the Spirit on the Apostles,[3] the miracles of Jesus, his death, resurrection and ascension are described as events foretold in the Old Testament and the conclusion is drawn that God has appointed Jesus Lord and Christ. In this dual capacity he has been raised from the dead, sits at God's right hand and has fulfilled the Father's promise by pouring out the Spirit on the Apostles. This complex of ideas is a mixture of reflections on Jesus' miracles, the Resurrection, the Lucan view of Pentecost and the apocalyptic notion of the Son of Man. At the conclusion of his address Peter enjoins repentance, baptism in the Name of the Lord Jesus for the remission of sins, and promises as a consequence the gift of the Spirit and salvation. All this is represented as news to his hearers, indispensable knowledge for all those who wished to be saved.

The next address ascribed to Peter in Acts iii. 12ff. resumes the theme of the passion, death and resurrection of Jesus. Instead of being a thwarted revolutionary, as the Jews had supposed, Jesus had carried out God's design, foretold by the prophets, and was the ἀρχηγὸς τῆς ζωῆς, the foreordained Messiah, the child of God. Repentance is again enjoined but no mention is made of baptism.

The speech ascribed to Stephen in Acts vii. 2ff. is a long one and is not properly a missionary address but, like that of Peter in

[1] Cadbury in *Beginnings*, vol. v, p. 402. Cf. Dodd, *Apostolic Preaching*, p. 30.

[2] Acts i. 16ff.

[3] Dodd rightly draws the distinction between κήρυγμα and διδαχή (*The Apostolic Preaching*, London, 1939, pp. 1ff.), but it would appear to apply more to the spirit in which instruction was sometimes given than to the form or the occasion.

Acts iv. 8ff., is a reply to his accusers and judges. It contains an interpretation of Old Testament history roughly parallel to those in Romans and Hebrews. At the end there is a brief allusion to Jesus as 'the Righteous One' whom the Jews had betrayed. As he was being stoned to death, however, Stephen experienced a vision and exclaimed, 'Lo, I see the heavens opened and the Son of Man seated at God's right hand.' Here the title 'Son of Man' appears in its traditional apocalyptic setting.

In his instruction to Cornelius, Peter makes the following points: that Jesus' mission was not to the Jews only but to all who were acceptable to God; that he was Christ and Lord of all; that he was baptized with John's baptism, came from Nazareth, was 'anointed' by God with the Holy Spirit and with power and had healed those who were under the devil's sway; that God had been with him; that the Apostles had been witnesses of his deeds in Judaea and Jerusalem; that he had been crucified but that God had raised him on the third day and revealed him not to all the Jews but to foreordained witnesses, viz. the Apostles, who had eaten and drunk with him after his resurrection; and finally that he had directed the Apostles to testify to the people that he had been appointed by God judge of the living and the dead. The prophets had all borne witness that everyone who believed in Jesus would receive remission of their sins 'by his Name', i.e. by baptism.

An analysis of this fragment of apostolic teaching is instructive. The description of Jesus' activities is a summary of events already described in the Gospel of Luke. The titles 'Christ' and 'Lord' are juxtaposed as in Acts ii. 36 and the Spirit is associated with power as in Luke xxiv. 49. The divine anointing which made Jesus the Anointed One and enabled him to perform miracles is the Baptism. The appointments of Jesus and of the Apostles were both features of God's plan; the one assigned to Jesus the functions attributed to the Son of Man, the other led to the apostolic mission, the acceptance of Christ, the forgiveness of sins and initiation through baptism into the sacramental life. The notion that Jesus' mission was not to the Jews only but to the elect is characteristically Lucan. Here is the skeleton of Christian *gnosis* as conceived by Luke. Its attribution to Peter is merely a literary device. That such a body of knowledge essential to Christians existed and that the Apostles had been trained and commissioned to transmit it is affirmed by Luke in xxiv. 46 and Acts i. 3.

In Paul's address in the synagogue at Pisidian Antioch a similar use is made of materials derived from Luke's Gospel. Jesus' descent from David affects his Messiahship; he is Israel's promised Saviour but 'Paul' includes the 'God-fearers' in his appeal. The familiar insistence on the interpretation of Jesus' death in the light of the resurrection and on its significance for the remission of sin recurs. In view of the setting of the speech the absence of Christian titles for Jesus is not surprising.

The knowledge required of Christians in Acts was, however, not confined to ideas; it included an acquaintance with the significance of sacramental acts. Luke's sacramental views and those of his sources were not always identical and Luke did not always edit his sources into conformity with his own convictions. Both, however, reckoned with sacraments and both regarded their administration and comprehension as essential to life in the Spirit. Baptism, the laying on of hands, healing, active membership in the Christian community, participation in its devotional life and the breaking of bread, all these were channels of the Holy Spirit's beneficent influence. Simon Magus perceived the value of this kind of *gnosis* and thinking it to be some hidden form of magic, offered to purchase its secrets.

If Acts presents us with anything like a fair picture of apostolic teaching, it must be concluded that its exponents varied considerably in their views of what was necessary to hold and practise. They were as much concerned with sound teaching about the Church and the sacraments as they were with the redemptive significance of the Passion and resurrection and they were equally preoccupied with sacramental and ecclesiastical administration. Paul and his converts paid scant attention to the Jesus of history, but Acts x. 37–42, Papias' account of Peter's addresses, and the Gospels themselves, show that this was an idiosyncrasy of the Pauline gospel, offset by Peter and no doubt the rest of the Twelve.[1]

Paul no less than Luke was aware of the importance of knowledge

[1] Cf. Acts ii. 22, iii. 22. It is curious how Peter stands out in the available evidence as the protagonist of the Jesus of history. It may be suspected that his 'gospel' is more faithfully reproduced in Mark than in the speeches in Acts. Cf. Dodd, *Apostolic Preaching*, pp. 57, 63.

to the Christian profession. His own experience had caused him to change his mind about Jesus and most of his Christian career was spent in changing the minds of others in the same direction. His conception of Christian knowledge was, however, more subtle and more highly differentiated than Luke's. He was acutely conscious that his theology differed substantially from that of many of his Christian contemporaries, some of whom had known Jesus in the flesh but he did not hesitate to impose his own views upon his converts and charges with doctrinaire insistence. If there was one thing of which he was convinced, it was that his gospel, the good news as he had received, formulated and proclaimed it, was the only adequate one.

Paul, however, seems to have regarded it as natural that his εὐαγγέλιον should evoke responses of different kinds in those who received it: σοφία, the practical wisdom it inculcated and encouraged, πίστις, the confident grasp of its content, and γνῶσις, its deeper understanding and assimilation. Γνῶσις is the theoretical apprehension of the Gospel and its implications but like all Paul's terminology, it is never merely abstract.[1] Knowledge is mediated by the Spirit and is therefore a factor in the living relationship between man and God. It does more than reveal; it confronts and unites. Paul's gospel is a part of himself but it is also a part of his experience of God which he transmitted to others and shared with them. Knowledge, however, plays a role of its own in the total Christian experience, seeks its own objects and deals with them in its own way. Anything that is revealed by God commands the assent of the Christian mind, the Old Testament first of all, the misapprehension of which had left the Jews without excuse, for to them had been committed the oracles of God. But the Spirit chose to illuminate minds in the present as well as in the past. The Incarnation added to knowledge and much depended on its acceptance and right understanding. The Church was the Second Body of Christ and inasmuch as Christians were members of this body they must keep in harmony with it. The outlines of Christian truth were emerging ever more clearly from the background of tradition, and Christian minds must contribute to this process and become a part of it. Special revelations were not unknown. Paul had had more than one. Glossolaly was a current

[1] Paul's usage even of key words is not always consistent.

indication of the revealing activity of the Spirit. Paul did not question its validity but insisted on its interpretation at public worship, that edification might be better served.[1]

For Paul, however, Christian knowledge could be expounded with varying degrees of assurance and with different degrees of authority. On the basis partly of ecclesiastical tradition and partly of inner criteria which he does not elucidate[2] he distinguished between what he had 'received from the Lord'[3] and what he regarded as plausible good sense.[4] The former included not only doctrine but also sacramental regulations.

In I Cor. xi he congratulates the Corinthians for holding fast the traditions he had transmitted to them but criticizes the manner in which they celebrated the Eucharist. They treated it like an ordinary meal, brought what they could severally afford without regard to the feelings of others and ate and drank what they liked, sometimes to excess. All this was consonant with the conventions of pagan feasts dedicated to the gods but Paul points out that it was one thing to eat at the table of the Lord, another to eat at the table of demons.[5] If Christians wished merely to dine together they were to do it at home. The Eucharist was another matter. 'For I received of the Lord that which I also handed on to you, that the Lord Jesus in the night in which he was betrayed took bread and having given thanks broke it and said "This is my body which is ⟨given⟩ for you, do this in remembrance of me." Likewise also the cup after supper saying, "This cup is the new covenant in my blood. Do this, as oft as ye

[1] I Cor. xiv. 23. K. Lake, *The Earlier Epistles of St Paul* (London, 1914), pp. 208, 241.

[2] The combined sense of otherness and unity which the sense of interaction between human personalities and divine influences produces has always proved difficult to describe. The simplest notion is that of possession in which the god or demon takes over the human personality and either suppresses it and replaces its activities by his own or dominates it to a lesser but still noticeable degree. In Judaism this view proved inadequate as theology became more refined. Ordinary prophets had their familiar spirits but the Spirit of the Lord was Yahweh himself and contact with him was a more majestic experience. For Paul the Lord, i.e. Christ, was the Spirit but this explained only some aspects of the inner relationship between Christ and the Christian. Paul, like the Prophets, appears to have had an intuitive perception of the difference between usual and charismatic states of mind, but like them he failed to produce an illuminating account of this difference.

[3] I Cor. vii. 10, xi. 23.

[4] I Cor. vii. 12, 35, x. 15.

[5] I Cor. x. 21.

drink ⟨it⟩ in remembrance of me."' This text contains no admonitions as to how the Corinthians were to mend their ways. It is evidently a reminder that at the Eucharist they were present at a solemn rite in which the Last Supper was re-enacted. Comparison of I Cor. xi. 23–5 with Mark xiv. 22–4 shows the former in all probability to be a liturgical text, a fragment of an early Canon. Paul continues with an exposition of Eucharistic doctrine in which he says, 'As often as you eat this bread and drink this cup, you proclaim the Lord's death till he come.'[1] The point of the words of Institution is that the death of Jesus was not to be in vain but would constitute the new covenant on which the Church rooted its claim to be Israel's successor to the promises of God. The eating and drinking of the Elements in which Christ's presence could be spiritually discerned proclaimed the true significance of Christ's sacrificial death, reaffirmed the covenant and united participants in the rite with both.

The word καταγγέλλειν means 'to proclaim' and is practically synonymous with κηρύσσειν. It has been recently maintained that the proclamation to which Paul here refers was not made by the liturgical acts of eating and drinking and by the recitation of the Words of Institution but by Scripture readings accompanying the ceremony.[2] Advocates of the theory that Passion narratives circulated before our Gospels were compiled urge that these were read at gatherings like those described in I Cor. xi and contained the proclamation of the Lord's death till he come.[3] If this be so, it is curious that self-examination (I Cor. xi. 28) and the discernment of the Lord's Body, the recognition of Christ's presence in the Elements, is connected so directly with the act of communion. Some offenders who had consumed the Sacred Species unworthily had sickened and died. It is not suggested that they died of inattention or disrespect during the reading of Proto-Q.

The Eucharist is, however, not the only sacrament the knowledge and understanding of which Paul regards as essential to the Christian profession. His teaching about baptism is also an integral part of his

[1] I Cor. xi. 26.

[2] J. Schniewind in G. Kittel's *Theologisches Wörterbuch zum Neuen Testament*, vol. 1 (Stuttgart, 1933), p. 69; H. Lietzmann, *Messe und Herrenmahl*, Arbeiten zur Kirchengeschichte 8 (Bonn, 1926), p. 222 n. 1.

[3] C. H. Dodd, *History and the Gospel* (London, 1938), p. 82.

gospel. The formula was in the Name of Jesus[1] and its effect was also to unite participants in the rite with the sacrificial death and triumphant resurrection of their Lord. In baptism the historical drama of redemption was repeated in the inner life of the believers.

A third sacrament described by Paul is Holy Matrimony.[2] Here no ritual prescriptions are given and Catholic doctrine has remained true to the primitive view of Christian marriage in affirming that both its matter and form inhered in the union of the contracting parties in love. This union was, however, no ordinary conjunction of the sexes. It was infused with a supernatural and sacramental quality, the closest analogy to which was the union of Christ and his Church. In both cases the bond was sacramental love, so that matrimony could be regarded as a special and intensified instance of that embracing affection which united all Christians with each other and with God.

The greatest sacrament of all in Paul's view was the Church itself.[3] Christ was its head, the faithful were its members, faith, hope, understanding and love constituted the fibre of its being and conditioned all its actions. This is the main theme of the Epistle to the Colossians in which cosmology, christology, sacraments, ritual and moral prescriptions all stem from the central conviction that the Church is the Body of Christ, a living organism of which the elect are functioning members. This is the heart of the mystery which has been revealed, the point of the proclamation, the burden of the teaching, the essence of Christian *gnosis* that only in this corporate social union with Christ can men achieve completeness.[4] Paul insisted that his gospel depended not on human conjecture but on divine revelation, whether mediated by tradition or by special revelation or by sanctified reflection. Paul leaves no doubt about the credentials he attaches to his message, 'For I would have you know, my brethren, that the gospel preached by me is not any man's version nor did I receive it from any human being nor was I taught it but I came by it through Jesus Christ's revelation.'[5] This revelation first burst upon the Apostle's mind in the vision described in Gal. i. 15–16, but it was not

[1] I Cor. i. 13, 15; Acts ii. 38; *Beginnings*, vol. 1, p. 335.

[2] I Cor. vii. 1–17; Col. iii. 18–19; Eph. v. 22–3.

[3] Rom. xii. 5; I Cor. xii. 12ff.; E. Mersch, *Le corps mystique du Christ*², vol. 1 (Bruxelles, 1936), p. 148; Bousset, *Kyrios Christos*², p. 116.

[4] Col. i. 13ff.

[5] Gal. i. 11–12.

confined to any one experience. It widened and deepened during the sojourn in Arabia and in the course of the missionary journeys; it was enriched and clarified by the illuminating years of pastoral experience and responsibility.

We have so far dealt with the absolute component in Paul's conception of Christian knowledge. He had, however, the great merit of distinguishing between what presented itself as a certainty to the Christian mind and what could only be judged by Christian good sense.[1] In dealing with the vexed questions of the care of 'virgins',[2] Paul admits that he has no commandment from the Lord but is willing to express his opinion as a loyal believer. So, too, in his moral instructions, the principles on which his prescriptions rest are dogmatic and gnostic but his recommendations are offered as natural deductions from the truth revealed.

In the last analysis, however, Paul recognizes that the *gnosis* of the Church militant could only be partial and approximate. In his sweeping definition of the Christian ethos in I. Cor. xiii, love is the link which binds limited earthly experience with the full vision of the truth which is to come. 'Then I shall know, even as also I am known.' The inadequacy of prophesies will be shown up, babbling glossolalies will cease, the limitations of *gnosis* will become apparent. Trust and hope will be superfluous, for all uncertainty will be done away. Only love will remain when that which is perfect is come and Christ will be all in all.

The outstanding features of Christian *gnosis* in the Johannine writings are its close association with the Incarnation and its relevance for salvation. The Christ of the Fourth Gospel is essentially a revealer and the elect are distinguished by their knowledge and acceptance of Christian doctrine. In this Gospel Jesus begins his ministry by attaching to himself disciples of John who are impressed by the superiority of his teaching.[3] He reveals his unity with the Father

[1] I Cor. vii. 12, 17. The ruling on divorce derives from revelation but the solution of the problem of mixed marriages rests on Paul's own decision.

[2] Lake, *Earlier Epistles*, p. 184. The question as to what was meant here by 'virgins' has never been satisfactorily answered. The difficulties seem to be most satisfactorily resolved by the assumption that they were young wards entrusted to men of senior years and mature discretion. An exact parallel to the situation envisaged in I Cor. vii. 36–8 is found in the Protevangelium of James 8–16.

[3] John i. 37.

and tells his disciples that they have seen the Father in him.[1] He foretells the coming of the Holy Spirit as his representative on earth and guardian of the Christian tradition.[2] He discloses his mission to the elect and explains that the unity of the Godhead extends to those predestined to salvation.[3] He discourses at length on dogmatic questions and reveals the nature and mysterious operation of the sacraments in terms baffling to the Jews and even to his own disciples. 'Unless a man be born again of water and the Spirit, he cannot enter into the kingdom of God.'[4] 'Unless ye eat the flesh of the Son of Man and drink his blood you have no life in you. He who eats my Flesh and drinks my Blood has eternal life and I will raise him up at the last day.'[5] In spite of the eschatological references this language would have been unintelligible to Jews and out of context at the stage of Christian development to which they are assigned. The author of the Fourth Gospel, however, does not present the mind of Christ as a Jewish mind but as a Christian mind steeped in later Pauline thought and deeply impregnated with sacramentalism.[6]

Γινώσκειν is used not only more frequently in the Fourth Gospel and in I John than in other writings of the New Testament but also with characteristic meanings.[7] It describes a grasp of the truth which neither the world nor the Jews possess. It is used of Jesus' knowledge of the Father and the Father's knowledge of him, a usage reminiscent of the logion in Q.[8] It is used also of Jesus' foreknowledge of events[9] and his ability to distinguish the elect from others who were not included in the plan of salvation.[10] It not only implies factual knowledge but establishes a bond of intimacy and union between the knower and the known. Oddly enough, although γινώσκειν is a key word in Johannine vocabulary, the noun γνῶσις is never once used. This is perhaps due to a certain dynamic quality, a kind of vivacity in the Johannine conception of religion. In spite of the author's fondness for semi-philosophical abstractions like life, light and

[1] John x. 30; xii. 45; xiv. 7–8.
[2] John xiv. 16, 26.
[3] John xv. 4ff.
[4] John iii. 5.
[5] John vi. 53–4.
[6] The most striking difference between the Synoptic and Johannine pictures of Jesus lies not in details but in their presentation of his personality as a whole. The Jesus of Mark and the Jesus of John are quite different persons.
[7] Dodd, *Fourth Gospel*, p. 151.
[8] John x. 15; xvii. 25. See above, p. 63.
[9] John ii. 25; vi. 6.
[10] John x. 14, 27.

truth,[1] his abstractions are implausible and unsustained and are translated promptly into movement and the flow of events: Jesus' dramatic life, death and resurrection, the practice of the Christian religion, its active inner life and its concrete expression in sacramental worship.

The Johannine view of Christian knowledge is the most luminous and richly developed in the New Testament. As in Paul three factors are constitutive in it: the truth revealed in the Old Testament, the truth revealed currently in the Church by valid Christian experience and the guidance of the Holy Spirit, the truth revealed in the sacraments. Each carries with it its own realization and mode of representation in the history of the chosen people, in the new phase of redemptive activity initiated by the Incarnation and sustained by the Spirit's operation in the Church and in the sacraments in which the lives of the elect and the life of Christ merge in a sense detrimental to the integrity of neither.

A brief word must be added on the knowledge made available in the Apocalypse of John. This disquieting document has caused much searching of hearts in recent criticism. A generation ago it was still possible to regard Revelation as a work of scissors and paste which included (1) the seven introductory letters; (2) the central action, the apocalypse proper, which differed as little from similar compositions by Jews and Christians that it, like Mark xiii, might be conjectured to be an originally Jewish source retouched by Christian hands; and (3) an editorial conclusion. R. H. Charles' monumental work was the last great effort in this direction.[2] But as has happened with each of the Johannine writings perplexities have remained. The style is not merely barbarous but eccentric, the vocabulary contains characteristically Johannine elements which distract the reader's attention from the more conventional apocalyptic imagery. There are disconcerting glints of thought not wholly in keeping with the rambling imagination exhibited by Enoch, the Ascension of Isaiah, the Apocalypse of Peter or the Visio Pauli. Could it be that in substance and in manner the author has evolved an idiom of symbolism

[1] Dodd, *Fourth Gospel*, pp. 201, 318ff.; Bousset, *Kyrios Christos*[2], p. 172; J. Grill, *Untersuchungen über die Entstehung des vierten Evangeliums*, vol. 1 (Tübingen, 1902), pp. 206ff.

[2] R. H. Charles, *Revelation of St John*, International Critical Commentary (Edinburgh, 1920).

in which the imaginative forms serve as the vehicle of profound sense? Allo and Farrer both think so and have produced a strong case for their view. Allo's study of the language[1] and Farrer's suggestive interpretation of the ideas[2] encourage a suspense of critical judgment and a broader view of the psychology of the whole piece. It is one of many indications that the Johannine riddle will be solved only after the point of the entire Johannine corpus has been discovered. It is enough for our purpose to draw attention to current doubts and novel approaches to this vexed question and to note that if the Revelation of the Patmos seer is more than ordinary apocalyptic, it has proved a less acceptable and convincing version of Christian *gnosis* than is offered by the Fourth Gospel and the three Epistles. The reserves with which its candidacy for canonical status has been met reinforce the critic's caution in dealing with its literary and exegetical problems.

We must now turn to another question of equal delicacy: What is the relation, if any, of the literature and thought of the New Testament to those of the movement commonly called 'Gnosticism'? This term describes not an ancient but a modern historical category and its fluctuating use has often confused issues.[3] The early Church was familiar with heretics and schismatics as people who rejected Catholic truth and broke away from Catholic discipline but drew no distinction in kind between an Arius, a Sabellius or a Paul of Samosata and a Valentinus, a Marcion or a Basilides. The modern use of 'Gnosticism' to denote a particular development of religious thought has, however, a practical use, if employed to distinguish aberrances from the Catholic norm in points of detail from rival systems which challenged Christian theology on a broad front. Such were the systems of Marcion, Valentinus, Basilides and a host of others, some of whom were founders or continuators of sects, some of whom were mere theosophical pamphleteers. Direct evidence for the existence of such rival systems is contemporary with the rise of Catholic systematic theology and appears to be connected with it.

[1] A. B. Allo, *Saint Jean. L'Apocalypse* (Paris, 1933), pp. cxlv, cxcix.

[2] A. Farrer, *A Rebirth of Images* (London, 1949). Cf. Allo, *op. cit.* pp. xxxvff.

[3] In the following paragraphs I have made liberal use of two articles I have already published: *J.T.S.* vol. XXXVI (1935), p. 45; *J.T.S.* vol. XXIX (1928), p. 40.

The history of first century and pre-Christian Gnosticism has been reconstructed by conjecture from later evidence. The approximate dates of the earliest Gnostic teachers of note are known: Marcion (in Rome 139), Valentinus (135–60), Basilides (120–45), all figures little earlier than the middle of the second century. The heresiologists' genealogies of these systems list their supposed antecedents and descendants, but are artificial schemes which derive ultimately from Justin's lost Syntagma. Neither it nor its elaborations possess much historical value and they are often contradicted by the fragmentary Gnostic sources which have survived. The Hermetic literature which has served as the basis for so many venturesome hypotheses, is in its present form scarcely earlier than the third century[1] and was compiled, if not composed *in toto*, to serve the interests of a particular sect the earlier history of which is not known. The Mandean literature in its present form is post-Islamic; the origins of the sect are assigned on good evidence to the fifth century.[2] Lietzmann has demonstrated the influence of Syriac Christian liturgy on the Mandean baptismal formulae[3] and Burkitt has pointed out that the Mandeans were acquainted with the Peshitto.[4] This is the evidence on which the hypothetical reconstruction of early Christian and pre-Christian Gnosticism is based.

A second line has been pursued in the history of philosophy in the Hellenistic and early Christian periods. Social and economic insecurity under the rule of the Diadochoi and later of the Romans, especially in the Near East, encouraged a return to religion and a disposition to asceticism. The lack of confidence in the normal processes of history which produced apocalyptic Judaism in Palestine, was paralleled elsewhere by a lack of confidence in the normal processes of thought and this accounts for the philosophical stirrings subsumed under the heading 'Neo-Pythagoreanism'. Revelation supplied the deficiencies of the natural reason. Ideas were held in

[1] The date of the Hermetic literature remains uncertain (Dodd, *The Bible and the Greeks*, p. 201; W. Kroll, 'Hermes Trismegistos', in *Realencyclopaedie der klassischen Altertumswissenschaft*; J. Kroll, *Die Lehren des Hermes Trismegistos* (Münster, 1894); R. P. Festugière, *La révélation d'Hermès Trismégiste* (Paris, 1949–50).

[2] A. Loisy, *Le mandéisme* (Paris, 1934), p. 19.

[3] *Berlin Sitzungsberichte* (1930), p. 596.

[4] *J.T.S.* vol. XXIX (1928), p. 228.

common by sectarian groups and sanctified by association with ritual acts and with public and private devotion. There was a marked tendency to reduce the philosophically abstract to the religiously concrete but unlike early Christianity there was little originality, little freshness and no greatness in these attempts. Some of the catchwords of these eclectic forms of speculation found their way into the later New Testament literature, notably the Johannine corpus, but even John was groping for words and forms of thought by which the new Christian experience could be made articulate and it is not surprising that the experience consistently transcended its expression. The knowledge proclaimed by the historic Jesus or conveyed by the Johannine Christ has little resemblance with the laboured allegories of Philo and Cornutus or the dismal encounters of the devotees of the *Hermetica* and the magical papyri with their gods. The early Christians were committed to sacramental worship but this did not include breathing exercises and the repetition of meaningless formulae.

It may be claimed with some justice that the early Christians were more at home with imagination than with abstract speculation and this, up to the end of the second century, seems to have been conspicuously the case. The contrast, however, between the Catholic and the Gnostic use of imagination is hardly less than their respective ways of thinking. The philosophical myth was a creation of Plato's. It remains an open question whether his myths reproduce Orphic originals or were adaptations of them or were, in whole or in part, his own inventions. What remains certain is that their imaginative content possessed integrity. Plato recognized this fact and makes Socrates observe at the end of the myth in the *Phaedo*, that if his account of the other world was not accurate, something like it, conveying a meaning approximate to it, must be true.

The Gnostic myths were of a different sort altogether. With the exception of Marcion's, they did not attempt to distil thought from imagination but imagination from thought. In some of the latest systems, like those of Pistis Sophia, a third stage may be detected in which imagination distilled from thought underwent a second process of degeneration and became the crudest dregs of fancy. Valentinus and Basilides, however, were philosophizing theologians who through mere feebleness of thought and imagination failed to produce what Bunyan with consummate art succeeded in realizing, a philosophical allegory, deep in meaning and luminous in form. The modern habit of transliterating, instead of translating the abstract nouns which serve as heroes and heroines of these pieces and the relationship of which to one another depends upon their natural sense, has obscured this obvious fact. The liveliness and colour of their plots as described in the text-books depend in large measure upon this pseudo-scientific distortion of their significance. Marcion's system is an exception to the Gnostic rule for its theology described events in heaven and earth as they presented themselves not to abstract intelligence but to the imagination. In this respect he remained more loyal to the Jewish-Christian materials from which he drew and on this ground Harnack claimed he was no Gnostic at all.[1]

In the New Testament there are no traces of Gnostic myth-making and little philosophizing of the professional sort. The ambiguous use of λόγος in the Prologue to the Fourth Gospel, the mystical overtones of such terms as life, light and truth, which hold their mysticism well within Christian bounds, the cosmology of Colossians and Ephesians, which must have occasioned as little surprise to their Gentile public as Mark xiii or Revelation did to their Jewish readers—this is the New Testament's slender yield to the harvester of Gnostic ideas in the field of Christian origins. Paul's use of γνῶσις and μυστήριον reveals a terminology common to pagan or Christian authors of the period but with transparent differences of sense. The clearest indication of a philosophic trend in the mind of any New Testament author is to be found in John, but it is Stoic rather than Platonic, and reached a dead end in Tertullian.[2] Origen, whose concessions to Valentinian speculations led to his condemnation, was put to no little embarrassment to explain that the Johannine λόγος was really the Platonic νοῦς and that πνεῦμα was ἀσώματον,[3] though John was repeating a Stoic catchword when he wrote πνεῦμα ὁ θεός.[4]

The conclusions of this essay are not new, but their restatement may serve to counter a trend in which the terms 'Gnosis' and 'Gnosticism' threaten to lose any precise meaning which can be controlled by the evidence at hand. What appears most certain is that the New Testament offers no ground for using documents of

[1] *Lehrbuch der Dogmengeschichte*, vol. I⁴, p. 292.

[2] *Harvard Theological Review*, vol. XVIII (1925), p. 81.

[3] *Ibid.* p. 83.

[4] J. von Arnim, *Stoicorum veterum fragmenta*, vol. II (Leipzig, 1903), pp. 112, 299.

the second and third centuries A.D. to explain it. The New Testament requires no explanation, either as a whole or in any of its parts, in terms of an hypothetical primitive Gnosticism. The early Christians valued religious knowledge not because it was esoteric and bizarre but because it was an essential component of their Christian sense of values and way of life and essential to their public teaching. Most of the Gnostics did not preach publicly. The fascination of their revelations and their own livelihood depended on a show of secrecy, though unlike the earlier mysteries this secrecy could be penetrated with relative ease. Irenaeus, Hippolytus and Epiphanius all had Gnostic literature at their disposal and possessed knowledge of Gnostic rituals derived from eye-witnesses.

The New Testament and Gnosticism occupy narrow strips of common ground but this is partly to be explained by their joint heritage of Greek philosophical ideas, partly by the indebtedness of the Gnostic theologians to the New Testament. The remarkable thing about the earliest Christian literature is not what it perpetuated but what it created. It was not a creation *ex nihilo* but old materials were miraculously transformed. Its authors might with justice have asserted the claim of the Christ of the Apocalypse, 'Behold I make all things new.'

THE MYTHOLOGICAL BACKGROUND OF NEW TESTAMENT CHRISTOLOGY

H. RIESENFELD

ABOUT half a century ago it was believed that a key had been found to the main questions of the New Testament. The opinion prevailed among more advanced scholars that primitive Christianity had been largely influenced by mystery cults of the Hellenistic age. It was supposed that the person and life of Christ were moulded, in the writings of the New Testament, after those of Eastern and Greek heroes or gods. It was then that W. Bousset wrote his acute and learned book *Kyrios Christos*, where the christology of the primitive Church was explained by supposing that mythological elements from the religions in the Mediterranean world had been condensing around the traditions about the person of Christ. This point of view cannot, in its entirety, be maintained any longer, because it seems to be, in spite of its learned argumentation, a construction which, when all is said and done, merely raises questions instead of answering them.

Nowadays, scholars of christology, if they are anxious to isolate not only the specific outlines of primitive Christianity but also its genetic relation to Judaism, can, of course, consider Bousset's ideas to be a temporary tendency in New Testament study. There is, however, an important factor which, apart from the relativity that is always to be found in the conception of a scholar or of a group of scholars, gives one the feeling of being on solid ground. This is that the writings of the New Testament bear such clear witness of the connection of primitive Christianity with the Old Testament and the religious history of Israel on the one hand, and with Palestinian Judaism on the other. If one wishes to deal with the forms and contents of New Testament christology, it seems to be necessary to return to the elements of Jewish Messianism.

In studies of the Old Testament and of later Judaism there has been a keen interest in the figure of the Messiah and of its place in eschatology. The importance of the annual cycle of worship for the formation of the religious conceptions of the Jewish people has often been pointed out. Following on this it is apparent that the king, in pre-exilic times, held a central position in Israelitic cult. He represented God to the people and the people to God. Because of his religious function as a mediator it was around his person that many of the ideas of salvation belonging to all cult and to all belief crystallized. To the extent to which the figure of an ideal king and the conceptions bound up with this figure were projected into the future—a procedure to which the exile itself and the conditions which it brought to the people undoubtedly contributed—there grew up the eschatological hope, the waiting for a king of the Davidic dynasty who would restore, after a period of humiliation and visitation, the Palestinian kingship, and reign over it in a time of victory and peace, justice and security. This king for whom the people were waiting was called the Messiah. In fact the faith in an ideal king was in no way confined to Israel or to the peoples of the ancient Near East, but it cannot be denied that these conceptions have been formed, in the Old Testament and in later Judaism, in quite a special way. It is necessary, therefore, to analyse the forms of this messianic hope, and in so doing one will realize that there is a natural connection between belief in the Messiah and belief in God. Life, justice, salvation to be brought by the Messiah, the judgment held by him and the people gathered by him—all these are fundamental conceptions of the Israelitic faith which occur constantly in Old Testament texts. The Messiah is the representative of God, sent by him in order to mediate and to carry into effect the final justification and beatitude of mankind. As Yahweh is the Living God, life will flourish in all its fullness in the reign of the Messiah. The hope of a paradise arises from the belief in a perfect life. And because God has chosen for his purposes a nation, the people gathered and led by the Messiah will show themselves to be worthy of this election by living up to the claims of obedience and perfection which God has set up. At the same time, however, the people will share in the divine mercy and blessing which are a logical result of the election. The promises, which with their various pictures and colours give a characteristic mark to the prophetic books of the Old Testament, will reach their fulfilment, but this cannot happen until a presumption has been realized, and this is that the powers, the nations and the individuals inimical to Yahweh are judged and doomed.

When accounting for the messianic hopes of the Jewish people in post-exilic and New Testament times, scholars have customarily presupposed two different kinds of saviour. They have distinguished sharply between the immanent and anthropomorphic national king Messiah and the transcendent Son of Man borne on heavenly clouds, and have treated them as representing thoroughly different features. That is to say the roots of the latter idea have been sought exclusively in Iranian eschatology, which in various ways, especially during the exile, could have influenced Jewish religious conceptions. But in making such a supposition one has to ask oneself—as, for example, when dealing with Jewish belief in the resurrection of the dead—if it is possible to postulate influences from other peoples and other religions without making clear such points of contact within Jewish belief as necessarily must have existed before any influence from outside could have gained ground within Judaism. A more profound investigation of the texts shows that the distinction between the immanent Messiah and the transcendent Son of Man is not absolutely clear-cut. There are, on the contrary, transcendent features to be found in the national type of Messiah characteristic of the Psalms of Solomon and the Testaments of the Twelve Patriarchs, whilst the Son of Man of the First Book of Enoch or of the Apocalypses of Baruch and Ezra is depicted in such a manner that several details can be called 'messianic' in a stricter sense. When reading about the enthronement of the priestly Messiah in the Testament of Levi (chs. viii and xviii), one becomes aware that the earthly immanent perspective passes into a heavenly and cosmic one, just as, in all worship, the wall between heaven and earth tends to be broken down.

It seems therefore to be reasonable to assume—though it cannot be demonstrated here in detail—that the difference between the Messiah and the Son of Man is not only due to influences from abroad in the latter case, but that there have been tendencies leading to a differentiation of eschatological conceptions within post-exilic Jewish religion. This differentiation takes its departure from the two aspects which are to be seen already in pre-exilic cult and eschatology: the immanent and the transcendent. The same duality is to some extent characteristic also of the idea of a coming Messiah from the very beginning of this conception. This more advanced process of differentiation has its place in the spiritual life of post-exilic Judaism with its different currents of piety. There was on the one side a realistic nationalism, the eschatological hope of which centred around the ideal king and the political liberator. This saviour was supposed to effect, as regards the religious life of the people, a cleansing and intensification of the national worship which was concentrated in Jerusalem, though the growing institution of the synagogues led to a certain decentralization of ordinary worship. Quite the same tendency is to be detected in the priestly aspirations of the sectarians who in New Testament times were centred about the western shore of the Dead Sea. On the other side there were circles, probably localized chiefly in Galilee, in which apocalyptic ideas together with a transcendental understanding of eschatology were developed. There was the place where the figure of the heavenly Son of Man was evolved and the related belief in the universality of salvation, which was lacking in the conception of a national Messiah. Thus, it is probable that certain ideas incorporated in the conceptions of the Son of Man have evolved from the belief in a heavenly saviour which, having originated in ancient Persia, spread over the countries of the Near East; but nevertheless it seems to be not impossible to suppose that the two figures, the Messiah and the Son of Man, still had so much in common in New Testament times, that Jews belonging to different opinions were aware of the fact that they expected the same saviour, whether they spoke of the Messiah-to-come or of the Son of Man.

We shall not deal with details of the messianic hope of the Jewish people. It is, however, obvious that it has grown up from ideas belonging to Israelitic kingship. But, in order to underline an important point of view, why is it necessary, even for the New Testament scholar, to work out not only the connections of christology with the messianic conceptions of Judaism, but also the lines from these conceptions backward to pre-exilic kingship? The answer lies in the acquisition, by this method, of the key to the pictorial language, to the metaphors and thus to the ideas belonging to the messianic hope, and having understood the language we can proceed to the understanding of the religious thoughts. Every effort to express experiences belonging to the realm of faith is dependent on metaphorical language; word pictures are used as garments with which the thoughts are clothed. But these pictures are derived from realities which have been experienced visually. As to religious metaphors, they are drawn to a large extent from the cult and from its different rites, an important function of which is to make visible the invisible. During the last decades Old Testament scholars have laid stress upon the role of the king in the rites belonging to the yearly cycle of festivals in the religious and national life of Israel, and they have investigated ritual patterns and their substance, thus laying a valuable foundation for the understanding of the vocabulary used to express different lines of thought in eschatology, and especially in the messianic hope. There are of course fluctuations in terminology and in the application of pictures and metaphors, and all alterations have to be analysed. But in the main there is a very conservative tendency in the pictorial language and in the metaphors, and alterations of thought are mostly expressed by new combinations of motifs. When dealing with such a complex of religious ideas as the messianic hope, one has to take into consideration a double problem: what motifs are used to express the belief in a Messiah, and what ideas are expressed by the various motifs employed?

Let us return for a moment to some dominating features in the conceptions of the Messiah. The saviour to come is described as a king, a term which is meant both to express a political reality and also, as far as transcendent events are concerned, to have a metaphorical content. The kingship of the Messiah helps to underline his majesty and power, but there are even more important associations to be found in the term. It is obvious that a king has a kingdom, a dominion where he reigns and where he realizes his intentions. Therefore there exists a fundamental relation between the Messiah and the Kingdom of God. For even if in some parts of later Jewish literature the Messiah is not mentioned in texts dealing with eschatology, whilst Yahweh himself appears as the final king, it has to be remembered that there is in no way a rivalry between Yahweh and his Messiah, but that the latter is always regarded as the visible representative of God, and that he reigns endowed with divine authority. The kingdom, on the other hand, has its *raison d'être* because of the people living within its borders. The king reigning over a people has to exercise his authority in such a way that he furthers the welfare of his subjects. The obligations of the governing and the governed are reciprocal. This is so also in the kingdom of the Messiah. He and the people of God are inseparable: the Messiah redeeming his people in order to procure new conditions of life, the people serving their king in righteousness and thus glorifying him.

The idea of the king is only one of the many motifs bound up with Jewish messianology, but it is sufficient to analyse one such motif and its background in Israelitic history and worship in order to receive an impression of the continuity which is characteristic of religious terms and conceptions in the Old Testament and in later Judaism. It is certainly not out of the way to speak of the history of the people of God even on the spiritual level. The Israelitic kingship, the sociological structure of the Israelites, their religious life, condensed in holy scriptures, their worship and rites, all these are elements in a long process which—from the point of view of the New Testament—can be characterized as a preparation or prefiguration, a time of forming and moulding of the terms and metaphors and thoughts, the existence of which was a necessary condition for the proclamation of the gospel by Jesus and for the belief of the Church from its very beginning. In this process a dominating place is occupied by messianology, which covers the evolution from the Davidic kingdom to the very point where christology begins. But in order to catch the nuances of christology—as well as of other New Testament ideas—it is necessary first to investigate the previous history of the 'motifs', especially in Jewish messianology.

There are reflections of the same kind to be made when dealing with the figure of the Son of Man. In Dan. vii his appearance is described in terms drawn from the royal enthronement. Behind the Son of Man as well as behind the Messiah there is the idea of the king. But in addition, modern commentators on Dan. vii have discussed the question whether the heavenly saviour is to be interpreted as a symbol of the saved people or as an individual ruler. Now there is a certain ambiguity in the text itself. In the description of the vision (*vv.* 13 f.) the individual traits prevail, whilst in the following comment a collective sense is stressed (*v.* 28). It has been justly remarked that there need not be an absolute antithesis between the two interpretations. In the figure of the Son of Man individual and collective features are to be found beside each other, and this is not an accidental conjunction but is due to traditional ideas. In ancient Israel—as well as elsewhere in the ancient Near East—the king was thought of as summing up and representing the people. That is why it is not surprising to find composite traits in the figure of the Son of Man, and that is the case also in other apocalyptic writings in later Judaism. The clue to this ambiguity lies again in the fact that the king and his people as well as the saviour and the saved community are indissoluble.

As we have already said, the figure and thus the term of the Son of Man express in a higher degree than those of the Messiah the notion of universality which evidently, in spite of all national limitations, existed even in Israelitic conceptions of the king and the chosen people. But in Jewish apocalyptics the Son of Man has a bearing not only upon the people of Israel but upon mankind; his reign is not confined to a flourishing Palestine but comprises a new world.

Closely connected with the function of king was that of high priest. This was so from the time when the Davidic king was also the highest sacral official of the people, the leader of cult performed in the temple. It is a characteristic fact that the robe of the high priest in the post-exilic period was that of the king in pre-exilic times, and that the high priest was inaugurated into his office, at any rate during the first centuries of its existence, by anointing. Therefore it is rather natural that the Messiah to come is described also as the ideal high priest. A special importance was given to this idea when the Hasmonaean dynasty was reigning in Palestine. Its members belonged to a priestly family and were therefore lacking in the royal qualifications restricted to the Davidic family. This resulted in the priesthood of the Messiah being underlined in accounts from that time of the eschatological events. There are striking examples in the Testaments of the Twelve Patriarchs, especially in that of Levi. Also in the Damascus Document as well as in the Dead Sea Scrolls the importance of the ideas connected with the eschatological priesthood is evident. The principal task of the priestly Messiah will be the establishment of definite and perfect temple worship. After the fall of Jerusalem and of the Herodean temple there are to be found, in Jewish prayers, supplications that God might send his Messiah to restore the temple and its worship. This association of the person of the Messiah with the temple of Jerusalem and with the cult performed there is in no way strange. On the contrary an important fact is here expressed. Cult is the visible form in which the relation between God and mankind takes shape. The duty of the priest and especially of the high priest is to be responsible for this cult and to present, on behalf of the people, the offerings prescribed by God himself, all that is necessary in order to eliminate the disorder in the relation between God and man caused by the guilt of man. The person of the Messiah stands as a mediator, restorer and saviour at the very point where the confrontation of man with God becomes most evident.

There is one more function of office of the Messiah which ought to be mentioned in addition to the two discussed hitherto. Even in this case it is possible to establish historical relations to the other ones from far remote times. This function is the prophetic one. When Josephus wanted to pay homage to the memory of the great Hasmonaean prince John Hyrcanus, he characterized him as ruler (i.e. king), high priest and prophet, endowed by God with these three charges.[1] In the Testamentum Levi (ch. viii) there is another proof of the combinations of the three offices in the person of the Messiah. There are of course other functions to be detected in the descriptions of the Messiah, but there is no doubt that the three mentioned are the most important ones. If the Messiah is a prophet or *the* prophet who sums up and fulfils the work of all prophets who have come before, that means that he is a messenger sent to mankind from God in order to let them know and to interpret to them in a final way the will of God, which otherwise is hidden to their minds. The prophet acts by demonstrating in words and deeds. In ancient Israel the functions of the prophets were in some respects closely connected to the kingship as well as to the priesthood, and these offices had several traits in common. Prophecy is, for instance, based on the possession of the divine spirit. The same spirit, conveyed by anointing, is, however, the attribute of the king and later on of the high priest. It is the same with the law, which was proclaimed by the king and also by the prophet—we need only think of Moses

[1] Jos. *Ant.* XIII, 299; *Bell.* I, 68.

and of the role attributed to him in later Judaism. The Messiah will thus be equipped with the spirit, the abundance of which is one of the signs of the coming age, and he will also promulgate the new or rather the definite law, and that means the regulating of human relations and of human conditions of life according to the will of God.

In Jewish messianology in New Testament times there are thus to be found an abundant number of motifs—of which only a few have been mentioned here—and these motifs can all be traced back to concrete features in the political or religious life of the Jewish people, and one has always to remember that there were no strict borders between the national and the sacral sphere. The expectation of the messianic age was at a high pitch in the time of the Herods, which was also that of the Roman occupation. But at the same time the messianic hope was a disparate phenomenon, two different forms of which were the idea of the national Messiah and that of the Son of Man. It is to be noted that the different conceptions of the Messiah as they meet in various situations or texts are formed by varying combinations of metaphors or motifs which were traditional. It seems that the conception which was adopted to a greater extent by the Jewish population in New Testament times was that of the specifically national Messiah, which was, however, after the serious adversities and the bitter disappointments of the first and the second centuries A.D., to fade away. Quite as important as the combinations of traditional elements in the different forms of the messianic hope in Jewish eschatology is the very existence of these elements—at least it seems so from the point of view of the New Testament scholar. For he may be interested not so much in the actual result of those Jewish combinations as in the elements and motifs, in their meaning and in their ability to express religious ideas. Therefore it appears to be an attractive task to investigate the history of these elements and thus to penetrate into their meaning and into their associations with central points in the religious life of the Jewish people: the idea of God, the Scriptures, the temple cult, the ideas of election and of the covenant and finally the hope of salvation.

When Jesus proclaimed his gospel he did not preach abstract religious or moral thoughts but presented himself as the centre of the coming kingdom of God. By means of the metaphorical language and of the traditional symbols which he used in his words and his deeds he proclaimed, if his listeners were willing to understand, that he was no less a person than the Messiah. By his own activity he laid the ground for the faith, i.e. for the christological belief, of the Church which was to grow up after his death and resurrection. The centre in all christology is Jesus Christ, not only because he is the object of the theological and dogmatic thinking of the primitive Church, but above all because he himself has created christology in its very kernel. For to the question: 'What manner of man was Jesus?' we feel obliged to answer not only: 'He was the Messiah'—which is an answer of faith—but also: 'He thought himself to be the Messiah'—a reply which emerges from the study of the texts. This is not the place to enter into a discussion of the messianic consciousness of Jesus, we only want to point out that the way in which Jesus is described in the Gospels cannot be finally explained without assuming a messianic conception in the mind of Jesus himself. For by means of the metaphors and symbols which Jesus used—and which in the main at least were not combined with his person secondarily, i.e. after his death and in the faith of the Christian Church—we can get an insight into the purpose of his activity and thus into his self-consciousness. Neither is it necessary to demonstrate here the Palestinian and Old Testament background of the terms and symbols used by Jesus. As to the formal side of his preaching and acting, he was deeply rooted in the milieu where he lived.

It is, on the other hand, a question of extreme pertinence to elucidate the relation of the messianic intentions of Jesus to the eschatological hope of the Old Testament and of the Jewish people in New Testament times. One could assume that the role of the Galilean preacher was that of an epigone or of a reproducer. He said himself that he had come in order not to destroy but to fulfil, but what is the meaning of these words? The connections with the religious history of Israel are evident, but it becomes clear that the continuity was not straight or uncomplicated. There has to be supposed something which perhaps can be most strikingly described as a re-creation, whereby the different elements in Jewish messianology which were taken over—conceptions, terms, symbols, social orders, forms of worship—but were selected, combined and transformed in such a way that the result of this process appears as quite a new unit. We shall try to sketch briefly the process of re-creation by means of the notions of selection, combination and transformation.

It is not difficult to notice a conscious *selection* in the attitude of Jesus towards the messianic hope of his compatriots. Many of the components of the Scriptural references to the person of the Messiah or of later Jewish conceptions about the saviour to come were eliminated or accused of being inadequate. Here it is worth mentioning that Jesus emancipated himself from the purely national and immanent idea of the ideal king. This is evidently the reason why he rejected the open use, when speaking of his own person, of the traditional title of Messiah, the Anointed One. On the other hand we find a markedly selective tendency towards the jungle of speculations which had grown around the more transcendent figure of the saviour as it was proper to Palestinian apocalyptics. Certainly Jesus used the title of Son of Man with regard to himself, certainly he placed his person and his activity in a wide eschatological perspective, but the occurrences of the last days, the whole scheme of events, the details of which were in the mind of the apocalyptists, are only touched upon in his utterances, and that in order to interpret the meaning and the consequences of eschatology. There is nothing in the Gospels of the products of a vivid imagination which is characteristic of Jewish apocalypses. We need only point at the discretion which distinguishes the scene of the last judgment in Matt. xxv. 31–46. All that is said there has reference to man in an essential way. On the other hand nothing is told about impersonal cosmic events. Thus it is obvious that the messianic terms used by Jesus are to be found in the Old Testament and in later Jewish literature, and there they have, as a matter of course, to be analysed in their context. The decisive feature, however, lies in the manner in which certain elements have been taken over, whilst others have been rejected.

Further, the teaching of Jesus about his own nature has received its individual characteristics from the *combination* of traditional elements and ideas. There is a good deal of creative work in the way in which extant data are put together. Three currents of Jewish messianic conceptions have been united or reintegrated in a manner to which there is no analogy in the history of Israelitic religion. These currents are the figures of the Messiah (in a narrow sense of the word), of the Son of Man and of the Ebed Yahweh. Without entering into the question of whether the Son of Man in single passages in the apocalyptic literature has been connected with the Servant of the Lord of Deutero-Isaiah, we can establish that the combination of the motifs of victory and suffering characteristic of New Testament christology, and thus undoubtedly of the teaching of Jesus, is distinguished by its radical and concrete form from all previous messianology. Variations of the same antithetical combination are martyrdom and glory as well as humility and authority.

One of the results of this combination of the ideas of the Messiah and of the Son of Man is that we can trace, in the person of Jesus and in his words about himself, the concrete realism of the immanent hope of the Messiah and also something of the transcendence characteristic of the idea of the Son of Man. In spite of its supranational breadth which is proper to the gospel of the Kingdom of God, the life and activity of Jesus is bound up with and restricted to the Jewish people. The messianic hope of Israel must first be accomplished, and that is the presupposition for the fulfilling of the real aim of Christ's coming: the proclamation of the gospel of salvation to the whole world. Having this goal in view he gathered around him the chosen people, the new Israel, and had already organized it during his lifetime as a real community, a social body, in the midst of this world. In this community, which at the same time represents the new covenant between God and mankind, the blessings of the coming age are given to its members, certainly not yet in their fullness but anticipated as first-fruits. In the mighty works and miracles performed by Jesus during his ministry—and succeeded later in the Church by the sacraments—in the salvation of judgment actualized by the preaching of the gospel, eschatology is already 'realized', i.e. life released from its limitations is being experienced, changing human beings and their mutual relations. That means that some of the features of the 'immanent' messianic hope are actualized, though bearing a mark of transcendence. On the other hand the waiting for the second coming of Christ, the belief in cosmic revolutions preceding the appearance of the heavenly saviour, in the realization of the age to come by catastrophes annihilating heaven and earth, in the resurrection of the dead, the last judgment and a new existence—all these elements associated with christology have their background in the Jewish conceptions of the transcendence of the Son of Man, though the sayings of Jesus about these events take into consideration in a much clearer way the relation of eschatology to actual human life.

The third creative process, that of *transformation*, has operated upon all the motifs and elements which in the words and deeds of Jesus have been selected from Jewish eschatology and which, having been combined in a unique way, constitute the picture of Jesus the Christ which emerges from the texts of the New Testament. Here we still presuppose that Jesus himself was the author of this christological conception. Transformation is in reality the essence of the re-creation which in New Testament terminology is called fulfilment. If we take the motif of kingship, we see in what a radical way it has been changed. Christ is really king in the fullest sense of the word, but apart from the nature of his kingdom, his glory is the result not of his power but of his service. His victory is won not in a fight against nations or cosmic powers but by obedience and suffering. The priestly function of Christ is performed not in the temple of Jerusalem or in an ideal sanctuary of a similar kind but in the sacrifice of the cross, interpreted and communicated by the sacrament of the Last Supper. The three functions mentioned, those of the king, the high priest and the prophet, break all national boundaries without losing their immediate relation to the life of men. The organism of the Church as it takes shape after the resurrection is clearly conceived and prefigured, with its specific features, during the ministry of Jesus. And yet both the activity of Jesus and the function of the Church point forward to a final consummation.

The most sublime and most essential result of the creative process which has formed christology is the conception of the mission of Christ in its entirety. The outlines of this conception are to be found in the sayings of Jesus about the Son of Man, and there is no need to suspect these sayings of being spurious or to doubt that Jesus identified himself with the Son of Man. According to the words of Jesus, the Saviour is a heavenly being, the Son of God who has assumed humanity, who is to suffer and to die, who will be raised from the dead, exalted to a heavenly dominion, and who will return for a final judgment. The ingredients of this soteriological drama have likewise been preformed in Israelitic cult and in later Jewish eschatology, and still there is no equivalent to it within Judaism. In this conception of the mission of Christ there are of course very distinct transcendental elements which are withdrawn from every attempt at a historical proof of what really happened. The New Testament scholar can only establish that this soteriology, this outline of the mission of Christ, is indissoluble from the gospel of Jesus as a whole. On the other hand he is obliged to analyse the meaning and the religious message of this kind of christology including the partly transcendental mission of the Son of Man.

The interpretation of the content of the christology created and taught by Jesus had already been begun in the preaching of the primitive Church from its first days. We can trace this work in the witness of the disciples of Jesus referred to in the first chapters of the Acts of the Apostles. Perhaps the main contribution of St Paul to Christianity is his evolution of christological thinking. His everlasting merit is to have carried out the translation—which of course had been inaugurated in the Church of Jerusalem from its beginnings—of the gospel of Christ and the gospel about Christ not only into Greek language but above all into modes of thought intelligible to the Greek. The title of Messiah, central in Jewish eschatology, has in its Greek equivalent become a mere proper name, *Christos*. In its place another characterizing epithet appears which is given a specific theological content all over the Hellenistic and Roman world. It is the term *kurios*, 'Lord', which certainly renders the Aramaic *maran* or *marana*, but which because of its suitableness gained a special importance. The sentence 'Jesus Christ is Lord'—or 'Our Lord is Jesus Christ'—was fitted to transcend all frontiers and thus made the world mission possible. What is meant by the term 'Lord' has to be expounded by preaching and teaching, the basis for which is being laid by theological reflection.

What about the title of Son of Man in the history of the primitive Church? We find it, apart from the Gospels, only once in Acts (vii. 56) and twice in the Revelation (i. 13; xiv. 14). The reason for this fact seems to be that during the ministry of Jesus the messianic or christological dogma was involved in this name, which from different points of view was fitted to be employed by Jesus. In the situation of the Church the term became superfluous. For the mystery of the Son of Man had been succeeded by the witness about Jesus

Christ, his incarnation, suffering and resurrection. With a slight exaggeration one could say that the Son of Man christology of the Gospels has given place to the preaching and creed of the Christian Church. At the same time we notice that there is a solid tradition in the Gospels, in many respects older and more primitive than the theology of the Church at the moment when they were written down. This comes out from the very fact that the primitive mystery of the Son of Man has been so clearly preserved in the Gospels.

Thus it is, and it has always been, the task of New Testament exegesis to work out the components of christology in order to understand and to interpret the intention of Jesus and the meaning of his sayings and actions. But the very essence of these components will appear more clearly in the measure that we are able to elucidate the process of development which they have undergone, in Old Testament times and in later Judaism, before being incorporated in the christological synthesis. The study of the mythological background of the christology of Jesus and of the primitive Church is therefore necessary for a thorough understanding of the gospel itself.

5

THE ECONOMIC BACKGROUND OF THE NEW TESTAMENT

F. C. GRANT

NEAR the beginning of one of his latest and greatest works, *The Interpretation of the Fourth Gospel*, Professor Dodd reminds us of a passage in a book which was popular forty years ago, *The Call of the Carpenter*, by Bouck White (Doubleday, 1911). The passage, quoted from memory, gives White's translation of John v. 17, 'My father is a working-man to this day, and I am a working-man myself.' White explained that Jesus 'even seems to have taken pride in the workmanlike qualities of his father, and of his descent from artisan loins' (pp. 36f.). Professor Dodd notes that the Greek words thus translated could quite well have borne this meaning, and that 'if one insists on placing them in the context of a philosophy dominated by the idea of the class-war, then such an exegesis is natural. But', he rightly adds, 'we have no reason to suppose that John or his readers had ever heard of that philosophy.'[1]

The reference recalls a whole school of interpretation whose *floruit* spanned the first two decades of this century, and whose views, not only of the New Testament but also of the economic conditions of the first century, strongly influenced what was called in those days and later the 'social gospel'. After the end of the First World War, the school declined, and in the realm of New Testament interpretation other interests crowded out its too sanguine, too puerile views. The new school of Form Criticism on the one hand and the rise of the Neo-orthodox theology on the other beamed the attention of New Testament students in another direction—or other directions. But around 1920 there was much discussion of the relation between economic conditions in the Mediterranean world under the early Empire and the spread of primitive Christianity—and not only its

[1] *The Interpretation of the Fourth Gospel* (Cambridge, 1953), p. 4 n.

spread but even the form it took, its content as well as its outward expression. The 'religious historical' school was still widely influential, and what the economic conditions did not seem to account for, the influence—at least the enchanting example—of the 'mystery religions' explained. Christ was 'the Carpenter God', the 'God of the underprivileged, the vast submerged masses in the Roman Empire, seething with revolt'; or he was the wistful, far-off projection of the frustrated hopes and dreams of the oppressed millions of slaves and freedmen throughout the Near East, southern Europe, and northern Africa; the one who enabled them to exchange their dismal, hopeless present for a bright and more-than-compensatory vision of a glorious life to come, in which servitude and hunger, the master's lash and the gaoler's stocks and shackles would for evermore be unknown. Parallels were found in other religions, parallels not only to the ideas expressed in the early Christian writings, but also to the 'psychological' roots and backgrounds of the ideas.[1]

Now there can be no question that every open and public religion, every organized cult—every religion except the most withdrawn and private kind of religiosity—has a real relation to the world in which it exists, including the economic factors and conditions prevailing in that world: and even the most private type of piety itself is perhaps also conditioned by the prevailing conditions. If a religion has relevance for life, it must take the risk of rubbing elbows in the market-place. If it has a message for men as they actually are, and for people where they actually live, then it cannot escape the reflex influence of its surroundings. It must address itself to men and women in their world, not in some dreamland of wish-fulfilment, and the auditors of its gospel are certainly conditioned by economic factors—and by many others as well.

The main question, then, is this: What were the economic conditions of the first century which favoured or impeded the expansion and development of early Christianity? Did those factors contribute

[1] See the references in my *Economic Background of the Gospels* (Oxford, 1926), p. 117 n. Professor Rostovtzeff criticizes this once-popular but wholly exaggerated Marxian view of the conditions of the labouring classes in the Empire, and its accompanying theory of the class-war. See his *Social and Economic History of the Hellenistic Age*, vol. II, p. 1258; *Social and Economic History of the Roman Empire*, pp. 99 f. The trouble with the Marxian historians is their subjectivism: they tend to read all history by the dim light of their own frustrations.

positively to the structure or content of the new religion; or did they warp and turn aside its normal course of growth, so that (for example) a purely eschatological type of Palestinian Judaism was transformed presently into one more current in that flood of 'Oriental mysteries' which was sweeping westward over the Empire? Was the outlook of the average man and woman—as far as this world went—so hopeless that the only alternatives seemed to be either violent revolution or a retreat into other-worldliness? What was the social-economic status and condition of the leaders of the early Christian movement: Jesus himself, his apostles, Paul, Apollos, Barnabas, and the rest? Were they members of the hungry proletariat, or of the middle class? Certainly none of them belonged to the aristocratic or well-to-do class. And what of their first hearers and converts, the earliest members of the church in Palestine, in Syria—say in Antioch, which was a key centre in the propaganda of early Christianity and the point of departure for the Gentile mission; or in Asia and Greece and Italy—say in Rome, under the very shadow of the imperial throne (Phil. iv. 22)?

The researches of classical scholars and of economic historians, especially since 1920, have done much to clear up the obscurity surrounding the economic life of the ancient world—an obscurity due in part to limited and fragmentary information, but also to a one-sided interpretation of the ancient data, the kind of 'modernizing' that consists of reading-in modern views, formulas, slogans, enthusiasms or resentments into the records of the past. The success of these scholars in recovering and reconstructing the past is among the proudest achievements of sheer learning and good judgment in the whole long history of scholarship. It has been like the putting together of a broken mosaic which has been smashed into the tiniest fragments; or it is like the solving of a jig-saw puzzle whose pieces have been further broken up and subdivided. The data provided by the classical authors in that small fraction of their work that has come down to us, together with the information contained in or to be inferred from the surviving inscriptions, or read between their lines (many of them fragmentary); together with the surviving papyri, as far as they have been discovered (chiefly, of course, in Egypt, and therefore containing data primarily relevant to that land); coins, especially when discovered in remote and unexpected places; sculptures, architecture, in brief all kinds of archaeological data, uncovered in increasing quantity, and given the most thorough and detailed sifting, criticism, and interpretation by experts and specialists in many different fields—all this fragile body of factual information has been studied and restudied, fitted together to form one trial solution after another, until finally the general or 'over all' picture has begun to emerge more clearly.

Among the more important works in this field which have been published during the past quarter-century may be mentioned the great series, *An Economic Survey of Ancient Rome*, edited by the late Professor Tenney Frank (Baltimore, Maryland: The Johns Hopkins Press, 1933–40): I. *Rome and Italy of the Republic*, by T. Frank; II. *Roman Egypt to the Age of Diocletian*, by A. C. Johnson; III. *Britain, Spain, Sicily, La Gaule Romaine*, by R. G. Collingwood and others; IV. *Africa, Syria, Greece, Asia Minor*, by R. M. Haywood and others; V. *Rome and Italy of the Empire*, by T. Frank; VI. *Index*. The bibliography in vol. v comes down to 1939. The aim of this work is primarily that of scientific fact-finding and fact-establishing, with no theories to propound or advocate—hence its great and permanent value.

Two other works of first-rate importance are *The Social and Economic History of the Hellenistic World*, by the late Professor M. Rostovtzeff of Yale (Oxford, 3 vols. 1941), and his equally important *Social and Economic History of the Roman Empire* (Oxford, 1926; 2nd ed. 1941). The literary and pictorial illustrations in these two works add greatly to their interest and value.

The volumes devoted to economic history in *The History of Civilization* series should also be mentioned, such as Jules Toutain's *The Economic Life of the Ancient World* (London, 1930); G. Glotz's *Ancient Greece at Work*; J. Jouguet's *Macedonian Imperialism*; Paul Louis's *Ancient Rome at Work*; Victor Chapot's *The Roman World*. These are only a few of the many recent works dealing with the subject—merely some of the volumes contained in one series. Other and independent works are W. E. Heitland's *Agricola: A Study of Agricultural and Rustic Life in the Graeco-Roman World from the Point of View of Labour* (Cambridge, 1921—which is more than a quarter-century ago), a supplement to his brilliant *Roman Republic* (3 vols. 1909; 2nd ed. 1923). Another is F. M. Heichelheim's *Wirtschaftsgeschichte des Altertums* (1938). W. W. Tarn's valuable *Hellenistic Civilization* (1927) has appeared in a revised and rewritten edition, in preparing which he has had the aid of G. T. Griffith (Arnold, 1952).

Another recent work is David Magie's *Roman Rule in Asia Minor to the End of the Third Century after Christ* (2 vols., Princeton, 1950), where the student will find chs. 2 and 21–7 especially rewarding. One must also mention the continued publication of inscriptions and papyri,[1] as well as archaeological remains of other kinds, together with many articles in learned journals all over the civilized world; the articles in the more recent volumes of Pauly-Wissowa; the editions and translations of classical authors in such a series as the indispensable Loeb Classical Library. Even the short articles on economic history in the ever-useful *Oxford Classical Dictionary* (Oxford, 1949) with their brief but up-to-date bibliographies are extremely valuable guides to the student: see the list of articles on p. 304. One must not overlook the equally up-to-date and even more comprehensive bibliographies in the volumes of the 'Clio' series, *La Grèce et l'hellénisation du monde antique* (new ed. 1948), by Robert Cohen, and the *Histoire de Rome* (1949), by André Piganiol.

Finally, as the most important and most comprehensive gathering together of all modern learning on the subject, one must mention the relevant chapters in the *Cambridge Ancient History*. In addition to the many scattered paragraphs and sections in other chapters, where the subject naturally comes under observation, there are the following major contributions:

Vol. v (1927), ch. 1, The Economic Background of the Fifth Century, by M. N. Tod.

Vol. viii (1930), ch. 11, Italy, by T. Frank.

Vol. ix (1932), chs. 1–4, on the Gracchi, Marius, and the Enfranchisement of Italy, by H. Last; ch. 6, on Sulla, ch. 7, on the Breakdown of the Sullan System and the Rise of Pompey, by H. Last and R. Gardner; ch. 10, The Provinces, by G. H. Stevenson; ch. 19, Ciceronian Society, by J. W. Duff.

Vol. x (1934), ch. 7, on the Imperial Administration, by G. H. Stevenson; ch. 13, The Economic Unification of the Mediterranean Region: Industry, Trade and Commerce, by F. Oertel; ch. 14, The Social Policy of Augustus, by H. Last.

Vol. xi (1936), ch. 1, The Flavian Dynasty, by M. P. Charlesworth; ch. 5, Nerva and Trajan, by R. P. Longden; chs. 11–16, a survey of the provinces by H. Last, E. Albertini, R. G. Collingwood, K. Stade, A. Alföldi, J. Keil, F. Cumont, H. I. Bell, and P. Romanelli; ch. 19, Social Life in Rome and Italy, by J. W. Duff.

[1] See the lists in the new edition of Liddell and Scott, *Greek-English Lexicon* (Oxford, 1940), pp. xli–xlv.

Vol. XII (1939), ch. 7, The Economic Life of the Empire, by F. Oertel; ch. 8, Britain, by R. G. Collingwood; and ch. 11, the Reforms of Diocletian, by W. Ensslin. One must read these later chapters in order to get the full picture of the development under the Empire. The bibliographies in all these volumes are extensive, reliable, and up-to-date.

One sees at a glance that the 'literature' of our subject is vastly greater in quantity and more wide-ranging in extent than that which was available to the student in, let us say, 1920. Not that the earlier work was ineffective—the pioneers mapped out the area, and some of their works are of permanent value; not least that which went into the editing and interpretation of the inscriptions in the various great series begun in the nineteenth century. It is especially the New Testament student with whom we are concerned at present; and it can be said at once that the conception of the economic background of early Christianity which these modern studies force upon us is one that is totally different from the more or less Marxian and certainly melodramatic *mise en scène* with which the student of the early 1920's was provided. It is less than ever possible, nowadays, to represent early Christianity as a revolutionary social (or social-economic) movement. Although, as we insist, religion is always conditioned by the world in which it lives, including the economic factor in that world, it is clear that Christianity was from the very beginning a purely religious movement, a cult, a body of beliefs and practices centred in something else than the economic welfare or well-being of any racial, national, or social group.

In order to see the economic background in its totality, even by a bird's-eye-view—and the bird must take swift flight in this brief paper—we should go back to the beginning of the Hellenistic age. This age began even before Alexander, according to Professor Bengtson and others, perhaps as early as 360 B.C. There was a growing crisis in the Greek world at least from that date onwards—and perhaps we should go back to the catastrophe of the Peloponnesian War with its disastrous consequences for all concerned. An earlier economist, Brooks Adams, theorized that the desperate lunge of Alexander at the throat of the Persian Empire was motivated by economic exhaustion—the mines at Laurium had given out.[1] Be

[1] See his *The New Empire* (New York, 1902).

that as it may (one suspects that this is too narrow an explanation), it is certainly true that Alexander's conquest of the Near and Middle East relieved Greece and the Islands of an acute economic and social crisis.[1] The treasure of the East, chiefly that which had formerly been possessed by the Persian Great King, was removed to the West: it was the first time in history that a whole empire had been looted by a totally alien people. What this injection of fresh blood might have done to stabilize the West, and ultimately the whole civilized world, we do not know; for presently Alexander's empire broke up, and the endless wars of the Successors, and of their successors, and eventually of the Romans, occupied the stage for the following three centuries, until the peace established by Augustus after the battle of Actium in 31 B.C.

The great curse of the Hellenistic age, as of the last two centuries of the Roman Republic, was the ceaseless warfare which characterized the period, warfare conducted in the East as a rule by mercenary armies, since the population of Greece and other countries about the eastern Mediterranean soon proved unable to produce sufficient excess man-power for the purpose. At least this is one reason: but another is that this was also a well-established precedent (which throws some added light on economic conditions at home), since when Alexander began his conquest of Asia Minor, the Macedonian and Persian armies alike were largely Greek.[2] The casualties in these wars were sometimes almost incredible. At the battle of Sellasia in 221 B.C.,[3] of 6000 Lacedaemonians engaged only 200 survived. The destruction of whole cities, like Alexander's razing of Thebes, was unusual, though the massacre of men and the enslavement of women and children was an age-old, even prehistoric custom, still followed in many wars: the Roman conquest of Italy provides examples enough. When Mantinea fell, in 223 B.C., Antigonus Doson sold the inhabitants to the Achaeans. Philip V and Philopoemen and the Romans after the war with Pyrrhus followed a like procedure. One can never forget Pausanias' repeated description of the deserted areas in Greece; where populous cities once flourished was now, in the second century A.D., only ruin, destruction, and desolation. Equally

[1] See Rostovtzeff, *Hellenistic World*, vol. II, p. 1026.

[2] See W. W. Tarn, *Alexander the Great* (Cambridge, 1948), vol. I, pp. 8–26.

[3] Plutarch, *Cleomenes* XXVIII, 5.

unforgettable is the letter of Servius Sulpicius Rufus to Cicero (*Ad Fam.* IV. 5. 4), written from Athens about 15 March 45 B.C.

> On my return from Asia, as I sailed past Aegina towards Megara, I began to observe the neighbourhood. Behind me lay Aegina, on my right the Piraeus, on the left Corinth. These once flourishing towns [*oppida*] now lay prostrate and in ruins, before my very eyes. And I began to think to myself, 'So—have we puny mortals, shorter lived than they, any right to resent it if one of us dies, or is killed [in battle]?—when
>
> here within this narrow space
> The corpses of great cities lie.'

Of course the letter is one of sympathy and condolence on the death of Tullia, Cicero's beloved only daughter, and this accounts for some of the language used, and for the letter's general tone, but certainly not for the facts referred to. The devastation wrought in the East, and the decline in population, was one of the major tragedies of history. As Professor Martin Nilsson remarks, 'Asia's prosperity was ruined for generations, that of Greece for ever.'[1]

Greek warfare aimed at the plunder and destruction of the food supply of the enemy—too often the people of a neighbouring Greek state. Thucydides describes the Theban and Spartan invaders of Attica destroying the standing crops in almost the language used by the Old Testament of the 'bands' of Syrian and Moabite marauders who swept over Palestine year after year (II Kings vi. 23, xiii. 20). The cost of maintaining and equipping huge armies on land and large fleets at sea, for generation after generation, likewise taxed the productive resources of the Mediterranean countries. Even the temples of the gods were not exempt from plundering in the Hellenistic age.[2]

Added to this was the constant loss of property and the decimation of the population by piracy, especially along the coasts and on the islands.[3] At times the pirates were in the pay of the kings, as in more modern times in the Caribbean; or as in the case of the barbarians hired to defend the Roman Empire in the fourth and fifth centuries. The ruined watch-towers on every Mediterranean headland still remind us of this perennial scourge of life in ancient times throughout

[1] *Geschichte der griechischen Religion*, vol. II (1950), p. 48.

[2] See the opposing speeches of Chlaeneas and Lyciscus in Polybius IX, 28–39. Cf. M. P. Nilsson, *Geschichte der griechischen Religion*, vol. II (1950), p. 40.

[3] Cf. H. A. Ormerod, *Piracy in the Ancient World* (1924).

the whole Mediterranean world. The capture and sale of slaves mounted steadily in numbers, especially after the Roman expansion in Italy and the consequent emergence of the *nouveaux riches*, with what Eduard Meyer called their 'burning, insatiable hunger' for slaves.[1] It is said that on the Island of Delos, which was the central slave market, as many as 10,000 slaves would be sold in a single day, and at prices ranging from 3 or 4 minas (say 15 to 20 dollars or 5 to 6 pounds) for a manual labourer to 100 or 120 for a highly skilled or well educated adult man. The capture and shipment of young children and even of older citizens, free born, to some distant place was a popular theme in current literature. Even more popular was the gathering up and rearing of unwanted children who had been exposed and left to die outside the cities. Generous men sometimes provided funds for the ransom of unfortunate captives of the slavers, as the inscriptions relate. Of course the interested governments, first the Rhodians and after them the Romans, undertook to curb the depredations of the pirates: the safety of their sea-borne commerce was at stake. As Professor Nilsson notes,[2] the inscriptions reflect the uncertainty of life in the Hellenistic age: the *proxenoi* were guaranteed safety in time of war and immunity from plunder in peace; city after city was designated as an asylum of refuge whose neutrality must be recognized and respected by both sides, as sanctioned by divine decree. But even Delphi had great difficulty in guaranteeing the safety of the *theoroi* sent thither on sacred missions. Under these conditions, we are not surprised to find here the beginnings of that steady depopulation and impoverishment of the Greek mainland which reached such terrible proportions in the second and third centuries of our era. The beginning of the decline took place early in the Hellenistic age, when ceaseless warfare, piracy, and brigandage destroyed what little survived of the old prosperity. This condition very seriously affected the middle class, which had been the mainstay of the ancient *polis*, though the old patriotic fervour and public spirit, including public generosity, were still far from dead. And, as Nilsson further notes, it all but destroyed the lower classes: cheap labour (slaves), cheap products (their handiwork), and low wages (the result of competition with slave labour) reduced the

[1] *Kleine Schriften* (1910), p. 192.
[2] *Op. cit.* p. 41.

artisan class to a half-starved proletariat.[1] Polybius, for example, disputes the high figure given for Cleomenes' assessment of Megalopolis, 6000 talents—it never could have been paid! (The entire assessment of Mantinea, including the receipts from the sale of the whole population by Antigonus Doson, amounted to only 300 talents.)

> For, not speaking of those times, when the Peloponnese had been utterly ruined by the Macedonian kings and still more by continued internecine wars, but of our own times [*c.* 150 B.C.], when all are in complete unison and enjoy, it is thought, very great prosperity, I assert that a sale of all the goods and chattels, apart from slaves, in the whole Peloponnese would not bring in such a sum.[2]

Megalopolis, it will be recalled, was Polybius' birthplace, and he must have known what he was talking about.

Along with poverty and depopulation went the threat of revolution—a constant danger from the very beginning of the Hellenistic age. Alexander himself, in his treaty with the cities of the Corinthian League (335 B.C.), forbade not only the steps that always meant revolution, viz. the repudiation of debts and the redistribution of land, but also the preliminary steps that invariably led to revolt, viz. the confiscation of property and the release of slaves for the recruitment of revolutionary armies.[3] And in fact we know of four slave revolts in the fourth and third centuries. The philosophers—especially the Stoics and Cynics—shared the mood of revolt, and pictured utopias which would be possible if slavery were done away. As in Jewish apocalyptic and other idealizations of human life, the conditions pictured are the opposite of those actually existing.[4]

There is a curious view abroad in some quarters nowadays that the life of a slave in ancient times, except perhaps in Italy among the families of the newly rich in Republican times and under the early Empire, was pleasant enough to be acceptable, even enjoyable, in

[1] See also Rostovtzeff, *Hellenistic Age*, vol. II, pp. 1132–4.

[2] Polybius II, 62.

[3] Nilsson, *op. cit.* vol. II, p. 44; G. Busolt, *Griechische Staatskunde* (3rd ed. 1926), vol. II, p. 1392; [Demosthenes], *Orat.* XVII, 15.

[4] The later opposition, under the Caesars, was also shared by the philosophers, but it included many more than the slaves; it was, in fact, centred in the nobility, who were now increasingly powerless, rather than in the proletariat or the slaves: see the epitome of Bk. 65 of Dio's *Roman History*.

spite of the condition of servitude. But one has only to read Menander, that incomparable sketcher of *genre* scenes, to realize what slavery meant, even under the best of circumstances. Take for example the words of Abrotonon, the harp girl in the *Arbitrants* (ll. 331 ff.):

> Oh, if I could only be free! O gods,
> Let me get free as my reward for this!

(Compare l. 731.) Or read l. 375 in *The Girl from Samos*: one could take a stick and beat a woman slave. Or compare *The Girl with Clipped Hair*, ll. 601 f.:

> He did unholy things to me—
> The way one might treat a slave girl.

And that was Hellas, in the late fourth century. The condition in Italy, in the last century of the Republic and the first century of the Empire, was far worse, as Eduard Meyer showed in his famous essay, *Die Sklaverei im Altertum*.[1]

What Strabo, Dio Chrysostom, Plutarch, Pausanias, and others say of the poverty and depopulation of Greece is unanimous testimony. What we know of Asia Minor, Syria, Egypt and other parts of the eastern Mediterranean basin tallies with it, though not to the same degree. Hence it is little wonder that the *pax romana*, when it came, was hailed by the East as a gift from heaven, and the bringer of this peace a god worthy of divine honours—honours which were duly paid at Priene and Halicarnassus and elsewhere.

Meanwhile, in the West, a century of foreign wars (264–146 B.C.) had been followed by a century of civil wars (133–31 B.C.), and although the civil wars were sometimes fought abroad (with the devastation of other countries as a consequence), and although the wealth of other countries poured into Italy as the Republican Empire expanded and its provinces increased, all was not well in the Italian peninsula. In spite of its increasing wealth, there was the most serious economic imbalance. Estates grew larger and larger. Hereditary land-holdings were confiscated by the government in order to re-

[1] *Kleine Schriften* (1910), pp. 169–212. Cf. W. L. Westermann, 'Sklaverei', in Pauly-Wissowa, *Realencyclopaedie für Altertumswissenschaft*, Suppl. VI (1935), cols. 894–1068; also in *Encyclopaedia of the Social Sciences*, vol. XIV (1934), pp. 74–7.

settle the veterans of the vast armies required by two centuries of ceaseless conflict. The landless and workless poor congregated in Rome, supported in idleness by the ever-growing dole. Slave workers took the place of the ancient freemen on what were now the huge estates of the South Italian and Campanian latifundia. The evil was recognized even then. As Pliny observed, in words that have been—and deserve to be—often quoted:

> In olden times it was thought that moderation in the size of a farm was a matter of primary importance, since it was thought better to sow less and plough it the more; and I find that Virgil was of the same opinion [*Georgics* II, 412, 'Praise a large farm, cultivate a small one']. And if the truth be told, it is the large estates that have been the ruin of Italy, and are now [middle of the first century A.D.] proving the ruin of the provinces too [*latifundia perdidere Italiam, iam vero et provincias*]: six landlords owned half of Africa, when the emperor Nero had them put to death. Pompey, on the other hand, must not be deprived of this sign of his greatness—he never bought land belonging to an adjoining estate. It was Mago's opinion that upon buying a farm the owner ought to sell his town house [and live on the land]...a rather rigid view, and one really not in the public interest, but showing nevertheless the importance he assigned to personal supervision.[1]

Mankind makes such tragic blunders at the economic level that one wonders sometimes if economic prosperity is not more often the result of divine benevolence and of natural abundance than of anything else, even of human thrift and enterprise. The prosperity of the Augustan age was the result partly of the cessation of war, and partly of the acquisition of the wealth of Greece (what was left of it!) and the East, which consisted chiefly of the artistic treasures of Greece and the monetary treasure of Egypt and its rich grain-producing soil. But the Augustan land allotments sowed the seeds of future disaster. As early as the land allotments of Sulla there had been bitter protest, as in the famous prophecy of the Seeress Vegoia, ostensibly taken from the Etruscan ritual books given to Aruns Veltymnus. The dictator's redistribution of land to his troops fell with special severity upon Etruria.

[1] Pliny, *Natural History*, XVIII, 35. Mago was a much-quoted Carthaginian expert in agriculture.

When Jupiter took the land of Etruria into his protection he specifically commanded that the commons should be surveyed and the fields marked off. Since he knew the greed of men and earthly covetousness, he willed that everything should be surrounded with boundary stones. These were some day to be purposely disregarded by men, seized, and moved away, through the greed of the eighth world age, near its end. But whoever lays hands upon and removes them, in order to increase his property, thus decreasing that of another, will for this offence be condemned by the gods. If slaves do it, they will have a change of masters, for the worse. But when it takes place with the knowledge and consent of their master, his house will soon be destroyed and his family will come to ruin. The one who has proposed it will be visited with the severest sicknesses and wounds and lose the use of his limbs. The land itself will cave in, in many places, amid storms and tempests [earthquakes?]. The fruit will often be damaged and knocked off by rain and hail, dried up by the heat, or destroyed by blight. Much dissension among the people. Know that all this comes to pass when such an offence is committed. Therefore do not be deceitful nor double-tongued. Safeguard the teaching in your heart![1]

The same note is sounded, though not so harshly, in Virgil's *First Eclogue*, where Meliboeus and Tityrus discuss their varying fortunes. Both of them are dispossessed of their ancestral acres, but the latter is successful in regaining his title through imperial favour, while the former faces exile in Africa, Scythia, Parthia, or Britain (there seems to be little choice). Meanwhile a foreigner reaps his fields, and a blaspheming veteran occupies his acres. One suspects that, after all, Meliboeus will not go to far-away Britain or Scythia, but will wander off to Rome, to join the growing proletariat of the great city. One also suspects that it will not be long before the transplanted veteran, who for twenty years has seen service in camp, and is no farmer anyway, will tire of his new surroundings, give up the toil of agriculture, sell out to the neighbouring rich landowner (i.e. to the landowner's steward), and join the former owner of his farm in one of the cheap flats in the swarming 'islands' on the Aventine. This is of course not the whole picture, bad as it is, and serious as a portent for the future. There are the charming scenes suggested in Horace's *Ode to Apollo*, each line a vignette, warm with

[1] K. Lachmann and A. Rudorff, *Die Schriften der römischen Feldmesser = Gromatici Veteres* (1848–52), vol. I, p. 350. Compare the prophecy in Isa. v. 8–10.

the amber glow of a Claude Lorraine landscape or the background of a Medicean portrait.

> What prayer should one offer Apollo, even a poet,
> Pouring fresh wine from the bowl? For harvests abundant,
> Wains groaning and slow amid sunny Sardinian grain-fields,
> Calabrian cattle, well nourished and sleek, or gold
> From far-away Ind, with ivories cunningly carven,
> Or fields by that beautiful stream, the smooth-flowing Liris?...
> But grant me, O Son of Latona, thy gift of contentment,
> With soundness of body and mind, though age be advancing—
> Let age be with honour, and ever the song of the lyre![1]

Diverse as they are, the prophecy of Vegoia, the eclogue of Virgil, and the ode of Horace all express the ancient Italian's love of the land, a love which Virgil also sang in his praises of Italy (*Georgics* II. 136–76) and made the theme of his agrarian protest against the luxury and debility of the city.[2]

The early slave revolts in southern Italy and Sicily had been serious enough. But even as late as the reign of Nero, his aunt, Domitia Lepida, was accused of attempting the life of the emperor's consort by the use of magic arts, and also of neglecting to 'coerce' the slaves on her vast estates in Calabria—thus disturbing the peace of all Italy.[3] And this in spite of the (not improbable) decline in the number of slaves under the Empire, due to manumissions and the approaching exhaustion of the old source of supply in the East. What was the ratio of slaves to free citizens in Italy at this time? The total figures for citizens, at the beginning of the Empire, may be taken from the *Monumentum Ancyranum*, where Augustus gives his own census records (*Res Gestae* 8):

> In 28 B.C. there were 4,063,000 Roman citizens.
> In 8 B.C. there were 4,233,000 Roman citizens.
> In A.D. 14 there were 4,937,000 Roman citizens.

Whether this increase of almost a million in forty-one years was due to the natural increase of the population or to the extension of

[1] *Odes* I. 31.

[2] *Georgics* I, 121–59. See my *Introduction to New Testament Thought* (1950), pp. 303–7. There is a whole series of such protests in the literature of the late Republic and early Empire.

[3] Tacitus, *Annals* XII, 65, 1.

citizenship is not clear; but—in spite of complaints about unfruitful marriages and preference for bachelorhood among the élite—one suspects that it is probably the former; an extension of citizenship by 25 per cent in the days of Augustus is most unlikely. Professor Tenney Frank estimated the number of free adult males in Italy at the time of the first imperial census at 3,500,000, and the total population of Italy (free and slave) at 14,000,000; the latter figure he divided between 10,000,000 free and 4,000,000 slave. This is an enormous ratio of slaves to free citizens; no wonder the dangers of slave uprisings were constant![1] One may guess that Professor Frank's ratio must have changed by the sixties, the period of Nero's aunt's neglect to 'coerce' her slaves. The rising curve of total population may not have continued (Tacitus would lead us to think otherwise), but the actual number of slaves may have fallen off by then.

And how was this new Empire financed? What was the basis (apart from the two private fortunes which Octavian contributed) for the widely hailed Augustan prosperity? The approximate figures for public finance, e.g. the expenses borne by the aerarium (controlled by the Senate), are now ascertainable. As estimated by Professor Frank,[2] the division was as follows:

Total costs	Million HS
Army and navy, under Augustus .	*c.* 240
Praetorian and urban cohorts .	35
The dole	60
Public buildings and roads . .	5
Games	2
Civil service	50
Total	*c.* 400
Income, approximately . .	450

This tidy margin spelled prosperity, under Augustus.[3]

But the later Julio-Claudians were spendthrifts. Caligula, with his games, lavish entertainments, and building programme, used up the accumulated savings of Tiberius (2,700,000,000 HS, according to

[1] See *Economic Survey*, vol. v, p. 1. [2] *Economic Survey*, vol. v, pp. 4ff.

[3] The figures do not include the totals of outright gifts made by Augustus—approx. 2400 million HS—of which 600 million were contributed to the aerarium, the plebs, and the soldiers: see *Res Gestae*, *ad fin.*

Suetonius, *Caligula* 37. 3) and proceeded to confiscation in order to meet his deficit—a programme which Claudius continued.[1] Nero, with his Golden House and other extravagances, seized half the province of Africa,[2] and compelled both the leading cities and the leading citizens of the Empire to contribute toward the cost of rebuilding Rome after the Great Fire.[3] Lyons in Gaul, for example, contributed 4 million HS, an amount which was returned when a similar disaster overtook that city in the year 65.[4]

It was Vespasian who turned the tide and brought back something like the old Augustan prosperity. When he took over, in the year 70, the Roman treasuries (both aerarium and fiscus) were empty, and it was estimated that it would take 40,000 million HS to meet the current needs.[5] Accordingly, the Julio-Claudian properties were all transferred to the fiscus (they were no longer to be the private property of the emperor and his family), the armies were paid up and many legions pensioned off, and the military budget balanced.[6] Estates and palaces in the provinces were sold, for example, in Egypt and Africa, in order to realize funds—a step which earned for the emperor the reputation of penuriousness; but he kept the empire solvent.[7] For the purposes of comparison with the income and expenditures of Augustus, Professor Frank estimated Vespasian's budget.[8] His chief sources of income were: the tribute (the old tithe) paid by the imperial provinces; sale or rental of public land; port dues, averaging 2·5–5 per cent; inheritance taxes, 5 per cent; sales tax at public auctions, 1 per cent; sales tax on slaves, 4 per cent, used to pay the city police; manumission tax, 5 per cent; income from mines, 50 per cent of the ore mined. On the basis of this schedule, Professor Frank estimated that while in the middle of Augustus' reign the government income was *c.* 500 million HS (=125 million denarii), the combined imperial and senatorial income in Vespasian's time was 1200–1500 million HS.[9]

[1] *Economic Survey*, vol. V, p. 42.
[2] Pliny, *N.H.* XVIII, 35, *ut sup.*
[3] Tacitus, *Annals* XV, 45, 1.
[4] *Ibid.* XVI, 13, 3.
[5] Suetonius, *Vespasian* XVI, 3.
[6] *Economic Survey*, vol. V, p. 45.
[7] Vespasian's frugality was notorious. He even refused to adopt labour-saving devices, in order to make jobs and 'feed his poor' (Suetonius, *Vespasian*, 18). He also authorized public works for the same reason; the Colosseum was an ancient Works Progress Administration project.
[8] *Economic Survey*, vol. V, pp. 47–55.
[9] See the table of estimates, *ibid.* p. 54.

One must not exaggerate. There was no doubt a general improvement of conditions during the period between Tiberius and Vespasian.[1] The colossal expenditures, the wastefulness and extravagance of emperors was possible only because there was a rising tide of prosperity: what they did was live beyond their income and leave to their successors, chiefly to Vespasian, a monstrous accumulation of debt. But growing national debts which accumulate *pari passu* with a rising prosperity are not unknown today: the general prosperity disguises the fact that the public at large is headed for insolvency. It has often been pointed out that the Roman government had no trade policy.[2] The old Roman aristocracy which had governed Italy down to the end of the Republic was 'almost wholly agrarian and militaristic.' The new aristocracy, under the Empire, were not farmers, and though they owned vast estates had no fixed policy, agricultural, industrial, or commercial. Even so it remains true that the ancient world as a whole never got far from the soil, and its income was mainly produce (or income from sale of produce), not the fruits of industry or commerce. The small artisan in his tiny, dimly lighted shop (one may see him there still, in Sicily and in southern Italy) was no competitor for the large factory operated by slaves: but the factories were few and far between, and there was no government-supported plan for handling exports. Capitalism existed, but again it was of limited operation; there was nothing like modern capitalistic production, for the simple reason that power-driven machinery had not been invented. One may walk along the desolate streets of Pompeii and visualize the ancient craftsmen and small manufacturers at their work; one may drop down the cross-street beside the theatre in Ostia and look into the old offices of the shipping companies (mainly second-century) or read their names and interpret their trade marks in the inlaid sidewalk before the doors, or gaze across to the huge warehouses, *horrea*, where the shipments from overseas were stored before being transferred by barge up the Tiber to Rome—it was a small world, after all, and the customs handed down from time immemorial still prevailed. Our modern world of manufacture, industry, trade and commerce simply did not exist, though in principle some of its main features were already present. In the words of Professor Rostovtzeff,

[1] Rostovtzeff, *Roman Empire*, p. 99. [2] *Economic Survey*, vol. v, pp. 294 f.

A policy of *laissez-faire* prevailed. In times of great catastrophes the state felt obliged to help the victims, as for example after the great earthquake in Asia Minor under Tiberius. Some measures were taken which might have had an influence on economic life in general, for instance measures for the improvement of tax-collection, measures introducing new taxes, measures relating to the conditions of transport, and so forth. But such measures were always taken from the purely fiscal point of view; they aimed at the improvement of the state finances, not at the betterment or readjustment of economic conditions. Economic development went on almost undisturbed by any interference on the part of the state. Its main features were those which characterized the Augustan period, but with the free play of natural forces they became more strongly marked.[1]

The truth of the saying of Jesus, 'All who take the sword will perish by the sword' (Matt. xxvi. 52), is writ large all over the history of the ancient world—and the modern as well. The fate which Rome meted out to Greece and the East overtook Rome herself in the end. After systematically weakening the defences of the whole Mediterranean world, there were no resources left, nor resilience of spirit, to meet the mounting crisis of barbarian invasion from the second half of the second century onwards. A large part of the tragedy was economic in character. Such real prosperity as existed, under Augustus and Tiberius, and again from Vespasian to Marcus Aurelius, was achieved in spite of Rome's economic blunders—or of this very *laissez-faire* of which Professor Rostovtzeff speaks—rather than as the consequence of any wisdom on her part. The prosperity was manifested superficially in Rome itself, in the construction of vast buildings and in the continued dole to the proletariat (no one went hungry in Rome), but its true realization was out in the provinces. Here the good government established with the Empire bore rich harvests of loyalty and good will as well as of financial prosperity. Yet underneath and behind the brilliant façade were two factors, two traits of human character, which poisoned the economic history of antiquity: the incurable mutual jealousy of cities and districts which had led Greece to ruin, and the insatiable greed of Rome, which seized what it wanted anywhere in the world, and took no thought for the morrow when the outer world, the hungry have-not peoples, would be sure to seek revenge—or to follow Rome's own example

[1] *Social and Economic History of the Roman Empire*, pp. 89f.

and take what they wanted. Just as the looted treasure of the Incas, seized and squandered by Spain, did nobody any good but wrecked Spain herself in the end, so the looted treasure of the Great King, which might have stabilized the whole Greek-Macedonian-Near-Eastern economy, instead was squandered and dissipated; so too the wealth of whole kingdoms and even empires was channelled off to the West by Rome, but remained in too few hands, was expended upon luxuries and lavish, wasteful extravagance, and upon an unproductive dole to the indolent; it likewise did nobody much good, but many persons, many peoples, many generations of men much harm.

These things of course were hid from the eyes of the first century, for the most part; and it can be said with confidence that the economic background of the New Testament is one of a rising tide of general well-being—except for the little land of Palestine with its poverty, over-population, declining food-supply, wasteful government, and recurrent rebellion. The Marxian reading of history which would equate the economic outlook of the first century with that of the fourth or fifth, or with that of the huge industrial centres of Europe in the nineteenth, simply will not bear inspection. As an explanation of the rise of Christianity, the theory is as impossible as the pseudo-facts upon which it is based. Christianity was not a social revolution disguised as a cult, perhaps as a 'mystery religion'. It was a religion, pure and simple; with a cult; with a body of doctrine, a faith, a *didache*, as well as with a *kerygma* (Professor Dodd has taught us to use these words); with a message of hope for men and women living in this impermanent and not too secure world; with means of grace for those who realized their inability to master themselves or to rise above their surroundings; with an assurance of forgiveness for the penitent, and of release from the burden of sin and guilt; above all with a spirit of tenderness and compassion, 'the lovingkindness of God our Saviour and his good-will toward man' combined with 'the meekness and gentleness of Christ'—these are among the factors, unique and powerful and universally attractive, which must be taken into account by anyone who seeks to understand the rise of the Christian religion and its swift spread to the far corners of that ancient world of the early Roman Empire.

6

DIE EBIONITISCHE WAHRHEIT DES CHRISTENTUMS

H. J. SCHOEPS

Wenn ich den religionsgeschichtlichen und systematischen Ertrag meiner Untersuchungen über das Judenchristentum oder den Ebionitismus zusammenfassen soll,[1] komme ich zu folgenden für Wesen, Wahrheit und geschichtliche Entwicklung des Christentums nicht unwichtigen Ergebnissen:

Bestimmte Quellenschriften des pseudoklementinischen Romans, vorliegend in *Hom(iliae)* und *Rec(ognitiones)*, die Bibelübersetzung des Symmachus, Reste apokrypher Evangelien, patristische und rabbinische Nachrichten erschließen uns die Theologie judenchristlicher Religionsgemeinschaften des mittleren und späten zweiten Jahrhunderts. Das Judenchristentum ist offensichtlich vielgestaltig gewesen (Epiph. Ἐβίων πολύμορφον τηράστιον) und dislociiert. Die genannten Quellen aber beziehen sich fast ausnahmslos auf Gruppen in Coelesyrien oder Transjordanien, die sich aus der Nachkommenschaft der emigrierten Jerusalemer Urgemeinde und wohl noch anderer kurz vor 70 und um 135 aus Palästina aufgebrochener Gemeinden zusammensetzen. Diese haben nun auch Nachrichten und Traditionen aufbewahrt, die bis in die Mitte des ersten Jahrhunderts hinabreichen und den Gegensatz ihrer Väter zu Jerusalem gegen Paulus und gegen die sich herausbildende heidenchristliche Kirche erkennen lassen. Dieser in den ältesten Schichten des pseudoklementinischen Romans reflektierte Gegensatz hat für diese Gruppen Tagesaktualität gewonnen, weil die Argumente ihrer Väter sich auch für den eigenen Abwehrkampf gegen Marcion und die christliche Gnosis verwenden ließen.

[1] *Theologie und Geschichte des Judenchristentums* (Verlag J. C. B. Mohr, Tübingen, 1949), sowie *Aus frühchristlicher Zeit* (Religionsgeschichtliche Untersuchungen, Verlag J. C. B. Mohr, Tübingen, 1950).

Wir wollen im folgenden in gedrängter Kürze[1] ihre Glaubenspositionen skizzieren hinsichtlich Christologie, Paulusgegnerschaft und Stellung zum biblischen Gesetz, soweit dies sich aus negativen Abgrenzungen und positiven Setzungen erkennen läßt. Wir haben dabei keine Wahrheitsaussagen zu machen oder Werturteile zu fällen, meinen aber, daß die 'ebionitische Wahrheit des Christentums' eine ebenso legitime Position ist wie die kirchliche. Denn 'Haeresie' wurden sie nur deshalb, weil sie im Kampfe unterlegen sind, wobei das Unterliegen freilich seine Gründe hat, womit die Frage ihrer geschichtlichen Standortsbestimmung aufzurollen ist. Der kritische Forscher wird dabei auch keinen Augenblick vergessen dürfen, daß das ebionitische Quellenschrifttum einen durch und durch tendenziösen Charakter hat. Aber schon der Tübinger Schule ist klar gewesen, daß dies in gleichem Maße auch für das großkirchliche Schrifttum gilt und die Tendenzkritik aus falsch verstandenen Glaubensinteressen heraus auch nicht vor den kanonisierten Schriften des Neuen Testaments halt machen darf.

I. DAS EBIONITISCHE BILD VON JESUS CHRISTUS

Die Ebioniten haben in Jesus den Lehrer und das Vorbild vollkommener Chassiduth gesehen. Wegen seiner ἀρετὴ βίου sei er von Gott zum Christus, d.h. zum messianischen Propheten berufen worden. 'Hätte ein anderer die Vorschriften des Gesetzes ebenso erfüllt, wäre er ebenso Χριστός geworden, denn bei gleichen Taten können auch andere Χριστοί werden', berichtet Hippolyt (*Philos.* VII. 34. 1f.) über ihren Glauben. Die Ebioniten sahen in Jesus den Saddiq, der das Gesetz als einziger Mensch vollkommen erfüllt habe. Er habe es aber als *Mensch* erfüllt, nicht als υἱὸς θεοῦ, sondern als υἱὸς ἀνθρώπου, der nicht durch reale Präexistenz oder mit der Geburt, sondern erst am Tauftage durch den mit Ps. ii. 7 angesagten Adoptivakt der Taufe, nämlich durch den im Wasser des Taufbades präsenten Heiligen Geist zum Messias geweiht und mit Kraft von Gott ausgestattet worden ist. Diese 'adoptianische Christologie' hat sich bei ihnen mit der apokalyptisch-urgemeindlichen Menschensohnerwartung verbunden, daß Rabbi Jeschu ha-Nozri, verwandelt in die

[1] Die genauen Quellenbelege und alle Details sind in den beiden S. 115, Anm. 1 genannten Büchern gegeben worden.

visionale Engelsgestalt des Menschensohns auf Himmelswolken, in Bälde wiederkommen werde zum heilszeitlichen Endgericht über Lebende und Tote. Das Enttäuschtwerden dieser Erwartung: das Faktum der 'Parusieverzögerung' trägt die Schuld daran, daß das Abflauen der eschatologischen Spannungen im vierten und fünften Jahrhundert zum Ende ihrer Bewegung überhaupt geführt hat. Die Parusieverzögerung hat zwar die Ausbildung der katholischen Kirche gefördert; die Weiterbildungen der Jerusalemer Urgemeinde aber haben dieses factum brutum wegen des Festhaltens an einer primitiven Stufe der Christologie—eben der Menschensohnerwartung—nicht überdauern können.

Das ebionitische Bild Jesu ist aber—von dieser Erwartung abgesehen—noch durch eine ganz andere Qualität bestimmt gewesen: nämlich die, daß er der von Moses verheißene wahre Prophet, der messianische Prophet gewesen sei. Ein solcher Prophet war in weiten Kreisen des Judentums der Zeitenwende erwartet worden, und die Urgemeinde charakterisiert das messianische Glaubensurteil, das in Jesu ὁ ἀληθὴς προφήτης gekommen sei. Dieses verbindet sie mit dem Judenchristentum des Epiphanius und der Pseudoklementinen, wie es sie genauso und definitiv von den weiterhin futurisch ausgerichteten Juden unterscheidet.

Ihr Glaube, daß Jesus ἀληθὴς προφήτης sei, nämlich der von Moses verheißene messianische Prophet, den Gott aufstellen werde 'gleich mir' (Deut. xviii. 15), hat bei ihnen zu einer völligen Parallelisierung beider Gestalten geführt. Beide wurden von Gott gesandt, um *Bünde* zu schließen mit der Menschenwelt. Wie Moses der Juden οἰκονόμος gewesen sei (Luk. xii. 42), so Jesus der für die Heiden (*Hom.* ii. 52). Da aber beider Lehre identisch ist, nimmt Gott jeden an, der einem von ihnen glaubt (*Hom.* viii. 6: Μιᾶς γὰρ δι' ἀμφοτέρων διδασκαλίας οὔσης τὸν τούτων τινὶ πεπιστευκότα ὁ θεὸς ἀποδέχεται). So werden ihnen die Bekehrung zu Christus und die Bekehrung zum heiligen Gott und zum Gesetz der Juden (*Hom.* iv. 22) ein und dieselbe Sache.

2. DIE EBIONITISCHE PAULUSGEGNERSCHAFT

Von dieser Grundposition aus mußten die Ebioniten in eine prinzipielle Gegnerschaft zu Lehre und Person des Apostels Paulus geraten. In den uns erhaltenen Quellen sind keine direkten Lehraussagen gegen die paulinische *Theologie* bewahrt worden, dafür aber eine umso heftigere Polemik gegen das Apostolat Pauli, die den Apostel als Irrgeist (πλάνος τις — II Kor. vi. 8), als Feind (ἐχθρός — Gal. iv. 16), ja als den Bösen schlechthin (ἀντικείμενος — II Thess. ii. 4) diffamieren will, der in der Kirche Christi Haeresie gestiftet habe. Seine Lehren verunglimpfen sie als τὸ εὐαγγέλιον ψευδές. Die Ebioniten des Pseudoklemens haben hier nur Vorwürfe ihrer Väter, der 'Judaisten' in den paulinischen Missionsgemeinden, wieder erneuert und lassen so deren Standpunkt erst ganz deutlich werden. Insbesondere aus dem Stück *Hom.* xvii. 13–20 ist zu erkennen, daß die Ebioniten und ihre Vorfahren Pauli Berufung auf eine Vision des Auferstandenen als dämonisches Blendwerk verurteilt haben. Sein auf ὀπτασίαι καὶ ἀποκαλύψεις begründetes Apostolat sei illegitim, da nur der persönliche Umgang mit dem irdischen Jesus zum Apostolat legitimiert habe.

Offenbar haben schon der Zwölferkreis mit Jakobus und die Jerusalemer die Augenzeugenschaft des Erwählten, d.h. das leibliche Zusammensein als konstitutiv für Apostelwürde und Lehramt erachtet und dem Paulus höchstens die Funktion eines σύνεργος ἡμῶν zugebilligt, wie es der klementinische Petrus (*Hom.* xvii. 20) ausdrückt. Oder *Rec.* ii. 55: 'Wer das Gesetz nicht von Lehrern lernt, sondern sich selbst für einen Lehrer hält und den Unterricht der Jünger Jesu verschmäht, der muß notwendig auf Absurditäten gegen Gott geraten.' Ja, Petrus urteilt noch darüber hinaus, Saulus-Paulus habe eine Vision bekommen, wie sie Jesus seinem Widersacher im Zorn (ὡς ἀντικειμένῳ ὁ 'Ιησοῦς ὀργιζόμενος) zuteil werden ließ (*Hom.* xvii. 14). Daher wird Pauli Denken das *Gegenteil* von Jesu Lehre genannt (xvii. 18).

Diese uns nur verstümmelt vorliegenden Polemiken dürften alten ebionitischen Apostelakten entstammen, die eine sehr gehässige Schilderung des antichristlichen Wirkens Pauli bis zum Stephanusmartyrium, seiner Konversion sowie der Vorgänge in Antiochia gegeben haben. Wie der ἐχθρὸς ἄνθρωπος in seiner jüdischen Periode für den kultisch verfälschten Mosaismus agitiert habe, so sei er später ein Feind jedes Gesetzes geworden. Hatte er schon die Bemühungen der Urgemeinde und des Jakobus um die Bekehrung der Juden zur lex mosaica per Jesum prophetam reformata durch sein Dazwischentreten vereitelt, so ist er auch nach der Bekehrung der Verfolger des *wahren* Gesetzes geblieben.

3. DAS EBIONITISCHE GESETZESVERSTÄNDNIS

Die Ebioniten des zweiten und dritten Jahrhunderts waren genauso wie ihre Väter, die τινες τῶν ἀπὸ τῆς αἱρέσεως τῶν Φαρισαίων πεπιστευκότες (Acta xv. 5) klare und erklärte ζηλωταὶ τοῦ νόμου (Acta xxi. 20). Sie nennen ihre Lehre τὸ νόμιμον κήρυγμα, haben aber das mosaische Gesetz noch erheblich verschärft und extremisiert durch ihren prinzipiellen Vegetarismus, der die Halbheiten der jüdischen Schechitha überwinden sollte, durch das Gebot der Armut und Gütergemeinschaft sowie durch eine rigorose Kathartik, die von rituellen Waschungen bis zu einer im Taufakt kulminierenden seltsamen Wassermystik reicht. Aber in einer entscheidenden und religionsgeschichtlich recht bedeutsamen Partie haben sie eine systematische *reductio legis mosaicae* durchgeführt: Sie haben nämlich den blutigen Tieropferkult, alsdann das Institut des israelitischen Königtums, ferner die falschen resp. nicht eingetroffenen Prophetien der Schrift sowie endlich die anthropomorphen Gottesaussagen als 'falsche Perikopen' gestrichen, die nachträglich in die Thora Mosis eingeschoben worden sind. Jesus war ihnen der Reformator des jüdischen Gesetzes, dessen διδασκαλία die Thorakritik als Verbreitung der Kunde gewesen ist, was das Wahre und was das widerrechtlich hineingekommene Falsche im Gesetze sei.

Die jesuanische Gesetzesreformation hat sich also nach dem Glauben der Ebioniten hauptsächlich auf den Opferkultus bezogen, und es könnte sein, daß sie darin tatsächlich Jesu rechtgläubige Schüler waren, die den Opferkultus deshalb so scharf verworfen haben, weil ihr Meister das bereits getan hatte. Nun hat in der modernen NT-Forschung Ernst Lohmeyer[1] tatsächlich die Behauptung aufgestellt, daß die im Kanon bei Matthäus und Marcus vorliegende Jesustradition strikt antikultisch gewesen sei, 'weshalb wir niemals

[1] *Kultus und Evangelium* (Göttingen, 1942), S. 125.

in der evangelischen Überlieferung eine Bemerkung darüber lesen, daß das gleiche Gesetz, das man als Willen Gottes verehrt und erfüllt, auch die Ordnung des Kultus enthält, die man verwirft.' Ebenso dürfte dann die Tendenz der Stephanusrede in Acta vii als gut jesuanisch zu erklären sein.

Bei einer solchen Einschätzung der Gegnerschaft Jesu zum blutigen Sühnopferkult wird ein weiterer Grund deutlich, warum die Ebioniten die paulinische Lehre ablehnen mußten. Denn Pauli soteriologische Wertung des Todes Jesu als Sühnopfertod ist—ebionitisch gesprochen—das größte Paradox, das gedacht werden kann, eine Lästerung solchen Stils, daß sie allein schon ihn als Typus des falschen Propheten erweist. Nicht durch das alles umfassende Opfer des Gottessohnes, wie die Kirche in Pauli Nachfolge lehrt, ist die Christenheit vom jüdischen Opferdienst frei geworden, sondern durch die Wasser der Taufe hat Jesu die Feuer des Opfertodes—so ist ebionitischer Glaube—zum Verlöschen gebracht. Jedenfalls war in der ebionitischen Theologie die Aufhebung der Opfer geradezu Jesu Auftrag, mit dem er sich als der 'wahre Prophet' ausgewiesen hat, daß er die Opferthora—bei aller sonstigen Treue und Bejahung des mosaischen Gesetzes—zur Auflösung bringt.

Alle von Jesus befohlenen ebionitischen Streichungen und Vermehrungen, Erleichterungen wie Erschwerungen im Gesetz geschehen aber nur, um den Willen Gottes als die Instanz *hinter* den Schriften (τὰ ἀληθῆ τῶν γραφῶν — Matt. xxii. 29) zum Ausdruck zu bringen, um die zerstörte Einheit zwischen dem Gesetz und dem Willen Gottes wieder herzustellen. Im Letzten haben sie das Gesetz von Jesus her beurteilt; in seinem Leben und in seiner Lehre sahen sie die rechte Erfüllung des mosaischen Gesetzes. Das Göttliche in ihm habe er bestätigt, das Widergöttliche vernichtet. Ebionitische Theologie zu betreiben, hieß für sie nichts anderes, als dies im einzelnen festzulegen. In Wendung gegen die paulinische Lehre war dabei ihr Ziel, als Inhalt der wahren θρησκεία: τὸ μόνον αὐτὸν σέβειν, μὴ ἀκαθάρτως βιοῦν, εὐποιεῖν, μὴ ἀδικεῖν (*Hom.* vii. 8). Durch δικαιοσύνη ἐξ ἔργων (justitia in operibus—*Rec.* ii. 36) werde man zu der von Jesus, dem wahren Propheten, geforderten 'besseren Gerechtigkeit' gelangen.

4. GESCHICHTLICHE STANDORTSBESTIMMUNG

Besonders auffällig ist die Feindseligkeit der Ebioniten gegen den jüdischen Opferkultus, der sich auch gegen die Kultstätte des Jerusalemer Tempels gerichtet hat, weil er eine Depravation der alten von Gott gewünschten Stiftshütte darstelle. Da es in der jüdischen Religionsgeschichte von den nomadischen Rechabiten durch die Makkabäerzeit hindurch bis zu den Essäern der Zeitenwende immer wieder Oppositionsbewegungen gegen den Opferkultus der jerusalemer Priesterschaft gegeben hat, sind die Ebioniten in einen deutlich aufzeigbaren ideengeschichtlichen Zusammenhang hineinzustellen; zumal zu den Essäern erscheint die innere Verbundenheit eng. Offensichtlich gehören in ihre Ahnenreihe bevorzugt auch *die* Gruppen hinein, welche hinter den Schriften stehen, die durch den Höhlenfund der Papyrusrollen von 'Ain Feshkha—nach Abfassung meiner Bücher—bekannt geworden sind. Zumindest ergibt der Vergleich ihrer Anschauungen eine sehr ähnliche Christologie (more ṣedeq — ἀληθὴς προφήτης), die gleiche Lobpreisung der Armen und wohl auch (*Sektenkanon* IX, 3) eine gemeinsame Reservation gegen den blutigen Tieropferkult.[1] Wie ich bereits a.a.O. zeigen konnte,[2] dürften die Sadoqitengruppe von 'Ain Feshkha, die Gemeinde von Damaskus, Essäer und Ebioniten in einem glaubensgeschichtlichen Zusammenhang gestanden haben. Ermöglicht wurde dieser durch den Exodus der Urgemeinde nach Ostjordanien, wo seit alters zivilisations- und zumal kultfeindliche jüdische Minderheitsgruppen gesiedelt hatten.

Daß die Ebioniten der Kirchenväter und des klementinischen Romans tatsächlich die leiblichen Nachkommen der jerusalemer Urgemeinde sind, ergibt sich übrigens, von den Zeugnissen des Eusebius und Epiphanius abgesehen, aus zwei bisher meist übersehenen Erklärungen der ebionitischen Quelle des pseudoklementi-

[1] Innerhalb der bereits sehr angeschwollenen Literatur zu den 'Ain Feshkha-Rollen ist auf die Arbeit von Kurt Schubert, 'Die jüdischen und judenchristlichen Sekten im Lichte des Handschriftenfundes von En Fescha' (*ZKTh.* (1952), Heft 1) hinzuweisen, der die uns interessierende Vergleichung systematisch und bisher am besonnensten durchgeführt hat.

[2] H. J. Schoeps, 'Handelt es sich wirklich um ebionitische Dokumente?', *Zeitschrift für Religions- und Geistesgeschichte* (1951), Heft 4, sowie 'Das gnostische Judentum in the Dead Sea Scrolls', *ibid.* (1954), Heft 3.

nischen Romans (*Rec.* i. 37 syr.; *Rec.* i. 39): Die Weisheit Gottes habe sie zu einem sicheren Ort der Landschaft zur Rettung weggeführt, und dies vor Ausbruch des Krieges, der den ungläubigen Juden zum Verderben ausschlagen werde.[1]

In ihren vom Weltverkehr abgelegenen neuen Heimatorten haben sich die Nachkommen der Jerusalemer Urgemeinde kaum länger als 350 Jahre halten können. Nach gewöhnlichem Sektiererschicksal scheinen sie sich in ihrer Spätzeit gespalten oder doch viele Sonderrichtungen hervorgebracht zu haben. Soweit sie nicht zur Katholischen Kirche zurückfanden, sind sie schließlich in dem bunten Religionsgemisch Vorderasiens untergegangen, nachdem ihre Losungen und Lösungen der jüdischen Gesetzesreform auf keiner Seite Anklang gefunden hatten und die Kraft ihrer eschatologischen Erwartung durch das Faktum der Parusieverzögerung allmählich gebrochen worden war, da sie durch keine besondere Sakramentsmystik wie in der Großkirche ausgeglichen wurde. Was aber ihre Religionslehren und Glaubenssätze betrifft, so sind diese mehr oder minder abgewandelt und umgeschmolzen—über mehrere Verbindungsgelenke hin—in der dritten, bisher zeitlich letzten Offenbarungsreligion der Weltgeschichte, dem *Islam*, wieder ans Tageslicht gekommen.

Die Frage aber muß zu stellen erlaubt sein, ob nicht diese vom lebendigen Strom der Entwicklung abgeschnittenen und zur Sekte erstarrten späten Nachkommen der Urgemeinde trotz aller Entstellung und Verzerrung genauso legitime Zeugen und Künder der Botschaft Jesu gewesen sind, wie die Vertreter der überwiegend heidenchristlichen Katholischen Kirche. Ob sich nicht im Geschlech-

[1] Vgl. meine Bemerkung in *Theologie und Geschichte des Judenchristentums*, S. 477: 'Wer sollte anders sonst in der ganzen Christenheit ein Interesse daran haben, sich auf diesen Vorgang zu berufen und ausgerechnet ihn in das Zentrum eines heilgeschichtlichen Berichtes zu rücken, wenn nicht eben die Nachkommen dieser Exulanten, die separierten Judenchristen oder Ebioniten, die von ihrer Separation freilich schon durch einen größeren Zeitabstand getrennt erscheinen. Aber sie zehren noch von den Traditionen der Jerusalemer Zeit und halten den Kirchenprimat des Jakobus auch noch für seinen Nachfolger auf dem Bischofstuhle aufrecht (*Rec.* IV, 35).' — Aus einer weiteren Stelle (*Hom.* ii, 17), die besagt, daß das wahre Evangelium erst nach der Zerstörung der Heiligen Stadt zur Widerlegung kommender Haeresien ausgesandt worden sei, hat auch der sehr kritische B. Rehm (*ZNW* (1938), 154) geschlossen, daß hier eine Gruppe Menschen das Wort nehme, 'die sich selbst von den vor und nach der Zerstörung Jerusalems geflüchteten Judenchristen ableiten'.

terverband der leiblichen Nachkommenschaft der ersten Apostel einschließlich der Sippe Jesu manche urchristliche Lebens-, Lehr- und Glaubensweise erhalten hat, die in der Großkirche früh vergessen wurde oder dem Drang in die Weite der Welt zum Opfer fiel, im engen Horizont syrischer Sektenkirche aber bewahrt und konserviert worden ist? Ob sich also nicht gerade ein Stück der urchristlichen Botschaft nach ihren ursprünglichen Tendenzen unter diesen versprengten Palästinensern entwickelt hat? Haben sie die Fortschritte der Kirche auf dem Boden der heidnischen Diaspora, die sogenannte 'Hellenisierung des Christentums' nicht mit Recht als Entfremdung von ihren palästinensischen Ursprüngen angesehen? Waren sie am Ende doch die wahren Erben, auch wenn sie untergingen?

Ich sagte in meinem Buch und wiederhole es hier: 'Es ist nicht das Amt des Historikers—auch nicht des Historikers der Religionen—Wertantworten zu geben und anstelle nüchterner Konstatierungen Glaubensentscheidungen zu treffen' (321). Aber er wird in jedem Fall mit Nachdruck auf das in Vergessenheit geratene Faktum hinzuweisen haben, daß es in der Frühzeit des Christentums und noch ziemlich lange in der alten Kirche neben der katholischen auch eine *ebionitische Wahrheit des Christentums* gegeben hat.

REFLECTIONS ON ARCHBISHOP CARRINGTON'S 'THE PRIMITIVE CHRISTIAN CALENDAR'

W. D. DAVIES

FOR some time criticism has been concerned to understand the documents of the New Testament not only in the light of their setting in life, conceived in a broad sense, but also especially in the light of the worship of the Church from which they emerged. A slight but stimulating volume by the Archbishop of Quebec, *The Primitive Christian Catechism* (Cambridge, 1940), brilliantly and fruitfully exemplified and served this concern. Primitive Christian baptismal and other practices he there exploited to illumine certain patterns of ethical exhortation which often recur in the New Testament. In a recent volume, *The Primitive Christian Calendar* (Cambridge, 1952), the same author has turned to what he considers to have been the lectionary needs and practices of the early Church as a key to the compilation and structure of some of the New Testament and other early Christian documents; in particular, he has sought to prove the relationship of the Gospel of Mark not only with the Jewish lectionary tradition but also with the primitive Christian calendar.

Since it was not likely that Christians should remain uninfluenced by their religious environment (any more than Carrington himself by the contemporary 'Myth and Ritual School', indebtedness to which he acknowledges), the tradition of evangelical teaching was moulded in such a way that it reflected the festal tradition of the surrounding Jewish community (this in turn was influenced by age-long mythological forms which thereby entered the Christian tradition itself: it is here that Carrington shows the influence of the 'Myth and Ritual School').[1] Not less than fifteen years after his

[1] *The Primitive Christian Calendar*, pp. xiv, 8ff.

death,[1] the tradition about Jesus became fixed in its main outlines around certain central days such as the Passover, Pentecost, Tabernacles, the New Year, the Day of Atonement. Carrington begins by pinning down the Feeding of the Five Thousand to Passover activity, in the light of John vi. 4. With this as a starting-point,[2] he is able to fit the rest of Mark into a lectionary scheme arranged to cover one whole year. The Passion narrative proper, which he takes to begin at Mark xiii. 1, he regards as a distinct lectionary unit for reading at the annual Christian Passover. It is preceded by what Carrington calls Mark I[3] or the Galilean Mark, which was not primarily an account of the life and teaching of Jesus, but of the origins of Christianity in Galilee,[4] in emphasizing the importance of which Carrington follows Lohmeyer. But Mark I and the Passion narrative are interlocked by an intricate system of triadic key-words, a triadic structure which is also apparent, in a minor pattern, in the various pericopae both of Mark I and the Passion narrative.[5] What is here to be emphasized, however, is that Carrington regards the whole of Mark, i.e. the Galilean Mark, and the Passion narrative, as through and through liturgical in its structure and intention. It is not merely that Mark has certain liturgical characteristics, but that it *is* a lectionary.[6] That this is the case, it is claimed, is supported by the fact that the lectionary units from which Mark was composed are reflected in the lectionary and script divisions of some of the oldest manuscripts of the New Testament.[7] It is not claimed that these divisions preserve the original lectionary arrangement of Mark; indeed, the text of Mark which we now have does not represent the original Mark, which was fitted into the Hebrew calendar of agricultural festivals, but a revised Mark which was made to fit the Julianic calendar at Rome.[8] Nevertheless, Carrington claims that the manuscripts enable him to underpin his thesis with factual evidence which he regards as mathematical in its cogency. This understanding of Mark as originally composed to serve as a lectionary, according to Carrington, explains why Form-Criticism has been able to isolate self-contained

[1] P. 85. Direct page references in these notes are to Carrington's book.
[2] P. 15.
[3] See pp. 18ff.
[4] P. 81.
[5] Pp. 9ff., 80.
[6] P. 87.
[7] Pp. 23ff.
[8] Pp. 78–80.

units of the tradition, which retained their opening and closing formulae *after* their inclusion in a full-length Gospel. This was so because they were intended as lectionary units in the services of the Church.[1]

Finally, the structure of Matthew is to be understood in the same light as that of Mark. It came into being, probably at Antioch or at any rate some other Syrian city, on the arrival of the Gospel of Mark from Rome. Mark was combined with Q and an old Aramaic Matthew, which was now translated into Greek and was itself a full liturgical gospel like Mark,[2] as is shown, according to Carrington, by the evidence of Papias.[3] Thus there emerged the canonical Matthew to form a kind of omnibus volume, a new lectionary which in its main divisions followed those of Mark. We shall deal with the details of Carrington's argument as we proceed. His study, which is marked by learning, ingenuity and a massive industry, raises, in an acute form, the question whether it was through the medium of a Christian lectionary that the Christian tradition was most transmitted. We shall now examine his thesis in order to discover whether it helps us to assess the significance of the lectionary factor in the transmission and formation of that tradition. It rests on what we can conveniently call a triad, namely, certain underlying assumptions, certain secondary supports, and, lastly, a certain external mathematical confirmation of these, derived, Carrington claims, from the manuscript evidence.

The main assumption behind Carrington's work is that the very early evolution of a fully developed lectionary, immensely complicated in its inner connections, was probable and possible in the early Church. This in turn rests, implicitly if not always explicitly, upon his view of that Church as a well-organized community which was so closely parallel to the Synagogue that the lectionary practice of the Synagogue found a natural counterpart in a lectionary concern within the Church. To Carrington it has become 'clear that the vigorous organization of the Christian ecclesia was not a new creation which evolved slowly out of nothing, but *simply the normal organization of the old Jewish Synagogue transformed by the injection into it of the Christian gospel and apostolate with its faith in Jesus and its*

[1] P. 18. [2] Pp. 59ff. [3] Pp. 58f.

possession of the Holy Spirit' (my italics).[1] Insisting on the 'system of readers, teachers, evangelists and so forth' in the Church, he holds that among other things the Church would certainly observe all the festivals of the Jewish liturgical year, so that its literature would be connected with the sacred Jewish calendar and thus subserve a lectionary purpose.[2] Nor is it necessary or possible to deny outrightly the synagogal connections upon which Carrington thus so strongly insists. The Jewish year doubtless continued to be followed for calendrical purposes at least by Christians who had once been Jews; the Jewish festivals supplied the Church with a wealth of imagery or symbolism,[3] features of synagogal worship reappeared in that of Christians;[4] it has been possible to claim that the organization of the Synagogue was the pattern for that of the Church.[5] It is not for nothing that in some parts the Church was actually designated a synagogue,[6] and we know that the separation of Church and Synagogue was a gradual process.

Nevertheless, certain factors must be recognized. First, at this point, it is highly pertinent to note the difference between the ethos of Christian and synagogal worship. The Synagogue was primarily a *beth midrash* which centred in the reading and interpretation of the Torah,[7] so that for the Synagogue the eventual evolution of some

[1] P. 17. It should be noted that to many who do not share Carrington's view of the early Church, but who regard it as a society altogether more free in its forms than Carrington would probably concede (see, for example, the salutary article by H. J. Cadbury in *The Crozer Quarterly*, vol. XXI (1944), pp. 246ff., on 'The Informality of Early Christianity'), it may seem sufficiently cogent to reject his thesis on general grounds. We have here attempted, however, to deal with specific points without prejudging the general issue as to the character of the early Church; see W. D. Davies, *A Normative Pattern of Church Life in the New Testament: Fact or Fancy?* (London, 1951), on the broad outlines of this problem.

[2] P. 17.

[3] This need not be illustrated because it is so obvious.

[4] See, for example, C. W. Dugmore, *The Influence of the Synagogue upon the Divine Office* (1944), pp. 1ff. For details see W. D. Davies, *op. cit.* pp. 15f., where the debt to the Synagogue is recognized.

[5] E.g. *The Ministry and the Sacraments* (ed. R. Dunkerley, 1937), pp. 368ff., E. J. Palmer on 'A New Approach to an Old Problem: The Development of the Christian Ministry'.

[6] See the evidence for this in C. W. Dugmore, *op. cit.* p. 5; K. L. Schmidt, *Theologisches Wörterbuch*, Bd. III, p. 521.

[7] See, for example, T. W. Manson in *Christian Worship*, ed. N. Micklem, pp. 35ff.

kind of lectionary system was a necessity, although, even so, that evolution, as far as we can gather, proceeded very slowly over centuries.[1] In the earliest days, to accept Carrington's dating,[2] these would last up to the sixties of the first century, but we can safely think of them as lasting longer, Christians frequently participated in the synagogal services with their concentration on the lessons. But it is easily possible to exaggerate how far they transferred any such concentration into their own services. The Church, it must be remembered, was not always imitative of the Synagogue; there was not only assimilation to synagogal forms of worship among Christians but also a deliberate cultivation of differences.[3] The multiplicity of forms which the specifically Christian services developed should warn us against elevating any lectionary concern to any such place as would demand a fixed lectionary as early as Carrington maintains.[4]

An assessment of the references to the reading of documents in the services of the Church confirms this warning. That there was much lectionary activity in the services is very probable,[5] nevertheless, the explicit references to this are surprisingly few. In his lengthy discussion of the necessity for order in worship, Paul never once refers in I Cor. xi ff. to the reading of the Scriptures. This is a difficulty for Carrington's theory whose emphasis is that such reading was

[1] The early lectionary practice of the Synagogue is wrapped in obscurity. Büchler's treatment in *J.Q.R.* vols. v, pp. 420ff., vi, pp. 1–73, is now antiquated; see Jacob Mann, *The Bible as Read and Preached in the Old Synagogue* (Ohio, 1940), p. 6. In addition consult Elbogen, *Der Jüdische Gottesdienst* (1931).

[2] P. 17.

[3] On the caution necessary in dealing with the relations between Church and Synagogue see O. S. Rankin, *Journal of Jewish Studies*, vol. 1, no. 1 (1948). The history of fasting in the Church, of the recitation of the Decalogue in the Synagogue, the *Birkath ha-Minim*—to note only the most obvious factors—show how the Church and Synagogue reacted against each other; I hope to deal with this problem elsewhere. Cf. C. W. Dugmore, *op. cit.* p. 6.

[4] On this see, for example, O. Cullmann, *Early Christian Worship* (Eng. trans. 1953), pp. 12ff.

[5] W. L. Knox, *The Source of the Synoptic Gospels* (1953), p. 5, '"In the beginning was the sermon" (Fascher) needs to be supplemented by the words, "The lesson was a close second..."'. Knox is writing of specifically Christian lessons. R. M. Grant, *The Bible in the Church* (1948), is not concerned with lectionary activity; A. Harnack, *Bible Reading in the Early Church* (Eng. trans. 1912), deals specifically with the private reading of Scripture. Although he does not find much evidence for this in the period before Irenaeus (p. 47), nothing that he writes suggests that the Gospels could have been intended primarily for public reading.

from the first κατὰ τάξιν. At least in the Gentile churches of Paul's acquaintance this was not so. That Paul could expect his own Epistles to be read at length in the services points to much flexibility.[1] Such reading for the Sabbath, i.e. our Saturday, as we find in the lectionaries at a far later date than Paul may well be a direct inheritance from the Synagogue,[2] but not the reading of the Epistles of a living person like Paul. Moreover it is difficult to imagine that a fixed lectionary comports in any way with such scenes as are implied in I Cor. xi or Acts xx. The reference in I Tim. iv. 13 is probably to the public reading of documents in the Church, but it does not provide any evidence as to *how* such reading was conceived.[3] The first fairly full description of a church service comes to us from Justin Martyr. Carrington has not noticed the point that the implications of this passage are directly opposed to his theory. The passage, the *First Apology*, I. 67, reads: 'And on the day called Sunday, all who live in cities or in the country gather together to one place, and the memoirs of the apostles or the writings of the prophets are read, as long as time permits; then when the reader has ceased, the president verbally instructs, and exhorts to the imitation of these good things....' It seems to us that the phrase μέχρις ἐγχωρεῖ, which Cullmann renders *so lange es die Zeit erlaubt*, i.e. as long as time

[1] I Thess. v. 27; Col. iv. 16. Too much, however, should not be made of this point. It would be customary for a *shaliach* to read letters from Jerusalem and elsewhere at various synagogues (cf. Acts ix. 1), (see Rengstorf, *Theologisches Wörterbuch*, Bd. I, pp. 416), and a similar custom would of necessity develop in the Church, though we need not, therefore, take the *shaliach* to be the strict prototype of the *apostolos* (see T. W. Manson, *The Church's Ministry* (1948), pp. 31 ff.). Professor Nock also pointed out to me the very significant fact that 'in the fixed pattern of the Roman Mass the Pastoral Letter of a Bishop is read'. So too M. Goguel, *L'Église Primitive* (Paris, 1947), pp. 292 ff. insists that it is erroneous to find in Col. iv. 16 a reference to such a strictly lectionary practice as we find in the Synagogue. He connects the introduction of the Gospels into the public reading of the Church with its edificatory needs and with the necessity of establishing its authority. The desire to see in the Christian cult no improvised novelty but a transcendent reality, which had been prefigured in the cult of the Old Israel, led the New Israel to seek conformity between its cult and that of the Old. This, Goguel thinks, contributed to the establishing of lectionary activity in the Church. But we have seen reason to question this emphasis on imitation, certainly in the early period in which Carrington finds it.

[2] See C. R. Gregory, *Canon and Text of the New Testament* (1912), p. 387. The whole section (pp. 384–93) is relevant to a discussion of Carrington.

[3] The context of I Tim. iv. 13 favours making it refer to public reading.

allows, makes the conception of any fixed lectionary improbable.[1] The length of the reading would depend not on a prearranged *schema* but on the exigencies of time. Had Justin Martyr had a fixed lectionary in mind he would have used some such phrase as κατὰ τάξιν. Notice also that the Old Testament prophets were read, how it is not stated, but this points again, however, to the *varied* character of lectionary activity, as of other forms, in the services. The whole section in Justin does not suggest rigidity of any kind. 'The president *verbally* instructs' probably implies that he instructs freely according to his own discretion; similarly he 'offers prayers and thanksgivings according to his ability'. In I, 65 it is not stated, that the prayers are of a fixed length but of a 'considerable length' (εὐχαριστίαν ὑπὲρ τοῦ κατηξιῶσθαι τούτων παρ' αὐτοῦ ἐπὶ πολύ). Again the evidence of I Clement XL, 1 ff., to which Carrington appeals,[2] equally points not to a fixed or formalized order of worship, however much the author may have desired such, so much as to a disorder or formlessness which needed to be corrected. (We shall return to this below.) It is pertinent, finally, to point out that Cullmann is probably to be followed in rejecting the older view that gatherings for the proclamation of the Word and gatherings for the Lord's Supper, were to be sharply distinguished as were in Judaism the synagogue service and the temple cult.[3] There was little that Christianity took over neat from Judaism and particularly in its worship is this the case. Historical probability does not favour Carrington's lectionary emphasis.

To illustrate further how, by implication at least, Carrington exaggerates the parallelism between Church and Synagogue we turn to his treatment of the development of the Christian Calendar. His contention—as it applies to Jewish Christians, at least—that the Church took over the Jewish Calendar would seem to be probable.[4] (How far the bulk of Gentile converts to the Church would be sufficiently familiar with the Jewish year to 'take it over' for their

[1] So too L. Pautigny, *Justin, Apologies* (Paris, 1904), p. 143, translates 'autant que le temps le permet'.

[2] P. 41.

[3] *Op. cit.* pp. 26–32.

[4] Carrington's use of I Cor. xvi. 8, Acts xx. 16, xxvii. 9 is pertinent and valid here, *op. cit.* p. 17. It should be noted, however, that the festivals of the Gentiles attracted some Jews very strongly (see Mishnah, Abodah Zarah), as indeed Carrington is fully aware.

own use is more questionable; it is probable that the Church became increasingly full of people who had little awareness of the Jewish festal tradition.) But it is probably erroneous to regard this as a deliberate process as if Christians formally decided to do so; rather there was among the earliest Jewish Christians at least an unconscious or quite natural maintenance of the calendrical tradition of Jewry.

Carrington's over-emphasis appears in his treatment of the emergence of the Lord's Day.[1] He searches for a parallel to, or precedent for, the celebration of the day we term 'Sunday' and early Christians 'the first day of the week' and later 'the Lord's Day', in the Jewish Calendar and finds it in the Firstfruits when it was traditional to bring offerings. It is in the light of the Firstfruits that the Christian Sunday, he seems to imply, is to be understood; this in turn explains why Paul arranged for the collection of money for the poor of Jerusalem on the first day of the week. But it is far more probable that the Christian Sunday which was designed above all to commemorate the resurrection of the Lord, emerged not indeed in parallelism to any Jewish observance like Firstfruits, but actually in conscious opposition to or distinction from the Jewish Sabbath.[2] Nor need we find any deeper motif for making arrangements for the collection of money on the first day of the week than that of simple convenience: probably it had nothing to do with the custom of offering firstfruits, any more than with the Temple tax.[3]

[1] *Op. cit.* pp. 38ff.

[2] Compare O. Cullmann, *op. cit.* pp. 10–12, where the evidence is sifted. There seems to be little, if any, evidence that the Christian Sunday was, for instance, a day of rest, as was the Jewish Sabbath. On this point contrast Cullmann, who (*op. cit.* pp. 87, 91) suggests that the first day of the week (our Sunday) was a day of rest for early Christians according to John v; it replaced the Jewish Sabbath as such. He finds support for this view from the Epistle of Barnabas xv. 9. But here the eighth day is stated to be kept in joyfulness not in rest, it being implied that the true rest can only be regarded as a future gift at the Son's coming again. (Cullmann finds an eschatological idea analogous to this in John v. 17 and compare also Heb. iv. 10.) The tone of the Epistle to Diognetus iv, does not suggest that Christians observed any day as a sabbath, as Professor H. J. Cadbury pointed out to me. See also C. H. Dodd in *Journal of Ecclesiastical History*, vol. iii, no. 3 (Oct. 1952); J. Daniélou, *Bible et Liturgie* (Paris, 1951), pp. 305ff; B. S. Easton, *The Apostolic Tradition of Hippolytus* (1934), p. 5 n. 2; R. Bultmann, *New Testament Theology*, vol. i, p. 123; A. D. Nock, *St Paul*, pp. 58 f.

[3] See K. Holl, 'Der Kirchenbegriff des Paulus in seinem Verhältnis zu dem der Urgemeinde', in *Sitzungsb. Preus. Akad. Wiss.* vol. liii (1921), and the discussion in R. N. Flew, *Jesus and his Church* (1938), *ad loc.*

So too in Carrington's treatment of the Christian Passover he has rightly recalled us again to the debt of early Christian sources to the festal tradition of Judaism, but that debt has to be carefully assessed. Paschal imagery does invade I Corinthians and so too II Corinthians may well reflect Pentecostal and Tabernacle motifs, as Carrington and T. W. Manson have affirmed, and it may well be that other New Testament documents are to be illuminated by reference to Jewish festivals, as is Romans, for example, by the Day of Atonement.[1] But it is quite another thing to ascribe to such imagery as we have referred to any strictly calendrical intention. Thus to take I Cor. v. 7 as implying a deliberate calendrical adherence to the Jewish Passover in a new Christian dress is to press the imagery too far. Paul's intention here is to emphasize that the *whole* of the Christian life is a Passover, Christ, the Passover Lamb, having been slain; he is not thinking of a specific Christian Passover day but of the Christian dispensation as such as a feast.[2] Again that the Pentecostal imagery in II Cor. i–v must not too certainly be taken to indicate the Pentecostal dating of that section appears from the fact that in II Cor. v the imagery may be interpreted as suddenly changing to that of Tabernacles.[3] All this means that the strictly calendrical significance of the festal symbolism or imagery of the New Testament documents should not be over-emphasized. What that imagery shows is that early Christians exploited the festal tradition of Judaism for their own evangelistic and hortatory ends; with its calendrical import they were not consciously concerned and still less were they seeking to base a Christian calendar upon it. Much as a modern poet, Dylan Thomas, made use of images born of the Christian tradition, because they were his *necessary* medium of communication in his own particular environment, which had been largely conditioned by Christianity, even though he himself had never embraced that

[1] For references see *Paul and Rabbinic Judaism*, pp. 240ff., 313. See also J. Munck, *Paulus und Die Heilsgeschichte* (1954), pp. 137 ff.

[2] It is important to realize that *every* Sunday commemorated Easter. How soon did the Church fasten on one day to commemorate the death of Jesus? There is no real evidence for thinking that Jesus intended his death to be commemorated annually. On the interpretation of I Cor. v. 7, see J. Weiss, in Meyer, *Kommentar: Der Erste Korintherbrief* (1924), *ad loc.*; A. D. Nock, *St Paul* (1938), p. 53.

[3] It is to be noted that T. W. Manson does not find Pentecostal motifs in II Cor. v but Tabernacle ones: see *Journal of Theological Studies*, Jan.–April, vol. XLVI (1945), pp. 1–10; Carrington, p. 43.

tradition, so too early Christians could use Jewish festal imagery without being aware in any way that they were thereby contributing to the establishment of a Christian calendar.

For example Carrington takes the passage I Clem. XL, 1 ff. to prove that 'a liturgical year of the Hebrew type must have been well established in Rome and in Corinth by the 90's'. The passage reads: πάντα τάξει ποιεῖν ὀφείλομεν, ὅσα ὁ Δεσπότης ἐπιτελεῖν ἐκέλευσε[ν] κατὰ καιροὺς τεταγμένους· τάς τε προσφορὰς καὶ λειτουργίας ἐπιτελεῖσθαι, καὶ οὐκ εἰκῇ ἢ ἀτάκτως ἐκέλευσεν γίνεσθαι, ἀλλ' ὡρισμένοις καιροῖς καὶ ὥραις κ.τ.λ.[1] Carrington notes that it is a feature of the style of I Clement to avoid precise detail: this makes it difficult to determine the exact connotation of his words. What do the phrases κατὰ καιροὺς τεταγμένους, ὡρισμένοις καιροῖς καὶ ὥραις, and προστεταγμένοις καιροῖς (XL, 4) mean? Because of the reference to the high priest, priests, Levites and laymen, Carrington interprets them to refer to a liturgical year of a Hebrew type, i.e. the seasons refer to Passover, Tabernacles, etc. But this is to draw far more rigid a parallelism between the Old and the New Dispensation than is intended by I Clement. Doubtless there is a parallelism to be seen between the 'ministers' of Judaism, the high priest, priests, Levites and laymen and those of the Church, apostles, bishops, deacons, but, as Lightfoot[2] long since pointed out, no *direct* reference to or identity with Christian ministers is suggested: it is only by *analogy* that they are referred to. Not only is a direct reference made improbable by the fact that while the high priest, priests and Levites constitute three orders, the Epistle only recognizes two, presbyters and deacons, but any attempt to identify Jesus with the high priest, the presbyters with the priests and the deacons with the Levites must fail, because this would be to blur the distinction between the high priesthood of Christ and any other. Just as the offerings, sacrifices and gifts presented by the presbyters are not a literal reference to Jewish sacrifice but are to be understood as prayers, thanksgivings, alms, eucharistic elements and gifts,[3] so too there is no identification

[1] The text used is from Hippolyte Hemmer, *Clément de Rome* (1926), pp. 83 f.

[2] *The Apostolic Fathers*, vol. II, pp. 122 ff.

[3] See Lightfoot, *op. cit.* pp. 134 f.; H. Hemmer, *op. cit.* p. 85 n., notes on the use of προσφερόνται in I Clem. XLI, 2, 'Clément de Rome emploie le présent pour décrire une institution demeurée dans son souvenir; mais il ne trace de parallèle

of the appointed seasons of I Clem. XL with the Levitical seasons: they refer rather to the Lord's Day, the first day of the week. Carrington's understanding of I Clem. XL is far too literal. Moreover, in any case, even if I Clement did intend to refer to a fixed Christian calendar following the pattern of the Hebraic, which is most improbable, as we saw, what the text points to is a disorder and formlessness in the Corinthian Church, a formlessness which must have ignored such a calendar, if it was intended to be followed, and demanded correction. Such evidence as we have in the New Testament, to which Carrington refers in the Pauline Epistles, does not point to a desire for such a calendrical imitation of Judaism. Rom. xiv. 5 and Gal. iv. 10, 11 certainly lend no support to this. In both we know Paul's attitude; he himself doubtless failed to achieve logical consistency in his life, and continued to observe days, but he is far from wanting Christians to follow any calendar. To see Christians, taught by him, insisting that days, months and years should be observed, prompts him to fear that he has laboured in vain in Gal. iv. 10, 11. It is true, as Carrington points out, that he is more tolerant in Rom. xiv. 5, and the same tolerant attitude lies behind Col. ii. 16f., but he makes no secret of the fact that he himself is 'among the strong' in such matters as meats and, by implication, the calendar. Justin's *Dialogue with Trypho*, X is very explicit in its assertion that Christians observe no festivals or Sabbaths: both Justin and Trypho refer to this. Nor is it irrelevant to point out in this connection that were the calendrical interests of the early Christians as strong as is suggested by Carrington it is unlikely that the controversy on matters of chronology to which he refers, the Quarto-decimian controversy, would have arisen at all. Surely such interests would have helped to preclude the development of any such.[1]

The same hesitation arising from historical probabilities makes it difficult to believe that early Christians were concerned to set forth the life and teaching of Jesus in the intricate triadic form discovered by Carrington in Mark, which he makes quite integral to his lec-

entre les deux sacerdoces que parce que la disparition de l'un fait valoir l'autre.' He cites a parallel usage of the present tense in Josephus, *Antiquities*, III, 7–11; Barnabas, VII–IX; *The Epistle to Diognetus*, III; Justin, *Dialogue*, CXVII.

[1] Pp. 39f.

tionary theory.[1] Apart from the difficulty of accepting the view that the Gospel which found its way into the canon is the product of what Carrington seems to regard as a kind of esoteric and poetic group in the early Church,[2] this hesitation is amply sustained by an examination of the facts.

Let us first take what Carrington calls the Major Triads in Mark.[3] His most important triad is that of the three mountains at iii. 13 f., vi 30 f., ix. 2 f. At the first mountain, iii. 13 f., the death and resurrection of the Son of Man is announced in parables. Carrington takes all the three parables in iv. 1–20, 26–9, 30–2, to be concerned with this one theme. But, if they were intended to be triadic, why should iv. 21–5 be inserted to break their continuity? Moreover, the explanation of the parable in iv. 1–8 is appended in *vv.* 13 ff. where the experience of the Church in its missionary activity is reflected. Whether or not this is the correct explanation of the parable, it *is* the one accepted by Mark and it does not coincide with Carrington's. Is it really conceivable that Mark had another explanation than the one he provides in his text? In any case, the close connection of these parables, even if Carrington's explanation of them be accepted, with the mountain mentioned in iii. 13 f. is doubtful. Thus iv. 1 does not follow immediately after iii. 19. Carrington ignores the intervening material in iii. 20–30 and iii. 31–5. The parables are uttered not at the mountain but by the sea; they do not follow directly the choice of the Twelve.

The episode of the so-called second mountain, where the death and resurrection of Jesus is claimed to be enacted sacramentally is equally misrepresented by Carrington. It is only *after* the feeding of the five thousand that the Lord goes up to a mountain, there to pray. No mountain is mentioned in connection with the feeding at all: we have to wait till vi. 46 for it, and there it is more closely connected with the walking on the sea than the feeding of the five thousand. Equally significant is the fact that in the feeding of the four thousand in viii. 1–10, which Carrington regards as a lectionary duplicate of vi. 30–44, designed for Pentecost, there is no reference to a mountain,

[1] Pp. 8 ff. On p. 9 Carrington writes: 'A recognition of the triads is equivalent to a recognition of the structure of the Gospel.' He reiterates this in the *Church Quarterly Review* (April–June 1953), no. 311, vol. CLIV, p. 216.

[2] Pp. 92 f.

[3] These Major Triads are listed on pp. 94 ff.; see also the whole section in pp. 6 ff.

which is inconceivable if that phenomenon was as central as Carrington insists.

When we turn to the third mountain, when the death and resurrection of Jesus is revealed openly, Carrington finds even more points of triadic significance. He takes the episode of the third mountain to open at viii. 27 ff. where the reference to John the Baptist (viii. 28) looks back, Carrington thinks, to vi. 14 ff. which precedes the feeding of the five thousand, whilst the reference to Herod in vi. 14 ff. similarly looks back to the reference to the Herodians in iii. 6. Assuming that the episode of the first mountain begins at iii. 7, of the second mountain at vi. 7—although Carrington does not always make it clear where the various episodes begin; thus on p. 6 it seems to begin at vi. 7, but on p. 7 at vi. 14 ff., where we read of 'echoes of those words of Herod which open the Episode of the Second Mountain'—and of the third mountain at viii. 27, it will appear that within these episodes the references to the Herodians and Herod do not constitute a triad. The term Herodians at iii. 6 occurs *outside* the first episode.

The Major Triad to which Carrington attaches most importance, in the light of the above, cannot be regarded as very convincing; indeed only by a *tour de force* can it be established as a triad at all. Nor are his other Major Triads more convincing. He himself admits that there are difficulties in identifying them because 'we often have to distinguish the significant uses of a word from the non-significant'.[1] Since this virtually amounts to an admission that what Carrington treats as triads are actually not triads, the difficulty he mentions is a real one indeed. In a list of Major Triads given on pp. 94 ff., there are seventy-three cases mentioned in all; of these six are regarded by Carrington himself as dubious and seven as merely significant repetitions, not triads, and by any strict triadic standard twenty-five other cases, it seems to me, on examination, must be rejected. This means that of the seventy-three cases only thirty-five are admissible. More important still is it that the Major Triads on which Carrington places the greatest emphasis—the Three Mountains, the Three Predictions of the Passion, the Three Parables—are all inadmissible.[2]

[1] P. 91.

[2] It should be noted that the employment of various sources by Mark, which might account for the frequent incidence of certain words, is not seriously considered by Carrington; for example, contrast the use made of the incidence of the term 'Twelve' by W. L. Knox, *op. cit.* pp. 17 ff., with that by Carrington.

The same negative verdict follows an examination of the minor triads isolated by Carrington in the various lections.[1] He divides Mark into sixty-two lections plus a supplemental Resurrection and Ascension lection (the spurious ending of Mark xvi. 9–20). In some of these he finds no minor triads, namely, in lections 7, 22, 23, 27, 39, although this last is a very important lection, though short (Mark ix. 30–2). No reason is given why these particular lections should be thus devoid of minor triads. An examination of the other lections where Carrington finds such reveals, in my judgment, only nine cases where straightforward minor triads are admissible, in lections 8, 17, 19, 30, 32, 33, 36, 50, 51. In the remainder it is only by special pleading that the minor triads proposed by Carrington can be established at all. It can be asserted that Carrington's understanding of the structure of Mark, if it rests only on the recognition of the triadic structure which we have above examined, must be rejected. We can only regret that he has confused his discussion of the lectionary character of the Gospel with an improbable and unproven theory of its literary character.

Were that theory accepted, it is further to be stated that Carrington's work then suffers from a deep inner contradiction which arises from the last assumption which we note. Throughout his treatment Carrington emphasizes the deliberate and highly intricate artistry with which the Gospel units and the total structure of Mark have been composed, this artistry, triadic in pattern, being linked to a specific liturgical purpose. In his last section, however, he describes the origin of what he calls the Galilean Gospel.[2] Accepting Lohmeyer's claim that there was a Galilean Christianity which is to be sharply distinguished from that of Jerusalem, Carrington pictures the convocations of Galilean Christians, which, it is suggested, in a phrase which it is difficult to understand precisely, 'came into being as a continuation of the ministry of Jesus in the churches which he had himself created'.[3] At these convocations one or more of the Twelve would stand up to recite their memories of Jesus, and thus the liturgical Gospel was given to the world. This Carrington supports by the somewhat amazing statement, in view of his previous

[1] The minor triads are noted after each lection, which Carrington isolates, on pp. 118–230; this is a monument of industry.

[2] Pp. 75ff.

[3] P. 87.

treatment, that 'the Gospel units have the *character of a local tale*, and are the work of someone who could tell a story effectively'[1] (my italics). Can anything be further from a local tale than the intricacies of the triadic structure of Carrington's units, not to speak of his lectionary? We cannot examine Lohmeyer's thesis here that there was a distinct and influential Galilean Christianity. Nor need we, because the importation of the Jerusalem-Galilee antithesis into the discussion of lectionary factors is not necessary. But we may at least safely assert that the popular Galilean activity of Jesus is not the only background to his ministry. Synagogal activity and other more private meetings all had their place. The festal element in the ministry cannot be made the dominant one.

Carrington supports the above broad assumptions with which we have dealt by certain secondary considerations which must now be examined. These are as follows.

(*a*) In a section entitled 'The Dodekad of Preaching' there is offered a thrice-twined argument. First, the view is stated that there could only be one gospel in a given Church, Mark was the Gospel for Rome and constituted a lectionary based on the Julianic calendar used there. Matthew was the one Gospel at Antioch.[2] Marcion clung to this principle and used a mutilated form of Luke which had been assimilated to Mark at some points and given a Marcan title.[3] Secondly, it is pointed out that Mark at an early date was the one Gospel in use at Alexandria. This is affirmed on the ground that the original theology of the Alexandrian heretics, such as Cerinthus (he is supposed by Carrington to have received an Egyptian education, although he taught in Asia), Valentinus and Basilides, who held that the Divine Christus became incarnate at the Baptism, must have depended on a Gospel like that of Mark which begins with the Baptism.[4] And, thirdly, because Mark had been read from the earliest times in the Church as an annual cycle of liturgical lessons, the idea would naturally grow that the events which were thus chronicled had taken place within a single year.[5] Thus Mark became associated with the view that the ministry of Jesus lasted twelve months, a view

[1] P. 88.
[2] Pp. 44ff.
[3] Pp. 46f.
[4] Pp. 48ff.
[5] P. 53.

also associated with the heretics and strongly attacked by Irenaeus.[1] In addition, this explains the famous reference to Mark in Papias.[2] Papias, Carrington points out, preferred to hear the Gospel orally transmitted. Nevertheless he did not criticize Mark for *what* he wrote but for the *order* in which he did so, and Carrington argues that the order here referred to is neither chronological nor topical nor historical but lectionary.[3] By implication he argues that the connection of Mark with Alexandrian Gnosticism would naturally predispose the Great Church against Mark and that Papias' disapproval of the twelve months' ministry which was, according to Carrington, as we have seen, closely connected with the arrangement of the Marcan lectionary, led him to look askance at the Marcan order.[4]

The position here adopted by Carrington is open to much doubt. First, does the evidence support the view that each Church had one gospel? Since Carrington himself regards his treatment of Marcion with uneasiness[5] we need not stay with it, except to point out that it is indeed hard to believe that we can make a list of its chapter divisions when we cannot satisfactorily reconstruct the Marcionite Luke itself.[6] The exclusive connection of Matthew with Antioch cannot be certainly established. While it is true that Ignatius was certainly acquainted either with our Matthew or with a Gospel very closely akin to it, he is also very probably dependent on the Fourth Gospel, and indeed emphasizes the Johannine doctrine of the pre-incarnate activity of the Logos.[7] Carrington supplies little evidence for the continued sole use of Mark at Alexandria as its one Gospel,[8]

[1] On this see *Adv. Haer.* II, xxi. The passage is dealt with by G. Ogg, *The Chronology of the Public Ministry of Jesus* (Cambridge, 1940), pp. 48ff.

[2] See Eusebius, *Ecclesiastical History*, III, 39.

[3] Pp. 58f. [4] *Ibid.* [5] P. 48. [6] P. 47.

[7] See E. Massaux, *Influence de l'Évangile de Saint Matthieu sur la littérature chrétienne avant Saint Irénée* (Louvain, 1950), p. 134; *The New Testament in the Apostolic Fathers* (Oxford, 1905), p. 83, 'Ignatius' use of the Fourth Gospel is highly probable' though it 'falls some way short of certainty'. G. D. Kilpatrick rejects the association of Matthew with Antioch; see *The Origins of the Gospel according to St Matthew* (Oxford, 1946), p. 134.

[8] Pp. 50f. Carrington refers only to Eusebius, *op. cit.* II, 16 (on which see Lawlor and Oulton, *Eusebius: translation, introduction and notes*, vol. II, 1928, p. 66). He writes: 'The form of the Alexandrian heresy which now begins to emerge is obviously Marcan, and is best explained by a theory of an early ascendancy of Mark in Alexandria, which went on later and was perhaps more influential there than elsewhere' (p. 51). It is difficult to follow Carrington in his

nor should he assume as settled the Roman provenance of Mark. *The Shepherd* of Hermas normally turns to Matthew rather than Mark; I Clement shows no trace of Mark.[1]

Again can we associate Mark so closely with Alexandrian Gnosticism as does Carrington? Had that association been very close it is difficult to understand why Mark so easily achieved canonicity. The case of the Fourth Gospel is instructive here: that Gospel's alleged *gnostic* affinities constituted a barrier to its canonicity.[2] Moreover, the arguments put forward by Carrington why Alexandrian Gnosticism would be specially drawn to Mark[3]—namely because it omitted a nativity story—would also apply to the Fourth Gospel. There seems no evidence for associating Mark peculiarly with Alexandria.[4] Nor need we turn to its Alexandrian Gnostic and calendrical affinities to account for the paucity of references to it. The incorporation of Mark into Matthew and Luke would sufficiently account for this.

However, Carrington's speculations on Mark and Gnosticism need not further concern us because there is nothing in the context of Papias' statement to which he refers to support the view that Mark was necessarily a liturgical Gospel. The term τάξει refers to the

understanding of Irenaeus and other authors here. The impression gained from Irenaeus is that it was the Simonians who were the well from which the rank growth of Gnostic heresy developed (see *Adv. Haer.* I, xxiii–xxv). Basilides is connected therewith although he promulgated his views in Alexandria: Valentinus, as Carrington himself points out (p. 48), is specifically connected with the Fourth Gospel (*Adv. Haer.* III, xi). Cerinthus according to the text preserved by Hippolytus was indeed trained in the wisdom of the Egyptians but the Latin text merely describes him as a 'certain man in Asia' (*Adv. Haer.* I, xxvi). Is there any real evidence for what Carrington calls a pre-Gnostic theology based on Mark in Alexandria? (p. 51). For Hippolytus, see W. H. Harvey, *Sancti Irenaei*, tom. I, p. 221.

[1] E. Massaux, *op. cit.* pp. 324f.; on I Clement Massaux (p. 65) writes: '...des évangiles seul celui de Mt. a exercé une influence littéraire certaine sur Clément de Rome: il ne dépend jamais des autres évangiles.'

[2] On this see B. H. Streeter, *The Four Gospels* (1926), pp. 13, 436ff.

[3] How subjective such judgments can be emerges with peculiar force in S. G. F. Brandon, *The Fall of Jerusalem and the Christian Church* (1951), pp. 217ff., who traces the origin of Matthew to Alexandria.

[4] See V. Taylor, *The Gospel according to St Mark* (1952), p. 32. In a penetrating discussion R. P. Casey, *Theology*, vol. LV, no. 38 (October 1952), p. 366 n. 4, also dismisses Carrington's understanding of Alexandrian Gnosticism. This article came into my hands after I had long pondered Carrington's thesis and on all points independently reached the same conclusions. As will emerge from the above, I am not sure that we can dismiss the lectionary significance of the divisions in the manuscripts as surely as does Casey.

things which had been spoken and done by Jesus. Mark had not been able to record these in the strict chronological order in which they happened because he himself in person did not always hear or follow Jesus, but had to rely on the account given to him by Peter. The context favours taking τάξει to refer quite simply to chronological order. (Compare how Luke uses a compound verb ἀνατάξασθαι, which is closely related to τάξις, to describe his method of compiling a gospel;[1] but Carrington does not take Luke as originally composed as a lectionary.)[2] Similarly Carrington's further identification of the λογία to which Papias refers with an Aramaic lectionary Gospel[3] carries no conviction; two comments are apt at this point. First, it is by no means certain that the phrase τὰ λογία refers to an Aramaic Gospel.[4] Secondly, the one thing about which many scholars seem to agree is that Papias at least meant by τὰ λογία our canonical Matthew, which had been translated into Greek.[5] But if Papias meant by τὰ λογία the Aramaic original of the canonical Gospel then Carrington is in difficulty because he has urged that the canonical Matthew follows more or less the lectionary order of Mark, so that if Papias rejected the lectionary order of Mark he would also have to reject Matthew (τὰ λογία) for the same reason: that Papias meant another lectionary Gospel than Matthew the text probably does not indicate and so Carrington from the point of view of Papias himself is probably involved in a contradiction.

(*b*) Carrington refers to Irenaeus' quotation of a 'piece of traditional mysticism which assigns to each gospel as an interpretative symbol one of the four "beasts" or rather living things (*ḥayyoth*) of the Revelation; the face (πρόσωπον) of the man is assigned to Matthew, the eagle to Mark, the calf or bull to Luke, and the lion to John'.[6] He suggests that the four zodiac figures referred to may 'have denoted the seasons of the year to which the four gospels

[1] Luke i. 1. [2] P. 48. [3] P. 59.

[4] See, for example, the exhaustive treatment of τὰ λογία by T. W. Manson, *Bulletin of the John Rylands Library*, vol. xxix, no. 2 (Feb. 1946), especially the appendix, pp. 22ff. One of the most recent Roman Catholic treatments (A. Wirkenhauser, *Einleitung in das Neue Testament*, 1953) takes τὰ λογία to refer to Q., i.e. the original Aramaic document translated into what is designated Q (I depend on G. D. Kilpatrick, *J.T.S.* vol. iv, Pt. 2 (1953), p. 229, for this).

[5] T. W. Manson, *op. cit.* pp. 4f. points out that B. W. Bacon and J. Donovan who discussed τὰ λογία recently agree on this, as does T. W. Manson himself, p. 5.

[6] Pp. 65f.

were allotted in the new four-gospel lectionary which succeeded the one-gospel lectionary'.[1] But a very strong argument against this is the fact, pointed out by Carrington, that the order of the Gospels which it attests is Matthew, Luke, John, Mark, but no list of the Gospels gives this order[2] and what is particularly damaging to Carrington's view is that Irenaeus himself has the order Matthew, Mark, Luke, John.[3] Moreover, in the lectionaries which later emerged in the Church, Matthew is assigned for reading not to 25 December as is the case, on Carrington's theory, in Irenaeus' intention, but to the period following Pentecost.[4] It is not likely that the later tradition is radically different from the earlier in lectionary matters. Moreover, Pentecost, which was associated with the giving of the Law,[5] is precisely the time at which we should expect Matthew to be read. (Carrington himself points to the use of Matthew after Pentecost in the Greek calendar.)[6] But apart from this, to interpret the 'faces' in Irenaeus calendrically is to import into his words an idea wholly alien to the context. Irenaeus is concerned to emphasize the universal scope of the Gospel. In the relevant passage, *Against Heresies* III, xi, 8, Irenaeus interprets for us the cherubim in Ezek. i. 5 ff. and/or Rev. iv. 7; their four faces were images of 'the dispensation of the Son of God'. This means that each face symbolized some aspect of the character or activity of the Christ. Similarly each of the four Gospels were severally concerned to express this in different ways. Thus the connection between the Gospels and the various beasts has to do with their particular emphases in presenting the life of Jesus, and by a logic strange to us moderns these four emphases are somehow related in Irenaeus' mind with the four zones and the four principal winds of the world which suggests the propriety of the fact that there should be four pillars (Matthew, Mark, Luke, John) for the Gospel. To find here an allusion to the calendar, even though the connection of the beasts with the Zodiac in Rev. iv. 7 be established,[7] is to drag in an idea irrelevant to the context.

[1] P. 66. [2] P. 67. [3] Irenaeus, *Adv. Haer.* III, i, 1.

[4] See C. R. Gregory, *The Canon and Text of the New Testament* (New York, 1912), pp. 389ff.

[5] See G. F. Moore, *Judaism*, vol. II, p. 48. [6] P. 58.

[7] See R. H. Charles, *Revelation*, International Critical Commentary, *ad loc.* See also J. Lawson, *The Biblical Theology of St Irenaeus* (1948), pp. 43 f. Irenaeus seems to have combined Ezek. i. 5 ff. and Rev. iv. 7 in his thinking here.

(*c*) There is a third minor point which remains to be noticed. Carrington argues that already in the New Testament the phrase 'to proclaim the Gospel' meant the delivery of a form of words with some solemnity in the Ecclesia, i.e. among other things it included the reading of a lection. He takes Mark xiv. 9, 'Verily I say unto you, wheresoever the Gospel shall be preached throughout the whole world, that also which this woman hath done shall be spoken of for a memorial of her', to mean 'Wherever this lection is read'.[1] But this is hardly tenable. If this was Mark's meaning there was nothing to prevent his saying 'wherever the Gospel shall be *read*'. Moreover, Carrington's interpretation demands the pronoun τοῦτο (so Matthew) to make it at all possible that the meaning is 'wheresoever *this* lection is read'. Further, the words 'that also which this woman hath done shall be spoken (λαληθήσεται)' become tautologous if the reference is to reading *this* lection, nor is it appropriate to refer to a lection read in the Ecclesia as being directed to the whole world, εἰς ὅλον τὸν κόσμον. This is far better taken as a reference to the general evangelistic or preaching (κηρυχθῇ) activity of the Church.[2]

The passages to which Carrington appeals in support of this interpretation of τὸ εὐαγγέλιον in Mark xiv. 9, i.e. I Cor. xv. 1–5 and I Cor. xi. 23 are not strictly concerned with lections as such. The first, I Cor. xv. 1–5, presents the Gospel in what is probably a kind of 'credal' summary of it; I Cor. xi. 26 refers to the *recital* not the reading of the Passion narrative. Despite the close connection with the acts of breaking of the bread and taking of the cup, the verb καταγγέλλειν is probably best understood of the recital of the story of the death of Jesus,[3] not of the acts themselves, but Carrington goes too far in thinking of this recital in lectionary terms. The analogy of the Passover would seem to point to a procedure more elastic than the reading of a Passion narrative: it suggests rather free *haggadah*. Neither I Cor. xv. 1–5 nor I Cor. xi. 23 f. can be urged as evidence for an early lectionary or for early lectionary units.

[1] Pp. 18f.

[2] So V. Taylor, *ad loc.* For another view of Mark xiv. 9, different from Carrington's, see J. Jeremias, *Zeitschrift für die neutestamentliche Wissenschaft*, Band 44, Heft 1/2.

[3] See *Paul and Rabbinic Judaism*, p. 252, n. 3; J. Schniewind, *Theologisches Wörterbuch* (ed. Kittel), vol. 1, p. 70; H. Lietzmann, *Messe und Herrenmahl*, p. 222 n. 1.

We next turn to the use that Carrington makes of manuscript evidence in support of his theory. Having satisfied himself that he can divide Mark i–ix into a series of lections beginning with the Jewish New Year (placing the Feeding of the Five Thousand at Passover and that of the Four Thousand at Pentecost), and further that the chapter divisions of the Vaticanus (B) fit in very well with this scheme, which he has imposed upon or discovered in Mark, Carrington concludes that the purpose of the chapter divisions was precisely to indicate the incidence of the lections.[1] He thus finds an 'external mathematical confirmation' of his theory.[2]

Two difficulties at least have to be noted. What is the exact purpose of the divisions in both the Vaticanus (B) and other Greek manuscripts of the New Testament? In all manuscripts Carrington, as we stated, takes their purpose to have been lectionary, and he assumes that the system of division in B is earlier than that found in non-B manuscripts.[3] But as far as I am aware students of the manuscripts of the New Testament have not found in the divisions of the text any lectionary significance. Von Soden takes the divisions in the Vaticanus to be the work of some commentator[4] to mark passages in the Gospels merely for purposes of dividing the text satisfactorily;[5] the non-B divisions, on the other hand, he takes to be earlier than those of B and designed, as were the Eusebian canons and the Ammonian sections for purposes of synopsis.[6] He notes the fact that in the Passion narratives of the Gospels only those sections which are peculiar to each Gospel seem to be noted by the division

[1] Pp. 20ff.

[2] P. xiii. Note that Carrington does not actually identify the lection system that he discovers in B in all respects with the original system.

[3] Pp. xi, 27.

[4] H. von Soden, *Die Schriften des Neuen Testaments*², vol. I (1911), p. 440.

[5] *Op. cit.* p. 432. The divisions in B arose because the divisions of the non-B manuscripts were unsatisfactory in the division of the material according to content.

[6] *Op. cit.* pp. 432, 426ff. Note that F. H. A. Scrivener, *A Plain Introduction to the Criticism of the New Testament*⁴, vol. I (1894), p. 56, takes B to present the oldest divisions. On p. 55 Scrivener writes: '[The sections] seem to have been formed for the purpose of reference, and a new one always commences where there is some break in the sense.' For a convenient statement, see W. H. P. Hatch, *Facsimiles and Descriptions of Minuscule Manuscripts of the New Testament* (1951), pp. 22ff. C. R. Gregory, *op. cit.*, is very unsatisfactory in his treatment; indeed he largely ignores the problem (p. 469).

lines: and since it is likely that the Passion narratives in themselves constituted lectionary units, the peculiar sections marked probably served a synoptic purpose.[1] When we turn to the divisions in B, moreover, many of them delimit sections which are either too long or too short as lectionary units.[2]

But, secondly, even if it should be proved that the divisions of the Vaticanus were lectionary, this evidence refers merely to the fourth century. The divisions also occur in Codex Zacynthius, a palimpsest containing the greater part of Luke i. 1–xi. 33 which is dated in the eighth century and in Cod. 579 from the thirteenth century.[3] Carrington claims that they do not appear in the Sinaiticus (א), from the second half of the fourth century.[4] Kirsopp Lake, however, found that at least in the first seven pages of Matthew in the Sinaiticus we are to find 'either the same or nearly the same system of division'.[5] A. Schmidtke, cited by Kenyon, found traces of the divisions in the Sinaiticus and 579 and argued that the divisions went back to the Gospel harmony of Ammonius, which is to be dated in the third century.[6] It is specially noteworthy that the Chester-Beatty Papyri, which may go back even to the beginning of the second century, show no traces of the divisions.[7] Carrington claims that the Diatessaron of Tatian, already in the second century, points to the existence of a strong tradition in favour of reading particular lections at a particular time and that time and time again the non-B order of lections appears in it.[8] But all this is built on the assumption that the divisions found in an eleventh-century Arabic version of the Diatessaron are a safe guide to divisions in the second-century original, and ignores the simple fact that the only fragment of the Greek Diatessaron which we possess, that from Dura-Europos, does not

[1] *Op. cit.* pp. 426ff.

[2] Thus, for example, Mark i. 12–13 is taken as a lection by Carrington, p. 120. Again can a long discourse like the Sermon on the Mount have been a single lection? (See Carrington, pp. 20, 123.)

[3] See F. G. Kenyon, *Handbook to the Textual Criticism of the New Testament*[2], (1912), pp. 80f.

[4] P. 23.

[5] *Codex Sinaiticus Petropolitanus* (Oxford, 1911); photographs by Helen and Kirsopp Lake, with description and introduction by Kirsopp Lake, p. xxi, col. a.

[6] See F. G. Kenyon, *op. cit.* pp. 80f.

[7] *The Chester Beatty Biblical Papyri*, ed. F. G. Kenyon (London, 1933), etc.

[8] Pp. 29ff.

show any traces of chapter divisions.[1] Nor must it be forgotten that the date of the Diatessaron, even if it did contain the divisions, is about A.D. 160–70, whereas Carrington's thesis requires textual evidence in the first century to supply us with 'mathematical' proof.

In addition to the above two major difficulties there emerge other minor ones. One is that it is very surprising, if Mark was intended from the first as a lectionary, that there are no marks of this intention in the text itself. For example, in discussing lection 23 (Mark vi. 7–13)[2] Carrington points out that in the parallel section in Q 'the sending out of the Twelve was preceded by a liturgical formula, "Pray to the Lord of the Harvest", etc.' It is curious that such formulas should be missing in Mark were its intention lectionary. Where Carrington discovers one such lectionary formula in Mark one must be sceptical. In Mark xiii. 32 Carrington is tempted to take the words 'Concerning that Day and that hour'[3] to be the title of the lection which has been incorporated into the text. Thus one of Schmiedel's foundation texts turns out in Carrington's view to be merely a lectionary title. Moreover, it may not be irrelevant to point out that in the Vaticanus and the Zacynthius chapter divisions occur in the text of Luke, but Carrington does not regard Luke to have been originally intended as a lectionary. But does not this mean either that the divisions are not lectionary or that they are much later than Carrington would have us believe?[4]

Finally, we have to point out that the divisions in the Vaticanus constitute a lectionary for one year of Sundays. Two factors are noteworthy. It follows, in the first place, that whatever the actual length of the ministry of Jesus it is compressed on Carrington's theory to a year of lections. It is hardly likely that the ministry lasted only one year;[5] history would not, therefore, suggest the lectionary arrangement that Carrington finds in the Vaticanus and

[1] See G. H. Kraeling, *A Greek Fragment of Tatian's Diatessaron* (London, 1935).

[2] Pp. 150f.

[3] P. 211. The title of the section given in the Codex Alexandrinus is περὶ τῆς ἡμέρας καὶ ὥρας; this has, according to Carrington, become the περὶ δὲ τῆς ἡμέρας ἐκείνης ἢ τῆς ὥρας of Mark xiii. 32.

[4] See p. 48.

[5] See G. Ogg, *op. cit.* p. 323. Only by concentration exclusively on a Galilean ministry can that of Jesus be reduced to a single year. Compare V. Taylor, *op. cit.* pp. 24f.

that arrangement had necessarily to do violence to history. On the other hand, the practice of the Synagogue which on Carrington's theory, as we saw, exercised a heavy influence on the practice of the Church would suggest not an annual cycle of lections but a triennial one; the Palestinian Jewish lectionary was almost certainly triennial.[1] Thus in the present state of our knowledge of the divisions of the manuscripts, it has to be asserted that it does not seem possible to accept Carrington's understanding of their purpose.

From all the above it will have emerged that the three supports upon which Carrington's lectionary or calendrical theory rests have all in turn failed to satisfy. Nevertheless, his study, by its thoroughgoing challenge and scope, has thrown into relief two necessities. First, it may be permitted to one who is not primarily a textual critic to voice a doubt. Casey[2] in a review to which I am very greatly indebted and at all of whose conclusions I had independently arrived, has dismissed Carrington's understanding of the divisions in B outright. But von Soden pointed out that even in the case of the non-B manuscripts only an increased knowledge of the liturgical practice of the early Church can further enlighten us on the purpose of some of the divisions.[3] For example that the use of such lines as those found in B, etc.,to divide the text may well go back to the earliest days of the Church, despite the lack of actual textual evidence in manuscripts of the New Testament, may be suggested by the Isaiah scroll from Qumrân. The dissident sect which used that scroll used lines in their text which are very similar, if not identical, with those found in B, etc. These lines were noted by Millar Burrows[4] who apparently takes them

[1] See J. Mann, *op. cit.* pp. 3ff. On the other hand it is not impossible that even within Palestine the practice varied; see R. Marcus' introduction to his translations of Philo's *Questions and Answers on Genesis* (Cambridge, Mass., and London, 1953), p. xiii. (I owe this reference to Professor Nock.) How varied calendrical practice in general must have been emerges from the fact that the sages at Jamnia had to regulate the calendar. It is erroneous to speak of a single utterly fixed Jewish Calendar therefore before Jamnia; see, for example, Mishnah, Rosh Ha-Shanah, ii. 9, *et passim*; an astronomically fixed calendar was adopted only about the middle of the fourth century, see G. F. Moore, *op. cit.* vol. II, p. 23 n. 3.

[2] *Op. cit.* pp. 367f.

[3] *Op. cit.* p. 428.

[4] *The Dead Sea Scrolls of St Mark's Monastery*, vol. I (1950), p. xvi. The lines in the Isaiah scroll are short and horizontal; some bend slightly on the left: they are placed at the edges of columns. I counted—including doubtful instances—about

to refer to lections (as does Carrington the *paragrapha*[1] in B, etc.). The grounds on which Millar Burrows takes this view are not stated, but if his conjecture is correct that the lines in *D S Isa.* are meant to serve a lectionary purpose it is difficult to think that the somewhat similar lines found in B, etc., may not have served the same purpose at least at some stage. Until the lines in both the Isaiah scroll and in manuscripts of the New Testament have been more thoroughly examined all this must remain highly conjectural, but there is no justification for any outright dismissal of Carrington's understanding of the divisions concerned.

But in the second place, not only is it necessary to examine the textual evidence more thoroughly than has hitherto been done, but also the influence of liturgical practice must still further be considered in the formulation and transmission of the tradition, although Carrington's study suggests that this is to be traced more along the lines pursued by G. D. Kilpatrick in his work on *The Origins of the Gospel according to St Matthew*, where there is intensive examination of the text itself, than by the more mechanical method of Carrington. That that influence is a real factor in the process referred to can hardly be questioned, but it is not likely to have dominated the creation of the Gospels of Mark and Matthew in the way that Carrington implies.[2]

sixty-one instances of their use. In some instances their incidence coincides with a break in the sense, i.e. they mark new sections, but in others they break across the sense of a passage. They do not cover the whole of the text but only certain sections. Bleddyn J. Roberts (*Bulletin of the John Rylands Library*, vol. XXXVI, no. 1, Sept. 1953, p. 91) claims that there are 'open' and 'closed' paragraphs in *D S Isa.* It has been customary to regard the identification of 'open' and 'closed' paragraphs as due to lectionary interests (see Bleddyn J. Roberts, *The Old Testament Text and Versions* (Cardiff, 1951), p. 36), in which case there would be no need for a special line to mark lectionary divisions and it may be that the lines under consideration in *D S Isa.* were merely designed to draw attention to certain particular passages frequently used. It should be noted, however, that the significance of the 'open' and 'closed' sections in manuscripts is not fully established. (See M. Gaster, *Hebrew Illuminated Bibles of the Ninth and Tenth Centuries* and *A Samaritan Scroll of the Law* (London, 1901), pp. 32, 34.)

[1] For these see Fig. 1 in Carrington, p. 121. It should be borne in mind that the Vaticanus is a far more finished manuscript than *D S Isa.*

[2] Compare the restrained treatment of the problem in G. Delling, *Der Gottesdienst im Neuen Testament* (1952), p. 91.

NOTE ON LEVERTOFF'S TREATMENT OF MATTHEW

In the course of his argument, p. 15, Carrington refers to the work of P. Levertoff in *A New Commentary on Holy Scripture*, ed. Gore, Goudge, Guillaume (London, 1928), pp. 128 ff.; and, since Levertoff's work was an early attempt to trace a connection between the Gospels and the Jewish year, it may be well to examine it. He claimed in particular that Matt. iii. i–vii. 13 is to be interpreted in the light of the liturgical seasons of the Synagogue. Apart from those places where he obviously follows Mark, it is these liturgical seasons, according to Levertoff, which determine the sequence of events for Matthew. Moreover this is so not because Matthew happened to be concerned so to arrange his material, but because of the simple fact that the material was, as a matter of history, connected with certain pivotal points in the liturgical schema of the Synagogue, i.e. the liturgical sequence of the material is historical and not merely editorial.

Nor can it be denied that the Synoptics make it clear that the Jewish festivals did play a significant part in the ministry of Jesus. It was at the Passover season that Jesus did set himself to die at the geographic and spiritual centre of the nation's life (Luke xxii. 15, cf. xiii. 33). As for the Fourth Gospel, it has been possible to claim that it presents the ministry of Jesus as a series of circles, so to speak, revolving round various Jewish festivals. (Thus J. Lowe in an unpublished paper communicated at Oxford, 1949.) The connections between these last and the Fourth Gospel have been forced (the identity of the various feasts referred to in the Gospel is by no means always clear), but at least they do serve as a reminder that the possibility is a real one that much of the course of the ministry would be influenced, if not determined, by the incidence of the important Jewish festivals.

With this preliminary let us examine Levertoff's case. He begins by placing the ministry of John the Baptist in the 'month' of Elul (i.e. in the end of August and the beginning of September). At this time of the year preparation was being made in the Synagogue for the New Year's Day on the first of Tishri (i.e. about 14 September); following this there were ten days of penitence leading, on the tenth of Tishri, to the Day of Atonement, which again was followed on the fifteenth of the same 'month' by the Feast of Tabernacles. During the period when the Baptist is presumed to have begun his ministry, Levertoff finds certain emphases in the Synagogue liturgy—on repentance, the Kingdom of Heaven, the descent of Jewry from Abraham, in short, on those elements which according to Matthew were prominent in the Baptist's teaching; moreover, what Levertoff calls the Baptist's allusion to Isa. xl (Matt. iii. 3) is due to his familiarity with the synagogal lessons of the time which were derived from Deuteronomy and Deutero-Isaiah; the very act of baptism itself is connected with another synagogal lection, namely, Mic. vii. 19 which reads 'and thou wilt cast all their sins into the depths of the sea'. Thus the activity and the message of the Baptist were, according to Levertoff, directly moulded by the synagogal practice at the time at which presumably he began his ministry.

The criticisms of this position are fairly obvious. First, Levertoff's assumption that John the Baptist began his ministry in Elul cannot in the nature of the case be proved or disproved. It is probable that the ministry took place between Nisan A.D. 28 and Nisan A.D. 29, but even this is not universally accepted.[1] Even if it were proven that Elul was the month which saw the beginning of the Baptist's ministry, there still remains the twofold problem: (1) whether we can with certainty establish the synagogal lessons for the months of Elul and Tishri, and (2) whether the Matthaean account of the ministry of the Baptist justifies the assumption that it was these same lessons which governed the particular time and form which that ministry assumed.

To deal with (1) first. We can be fairly confident that the Pentateuchal and Prophetic lessons were in use in the first century (see J. Mann, *op. cit.* pp. 4ff.; so Büchler, *J.Q.R.* vol. v (1892–3), pp. 420ff.; vol. vi (1893–4), pp. 1ff.; Elbogen, *op. cit.* p. 176. In the *J.E.* vol. vi, pp. 136f. the view is given that the *Haftaroth* for the feast days were first determined in the middle of the second century, and that there followed *Haftaroth* for the special sabbaths and later still those for ordinary sabbaths only a few of which were fixed). Levertoff claims that Deutero-Isaiah was the source of the prophetic lessons for the period following Elul when John the Baptist appeared. According to *J.E.* vol. vi, *ibid.*, Isa. lvii. 14–lviii. 14 was a *Haftarah* for the Day of Atonement in the second century when the *Haftaroth* for the various festivals were formally fixed and was probably also on this supposition the *Haftarah* for the same day in the first century, but this is conjectural. We cannot be as certain as Levertoff assumes as to the exact *Haftaroth* used in the first century. (Thus the use of Isa. xl–lxi for the *Haftaroth* of consolation on the sabbaths extending from the ninth of Ab to the Day of Atonement is later than the early first century according to Thackeray, *The Septuagint and Jewish Worship* (1923), p. 83. Unfortunately Mann's work, cited frequently above, was not completed.)

The other problem (2) demands an answer equally unfavourable to Levertoff. He claims, as we saw, that John applied to himself a passage

[1] Ogg, *Chronology of the Public Ministry of Jesus* (1940), p. 300.

which was one of the current *Haftaroth* namely Isa. xl. 3. Assuming that we know that Isa. xl. 3 was a *Haftarah*, is this position of Levertoff's likely? One thing we may safely assume, that the name, the Baptist, by which John came to be known probably affords the best clue to what historically was most noteworthy about his activity, namely, his emphasis on baptism.[1] With this agrees the contrast found in Mark and Q between his baptism which was with water and that of the coming One which was to be with Holy Spirit and fire.[2] Note, however, that the emphasis supplied by the quotation from Isa. xl. 3 is not upon the ministry of baptism at all, so much as upon the significance of John as an eschatological figure, the forerunner of Christ. Moreover this emphasis, as Dibelius has shown, is the outcome of the Church's reflection on the meaning of the Baptist's ministry: the presentation of John in all the Four Gospels is coloured by the desire to clarify the mutual relationship of John and Jesus. It was this desire that probably occasioned the juxtaposition of Isa. xl. 3 with the ministry of John: it supplied scriptural support for the Church's understanding of John the Baptist as the forerunner of Jesus, the beginning of the Gospel.[3] Levertoff fails to perceive that Isa. xl. 3 does not really illumine John's understanding of his own ministry; historically it was possibly not particularly relevant to that ministry; rather does it reflect the understanding of it which the early Church came to cherish. We may further suggest that if, as Levertoff holds, John saw a direct connection between his activity and the Synagogue lectionary, he had to hand a most pertinent quotation from Ezek. xxxvi. 25 which was used in the liturgy of the Day of Atonement; and which reads: 'Then will I sprinkle clean water upon you and ye shall be clean'.[4] This rather than Isa. xl. 3 we may surmise would have been used by John were he himself responsible for any quotation from Scripture. One thing is indeed suggested by our treatment of John, that the tradition probably came to be formulated under the impact of the Scripture reading in the Church and its exegesis. Thus the emphasis on the location of John's baptism in the desert probably reflects the influence of Isa. xl. 3[5] and Lohmeyer[6] sees the same influence at work in the statement in Mark i. 5 that 'there went out unto him all the land of Judaea, and they of Jerusalem' which is further expanded in Matt. iii. 5; this insertion was dictated by the necessity to fulfil Isa. xlviii. 20,

[1] Lohmeyer, *Das Evangelium des Markus* (1937), p. 13.
[2] Mark i. 8 and parallels.
[3] *Die Urchristliche Überlieferung von Johannes dem Taufer* (1911), p. 47.
[4] See Abrahams, *Studies in Pharisaism and the Gospels*, second ser. p. 35; Danby, *The Mishnah*, p. 172.
[5] Bultmann, *Geschichte der Synoptischen Tradition*, p. 261.
[6] *Op. cit.* p. 15.

and lii. 11. In Mark the account of the Baptist's ministry is largely derived from a traditional exegesis of Scripture, what Lohmeyer calls 'ein altes Stück urchristlicher Schrifttheologie', and although Matthew, like Luke, has redressed this by giving the actual teaching of John as presented in Q, he too has retained this exegetical matter. This is the element of truth in Levertoff's position, that the 'lectionary' activity of the Church—not as he thinks, however, of the Synagogue—has left its mark on the tradition. But his attempt to determine the chronology and character of John's ministry by means of the synagogal lectionary must be rejected.[1]

He carries the same method through to Matt. xvii. 1–13 but it is only by the same kind of violence to his sources that he manages to do this. We need not further examine his position in any detail. Let us note only one point by way of illustration. According to Levertoff behind the Sermon on the Mount we are to see the influence of the Synagogue lectionary such as we saw behind the account of the Baptist's ministry; if we understand him aright he would seem to connect the 'Sermon' with the lections of the period around about Tabernacles; but his argument really demands that the Sermon on the Mount which contains what we may be allowed to call 'the New Law' should be connected with Pentecost, which was the festival of the giving of the Law, as we argued above.

[1] New light on the *Schrifttheologie* of the early Church has probably been supplied by the Qumrân Scrolls; see K. Stendahl, *The School of Matthew* (Uppsala, 1954); on Matt. iii. 3f., see pp. 47ff. If Stendahl is correct in tracing in parts of Matthew a method of Biblical interpretation similar to that found in the *DSS* this perhaps gives added force to our suggestion above that the textual works in *DSIsa. may* be relevant to our understanding of New Testament manuscripts.

8

RECENT DISCOVERIES IN PALESTINE AND THE GOSPEL OF ST JOHN

W. F. ALBRIGHT

UNTIL 1949/50 the problem of the date of St John's Gospel and the authenticity of its contents seemed to be almost insoluble.[1] The external evidence was fragmentary and ambiguous; the internal evidence lacked external pivots and controls. The evidence of Hellenistic and early Roman papyri explained many features of the *koinē* language of the N.T., but not enough to be very helpful in solving the Johannine problem. The increasing recognition of the Aramaic substratum of Johannine Greek during the last three decades of this period was countered by opposition ranging from outright denial of such influence to a tempered scepticism with respect to the methods used by the proponents of Aramaic hypotheses.[2] The failure of the first series of efforts on the part of the *Religionsgeschichtliche Schule* to establish connection between the Gospel and the mystery religions was followed by a new and much more powerful onslaught by Bultmann, Bauer, and others, who endeavoured to prove Mandean influence on the Gospel.[3]

[1] No purpose is served by extended reference to the vast literature on the subject since K. G. Bretschneider inaugurated the debate with his *Probabilia*, published in 1820. Reliable and easily accessible surveys will be found in B. W. Bacon's *The Fourth Gospel in Research and Debate* (1910), and W. F. Howard's *The Fourth Gospel in Recent Criticism and Interpretation* (1931). The classical presentation of a radical approach to its historical criticism is P. W. Schmiedel's long article in the *Encyclopaedia Biblica*, vol. II (1903), cols. 2503–62, while the best presentation of a conservative scholarly position is probably to be found in M. J. Lagrange, *L'Évangile selon Saint Jean* (1925). In the autumn of 1951 the writer published a four-page summary of the position defended in the present paper, in the Methodist quarterly *Religion in Life*, vol. XXI, pp. 547–50.

[2] Cf. the writer's *From the Stone Age to Christianity* (1940), pp. 294ff., with references to the literature before 1940. The debate has since tended to die down.

[3] Cf. especially R. Bultmann, *Das Evangelium des Johannes* (1923; 11th ed. 1950) and W. Bauer, in the second and subsequent editions of his book, *Das Johannes-evangelium* (1925ff.). On the opposition to the Mandean hypothesis which soon arose cf. below, p. 154 and n. 1.

In 1940, the present writer, who had long been intensely interested in New Testament problems, though limiting his publication in the field to questions of topography and archaeology, presented his views in the first edition of his book, *From the Stone Age to Christianity*, pp. 292–300. Since they naturally made little impression on professional specialists, they might have only a remote historical interest for us here but for the fact that these views were a symptom of the new period in Johannine criticism which was beginning to emerge; I should still endorse them throughout with emphasis. In this book the fact was stressed that the conceptual imagery and background of ideas reflected in the Gospel were not Gnostic but at best proto-Gnostic: 'The slight dualistic element was already present in Judaeo-Hellenistic literature as a legacy from Iranian religion' (p. 300). Particular emphasis was laid on the fact that the accumulating indications of Aramaic rather than Greek background made a second-century date exceedingly difficult, and that the remarkable papyrus finds published in 1935 by C. H. Roberts and H. I. Bell made wide circulation and use of the Gospel before the middle of the second century practically certain. It must be remembered that outstanding theologians had denied any indications of the use of the Gospel in extant Christian literature antedating the last decades of the second century. Emphasis was also laid on the convincing rejection of Lidzbarski's extremely early date for the origin of Mandeanism by E. Peterson, F. C. Burkitt, H. Lietzmann, and others (*op. cit.* p. 281), who proved that this sect cannot antedate the fifth century A.D. (though its sources are naturally much older, as recently shown by T. Säve-Söderbergh).[1]

In 1949, the present writer returned to the subject in his Pelican Book, *Archaeology of Palestine* (pp. 239–48), continuing a vein which he had tapped very lightly in 1924.[2] He preluded his discussion by a new treatment of the question of Aramaic gospels (pp. 198–203),

[1] See his brilliant study in *Studies in the Coptic-Manichaean Psalm Book* (1949), pp. 156–66, where he proves the dependence of a Manichean hymn on an older hymn of strong Mandean colouring. As a matter of fact, however, this merely proves the correctness of my remarks in *From the Stone Age to Christianity*, p. 282 (compare the literature cited on p. 281); the Mandean system is both older and younger than Manicheanism (cf. W. Baumgartner, *Theologische Rundschau*, 1951).

[2] *Harvard Theological Review*, vol. XVII (1924), pp. 193 ff.

in which he laid particular stress on a never before emphasized point: the demonstrable eclipse of Aramaic literature under the Hellenistic successors of Alexander, especially the Seleucids of Syria. There are no Aramaic inscriptions worth mentioning from the Seleucid Empire before it fell to pieces in the last century B.C.; almost all Aramaic inscriptions from the Hellenistic period proper come from Egypt, the Arabian fringes of Greater Syria, southern Babylonia, and the lands to the east and north-east. Moreover, there is absolutely no trace so far of a continuous Aramaic literary tradition spanning the interval between the Achaemenian and earliest Hellenistic period on the one hand, and the second century A.D. on the other. For example, there is no demonstrable literary connection between the Aramaic Aḥîqar known from fifth-century Elephantine and the Christian Syriac Aḥîqar, though the latter is undoubtedly just as pagan in its background as was the Aramaic Aḥîqar. The obvious link between the two must have been transmitted orally. It therefore became, the writer thought, very hazardous to assume the existence of a written Aramaic prototype of the Gospel, as maintained by Torrey and Olmstead (*inter alios*). He accordingly insisted with renewed emphasis on the orally transmitted Aramaic background of St John.[1]

In his main discussion the writer emphasized the archaeological evidence for an almost total break in the continuity of occupation caused by the First Revolt (A.D. 66–70). All Jewish remains from Roman Jerusalem antedate the fall of the city and the destruction or dispersion of its Jewish population in the year 70. All synagogal remains from Palestine which have hitherto been discovered in place, belong to the second century A.D. or later; there was thus a complete or nearly complete destruction of Jewish synagogues in 66–70. The devastation created by the calculated ferocity and the accompanying vindictiveness of the Roman armies, alone sufficient to raze most

[1] It should be emphasized that these contentions have not been disproved by the extraordinary discoveries in the Dead Sea caves. It is true that we have documentary proof of the Aramaic origin of the Book of Lamech (which carries with it the 'Book of Noah' and part of Enoch), and that Aramaic fragments of Tobit and other known books have been found. However, the Hebrew literary texts which have been brought to light exceed the Aramaic by far in both number and extent—not counting Biblical manuscripts, which would still further accentuate the disparity.

Jewish buildings,[1] was enormously extended by the ruthless hostility of the native pagan population of Palestine, so graphically described—and exaggerated—by Josephus. Christians were treated by the Jews as traitors, and were persecuted or expelled; the pagans regarded them as Jews, and doubtless engulfed them much of the time in their war of extermination against the Jews. Later Christian tradition tells of the escape of some Christians from Jerusalem to Pella in Transjordan, where they were presumably tolerated as refugees from the Jewish rebels. It is significant that Pella alone is mentioned—perhaps this was the only Christian community made up of the descendants of refugees who fled at this time and survived more or less intact to the time of Eusebius' sources.[2] Even before the year 66, bitter persecution of the Christians by the increasingly intolerant Jewish majority had undoubtedly caused many Palestinian Christians (among whom tradition included St Peter and St John) to seek refuge among the freer Christian communities of the Diaspora.

We must, accordingly, recognize an almost complete break in the continuity of Christian tradition in Palestine itself; any reminiscences of the life of Jesus or of conditions in Palestine in his time must have been carried into the Diaspora by Christian refugees, either voluntarily or otherwise. This means that if there are correct data in the Gospels or Acts of the Apostles which can be validated archaeologically or topographically, they must have been carried from Palestine in oral form by Christians who left that land before or during the First Jewish Revolt. The importance of this almost universally disregarded fact is so great as to be basic to our conclusions. It is a great pity that the learned and original book of S. G. F. Brandon, *The Fall of Jerusalem and the Christian Church*, which appeared in 1951, did not concentrate on this vital point instead of so often reflecting wild ideas of the late Robert Eisler.[3]

[1] For example, the writer's still unpublished excavations of 1933 at Gibeah of Saul and of 1934 at Bethel proved decisively (with the aid of coins) that the occupation of both sites was brought to a sudden close by Vespasian's invasion of A.D. 69 (both towns are explicitly mentioned by Josephus as having been occupied by the Romans, though he says nothing specifically about their destruction).

[2] Cf. Brandon, *The Fall of Jerusalem and the Christian Church* (1951), pp. 68–73.

[3] We grant that the problem is difficult for non-specialists in Old Slavonic to master, but Brandon might at least have mentioned (in addition to the relatively

However, one must agree with most of Brandon's acute observations about the tendencies exhibited by the Christians of Palestine before A.D. 70[1] and applaud his recognition of the light shed on their beliefs by the Synoptic Gospels.[2]

In the writer's Pelican Book (pp. 244f.) he goes on to list numerous illustrations of the correct local colour of St John's Gospel. For example, there are a number of passages in John where Jesus is called by the Aramaic name *rabbi* (literally, 'my master') or the Greek equivalent *didaskalos* (literally 'teacher'). This was formerly cited as an illustration of the relative lateness of John as compared with the

mild criticisms which he lists on pp. 115ff. of his book) the devastating criticisms of S. Zeitlin in the *Jewish Quarterly Review*. It may be added that the present writer has followed the publications of Robert Eisler closely through several decades of the latter's activity. Eisler was very learned, fabulously ingenious—but he lacked disciplined self-criticism almost completely. Moreover, he had never been subjected to the rigorous schooling in philological method which was required by the nature of the problems which he tackled. As a result, not one in a hundred of his original ideas possessed any merit except to stimulate some more careful philologian to try his hand at the tiller. On Brandon's book and the untenable nature of Eisler's speculations, see further the admirable review by Elias Bickerman in *Bibliotheca Orientalis*, vol. x (1953), p. 37.

[1] On pp. 262ff. Brandon discusses H.-J. Schoeps' remarkable book, *Theologie und Geschichte des Judenchristentums* (1949), which he received too late to utilize in the body of his work. He is inclined to accept Schoeps' view that the Ebionite heresy 'is in the true line of descent from that of the original Christian church'. Without discounting the great importance of Schoeps' work, I consider it as a pity that Brandon made this concession, since his own view of the teaching of the Jerusalem Mother Church is generally reasonable. Moreover, the Dead Sea scrolls are now bringing a totally new body of evidence into the discussion. There can be no question that the Ebionites actually did continue Essene practices in many important respects, just as was formerly conjectured by various scholars. In fact, J. L. Teicher has gone so far as to identify the sectarians of Qumrân with the Ebionites. This is chronologically impossible, but Schoeps has recognized the existence of a close relation between the two sects (see his remarks, *Zeitschrift für Religions- und Geistesgeschichte*, vol. III (1951), no. 4). What complex relationships exist here may be easily seen by reading the study of the light shed by the Dead Sea scrolls on John the Baptist and the obscure movements that started with him, just published by Bo Reicke, *Religion och Bibel*, vol. XI (1952), pp. 5–18, as well as the comprehensive survey by A. Dupont-Sommer, *Nouveaux aperçus sur les manuscrits de la Mer Morte* (1953), pp. 191–213.

[2] My general agreement on this point does not mean, of course, that I should treat any of the content of the Synoptic Gospels as originating in the teaching of the early Church, but merely that the needs of the Church had a tendency to select what we have from a much more extensive body of oral tradition. Fortunately, the edited forms of different Gospels reflect different milieux and different needs, so they complement one another most happily.

Synoptics, since these terms are much more frequent, relatively speaking, in the former than in the latter. Some scholars even denied that a teacher would be called *rabbi* in the time of Christ, holding that this was a Tannaitic development. However, in 1931 E. L. Sukenik called attention to the fact that one of the ossuaries which he had found, dating from the generation or two before A.D. 70, used the term *didaskalos* of the person whose bones were interred in it.[1] It should be added that the treatment of this term in G. Kittel's *Theologisches Wörterbuch zum Neuen Testament*, vol. II (1935), p. 154 (and in general on pp. 150–62) needs further amplification archaeologically and linguistically; e.g. it should have been emphasized that ῥαββουνεί (John xx. 16), like the corresponding rabbinic expression, is a caritative of *rabbî*, standing for **rabbônî*, 'my (dear [or] little) master'.[2]

The ossuaries have demonstrated that the personal names of the Gospels, including again particularly those of John, were characteristic of the period from Herod the Great to A.D. 70. For example, the name Eleazar is quite common in the ossuary inscriptions in the same abbreviated form *La'zar*, 'Lazarus', that we find in John. The female names all occur commonly in the ossuary inscriptions: e.g. *Maryam* (Mary), *Martâ* (Martha), *Elisheba'* (Elisabeth), *Shalôm* (Salome). To be sure, these names were current in the early Christian tradition, but if the Gospel of John innovated as drastically as is often thought, we should expect to find at least a few names not taken from good tradition.

In the writer's Pelican Book (pp. 244–8) he has already discussed three striking topographical illustrations of good ancient tradition found only in John. The most remarkable is certainly the reference to the place where Pilate brought Jesus (John xix. 13) as called *Lithostroton* in Greek and *Gabbatha* in 'Hebrew' (i.e. Aramaic). Thanks to the work of L. H. Vincent, there can be no reasonable doubt that the place referred to lies in the court of the Tower of Antonia, where a splendid Roman pavement has long been known.

[1] *Jüdische Gräber Jerusalems um Christi Geburt* (1931), pp. 17f.

[2] Cf. Strack-Billerbeck, vol. II, p. 25, on Mark x. 51. Later the Aramaic word was borrowed in Hebrew in the form *ribbôn* (e.g. *ribbônô shel ha-'ôlam*, 'Master of the Universe'), used almost exclusively of God. Similar evolution of caritatives is by no means uncommon in the Semitic languages; e.g. *Yahu* is caritative of *Yahweh*.

Its extent has been shown by Vincent to have covered not less than about 2500 square metres. Moreover, he has demonstrated that it originally stood on a rocky elevation rising above the adjacent terrain, so that the name *gabbetâ*, 'ridge', was properly applied to it. Its age is proved by the fact that the foundations of structures belonging to the Hadrianic Aelia Capitolina were laid over this pavement, which was thus buried under deep masses of débris before A.D. 135.[1] It stands to reason that such correct tradition must have been handed down orally from before the First Jewish Revolt in A.D. 66–70.

Two very striking topographic references in John come from the region of Shechem. In iii. 23 we learn that John the Baptist was conducting his baptismal work at 'Aenon near Salim because there was much water there'. Later Christian tradition identified this Salim with a village of somewhat similar name (Salumias) south of Beth-shan in the Jordan Valley, and this identification is still accepted by a majority of scholars. Against it are many facts. South-east of Nâblus and Shechem lies the town of Sâlim, which figures in Israelite, Hellenistic, and Samaritan literature; the form of the name is identical.[2] Near it lies modern 'Ainûn, with a name unquestionably derived from an Aramaic *'*Ainôn*, 'little fountain'. Since these places lie near the headwaters of Wâdi Fâr'ah, with many springs in the neighbourhood, it could well be said that 'there was much water there'. Furthermore, as stressed many years ago by the writer and following him by the late B. W. Bacon, there is clear evidence for the influence exerted by John the Baptist on Samaritan groups.[3] If John was really baptizing in the area south of Scythopolis (which was then a pagan city), it would have been quite unnecessary to have commented on the fact that there was much water there. Again, in

[1] See Vincent, *Revue Biblique* (1933), pp. 83–113; (1952), pp. 513–30. The alternative view, that the Pretorium in question was at the Palace of Herod on the Western Hill is defended by P. Benoit, *Revue Biblique* (1952), pp. 531–50, who also demonstrates that the word would be the normal designation of a fine Herodian pavement like that of Antonia. It may be emphasized that Benoit's view would not appreciably affect our contention here.

[2] Cf. *Harvard Theological Review*, vol. XVII (1924), pp. 93f.

[3] See my remarks in *Harvard Theological Review*, vol. XVII (1924), pp. 193f., and especially B. W. Bacon, *Journal of Biblical Literature*, vol. XLVIII (1929), pp. 50–5, who develops this idea much more fully. It is a pity that these pages have been generally disregarded by more recent writers.

iv. 5f. we are told about Jesus' visit to the Well of Jacob, at Sychar, 'a town of Samaria'. Sychar has been identified with modern Arabic 'Askar, some distance from Jacob's Well toward the north, but this settlement is quite recent and the name means simply 'military camp' in Arabic. Until the German excavation of the site of Balâṭah beside the Well and the conclusive demonstration that it was the site of Biblical Shechem (Greek Sychem), there was some excuse for the 'Askar hypothesis, especially since a dubious Samaritan place-name could be brought into the argument at a pinch. Now it is obvious that we must follow the Old Syriac and read simply Συχέμ for Συχάρ, which has evidently been influenced by two immediately preceding references to Σαμαρεία (note the recurrence of the first and the fourth and fifth letters of both names). But since Balâṭah was continuously occupied until about A.D. 67 and then abandoned in connection with Vespasian's suppression of the Samaritan revolt and destruction of the temple on neighbouring Gerizim, mention of it must be based on correct tradition going back to the years before A.D. 67. The new site Flavia Neapolis (Nablus) was built two miles farther to the north-west, on the watershed. These are the most striking pieces of topographic evidence; the writer has at various times adduced others, but they cannot be called decisive, and thus they would tend to weaken our argument here rather than to strengthen it.[1]

Meanwhile, in 1942, the late A. T. Olmstead had come out very strongly as a historian against the usual late date attributed to the Gospel of John. In his *Jesus in the Light of History*, Olmstead insisted 'that the narratives proper are fully trustworthy while the interpolations agree with the long sermons in style and thought'—an observation which he credited to W. F. Howard and used as the basis for his book (p. 291). Olmstead based his early date for the supposed Aramaic original of the narrative passages in John before A.D. 40 (!) on general considerations, as well as upon an analysis of the accounts of the Passion and on miscellaneous lines of reasoning. He did not employ the materials on which the writer bases his insistence on the

[1] See J. Jeremias, *Die Wiederentdeckung von Bethesda* (1949) for one of the most plausible additional cases (my Ephraim, though accepted by B. W. Bacon and A. T. Olmstead, can scarcely be considered convincing, as long as we do not have independent toponymic confirmation).

origin of the tradition before A.D. 66–70. There can be no doubt that Olmstead had acquired a very good instinct for the degree of reliability to be attributed to ancient narratives; it is also clear that his lack of equal insight into the history of ideas led him to an indefensible separation of the words and sermons of Jesus from the narrative sections. It should be emphasized that Olmstead was not actuated by apologetic considerations.

Three years later E. R. Goodenough reacted along similar lines but devoted himself to an analysis of the relative age of the ideas contained in the words of Jesus, without expressing any definite opinion about the narratives.[1] It must again be stressed that Goodenough was even less moved by apologetic aims than Olmstead, and that his long and intimate specialization in Philo and Philonic questions has given him unrivalled feeling for just such problems as that of the relative age of John. He insisted in this paper on the fact that the Johannine Logos is more primitive in its metaphysical connotations than the Philonic and that both presumably go back to a common source in an early form of quasi-Gnostic Jewish thinking. What is true of the Logos is, Goodenough held, equally true of the other supposed late and 'Gnostic' elements in John. In stressing the Jewish origin of John, he disagreed sharply with the views of those who, like Gardner-Smith, maintained that John was composed in a centre of Greek learning, such as 'Athens, Ephesus, or Alexandria'. Despite this trenchant essay the protagonists of second-century Gnostic influence on the composition of the Gospel remained quite unconvinced. Thus, as late as 1950, Robert M. Grant wrote on 'The Origin of the Fourth Gospel', concluding: 'The environment in which he lives is no longer that of Judaism, but of a kind of gnosticism not unlike that of Ignatius [*sic*] and the Odes of Solomon....He lives between two worlds, the one that of the Palestinian Judaism out of which Christianity arose, the other that of Diaspora Judaism through which it reached the Gentile world....And in his effort to express the essence of the one in terms of the other he is compelled to reinterpret the gospel from beginning to end.'[2]

[1] 'John a Primitive Gospel', *Journal of Biblical Literature*, vol. LXIV, pp. 145–82.

[2] *Journal of Biblical Literature*, vol. LXIX, pp. 305–22. C. H. Dodd's important book, *The Interpretation of the Fourth Gospel* (1953), pp. 97–114, deals very well with the question of supposed Gnostic influence on the Gospel of John, recognizing

Meanwhile, in the same year (1948) announcement had been made of two entirely distinct discoveries of the greatest possible significance for our subject: the early Gnostic codices of Chenoboskion in Upper Egypt (originally found by natives in 1946), and the Hebrew and Aramaic scrolls from a cave near Khirbet Qumrân south of Jericho in the Jordan Valley (originally found by natives in 1947). The Gnostic codices were immediately dated by specialists in Coptic philology and palaeography in the late third and early fourth centuries A.D.; they had been previously translated from Greek into an early form of Coptic. Containing nearly forty (omitting duplicates and overlapping material) lost treatises belonging to the Sethians, Ophites, and Barbelo-Gnostics (with some material of Hermetic and still unidentified Gnostic origin), these codices are of inestimable value for the exact reconstruction of the pre-Valentinian and orientalizing theologies of the Gnostics.[1] Preliminary surveys by several highly qualified specialists have established their content and character, though we may have to wait for some time before any appreciable quantity of these priceless 800 pages appears in published form. It is already certain that the accounts of the earliest heresiographers, Hippolytus and Irenaeus, are much more accurate than they have been supposed to be by many recent writers. A brilliant survey of *Gnosis als Weltreligion* by the distinguished specialist Gilles Quispel (1951) turns the new information to very good account by showing why we can no longer accept the 'domesticated and manicured' Gnostics of E. de Faye and many other recent writers as historically justified representations. These early Gnostics were 'even worse heretics than the Church Fathers supposed'; they were almost pathological in their beliefs and practices. Against F. C. Burkitt[2] and

certain common interests but denying any direct influence. This work was completed before the discoveries at Chenoboskion and Qumrân had become generally known. Dodd's book was also finished before the appearance of the writer's pages in his Pelican Book, *Archaeology of Palestine*, a fact which adequately explains the absence of any comment on the new material by Dodd in his interesting pages on the 'Historical Aspects' of the question (pp. 444–53).

[1] See especially the valuable comprehensive survey of the new material by H. C. Puech, *Coptic Studies in Honour of Walter Ewing Crum* (1950), pp. 91–154. An excellent popular account of the finds, based on all available publications in the field, has been written by V. R. Gold for *The Biblical Archaeologist*, vol. xv (1952), pp. 70–88.

[2] *Church and Gnosis* (1932), pp. 40ff.

others he makes a very strong case for dating the emergence of the Barbelo-Gnostics and their congeners before the work of Valentine and the related Greek philosophical schools of Gnosticism.[1] He shows that structurally the system of Simon Magus is definitely the oldest of the known Gnostic theologies, and that there is no reason to doubt the unanimous testimony of the Church Fathers on this matter. In other words, Gnosticism had already developed some of its most pronounced sects well before the Fall of Jerusalem, and there is no reason to date the emergence of the Sethians and Barbelo-Gnostics after the end of the first century A.D. The supposed forms of mild Gnosticism which might have influenced John simply vanish from the picture, and the whole notion that the Gospel somehow reflects relatively harmless early forms of Gnosticism conjectured from the Odes of Solomon and a tendentious interpretation of St Ignatius and others, becomes incredible. Such common elements as do in fact exist—and few they are—prove to be a common inheritance from an earlier period.

The initial discovery of the Qumrân scrolls was followed by many additional finds of manuscript material in the Dead Sea Valley, especially an even more remarkable find at Qumrân in the late summer of 1952.[2] The clearance of the two caves at Qumrân, together with two seasons of excavation at the settlement itself, has fully confirmed the initial judgment of palaeographers.[3] Thanks to

[1] See also the excellent earlier study by Hans Jonas, *Gnosis und spätantiker Geist* (1934), pp. 351–75.

[2] So far little has been published except in the daily press about this latest group of finds, which will take years to put into shape for publication; on the recent finds see provisionally the convenient survey by A. Dupont-Sommer, *Nouveaux aperçus* (1953), pp. 215–18. Contrary to some reports, the numerous scrolls (believed to have numbered at least 300) found in 1952 are preserved in the form of an immense mass of fragments, which will have to be sorted and arranged in place before they can be adequately published.

[3] My original date (in early 1948) for the Isaiah scroll was about 100 B.C., that is, somewhere in the latter part of the second century or the first part of the last century B.C. This date was based on the material collected in my article on the Nash Papyrus in *Journal of Biblical Literature*, vol. LVI (1937), pp. 143–76, plus additional material which had come in since then. We now have an excellent (though highly polemic) discussion of the palaeography of the Qumrân scrolls in S. A. Birnbaum's *The Qumrân (Dead Sea) Scrolls and Palaeography* (1952), and a valuable survey of the progress of research in J. C. Trever's paper in the *Proceedings of the American Philosophical Society*, vol. XCVII (1953), pp. 184–93.

a combination of evidence from pottery,[1] coins,[2] and radiocarbon dating of the linen cloth in which some of the scrolls found in the first cave had been wrapped,[3] there is no longer the slightest doubt possible about the dating of the vast majority of the scrolls and fragments between the middle of the second century B.C. and the middle of the first century A.D. It was natural that scholars should be suspicious of the claims made by the writer and others—I would have been the first to discount the possibility of such extraordinary finds being made in Palestine. However, there never was any excuse for rejecting clear-cut evidence without thorough investigation.

This is not the place to discuss the contents of the new documents except in so far as they throw light on the Gospel of John and related

[1] When the original cave was completely cleared by G. L. Harding and R. de Vaux in January 1949, they were greatly impressed by the Hellenistic character of the bulk of the pottery shapes, and so dated the sealing of the cave much too early (about 100 B.C.). I reacted strongly against such a high date, but relied on the acknowledged ceramic competence of the excavators, and pushed my own preferred date for the sealing back from about the turn of our era toward the middle of the last century B.C. Since the end of 1951 the excavation of Khirbet Qumrân has yielded conclusive evidence from coins that the 'mother house' of the Essenes in this area had been occupied from about 100 B.C. to A.D. 68 with an interruption between *c.* 30 and *c.* 1 B.C. Pottery of the second phase like the jars of the first cave proved that the two were roughly synchronous. Meanwhile it had become clear that there were scrolls in the collection which were later than the Habakkuk Commentary, so the date for the sealing would have had to be lowered in any case. In August 1952, I had my first opportunity to see the fragments of a jar from the cave, which had been freshly broken in transit to Baltimore from Jerusalem and was being repaired at the Oriental Institute in Chicago. The texture of the pottery is characteristically Roman, not at all the familiar Hellenistic ware of Gibeah, Beth-zur, Bethel, and other sites that I had excavated. In other words, it is in any case later than the third quarter of the last century B.C., despite the Hellenistic appearance of the shapes. A date in the Herodian Age or immediately afterwards is thus clear from the ceramic point of view alone.

[2] See previous note. The second campaign in the spring of 1953 brought further numismatic confirmation of the previously obtained results.

[3] It will be recalled that the date fixed by radiocarbon (on which cf. A. Dupont-Sommer, *Nouveaux aperçus* (1953), pp. 29f.) was A.D. 33 plus or minus some two centuries. While the uncertainty is purely statistical, it should be recalled that the conditions of freedom from moisture in the cave were such that the hunks of linen which were used formed optimal material for an accurate count. Since the first cave was probably to some extent, at least, a *genîza* for the preservation of disused manuscripts, an average date about A.D. 33 would suit our present evidence for the probable time of deposit very well.

matters.[1] There can be no doubt that the sectarians to whom we owe the Scroll of Discipline (and the somewhat later Damascus Covenant), the Habakkuk Commentary, the Scroll of Hymns, and the War between the Children of Light and the Children of Darkness (to mention only published material) were Essenes.[2] Whether they were the Essenes proper, described by Josephus, or a splinter sect which emerged from them, will perhaps be debated for some time; opinion increasingly favours the former alternative. Birnbaum, Trever, and I—to mention only the scholars who have been active in studying the palaeography of the documents—agree in general about the dating of the scrolls mentioned above between the latter part of the second century B.C. (at most) and the first decades of the first century A.D. (in roughly the order of their listing above). My own preference is for dating these four Dead Sea scrolls between about 75 B.C. and A.D. 25, allowing a span of about a century to cover the evolution of the square Hebrew character which they exhibit. There can be no doubt that such documents as the Aramaic Book of Lamech are written in a later script which is very closely related to the script of most of the graffiti, dipinti, and lapidary imitations of cursive which we find on mortuary monuments and objects around Jerusalem, all dating from the last two or three generations before A.D. 70. The script of the written fragments from the time immediately preceding the downfall of Bar Cochba (i.e. between *c.* A.D. 100 and *c.* 135) is definitely later than anything yet found in the Qumrân caves.[3]

[1] In H. H. Rowley's book, *The Zadokite Fragments and the Dead Sea Scrolls* (1952), we have an extremely full bibliographical survey of the rapidly growing literature up to a few months before publication. Dupont-Sommer's book *Nouveaux aperçus* (1953), also provides recent bibliographical indications.

[2] On this question see especially Millar Burrows, *Oudtestamentische Studiën* (1950), pp. 165ff.; W. H. Brownlee, *The Biblical Archaeologist*, vol. XIII (1950), pp. 49–72; A. Dupont-Sommer, *Nouveaux aperçus* (1953), *passim*, etc. One of my recent students, Dr Joseph Baumgarten, has published a paper in the *Harvard Theological Review* in which he shows that the Essenes did not reject the sacrificial system, much less the Temple, but that they objected strenuously to the laxness and impurity of the priests who officiated there, and consequently refused to participate in the services under conditions as they were; see *H.T.R.* (1953), pp. 141–59.

[3] See now the illustrative plates of documents and fragments from this period published by G. L. Harding, *Palestine Exploration Quarterly* (1952), Pl. XXVIII, and by R. de Vaux, *Revue Biblique* (1953), Pls. XII–XIV.

The actual date of the compositions themselves, as distinct from that of our extant copies, is more uncertain. Most scholars who have expressed themselves favour a date in the Hasmonean dynasty, either in the latter part of the Maccabean period proper, about the time of Alexander Jannaeus, or shortly after the Roman conquest of 63 B.C. We lack space to go into details here, and it is not necessary for our purposes to date them exactly; the writer has oscillated between a pre-Roman and early Roman date, though he has never stated his views in print. He considers it as highly probable that the Book of Discipline and the Hymns are pre-Roman, while it appears to him that Dupont-Sommer is in general correct in dating the Habakkuk Commentary in the early Roman period; the War is now dated by Yadin between *c.* 60 and 30 B.C. In any case he is more and more convinced that the Sectarian documents hitherto published are in general later than the similar pseudepigraphical literature. Jubilees is definitely pre-Maccabean, and L. Finkelstein's date in the early second century (with preference for a date between 175 and 167 B.C.) commends itself; the writer's own earlier date in the third century was probably a little too high.[1] The Enoch-Noah-Lamech literature now looks like a product of the last two centuries B.C.; in any case the Aramaic of the two fragments of Lamech which I have examined, thanks to the kindness of Dr Trever, is definitely later than that of Daniel, though earlier than that of any extant rabbinic literature. The Testaments of the Twelve Patriarchs are closest of all to our new documents, but they lack the highly developed characteristics of the latter and must be either earlier or somehow different in background and associations. In view of E. Bickerman's rather convincing attribution of the Testaments to a date not far from 175 B.C.,[2] and the fact that Charles' date toward the end of the second century tends to conflict with the probable date of our new documents, I should not hesitate to follow Bickerman. It is now certain from the Qumrân discoveries that all the pseudepigraphical books we have mentioned were recognized as edifying by our

[1] L. Finkelstein, *Harvard Theological Review*, vol. XXXVI (1943), pp. 19–24; for the writer's view see his book, *From the Stone Age to Christianity* (1940), pp. 266f., where he proposed a date in the early third century. Later he lowered the date to the second half of the third century, which was still probably too high. However, a Maccabean date is most certainly too low.

[2] *Journal of Biblical Literature*, vol. LXIX (1950), pp. 245–60.

Qumrân Essenes, but whether they considered them as part of their own sectarian literature we do not yet know.

Turning from the relation between the new Essene books and the already known intertestamental literature to that between the former and the Gospel of St John, we note that they are in some respects very close. There are many parallels between the new scrolls and the Synoptic Gospels, the Pauline letters, and the remaining books of the New Testament, but these parallels are most numerous in the areas where the New Testament books in question parallel the Gospel of John most closely. The parallels between the new scrolls and the Pauline corpus are almost as important for our purposes as the others, since there has been a century-old tendency to put the Gospel of John as far as possible from the letters of St Paul. E. R. Goodenough protested against this tendency in 1945, and the new scrolls confirm his protests in the most striking way. In our following discussion we are heavily indebted to a series of brilliant essays by K. G. Kuhn since 1950.[1]

In these essays Kuhn has demonstrated that the new scrolls are characterized by a far-reaching ethical dualism of ultimately Iranian inspiration.[2] In Mazdayasnianism we find the two primordial representatives of good and evil, light and darkness, truth and falsehood opposing each other as Ahuramazda (Ormazd) and Angramainyu (Ahriman). These two opposing principles appear as clashing spirits of truth and perversity, light and darkness, etc., in the Essene documents from Qumrân.[3] Among the Essenes, however, these opposing spirits were both created by God at the beginning of time; their dualism is not only ethical but monotheistic, as is to be expected of a sect which was more rigorous in its adherence to the moral laws of the Old Testament than were even the Pharisees. The same ethical dualism appears throughout the New Testament, but again it is most strongly expressed by John and Paul. In John the militant aspect of ethical dualism is not nearly so much emphasized as in Paul's epistles;[4] on the other hand, a more static opposition of

[1] Note particularly his essays in the *Zeitschrift für Theologie und Kirche*, vol. XLVII (1950), pp. 192–211; vol. XLIX (1952), pp. 200–22, 296–316.

[2] Cf. especially *Z.T.K.* (1952), pp. 296ff.

[3] See especially *Z.T.K.* (1950), pp. 199f.; (1952), pp. 308f.

[4] Cf. particularly *Z.T.K.* (1952), pp. 200ff., 212ff.

dualistic pairs is very common, and is, in fact, the dominant note of the Gospel, speaking from the standpoint of the history of ideas.

We have a very clear statement of this basic Essene creed in the Scroll of Discipline, iii. 13–iv. 26.[1] Here we read that God planned and foreordained all creation, fashioning man to rule over it and assigning the two spirits of truth (*'emét*) and perversity (*'awel*) to guide him until the final accounting in the Day of Judgment. 'From a fountain of light are the generations of truth and from a spring of darkness are the generations of perversity' (iii. 19). All men are either sons of light or sons of darkness, predestined (though the possibility of election is more than once offered by our texts) by God from the beginning. Comparing the terminology (not necessarily the theology) with that of John, we note that the new documents greatly increase the widely recognized resemblance between both theology and wording of the Gospel and the First Epistle of John. For instance, the spirit of truth (τὸ πνεῦμα τῆς ἀληθείας) of John, chs. xiv–xvi, and I John iv. 6 is a direct translation of the Hebrew *rûaḥ ha-'emét*, and the opposite spirit in the latter passage is called τὸ πνεῦμα τῆς πλάνης, which is identical with **rûaḥ hat-ta'ût* (*ta'ût* is a frequent synonym of *'awel*, 'perversity', in the new scrolls).[2] The spirit of perversity is, of course, identical with the often mentioned Belial; we do not seem to be given any special name for the spirit of truth (the Paraclete of the Gospel).

The contrast of light and darkness plays a very striking role in the Essene documents, as well as in the New Testament, again particularly in John. For instance, the 'sons of light', who appear so frequently in the scrolls (note here especially the key passages in the Scroll of Discipline, i. 9, iii. 24f.), also appear as υἱοὶ φωτός in John xii. 36. In the Scroll of Discipline, iii. 7 we have *'ôr ha-ḥayyîm*, 'the light of life' = τὸ φῶς τῆς ζωῆς (John viii. 12) and ὁ περιπατῶν ἐν τῇ σκοτίᾳ (John xii. 35) corresponds almost word for word with the Scroll of Discipline, iii. 21: *b^e-darkê ḥoshek yithall^ekû*, 'and in ways of darkness they continue to walk', with which compare the same expression in John viii. 12.[3]

[1] See W. H. Brownlee, *The Dead Sea Manual of Discipline* (1951), pp. 12–18; H. G. Kuhn, *Z.T.K.* (1952) pp. 297–303.

[2] See Kuhn, *Z.T.K.* (1952), p. 205 n. 1.

[3] See Brownlee, *op. cit.* pp. 14f.

The parallels between the use of 'truth' in the Scrolls and in the Gospel of John are just as close, though the latter, in keeping with its habitual emphasis on the positive rather than the negative, does not mention the opposite word for 'lie', which appears so often as *drauja* and *druj* in the Iranian literature of the Mazdayasnian movement and as *kazab* in the Scrolls. Striking is the parallel between the expression 'to "do" the truth' (i.e. to practise righteousness) in the Scroll of Discipline, i. 5 (*la-'asôt 'emét*) and John iii. 21 (ὁ ποιῶν τὴν ἀλήθειαν).[1] In this connection note the parallelism between 'the works of God' (*ma'aśê 'Ēl*) in the Scroll of Discipline, iv. 4 and John vi. 28f.[2]

Perhaps the most important service of the Dead Sea scrolls will be the demonstration which may be brought from them that John, the Synoptics, St Paul, and various other books draw from a common reservoir of terminology and ideas which were well known to the Essenes and presumably familiar also to other Jewish sects of the period. In future these reminiscences must be studied in their genetic context, and much of the artificially created contrast and conflict between the point of view of different early New Testament sources will vanish. It is noteworthy that Kuhn, who began with a position not too far from that of Bultmann, has rapidly changed his mind under the weight of the new material, and particularly of his clear recognition of the gulf between the basically physical dualism of the Gnostics and the ethical dualism of the Gospel of St John.[3]

In view of the preceding paragraphs it should be clear to all students by now that the books of the Essenes from the first century B.C. provide the closest approach to the Gospels (particularly St John) and the Pauline Epistles, so far as conceptual background and terminology are concerned, that has yet been discovered—far closer than post-Christian gospels such as the Hermetic writings, Philo, Rabbinic Judaism, Gnosticism, or Mandeanism.[4] The direct link between the

[1] See Kuhn, *Z.T.K.* (1950), p. 210. [2] Cf. Brownlee, *loc. cit.*

[3] Contrast Kuhn's remarks in *Z.T.K.* (1950), pp. 203f., with *Z.T.K.* (1952), p. 213 n. 1, and especially *Z.T.K.* (1952), pp. 313–16. On the question of possible 'gnostic' influence on New Testament thinking, see the excellent paper by W. D. Davies in the *Harvard Theological Review*, vol. XLVI (1953), pp. 113–39. on '"Knowledge" in the Dead Sea Scrolls and Matthew xi. 25–30.'

[4] See particularly the valuable pages devoted to a survey of this material, in the order I have indicated, in C. H. Dodd, *The Interpretation of the Fourth Gospel*

Essenes and the Gospels has long been conjectured to be represented by the teachings of John the Baptist; this can now be made much more plausible than ever before. There is, on the other hand, less evidence than ever to support the claims of Gnostic influence on Paul and John.[1] There is no fundamental difference in teaching between John and the Synoptics; the contrast between them lies in the concentration of tradition along certain aspects of Christ's teachings, particularly those which seem to have resembled the teaching of the Essenes most closely.[2] And yet, with all this superficial similarity, there is a wide gulf between the doctrines of the Essenes and the essentials of Johannine teaching, which the latter shares with the Synoptics and Paul. These essentials may be listed as follows (with some simplification):

A. Role of the Messiah. The Messiah appeared on earth to suffer and die a miserable death, not to reign in earthly splendour.
B. Soteriology. Christ came to save sinners, not (merely) the elect.
C. Ministry of Healing. Christ came to heal the physically and spiritually sick, not (merely) to sanctify his followers.
D. The God of love. Christ taught the Gospel of love, not merely the gospel of righteousness.

We have seen that both narratives and *logia* of John's Gospel certainly or presumably date back to oral tradition in Palestine, before A.D. 70; they were probably transmitted orally in the Diaspora for at least a decade—possibly two decades—before being put into writing. It stands to reason that there has been rearrangement of

(1953); see above, p. 161 n. 2. It may be added that several Hermetic books were found bound with the Gnostic treatises of Chenoboskion. It may further be observed that there is at most only the faintest echo of the Philonic or Hellenistic Logos (on which see Dodd, *op. cit.* pp. 263–85) in the Gospel of John, for which Dodd might have consulted the indispensable book of Lorenz Dürr, *Die Wertung des göttlichen Wortes im Alten Testament und im antiken Orient* (*Mitt. der Vorderasiatisch-aegypt. Ges.* vol. XLII, 1938). On Dürr's work cf. my detailed review, *Journal of Biblical Literature*, vol. LX (1941), pp. 206ff., and the remarks in my book, *From the Stone Age to Christianity* (1940), pp. 146, 285.

[1] In this connection see the judicious treatment of the material already available before the discovery of the Dead Sea scrolls by W. D. Davies, *Paul and Rabbinic Judaism* (1948), especially ch. I on 'Palestinian and Diaspora Judaism'.

[2] On the points in which the Gospels—and again particularly John—agree closely with Essene teaching see the useful summary by H. G. Kuhn, *Z.T.K.* (1950), pp. 209f.

material, concentration of *logia* into sermons, refraction of parables in passing from spiritual to factual truth. But there is absolutely nothing to show that any of Jesus' teachings have been distorted or falsified, or that any vital new element has been added to them.[1] That the needs of the early Church influenced the selection of items for inclusion in the Gospel we may readily admit,[2] but there is no reason to suppose that the needs of that Church were responsible for any inventions or innovations of theological significance.[3] Whether the Gospel was edited by John the Presbyter of Papias and the First Epistle of John, or whether some other reconstruction is more probable, we may rest assured that it contains the memories of the Apostle John—regardless of whether he died in Jerusalem or in Ephesus, though the latter is so well attested by tradition that it remains most plausible.[4]

[1] One of the strangest assumptions of critical New Testament scholars and theologians is that the mind of Jesus was so limited that any apparent contrast between John and the Synoptics must be due to differences between early Christian theologians. Every great thinker and personality is going to be interpreted differently by different friends and hearers, who will select what seems most congenial or useful out of what they have seen and heard. From Socrates to the most recent men of eminence there are innumerable examples. The Christian might *a fortiori* suppose the same to be true of his Master.

[2] Cf. *From the Stone Age to Christianity* (1940), pp. 292–4, 297–8.

[3] Cf. *ibid.* pp. 304ff.

[4] The thorough and sympathetic treatment by J. H. Bernard in his commentary on the Gospel of St John in the *International Critical Commentary* (1928), vol. I, pp. xxxiv–lxxi, has never been superseded. In this connection I should like to direct attention to an excellent little book by the lamented J. A. Montgomery, *The Origin of the Gospel According to St John* (Philadelphia, 1923), which deals very intelligently with the limited material then available for the background of the Gospel. I subscribe unreservedly to his conclusions (p. 30): 'That the Gospel of St John is the composition of a well-informed Jew, not of the Pharisaic party, whose life experience was gained in Palestine in the first half of the first century, and whose mother-tongue was Aramaic; and that this conclusion alone explains the excellence of the historical data and the philological phenomena of the book.'

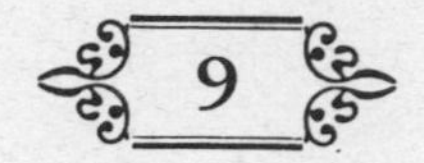

THE ACCOUNT OF THE ESSENES IN HIPPOLYTUS AND JOSEPHUS

M. BLACK

THE possibility that the new Zadokite documents from the region of the Dead Sea have some connection with the ancient Essenes[1] has sent a number of students of the Jewish background of the New Testament back again to the primary sources for our knowledge of that influential pre-Christian 'sect'. Our chief information about it comes from Josephus' *Bellum Judaicum* II, 8–13. From these chapters in Josephus descriptive passages have been apparently excerpted by patristic writers such as Hippolytus, Porphyry and Origen, of which by far the most interesting is the long 'version' of Josephus embedded in Hippolytus' *Refutatio Omnium Haeresium* (ix, 18–28).

That the Hippolytean description of the Essenes is substantially the same in contents (and in arrangement of topics) as that in Josephus is apparent from a comparison of the first few paragraphs of each account. But differences are as striking as agreements; Hippolytus gives us a number of fresh facts about the Essenes of which there is no trace in our Josephus text, and, together with a marked difference throughout in style and language, his whole account creates the strong impression of being a closely related but independent version. It would be quite impossible, for instance, to collate the 'variants' in Hippolytus and include them in a critical apparatus to Josephus: Duncker, in his edition of Hippolytus,[2] prints the entire Josephus text underneath his text of the *Refutatio*. Moreover, the introduction of fresh information by Hippolytus is difficult to reconcile with a theory of free adaptation and paraphrase, though such a view is tenable. It seems more likely, either that Hippolytus

[1] Cf. Millar Burrows, 'The Discipline Manual of the Judaean Covenanters', in *Oudtestamentische Studiën*, vol. VIII (Leiden, 1950), pp. 165 ff.

[2] Göttingen, 1859.

had a different edition of Josephus from ours, or that he is reproducing one of Josephus' own sources.[1]

In view of this second possibility, the points of greatest interest in Hippolytus' account are: (1) those where it supplements Josephus and gives fresh facts, especially on topics directly bearing on subjects of interest to the New Testament student; and (2) when his version contradicts the traditional account of Josephus.

One feature of Hippolytus' description, however, must first be noted, as it constitutes a strong argument for its independent origin. It is at once a much simpler, and, from the literary point of view, a less elegant version, and, at the same time (and in keeping with its literary plainness), a much more factual account. The Josephan version, in comparison, reveals a characteristic tendency to hyperbole and extravagance. An example of Hippolytus' literary style is the unadorned statement at § 20, οὐδὲν δὲ ὅλως οὔτε ἀγοράζουσιν οὔτε πωλοῦσιν, ὃ δ' ἂν ἔχῃ τις τῷ μὴ ἔχοντι δούς, ὃ οὐκ ἔχει λαμβάνει. Josephus confronts us with the following (somewhat prolix) period: οὐδὲν δὲ ἐν ἀλλήλοις οὔτε ἀγοράζουσιν οὔτε πωλοῦσιν ἀλλὰ τῷ χρῄζοντι διδοὺς ἕκαστος τὰ παρ' αὐτοῦ, τὸ παρ' ἐκείνου χρήσιμον ἀντικομίζεται. καὶ χωρὶς δὲ τῆς ἀντιδόσεως ἀκώλυτος ἡ μετάληψις αὐτοῖς, παρ' ὧν ἂν ἐθελήσωσι. It is arguable that here (and perhaps in other passages), Hippolytus is simplifying Josephus and at the same time adding a 'Christian touch'.[2] But why a Christian Father should thus deliberately assimilate his account of a 'heresy' to a Synoptic saying of Christ is difficult to explain—or why he should depart at all from the text of Josephus, if it lay before him in its present form.

Examples of Josephan hyperbole (and perhaps even of distortion of his source) occur more than once: thus the statement at § 18 in Hippolytus that the Essenes are φιλάλληλοι is in Josephus that they are φιλάλληλοι δὲ καὶ τῶν ἄλλων πλέον; where Hippolytus informs us about the Essenes' attitude to women, he tells us simply that even though women should want to become adherents of the sect, they are not admitted, since the Essenes in no way trust women (κατὰ

[1] Cf. Duncker, p. 471, l. 90 n.: *quae sequuntur* (IX, 18–28) *Hippolytus e Flavio Iosepho...hausisse videtur, nisi uterque unum eundemque auctorem secutus.* The first to draw the consequences of Duncker's second alternative for the study of the Essenes was Dr K. Kohler in his article on the Essenes in the *Jewish Encyclopedia.*

[2] Cf. Conybeare on the Essenes in Hastings' *Dictionary of the Bible*, p. 770.

μηδένα τρόπον γυναιξὶ πιστεύοντες); in Josephus we are told that they take special precautions against the wantonnesses of the sex, καὶ μηδεμίαν τηρεῖν πεπεισμένοι τὴν πρὸς ἕνα πίστιν.

If Josephus has introduced something of himself into this last passage, it is probably not the only occasion. Thus the statement that the Essenes were sun-worshippers is based on *B.J.* VIII, 5, πρὶν γὰρ ἀνασχεῖν τὸν ἥλιον οὐδὲν φθέγγονται τῶν βεβήλων, πατρίους δέ τινας εἰς αὐτὸν εὐχὰς ὥσπερ ἱκετεύοντες ἀνατεῖλαι: over against this Hippolytus has simply παραμένουσι δὲ εὐτάκτως καὶ ἐπιμόνως εὐχόμενοι ἕωθεν, μηδὲν πρότερον φθεγξάμενοι εἰ μὴ τὸν θεὸν ὑμνήσωσι.

Hippolytus' version in general is a much fuller and circumstantial account, occasionally adding a fresh detail which has a ring of authenticity, such as the statement that some of the stricter members of the sect refused even to leave their beds on the Sabbath (§ 25, τινὲς δὲ οὐδὲ κλινιδίου χωρίζονται). The longest 'interpolation' occurs at § 26 where Hippolytus goes on to describe some further traits of the stricter *renuntiantes*. Some of these will not even carry a coin about with them, declaring that it is wrong even to look on an image, and for the same reason refusing to enter a city gate over which a statue stands. Others still, if they heard any Gentile discussing God or his laws would lie in wait for him and threaten him with death if he refused to be circumcised, an excess of zeal which earned for them the name of Zealots or Sicarii.

None of this information is contained in Josephus, whose brief account of the Zealots (*Ant.* XVIII, 1, 6) is confined to a statement, the gist of which is given in a single sentence in Hippolytus, that their love of liberty is such that the fear of death itself would not induce them to call any man lord, since God is their only Lord (Hippolytus § 26, ἕτεροι δὲ αὐτων οὐδένα κύριον ὀνομάζουσι πλὴν τὸν θεόν, εἰ καὶ αἰκίζοιτό τις ἢ καὶ ἀναιροῖτο).

An instance where Hippolytus introduces another unexpected and perhaps a 'Christian touch' is in his account of the Essenes' attitude to those who wrong them. Josephus (VIII, 7) tells us that among their 'fearful oaths' is a promise μήτε κατὰ γνωμην βλάψειν τινὰ μήτε ἐξ ἐπιτάγματος, μισήσειν δὲ ἀεὶ τοὺς ἀδίκους καὶ συναγωνιεῖσθαι τοῖς δικαίοις. Hippolytus has (they swear) κατὰ μηδένα τρόπον ἀδικήσειν τινα, μηδένα δὲ μήτε ἀδικοῦντα μήτε ἐχθρὸν μισήσειν, προσεύχεσθαι δὲ ὑπὲρ αὐτῶν, συναγωνίζεσθαι ἀεὶ τοῖς δικαίοις.

The passage which stands in direct contradiction to Josephus' account and which is of greatest interest to the New Testament student is Hippolytus' version of the Essene doctrine of immortality.

JOSEPHUS, *B.J.* VIII, 11: Now the following opinion is firmly held among them (καὶ γὰρ ἔρρωται παρ' αὐτοῖς ἥδε ἡ δοξα) that while bodies are corruptible and their material substance has no permanency, souls are immortal and continue for ever; and that, emanating from the finest atmosphere, they are bound up in their bodies as in prisons, into which they are drawn by a certain natural attraction: but when they are released from the bonds of the flesh, they rejoice and are borne upwards, freed from a long slavery.

HIPPOLYTUS, 27: Now the dogma (word) of the resurrection also is firmly held among them (ἔρρωται δὲ παρ' αὐτοῖς καὶ ὁ τῆς ἀναστάσεως λόγος). For they confess that the flesh also will rise and be immortal as the soul is already immortal, which they now say, when separated from the body, enters a place of fragrant air and light, to rest until the judgment... for they say that there will be a judgment and a conflagration of everything, and that the wicked will be eternally punished.

There are two possible interpretations of this last evidence: (1) that Josephus is adapting and conforming his account to Greek conceptions, whereas Hippolytus is remaining faithful to his source; or (2) that it is Hippolytus who is conforming his report of Josephus to Christian ideas and attributing such beliefs wrongly to the Essenes. In the first case the motive is plain enough; in the second it is more difficult to discern; moreover, it is the Jewish doctrine, not the Greek, that we would expect in a Jewish sect. At one point at least the new scrolls agree with Hippolytus' account; there is little doubt that the Zadokites believed in a final 'conflagration of everything'.[1] But whether the Essenes taught a resurrection of the body (or prayer for enemies) must still remain in doubt. Hippolytus may equally well, however, be faithful to his source, and the ancient Essenes may have taught both.

[1] Cf. G. Vermes, *La Communauté de la Nouvelle Alliance* (*Analecta Lovanensia Biblica et Orientalia*, ser. II, fasc. 22).

SEPTUAGINTAL STUDIES IN THE MID-CENTURY

THEIR LINKS WITH THE PAST AND THEIR PRESENT TENDENCIES

P. KATZ

One hundred and thirty years ago J. F. Schleusner was able to produce extensive Lexica both of the Septuagint (LXX) and the New Testament. Today such a feat seems almost to belong to the realm of fairy tales. No N.T. student is now prepared to follow his example. In this age of specialization both O.T. and N.T. studies have been branching out widely, without much regard for the LXX, though the LXX is by nature a connecting link between them both.

The contributors to this symposium, however special their chosen subjects may be, all enjoy a common privilege: they are addressing a body of fellow-students who are familiar with their problems and know how to assess the possible value of forthcoming solutions. The field of N.T. studies is well circumscribed. Its map therefore is always before the eyes of the writers, to whatever great lengths their special subject may carry them. They are geared to a common task of teaching, which links them both to the past and future. There is continuity, due to a large extent to the necessity of elementary instruction and its requirement for handbooks at all stages. There are examinations and there are chairs.

This is not so, however, in the field of Septuagintal studies. The absence of professorships limits regular teaching and deprives Biblical scholars of useful neighbourly consultation. Hence a note of uncertainty is sounded whenever the LXX is touched upon. Even when problems are rightly seen and fully treated, it is often forgotten that, seen primarily from the point of view of the LXX, these problems may present very different aspects. The learned literature provides, alas, little guidance. It is significant that Swete's *Introduction* was never brought up to date nor replaced.[1] No wonder that studies published in monographs are frequently erratic, a fact that can make reviewing an invidious task. This fact points to an absence of co-ordination and common understanding, and much of real promise fails to find a ready response in the wider circles of Biblical scholarship. There will certainly be a change for the better as soon as the basic principles which have led to recent progress have been stated in an up-to-date introduction to the study of the LXX.

It would be to no purpose merely to pass in review a number of important publications and attempt to assess what is new and useful in them. Rather we should try to fix some point from which a new departure will be readily understood by the N.T. student. If that point is well chosen, juxtaposition of past and present methods will expose their differences in full relief.

There is a period that will serve us well in this respect. In the 1880's there was a definite break both in the study of the N.T. and that of the LXX. Those years saw the conclusion of Westcott and Hort's N.T. Text and Introduction, the first critically established and carefully substantiated edition, which brought to an end the domination of the Received Text. Text and grammar had been examined with great circumspection, their rules being laid down in a masterly poised code of law, as it were. This work left its impression on all subsequent study, for it was the first to offer definite standards with which to contend. What has been done textually since then is adjustment rather than refutation. It has been different with the grammatical factors. Here the reaction was bound to be more violent.

The same 1880's witnessed a break in Septuagintal work. Again it was Hort who gave the first impulse. As soon as his mind was set free from the 'many long years' preparation of the N.T., he turned to the LXX and eventually drew up a scheme which resulted in the Cambridge editions of Swete and of Brooke and McLean. There was, however, a great difference in method. While the N.T. was

[1] A promising first step has been taken in Part II of B. J. Roberts' book, *The Old Testament Text and Versions* (Cardiff, 1951), pp. 101–87. Cf. E. Vogt's review in *Biblica*, vol. XXXII (1951), pp. 441 ff., and mine, in *T.L.Z.* vol. LXXVI (1951), cols. 535 ff.

issued in a critical edition, the LXX, a long neglected text, was to be edited in the provisional form of a reliable collection of the evidence, leaving the reconstruction of a critical text to subsequent endeavours. Caution was certainly well advised, and the edition was timely, as it involved a break with the Received Text of the Sixtine, the place of which was to be taken by the true text of Vat. B,[1] or its next best substitute. It was Hort's hope that each of the four volumes of the larger edition might take no more than five years' preparation, and if this edition could have been completed in this time, a solid basis for work on a critical text would have been created. Hort's assumption, however, that the collations of minuscules in the Holmes and Parsons edition, together with those done by Lagarde, might suffice, proved mistaken, and the necessary search for MSS. and their collation took much more time, so that by 1940 the edition was only half finished.

Nevertheless, Hort's feeling that there was need for an edition to be completed within a short space of time was correct; for there were early forebodings of a development in the direction of a definitively constituted text in the same 1880's. In 1883 Lagarde's first and only volume of Lucian's recension was published.[2] As we can see now, its shortcomings vindicated Hort's more cautious plan. It was, however, the first sign of a development which, as soon as it achieved maturity, was bound to make mere collections of evidence obsolete.

Thus the common denominator of both N.T. and LXX studies was their interest in establishing the text. As this interest receded in N.T. studies, concern for the problems of the LXX correspondingly waned. Texts are, however, tools of primary importance. It is therefore worth while devoting more space to these two types of LXX editions, for they point to different lines of procedure, neither of which can be said wholly to belong to the past.

[1] The Sixtine was printed from a still existing copy of the Aldine with superficial corrections from Vat. B and other MSS. (A. Rahlfs, *Z.A.W.* vol. XXXIII (1913), pp. 30–46; M. L. Margolis, *J.B.L.* vol. XXXVIII (1919), pp. 51 f.; J. Ziegler, *Biblica*, vol. XXVI (1945), pp. 49ff.).

[2] *Librorum Veteris Testamenti Canonicorum Pars Prior Graece* (Göttingen, 1883).

Septuagintal studies in the mid-century

I. THE FIRST GENERATION

(a) The Cambridge Procedure

Hort's scheme provided for two editions, each to be done by a distinguished Cambridge N.T. scholar, H. B. Swete. The first was to be 'portable'. It was to give to the ordinary reader for the first time a text based on the MSS. and, at the same time, to serve as an instrument for collation. The second 'larger' edition was to present the same text but, in addition, 'to give the variations of all the Greek uncial MSS., of select Greek cursives, of the more important Ancient Versions, and of the quotations made by Philo and the earlier and more important ecclesiastical writers'. The text was to attempt no approach to an hypothetical original text behind the evidence. Whenever it departs from the leading MS. where this is corrupt, this is done merely to shorten the annotation. Brooke and McLean (BM), who were entrusted with the task after Swete had felt unable to do also the larger edition, gradually introduced more departures from the MS. than Swete had done; but they stopped half-way. What has been shown for I Esdra[1] applies to all books: in many passages they retain individual corruptions of B* in close proximity to other similar corruptions which they correct, though all equally demanded correction. It is, however, intelligible why the editors refrained from broadening their approach. They avoided the temptation of emendation. The result is an uneven compromise between diplomatic reproduction and the exclusion of the most obviously intolerable readings. In rare instances Swete and after him BM took the desperate step of 'emending' singular readings of B* without regard for the correct reading of the other MSS.[2]

The true test of diplomatic reproductions is reliability. Swete's second and third editions were much improved by fresh collations by E. Nestle; yet M. L. Margolis in preparing his edition of the Greek Joshua considered it 'desirable, in view of the inaccuracies in Swete's apparatus', to base his work on entirely fresh collations.[3] Rahlfs found Swete's collations of the Psalms 'fairly reliable', but inferior

[1] *T.L.Z.* vol. LXII (1937), cols. 341 ff.

[2] *Ibid.* col. 343. In I Esdr. viii. 67 (71) B reads τας, an obvious corruption of γάρ. Both editions insert an unwarranted †τινας† into the text.

[3] *J.A.O.S.* vol. XXXI (1911), p. 366.

to those of Lagarde's *Psalterii Graeci Quinquagena Prima.*[1] J. Ziegler expresses his disappointment that Swete's edition, so beautiful in appearance and so full of the most detailed information, should be marred by many mistakes.[2] Nevertheless, it represented real progress at its time. The remarkable thing is that the criticisms quoted above all came from editors of critical texts. Their evaluation of individual MSS. was based on first-hand study and their work on MSS. groups accustomed them to recheck all strange readings in the collation of individual MSS. Even a diplomatic edition can be done to perfection only by those whose work enables them to look behind the façade.

Brooke and McLean based their edition on fresh collations (many provided by Rahlfs' Göttingen LXX Bureau which they checked), attaining a much higher standard of accuracy. Nevertheless, Margolis published thirty pages of 'Corrections in the Apparatus of the Book of Joshua' alone.[3] At times their demarcation of the lemmata in the apparatus could have been improved by a knowledge of the recensional problems. In spite of these defects their presentation of the evidence is a solid piece of work, and many students have gratefully profited by its merits.

There are, however, some points in which the methods chosen

[1] *Sept.-Stud.* vol. II, p. 4.

[2] 'The text is tolerably well reproduced; among the MSS. the collations of B and S (after Tischendorf) are the best; A is frequently recorded inexactly. The collation of Q is completely insufficient, in spite of its great importance for the prophetical books; for it offers a good text of Isaiah, Jeremiah and the Minor Prophets, and subsequently was worked over after a hexaplaric MS. by a corrector, who has marked the hexaplaric additions and omissions by asterisks and obeli and himself has added plenty of hexaplaric readings and, more especially, those of the more recent translators. Swete certainly has many notes about Q^{a} and Q^{mg} (=corrector of Q), but many are omitted or wrongly recorded; frequently the hexaplaric notes are not given, and the signs for transposition are not even recognized. In Jon. ii. 3 ειπεν] + ως Q^{mg} should read ειπεν] + ωδη ϛ′ Q^{mg}: it is the superscription of the sixth Ode, =Jon. ii. 3–10.' After giving his re-collation of Amos, he comes to the conclusion that 'Swete's edition is insufficient a basis for scholarly investigation, since textual criticism calls for the most extreme accuracy....If only he had checked his collations with the edition of Cozza-Luzi these mistakes could have been avoided from the very first, and much additional material added. Unfortunately, reviewers did not consult the MSS. either and consequently the new editions and reprints have been published in this deficient form to this very day' (*Z.A.W.* vol. LX (1944), pp. 126ff.).

[3] *J.B.L.* vol. XLIX (1930), pp. 234–64.

were regrettable. One was taken over from Swete. Both Cambridge editions professedly based their text on B. But the evidence of B is often distorted by the inclusion and treatment on an almost equal footing of its correctors, the latest of whom may be dated in the fourteenth century. When the readings of B* appear implausible, three of his correctors are cited as substitutes. Often the work of a corrector cannot be dated, but it is of a much more recent date than other MSS. which, according to the principle underlying the editions, should be preferred to B*. More particularly, there are sets of corrections which, far from merely restoring a blunder of the first hand, replace its text by that of a different recension. In such instances the corrector's reading merely attests a recension for which there are earlier and more reputable witnesses. This has been overlooked by the editors who have neglected the truly editorial problems. Once the strict reproduction of evidence was abandoned, the Cambridge editions became involved in the meshes of the LXX recensions and the editors were caught unawares. But how could they be aware? Unless the basic problems posed by a text are constantly in the mind of an editor, not even a pre-critical edition can be done to perfection.

If subjectivity enters the field here where one would least expect it, in the treatment of the secondary versions of the LXX objectivity goes much too far. The reason for their use is to make available to the critic forms of the Greek text which have survived only in translations. All we want to know is what Greek underlay them. All the secondary versions are at points corrupt and remote from the original Greek. Here the student requires critical conjectures about the underlying variants. It is unfortunate that BM cite only the corrupt texts, even when the original editors have intimated solutions which might appear quite natural to those familiar with the language in question.

I give an example from the Old Latin. For II Reg. vii. 14 BM record 'αφαις] *actibus* Tyc-codd'. Here 'codd' points to a different reading in the edition. Burkitt has suggested the obvious emendation *tactibus* = ἁφαῖς. No reference therefore to Tyconius is required, for an edition of the LXX is not concerned with the incidental corruptions of the versions, but only with evidence for Greek variants. The Lyons Old Latin abounds with similar corruptions, most of which have been corrected by U. Robert. BM ignore this and inflate their apparatus with superfluous 'variants'.[1] The student who knows Latin finds an easy solution but Latin renderings of readings from the Oriental versions pose a different problem. Are they errors or variants? The editor, not the unfortunate student should give the answer. In an edition done on recensional lines it would be indicated whether the Oriental witness be supported by some Greek evidence. This should have been indicated in BM too.

In spite of Nestle's warning, Swete's edition was taken by many readers to be *the* Septuagint and gave the impression that in fact there are two rival texts, those of B and of A. These MSS. came to be considered as individual quantities, homogeneous throughout the LXX and consequently offering a clear-cut choice to the 'critical' reader. N.T. students will be reminded here of attempts to define the characteristics of MSS. which in fact reflect the work of generations of copyists with their varying whims and idiosyncrasies. The same conception underlies Procksch's strange imagery about the path to the source of the LXX leading through a porch, the two pillars of which are B and A.[2] When the early Chester Beatty papyri of the LXX were first discussed scholars asked: 'Do they give a B-text or an A-text?' *Tertium non datur*. This fallacy sprang from a misunderstanding of Swete's purpose in selecting only a few MSS. for his text. Much of this misunderstanding survives in the apparatus of *Biblia Hebraica* (*BH*3). BM's presentation of an abundance of deliberately unanalysed information had the opposite effect. L. Koehler described it as 'but a roaring sea of variants', in which cabin boy and master mariner alike perish; for the number of seamen able to navigate through this material is small. Swete's Introduction indicates that a reliable chart was not yet available in spite of the wide range of information at hand, which was a kind of antiquarian stocktaking. The student of the O.T. or N.T. cannot, however, dispense with critical guidance which must necessarily come from quarters

[1] In using Field's Hexapla, they draw on his text only and neglect the rich notes in which he offers his observations and emendations. This shortcoming was anticipated by the Concordance.

[2] Elsewhere he alleges many more supports. In his attempt to restore a metrical text of almost the whole of Genesis he selects any group of LXX MSS. which yields what he requires, retranslates their readings into Hebrew and presents them as the original Hebrew text!

the learned editors were bound to shun, by virtue of the very principles which they chose to adopt.

The Cambridge editions of the LXX are younger sisters of Westcott and Hort's N.T. They are the Cinderellas of the family. In the N.T. choices of readings were based on firmly established principles. Each decision rested on appropriate references to the introductory volume. The editors of the LXX had nothing of the kind to rely on and trusted vague analogies applied to a text centuries older and of a very different character. This is most noticeable when we now consider the grammatical aspect of both editions.

Grammar

Hort's Introduction devotes as much attention to matters of spelling as to recensional problems, for he regards them both as connected in a peculiar way. In his study of the N.T. recensions he had come to the conclusion that the group headed by BS (א) was far superior to the rest. In it he saw the pre-recensional, 'neutral' text. In matters of orthography he made some reservations,[1] but these do not prevent him from dealing with matters of spelling in close connection with the problems of textual criticism. To him spellings form as much a part of the evidence as variants in readings, so that he placed a high estimation on the spelling of MSS. which he regarded as textually superior. It never occurred to him that he was moving in a vicious circle when he believed his grammatical standards confirmed by the 'neutral' text from which they were taken. Text and editor had much in common; both deliberately refrained from extremes (which, in a text, is the unmistakable mark of *recension*). In fact spelling, except for the deliberate Atticizers of a later period, was obviously a matter of minor concern to ancient authors and copyists, and no one can distinguish spellings of copyists from those transmitted from the archetype.

In practice Hort's attitude was an uneasy compromise between his knowledge of Attic spelling and the evidence of MSS. which for other reasons had a just claim on his favour.[2] This uneasiness, which

[1] § 403; § 399 about B and S.

[2] He justified his own inconsistencies by the maxim: 'absolute uniformity belongs only to artificial times' (Intr. p. 308). Editing, however, involves a certain amount of standardizing, especially when it is claimed that itacisms have been corrected.

does him credit, has a curious way of upholding forlorn causes: 'Tabulation renders it morally certain that ἱστήκειν is nowhere a mere itacism.'[1] Here, if anywhere, we have 'the mistake of assuming the identity of the morally-acceptable with the historically-true.'[2] J. H. Moulton long ago gave the right answer: 'It is perfectly futile to follow our best uncials in printing abnormal forms like ἴδον for εἶδον and ἱστήκειν for εἱστήκειν.... The MS. evidence is not adequate proof that such forms really existed.'[3]

It is useful here to glance at the work of H. St J. Thackeray, the grammarian of the school. In fact he was much more than that: he was a co-editor with Brooke and McLean and a loving connoisseur of the whole range of Jewish Hellenists, was versed in Josephus and familiar with the papyri as well as with the grammars of Blass, Mayser, and J. H. Moulton but a thorough Hortian. Though he disposes of Hort's ἱστήκειν, yet on the same page (201) he tries to justify ἴδον and even offers alternative explanations for it. He considers the itacistic participle ἰδώς acceptable,[4] and is able to explain the slip ΑΝΟΡΑΣ (I Reg. viii. 22*a*) as 'a relic of the Epic ΑΝΕΡΑΣ'.[5] It was not by chance that he chose to postpone writing his chapter on word formation. Had he considered its problems in time, much of his chapters on phonetics and accidence would have read very differently. He made some attractive suggestions; for example, that for the translation some books were divided among two translators. Some of his observations, however, are based on Swete's edition, and earlier papyri which have since come to light change the picture. We now see that phenomena which Thackeray attributed to translators arose at a later stage of transmission and the same holds good of some of his grammatical points; for he regarded the Cambridge LXX as representative of primitive usage. For this reason also a new edition of his grammar would have to undergo far-reaching alterations.

Swete's few introductory remarks about spelling should be read in the light of Hort's principles. Brooke and McLean do not touch this point, for their text is usually Swete's. Swete's spelling and accentuation reveal much care and erudition. He candidly states,

[1] Appendix, p. 162b.
[2] C. J. Cadoux, *The Historic Mission of Jesus*, p. 3.
[3] *Grammar*, vol. II, p. 77. [4] *Ibid.* p. 278 n. 2. [5] *Ibid.* p. 150.

'It is premature to enter upon a detailed examination of the principles which direct the judgement in the acceptance or rejection of particular forms; and it is possible that not a few of the results to which the Editor has been led may be modified by further consideration'.[1] But when he further assures us that itacisms have been corrected, he is obviously unaware that numbers of sheer mistakes are left untouched. In fact, a list of them would amount to a fairly complete treatise on phonology. The rules underlying word formation are likewise ignored, in favour of traditional spellings, especially if those spellings are found in B*. This is a survival of another Hortian peculiarity: an exaggerated confidence in the first hand of B in matters of spelling, for in the last analysis their idea about what is correct derives from B*. Actually B* ought to be abandoned much more frequently. For example ἑώρων⟨ἠϝόρων and ἑόρακα⟨ϝεϝόρακα, though different, are the correct forms. Thackeray, relying on W. Veitch's rich and useful but philologically uncritical compilation,[2] considered ἑώρακα the 'older Attic form' and admitted both. He maintained that ἑώρακα is 'universal in the Pentateuch', but this can no longer be maintained in view of the Chester Beatty papyri. Here instances of the correct spelling have survived, and Sir Frederic Kenyon accordingly should not have supplied the lacunae from Swete. Our texts betray Hort's dislike of uniformity, III Reg. xx. 29 ἑώρακας; xxi. 13 ἑόρακας, both with B*. The rejected correct form of xx. 29 is duly recorded in BM's first apparatus of 'mistaken' spellings. Unfortunately, this edition never indicates what other MSS. share the mis-spellings noted in the first apparatus. Hence this edition, which purposely confines itself to a reliable record of all the details, nowhere enables the student of grammar to make sure how widely this kind of mistake is spread. The irony of it all is that there are all sorts of correct forms listed as mistaken spellings in the first apparatus.

The two determinants of Swete's orthographical presentation, grammar and his preference for the first hand of B, conflict. This was perhaps excusable in his first edition but with the rapid increase in knowledge it is hard to understand what purpose is served by perpetuating error in edition after edition. Such as it is, the larger

[1] *The Old Testament in Greek*, vol. 1, p. xii.
[2] *Greek Verbs Irregular and Defective*.

edition would also have been a real boon if it had been completed before the First World War. If it is ever resumed the least to be hoped for is a thorough revision of these blemishes.

(*b*) *The Göttingen Procedure*

This all began with one man and one book, Lagarde's *Lucian*. His faithful pupil, who carried on the master's work after his premature death, judges that it was Lagarde's biggest failure. Rahlfs bases his judgment both on its leading principles and on the way in which it was produced.

Over a period of many years Lagarde was again and again attracted to the study of the LXX, but his approach to its problems underwent several radical changes. What is generally considered 'Lagarde's method' was only the last phase. The earlier ones became better known when, a hundred years after his birth, his personal papers and correspondence were opened.[1] As a young student he used to correct the Greek by the Hebrew which, he thought, had never undergone change. His *Anmerkungen zur griechischen Uebersetzung der Proverbien* (1863) started with his renowned axioms[2] and was a sober and penetrating critical work. In 1868, when editing *Hieronymi quaestiones hebraicae in libro Geneseos* and *Genesis graece*, he developed a plan for an edition of the LXX, worthy of an admirer of K. Lachmann whose edition of the N.T. was the first to ignore the Received Text and to substitute for it a fourth-century text. The plan was as follows. Because of the scarcity of uncials, full use was to be made of the early versions, but only after a thorough study of their methods of translation, as otherwise inferences about their originals would be rash. Related minuscules were to be grouped with a view to tracing the ancient uncials which were their direct or indirect parents.[3] All this sounds very familiar to the N.T. student of our

[1] A. Rahlfs, *Paul de Lagardes wissenschaftliches Lebenswerk, im Rahmen einer Geschichte seines Lebens dargestellt*, *Mitteil. d. Sept.-Unternehmens* (Berlin, 1928), Band 4, Heft 1.

[2] Quoted in Swete's *Introduction*, pp. 484ff.

[3] There were to be three editions: (1) the pre-hexaplaric text of the LXX, without apparatus; (2) the hexaplaric text together with the remains of the more recent translations, fresh collations of which were to yield a rich harvest; and (3) a complete edition of the pre-hexaplaric text, giving the readings of the small or larger groups, with the mistakes of individual MSS. forming a second apparatus in smaller print.

day, whose work is done on identical lines. He cannot but be struck by this anticipation of modern principles and by the fact that they were boldly applied to the much neglected LXX.

The fresh material to which Rahlfs gives us access reveals the sad story how this plan came to be abandoned. Lagarde's ideas appealed to the great O.T. scholar Justus Olshausen who, in his capacity as a civil servant, recommended them to his chief, and the Minister offered Lagarde money to employ an assistant. During and immediately after the war of 1870, however, Lagarde could find no one to train and, being both impatient and impetuous, declined the offer which was never renewed. Similarly he declined repeatedly offers by British scholars, made at the suggestion of William Wright, to provide a yearly sum towards the formation of a bureau. He may have felt that his plans and ideas were far from final and, in fact, they were constantly changing.

In 1870 he advanced the novel idea of local, provincial texts but emphasized that this did not imply a preference for one recension to the exclusion of others, since each province merely perpetuated the text with which it was familiar. A few years later, however, he suggested printing the recensions of Lucian and Hesychius in parallel columns and referred to Jerome's statement in the *prologus galeatus* that about A.D. 400 there were 'three editions' or, as we would say, 'recensions' of the LXX: those of Hesychius in Alexandria and Egypt, of Lucian in Constantinople 'usque Antiochiam', and of Origen in Palestine. He not only abandoned his earlier view that this differentiation occurred spontaneously through force of circumstances, but, contrary to the historical evidence, he gave Jerome's words a meaning which Jerome never intended; he claimed that the provincial churches had official texts, imposed upon them 'under the control of the bishops'.

Lagarde's *Lucian* remained a torso. There never was a second volume nor an edition of the remaining recensions. The preparation of this volume was involved in awkward changes of plan, characteristic of Lagarde. He lived in deliberate isolation, yet longed for agreement and appreciation. He consulted no one but himself—worked hard and at an astounding pace, but was given to moods. His first plans were frequently too ambitious and required modification. The swing of the pendulum could be amazingly broad.

While doing the collations for his *Lucian* he became so satisfied that he had found the solution that he failed to sort his material and rushed prematurely into print. He began with an enormously inflated apparatus and when he saw its impracticability—he was his own publisher—he first reduced the annotation and finally abandoned it.[1] Thus his text 'could not be checked' (E. Nestle). As printer's copy he used one of his MS. transcriptions. The printing was done quickly and, as Rahlfs points out, the spacing still indicates the many changes which were introduced in the course of printing. He was half submerged in his material and in the end some of it was not used at all and instead of checking it carefully, he disfigured his text by many mistaken conjectures. He had fits of weariness with his work and disposed of it with undue haste.

The published text was welcomed by some as the true LXX, by others as the true Lucianic, but sober students sensed that it had something erratic about it. This was the root of the repeated assertion, even in our day, that 'Lagarde's method' has failed. In fact the edition was a distortion of the best that Lagarde had to teach. He never returned to these problems but went on publishing most useful detailed information. He complained himself that his 'Septuagint Studies have eaten up the Septuagint'.

So much for the story of the 1880's and it is amazing how remote it sounds. There were, however, things in common between the Cambridge and the Göttingen efforts. Nowhere was it recognized that MSS. are far from homogeneous throughout. Hence the reliance on B in Cambridge[2] and that on the Lucianic MSS. in Göttingen.[3] In both distinguished scholars worked tirelessly in isolation, without dividing work which even now that photographs of MSS. are readily available, seems to us indispensable.

[1] Lagarde tells the full story himself in *Ankündigung einer neuen Ausgabe...* (Göttingen, 1882).

[2] B is hexaplaric in Isaiah. Its text of Judges is unknown to Origen and may not have been in existence when he composed the Hexapla.

[3] Lagarde's *Lucian* becomes Lucianic first on p. 259, where there is a change in text between Ruth iv. 10 and iv. 11 (Rahlfs, *P. de Lagardes wiss. Lebenswerk*, p. 77).

2. THE SECOND GENERATION

Compared with the zeal with which N.T. students set to work to check, refine, or undo the results achieved by Westcott and Hort's N.T., there has been nothing in the field of the LXX except the painfully slow progress of BM. The amazing thing, however, is that after the apparent failure of Lagarde's long sustained efforts and extravagant claims, work along his lines was in fact not at its end. There was at first a period of apparent unresponsiveness but actually of serious preparation. Rahlfs tells the moving story of how Lagarde, immediately before his fatal operation, showed him all his unfinished work and developed his ideas as to how it should be continued. Rahlfs did not fully understand but learned soon afterwards that he was given the task of completing and editing Lagarde's last works.

It took the young Göttingen lecturer years before he got a firm hold of this vast field. It was not until the end of the century that his first two short articles appeared in the Göttingen *Nachrichten*.[1] In the second[2] he proved that the date of B must be later than 367 by observing that its content followed the Bible canon of Athanasius' 39th Festal Epistle. In 1901 he edited the Berlin MS. of the Sahidic Psalter with an extensive commentary. In 1904 he began his series of *Septuaginta-Studien*, 'dedicated to the memory of Paul de Lagarde'. Here he came to grips with Lagarde's unsolved problems. The first essay showed that min. 82 (=o BM) displays a text that is a mixture of Lucian (*L*) and the real LXX (𝔊), and that the 𝔊 readings are confined to one or more double pages each. The parent MS. had been a defective *L* MS., supplied from a 𝔊 MS. The second volume analysed the different recensions of the Greek Psalter, the third was a study of the Lucianic text of Kings. In both volumes the versions, especially the Old Latin, and the patristic quotations were treated with exemplary lucidity. Meanwhile the Septuaginta-Unternehmen of the Göttingen Academy had been founded on the initiative of R. Smend and J. Wellhausen, and the *Mitteilungen des Septuaginta-Unternehmens* took the place of Rahlfs' *Septuaginta-Studien*. Its

[1] Cf. Walter Bauer's obituary in *N.G.W.*, Jahresbericht 1935, pp. 60ff.

[2] 'Alter und Heimat der vaticanischen Bibelhandschrift', *N.G.W.*, Philos.-hist. Klasse (1899), pp. 72–9.

volumes reveal Rahlfs' skill as a teacher and director of research. Half of the contributions are by his pupils and none of them immature. The second volume gives a full account of the extant LXX MSS. with most useful additional lists.[1] In the first, which was published in the years 1909–15, Rahlfs' 120 pages on *The O.T. Lessons of the Greek Church* provide much more than its title would suggest (Ch. v, 'Contributions to an understanding of the Greek lectionary system'). Further, there are several editions of newly found MSS., all with full comment, including the edition of the hexaplaric marginal notes to Isa. i–xvi from min. 710. Its 582 footnotes form an incomparable introduction to the study of the more recent translators. The third volume offers Rahlfs' model of an analysis of all extant forms of the text of a single book and contains the important discovery of an hitherto unknown recension *R*, a source of the Catenae-recension *C*. To cover all the details Rahlfs chose the Book of Ruth which contains eighty-five verses only. There is no better introduction to the recensional problems of the LXX than this painstaking and unassuming study.

All this was done with a critical edition in mind. Its fate was more than once in the balance, owing to war and post-war conditions.[2] Rahlfs therefore had to do his editions of Ruth and Genesis on a reduced scale,[3] and it is evident that even the fuller edition of the Psalms[4] was originally planned as an *editio minor*. After the First World War he began an edition of the whole LXX on a much smaller scale, a 'German Swete', which was published immediately before his death in 1935. The plan was to base the text on the uncials BSA, but increasingly Rahlfs used additional sources, including the versions, all of which were at his command, and he set out to give the nearest possible approximation to the original at all points. In contrast to his master Lagarde he had no illusions, was an exact analyst and governed by a sure sense of what was possible. He never lost himself in speculation and knew how to get things done in time.

[1] *Verzeichnis der griechischen Handschriften des Alten Testaments*, Beiheft zu *N.G.W.*, Philos.-hist. Klasse (1914). The first volumes contain matter that can be found in *N.G.W.* too. From vol. IV onward there is only the separate edition, in *Mitteil. d. Sept.-Unternehmens*, which perished in the war.

[2] Cf. Rahlfs' Preface in the Stuttgart edition.

[3] *Das Buch Ruth griechisch*... (Stuttgart, 1922); *Genesis* (Stuttgart, 1926).

[4] *Psalmi cum Odis* (Göttingen, 1931).

He therefore did his work on the Psalms without first collating afresh the mass of late MSS., and his Stuttgart edition, though marking enormous progress in grammar and the constitution of a critical text, left much for his successors to do.[1] The wisdom of his policy was realized after his sudden death. L. Koehler, commenting on his Stuttgart edition, says: 'There are pieces of work in which all labour is lost, unless the author himself is able to complete them.'[2] Rahlfs left a complete edition. Its basic foundations are thoroughly sound, others can build on it. He was furthermore the only one among the specialists of the LXX who left behind him a school to continue his work.

There was a second editor who followed Lagarde's lead but quite independently of Rahlfs, his contemporary M. L. Margolis. His early publications were in German, but his main work was done in America where he taught at Dropsie College. His erudition was exceptionally wide, for he combined a first-hand knowledge of rabbinic exegesis with an expert's handling of classical philology, and could read the Oriental versions in their originals. He was almost forty when he began a series of brief studies on the LXX and its relation to the Hebrew text.[3] They are models of an intelligent use of the Concordance for the study of the Greek and Hebrew Bibles. For him the pursuit of single Greek words throughout the LXX and the comparative treatment of Greek and Hebrew idioms was the way to look over the translators' shoulders and become familiar with their difficulties and techniques. He felt strongly about the shortcomings of the big Concordance in the imprecise indication of Hebrew and Aramaic equivalents, the false economy of space in the Hebrew Index which gives hopelessly long arrays of sheer numbers instead of the Greek equivalents themselves, and the niggardly presentation of the hexaplaric material. This last item he planned to

[1] *T.L.Z.* vol. LXI (1936), cols. 265–87.

[2] *Neue Zürcher Zeitung*, 14 April 1935, no. 656.

[3] For the titles and much more detail I refer to H. M. Orlinsky, 'Margolis' Work in the Septuagint' (in *Max Leopold Margolis—Scholar and Teacher* (Philadelphia, 1952), pp. 35–44); to his monograph 'On the Present State of Proto-Septuagint Studies', *J.A.O.S.* vol. LXI (1941), pp. 81–91, also separate; and to his 'Current Progress and Problems in Septuagint Research' in *The Study of the Bible Today and Tomorrow* (Chicago, 1947), pp. 144–61, a survey not superseded by the present essay.

have redone on new lines by his students. Only Joseph Reider's Aquila Lexicon was completed and its manuscript was stored until the other portions of the work should be completed. We have therefore nothing but Reider's excellent thesis[1] and can only regret that Margolis' example has not encouraged other students to bring his original plan to completion.

He next turned to the study of the transliterations found in the LXX. From them, especially from the place-names of which there is an accumulation in Joshua xv and xvi, he discovered definite groups within the LXX MSS. and collected evidence for the pronunciation of the Hebrew.[2] He then decided to do a critical edition of the Greek Joshua, and thus became the first in the field to check Lagarde's brilliant surmises by a careful inductive procedure. A report of his first results dates from 1910;[3] another in 1927 is more detailed.[4] In the meantime he transcribed the elaborate edition, which was complete at his death in 1931. Four parts were published posthumously, in an autograph edition,[5] but the fifth, including his Introduction, appears unhappily to have been lost, as was a monograph on Masius' excerpts from the lost Syro-Hexaplar which Margolis' edition frequently quotes. Once again we must deplore the absence of any organization which could have spared this brilliant scholar many years of purely mechanical labour and enabled him to carry on his work. Posterity has been thus deprived of much that he could otherwise have achieved.

It is useful to compare Margolis' grouping with Rahlfs' in Ruth (1922), a work of which he betrays no knowledge.[6] The BOL groups are the same but the others differ and Margolis would have

[1] *Prolegomena to a Greek-Hebrew and Hebrew-Greek Index to Aquila* (Philadelphia, 1916).

[2] His pupil E. A. Speiser wrote an early thesis on 'The Pronounciation of Hebrew based chiefly on the Transliterations in the Hexapla', *J.Q.R.* 1925–6 ff.

[3] 'The Grouping of the Codices in the Greek Joshua', *J.Q.R.* vol. 1 (1910), pp. 259–63.

[4] 'Specimen of a new Edition of the Greek Joshua', in *Jewish Studies in Memory of Israel Abrahams* (New York, 1927), pp. 307–23.

[5] Paris, 1931–8.

[6] Margolis' E(gyptian) group is the pre-hexaplaric B q r (h o) 𝔈𝔅ℭ; his S(yrian) the Lucianic recension including 𝔏; his P(alestinian) Origen's recension which he divides into hexaplaric (G b c) and tetraplaric (x 𝔖 Onom.(d_2)). He adds a C(onstantinopolitan) group (A M N W l y b_2 122 68 71 (h o u) 𝔄, and a M(ixed) group, comprising F a i k m 64 18 128 461, the Catenae-MSS. e f j s v z 343 730 (=*C*), and u 509 (=E/a_2) 661 (=Δ_8). For the benefit of the reader I have transferred his

greatly profited by Rahlfs' analysis of Ruth,[1] and the apparatus criticus in his edition of Ruth (1922). Apparently there was no contact between the two scholars whose methods and aims had so much in common. Margolis devised a needlessly complicated presentation of the evidence, an elaboration of Lagarde's idea of printing the several recensions in parallel columns.[2] Its nine separate sets of annotation can be reduced to three without loss.[3] Rahlfs had demonstrated that the single apparatus used by classical students is able with careful arrangement to indicate at a glance even the most minute sporadic variants. His example would have greatly simplified Margolis' presentation.

Some of the finest American scholars adopted his method, foremost among them J. A. Montgomery, whose commentary on Daniel has an excellent chapter on the versions.

notation, which is on a par with von Soden's in the N.T., into that of BM and those MSS. not in BM into Rahlfs' symbols. *OLC* are the recensions as in Rahlfs, 𝔏 is the Old Latin, 𝔅 the Bohairic, ℭ the Coptic, 𝔈 the Ethiopian, 𝔖 the Syriac version.

[1] In Ruth, together with other MSS., M N y b_2 71 h u 𝔄, the majority of Margolis' Const. group, form a definite recension *R* which Rahlfs proved to be the source of the *C*(atenae) recension (cf. p. 190). Rahlfs further traced this recension *R* in Judges and Reg. In my *Philo's Bible* an effort has been made to show that the aberrant set of Pentateuchal quotations in Philo is identical in method with *R*. The fact that Margolis singled it out for Joshua was concealed by his unconventional notation. It provides, however, valuable addition to our knowledge and encourages us to study his edition. That Alex. A should form part of this group is astonishing and should be checked. It would also seem advisable to find out whether the Catenae-MSS., instead of being relegated to the limbo of 'Mixed' texts, do not rather represent a recension of their own, as they do elsewhere. It is generally 'mixed', but distinctive. Commenting upon his Const. group Margolis surmised that it may have 'made use of the common text prevalent in Palestine. This Pal. *koine* was only slightly touched upon by Theodotion—*Urtheodotion* would accordingly be nothing but the Palestinian *koine*'. This argument is particularly infelicitous. Theodotion lived no later than the end of the second century and it is advisable not to speculate about his archetype in terms of a serious hypothesis. The *R* recension is unmistakably post-Origenic, for it is based on a late and independent approach to the Hexapla as a whole. As Rahlfs has seen, the use made of it in Ruth by the Latin and Armenian suggests a date not later than the second half of the fourth century, i.e. two centuries after Theodotion! Since it is certainly much later than the Caesarean edition of Origen's hexaplaric LXX-column, it can hardly be as early as the third century.

[2] Cf. p. 187.

[3] Only the last two must remain separate, for they contain the remains of the late translators (8) and Margolis' comments on the relation of the Greek to the Hebrew (9). But the first seven ought to be one only.

He follows Margolis even where the latter is mistaken. In section 14 of his Introduction he discusses the relative value of the two branches constituting the hexaplaric recension. Montgomery distinguishes two Origenic groups, a Palestinian O^P (V 62 147) and a Constantinopolitan O^C (A-group, Arab., Bohair.). His conclusion is that O^P represents the earlier form of Origen's revision of Theodotion's version which was subjected to a subsequent revision as extant in O^C—'critically retrograde in its approximation toward the elder Textus Receptus'. This retrograde development is in itself most implausible and the designation 'Const.' rests merely on the precarious assumption that descendents of the fifty copies of the Bible ordered by Constantine for the metropolitan churches must have survived. Montgomery himself realizes that 62 147 are 'degraded and contaminated types' and that 'the group is Aquilanic in the secondary sense that it presents Origen's work in its closest approximation to his Jewish master'.[1] Now 62–147(–407) form a distinct group within the Origenic recension of the preceding book of Ezekiel[2] which here also draws largely on Aquila in about 800 individual readings. Ziegler considers them a sub-group *o* beside O (=Q-88-$\mathfrak{S}^h$). There are, indeed, instances in which the genuine O follows Theodotion, but *o* Aquila: so xiii. 4 Ισραηλ] + ⋇ησαν 88-$\mathfrak{S}$=θ′; +εγενοντο 62=α′ σ′. So extensive a transformation is, however, inconceivable. My inference therefore is that the latter is neither O nor *o*, but *R* whose preference for Aquila we have come to know. In my opinion the same applies to Montgomery's O^P in Daniel: it is not Origen's revision and certainly not its earliest form. It was done independently of him, at least a century later. Only O^P can properly be styled Constantinopolitan, as Margolis understands it. Montgomery's O^C, though not uniform as a group, is more in the nature of O (or P after Margolis), but certainly does not reflect it faithfully. In his edition of the Greek Daniel Ziegler too reverses Montgomery's grouping; but his argument is different.

Thanks to Montgomery a succession of students have been working on Margolis' line, H. S. Gehman in the second generation, and J. W. Wevers, now in Toronto,[3] in the third.

[1] Pp. 51f. [2] Ziegler, *Ezechiel*, pp. 34ff.

[3] Cf. Wevers' bibliographical notes in the *Catholic Biblical Quarterly*, vol. XIV (1952), p. 40, and vol. XV (1953), p. 30. Here he refers to 'a Gehman School of

By this time the climate had completely changed. It was no longer a question of doing merely preparatory work. The reconstruction of a critical text which had been considered rash only a few years earlier was confidently and methodically undertaken. Once again after K. Lachmann, the dividing walls between theological and classical texts and methods were broken down. As more reliable texts were established theology gained a much firmer foothold for exegesis, for as long as it had to rely on a pre-critical text its results were inevitably haphazard.

I give an example to show that the textual basis of some of today's typological work must be more critically examined before the far-reaching inferences now drawn from it can be justified.

In a note on 'The Choice of Matthias',[1] Dr L. S. Thornton considers ἔλαχεν, Acts i. 17 (Luke i. 9), and observes, 'The solitary analogy for this use of λαγχάνω in the LXX is I Sam. xiv. 47, which states that Saul obtained the kingdom by lot. The reference is to the incident already described in x. 21' (p. 52). And 'Like Saul, Judas, as one of the twelve princes of the new Israel (Luke xxii. 30), obtained a "kingdom" by lot. But in I Sam. xiv. 47 ἔλαχεν renders לָכַד which appears to mean that Saul "took" the kingdom by force of arms' (p. 54). It is useless to try to reconcile these two interpretations. λαγχάνω would be unique in the LXX proper and is, indeed, not 'LXX' at all, except in Swete's text. It is the reading of B* and derives from a hexaplaric insertion by which the misreading מְלָאכָה for מְלָכָה was corrected. If Origen took it from one of the more recent translators its choice might be due to similarity in sound, without regard to the meaning. If, however, the insertion is Origen's own, he can very well have chosen the word with the same N.T. passages in mind which Dr Thornton would like to explain by it. Origen is not averse to typology either. Rahlfs' apparatus precludes any mistakes: κατακληρ. (+το *L*†) εργον B*L* (†)] +του βασιλευειν *L*†, ελαχεν του βασιλευειν *O*, pr. ελαχεν του βασιλευειν B†. His edition abounds with such unobtrusive helps. Accordingly, W. Bauer,[2] who uses Rahlfs' text, avoids this pitfall.

LXX studies'. The leading authority on the LXX in America, H. M. Orlinsky, owed his original inspiration to Margolis but has long outgrown the limits of any school. His book on the Greek Job is still under revision, but the specimens published raise high hopes.

[1] *J.T.S.* vol. XLVI (1945), pp. 51 ff.   [2] *Wörterbuch*[4], 1952, col. 837.

3. THE PRESENT GENERATION

Here again the most significant achievement is in an edition, J. Ziegler's Göttingen edition of the Prophets.[1] Each volume has a full Introduction which presents and discusses the evidence and then proceeds to its analysis. He gives a sober account of the groups and their nature and is equally candid about any residual difficulties. Good use is made of the patristic evidence and each volume has full lists of the abundant variants in spelling which would have unduly enlarged the apparatus and are therefore put in the Introduction, following Thackeray's paragraphs. Ziegler's methods have been refined in each succeeding volume so that increasingly everything noteworthy is recorded. The list of grammatical variants includes even those of late minuscules. The remains of the hexaplaric translations are edited afresh from the MSS. with much new material added and not from old collations as in Field. There is some emendation, which increases with each volume but is never extravagant.[2] The extreme usefulness of his edition is everywhere recognized, even among those who do not approve of the Göttingen method.

Ziegler is publishing a number of small monographs on special points which cannot be included in his introductions and these cover a very wide range.[3] He has developed a master method of deter-

[1] *Isaias* (1939); *Duodecim Prophetae* (1943); *Ezechiel* (1952); *Daniel* (1954), all published in Göttingen. *Jeremias* is under preparation.

[2] At times Ziegler's judgments are perhaps unduly influenced by the impressive strength of the evidence. This evidence may, however, prove misleading if we clearly distinguish two stages, that of the translator, however mistaken, with the Hebrew before him, and that of later copyists who had only the Greek to rely upon. An obvious example which, of course, does not deceive Ziegler, viz. the frequent confusion of ἡμ- and ὑμ-, is secondary; for ־ֵנוּ and ־ְכֶם could not be confused by any translator but ἡμ- and ὑμ- were both pronounced *im-* at a later date. Grabe had corrected them throughout but Rahlfs overlooked a number of his corrections. We may compare the impossible dialectal changes in the entire evidence and the editions of Herodotus (F. Bechtel, *Die griech. Dialekte*, III, 1924, pp. 10–20). I refer to the discussion 'Zur Textgestaltung der Ezechiel-Septuaginta' in *Biblica*, vol. XXXIV (1953), pp. 435 ff. (Ziegler); vol. XXXV (1954), pp. 29 ff. (Katz).

[3] 'Textkrit. Notizen zu den jüng. griech. Uebersetzungen des Buches Isaias', *N.G.W.* (1939), pp. 75–102; 'Beiträge zum griech. Dodekapropheton', *N.G.W.* (1943), pp. 345–412; *Die jüng. griech. Uebersetzungen als Vorlagen der Vulgata in den prophet. Schriften* (Progr. Braunsberg, 1943); 'Beiträge zur kopt. Dodek.-Ueber-

mining whether more than one translator worked on a single book.[1] In his monograph on Isaiah he was the first to study the general attitude of translators toward the original and their degrees of competence. Since it is not sufficient to deal with isolated words, he always considers contexts and assesses Greek words representing several Hebrew words or Hebrew words translated in various ways. By widening the range of observation he has demonstrated that even in the Minor Prophets the apparent existence of more than one translator is illusory. His remarks about the translators' range of vocabulary are illuminating. It must be earnestly hoped that collaborators will be found to complete the Göttingen edition.

4. PROBLEMS

So far we have mainly emphasized editions, for they are tools with which the student of the Bible must be familiar. Their planning is based on definite principles, some of which we shall now consider.

First comes the Greek text, the presentation of which has been so improved by Rahlfs and Ziegler that only isolated points remain to be cleared up. This is an important, if unsensational task. Once Atticism had consigned Hellenistic literature to oblivion and post-Aqiban Judaism had done the same to its own Hellenistic literature, the LXX as adopted by the Church remained the most comprehensive body of Hellenistic writing to survive. Neither its contribution to our knowledge of Hellenistic speech in general nor its peculiar reflection of Hebrew idioms have been fully explored.[2]

Then comes the question of the critical value of the LXX for emending the Hebrew text. For well-known reasons the Hebrew

setzung', *Biblica*, vol. xxv (1944), pp. 105–42; 'Der griech. Dodek.-Text der Complutenser Polyglotte', *ibid.* pp. 297–310; 'Der Text der Aldina im Dodek.', *ibid.* vol. xxvi (1945), pp. 37–51; 'Die Bedeutung des Chester Beatty-Scheide Papyrus 967 für die Textüberlieferung der Ezechiel Septuaginta', *Z.A.W.* vol. LXI (1945/8), pp. 76–94; 'Der Bibeltext im Daniel-Kommentar des Hippolyt von Rom', *N.G.W.* (1952), pp. 165–99; 'Die Septuaginta Hieronymi im Buch des Propheten Jeremias' in *Festschrift Alban Dold* (1952), pp. 13–24.

[1] 'Der textkrit. Wert der Septuaginta des Buches Job', *Miscellanea Biblica*, vol. II, pp. 277–96; *Die Einheit der Septuaginta zum Zwölfprophetenbuch* (Progr. Braunsberg, 1934); *Untersuchungen zur Septuaginta des Buches Isaias*, 1934.

[2] My forthcoming *The Text of the Septuagint* will contribute to the elucidation of this subject.

Bible is almost without variants but to what extent can we recover variants from the LXX and how should we decide which is right in places where the original and the versions differ? If we neglect, as well we may, Philo and St Augustine, to whom the LXX was an inspired text, there seem at first sight to be two alternatives.

The first accepts nothing but the *Hebraica veritas*. Origen, Jerome, Grabe, and Z. Frankel, to mention only a few examples, ignore the fact that the Hebrew underwent development, and therefore underestimate the LXX when it derives from a variant Hebrew text. Grabe demonstrated that in many instances the Greek variants are due to corruption.[1] In many more passages emendation of the Greek merely restores its original identity with the Hebrew.[2]

The opposite idea that 𝔐 might be emended from 𝔊 is relatively new. Bishop Lowth was the first to make wide use of this for the text of Isaiah. In his later years Lagarde became convinced that 𝔐 was so corrupt that it could not be used with a good conscience until an emended text of 𝔊 was forthcoming. I mention this gross exaggeration only because it strongly influenced Duhm and his school. Contrary to Lagarde's intentions they confined their interest in the LXX to those passages which seemed hopeless in the Hebrew. One may say with truth: Never was the LXX more used and less studied! Unfortunately much of this misuse survives in BH3. I have long given up collecting instances. Ziegler, after ten pages of corrections from the Minor Prophets alone, rightly states that all the references to 𝔊 must be rechecked.[3] H. M. Orlinsky who comes back to this point time and again is not very far from the truth when he says that not a single line in the apparatus of BH3 is free from mistakes regarding 𝔊.

However, the alternative '𝔐 or 𝔊' is not the whole problem, as Wellhausen realized better than any one. He attempted an answer

[1] In others he unduly approximates 𝔊 to 𝔐.

[2] I refer to ⟨στ⟩ε⟨ι⟩ρωσ⟨ις⟩ Prov. xxiv. 51 (xxx. 16), as mentioned on p. 204 n. 3, further to Prov. xxvi. 7, where the nonsense ΑΦΕλου ΠΟρεΙΑΝ σκελων και παρανομιαν must be read ΧΩλου ΠΑρεΣΙΣ σκελων και παροιμια in complete agreement with 𝔐, and to Num. x. 31 in which the confusion of οἶσθα and ᾔσθα (which is found also in Deut. ix. 2 ΑΘ ... and in the Menander Papyrus) led to the corruption of the whole verse, worst of all in the last word ΠΡΕΣΒΥΤΗΣ which, through a frequent corruption, due to popular etymology, into ΠΡΟΣΒΥΤΗΣ, is a distortion of ΠΡΟΣ ΟΨΕΙΣ = לְעֵינָיִם.

[3] *Z.A.W.* vol. LX (1944), pp. 107–20.

by telescoping 𝔐 and 𝔊 into one. They have many aspects in common. Both are in a state of flux, and it is hard to tell when this ended.[1] Where there are quantitative differences nothing that is in the Hebrew alone should for that reason be given preference; conversely nothing that is in the Greek alone should be condemned on that account. Both indulge occasionally in additions and embellishments and the choice between them does not lie in a simple preference for the 'original' against the 'translation', but must be governed by a strict interpretation of the context. For example, Wellhausen observes that subjects and objects are frequently implicit. If 𝔐 and 𝔊 have different *explicita* both are likely to be later additions.[2] This observation lends itself to fruitful application.[3]

Only after careful consideration of all the possibilities are we in a position to decide whether the Greek actually supplies a variant of the Hebrew. Influence from parallel passages or a translator's mannerism may produce divergences that are not 'variants'.

Even before BH3 was complete H. S. Nyberg strongly objected to unjustified confidence in the Greek and Syriac versions.[4] He emphasized that their *Vorlage* was greatly inferior to 𝔐 and that the translations abound with facile misunderstandings. Such blunders do not become emendations through being reiterated by modern scholars, who succumb to the same temptations as the ancient translators. Agreement in misunderstanding is suspect However timely, Nyberg's defence of 𝔐 is on occasion a *tour de force* and cannot therefore obviate the need for emendation, even if the emendations have no support from the translations. The translation of the Minor Prophets from which Nyberg derives his results is among the most incompetent. I doubt whether he could have attained the same results from the Books of Samuel. We should beware of generalizing.

[1] *Der Text der Bücher Samuelis* (Göttingen, 1871). Wellhausen's conclusions, which he never applied to other books than those of Samuel, have been brilliantly vindicated by the discovery of fragments of a pre-Christian Hebrew text of I Samuel (Frank M. Cross, Jr. in *B.A.S.O.R.* vol. CXXXII (Dec. 1953), pp. 15–25).

[2] Accordingly not even such *explicita* as fit the context are above suspicion.

[3] Even passages in which 𝔐 and 𝔊 are corrupt in divergent directions permit emendation in an analogous way. After Galling had restored Isa. viii. 1 by changing גִּלָּיוֹן גָּדוֹל to גִּלָּיוֹן גּוֹרָל, it was easy to see that in καινου μεγαλου the former must be κλήρου and the latter cancelled as deriving from the corruption of 𝔐 (*J.T.S.* vol. XLVII (1946), pp. 130f.).

[4] *Z.A.W.* (1934), pp. 241–54; *Studien zum Hoseabuche* (Uppsala, 1936).

More recently doubts have been raised as to the extent to which 𝔊 is strictly a translation. Translation always involves transposition to a new period and *milieu*. There are always two voices speaking and the minds behind them may clash every now and then. The translator may do his work conscientiously and yet never be aware that he is really interpreting.[1] All this, however, matters practically very little when we are given in the main a true reproduction of the original, as in most books of the LXX. The books, however, vary in their reliability. The translators of the Pentateuch sometimes call to mind the Bible histories for children done by men of the period of eighteenth-century Rationalism. God and his Word meant everything to them, but they had their peculiar ideas about what was suitable and seemly for God's Word. They deleted everything they considered crude or unworthy and replaced it by something 'better'. The LXX was, however, not as consistent in this respect as were the Targums. At times the Greek has crude, 'anthropopathic' modes of speech even when they are not in the Hebrew.[2] Orlinsky is therefore right in flatly denying that any 'antianthropomorphism' is characteristic of the LXX.[3]

Elsewhere the difference between 𝔐 and 𝔊 which is sometimes considerable is due to mere incompetence on the part of the translator. As was shown by Thackeray,[4] Ottley, and Ziegler, the translator of Isaiah who worked at an early date was completely unequal to his task. Many Hebrew words were unknown to him and 'often we can see him reduced to guessing or a stop-gap

[1] I. L. Seeligmann, *The Septuagint Version of Isaiah. A discussion of its problems* (Leiden, 1948), cites instances in which the translators, when faced with prophecies, had in mind events of their own time, an association of ideas that led to subtle modifications. This is an excellent suggestion, but convincing demonstration is difficult owing to the evasiveness of the allusions. Seeligmann's first contribution to LXX studies is the illuminating survey 'Problemen en Perspectieven in het moderne Septuaginta-Onderzoek', *Jaarbericht No.* 7 *van het Vooraziatisch-Egyptisch Gezelschap, Ex Oriente Lux*, 1940, pp. 359ff.

[2] This confirms Wellhausen's assertion that 𝔐 and 𝔊 were under identical influences, but at times in different places.

[3] Review of *The Anti-Anthropomorphisms of the Greek Pentateuch* by Ch. T. Fritsch, in *The Crozer Quarterly*, vol. XXI (1944), pp. 156–60; of Gerleman, *Book of Job* in *J.B.L.* vol. LXVII (1948), p. 385; and 'The Treatment of Anthropomorphisms and Anthropopathisms in the LXX of Isaiah' (*Eretz Israel III*, Casuto memorial volume).

[4] *J.T.S.* vol. IV (1903), p. 583.

rendering,... falling back on certain favourite words and using them almost at random'.[1] One of his favourites is παραδιδόναι. It is therefore bad method to change παραδῶ, Isa. xlvii. 3, to παρίδω (BH3) in order to make sense where the translator was unable to do so. Instances occur in which the translator proceeded in happy ignorance that an initial misunderstanding had led him completely astray.

In some books the emphasis shifts markedly from translation to interpretation, as has been demonstrated by Gerleman for Job and Proverbs.[2] The original Greek Job is shorter than the Hebrew by a sixth. Gerleman has shown that this is not merely a question of omission. The translator frequently contracts his text. A line or two may stand for a longer text in 𝔐, and here the Greek is of no use for the reconstruction of the Hebrew. This shortening is due neither to incompetence nor to any exception taken to the content. It is rather a matter of style and taste. As L. Koehler has seen,[3] the Book of Job is not a Platonic symposium, but a forensic exchange of pleas, hence its redundancies and repetitions. The translator disliked these and so weeded out parallels and synonyms not without discrimination. Elihu's speeches are the most ruthlessly curtailed; God's are treated with more respect. Metaphors are frequently transformed into non-figurative language. In ch. xxviii, which concerns divine wisdom, the description of mining is replaced by moralistic platitudes. In ch. xxiv the original pictures the poor man's lot out of pure delight in portrayal, but the Greek produces accusations against oppressors, interlaced with sentences about the ways of divine justice. Gerleman is not always right, e.g. when he states that the doctrine of strict retaliation as taught by Job's friends is toned down by the translator. Gerleman's only proof is the use of the optative aorist for a Hebrew future, but in this he is mistaken. Job reproduces in an idiomatic rendering the Hebrew jussive by an optative aorist, which is impossible in Greek. It has recently been demonstrated that there is Jewish

[1] R. R. Ottley, *Isaiah according to the Septuagint*, vol. I, p. 50.

[2] G. Gerleman, *Studies in the Septuagint, I. Book of Job* (Lund, 1946). 'The Septuagint Proverbs as a Hellenistic Document', *Oudtestamentische Studiën*, vol. VIII (1950), pp. 14–27. As to Proverbs some of his observations were anticipated by G. Bertram, *Z.A.W.* N.F. 13 (1936), pp. 153 ff.

[3] *Die hebräische Rechtsgemeinde* (Zürich, 1931), reprinted in *Der hebräische Mensch* (Tübingen, 1953).

evidence for this outside the Bible.[1] There are other fine observations in Gerleman's essay. The picture of Job in the N.T., the Fathers, and the arts, not as the Promethean rebel, but as the martyr hero, derives from the LXX, not from the Hebrew.

The translator of Proverbs also adapts much of the Hebrew to Greek standards of style. Where the Hebrew employs parallelism, the translator prefers antithesis and this involves him in more alteration. He obviously shuns tautology and reads his text with a townsman's eyes. Thus x. 5, 'He that gathereth in summer is a wise son' becomes: 'A wise son is protected from the heat'; xxiv. 30ff. which describes the dismal appearance of 'the field of the slothful', is transformed into a lame parable: 'A fool is like a field.'

Where this kind of translation prevails not much can be hoped for in emending the Hebrew. In Proverbs the quotations found in Clement of Alexandria indicate that the Greek text long remained fluid. The text of the Greek Job, however, is attested by an author of the second century B.C.[2] We should not forget that we are moving here on the fringes of the canonical literature.

As early as 1912 a promising student soon to become a victim of the First World War, M. Flashar,[3] observed extensive rephrasing caused by an 'advanced' theology in the Greek Psalter. Among many good things in his essay, the most important is perhaps the observation that wherever the translator could see his way clearly he advanced securely, but when baffled he was like a schoolboy following literally his original. Each Greek word equates the Hebrew, but the total result makes no sense. There are parallels in other books.[4] Hence we should take the warning: where betrayed to bungling literalness, a translation is no guide, however desperately it be needed for understanding the Hebrew.

It might appear that the translation of the Deutero-canonical *ketubim* offered a wider scope for the idiosyncrasies of unofficial translators. Similar claims, however, are made for Samuel and

[1] P. Katz, 'Papyrus Fuad 203 und die Septuaginta', *T.Z.* vol. IX (1953), pp. 228–31.

[2] Schürer III[4], p. 480. Gerleman, *Book of Job*, pp. 73f.

[3] 'Exegetische Studien zum Septuagintapsalter', *Z.A.W.* vol. XXXII (1921), pp. 81–116, 161–89, 241–68.

[4] Ziegler observes the same for the Minor Prophets in *Z.A.W.* vol. LX (1944), pp. 107f.

Kings.[1] I cannot here go into the detail, however interesting. A number of conclusions have been based on pre-critical texts and can be eliminated by emendation.[2] Others, however, stand the test better. Here I confine myself to P. A. H. de Boer's painstaking *Research into the Text of I Samuel*.[3] The first part has a useful Historical Introduction in which the value of Wellhausen's contribution is freely acknowledged but the notions that the 'history of the text' can be established only by a quantitative comparison of the versions with the Hebrew and that, only when this has been done, 'the actual criticism of the text can be embarked on' preclude the author's use of his predecessors' valuable results in the first stage of his work, the comparison of the text and versions.[4] It would be a pity to under-

[1] H. S. Gehman, 'Exegetical Methods employed by the Greek Translators of I Samuel', *J.A.O.S.* vol. LXX (1950), pp. 292ff.; J. W. Wevers, 'Exegetical Principles underlying the Septuagint Text of I Kings ii. 12 – xxi. 43', *Oudtest. Stud.* vol. VIII, pp. 300ff.; 'Principles of Interpretation guiding the Fourth Translator of the Book of the Kingdoms', *Cath. Bibl. Quart.* vol. XIV (1952), pp. 40ff.; 'A Study in the Exegetical Principles underlying the Greek Text of II Sam. xi. 2 – I Kings ii. 11', *C.B.Q.* vol. XV (1953), pp. 30ff.

[2] In III Reg. viii. 46 ἐπάξεις αὐτούς does not 'avoid attributing anger to God' (*Oudtest. Stud.* vol. VIII, p. 318), as it cannot be translated *thou shalt lead them on.* Rahlfs rightly reads ⟨ἐπ'⟩ αὐτούς, against Bq. This intransitive use *to fall upon somebody as an enemy* occurs in I Reg. v. 6 (= שׁמם Hiphil) and in Polyb. II, 29, 2 τῶν πολεμίων ἐπαγόντων αὐτοῖς, X, 21, 7 αἱ ἐπαγωγαὶ αἱ ἐπὶ τοὺς ἐναντίους and is an appropriate translation of אָנַפְתָּ *art angry with them.* πατάξεις, the reading of the parallel text II Par. vi. 36 and of a_2 in our passage, looks like a corruption of ἐπάξεις for which there are parallels elsewhere.

[3] *Research into the Text of I Samuel i–xvi* (Amsterdam, 1939). Continued in *Oudtest. Stud.* vol. I, pp. 79–103 (ch. XVII) and vol. VI, pp. 1–100 (chs. XVIII–XXXI).

[4] I give a few examples. In I Reg. xi. 7 ἐβόησαν is not an 'exaggeration' of יֵצְאוּ, but stands for יִצְעֲקוּ which is required by the context. In xv. 29 διαιρεθήσεται εἰς δύο certainly 'anticipates the history', but it does so only because the translator did not understand the unique נֵצַח יִשְׂרָאֵל and ventured—or repeated from a source—a guess נֶחֱצָה. It reveals an embarrassment which is shared by modern expositors but is not 'an exegetical enlargement'. The mistranslation ἐν ἐμοί for בִּי i. 26 betrays sheer ignorance; too much honour is done to the translator by rendering his nonsense by 'the responsibility of the following rests with me'. Accordingly one should not speak of a 'difference' between 𝔐 and the *Vorlage* of 𝔊. Unfortunately de Boer scatters his observations by grouping them under the headings 'Minus', 'Plus', 'Difference'. To get at his interpretation of a verse one has to piece them together from many places. Thus it remains obscure whether he intends to suggest a solution of the difficulties offered by iv. 14f. other than those of Wellhausen and A. Klostermann. On xv. 23 he

estimate his careful observations, but this preliminary part of his investigation, which postpones evaluation of the variants, implies a finality impossible without such evaluation. The translator, he claims, is an independent story-teller, his Hebrew text identical with 𝔐, and his translation is 'of little value for the determination of the "original" Hebrew text'.[1] These sweeping statements and the way in which they are obtained are remote from Wellhausen's '*discriminating* use of the ancient versions for purposes of textual criticism',[2] but I am unable to see how they could ever supersede it. Especially in II Samuel there are a number of passages in which Wellhausen, with his fine flair for emendation, found that a special group of LXX MSS. (the Lucianic, as he realized later) reflected a Hebrew better than ours. In I Samuel the *L* group offers at least one unexceptionable reading which the others have mutilated: xx. 11 נֵצֵא ἐξέλθωμεν *L*] μενε rell.[3]

In conclusion, signs of incompetence are found in many books, least in the Pentateuch, and translation is more interpretative in some of the 'Writings'. None of the latter, however, forfeit their value as evidence for the Hebrew even in passages where they transform it in accordance with their own bias. The problem is not the absence of individual traits, but their preponderance. This is, however, contested by those scholars who deny that the LXX is a translation

has comments under each of his three headings: 'gives a free translation' ('Minus', p. 54); 'πόνους and θεραφιν probably explanation' ('Plus', p. 56); '23ª is a paraphrase of the pregnant mašal-text' ('Difference', p. 67). Everything essential is, however, contained in Wellhausen's short sentence (p. 100): 'The divergences of the versions rest on misunderstanding of הפצר.' Moreover the Old Latin and the 𝔊 half of Lucian's doublet (the other half is Theodotion) indicate that neither θεραφιν nor even its late Grecizing θεραπειαν (Bvy) was in the original Greek.

[1] P. 69.

[2] Quoted from S. R. Driver's *Notes on...Samuel*², p. VII. The whole page seems to me as true as ever.

[3] *T.L.Z.* vol. LXI (1936), col. 276. Wellhausen's ἴωμεν is not LXX Greek. This μενε, with which we may compare other mutilations such as ερως for στείρωσις = עֹצֶר *barrenness* Prov. xxiv. 51 (xxx. 16) (*T.L.Z.* vol. LXIII (1938), col. 34), was one of the ever repeated arguments for the mistaken theory of F. Wutz according to which the LXX was translated from a Hebrew text written in Greek characters (MENE < ΝΕΣΕ!). In the end this theory was tacitly given up by its author and is now duly forgotten. Its obituary was written by P. Kahle who had favoured it for many years (*Z.D.M.G.* vol. XCII (1938), pp. 276ff.) and by H. M. Orlinsky, 'Current Progress and Problems in Septuagint Research' in *The Study of the Bible Today and Tomorrow* (Chicago, 1947), pp. 155ff.

in the strict sense of the word and insist that it is merely a Greek Targum.

P. Kahle is the champion of this theory which he has propounded many times since 1915.[1] He argues that the LXX was formed in the same way as the Aramaic Targums, and that uniformity was attained only at the end of a long process of assimilating isolated fragments of translation.[2] Consequently any search for the 'original' behind the variants, following the methods developed by classical students, is useless.[3] Instead we must tackle in earnest the wealth of variants, including those found in the indirect evidence of later quotations, with a view to unearthing any survivals of hypothetical early rival translations which merged in the 'LXX'. The pursuit of remnants of this kind was begun,[4] often in complete neglect of the results established by solid investigation of recensional problems which this school of thought considered superfluous. Struck by the obvious irrelevance of this new branch of study as presented in *The Cairo Geniza*,[5] I subjected it to a searching study,[6] only to find out that it involved no cogent argument,[7] but merely a mass of uncoordinated information. The chapter on the LXX is an impassioned plea for an arbitrary choice of authorities, omitting anything that might prejudice the author's case. In reply I undertook to demonstrate that the comparison with the Targums rested on loose analogies, that the several books of the LXX at their first stage disclose the individual traits of their authors, that the wealth of variants is perplexing only as long as they are neither grouped nor analysed, and that most of them, including the indirect quotations, derive from well-known secondary recensions and are neither LXX nor early. For example the quotations found in the branch of Philonic evidence, from which Kahle's repeated argument is taken,

[1] 'Untersuchungen zur Geschichte des Pentateuchtextes', *Theol. Stud. u. Krit.* vol. LXXXVIII (1915), pp. 399ff.

[2] It is not clear whether Kahle realizes that this would also imply that the LXX, owing to its composite nature and the late date of its final formation, would be almost valueless as a witness for the early Hebrew text.

[3] 'A wild-goose chase' (T. W. Manson in *Dominican Studies*, April 1949).

[4] 'A wild-goose chase' (H. M. Orlinsky in *J.A.O.S.* vol. LXIX (1949), p. 165).

[5] *The Schweich Lectures for 1941* (London, 1947).

[6] For the titles see below, p. 207 n. 2.

[7] This confirms Orlinsky's statement in 'On the State...', pp. 86, 91.

are confined to the *lemmata* unconfirmed by Philo's own comments.[1] Actually they draw freely on Aquila.[2]

These secondary Philonic quotations and others claimed by Kahle as pre-LXX translations are all closer to the Hebrew than is the LXX. It has been demonstrated that they possess characteristics of very late recensions of the LXX, but the fact remains, texts exist which reveal early, pre-hexaplaric approximations to the Hebrew, among them Upper Egyptian translations and the Greek Washington papyrus of the Minor Prophets (third century A.D.). This raises the question whether there were not repeated consultations of the Hebrew, before and after Origen,[3] and if there were, to what extent they can be distinguished. A recent discovery may assist us to a solution but since it has not yet been published in full we can only estimate it provisionally.[4]

Fragments of a Greek Dodekapropheton, said to be buried in a cave during the reign of Bar Kochba, have a LXX text approximated to the Hebrew, and this text has very much in common with Justin's quotations[5] (though it does not contain any of those few which

[1] This observation has been accepted by G. D. Kilpatrick, who in other respects is close to Kahle's theory (*J.T.S.*, n.s. II (1951), p. 88).

[2] Patrick W. Skehan, reviewing Kahle's *Die Handschriften aus der Höhle* in *J.B.L.* vol. LXXI (1952), remarks on p. 121: 'The observations on P. Katz' *Philo's Bible* which this section contains prescind from the point made by the latter, that the variant tradition of text in some of the MS. evidence for Philo shows a dependence on Aquila.' Thus Kahle's only answer to my list of his misquotations is a fresh example of the same. His latest contribution (*T.L.Z.* vol. LXXIX (1954), col. 91) dates the Aquila readings back to Philo's lifetime. If only he could bring himself to check Philo's expositions as to the underlying form of quotations he would soon realize that they do not support his theories.

[3] *T.Z.* vol. V (1949), p. 22; *Actes*...(cf. p. 207 n. 2), p. 181; W. G. Lambert in *Vet. Test.* vol. II (1952), p. 185.

[4] D. Barthélemy, 'Redécouverte d'un chaînon manquant de l'histoire de la Septante', *Revue Biblique*, vol. LX (1953), pp. 18–29. Of this E. Vogt has given a full abstract in *Biblica*, vol. XXXIV (1953), pp. 423–6.

[5] A distinctive set of O.T. quotations in Justin, however, is not affected by this new perspective. There are numerous passages in which Justin takes a stand against 'Jewish falsifications of the Bible', passionately defending readings which are, in fact, early Christian interpolations. As was seen by Hilgenfeld, *Theol. Jahrb.* vol. IX (1850), pp. 394 f., 398 ff.; Hatch, *Essays in Biblical Greek* (Oxford, 1889), pp. 188 ff.; Bousset, *Die Evangelienzitate Justins des Märtyrers* (Göttingen, 1891), pp. 18–35; Rahlfs, *Sept.-Stud.* II (Göttingen, 1907), pp. 203–6, 223 f., but ignored in Swete's *Introduction*, pp. 417 ff., and in B. J. Roberts' *The Old Testament Text and Versions*, p. 118, these interpolations have disappeared from the long quotations

Justin professes to borrow from the Jews' own version), with the Upper Egyptian translations of the Minor Prophets,[1] and also with Aquila and Symmachus and still more with the Quinta. If this text could be demonstrated to be as early as its editor suggests it would prove the existence of a first-century revision of the LXX though not a rival translation, as rightly emphasized by the editor. The basis of this revision would be the Quinta, and Aquila and Symmachus could be seen as the final stages of a development rather than its inception. This would confirm the impression that quotations with a text closer to 𝔐 than the unaltered LXX are earlier than the hexaplaric recension but they would still be secondary to the LXX text into which they came as sporadic corrections by Jewish revisers. This would raise the question whether post-hexaplaric recensions such as *RC*, have an early basis.[2] Although nothing would be gained for the theory of early independent and rival translations, many of its defenders would be satisfied that their claim for the existence of a modified form of text, a 'revised version' of the first century A.D., was justified.

Barthélemy's dating, however, rests on the assumption that none of the MSS., coins, etc., were deposited later than *c.* 130. If, however, this cave, like others, served as a depository down to the period of the Arab conquest, the assumption of the early date of the Dodekapropheton papyrus and its text would require close scrutiny and the burden of proof would rest on those who made this claim. In this

heading Justin's expositions. Their place is taken by the ordinary text of the LXX as we read it now, and consequently the peculiar points which were closest to Justin's heart are no longer found in the *lemmata* to which he refers. The same applies to those long passages of which our single MS. gives only the first and last verses connected by καὶ τὰ ἑξῆς.

[1] And the Washington papyrus W!

[2] Ziegler, *Theol. Revue*, vol. XLVII (1951), pp. 202f. Similarly Kilpatrick, *J.T.S.* (1951), pp. 88f. and W. D. Davies in *Theology* (August 1950), all in reviews of *Philo's Bible*. With the final publication of the Greek Dodekapropheton fragments we shall be in a better position to investigate this problem, and it is therefore wiser to wait until then. For this reason I have concentrated in this paper on the texts and editions; but for what may be said at the present juncture on the question of recensions I would refer to earlier publications, copies of which are available to those interested: 'Das Problem des Urtextes der Septuaginta' (*T.Z.* vol. v (1949), pp. 1–24) and 'The Recovery of the Original Septuagint. A Study in the History of Transmission and textual Criticism', *Actes du 1er Congrès de la Fédération Internationale des Associations d'Etudes Classiques* (Paris, 1951), pp. 165–82.

case Justin's quotations could not by themselves prove an early date of the new MS. They would be another example of what has been shown for the inferior Philonic quotations. Nevertheless, if the text could be proved to be early we should welcome this fresh light on the century beginning with A.D. 30 which is so much in need of illumination.

The sequence of LXX recensions as worked out in accordance with Lagarde's suggestions will stand any fresh examination, for it is both solid and elastic. The preliminary investigations by which it was established should be much more carefully studied by the student of the N.T., for the problems of the two Greek Testaments are similar and frequently correlated. The seventy years since 1883 have seen as much progress in the field of the LXX as in that of the N.T., if we take into account their difference in scale. It will perhaps one day be recognized that work on the O.T. in Greek requires, and deserves, the same measure of security as has been allowed N.T. research.

PART II

*

TOWARDS THE UNDERSTANDING OF THE ESCHATOLOGY OF THE NEW TESTAMENT

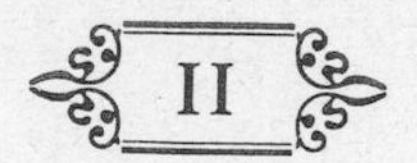

THE LIFE OF JESUS: SOME TENDENCIES IN PRESENT-DAY RESEARCH

T. W. MANSON

By far the longest, as it is by far the most important, chapter in Schweitzer's *Quest of the Historical Jesus* is the nineteenth, headed 'Thoroughgoing Scepticism and Thoroughgoing Eschatology'. Two works only are named in the bibliography to this chapter: Schweitzer's own *Das Messianitäts- und Leidensgeheimnis* and Wrede's *Das Messiasgeheimnis in den Evangelien*, both works of great importance for the study of the life of Jesus. According to Schweitzer's understanding of the situation, the two views embodied in the two books would unite to destroy the existing accounts of Jesus; and that being done, it would only remain to accept one or other of the victors.

> The inconsistency between the public life of Jesus and his Messianic claim lies either in the nature of the Jewish Messianic conception, or in the representation of the Evangelist. There is, on the one hand, the eschatological solution, which at one stroke raises the Marcan account as it stands, with all its disconnectedness and inconsistencies, into genuine history; and there is, on the other hand, the literary solution, which regards the incongruous dogmatic element as interpolated by the earliest Evangelist into the tradition and therefore strikes out the Messianic claim altogether from the historical life of Jesus. *Tertium non datur.*[1]

That is a drastic enough proposition; but, like all disjunctive propositions, it must exhaust all the possibilities if it is to stand: and time has shown that it does not exhaust the possibilities.

There is, however, this much in Schweitzer's statement of the case, that progress in this study since the *Quest* was written has been, in the main, a continuation along the lines of which the *Messiasgeheimnis*

[1] Schweitzer, *Quest of the Historical Jesus*² (1911), p. 335.

and the *Quest* were the termini a generation ago. If we consider the two most outstanding developments of our own day, Form-Criticism and Realized Eschatology, I think we may say that the first suggestions of Form-Criticism are already present in the work of Wrede[1] and others, and that Realized Eschatology is the logical sequel to Johannes Weiss and Schweitzer.

After thirty years it is possible at least to attempt a rough appraisal of Form-Criticism; and it may perhaps be suggested that it has by now done about all that it could do, and more than it ought. Strictly speaking the term 'form-criticism' should be reserved for the study of the various units of narrative and teaching, which go to make up the Gospels, in respect of their form, and that alone. It is concerned with the structure of these units; and it is certainly interesting to learn that there are a number of anecdotes in Mark, Matthew, and Luke, in which a brief statement of time and place leads up to a short conversation between Jesus and someone else, which is terminated by a dogmatic pronouncement from our Lord. It is interesting but not epoch-making. So far as structure goes, similar stories can be found in Boswell's *Life of Samuel Johnson* and elsewhere. We can list these stories in the Gospels. We can label them, and other units, when we are agreed about the terminology of the science. But a paragraph of Mark is not a penny the better or the worse as historical evidence for being labelled 'apophthegm' or 'pronouncement story' or 'paradigm'. In fact if Form-Criticism had been confined to this descriptive activity, it would probably have made little stir. We should have taken it as we take the forms of Hebrew poetry or the forms of musical composition.

But Form-Criticism got mixed up with two other things. One was K. L. Schmidt's full-scale attack on the Marcan framework;[2] the other was the doctrine of the *Sitz im Leben*. Of the former it may be said that it really asks us to believe that the earliest Gospel was produced by putting together a random assortment of disconnected anecdotes. Those dealing with the Passion clearly had to come at the end of the narrative, but the rest just had to be fitted together by the evangelist to the best of his ability. This is difficult to believe as literary history. The Gospel itself is clear evidence that

[1] See, for example, *Messiasgeheimnis*, p. 1.
[2] In *Der Rahmen der Geschichte Jesu* (1919).

by the time it was written (I should say between A.D. 58 and 65), there were people who wanted something more than disconnected anecdotes. They wanted the story of the Ministry as a whole; and Mark is the first to meet that demand. But if an outline of the Ministry had then to be created out of nothing for this purpose, it can only be that for the thirty years between the end of the Ministry and the composition of Mark, Christians in general were not interested in the story of the Ministry and allowed it to be forgotten. That leaves us with the question why the first generation were not interested, while the second generation demanded a continuous narrative. More than that, we need some explanation why it was possible for the details of the story to be remembered and the general outline forgotten. Our own experience is not remembered in that way. When I recall those periods in my own life which seem to me to be specially important, I find that I have two things: a clear picture of the main course of events in their proper order; and, along with that, a vivid recollection of a number of outstanding experiences which fit into the general picture at various points, give it focus and definition, and make it *my* apprehension of a set of events which was also apprehended by many others besides myself. It is, therefore, inherently probable that if there was a succession of events which can be called the 'Ministry of Jesus', the general outline of its progress would have a better chance of being remembered than the details, simply because the knowledge of the general outline was the common property of a considerable number of people.

Prolonged study of Mark goes to confirm this *a priori* probability. I am increasingly convinced that the Marcan story presents in the main an orderly and logical development; and that this development or framework has as good a title to be considered reliable historical material as any particular anecdote incorporated in it.

The *Sitz im Leben* introduces a new set of considerations, which again have little or nothing to do with Form-Criticism in the strict sense of the word. It is undoubtedly a good thing that the Gospels should be studied in the context—so far as we can know it—of the interests, problems, and practical needs of the people who first used them. No doubt the stories and sayings were useful to missionary preachers of the first century. No doubt they gave guidance to the early communities on questions of faith and conduct. But we shall be travelling much too far and far too fast if we infer from that that they were created by the community to serve these ends or to meet these needs. In most cases it is equally possible, and a good deal more likely, that the tasks, problems, and needs of the first-century Church affected the selection, and in some cases the interpretation, of what went into the Gospels out of a much larger mass of available material.[1] But even that may not be the whole truth of the matter. It is at least conceivable that one of the chief motives for preserving the stories at all, and for selecting those that were embodied in the Gospels, was just plain admiration and love for their hero. It is conceivable that he was no less interesting, *for his own sake*, to people in the first century than he is to historians in the twentieth. This makes it all the more urgent that we should be prepared to look first for a *Sitz im Leben Jesu* or a *Sitz im Leben des jüdischen Volkes*, and not resort automatically to a *Sitz im Leben der alten Kirche*, a procedure which may easily involve us in circular arguments; since the alleged modifications or inventions in the Gospels are used to define the positions of the early Church, and these positions are then used to account for the phenomena presented by the Gospels.

There is one simple test that can be applied to theories which suggest that the tradition about Jesus is in any considerable degree the creation of the Christian community. We possess a fair selection of the written works of one of the most influential figures in the Church during the period in which the Gospel tradition took shape. St Paul's letters were all, on the generally accepted dating,[2] written before the earliest Gospel. The Roman community—the traditional home of St Mark's Gospel—possessed the Epistle to the Romans before it possessed the Roman Gospel of St Mark. The Pauline letters abound in utterances which could readily be transferred to Jesus and presented to the faithful as oracles of the Lord.[3] But how many are? It seems a little odd that if the story of Jesus was the creation

[1] For admirable illustration of the way in which parables of Jesus could be reinterpreted and reapplied in the early Church, reference may be made to C. H. Dodd, *The Parables of the Kingdom* and Joachim Jeremias, *Die Gleichnisse Jesu*[2].

[2] Even if we take the earliest likely date for Mark and the latest likely dates for the Pauline letters, it will still be true that the greater part of our Pauline corpus antedates the Gospels.

[3] A few selections from I Cor. xiii would perhaps not look out of place in the Sermon on the Mount, for example.

of the Christian community, no use should have been made of the excellent material offered by one of the most able, active, and influential members of the community.

We have to beware lest historical study of the life of Jesus should come to consist in asking about any story in the tradition not, 'Is it credible in itself?', but 'What motive could the Church have had for telling this tale?'—which can easily become the question, 'What motive led the Church to invent it?' The danger is that what purports to be a historical account of Jesus of Nazareth should turn out to be in fact a psychological novel about a large number of anonymous members of the primitive Church; and, what is worse, that this brand of fiction should enjoy a greater credit than the Synoptic Gospels themselves. It is perhaps not unreasonable to suggest that these booklets do not profess to be theological treatises or manuals of Christian behaviour, but accounts of the public activities during the last two years, more or less, of the life of an extremely important and interesting person, known to his Jewish contemporaries as 'Jesus bar Joseph of Nazareth', to the Roman authorities as 'Jesus, domiciled in Nazareth, Pretender to the Jewish throne', and to his followers as 'Jesus, Messiah and Lord'. The career of such a person must have an interest of its own and for its own sake; and the openings of all three Synoptics seem to suggest that this interest was the most effective motive behind both the demand for and the supply of Gospel material. If so there is a good deal to be said for treating the Gospels as historical documents concerning Jesus of Nazareth rather than as psychological case-material concerning the early Christians.

It is at this point in the debate that a new factor is introduced by C. H. Dodd's work on the primitive Christian *kerygma*.[1] The nerve of the argument is that when we examine the early Christian convictions, which may be supposed to have shaped or even created the story of Jesus, we find a single and consistent story of Jesus in brief. We have abstracts of the propaganda speeches of the earliest Christians in Acts; and when we compare these with similar passages in the Pauline Epistles, we find a singular unanimity. It is natural to infer that such close agreement between men as different as Peter and Paul is the result neither of accident nor of design; that their

[1] *The Apostolic Preaching and its Developments* (1936).

claims for Jesus Christ tally because they are founded on facts. Whatever may be said about this or that detail in the Gospels, there was a total impression made by Jesus on those who came nearest to him and knew him best; and it is that total impression that is embodied in the *kerygma*. It is, of course, possible to say that the primitive *kerygma* is just the first stage in a process of mythologizing which it is the business of critical scholarship to reverse. It is possible; but it may be doubted whether it is useful. For the process of demythologizing may easily turn out to be another name for recreating Jesus in our own image;[1] and it may not be unjust to say, as Théo Preiss did, that the latest attempt at demythologizing issues in the myth of a Heideggerian Jesus. And it may not be altogether unjust to add that on closer inspection the 'Heideggerian Jesus' turns out to be Heideggerian robes with nobody inside them except the pale ghost, which is what thoroughgoing historical scepticism has left of the 'Jesus of History'.

The farther we travel along the Wredestrasse, the clearer it becomes that it is the road to nowhere. Do we fare any better if we take Schweitzer's turning?

It is true that Schweitzer's interpretation of the Gospel story is vulnerable at a number of points. It can be urged that it depends on uncritical use of the Gospels, particularly that of Matthew. It can be urged that, in spite of the moving eloquence with which the story of Jesus is told by Schweitzer, there is no escape from the conclusion that its hero was a deluded fanatic. But these are not the points that seem to me most impressive. The real answer to thoroughgoing eschatology was given by one of England's greatest New Testament scholars, one who was himself deeply impressed and influenced by the theory, F. C. Burkitt. In the Epilogue to his book, *The Earliest Sources for the Life of Jesus*,[2] he says,

> There is a sense, on the eschatological view, in which it is true to say that Jesus had radically changed the messianic ideal. He had changed it, not by 'spiritualizing' it, but by adding to it. The ideal of King Messiah, coming in glory on the clouds of heaven to judge the world and vindicate

[1] H. J. Cadbury's book *The Peril of Modernising Jesus* is very much to the point here.

[2] New and revised edition (1922), pp. 130f., quoting from an article by himself in the *American Journal of Theology*, vol. XV (1911), p. 193.

the elect of God, he left untouched, but he prefixed to it a Prologue. He prefixed to it not a doctrine about Messiah, but the actual course of his own career. We call it his *Ministry*—why? Because his view of the office of the Man who was predestined to be Messiah was that he should 'minister' to the needs of God's people (Mark x. 45). According to Mark, Jesus went up to Jerusalem to die, to be killed, believing that thereby the Kingdom of God would come. And his great resolve has to be judged in the light of its amazing success.

To that we must add the fact that Schweitzer himself was prepared to forsake all and go to Africa as a medical missionary in the service of the Jesus whom he found by thoroughgoing eschatological interpretation of the Gospels.

But when we come to consider these points seriously it emerges that what really matters is not the eschatological theory but the ministerial practice. The Prologue, of which Burkitt speaks, in fact makes nonsense of the expected sequel; so much so that it is no calamity but a positive relief that there is no Parousia of the conventional Jewish pattern. Similarly, the thing that really matters for Schweitzer, the thing of eternal import, is the thing that on his own theory he ought to call 'interim ethic'. The medical work in Africa, which commands our unstinted admiration and respect, is a continuation of what Burkitt calls the Prologue. In a word, the most significant thing about the Jesus of the eschatological theory, the permanently effective thing right down to the life of Schweitzer himself, is the non-eschatological, even the anti-eschatological element. The interim ethic is the abiding moral force: the Prologue has become the whole drama.

Something of the same sort was perceived by Feine in a criticism of thoroughgoing eschatology which was published in 1914.[1]

Wir dürfen es aber als ein Ergebnis der neuesten Forschung betrachten, mag Schweitzer dem zustimmen oder nicht, daß eine feste und geradlinige Gedankenverbindung von der synoptischen Verkündigung Jesu zu Paulus und Johannes hinführt, die gerade nicht eschatologischen Charakter hat. Es ist die Lehre, daß im Anschluß an die Person Jesu das Heil bereits in der Gegenwart genossen wird, anders ausgedrückt, daß das Reich Gottes nicht eine rein eschatologische Größe ist.[2]

[1] 'Die Konsequente Eschatologie' in *Neutestamentliche Studien für G. Heinrici* (1914), pp. 201–7.

[2] *Op. cit.* p. 204.

It is here that we make the transition from thoroughgoing eschatology to what has come to be known as Realized Eschatology.[1] The taking of this step, which I believe to be a real step forward, was made possible by two important works, which appeared almost simultaneously: C. H. Dodd's *The Parables of the Kingdom* and Rudolf Otto's *Reich Gottes und Menschensohn*.[2] The essential proposition in Realized Eschatology is that the Ministry of Jesus is not a prelude to the Kingdom of God: it *is* the Kingdom of God. Or as Dodd expresses it in one of his latest works, 'His [John's] formula ἔρχεται ὥρα καὶ νῦν ἐστιν, with the emphasis on the νῦν ἐστιν, without excluding the element of futurity, is, I believe, not merely an acute theological definition, but is essentially historical, and probably represents the authentic teaching of Jesus as veraciously as any formula could.'[3] The same thing is expressed in another way by Jeremias who claims that all the parables of Jesus compel the hearers to make up their minds about his Person and his Mission. 'For they are all filled with the "secret of the Kingdom of God" (Mark iv. 11)—namely the certainty of "sich realisierenden Eschatologie". The hour of fulfilment is present, that is their keynote.... The acceptable year of God has begun. For he has appeared, whose hidden glory shines through every saying and every parable, the Saviour.'[4] If this is the true state of the case, it means that we have to begin revising our ideas of the Kingdom of God—both what it meant to the Jewish contemporaries of Jesus, and what it must mean for his disciples then and now—in the light of the Ministry.

In attempting to recapture the visions that floated before the mind's eye of a first-century Jew in Palestine when words like 'Messiah' and 'Kingdom of God' were used, we shall probably be well advised to think in something very like Zionist terms, at least so far as the methods and results of the Messianic activity are concerned. The Kingdom for which the contemporaries of Jesus looked and longed was to be established on the ground floor of the three-storey universe,

[1] On the name, see C. H. Dodd, *The Interpretation of the Fourth Gospel* (1953), p. 447 n. 1; Joachim Jeremias, *Die Gleichnisse Jesu*[2] (1952), p. 162 n. 3.

[2] Otto's book was published in 1934. Dodd's study of the parables of the Kingdom was given as lectures at Yale in the spring of 1935 and published in book form later in the same year. I believe the two works were quite independent of one another.

[3] *The Interpretation of the Fourth Gospel*, p. 447. [4] *Op. cit.* p. 162.

however much its establishment might depend on intervention from above; and its establishment would be at the expense of existing world-empires and to the immediate advantage—physical, economic, and political as well as moral and spiritual—of the people of Israel. Such a consummation, devoutly wished by the Jews and as devoutly dreaded by those who stood to lose most by its achievement, is one of the decisive elements in the thinking of the contemporaries of Jesus.

But terms like 'Messiah' and 'Kingdom of God' meant something very different to Jesus. The Gospels give us a clear enough indication of where the difference lies; and there is ample justification for treating them with respect as historical documents. They reveal that Jesus stood alone between his friends and his enemies; and they show why it had to be so. The story they tell, in its main outlines and in much of its detail, fits with what we otherwise know about contemporary Jewish faith and life in Palestine. It makes sense in the context of Roman Imperial policy in the Near East. It gives an adequate explanation of the genesis of the Church.[1] It does not give a complete biography of Jesus, not even a full chronicle of the Ministry. His life lasted between thirty and forty years, and his public career not less than eighteen months; and all the records we possess can be read in a few hours. The gaps are enormous. But we have some details; and I think it is true to say that these short stories, parables, sayings, poems, and so on, which go to make up the Gospels, themselves epitomize the whole story. Each of them is, as it were, a little window through which we can survey the Ministry as a whole; or a vantage-point from which we can take a Pisgah-view of the authentic Kingdom of God.

All this means that we are driven back to the business of treating the Gospels[2]—as wholes and in detail—as historical documents, using

[1] I have tried to show some of these things in detail in my book *The Servant-Messiah* (1953).

[2] All four of them. Forty years ago it was possible to write off John as having been discredited once and for all by Strauss. See, for example, Schweitzer's *Quest*, pp. 85 ff. Today we are not so sure. There is a growing body of evidence that the Fourth Gospel enshrines a tradition of the Ministry which is independent of the Synoptic accounts, bears distinct marks of its Palestinian origin, and is on some points quite possibly superior to the Synoptic record. The question of the historical value of the Fourth Gospel is wide open again.

all the resources of exact scholarship and strict historical method for the task. We need not ask that the documents should be exempt from any of the tests that are applied to other ancient historical texts; but we must ask that they should be treated seriously as evidence for the events they purport to describe, and in the first instance as evidence for those events rather than for the states of mind of first-century Christians. We cannot completely eliminate those states of mind from the reckoning; but we can control them in some degree. We can in many cases work our way back from Gospel material as employed in the early Church to the same material in its *Sitz im Leben Jesu*. In the case of the parables Dodd and Jeremias have shown us the way.

That we are compelled to continue the quest of the historical Jesus is, I venture to think, a good thing. It is an excellent thing that we should not be allowed to reduce the Good News to ancient dogmas or modern speculations. There are those who like to think that 'rationalist criticism' has worked itself to a standstill in making the thoroughgoing scepticism of Wrede more thoroughgoing still; who feel that the supposed insolvency of historical criticism allows them to take refuge in the Councils of the undivided Church or in a revived or modified Calvinism or Lutheranism. Unfortunately for such policies the Councils of the undivided Church and Luther and Calvin had already assumed the general reliability of the Gospels as historical documents. These authorities cannot be used to solve the historical problem, but only to by-pass it. The clock cannot be put back to the sixteenth century or the fifth; and even if we take the wings of the morning and fly to Geneva or Chalcedon we shall still be haunted by historical questions which refuse to be silenced by dogmatic answers. There are others in our day who would find in the essential Jesus the reflection of their own chosen philosophy. It is easy to laugh at those who, a couple of generations ago, saw in Jesus a good nineteenth-century liberal humanist with a simple faith in a paternal deity. It is less easy to see the joke when the Jesus of history is a twentieth-century existentialist, a kind of pre-existent Heidegger. But the Good News was not the clever anticipation by the carpenter of Nazareth of the most up-to-date philosophical ideas.

The Good News is the announcement of a historical event, as that 'God so loved the world that he gave his only-begotten Son'; or that 'God was in Christ reconciling the world to himself'; or that 'If I by the finger of God cast out demons, why then the Kingdom of God has come upon you'. What is claimed by Jesus, and by his followers on his behalf, is that in his Ministry God has revealed himself in saving action. This revelation does not stand by itself. It is unique in quality, but it is not solitary. It is the crowning example of something which, the Bible declares, is always liable to occur in history. But if God does reveal himself in history, it is there if anywhere that we must find him. If God did in fact speak through the prophets we cannot absolve ourselves from the task of finding out as exactly as we can what was said and what it meant. If God did in fact speak to us through the life, death, and resurrection of Jesus it is vitally important to know as fully and as accurately as possible what sort of life and death and resurrection became the medium of the divine revelation. There is no escape from the historical inquiry. And there is no need to be despondent about its prospects. We may venture to hope that as it progresses, we shall find that the Ministry of Jesus is a piece of real history in the sense that it is fully relevant to the historical situation of its own time, to the hopes and fears, the passionate convictions and the gnawing needs of our Lord's own contemporaries. And just because it was so relevant to their life, we shall find it relevant to our own.

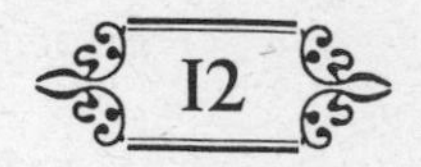

ENDERWARTUNG UND KIRCHE IM MATTHÄUSEVANGELIUM

G. BORNKAMM

Es gehört zu den gesicherten Ergebnissen der Synoptiker-Forschung, daß die ersten drei Evangelisten in erster Linie Sammler und Redaktoren überkommener Traditionen sind. Die stereotypen, historisch-pragmatisch durchaus unergiebigen redaktionellen Wendungen, mit denen Mk. Logien und Einzelperikopen rahmt und verknüpft, und die entsprechenden redaktionellen Mittel, deren Matth. und Lk. sich bedienen, speziell auch in der Verarbeitung und Gruppierung ihrer Quellen, lassen an der Richtigkeit dieses Urteils keinen Zweifel. Gleichwohl sind auch die ersten drei Evangelien Dokumente einer bestimmten, in jedem Fall sehr verschiedenen Theologie, die jedem von ihnen, unbeschadet des ihnen Gemeinsamen, eine eigene mehr oder weniger konsequent und planmäßig durchgeführte Thematik gibt.

Diese besondere Theologie und Thematik der drei ersten Evgll. reicht tiefer in die Substanz hinein, als es in der Regel angenommen wird und modifiziert ihre Botschaft nicht unerheblich, auch wenn ihre Traditionen auf weite Strecken die gleichen sind. Die Mittel, mit denen die Synoptiker ihre Theologie zur Darstellung bringen, sind freilich, wie besonders der Vergleich mit dem Joh.-Ev. zeigt, bescheiden und lassen jedem von ihnen nur einen begrenzten Spielraum. Hier liegt der Grund für die nicht selten erkennbaren Spannungen zwischen der verarbeiteten Tradition und den theologischen Anschauungen, denen sie dienstbar gemacht wird. Indessen erweisen die Synoptiker — alle drei und jeder in besonderer Weise — durch Redaktion und Komposition, durch Auswahl, Aufnahme und Auslassung und nicht zuletzt durch eine zunächst geringfügig erscheinende, bei näherem Zusehen aber doch charakteristische Abwandlung des überlieferten Stoffes, daß sie keineswegs nur

Tradenten und Sammler, sondern auch Interpreten der Überlieferung sind.[1]

Das soll in folgenden am Matth.-Ev. und zwar unter der speziellen Fragestellung 'Enderwartung und Kirchenverständnis' gezeigt werden.

I. DIE VERBINDUNG VON ESCHATOLOGIE UND EKKLESIOLOGIE IN DEN REDEN DES MATTH.-EVS.

Wir beginnen mit den Redekompositionen des Matth., die für den schriftstellerischen und theologischen Charakter des Evangelisten bekanntlich besonders bezeichnend sind. Sie zeigen durchgängig eine ihm eigentümliche Verbindung von Enderwartung und Kirchengedanken. Das wird bereits deutlich in der *Täuferrede* (iii. 1–12). Matth. unterscheidet sich in dem Täuferabschnitt nicht unerheblich von den Seitenreferenten. Mk. widmet Joh. dem Täufer überhaupt keinen eigenen Abschnitt, sondern faßt nur seine heilsgeschichtliche Funktion, seine Bußtaufe und -predigt, seine Wirkung und Gestalt und — in einem ersten Logion — die Ankündigung des erwarteten Messias in wenigen Sätzen zusammen, um dann schon i. 9ff. mit Taufe, Versuchung und Auftreten Jesu zu beginnen. Anders Lk.: er schildert das Auftreten des Täufers in einem historisch fixierten (Lk. iii. 1ff.) in sich abgeschlossenen Abschnitt (vgl. bes. *v*. 19f.) und weist seine Gestalt damit einer xvi. 16 ausdrücklich bezeichneten geschichtlichen und heilsgeschichtlichen Epoche zu.[2] Matth. dagegen verbindet den Täufer und seine Botschaft aufs engste mit der Botschaft Jesu. Die Predigt des Täufers und die Predigt Jesu werden nur bei Matth. in demselben Logion zusammengefaßt: μετανοεῖτε· ἤγγικεν γὰρ ἡ βασιλεία τῶν οὐρανῶν (iii. 2 und iv. 17). So wird der Täufer zum Prediger auch der christlichen Gemeinde. Unterschieden ist nach Matth. zwar seine heilsgeschichtliche Funktion von der Jesu.[3] Der ersten Stelle (iii. 3) wird darum die Weissagung von dem Wegbereiter zugeordnet (Jes. xl. 3), der zweiten Stelle dagegen

[1] Für Lukas zeigt das Entsprechende das ausgezeichnete Buch von H. Conzelmann, *Die Mitte der Zeit* (1954).

[2] Vgl. Conzelmann, a.a.O. S. 13ff.

[3] Auch der Taufe des Joh. erkennt Matth. keine Sünden vergebende Kraft zu; sie geschieht εἰς μετάνοιαν (iii. 11) nicht εἰς ἄφεσιν ἁμαρτιῶν (Mk. i. 4).

ein atl. Wort, das die Erfüllung der Weissagung ausspricht (iv. 15f.).[1] Die Ankündigung der kommenden βασιλεία und damit des nahenden Gerichtes und der in ihr begründete Bußruf sind jedoch hier und da die gleichen, wie auch die spätere Wiederaufnahme des Drohwortes von dem Baum, der keine Frucht bringt, abgehauen und ins Feuer geworfen wird (iii. 10), in der Bergpredigt (vii. 19) zeigt. An die Stelle der Pharisäer und Sadducäer (iii. 7) sind freilich vii. 15ff. die Pseudopropheten in der christlichen Gemeinde getreten. Beide hier wie da vertreten einen von Matth. scharf abgewiesenen Kirchengedanken, sofern jene sich in vermessener Sekurität auf ihre Abrahamskindschaft, diese sich auf ihre Jüngerschaft und die im Namen Jesu vollbrachten charismatischen Wundertaten berufen, aber nicht wahrhaben wollen, daß über die Zugehörigkeit zur messianischen Gemeinde der kommende Weltenrichter nach dem einen und gleichen Maßstab, ob nämlich die 'Frucht der Buße' erbracht und der Wille des himmlischen Vaters getan ist, entscheiden wird. Damit sind bereits in der Täuferpredigt die einfachen, von der Erwartung des kommenden Gerichtes geprägten Grundgedanken des matthäischen Kirchenverständnisses ausgesprochen. Sie durchziehen sein ganzes Evangelium.

Enderwartung und Kirchengedanke bestimmen auch den Aufbau der *Bergpredigt*. Mit Recht hat Windisch sie als 'Proklamation der von Gott verfügten Einlaßbedingungen durch den Mund Jesu' bezeichnet.[2] Schon die Seligpreisungen gestaltet Matth. zu einer Tafel von Einlaßgeboten aus[3] und gibt in den anschließenden Sprüchen durch das doppelte ὑμεῖς ἐστε dem Wort vom Salz und Licht (verknüpft mit dem Spruch von der Stadt auf dem Berge), dem von Mk. und Lk. völlig anders verwendeten Bildwort vom Licht, das auf den Leuchter gehört, und der Mahnung: 'so soll euer Licht leuchten...' eine klare Deutung auf die Jüngerschaft, die sich als solche vor der Welt durch ihre 'guten Werke' erweisen soll. Ihr gilt auch das programmatische Wort von der 'besseren Gerechtigkeit' (v. 20), ohne die keiner in die βασιλεία eingehen wird, und die Auslegung dieses Wortes in den Antithesen (v. 21–48), den

[1] Beachte dabei die von LXX abweichenden Tempora in dem Zitat aus Jes. ix. 1 φῶς εἶδεν μέγα gegen ἴδετε und φῶς ἀνέτειλεν αὐτοῖς gegen λάμψει.

[2] H. Windisch, *Der Sinn der Bergpredigt*, 2. Aufl. S. 9.

[3] M. Dibelius, *Botschaft und Geschichte*, 1 (1953), S. 92f.

Frömmigkeitsregeln (vi. 1 ff.) und allen weiteren Geboten bis hin zur goldenen Regel (vii. 12). Die eschatologische Ausrichtung der ganzen Rede, die von den ersten Seligpreisungen an (v. 3 ff.) über v. 20, die Sprüche vom Lohn (vi. 1 ff.), vom Trachten nach der βασιλεία und ihrer Gerechtigkeit (vi. 33), und die Worte vom Richten sichtbar ist, wird endlich durch die betont und neu einsetzenden Worte von der engen Pforte,[1] die Warnung vor den falschen Propheten (vii. 15 ff.), deren Auftreten, wie xxiv. 4 ff., 23 ff. zeigt, zu den Zeichen der Endzeit gehört, die Schilderung des Weltgerichts (vii. 21 ff.) und die Schlußgleichnisse mit allem Nachdruck zur Geltung gebracht.

Matth. konnte in dieser Anordnung der Motive weithin der schon vorgegebenen Ordnung der Sprüche in der Spruchquelle folgen, er ergänzt und profiliert sie aber erheblich und gibt dem Ganzen eine Art Katechismuscharakter. Das wird sofort deutlich, wenn man den Parallelismus des Aufbaus der Bergpredigt zu dem Aufriß der Didache beachtet. Seligpreisungen, Jüngersprüche und Antithesen haben ihre Parallele in der Zwei-Wege-Lehre von Did. i–vi (beide beschlossen mit dem Ruf zur Vollkommenheit, Matth. v. 48 und Did. vi. 2). Auch die daran anschließenden Gemeinderegeln über Fasten und Gebet (Matth. vi., Did. viii — hier auch das Vaterunser!) haben hier wie da ihre Entsprechung, in der Did. freilich ergänzt durch Anweisungen für Taufe und Eucharistie (unter Verwendung von Matth. vii. 6!). Endlich entsprechen sich an derselben Stelle im Gesamtaufbau die Warnungen vor den falschen Propheten (Matth. vii. 15 ff., Did. xi–xiii) und der eschatologische Abschluß des Ganzen (Matth. vii. 24 ff., Did. xvi). Der gleiche Aufriß ist in beiden Schriften so unverkennbar, daß man als Grundlage der Komposition ein festes Katechismusschema erschließen darf, das in der Did. geradezu den Charakter einer Kirchenordnung erhält. Hier wie da wird paränetisches Spruchgut als Einlaßtora an den Anfang gestellt, Weisung für konkrete Fragen des gottesdienstlichen und gemeindlichen Verhaltens gegeben und mit einem eschatologischen Ausblick geschlossen.

Ein eigentümlich eschatologisches Gepräge und Gefälle hat auch die *Missionsrede* des Matth., wobei wieder Kirchengedanke und Enderwartung streng aufeinander bezogen sind. Wir achten auch

[1] εἰσέλθετε διὰ τῆς στενῆς πύλης (vii. 13).

hier wieder auf die Komposition des Matth. und ihre theologischen Motive. Der Evangelist eröffnet die Rede mit dem Summarium, das Bergpredigt und Taten Jesu umklammert (ix. 35 = iv. 23), und stellt, indem er das Wort aus Mk. vi. 34 (dort im Zusammenhang der Speisungsgeschichte!) damit verbindet, die ganze Mission unter das Motiv des Erbarmens Jesu mit dem verschmachteten und führerlosen Volk.[1] Dann folgt nicht sofort die Aussendung, sondern die Mahnung an die Jünger, den Herrn der Ernte um Arbeiter zu bitten. Das Wort stand, wie Lk. x. 2 zeigt, schon in einer Missionsrede der Spruchquelle, lehrreich darum, weil hier bereits das für das Weltgericht geläufige Bild von der Ernte auf die Mission angewandt ist. Ja, man wird für den Spruch, wie ihn Q bot, sogar behaupten dürfen, daß er bereits die Heidenmission voraussetzt, denn das eschatologische Bild der Ernte denkt immer an das Völkergericht (Jes. xxiv. 13, Joel iv. 10ff., Apok. xiv. 15f.); Lk. stellt das Wort darum sinngemäß an den Anfang der Aussendung der Siebzig (x. 1ff.; im Unterschied zur Aussendung der Zwölf, c. ix), wie auch Joh. iv. 35 das Erntewort im Zusammenhang der Samaritermission erklingt. Matth. wendet den Spruch, wie der Fortgang seiner Rede zeigt, allerdings mit Betonung nicht auf die Heidenmission an und grenzt den Missionsauftrag der Jünger auf Israel ein (x. 5f.). Lehrreich ist das Wort bei Matth. aber auch darum, weil es zum Ausdruck bringt, daß die Jünger nicht eo ipso schon Missionare sind, vielmehr ihre Sendung der freien, im Gebet von der Gemeinde erflehten göttlichen Entscheidung vorbehalten ist (Vgl. Act. xiii. 1ff.).

Inhalt des Missionsauftrages der Jünger ist die Ankündigung des nahen Gottesreiches und die Aufrichtung seiner Zeichen in Heilungen, Totenerweckungen und Dämonenaustreibungen (x. 7f.). Ihr Weg steht im Lichte des in Bälde kommenden Menschensohnes (x. 23), des Weltgerichtes und der ihm vorangehenden Drangsale. Angesichts des heraufziehenden Endes haben die Jünger Verfolgung und Bekenntnis, Scheidung und Entscheidung zu bestehen (x. 17–39). Dieser letzte Teil der Missionsrede ist nicht mehr im eigentlichen Sinn missionarische Instruktion, sondern gibt der Kirche im Ganzen Weisung und Ankündigung dessen, was die Jünger Jesu insgesamt zu erwarten und zu bestehen haben. Wieder wird Wesen und Weg

[1] Hängt damit zusammen, daß in dem Missionsauftrag x. 7f., der doch sonst Matth. iv. 17 wieder aufnimmt, der Bußruf fehlt?

der Jüngerschaft hier ganz in eschatologisches Licht gerückt. Der Evangelist nimmt darum schon in den letzten Teil dieser Rede eine nicht geringe Zahl von Logien aus dem apokalyptischen Spruchgut von Mk. xiii und der Spruchquelle auf.[1]

Auch die Komposition der sieben *Reich-Gottes-Gleichnisse* (c. xiii) zeigt die Verbindung eschatologischer und ekklesiologischer Motive. Der Kirchengedanke des Matth. wird bereits in dem gegenüber Mk. stärker ausgestalteten Abschnitt über den Zweck der Parabeln Jesu sichtbar: die Jünger sind die 'mit den Mysterien des Himmelreiches' Vertrauten (xiii. 11)[2] und als solche die seliggepriesenen Augen- und Ohrenzeugen (beachte den entsprechenden Einsatz xiii. 16, 18 wie v. 13), im Gegensatz zu dem verstockten und nun für seine Schuld[3] gerichteten 'Volk' (xiii. 15).[4] Hier also derselbe Gegensatz zwischen Jüngerschaft und Israel, der für das ganze Matth.-Ev. charakteristisch ist. Aber auch der nicht minder für Matth. kennzeichnende Gedanke, daß die 'Kirche' nicht schon Sammlung der Auserwählten und ewig Geborgenen, sondern ein corpus mixtum ist, das der Scheidung zwischen Guten und Bösen[5] im Endgericht erst entgegengeht, ist in den Gleichnissen vom Unkraut unter dem Weizen (xiii. 24–30, 36–43) und vom Fischnetz aufs klarste ausgesprochen. Das kommende Gericht in seiner Bedeutung gerade für die Kirche ist Zielpunkt der ganzen Komposition.[6]

Gehen wir weiter zu der Komposition der *Gemeinderede* (c. xviii), so wird man bereits für das Verständnis ihrer Stellung im Ganzen beachten müssen, daß das Petrusbekenntnis und das Wort von der Gründung der Kirche (xvi. 13–23) mit den nachfolgenden, schon bei Mk. sachlich gruppierten Perikopen (Leidensweissagung-Leidens-

[1] Vgl. zu Matth. x. 17–22 Mk. xiii. 9ff.; Lk. xxi. 12ff.; xii. 11f.; zu Matth. x. 34ff. Lk. xii. 51ff.

[2] τὰ μυστήρια τῆς βασιλείας τῶν οὐρανῶν gegenüber τὸ μυστήριον τ. βασ. τ. θεοῦ (Mk.) offenbar auf die Lehre Jesu zu beziehen.

[3] Matth. xiii. 13 ὅτι statt Mk. iv. 12 ἵνα!

[4] Auch der hier von Matth. eingefügte Spruch xiii. 12 dient dieser Kontrastierung.

[5] Beachte auch hier das gleiche Motiv und Bild wie in der Täuferrede iii. 12.

[6] Offenbar soll das zwischen die Gleichnisse vom Unkraut und Fischnetz eingefügte Doppelgleichnis von Schatz und Perle im Sinne des Matth. das Verhalten derer illustrieren, die dereinst 'wie die Sonne im Reiche ihres Vaters' als 'die Gerechten' (xiii. 43) leuchten werden, das Verhalten der völligen Hingabe, des radikalen Gehorsams.

nachfolge der Jünger) bis zur zweiten Leidensverkündigung vorangeht. Aber auch die Tempelsteuerperikope (c. xvii. 24–7), unmittelbar vor der Gemeinderede eingefügt, steht unverkennbar im Dienst seines Kirchenverständnisses. Sie zeigt, daß die Gemeinde, die Matth. repräsentiert, noch im Verbande des Judentums steht und die Versteuerung der jüdischen Diasporagemeinden für sich selbst durchaus nicht ablehnt, sondern anerkennt, freilich im deutlichen Bewußtsein ihrer eigenen Sonderstellung: Jesu Jünger zahlen die Tempelsteuer als die freien Söhne, nur um nicht Ärgernis zu geben.

Daß die Rede selbst den Kirchengedanken wieder ganz in das Licht der kommenden βασιλεία stellt, zeigt sofort die Formulierung, die Matth. der Rangstreitfrage aus Mk. ix. 34 gibt: τίς ἄρα μείζων ἐστὶν ἐν τῇ βασιλείᾳ τῶν οὐρανῶν; (xviii. 1), sowie die Aufnahme des im Mk.-Ev. erst bei der Kindersegnung (Mk. x. 15) begegnenden Logions vom Umkehren und den Kindern Gleichwerden, durch das οὐ μὴ εἰσέλθητε εἰς τὴν βασιλείαν τῶν οὐρανῶν (xviii. 3) und den zu der Eingangsfrage zurücklenkenden Spruch xviii. 4 (οὗτός ἐστιν ὁ μείζων ἐν τῇ βασιλείᾳ τῶν οὐρανῶν) für den Zusammenhang trefflich geeignet. Das Motiv des Endgerichtes ist in dem weiterhin zunächst leitenden Zusammenhang der Sprüche bei Mk. bereits enthalten und brauchte von Matth. nur übernommen zu werden.[1] Seine eigene Komposition setzt erst mit xviii. 10 ein. Dabei ist die Umrahmung der Sprüche über die Durchführung der Gemeindedisziplin (xviii. 15–18) offenbar sehr überlegt und sinnvoll. Gerade die Anweisung für die Gemeindezucht umklammert Matth., indem er das Gleichnis vom verlorenen Schaf (xviii. 12–14) vorhergehen und die Worte über die grenzenlose Vergebungsbereitschaft mit dem nur von ihm überlieferten Gleichnis vom Schalksknecht folgen läßt (xviii. 21 ff.). Auch dieses Gleichnis — und damit die ganze Rede — endet mit dem Hinweis auf das Gericht, das die zur Vergebung nicht bereiten Glieder der Gemeinde unerbittlich treffen wird (xviii. 35).

Der charakteristisch matthäische Gedanke, daß auch der Jüngerschaft Jesu das kommende Gericht gilt (s.o. zu Matth. xiii), ist auch in dem *Winzer- und dem Hochzeitsgleichnis* ausgesprochen. Ist das

[1] Immerhin beachte das apokalyptische Drohwort, das er xviii. 7 noch einfügt.

erste auch zunächst gegen Priester und Pharisäer gerichtet, so macht Matth. doch in dem nur von ihm formulierten und am Ende noch einmal mit Nachdruck wieder aufgenommenen Satz, daß der Weinberg (xxi. 41) — die βασιλεία τοῦ θεοῦ (xxi. 43) — den bösen Winzern (Israel) genommen und denen gegeben wird, die 'gute Früchte erbringen werden', die Norm des künftigen Gerichtes geltend, an dem, wie das ganze Evangelium sagt, alle und gerade die vermeintlich zum Gottesvolk Gehörenden gemessen werden. Eben dies sagt, ausdrücklich auf die Gemeinde bezogen, auch die von Matth. angefügte Schlußszene des Gleichnisses vom königlichen Hochzeitsmahl (xxii. 11–13),[1] aber schon die xxii. 10 begegnende Wendung πονηρούς τε καὶ ἀγαθούς, die wie die letzten Gleichnisse von c. xiii auf die endliche Scheidung weist, schließlich auch die für Matth. so charakteristische Abschlußsentenz xxii. 14: 'Viele sind berufen, wenige aber auserwählt.'

Daß die *Pharisäerrede* mit ihrem siebenfachen 'Wehe' von dem Gedanken an das Endgericht durchzogen ist (xxiii. 13, 33 ff.), braucht nicht besonders betont zu werden. Die Klage über Jerusalem mit der Ankündigung des Kommens Jesu zum Weltgericht an ihrem Ende (xxiii. 37–9) und die Stellung der Pharisäerrede unmittelbar vor der eschatologischen Rede bestätigen die Zielsetzung schon von c. xxiii. Die Rede zeigt in ihren Eingangsversen wieder deutlich, daß die Gemeinde sich selbst vom Verband des Judentums noch nicht gelöst sieht (xxiii. 1–3), zugleich aber zeigt die Rede an dem Gegensatz zur Heuchelei der Pharisäer und Schriftgelehrten das Wesen der christlichen Gemeinde. Sie wird ausdrücklich im Anschluß an die Worte über die menschliche Eitelkeit der jüdischen Führer angeredet, in dem Verbot xxiii. 8–12 (ὑμεῖς δέ...), sich in der Gemeinde Jesu noch Rabbi, Vater und Führer zu nennen.

Eine starke Profilierung des Kirchengedankens und seine Ausrichtung auf das Ende zeigt endlich auch die letzte große Redenkomposition des Matth., die *apokalyptische Rede* von. c. xxiv mit den eschatologischen Gleichnissen in c. xxv. Anders als bei Mk. (xiii. 1–4) wird die Rede bei Matth. nicht als esoterische Belehrung der vier ersten Jünger, sondern als Jüngerbelehrung überhaupt eingeführt

[1] Vielleicht ein ursprünglich selbständiges Gleichnismotiv. Vgl. J. Jeremias, *Die Gleichnisse Jesu*, 2. Aufl., 1952, S. 35 und 134f., unter Hinweis auf b. Schab. 153a.

(beachte die stereotype Formel προσῆλθον οἱ μαθηταί wie v. 1; xiii. 10, 36; xviii. 1) und deutlicher als bei Mk. unter das Thema gestellt: τί τὸ σημεῖον τῆς σῆς παρουσίας καὶ συντελείας τοῦ αἰῶνος; (xxiv. 1–3). Dann folgt wie Mk. xiii. 5–8 der 'Anfang der Wehen' (xxiv. 4–8), nun aber nicht wie bei Mk. die Ankündigung der Verfolgung, die die Gemeinde von Seiten der jüdischen Gerichte erfahren wird (dieser Passus der Rede ist x. 17ff. schon vorweggenommen) sondern die summarische Ankündigung des Leidens (τότε παραδώσουσιν ὑμᾶς εἰς θλῖψιν καὶ ἀποκτενοῦσιν ὑμᾶς), wobei — für Matth. bezeichnend — die Jüngerschaft das Schicksal der *Juden* unter den Heiden erleidet (καὶ ἔσεσθε μισούμενοι ὑπὸ πάντων τῶν ἐθνῶν διὰ τὸ ὄνομά μου xxiv. 9);[1] dann die Ankündigung der Zeichen des kommenden Endes *innerhalb* der Gemeinde: Abfall, Verrat, Haß, Verführung durch falsche Propheten, Überhandnehmen der Gesetzlosigkeit, Erkalten der Liebe. Und endlich die Verheißung der Verkündigung 'dieses' (von Matth. repräsentierten) Evangeliums vom Reich in der ganzen Welt als Präludium des Endes.

Daß hier das Bild der judenchristlichen Gemeinde ersteht, die am Gesetz festhält und sich vom Verbande des Judentums noch nicht gelöst hat, vielmehr im scharfen Gegensatz zu einer gesetzesfreien (im Sinne des Matth. gesetzlosen) Lehre und Mission steht, ist hier völlig deutlich.[2] Diese judenchristliche Gemeinde teilt das Schicksal des jüdischen Volkes, die Entweihung des Tempels und die Schrecknisse der Flucht. Reicher ausgestaltet als bei Mk. ist bei Matth. auch die folgende Warnung vor den 'falschen Messiassen' und den 'falschen Propheten' und die Ankündigung der Parusie des Menschensohnes plötzlich und offenbar vor der ganzen Welt (xxiv. 23–8);

[1] Mit Recht beachtet von G. Harder, *Das eschatologische Geschichtsbild der sogenannten kleinen Apokalypse Markus 13*, Theologia viatorum, 1952, S. 80f.

[2] G. D. Kilpatrick in seinem ausgezeichneten Buch, *The Origins of the Gospel according to St Matthew* (1946), behandelt pp. 101–23 die Frage 'The Gospel and Judaism' eingehend und weist überzeugend nach, daß das gegnerische Judentum im Matth.-Ev. nicht einfach mit dem Judentum zur Zeit Jesu zu identifizieren ist, sondern in die Zeit zwischen 70 und 135 gehört, wo vom Rabbinat die jüdischen Sekten samt den Christen verketzert und ausgeschieden werden. Das erste Evangelium spiegelt deutlich den noch nicht abgeschlossenen Prozeß. Die Auseinandersetzung mit dem von den Pharisäern geführten Judentum ist in vollem Gange (scharfe Kontroversen, Verfolgung), aber noch ist die Verbindung nicht abgerissen und wird von der Gemeinde selbst, die sich als wahre Judenschaft versteht, zäh verteidigt.

desgleichen die Schilderung der nun erfolgenden Parusie, bei der unter kosmischen Katastrophen das 'Zeichen des Menschensohnes' am Himmel erscheint (vgl. xxiv. 30), alle 'Stämme der Erde' wehklagend den Menschensohn in großer Kraft und Herrlichkeit sehen, und seine Engel 'unter großem Posaunenschall' die Auserwählten aus allen Winden der ganzen Welt einsammeln werden. Die Mk.-Apokalypse braucht hier von Matth. nur durch wenige Züge verstärkt zu werden. Das so entstandene durchaus jüdische Bild läßt deutlicher noch als der Mk.-Text die Parusie zur Beschämung der Weltvölker erfolgen und zur Rettung der Erwählten aus aller Welt.

Die von Matth. hier unter Aufnahme des Stichwortes οὕτως ἡ παρουσία τοῦ υἱοῦ τοῦ ἀνθρώπου xxiv. 37, 39 angefügten eschatologischen Gleichnisse schildern im Bild der Sintflutkatastrophe das plötzliche Verderben, das über die Ahnungslosen und Sorglosen hereinbrechen wird (so auch im Gleichnis vom nächtlichen Einbrecher xxiv. 43). Matth. aber verwendet es sofort als Ruf zur Wachsamkeit und Bereitschaft an die Jünger (*vv.* 42, 44; xxv. 13),[1] denen an den Gleichnissen vom treuen und vom bösen Knecht (xxiv. 45–51), von den klugen und törichten Jungfrauen (xxv. 1–13) und den anvertrauten Talenten (xxv. 14–30) vor Augen gestellt wird, was Treue, Bereitschaft und Eifer im guten Werk (ἐργάζεσθαι xxv. 16) bedeuten. Es ist dabei lehrreich zu sehen, wie die Erfahrung der verzögerten Parusie sich deutlich in den Gleichnissen abzeichnet und das Verständnis der 'Klugheit' sich wandelt: xxiv. 48 wird das χρονίζει ὁ κύριος μου als Illusion des bösen Knechtes bezeichnet, xxv. 1–3 dagegen ist das Verziehen des Bräutigams die reale Erfahrung, an der sich die Klugheit der auf eine längere Wartezeit eingerichteten Jungfrauen bewährt, während die törichten nicht genug Öl für ihre Lampen mitgenommen haben.[2] Ihre Illusion ist also gerade das Rechnen mit seiner Nähe. Auch das Talentengleichnis rechnet, wie xxv. 19 zeigt, mit dem langen Ausbleiben des Herrn (μετὰ δὲ πολὺν χρόνον). Durchweg ist der Gerichtsgedanke in diesen Gleichnissen auf die Kirche angewandt. Mit der Gerichtsdrohung enden xxiv. 51 f., xxv. 12, 30, so gewiß das Gegenbild zum

[1] Die Übersetzung der Gleichnisse Jesu in die Situation der Gemeinde hat neuestens J. Jeremias in seinen *Gleichnissen Jesu* sorgfältig und umfassend untersucht.

[2] Vgl. G. Bornkamm, 'Die Verzögerung der Parusie' (*In memoriam Ernst Lohmeyer*, 1951), S. 119ff.

Gericht wenigstens im Jungfrauen- und Talentengleichnis (der Einzug ins Hochzeitshaus, die Auszeichnung der mit fünf und zwei Talenten betrauten) nicht fehlt.

Schwerlich wird man die Schilderung des Weltgerichtes, mit der — nicht mehr in Gleichnisform — die ganze Redenkomposition abschließt, nur auf das über die *Heiden* ergehende Gericht im Unterschied zu den Gliedern der Gemeinde Jesu beziehen dürfen.[1] Vielmehr ist für die Enderwartung des Matth. gerade kennzeichnend, daß hier unter einem großen, vom Judentum bereits vorgeformten Bild[2] das Weltgericht über 'alle Völker' angekündigt wird, nun aber so, daß jetzt zwischen Juden und Heiden, aber auch zwischen Gläubigen und Ungläubigen nicht mehr unterschieden wird. Alle vor dem Tribunal des Weltenrichters Versammelten werden vielmehr nach *einem* Maßstab gerichtet, nämlich nach der Liebe, die den Geringsten erwiesen oder versagt ist. Sie entscheidet, wer zu den Gerechten gehört, die in das ewige Leben eingehen, und zu denen, die in die ewige Strafe dahinmüssen. Noch einmal wird hier deutlich, daß auch die Jüngerschaft Jesu nicht schon die Schar der Auserwählten, sondern vorerst die Schar der 'Gerufenen' ist, über deren endliches Schicksal das Tun des göttlichen Willens entscheidet.

Die kurze Analyse der Reden des Matth. hat uns die enge Verklammerung von Kirchengedanken und Enderwartung gezeigt, aber auch immer wieder sichtbar gemacht, worin die Klammer zwischen beiden besteht, nämlich im Verständnis des Gesetzes und damit der neuen Gerechtigkeit, die die Jünger Jesu von Pharisäern und Schriftgelehrten unterscheidet, zugleich aber der Maßstab ist, nach dem die Glieder der Kirche selbst von dem kommenden Richter erst gerichtet werden.[3] Die Frage nach dem Gesetzesverständnis im Matth.-Ev. muß jetzt näher bedacht werden.

2. DIE BESSERE GERECHTIGKEIT

Das Gesetz ist verbindlich bis hin zu Jota und Häkchen. Matth. selbst gibt den Worten v. 17–19, deren Formulierung offensichtlich auf die judenchristliche Gemeinde zurückgeht und gegen eine

[1] So zuletzt J. Jeremias a.a.O., S. 147f.

[2] Vgl. Billerbeck IV, S. 1199ff.; Bultmann, *Geschichte der synoptischen Tradition*, 2. Aufl., 1931, S. 130f.

[3] Vgl. A. Schlatter, *Die Kirche des Matthäus* (1929), S. 29f.

gesetzesfreie Richtung polemisiert, einen repräsentativen Platz und einen programmatischen Sinn. Mit der unverkürzten Geltung der Tora steht für ihn grundsätzlich auch die schriftgelehrte Auslegung in Kraft, wie denn schon in den nachfolgenden Antithesen zunächst keineswegs Tora und schriftgelehrte Auslegung einander gegenüber gestellt werden, sondern das, was 'zu den Alten' gesagt ist, jeweils in der für den Juden selbstverständlichen Form zitiert wird, die die Überlieferung dem Schriftwort gibt.[1] Ja Matth. xxiii. 2 konzediert den Schriftgelehrten und Pharisäern, daß sie auf der καθεδρα des Mose sitzen, ihre Lehre wird nicht angefochten, sondern für verbindlich erklärt (xxiii. 3). Angegriffen wird die Diskrepanz zwischen ihrem Lehren und Tun, ihre Heuchelei (xxiii. 4 ff.; vi. 1 ff.).[2] Freilich ist diese Kritik xv. 3 ff. zu der Anklage radikalisiert, daß die Gegner auch ihre παράδοσις dazu mißbrauchen, das Gesetz Gottes ungültig zu machen und Menschengebote an die Stelle des göttlichen Willens zu setzen (xv. 6, 9); darum heißen sie blinde Blindenführer (xv. 14) und die Jünger werden vor dem 'Sauerteig', d.h. vor der Lehre der Pharisäer und Sadducäer gewarnt (xvi. 6, 11).

Die zwischen Jesus und seinen Jüngern einerseits und den jüdischen Gegnern andrerseits strittige Frage ist damit die Frage nach der rechten Auslegung des Gesetzes. Schriftgelehrte Auslegung muß es auch in der christlichen Gemeinde geben, daher wird der Titel des γραμματεύς auch für die Jünger verwendet (xxiii. 34), nur ist der Jünger ein γραμματεὺς μαθητευθεὶς τῇ βασιλείᾳ τῶν οὐρανῶν (xiii. 52). Was aber ist die rechte Auslegung?

Die Antwort auf diese Frage gibt schon die Antithesenreihe der Bergpredigt (v. 21–48). Ihr durchgängiges Motiv ist der Durchstoß durch ein in formale Rechtssätze verkehrtes Gesetz, hinter dessen Ordnung das ungehorsame Herz des Menschen sich in Ordnung wähnt, und damit das Dringen auf den ursprünglichen, radikalen Willen Gottes, der zur 'Vollkommenheit' ruft. Das spricht sich in dem durchgängigen gedanklichen Schema dieser Antithesen aus: 'nicht erst—sondern schon', schon der Zorn,...schon der lüsterne Blick,...schon die 'legale' Scheidung der Ehe,...schon die Liebe

[1] Dem Verbot des Dekaloges (Ex. xx. 15; Dtn. v. 18) wird die Strafbestimmung angefügt (v. 21), dem Gebot der Nächstenliebe als Komplement das Gebot des Feindeshasses (v. 43).

[2] Vgl. E. Haenchen, 'Matthäus 23', *Zeitschrift für Theologie und Kirche*, Jahrg. 48, S. 38 ff.

zum Nächsten, die doch dem Feindeshaß noch Raum läßt, sind wider Gottes Willen.

Matth. versteht diese Radikalisierung der göttlichen Forderung, die ja faktisch nur in der ersten, zweiten und vierten Antithese eine Verschärfung des Gesetzes, in der dritten, fünften und sechsten dagegen seine Aufhebung bedeutet, offensichtlich als Bestätigung der Gültigkeit des Gesetzes bis hin zu Jota und Häkchen, ohne die Diskrepanz dieser Antithesen zu der an Jota und Häkchen festhaltenden, also die Verbindlichkeit des *Wortlautes* aussprechenden jüdisch-judenchristlichen Formulierung von v. 18f. zu empfinden. Seine Bindung an Jesu eigenes Wort und an das Gesetzesverständnis der jüdisch-judenchristlichen Tradition stehen hier in unverkennbarer Spannung zueinander.

Antwort auf die Frage nach der rechten Auslegung des Gesetzes gibt vor allem auch die Diskussion der Ehescheidungsfrage (xix. 1–12). Ihre Fassung bei Matth. gegenüber Mk. ist in mehrfacher Hinsicht lehrreich. Nicht nur, daß er den ungeschickten Aufbau gegenüber Mk. 'ausgezeichnet korrigiert'[1] und das Logion xix. 12 anfügt, er stellt Jesu Entscheidung in die zwischen den Rabbinen umstrittene Frage nach dem zureichenden Grund der Ehescheidung hinein (κατὰ πᾶσαν αἰτίαν; xix. 3) und läßt Jesus durch die offensichtlich sekundäre Ehebruchsklausel (xix. 9, vgl. v. 32) im Effekt den strengen Standpunkt der Schammaiten vertreten. Das radikale Verbot Jesu, auf das auch bei Matth. die ganze Argumentation *vv.* 4ff. (Mk. x. 6ff.) abzielt, wird damit fraglos um seine Schärfe gebracht. Gleichwohl ist die Norm, an der nach Jesu Wort hier sogar die Tora des Mose (nicht nur ihre Auslegung) gemessen werden soll, auch bei Matth. noch erkennbar und der ursprüngliche Wille des Schöpfers im Gegensatz zu der mosaischen Konzession an die menschliche σκληροκαρδία als Prinzip der Auslegung ausgesprochen. Der in der Schöpfung manifestierte Gotteswille ist in Jesu Forderung ein geläufiges Argument (Matth. v. 45; vi. 26ff.), übrigens gerade in Matth.-Worten. Der Evangelist selbst pflegt, wieweit auch hier an Jesu eigenes Wort gebunden, stehe dahin, die Frage nach dem rechten Auslegungsprinzip als die Frage nach dem Inbegriff von 'Gesetz und Propheten', bzw. dem Wichtigen im Gesetz, zu stellen. So bei der Formulierung der goldenen Regel

[1] R. Bultmann, *Geschichte der synoptischen Tradition*, S. 25f.

nach Matth. (vii. 12), der Formulierung des Doppelgebotes (xxii. 40, wieder nur Matth.), des 'Wichtigeren im Gesetz' (xxiii. 23), das Schriftgelehrte und Pharisäer außer acht lassen (κρίσις, ἔλεος, πίστις). Hierher gehört auch das zweimalige Zitat aus Hos. vi. 6: 'Barmherzigkeit will ich und nicht Opfer' (ix. 13; xii. 7).

Unter den verschiedenen Wendungen, mit denen Matth. die Hauptsache des Gesetzes zusammenfaßt, erfordert die Trias 'Recht, Barmherzigkeit, Treue' (Matth. xxiii. 23) besonderes Interesse. Zweifellos knüpft sie an alttestamentlich-jüdische Wendungen an wie 'Recht und Erbarmen' (Micha vi. 8) oder 'Erbarmen und Treue' (Prov. xiv. 22), wenn sie auch wörtlich in dieser Formulierung meines Wissens weder im A.T. noch im Judentum nachweisbar ist. Ihre drei Glieder sind für das Matth.-Ev. von unterschiedlicher Bedeutung. Die erste Forderung, den Armen Recht zu schaffen, wohl angebracht in der Anrede an Pharisäer und Schriftgelehrte als Verwalter der Jurisdiktionsgewalt und reichlich im A.T. begründet, spielt im Ev. sonst keine Rolle. Das ist nicht verwunderlich in einer Gemeinde, die der allgemein jüdischen Jurisdiktionsgewalt noch untersteht und für sich selbst noch keine eigene Rechtsprechung entwickelt hat. Umso mehr aber durchzieht das Gebot der Barmherzigkeit, unter dem die Jüngerschaft Jesu steht, das ganze Evangelium (v. 7; xviii. 33; ix. 13; xii. 7 und — der Sache nach — xxv. 31 ff.). Matth. ruft es der Gemeinde mit Nachdruck in Erinnerung, wie wir sahen, sogar dort, wo die ersten Regeln für die Durchführung der Gemeindedisziplin gegeben werden. Was endlich den dritten Begriff der Trias (πίστις) angeht, so wird man ihn in der Verbindung mit den beiden andern zwar nicht ohne weiteres als 'Glaube', sondern als 'Treue' verstehen müssen, schwerlich aber als Treue zu anderen Menschen (diese Verwendung wäre im ganzen Ev. singulär) sondern im umfassenden Sinn als ein auf Gott gerichtetes Verhalten, d.h. als Treue zu seinem in Gesetz und Propheten dokumentierten Willen. Nur so fügt der Begriff den beiden andern ein neues Moment hinzu, und die Trias wird zu einer erschöpfenden Formel für die Hauptsache des Gesetzes. Vor allem aber läßt sich nur von dieser auf Gott bezogenen, umfassenden Bedeutung aus eine Brücke zu der sonstigen Verwendung von πίστις und πιστεύειν im Evangelium schlagen.

Überblickt man den Sprachgebrauch dieser Begriffe bei Matth.

so zeigt sich, daß der Evangelist an zahlreichen Stellen vom Glauben im Sinne der ihm vorgegebenen christlichen Tradition redet. Glaube meint hier das Vertrauen, das sich auf Jesu ἐξουσία richtet (viii. 10; ix. 2) und seine Wunderkraft erfährt (viii. 13; ix. 22, 28f.). Zu diesem Glauben an die rettende Wunderkraft Jesu (Gegensatz: der Zweifel xxi. 21) ist die Jüngerschaft gerufen. Jesus selbst stellt ihn unter die Verheißung, daß ihm nichts unmöglich sein wird, auch wenn er nicht größer ist als ein Senfkorn (xvii. 20; xxi. 21). Scharf zu unterscheiden von diesem Glauben ist der 'Kleinglaube' (ein Lieblingswort des Matth.), der gerade dann versagt, wenn es darauf ankommt — in Sturm und Wellen (viii. 26; xiv. 31), gegenüber der Sorge (vi. 30; xvi. 8) — und dem Ansturm dämonischer Gewalten nicht gewachsen ist (xvii. 20). Wie kein anderer Evangelist verwendet und illustriert Matth. dieses Motiv.[1] Gleichwohl redet er hier in der Sprache urchristlicher Paränese und Paraklese überhaupt. Auch die Entwicklung der dogmatischen Sprache des Urchristentums ist bei Matth. erkennbar. Das bloße πιστεύειν (Mk. ix. 42; xv. 32) verdeutlicht er durch πιστεύειν εἰς ἐμέ (Matth. xviii. 6), πιστεύειν ἐπ' αὐτόν (xxvii. 42). Dieser spezifisch christliche, auf die Person Jesu bezogene Begriff wird bemerkenswerterweise von ihm nicht vor dem Petrusbekenntnis verwendet.

An keiner dieser Stellen ist jedoch πίστις und πιστεύειν mit Gesetz und Enderwartung in Verbindung gebracht. Das geschieht erst an zwei Stellen, an denen wieder eine spezifisch matthäische Komposition und Interpretation erkennbar wird. Die erste Stelle ist xxi. 32, ein ursprünglich selbständiges, von Matth. abgewandeltes Logion (vgl. Lk. vii. 29f.), das er an das Ende des Gleichnisses von den beiden ungleichen Söhnen stellt. Er gibt damit dem Verhalten des Neinsagers und des Jasagers eine sehr bestimmte Auslegung: das erstere hat sich erfüllt in dem 'Glauben' der Zöllner und Dirnen gegenüber Johannes dem Täufer, der 'mit dem Wege der Gerechtigkeit' kam, das letztere in der Verweigerung von Umkehr und Glauben seitens der Pharisäer und Schriftgelehrten, die darum keinen Eingang in die βασιλεία finden.[2] Lehrreich ist an dieser Deutung,

[1] Der Ausdruck findet sich sonst nur Lk. xii. 28.

[2] Daß Matth. xxi. 32 eine sekundäre Ausdeutung des Gleichnisses ist, zeigt mit Recht J. Jeremias a.a.O., S. 62f. Ich glaube allerdings nicht, daß der Evangelist das Gleichnis schon mit dieser Deutung übernahm (so Jeremias), sondern sie selbst

daß sie (1) ein abgeschlossenes, heils- und unheilsgeschichtliches Geschehen ausspricht, daß sie (2) die beiden gegensätzlichen Entscheidungen schon gegenüber dem Täufer gefallen sieht und damit die Gültigkeit seiner Gerechtigkeitsforderung (wie schon iii. 1–12) in vollem Umfang statuiert und (3) daß sie den schon von Johannes geforderten Gehorsam als 'Reue' und 'Glauben' beschreibt und ihn zur Bedingung für den Eingang in die zukünftige βασιλεία macht.

Die zweite Stelle ist die Perikope vom Hauptmann von Kapernaum (viii. 5 ff.). Wieder ist das Mittel der Interpretation die Komposition. Erst Matth. fügt in den Rahmen der Erzählung das ursprünglich selbständige Logion viii. 11 f. ein (bei Lk. begegnet es in völlig anderem Zusammenhang xiii. 28) und gibt damit der Erzählung einen ins Eschatologische ausgeweiteten Sinn, dergestalt, daß nun der Glaube, den Jesus bei dem Hauptmann findet, aber in Israel vergeblich gesucht hat, als das Verhalten sichtbar wird, das über die Zugehörigkeit zum wahren Gottesvolk und den Eingang in das kommende Gottesreich entscheidet. Beide Stellen zeigen, wie Matth. den Begriff des Glaubens versteht und ihn mit seinem Verständnis der Gerechtigkeit sowie des Gottesreiches verbindet. Er entnimmt ihn zwar der urchristlichen Tradition, die ihn *nicht* am Gesetz entwickelte, aber er verankert ihn gerade an diesen Stellen, wo wir ihn als Interpreten der Tradition am Werke sehen, im Gefüge seiner von Gesetz und Enderwartung bestimmten Lehre.

In diesem Zusammenhang ist auch die Verwendung von πίστις in der Formel xxiii. 23 wichtig. Ohne seine alttestamentlich-jüdische Bedeutung zu verlieren, wird er zur Klammer zwischen dem vom Gesetz geforderten Verhalten und dem Glauben der Jünger, der sich auf Vollmacht und Person Jesu richtet. Der Evangelist kann nun gleichsam von beiden Seiten her das Wesen der besseren Gerechtig-

in Gestalt des Logion v. 32 hinzufügt, um so den illustrativen Sinn, den das Gleichnis auch im Zusammenhang der vorangehenden Vollmachts-Perikope (besonders für xxi. 25) hat, zu verdeutlichen. Die Wendung ἐν ὁδῷ δικαιοσύνης ist fraglos auf die Lehre des Johannes, die Forderung der Gerechtigkeit zu beziehen. So mit Billerbeck I, S. 866f.; Schrenk, *Th.W.* II, S. 201, Klostermann z.St. u.a. gegen Michel, *Th.W.* V, S. 90f. Übrigens bietet zu xxi. 32 der neugefundenen Habakukkommentar (VIII, 2f.) jetzt eine lehrreiche sachliche und sprachliche Parallele: 'Die Gott erretten wird aus dem Hause des Gerichts wegen ihrer Mühsal und ihrer Treue zum Lehrer der Gerechtigkeit.'

keit sichtbar machen, an der die Jüngerschaft Jesu zu erkennen ist: von ihrer Bindung an das Gesetz aus, das Jesus erfüllt, d.h. vollmächtig auslegt, wie auch von ihrer Bindung an die Person und den Weg des Messias her. Erfüllung der Gebote und Vollkommenheit ist nun nicht mehr anders zu verwirklichen als in der *Nachfolge* Jesu. Das zeigt sich am deutlichsten an der Perikope vom reichen Jüngling (xix. 16–30). Sie ist Matth. aus der Tradition vorgegeben, aber er ändert und unterstreicht bestimmte Züge, so wenn er die Antwort Jesu Mk. x. 18 τί με λέγεις ἀγαθόν; abwandelt in die Frage τί με ἐρωτᾷς περὶ τοῦ ἀγαθοῦ; (xix. 17) und damit Jesus selbst das von ihm Mk. x. 18 abgewehrte Prädikat wieder zuspricht, und wenn er gleich im Anschluß daran den Imperativ einfügt: εἰ δὲ θέλεις εἰς τὴν ζωὴν εἰσελθεῖν, τήρει τὰς ἐντολάς und *v.* 21 den für sein Verständnis des Gesetzes charakteristischen Ausdruck εἰ θέλεις τέλειος εἶναι (vgl. v. 48). In der Nachfolge Jesu also erfüllt sich die vom Gesetz geforderte Vollkommenheit. Seinen Jüngern, die alles verlassen haben und ihm nachgefolgt sind, gilt die Verheißung, daß sie in der 'Wiedergeburt', beim Erscheinen des Menschensohnes zum Gericht auf zwölf Thronen sitzen und die zwölf Stämme Israels richten werden. Durch den Kontext und das wieder erst von Matth. an dieser Stelle eingefügte Logion xix. 28 wird damit die Nachfolge fest mit dem Gesetzesbegriff und der dem wahren Gottesvolk geltenden Verheißung verbunden.

Lehrreich ist in dieser Perikope aber noch eine weitere, nicht unwichtige Abwandlung gegenüber der im Mk.-Text erkennbaren Tradition. Matth. nämlich sagt nichts von einem schon in diesem Äon auf die Jünger wartenden Lohn (so Mk. x. 30), sondern verheißt ihn nur für den kommenden Äon (xix. 29), und zwar der Jüngerschaft Jesu allein im ausdrücklichen Gegensatz zu Israel. In diesem Sinn versteht er das an die Perikope angefügte Gleichnis von den Arbeitern im Weinberg, wie die Schlußsentenz Mt. xx. 16 zeigt, die wörtlich xix. 30 wiederholt.[1] So werden beide Perikopen von ihm in den Dienst der ihm eigenen Anschauung der Heilsgeschichte gestellt.[2] Wichtig ist aber vor allem das radikal eschatologische Verständnis der den Jüngern gegebenen Verheißung. In diesem Äon erwartet die Jünger ausschließlich das Leidensgeschick der Propheten

[1] Vgl. J. Jeremias a.a.O., S. 20f.
[2] Vgl. hierfür besonders xxi. 33ff.; xxii. 1ff.

(v. 12; xxiii. 32ff.). Matth. hat darum die Sturmfahrt der Jünger (viii. 23–6) zu einem beispielhaften Bild der Nachfolge umgestaltet und ihr einen symbolischen Sinn gegeben.[1] Das wird daran deutlich, daß er in einem Zusammenhang, der sonst ausschließlich Wundergeschichten bietet, der Geschichte von der Stillung des Sturmes die aus Lk. ix. 57ff. bekannten Nachfolgersprüche voranstellt und beides ausdrücklich durch das Stichwort ἀκολουθεῖν (viii. 19, 22, 23) verklammert. Auch die nicht unerheblichen Umgestaltungen der Erzählung — die Tilgung novellistischer Einzelzüge, die Formulierung des Hilfeschreis der Jünger als Gebetsruf (κύριε, σῶσον, ἀπολλύμεθα), die Voranstellung des tadelnden Wortes Jesu an die Jünger vor dem Wunder selbst (unter Verwendung des Lieblingswortes ὀλιγόπιστοι), endlich auch die Bezeichnung der Seenot mit σεισμός, einem Ausdruck der sonst zur Schilderung der eschatologischen Drangsal gehört, — alles das zeigt deutlich, daß er der Szene eine für die Jüngerschaft und Nachfolge typische sinnbildliche Bedeutung gibt. Leidensbereitschaft (x. 17ff.; xvi. 24ff.), Armut (xix. 23ff.; vi. 19ff.), Niedrigkeit (xviii. 1ff.), Liebe (xxv. 31ff. und öfter), Verzicht auf weltliche Ehre (xxiii. 7ff.) und Dienst (xx. 20ff.) sind die Kennzeichen der Nachfolge. Nur den Jüngern, die sich darin bewähren und beweisen, ist, wie keine dieser Stellen ungesagt läßt, der Lohn im Reiche Gottes verheißen.

Wie stark und konsequent Matth. trotz aller spezifisch christlichen Motive, die auch er verwendet, alles, was er über das Wesen der Jüngerschaft sagt, an Gesetz und Gerechtigkeit orientiert, zeigt endlich das nur bei ihm sich findende Vorherrschen der Begriffe δίκαιος und δικαιοσύνη. Jesus selbst ist 'gerecht' (xxvii. 19), erfüllt 'alle Gerechtigkeit' (iii. 15), er ist wahrhaftig und lehrt den Weg Gottes in Wahrheit (xxii. 16), die Verfolgung der Jünger um seinetwillen ist gleichbedeutend mit der Verfolgung um der Gerechtigkeit willen (v. 10f.); Gerechtigkeit ist der zusammenfassende Begriff für die Frömmigkeit der Jünger überhaupt (vi. 1). Niemals aber ist die Jüngerschaft insgesamt und eo ipso schon gerecht. Vielmehr ist sie zu der besseren Gerechtigkeit gerufen (v. 20; vi. 33), im kommenden Gericht erst werden die Gerechten leuchten wie die Sonne (xiii. 43), wenn die Engel die Bösen aus der Mitte der Gerechten

[1] Vgl. G. Bornkamm, 'Die Sturmstillung im Matth.-Ev.', in *Wort und Dienst* (*Jahrb. der Theol. Schule Bethel*), 1948, S. 49ff.

ausscheiden werden (xiii. 49) Die Seligpreisung v. 6 gilt denen, die hungern und dürsten nach der Gerechtigkeit. Gerechtigkeit ist also das Verhalten, das dem Willen Gottes im Gesetz und damit dem Spruch des kommenden Richters entspricht, Forderung und eschatologisches Heilsgut zugleich. Er behält also bei Matth. formaliter seinen alttestamentlich-jüdischen Sinn; er bleibt darum das höchste Kennzeichen der alttestamentlichen Frommen (xiii. 17; xxiii. 29, 35; vgl. schon i. 19). Nur die Gerechtigkeit legitimiert die Jüngerschaft als das wahre Gottesvolk und macht sie zu Nachfolgern der Propheten und Gerechten des alten Bundes (x. 41; xxiii. 34ff.). Sie scheidet Jesu Jünger von dem Israel, das Pharisäer und Schriftgelehrte repräsentieren, und verbindet sie zugleich mit Israels Geschichte und seiner Verheißung.

Wir fassen zusammen: Matth. versteht das Gesetz in einer vom Judentum nicht prinzipiell oder besser gesagt prinzipiell *nicht* unterschiedenen Weise, d.h. er stellt sein Gesetzesverständnis bewußt in die jüdisch-schriftgelehrte Tradition hinein. Das Pathos seines Gegensatzes zum Judentum entsteht an der Diskrepanz von Lehren und Tun auf Seiten der Gegner, damit freilich auch an dem Mißbrauch und Versagen einer Gesetzesauslegung, die nicht nach dem ursprünglichen Sinn der göttlichen Forderung fragt und die Hauptsache des Gesetzes nicht wahrhaben will.

Inbegriff des Gesetzes ist nach Matth. das Liebesgebot in seiner doppelten Ausrichtung auf Gott und den Nächsten.[1] Das Kultgesetz wird zwar nicht grundsätzlich bestritten; Privatopfer (v. 23f.), Tempelsteuer (xvii. 24ff.), Sabbatgebot (xxiv. 20),[2] Almosen, Gebet

[1] Zum Verhältnis von Mk. xii. 28–34 zu Matth. xxii. 34–40 (und Lk. x. 25–8) vgl. G. Bornkamm, 'Das Doppelgebot der Liebe' in *Neutestam. Studien für Rudolf Bultmann* (1954), S. 85ff.

[2] Daß das Sabbatgebot für Matth. seine Gültigkeit nicht verloren hat, zeigt die Abmilderung des Mk.-Textes an verschiedenen Stellen: die Sabbatheilung Mk. i. 21–8 wird übergangen, so daß auch die Heilungen Mk. i. 29–34 bei Matth. (viii. 14–17) keinen Bruch des Sabbatgebotes mehr darstellen. Der Sabbatkonflikt Mk. ii. 23–8 = Matth. xii. 1–8 ist zwar von Matth. aufgenommen, aber durch Zufügung von ἐπείνασαν (xii. 1) wird dem Verhalten der Jünger der Makel der Willkür genommen und durch xii. 5f. ihm ausdrücklich eine Legitimation aus dem Gesetz gegeben. Mk. ii. 27, das einer laxen Haltung dem Gesetz gegenüber Vorschub leisten könnte, streicht Matth. Vgl. hierzu Kilpatrick a.a.O., p. 116.

Lehrreich ist übrigens auch, wie Matth. die Debatte über rein und unrein abmildert. Den drastischen Ausdruck κοιναῖς χερσὶν ἐσθίουσιν τὸν ἄρτον (Mk. vii. 2, 5) vermeidet er, läßt Jesus auf den Vorwurf der Pharisäer und Schriftgelehrten

und Fasten (vi. 1 ff.), ja nach xxiii. 16 ff. und 23 ff. sogar Eid und Zehntung, sind als gültig vorausgesetzt, sofern sie nicht heuchlerisch mißbraucht und darüber 'die gewichtigeren Bestimmungen des Gesetzes' nicht versäumt werden. Aber sie liefern nicht mehr den Maßstab für die Gerechtigkeit, die besser ist als die der Pharisäer und Schriftgelehrten.

Matth. gewinnt sein radikales Verständnis des Gesetzes, indem er es sub specie principii, im Lichte des in der Schöpfung kundgewordenen Willens Gottes, aber erst recht sub specie iudicii, im Sinne des universalen Weltgerichtes versteht, dem alle und gerade auch die Jünger entgegengehen. In den so gespannten Rahmen des Gesetzesverständnisses fügt Matth. erst die spezifisch christlichen Motive, die Wesen, Glauben und Leben der Jüngerschaft kennzeichnen, ein und gewinnt aus ihm für die Auseinandersetzung der Kirche mit Israel Legitimation und Waffe. Was aber bedeutet dabei Christus für sein Verständnis von Gesetz, Kirche und Endgericht?

3. CHRISTOLOGIE UND GESETZ IM MATTH.-EV.

Wie kein anderer Evangelist begründet Matth. den Christusglauben der Gemeinde mit der Schrift; Reflektionszitate durchziehen das ganze Evangelium. Die messianischen Titel, die das Ev. in großer Fülle verwendet, entstammen zwar keineswegs alle der jüdischen Messianologie, sondern — mindestens in dem Sinn, in dem sie verwandt werden — der vorgegebenen christlichen, und zwar gerade auch der in der hellenistischen Gemeinde vorgeformten Überlieferung (wie schon die Rezeption des ganzen Mk.-Ev. in Matth. zeigt). Für Matth. bezeichnend ist nur, mit welcher Energie und Konsequenz er alle messianischen Würdenamen Jesu, seine Lehre, seine Taten und seine Geschichte vor der Autorität der Schrift ausweist. Das gilt für alle Hoheitsbezeichnungen Jesu: Er ist der Davidssohn, der König Israels, bzw. der Juden, der Erfüller der Immanuel-, der Bethlehem-, der Galiläa-, der Gottesknecht-Weissagung, der Gottessohn, der Sach. ix. verheißene sanftmütige König, der in den Leidenspsalmen Geweissagte und endlich der Menschensohn-Weltrichter,

sofort mit dem Gegenvorwurf antworten, daß *sie* mit Hilfe ihrer παράδοσις das Gebot Gottes außer Kraft setzen, und kündigt ihnen als den Verführern das Gericht Gottes an (xv. 3–14).

der hier verworfen wird, leidet und aufersteht, schon hier auf Erden den Titel des Menschensohnes trägt, aber in Herrlichkeit im Gericht erst erscheinen soll.

Theologische Reflektionen über den Zusammenhang dieser Würdenamen untereinander läßt das Matth.-Ev. nur an wenigen Stellen erkennen; erstlich genügt ihm der Nachweis, daß sie alle in der Schrift begründet sind. Immerhin fehlen Spuren solcher Reflektion nicht, wenn auch Matth., wo er sie bietet, hier zunächst im Rahmen seiner Tradition bleibt. Hierhin gehört die Erörterung über das Verhältnis des Davidssohntitels und des Kyrios-Titels (Matth. xxii. 41 ff.), das mindestens von dem Evangelisten, der sonst die Davidssohnschaft Jesu reichlich zur Geltung bringt, nicht im Sinne eines Entweder-Oder verstanden sein kann. Die Frage εἰ οὖν Δαυὶδ καλεῖ αὐτὸν κύριον, πῶς υἱὸς αὐτοῦ ἐστιν; (xxii. 45) kann dann nur auf das paradoxe Miteinander beider Jesus zukommender Titel hinweisen wollen und darauf hindeuten, daß er in seiner irdischen Niedrigkeit Davids Sohn, aber als Erhöhter der Kyrios ist, als den David selbst ihn Ps. cx. 1 bezeichnet.[1]

Eine Reflektion über den Zusammenhang der Christus- und Gottessohnwürde Jesu und seiner Stellung als Menschensohn-Weltrichter verrät auch die Frage des Hohenpriesters im Verhör und Jesu Antwort (xxvi. 63 f.), in der er das erstere jetzt schon für sich in Anspruch nimmt und sein Kommen als Menschensohn mit Dan. vii. 13 ankündigt. Es ist bezeichnend, daß Matth. (ähnlich wie Lk. xxii. 69) den Mk.-Text durch das betonte ἀπ' ἄρτι ὄψεσθε (xxvi. 64) schärfer profiliert. Stärker als hier sieht man den Theologen und Interpreten Matth. in der Einzugsgeschichte am Werk (xxi. 1 ff.), sofern nur er ausdrücklich Sach. ix. 9 (verbunden mit Jes. lxii. 11)

[1] Schwerlich hat schon Mk., der ja auch von dem Davidssohntitel sonst in seinem Ev. Gebrauch macht (x. 47 f., vgl. auch xi. 9), die Frage xi. 37 so gemeint, wenn auch der ursprüngliche Sinn der Perikope die Ablehnung der Davidssohnschaft gewesen sein kann (Wrede, Bousset, Klostermann, Bultmann unter Hinweis auf Barn. XII. 10f.); denn die Frage müßte ja eigentlich, wenn von der Davidssohnschaft des Messias ausgegangen würde und im Schema Niedrigkeit/Erhöhung gedacht wäre, gefragt sein: ist der Messias Davids Sohn, wie kann er dann sein Herr sein? Der unangefochtene Gebrauch des Davidssohn-Titels in dem Ev. sonst, zwingt jedoch zu der Folgerung, daß sie ihn, wie die christologischen Formeln Röm. i. 3; II Tim. ii. 8; Ign. Sm. i. 1; Trall. ix u.a. zeigen, auf seine irdisch-menschliche Gestalt beziehen, im Unterschied zu seiner Erhöhung. Vorausgesetzt ist also christliche, nicht mehr jüdische Reflektion.

zitiert und Jesus so als den 'demütigen König' bezeichnet. Wie bei Mk. erklingt der Hosannaruf auch bei Matth. aus dem Munde der Jesus begleitenden Menge (*v.* 9), aber er tilgt die zweite Hälfte dieses Rufes (εὐλογημένη ἡ ἐρχομένη βασιλεία τοῦ πατρὸς ἡμῶν Δαυίδ Mk. xi. 10) und ersetzt die Volksmenge bald darauf durch die Schar der Kinder, in denen hier wie häufig in seinem Ev. die von den Hohenpriestern und Schriftgelehrten scharf abgelehnte Jüngerschaft Jesu vor- und abgebildet ist. Er vermeidet also offensichtlich die Gleichsetzung der von ihm konsequent eschatologisch verstandenen, universalen βασιλεία τῶν οὐρανῶν mit der 'Königsherrschaft Davids'. Gegenwärtig ist hier und jetzt der König der Niedrigkeit; das Reich Gottes, in dem er der Weltenrichter über alle Völker ist (Matth. xxv. 31), ist Zukunft.

Selbst dort, wo Matth. tatsächlich — ein einziges Mal — mit einem aus Q stammenden Wort das Schon-Gekommen-sein der βασιλεία τοῦ θεοῦ ausspricht ('wenn ich aber mit dem Geiste Gottes Dämonen austreibe, so ist die Gottesherrschaft schon zu euch gelangt' xii. 28), wird doch durch den Kontext die Gegenwart als die Entscheidungszeit gekennzeichnet (xii. 30), die Zukünftigkeit des Gerichts festgehalten (xii. 27, 36f.) und die Unterscheidung dieses (jetzt noch währenden) und des zukünftigen Äon nicht preisgegeben (xii. 32). Ja, man wird dem hier von Matth. eingefügten, aus Mk. entnommenen, aber durch die Q-Fassung ergänzten und christlich interpretierten Logion von der Unvergebbarkeit der Lästerung des Geistes im Unterschied zu der Vergebbarkeit eines gegen den Menschensohn gerichteten Wortes (xii. 31f.) sogar noch eine genauere Differenzierung der heilsgeschichtlichen 'Epochen' entnehmen dürfen. Wie Mk. iii. 28f. zeigt, ist der ursprüngliche Sinn des Wortes Jesu: alle Sünden und Lästerungen können vergeben werden, die Lästerung aber gegen den in Jesu Sieg über die Dämonen sich manifestierenden heiligen Geist nicht. Matth. (bzw. schon Q, Matth. xii. 32; Lk. xii. 10) differenziert zwischen Menschensohn und Geist und der Lästerung beider und unterscheidet damit zwischen einer Zeit, in der Jesus, noch ehe der heilige Geist da ist, als 'Menschensohn' begegnet (d.h. hier offenbar im Stande der noch zweideutigen Niedrigkeit), und einer Zeit, in der durch den heiligen Geist (also nach seiner Erhöhung) die Stellung zu ihm (und seiner Gemeinde) den Charakter eines eindeutigen Entweder-Oder annimmt. Jetzt erst gibt es Lästerung als unvergebbare Sünde, denn im Geist redet der sich offenbarende erhöhte Herr. Beide Zeiten gehören diesem Äon an. Sie sind noch einmal zu unterscheiden vom kommenden Äon, der das endgültige Gericht bringen wird. Im Sinne dieser heilsgeschichtlichen Periodisierung, in der die Erscheinung Jesu als Menschensohn der Periode seiner noch nicht erfolgten Erhöhung, dagegen der Geist der Periode der nun eindeutigen und verpflichtenden Offenbarung, also der Zeit der Kirche des Erhöhten, zugeordnet werden und das definitive Gericht den noch erwarteten Abschluß bildet, wird das Wort verständlich.[1]

Alle diese Stellen, in denen Matth. (zum Teil schon seine Quellen) theologisch die vorgegebene Tradition interpretiert, zielen auf die Unterscheidung der irdischen Niedrigkeit Jesu und seiner zukünftigen Erscheinung in Herrlichkeit zum Gericht.

Die irdische Funktion Jesu als des Messias ist nun aber — abgesehen von seinen Wundertaten, denen Matth. natürlich auch einen breiten Raum, aber hinter seiner Lehre den zweiten Platz einräumt (iv. 23; ix. 35 und öfter) — vor allem die *Auslegung des Gesetzes.* Hier erst wird die eigentlich matthäische Christologie greifbar. Es ist oft und mit Recht beobachtet worden, daß Jesus im Matth.-Ev. als ein zweiter Moses erscheint,[2] die Mosestypologie schon die Vorgeschichten beherrscht, möglicherweise der Berg der Bergpredigt in Analogie zum Sinai verstanden sein will und Jesu ganze Geschichte und Lehre unter das Motiv der Erfüllung des Gesetzes (v. 17), 'aller Gerechtigkeit' (iii. 15) gestellt wird.

Das Verhältnis Jesu zu Moses ist dabei nicht in dem Sinne der Antithese gemeint — wie etwa im Joh.-Ev. (i. 17; vi. 32ff.), sondern im Sinne der Entsprechung. Trotz des autoritativen 'Ich aber sage euch' wird Jesu Lehre ständig am Gesetz ausgewiesen und seine Autorität nicht einfach deklariert. Das ἐγὼ δὲ λέγω ὑμῖν (v. 22, 28 und öfter) spricht also keinen Anspruch aus, der auf Begründung verzichtet; est ist kein Offenbarungswort im Sinne der johanneischen

[1] Vgl. zum Verständnis der schwierigen Stelle auch C. K. Barrett, *The Holy Spirit and the Gospel Tradition* (1947), pp. 103ff.

[2] So vor allem B. W. Bacon, *Studies in Matthew* (1930); F. W. Green, *The Gospel according to St Matthew*[4] (1949); vgl. auch Kilpatrick a.a.O., S. 107f. — Bacons These, daß Matth. unter Nachahmung des Pentateuch seine Schrift in fünf Teile gegliedert habe, hat viel Beifall gefunden. Mir ist sie nicht überzeugend.

ἐγώ εἰμι-Sprüche. Wie die Schrift ihn in seiner messianischen Stellung und Würde legitimiert, so legitimiert das Gesetz seine Lehre und zwar gerade seine messianische ἐξουσία als Lehrer im Gegensatz zu Pharisäern und Schriftgelehrten.[1]

Fragt man nach dem Verhältnis der Aussagen, in denen von der Würde Jesu als des Χριστός, des Davidssohnes, des Königs von Israel, des Gottessohnes usw. die Rede ist, zu denen, die ihn als Gesetzeslehrer schildern, so zeigt sich, daß Matth. beides nicht unverbunden stehen läßt, sondern fest verklammert.

Lehrreich ist dafür bereits das von ihm gebildete, jedenfalls nur von ihm gebotene Gespräch zwischen Joh. dem Täufer und Jesus, mit dem er — das wird in der Exegese allermeist übersehen — nicht nur die Taufgeschichte einleitet, sondern sie zugleich mit der unmittelbar vorangehenden Ankündigung des Messias und *seiner* Taufe verbindet. (Schon das in Matth. häufige τότε dient dieser Verklammerung.) Nichts berechtigt, dieses Gespräch, wie schon das Hebr.-Ev. es tut, nur unter dem Gesichtspunkt der Sündlosigkeit Jesu zu verstehen, die den Sinn seiner Taufe zu einem Problem und ihre Übernahme zu einer demutsvollen Konzession an die fromme Übung des Volkes macht. Auch die Frage des Täufers besagt mehr, als nur eine respektvolle Anerkennung der Überlegenheit Jesu. In Wahrheit ist das Gespräch wieder Ausdruck einer theologisch-heilsgeschichtlichen Reflektion. Es stellt die Frage nach dem Verhältnis der von Johannes soeben angekündigten Messiastaufe (mit Geist und Feuer)

[1] Das Verhältnis Jesu zum Gesetz nach Matth. scheint mir nicht ganz zutreffend charakterisiert zu sein, wenn Kilpatrick formuliert: 'The central position that Judaism gave to the Law, the Gospel gives to Jesus' (a.a.O. p. 108) und behauptet, das Gesetz hätte bei Matth. 'an important, though subordinate, place in the Christian scheme' (p. 109). Das Logion Matth. xviii. 20 kann in der Tat von Jesus sagen, was das Rabbinat entsprechend von der Tora zu sagen wußte (Pirke Aboth III, 2 'wenn zwei (zusammen) sitzen und Worte der Tora sind zwischen ihnen, da weilt die Schekhina unter ihnen') wie Matth. auch Sophia-Worte Jesus in den Mund legt. Das bedeutet aber nicht, daß *an die Stelle* des Gesetzes (bzw. der Weisheit) Jesus gesetzt sei, sondern gerade im Sinne von v. 17ff. die Bestätigung des Gesetzes. Man wird zu beachten haben, daß es im Matth.-Ev. den Begriff der nova lex (Bacon, Kilpatrick u.a.) nicht gibt und nicht geben kann. Matth. xii. 6 steht: 'Größeres als der *Tempel* ist hier', — nicht: als das *Gesetz*; gerade für xii. 6 wird von Matth. das Gesetz selbst zum Zeugen aufgerufen (xii. 3–7), es legitimiert den Menschensohn als Herrn auch über den Sabbat (*v.* 8). Zur positiven Bedeutung des Satzes ὅτι τοῦ ἱεροῦ μεῖζόν ἐστιν ὧδε vgl. die treffenden Ausführungen von Schlatter in: *Die Kirche des Matthäus*, S. 31ff.

und der durch den Täufer an Jesus jetzt sich vollziehenden Taufe, damit zugleich nach der Funktion des nun angekommenen Messias, der überraschenderweise nicht als Täufer, sondern als Täufling, ohne die Wurfschaufel in seiner Hand, erscheint. Das Wort des Täufers: 'ich müßte von dir getauft werden, und du kommst zu mir?' also meint: meine Zeit und meine Taufe ist vorbei und die Stunde deiner (messianischen) Taufe ist da. Jesu Antwort lautet programmatisch: 'laß es jetzt; denn so ziemt es sich für uns, alle Gerechtigkeit zu erfüllen' (iii. 15).

Verkündigung und Erfüllung der von Gott geforderten δικαιοσύνη also ist die hier auf Erden dem Messias obliegende Funktion. Als der, der sie übernimmt, wird er als 'Sohn Gottes' proklamiert. Er erfüllt sie selbst im Gehorsam gegen das Gesetz und erweist sich gerade so in der Abwehr der Versuchungen des Teufels als der Sohn Gottes (wieder das charakteristische τότε iv. 1) gehorsam 'im Sinne der Frömmigkeit der Anawim'[1] oder, mit den eigenen Worten des Matth., als der πραΰς und ταπεινὸς τῇ καρδίᾳ (xi. 29).[2] Wird hier in der Versuchungsgeschichte also 'Jesus gegen einen Magier und christliches Wundertun gegen Magie abgegrenzt',[3] und damit das Verständnis seiner Gottessohnschaft von dem hellenistischen υἱὸς τοῦ θεοῦ, der in Wundertaten sich erweist, so entsteht mit Notwendigkeit die Frage, wie sich damit dieses hellenistische, im Mk.-Ev. ohne Zweifel wirksame und von Matth. durchaus rezipierte Bild des υἱὸς τοῦ θεοῦ zusammenreimt. Die Auseinandersetzung mit dieser Frage ist nicht erst im Matth.-Ev., sondern schon, wie die Versuchungsgeschichte zeigt, in der Spruchquelle erkennbar, Matth. aber führt darin weiter, wenn er Jesu Lehren und Heilen in Galiläa in den ihm eigenen Summarien iv. 12ff. und iv. 23ff., die die Berufung der ersten Jünger umrahmen, unter das Heilswort an die im Land und Schatten des Todes Wohnenden stellt (Jes. ix. 1f.; Matth. iv. 15f.), ihn ix. 36 als den sich erbarmenden Hirten der zerschundenen Herde schildert und in den Heilandstaten Jesu sich die Weissagung von dem Gottesknecht (Jes. liii. 4; xlii. 1ff.) erfüllen sieht (viii. 17;

[1] W. Sattler in der *Festg. f. A. Jülicher*, 1927, S. 10.

[2] Mit Recht haben Schlatter, *Der Evangelist Matthäus* (1933), S. 95ff. und Bultmann, *Geschichte der syn. Trad.* (1931²), S. 271ff. den messianischen Charakter der Versuchungen bestritten und die Bedeutung der Perikope für das Gesetzesverständnis überhaupt herausgestellt.

[3] Bultmann a.a.O., S. 273.

xii. 18 ff.). Die Wunder sind hier also nicht mehr Manifestation des θεῖος ἀνήρ, sondern seines Erbarmens und seiner Niedrigkeit. Die grundsätzliche Absage an das hellenistische Bild des Wundertäters ist damit ausgesprochen, ohne daß Matth. sich freilich durchweg seinem Banne entzieht.

Die πραύτης des Messias und seine Barmherzigkeit gegenüber den Geringen, beides verstanden als Erfüllung aller Gerechtigkeit, durchzieht das Evangelium des Matth. bis hin zu der Weltgerichtsschilderung (xxv. 31 ff.), in der der Menschensohn die Geringsten seine Brüder nennt. Eben dem entspricht genauestens, wie wir schon sahen, auch die Auslegung, die er dem Gesetz Gottes gibt ('Barmherzigkeit will ich und nicht Opfer', ix. 13; xii. 7), der Ruf zur Liebe, zum Kleinwerden, zur Demut, zur Leidensbereitschaft und so fort. Alles das umschreibt die 'bessere Gerechtigkeit', die Früchte, nach denen im Gericht gefragt wird, die Vollkommenheit, von der das Ende der Antithesen der Bergpredigt redet.

Die konsequente und radikale Rezeption des Gesetzes (in dem, worauf es eigentlich abzielt) steht für Matth. also in engstem Zusammenhang mit seiner Christologie. Bis Himmel und Erde vergehen, muß alles erfüllt werden, was das Gesetz sagt; bis dahin gilt die Verheißung der Größe im Himmelreich denen, die die neue Gerechtigkeit ohne Abstriche tun und lehren (v. 18 ff.), bereit, als νήπιοι (xi. 25) das Joch der Sanftmut und Demut des Herzen (xi. 29) auf sich zu nehmen und damit μαθητής dessen zu werden, der selbst sanftmütigen und demütigen Herzens ist, bis er in Herrlichkeit als Richter kommt, die Guten und Bösen nach ihren Werken scheiden und die Niedrigen erhöhen wird.

4. EKKLESIOLOGIE UND CHRISTOLOGIE

Kein anderes Evangelium ist so wie Matth. vom Kirchengedanken geprägt, für den kirchlichen Gebrauch gestaltet; es hat darum auch wie kein anderes in der späteren Kirche maßgebliche Wirkung geübt. Aussagen, in denen sich das eschatologische Selbstbewußtsein der Urchristenheit ausspricht, durchziehen das ganze Evangelium: nur hier heißt die Gemeinde die ἐκκλησία (Matth. xvi. 18) (d.h. der q^{e}hal jahwä der alttestamentlich-jüdischen Erwartung), die βασιλεία des Menschensohnes (xiii. 41); Jesu Jünger sind die freien Söhne

Gottes (xvii. 26); sie sind mit den Mysterien des Himmelreiches vertraut (xiii. 11), Augen- und Ohrenzeugen der Erfüllung dessen, was Propheten und Gerechte vergeblich zu sehen und hören begehrten (xiii. 16ff.); sie sind das Salz der Erde und das Licht der Welt, die Stadt auf dem Berge (v. 13). Und doch wird man allererst für das Matth.-Ev. feststellen müssen, daß trotz aller dieser Stellen eine eigentliche Ekklesiologie, orientiert an der Kirche als einer selbständigen, empirisch umgrenzten Größe nur in sparsamsten Anfängen zu erkennen ist. Der Fülle christologischer Titel und Aussagen entspricht in keiner Weise eine ebensolche Zahl ekklesiologischer Begriffe und Worte. Niemals heißt es: ihr seid 'das wahre Israel', die 'Heiligen', die 'Erwählten', die 'Gemeinde des Neuen Bundes'. Selbstbezeichnungen, wie wir sie aus der Damaskus-Schrift und den neu aufgefundenen Texten vom Toten Meer, aber auch aus dem Urchristentum kennen, finden sich im Matth.-Ev. nicht. Auch fehlen alle Anzeichen besonderer Ämter, wie sie etwa die 'Sektenrede' in genau abgestuftem hierarchischem Aufbau erkennen läßt.[1] Man wird solche Angaben zwar in einer Schrift, die zur Gattung der Evangelien gehört, von vornherein nicht suchen, doch ließen sie sich wenigstens dort, wo für die Durchführung der Gemeindedisziplin Anweisungen gegeben werden, durchaus vermuten (c. xviii). Aber auch hier fehlen sie, und das Verbot, in der Gemeinde Jesu einzelne als 'Rabbi', 'Vater' und 'Führer' zu betiteln, ist ausdrücklich ausgesprochen (xxiii. 8ff.). Auf Schritt und Tritt bestätigt das Matth.-Ev., daß die von ihm repräsentierte Gemeinde sich vom Judentum noch nicht gelöst hat. Die Messianität Jesu und die Gültigkeit seiner Lehre werden darum, wie wir sahen, noch durchgängig im Rahmen des Judentums vertreten und verteidigt, und die Jüngerschaft in dem Wort xxiii. 34, in dem bezeichnenderweise ein Sophia-Spruch Jesus in den Mund gelegt wird (vgl. Lk. xi. 49), nur mit alttestamentlich-jüdischen Ausdrücken als die von Jesus ausgesandten Propheten, Weisen und Schriftgelehrten bezeichnet. Der Kampf gegen Israel ist noch ein Kampf intra muros.

[1] Immerhin kann man aus der Polemik gegen falsche Lehrer (v. 18f.) und falsche Propheten (vii. 15ff. u.ö.), aus der Erwähnung von προφῆται, σοφοί und γραμματεῖς (xxiii. 34), aus der gewichtigen Hervorhebung der zwölf Apostel (x. 1f.) und des Petrus (xvi. 17ff.) und aus dem Verbot xxiii. 8ff. erschließen, daß die Gemeinde nicht ohne Ordnung und Träger bestimmter Funktionen war. Näheres s. Kilpatrick a.a.O., pp. 124ff.

So bleibt der Kirchenbegriff des Matth. der jüdischen Tradition verhaftet, zugleich aber bleibt er in Richtung auf die Völkerwelt eigentümlich geöffnet. Er entspricht darin der Christologie des Evangeliums: Jesus ist der messianische König Israels, zu den verlorenen Schafen vom Hause Israel gesandt (xv. 24), als Auferstandener aber betraut mit der ἐξουσία über Himmel und Erde, der nun durch seine Jünger alle Völker in seine Jüngerschaft rufen läßt (xxviii. 19) und als kommender Menschensohn sie richten wird (xxv. 31 ff.).

Die geläufigste Jüngerbezeichnung in Matth.-Ev. ist wie in den anderen Evangelien οἱ μαθηταί, der Korrelatbegriff zu διδάσκαλος.[1] Der Evangelist entnimmt diese Begriffe der ihm vorgegebenen christlichen Tradition. Ihre Abkunft aus dem Judentum ist bekannt; sie enthalten als solche nichts spezifisch Christliches, sondern knüpfen unmittelbar an die im Rabbinat ausgebildete Schulterminologie an. Freilich haben beide Begriffe längst vor Matth. einen neuen Inhalt bekommen. Jesu Jüngerschaft entsteht nicht auf Grund eines freien Anschlusses an einen Lehrer, sondern auf Grund der von Jesus ausgehenden Berufung in seine Nachfolge. Jesus selbst ist nicht um seiner Thora-Kenntnis willen für seine Jünger Autorität und nur Mittel zum Zweck der Erwerbung entsprechender Gesetzesweisheit. Die Stellung des μαθητής ist auch nicht ein Durchgangsstadium, darauf zielend, daß er selbst ein διδάσκαλος wird (xxiii. 8 ff.), sondern bezeichnet ein dauerndes Verhältnis zu Jesus. Nirgends diskutiert darum Jesus mit seinen Jüngern; seine Teilnehmer bei Gesetzes-Debatten sind immer seine Gegner. Auch werden die Jünger nicht zu Tradenten der von ihm hinterlassenen, von seiner Person abzulösenden Lehre, sondern — obwohl dieser Ausdruck bei Matth. sich noch nicht findet — zu seinen Zeugen.

Alle diese auch sonst für die Evangelien charakteristischen Züge im Begriff des μαθητής sind auch im Matth.-Ev. erkennbar. Nicht die Lehre Jesu, wie die Bergpredigt sie enthält, wird zum Motiv für die Jünger, in seine Nachfolge zu treten. Vielmehr geht ihre Berufung voraus, und die Unterscheidung zwischen der Jesus umgebenden Volksmenge und den Jüngern steht an ihrem Eingang. So ist der Auftrag der Jünger in der Missionsrede zunächst auch kein anderer

[1] Zum folgenden vgl. die Artikel διδάσκαλος und μαθητής von Rengstorf, *Th.W.* II, S. 154 ff. u. IV, S. 444 ff.

als dieser, die von Jesus in Vollmacht angekündigte Nähe des Gottesreiches auszurichten (κηρύσσειν x. 7), nicht seine Gesetzesauslegung zu tradieren; von ihm sind sie betraut mit der ἐξουσία über die unreinen Geister. Selbst da, wo sie wirklich mit der Lehre beauftragt werden, 'zu halten alles, was ich euch geboten habe' (xxviii. 20), geht der Ruf μαθητεύσατε πάντα τὰ ἔθνη voraus, begründet mit der Auferstehung Jesu und seiner Macht über Himmel und Erde, also seiner Kyrios-Würde. Und die Lehre seiner Gebote verbindet sich nicht mit der Berufung auf ihn als einen maßgeblichen Rabbi der Vergangenheit, sondern geschieht unter der Verheißung des Erhöhten: 'Ich bin bei euch alle Tage bis zur Vollendung der Welt' (xxviii. 20, vgl. xviii. 20).[1]

Diesem Verständnis der Jüngerschaft und ihres Verhältnisses zu Jesus entsprechen sehr konsequent weitere Eigentümlichkeiten des Matth. So wenn nur er (x. 25) die allgemeine Sentenz 'der Jünger ist nicht über den Meister' in dem parallelen Satz fortführt: 'und der Knecht nicht über seinen Herrn' und mit x. 25 b zeigt, daß dies nicht nur im Sinne einer allgemeinen Wahrheit, sondern von Jesus als dem Κύριος und οἰκοδεσπότης verstanden sein will. Jesus hört damit auf, ein διδάσκαλος im jüdischen Sinne zu sein.

Sehr bezeichnend wird von da aus die Tatsache, daß Matth. zwar den Titel διδάσκαλος und ῥαββί reichlich verwendet, aber niemals als Anrede aus dem Munde seiner Jünger, mit einer Ausnahme — Judas Ischariot[2]. διδάσκαλε nennen ihn die Pharisäer und Fremde. Seine Jünger nennen ihn κύριε.[3] Diese Beobachtung wiegt umso mehr, als die vorgegebene Tradition, wie Mk. zeigt, noch häufig und unbefangen die Anrede διδάσκαλε oder ῥαββί den Jüngern in den Mund legt. (Mk. iv. 38; ix. 5; ix. 38; x. 35; xiii. 1; auch Lk. macht von ihr Gebrauch, z.B. xxi. 7, wenn er nicht dafür den für griechische Ohren verständlichen Terminus ἐπιστάτης wählt, Lk. v. 5; viii. 24, 45; ix. 33, 49; xvii. 13.) Matth. dagegen ändert konsequent in κύριε (vgl. viii. 25 und Mk. iv. 38; xvii. 4 und Mk. ix. 5; xx. 33 und

[1] Die Herrenworte lassen sich darum niemals irgendwelchen 'Pirke Aboth' zuzählen.

[2] Vgl. xxvi. 49 und xxvi. 25; beachte, wie hier zwischen der Anrede κύριε seitens der andern Jünger (xxvi. 22) und ῥαββί bei Judas unterschieden wird. Mk. und Lk. bieten keine Parallele.

[3] Von Rengstorf *Th.W.* II, S. 156 übersehen; dagegen von Foerster *Th.W.* III, S. 1092 richtig beobachtet.

Mk. x. 51; ῥαββί Mk. xi. 21, wird ausgelassen). Die, die nicht zu den Jüngern gehören, sagen zu diesen 'euer Meister' (ix. ii; xvii. 24); ebenso wird er von den Jüngern Juden gegenüber als 'der Meister' bezeichnet (xxvi. 18), aber innerhalb der Jüngerschaft reicht dieser Titel für ihn nicht zu, sondern nur der Kyrios-Titel.

Es ist freilich umstritten, ob man die κύριε-Anrede der Jünger ohne weiteres als Hoheitsnamen verstehen darf, oder ob sie nicht einfach den Sinn einer respektvollen Anrede an einen Menschen hat. Sicher wird man, wie schon Bousset betont,[1] zu unterscheiden haben zwischen der durchaus vereinzelten Wendung ὁ κύριος, die nur Matth. xxi. 3 — Mk. xi. 3 für Jesus sich findet, und der Anrede κύριε, die 'einen viel weiteren Umfang' hat und im N.T. nicht nur gegenüber Gott, Christus und himmlischen Wesen, sondern, wie gerade Stellen des Matth.-Ev. zeigen (xiii. 27; xxv. 11, 20, 22, 24; xxi. 30), auch zwischen Knecht und Herrn, Sohn und Vater sich findet. Bousset stellt darum für Matth. fest, daß sein Sprachgebrauch aufs ganze gesehen der des Mk. sei. Nur die Anrede κύριε (nicht im titularen Sinn) sei an einer Reihe von Stellen eingedrungen. Tatsächlich zeigt etwa x. 24, daß das Verhältnis des Knechtes zum Herrn wie das des Schülers zu seinem Lehrer in einem allgemeinmenschlichen Sinn für die Stellung der Jünger wesentlich bleibt. Dennoch ist im Matth.-Ev. κύριε durchaus nicht nur Ausdruck menschlichen Respekts, sondern als Hoheitsname gemeint. Es ist die Anrede, die Jesus als wundertätigem *Heiland* zuteil wird (viii. 2, 6, 8; ix. 28; xv. 22, 25; xvii. 15; xx. 30, 33), sei es aus dem Munde Leidender, die ihn um 'Erbarmen' anflehen,[2] sei es aus dem Munde der Jünger, die ihn um 'Rettung' anrufen (viii. 25; xiv. 30) oder sonst mit dieser Anrede seine Hoheit aussprechen (xvi. 22; xvii. 4; xviii. 21; xxvi. 22). Vor allem aber gilt sie Jesus als dem kommenden *Weltrichter* (vii. 21f.; xxv. 11, 37, 44). Auch da, wo ὁ κύριος im Gleichnis gebraucht wird und also zunächst einen irdischen Herrn bezeichnet, spielt der Begriff doch sofort von der Bild- in die Sachhälfte hinüber und wird zum Titel des Menschensohnes. So deutlich z.B. Matth. xxiv. 42: 'Wachet, denn ihr wißt nicht, an welchem Tag *euer Herr* kommt', das (vgl. *v.* 44) an den Anfang des Gleichnisses

[1] W. Bousset, *Kyrios Christos*, S. 79f.

[2] ἐλέησον (ix. 27; xv. 22; xvii. 15; xx. 30), wiederholt in Verbindung mit dem Davidssohn-Titel (ix. 27; xv. 22; xx. 30).

vom nächtlichen Einbrecher gestellt wird (wo vom Hausherrn im irdisch-biblischen Sinn geredet ist).[1]

Aus dem dargelegten Befund ergibt sich: Titel und Anrede Jesu als des κύριος haben bei Matth. also durchaus den Charakter eines göttlichen Hoheitsnamens. Die Legitimation aus der Schrift liefert ihm dafür Ps. cx. 1 (xxii. 41 ff.).

Trotz der deutlich erkennbaren Distanzierung vom Titel des διδάσκαλος und seiner Überhöhung durch den κύριος-Titel überall dort, wo Matth. das Verhältnis der Jünger zu Jesus nicht von außen, sondern von innen her zum Ausdruck bringt, bleibt jedoch οἱ μαθηταί *die* eigentliche Bezeichnung der Jüngerschaft bis hin zum Missionsbefehl des Auferstandenen. Man wird darin nicht nur ein Haften an der nun einmal vorgegebenen Überlieferung, die das Verhältnis Jesu und seiner Jünger in jüdischen Kategorien ausspricht, zu erblicken haben; vielmehr bleibt der Begriff des Jüngers für Matth., nachdem die christliche Tradition ihn bereits mit neuen Inhalten gefüllt hatte (Nachfolge, Leidensbereitschaft etc.), als ekklesiologischer terminus erschöpfend und gültig, weil er beispielhaft zugleich mit der bleibenden Bindung an Jesus und seine Lehre, — dem beständigen 'lernen von ihm' (xi. 29), — das Motiv der Zukünftigkeit der βασιλεία und des Gerichtes festhält und ausspricht. οἱ μαθηταί ist die Bezeichnung der Jünger hier und jetzt, sie sind Jünger des *einen* Meisters und untereinander 'Brüder' (xxiii. 8), von ihm zur Nachfolge berufen und zur neuen Gerechtigkeit aufgerufen. In den Zukunftsaussagen dagegen wird nicht mehr von den 'Jüngern' gesprochen, nicht 'die Jünger', sondern 'die Gerechten' werden leuchten wie die Sonne im Reich ihres Vaters (xiii. 43) und im Gericht zur Rechten des Menschensohnes stehen (xxv. 31 ff., 37). Und nicht 'die Jünger', sondern 'die Erwählten' werden am Tage des Menschensohnes von seinen Engeln gesammelt (xxiv. 31). 'Erwählt' aber sind nicht die Glieder der Kirche schlechthin, sondern die υἱοὶ τῆς βασιλείας, die auf dem Acker der Welt als der gute Same ausgesät sind neben dem Unkraut, das auf demselben Felde

[1] Die Erfahrung der Verzögerung der Parusie des κύριος ist mit unmißverständlicher Allegorisierung in die Gleichnisse vom bösen Knecht (xxiv. 48) und von den anvertrauten Talenten (xxv. 19) — wie in das Gleichnis von den zehn Jungfrauen — hineingezeichnet. Der schon in den Gleichnissen selbst anhebenden Allegorisierung entspricht an ihrem Schluß die Androhung des ewigen Gerichtes, die jeweils den Gleichnisrahmen sprengt (xxiv. 51; xxv. 30).

der Teufel gesät hat (xiii. 36ff.).[1] Wir haben ständig darauf geachtet, wie dieses Motiv der erst zukünftigen Scheidung das ganze Evangelium beherrscht. Es spricht sich, worauf wir schon hinwiesen, mit aller wünschenswerten Klarheit im Matth.-Schluß des Winzergleichnisses aus, das noch bei Mk. xii. 1 ff. offensichtlich die *geschehene* Verwerfung Israels und die *erfolgte* Übertragung des Weinbergs an andere zum Inhalt hat, bei Matth. dagegen ins Zukünftige übersetzt wird, so daß nun die Jüngerschaft selbst in das Gericht einbezogen und ihr damit die vorerst noch offene Frage gestellt wird, ob sie das Volk ist, das seine Früchte bringt (xxi. 43). Nicht anders der von Matth. angefügte Schluß xxii. 11: auch hier wird am Ende die im Gleichnis vom Hochzeitsmahl dargestellte, geschehene und erfolgte Entscheidung überraschend in Richtung auf die noch ausstehende Zukunft des Gerichtes wieder geöffnet. Wie stark sich damit die Matth.-Perikope gegenüber Lk. xiv. 15–24 verschiebt, ist offenkundig.

Die gegenwärtige Kirche ist nach Matth. damit, wie xiii. 36ff. sagt, die βασιλεία des Menschensohnes, aber nicht identisch mit der Schar derer, die in die Gottesherrschaft eingehen. Die Terminologie dieser deutlich sekundären allegorischen Deutung der Unkraut-Parabel[2] ist in vieler Hinsicht bemerkenswert und sicher, wie Jeremias mit minutiösen Nachweisen gezeigt hat,[3] des Matth. eigenes Werk. Sie setzt die gerade für ihn selbstverständliche Gleichsetzung des irdischen Jesus mit dem Menschensohn voraus (der Sämann = der Menschensohn, *v.* 37), sie redet von der Kirche als seiner irdischen βασιλεία (*v.* 41)[4] — eine Wendung, die terminologisch sich sogar mit der eigenen Sprache des Matth. stößt,[5] wenn sie auch sachlich seiner Anschauung entspricht — und verwendet *v.* 41 den Titel

[1] Vgl. besonders xxii. 14 (xx. 16 *v.l.*).

[2] Diese hat zur Pointe die in der Auslegung übergangene Geduld.

[3] A.a.O. S. 63ff.

[4] So mit Recht Klostermann z.St., Dodd, *The Parables*, S. 183, Jeremias, S. 65. Bultmann bestreitet unverständlicherweise die Gleichsetzung mit der Kirche und versteht ἐκ τ. βασιλ. αὐτοῦ: aus dem *dann* erscheinenden Reiche (*Gesch. der syn. Trad.*, S. 203, A. 1). Zu dem *dann* erscheinenden Reiche gehören jedoch *nur* die υἱοὶ τῆς βασιλείας (*v.* 38), es ist das Reich ihres Vaters, nicht das Reich des Menschensohns. Vgl. z.St. auch C. H. Dodd, 'Matthew and Paul', *Exp. Tim.*, 1947, p. 294.

[5] xvi. 28 (vgl. auch xx. 21) ist von dem kommenden Menschensohn die Rede, der mit seiner (künftigen) Herrschaft erscheint.

υἱὸς τοῦ ἀνθρώπου anders als *v*. 37 (aber ebenso selbstverständlich) für den kommenden Weltrichter, hier also deutlich wieder seine irdische und künftige Gestalt und Funktion differenzierend und zugleich verbindend. Dieser christologischen Anschauung entspricht die Differenzierung und zugleich die Zuordnung von Kirche und kommender βασιλεία, mit anderen Worten der schon erfolgten Berufung der vielen und der zukünftigen Auswahl der wenigen Gerechten.

In den Zusammenhang dieser Matth. xiii. 36–43 ausgesprochenen, speziell für Matth. charakteristischen Anschauungen über Kirche und Enderwartung stellt sich auch sein berühmtes ἐκκλησία-Wort (xvi. 17–19). Die zahlreichen exegetischen und überlieferungsgeschichtlichen Probleme dieser Stelle können hier nicht erörtert werden. Wie weit das Urteil über die Echtheit des ἐκκλησία-Wortes heute in der Forschung auseinandergeht, zeigen zwei Sätze aus den neuesten Veröffentlichungen zur Frage. Während O. Cullmann in seinem jüngst erschienenen Petrusbuch die von ihm bereits früher vertretene These,[1] 'die Bestreitung der Echtheit von Matth. xvi. 17ff. könne wissenschaftlich nicht gerechtfertigt werden',[2] wiederholt und verteidigt, urteilt H. von Campenhausen:[3] 'daß die Kirchengründung auf Petrus im Munde Jesu undenkbar ist, sollte trotz der neueren Rettungsversuche nicht in Zweifel gezogen werden.' Auch ich halte den Spruch für ein nachösterliches Wort, aus vielen, oft und zur Genüge dargelegten Gründen, unbeschadet der sprachlichen und geschichtlichen Indizien, die für sein hohes Alter sprechen. Gegen die Argumente, die neuerdings vor allem Oepke[4] und Cullmann für die Echtheit des Wortes anführen, spricht m.E. vor allem die Tatsache, daß die ἐκκλησία von Matth. xvi. 18 sich nicht einfach mit dem traditionellen jüdischen Gottesvolk-Gedanken erfassen läßt, sondern durchaus institutionellen Charakter trägt, charakterisiert durch Lehr- und Disziplinargewalt eines bestimmten Apostels. Sie

[1] *Königsherrschaft Christi und Kirche*, S. 22.

[2] *Petrus* (1952), S. 214; R. Bultmann, 'Die Frage der Echtheit von Matth. xvi. 17–19' (*Theol. Blätter*, 1941, S. 265ff.) nimmt sie zum Ausgang seiner zum entgegengesetzten Ergebnis führenden Untersuchung. Bei ihm wie bei Cullmann u. Oepke, 'Der Herrnspruch über die Kirche Matth. xvi. 17–19 in der neuesten Forschung' (*Studia Theologica*, 1948/50, S. 110ff.) findet sich ein sorgfältiges Referat über die neuere Diskussion.

[3] *Kirchliches Amt und geistliche Vollmacht* (1953), S. 140f.

[4] Siehe Note Nr. 2.

ist, wenngleich eine eschatologische Größe, einer Zeit zugeordnet, die vom Zeitpunkt der Szene selbst aus Zukunft ist (das dreimalige Futur in *vv.* 18f. οἰκοδομήσω, οὐ κατισχύσουσιν, δώσω), gleichwohl aber eine irdische Zukunft, zu unterscheiden von der Zukunft der kommenden βασιλεία und des künftigen Gerichtes; auf diese Zukunft (des neuen Äon) bezieht sich erst das doppelte ἔσται (δεδεμένον-λελυμένον) ἐν τοῖς οὐρανοῖς (*v.* 19). Petrus erhält als Fels der Kirche das Schlüsselamt also für die Zeit nach der Auferstehung, aber vor der Parusie. Dies ist die Zeit der Kirche, die Jesus 'meine Kirche' nennt und der er die Verheißung des Bestehens gegen die Mächte des Todes gibt.[1] Die Kirche also ist irdisch, nicht himmlisch, von der βασιλεία τῶν οὐρανῶν unterschieden, aber engstens ihr zugeordnet, weil ihre Lehr- und Disziplinarentscheidungen, ihr Binden und Lösen, in der kommenden βασιλεία ihre Bestätigung finden, 'ratifiziert' werden.[2]

Matth. interpretiert diesen Text wieder mit dem einfachen Mittel der Komposition. Zum Verständnis dieser Interpretation ist darum zunächst nach Charakter und Umfang des Kontextes zu fragen, in den Matth. den ἐκκλησία-Spruch einordnet. Ohne Frage ist dem Kontext erstlich der durch Mk. viii. 27–33 vorgegebene Abschnitt Matth. xvi. 13–23 zuzurechnen (Petrusbekenntnis und erste Leidensverkündigung), aber nicht minder der anschließende Abschnitt über die Leidensnachfolge der Jünger (Mk. viii. 34–ix. 1; Matth. xvi. 24–8). Gewiß kann man mit einigem Recht sogar xvi. 20 als Schluß der Petrusperikope bezeichnen und mit dem betonten ἀπὸ τότε ἤρξατο..., *v.* 21 einen neuen Abschnitt beginnen lassen.[3] Aber diese engere Eingrenzung der Perikope darf nicht darüber hinwegtäuschen, daß schon xvi. 21–3, aber nicht minder xvi. 24–8, noch in engem sachlichen Zusammenhang zu dem Petruswort stehen. Der xvi. 21 markierte Einschnitt hat dann die Funktion, sozusagen 'Text' und 'Interpretation' voneinander abzusetzen, wobei selbstverständlich, was kaum gesagt zu werden braucht, der Begriff der Interpretation

[1] Der Ansturm der Todesmächte ist dabei fraglos im Sinne der Wehen und Drangsale zu verstehen, die der Erscheinung des Menschensohnes und seiner Herrschaft vorangehen (xvi. 28; xxiv. 8, 29ff.).

[2] Kirche und Gottesreich dürfen also ganz und gar nicht als gleichzeitig nebeneinander bestehende Reiche verstanden werden, sondern lösen zeitlich einander ab. Die Kirche wird so auf das kommende Reich und Gericht ausgerichtet.

[3] Vgl. H. Lehmann, 'du bist Petrus...', *Ev. Theol.* (1953), S. 47ff.

cum grano salis zu verstehen ist, da sie ja faktisch in der Anfügung anderer Traditionsstücke besteht, die auch ihre eigene Thematik und Pointe haben. Die von uns behauptete Bedeutung des Zusammenhanges von xvi. 13–28 muß zunächst genauer begründet werden.

Schon Mk. hat hier dem Matth., aufs beste vorgearbeitet; denn er bietet viii. 27–ix. 1 einen durchaus sachlich bestimmten, theologisch durchreflektierten Zusammenhang: (1) (viii. 27–33): Petrusbekenntnis und Schweigegebot; stattdessen offene Ankündigung des Leidens und Auferstehens des Menschensohnes; Zurückweisung des Petrus (beachte die Rahmung von viii. 27–33 durch die Stichworte οἱ ἄνθρωποι, *v.* 27 und τὰ τῶν ἀνθρώπων, *v.* 33). (2) (viii. 34–ix. 1): die Sprüche über die Leidensnachfolge[1] der Jünger, abschließend mit der Ankündigung des in Herrlichkeit kommenden Menschensohnes und des baldigen Kommens der βασιλεία.[2]

Matth. ändert diese Komposition nicht, strafft und verstärkt aber den Zusammenhang, indem er durch seine Lieblingskopula τότε[3] xvi. 13–23 und 24–8 noch enger miteinander verbindet, unter Weglassung der Volksmenge den umständlichen Neueinsatz von Mk. viii. 34 vermeidet und am Schluß die Ankündigung der Parusie des Menschensohnes in Herrlichkeit — zum Gericht nach den Werken — zwiefach ausspricht (xvi. 27!).

Blickt man zunächst auf den engeren Kontext (Matth. xvi. 13–23; Mk. viii. 27–33), so ist sofort deutlich, daß Matth. dem Petrus-Bekenntnis einen völlig anderen Sinn gibt und eine andere Wertung zuteil werden läßt als Mk. Streng genommen ist nur die Matthäische Perikope als 'Petrus-Bekenntnis' zu bezeichnen, während man die Marcinische etwa mit 'Abweisung des Petrus-Bekenntnisses' überschreiben sollte.[4] Der Skopus bei Mk., dem Theologen des Messiasgeheimnisses, ist der: Jesus ist jetzt der dem Leiden und Auferstehen erst entgegengehende Menschensohn, das Bekenntnis zu ihm als Messias

[1] Beachte das verbindende Stichwort ὀπίσω μου, viii. 33, 34; J. Sundwall, *Die Zusammensetzung des Markusevangeliums* (1934), S. 56.

[2] Die Verknüpfung von Leidensankündigung und Nachfolge in Niedrigkeit wiederholt sich in ix. 31ff., 33ff.; x. 32ff., 35ff.

[3] τότε zur Verknüpfung von einander folgenden Perikopen bekanntlich bei Matth. beliebt und häufig. Vgl. z.B. iii. 13 und iv. 1, wo es dem Evangelisten deutlich um einen *sachlichen* Zusammenhang geht, wie an der ersten Stelle das Stichwort βαπτίζειν (iii. 11, 13ff.), an der zweiten das Stichwort υἱὸς τοῦ θεοῦ (iii. 17; iv. 3, 6) zeigt.

[4] Vgl. dazu Lehmann a.a.O., S. 44ff.

kann und darf erst nach Ostern erklingen.[1] Für Matth. dagegen hat die Idee des Messiasgeheimnisses nicht mehr dieselbe bestimmende Kraft, obwohl das Motiv nicht einfach preisgegeben wird. Petri Bekenntnis wird darum zunächst bestätigt und ist der Grund, ihn zum Felsen der Kirche zu machen.

Die Seligpreisung des Apostels, die Verheissung der Kirchengründung auf ihn als Felsen und die schroffe Zurückweisung Petri unmittelbar darnach stehen nun bei Matth. in äußerster Spannung zueinander, die einen sachlichen Zusammenhang zwischen dem ersten und dem zweiten Petrus-Spruch überhaupt zu zerreißen droht. Gleichwohl wird man nicht sagen dürfen, daß Matth. nach dem Ekklesia-Wort an Petrus nur äußerlich in die Bahn des vorgegebenen Mk.-Zusammenhanges einlenkt. Er nimmt ihn sehr bewußt auf, ja er tilgt ihn nicht nur nicht wie Lukas, sondern profiliert die Szene noch schärfer als sogar Mk., wie die entrüstete Entgegnung Petri auf diese Leidensansage und erst recht Jesu Antwort: ὕπαγε ὀπίσω μου, σατανᾶ· σκάνδαλον εἶ ἐμοῦ ('Du willst mich verführen')[2] zeigt. Die Frage nach dem inneren Zusammenhang der ganzen Perikope ist also durchaus geboten; wir haben uns mit der Feststellung einer äußeren Verknüpfung disparater Überlieferungsstücke nicht zufrieden zu geben. Dann aber ergibt sich: die schon im Mk.-Text deutliche Dialektik zwischen der Christus-Würde Jesu und seinem Leiden als Menschensohn ist von Matth. in keiner Weise aufgehoben oder nur abgemildert. Aber sie ist für ihn kein apologetisches Theologumenon mehr, sondern für die Kirche selbst von höchster Bedeutung. Nun gilt — anders als bei Mk.: der, der jetzt schon Christus und Gottessohn *ist*, ist es als der hier auf Erden leidende Menschensohn. Als solcher stellt er auch seine Jünger in die Leidensnachfolge (xvi. 24ff.; bei Matth. reine Jüngerrede). Eben dieser leidende Gottes- und Menschensohn aber ist der in Bälde kommende Menschensohn-Weltrichter, der 'einem jeden nach seinem Tun vergelten wird' (xvi. 27f.).

Fragt man, was dieser ganze Zusammenhang für die Interpretation speziell des ἐκκλησία-Wortes ergibt, so wird man antworten müssen:

[1] Vgl. W. Wrede, *Das Messiasgeheimnis*, S. 115ff.

[2] σκάνδαλον, σκανδαλίζεσθαι sind wieder von Matth. am häufigsten gebrauchte termini, wiederholt verwendet für Verführung und Abfall *in der Gemeinde* als endzeitliche Erscheinungen (so xiii. 21, 41; xviii. 7; xxiv. 10).

est ist offenbar nicht nur überlieferungsgeschichtlich, sondern im Sinne des Evangelisten theologisch bedeutsam, daß Matth. das in nachösterliche Zeit weisende, möglicherweise sogar auf eine Ostergeschichte zurückgehende Wort in der vorösterlichen Geschichte Jesu und gerade im Rahmen des von Mk. vorgegebenen Zusammenhanges verankert. Die Kirche nach Ostern mit ihrem Leben und ihrem von Jesus autorisierten Schlüsselamt wird so unter das Lebens- und Leidensgesetz des irdischen Jesus gestellt. Sollen die von der Kirche getroffenen Entscheidungen in kommenden Gericht gültig sein, so ist klar, daß Sündenvergeben und Sündenbehalten damit unter den Maßstab gestellt werden, von dem xvi. 24–7 (κατὰ τὴν πρᾶξιν αὐτοῦ) reden: Leidensnachfolge und Lebenshingabe.[1]

Diese Interpretation wird bestätigt durch den Zusammenhang, in den Matth. in der Gemeinderede c. xviii das Wort vom Schlüsselamt stellt (dort ist die Gesamtgemeinde mit ihm betraut): deutlich ist hier mit der in c. xviii ausgesprochenen Forderung der Umkehr und Niedrigkeit, der Vermeidung des Ärgernisses, dem Gebot radikalen Gehorsams und unbegrenzter Bereitschaft zur Versöhnung unmißverständlich die Norm angegeben, unter der das ganze Leben der Jüngerschaft und damit auch die xviii. 18 ihr befohlene Verwaltung des Schlüsselamtes steht.

Matth. xvi. 17–19 darf also nicht isoliert, sondern will im Gesamtzusammenhang von xvi. 13–28 verstanden werden. Nun erst zeigt sich, daß das Wort vom Schlüsselamt des Petrus (bzw. der Kirche) nicht nur die Statuierung der formalen Autorität der kirchlichen Entscheidungen ausspricht, die ipso facto im Weltgericht übernommen werden, sondern daß es die Einsetzung des Schlüsselamtes durch den Messias-Menschensohn im Blick auf das von ihm nach klaren, unmißverständlichen Maßstäben in Bälde ausgeübte Gericht zum Inhalt hat. Das in xvi. 17–19 ausgesprochene Kirchenverständnis hat in der Christologie des Kontextes xvi. 13–28 seine Entsprechung

[1] Zu Matth. xvi. 19 bemerkt H. v. Campenhausen, a.a.O. S. 137, durchaus zutreffend: 'Das Wort geht nicht etwa von einer schon feststehenden himmlischen Entscheidung aus, nach der sich die Kirche ihrerseits zu richten hätte, sondern es setzt umgekehrt bei der vollmächtigen Wirklichkeit dieses kirchlichen Urteilens und Entscheidens ein und verheißt, daß Gott ihm am jüngsten Tage beitreten, es also gültig anerkennen und "ratifizieren" werde.' Doch schließt das in keiner Weise aus, daß Matth., durch Komposition interpretierend, das überkommene Logion zu dem künftigen Gericht und dem dort geltenden Maßstab in Beziehung setzt.

und Begründung. Von dem hier leidenden und auferstehenden und seine Jünger in diesem Äon in die Leidensnachfolge rufenden Christus kommt die Kirche her, in der Person des Petrus mit den Schlüsseln des Himmelreiches betraut, als Kirche gewappnet gegen die Mächte des Todes, aber in allen ihren Gliedern noch in der Erwartung des künftigen Gerichtes nach den Werken.

Unsere Untersuchung galt der theologischen Eigenart und Thematik des Matth.-Ev. Sie versuchte zu zeigen, in wie hohem Maße der erste Evangelist Interpret der von ihm gesammelten und geordneten Tradition ist. Dabei dürfte deutlich geworden sein, daß Tradition und theologische Konzeption in einem Wechselverhältnis stehen. Ebenso wie die Theologie in den Dienst der Überlieferung gestellt ist, gilt auch das Umgekehrte.

Matth. erscheint in seinem Ev. sicherlich allererst als Repräsentant einer Gemeinde. Indes genügt es nicht, sein Evangelium nur als Niederschlag einer Gemeindetheologie zu verstehen. Die Sorgfalt und Planmäßigkeit seiner Arbeit weist nachdrücklich auf eine individuelle Gestalt der urchristlichen Literaturgeschichte, auch wenn man auf Namenjägerei und biographisches Nachspüren verzichten wird. Will man ihn charakterisieren, so wird man ihn am besten mit den Worten seines Evangeliums einen Schriftgelehrten nennen, 'der ein Jünger für die Himmelsherrschaft wurde und, einem Hausherrn gleich, aus seinem Schatz Neues und Altes austeilt' (xiii. 52).[1]

Mit der Wendung 'Neues und Altes' sind der Forschung eine Fülle von Fragen gestellt, deren Lösung sie seit langem beschäftigt und weiter beschäftigen wird: nach den literarischen Quellen, die das Evangelium bearbeitet, wie nach Art und Zweck der ihnen voraufgehenden mündlichen Tradition; sodann die Frage nach dem Verhältnis des Evangeliums zur Gestalt, Botschaft und Geschichte des historischen Jesus. Alle diese Probleme lassen sich nicht von den weiteren Fragen lösen: nach der Abhängigkeit des Matth. vom palästinischen, aber auch — nicht zu unterschätzen — vom Diaspora-Judentum,[2] entsprechend nach seiner Stellung zur palästinischen und zur hellenistischen Urgemeinde und seinem Platz in der Geschichte

[1] Der Dativ τῇ βασ. τ. οὐρ. kann doch wohl nur ein dat. commodi sein.

[2] Auch sein Verhältnis zu den jüdischen Sekten, deren Erforschung jüngst in ein neues Stadium getreten ist, wird neu geklärt werden müssen.

der werdenden Großkirche und des kirchlichen und häretischen Judenchristentums.[1] Damit hängt engstens die schwierige Frage nach dem Kirchengebiet zusammen, aus dem Matth. stammt.[2]

Alles das sind Fragen, die keineswegs in Bausch und Bogen als hoffnungslos und theologisch belanglos abgetan und in billiger Weise dem Interesse an dem 'Kerygma' oder dem 'Lehrbegriff' des Evangeliums geopfert werden dürfen.[3] Haben wir hier alle diese Fragen weithin ausgeklammert, so nur darum, weil die Untersuchung unseres Problems, ohne eine bewußte Konzentration nicht durchführbar, auch für die Beantwortung jener Fragen eine unerläßliche Voraussetzung ist.[4]

[1] Mit Recht stellen J. Weiß, *Das Urchristentum*, S. 584 und H.-J. Schoeps, *Theologie und Geschichte des Judenchristentums*, S. 64f., 343ff., das Matth.-Ev. in die Nähe des Jakobusbriefes; beide werden von Schoeps richtig vom häretischen Ebionitismus abgesetzt. Zu Matth. und Paulus vgl. C. H. Dodd, 'Matthew and Paul', *The Expository Times* (1947), S. 293ff.

[2] Offenbar kommt nur ein Gebiet in Frage, in dem ebenso wie das Nochverbleiben der Christen im Verband des Judentums und das Fortwirken palästinischer Traditionen (jüdischer und christlicher) auch ein starker diasporajüdischer und hellenistisch-christlicher Einfluß vorstellbar sind. Gegen Jerusalem und Judäa selbst spricht schon die archaische, in der Jerusalemer Gemeinde schon sehr bald nicht mehr mögliche Petrustradition, die Matth. erhalten hat. Vieles spricht daher für Syrien (in einem weiten Sinne) doch wird dann das Erstaunen nur um so größer, was alles in diesem Gebiet von Paulus über Lukas (und Johannes?) bis zu Ignatius Raum hatte. Kilpatrick tritt mit beachtlichen Gründen für eine phoenizische Küstenstadt ein. A.a.O., S. 124ff.

[3] Diese Bemerkung richtet sich gegen eine in Deutschland verbreitete 'Stimmung' und will auch einem Mißverständnis der Absichten meiner Arbeit vorbeugen.

[4] Das Manuskript dieses Aufsatzes wurde bereits im Herbst 1953 abgeschlossen. Ich kann darum auf die später erschienenen lehrreichen Untersuchungen von K. Stendahl, *The School of St Matthew* (Uppsala, 1954), und H. Ljungman, *Das Gesetz Erfüllen* (Lund, 1954), hier nur hinweisen. Doch darf ich bemerken daß die letztere mich nicht in der Auffassung, daß Matth. v. 17 sich auf Jesu Lehre und iii. 15 sich auf Jesu Gehorsam bezieht, irre gemacht hat. Die These von Stendahl, hinter dem Matth.-Ev. stünde eine christliche Schriftgelehrten-Schule, ist mir durchaus überzeugend. Doch verrät die Verarbeitung der christlichen Tradition im Matth.-Ev. zugleich ein hohes Maß individueller theologischer Arbeit. Das meines Erachtens richtige und wichtige Ergebnis der Arbeit von Stendahl bleibt davon unberührt: 'Thus the Matthaean school must be understood as a school for teachers and church leaders, and for this reason the literary work of that school assumes the form of a manual for teaching and administration within the church' (p. 35).

LE SENS DU MOT PAROUSIE DANS L'EVANGILE DE MATTHIEU

COMPARAISON ENTRE MATTH. xxiv ET JAC. V, I–II

A. FEUILLET

DANS la plupart des écrits du Nouveau Testament, le mot παρουσία a un sens technique très précis: il désigne l'apparition du Christ à la fin des temps pour le jugement du monde entier. Dans les Evangiles, ce vocable n'est mis sur les lèvres de Jésus ou des disciples de Jésus que par Matthieu (xxiv. 3, 27, 37, 39), et l'on pense à peu près unanimement que là encore il revêt le sens de jugement final de l'humanité. On ne se donne même pas la peine de justifier cette position, tant elle paraît évidente.

C'est pourtant cette exégèse communément admise que nous voudrions ici remettre en question. A priori déjà cette interprétation de la Parousie de Matthieu à partir des Epitres pauliniennes paraît sujette à caution, car, ainsi qu'on l'a reconnu récemment,[1] le chapitre xxiv de Matthieu pris dans son ensemble ne trahit aucune dépendance par rapport au vocabulaire paulinien. C'est même le contraire qui est vrai: dans les deux Epitres aux Thessaloniciens, l'Apôtre a emprunté plusieurs traits de ses descriptions eschatologiques à l'apocalypse synoptique, qu'il paraît même avoir connue sous une forme semblable à celle que nous offre Matthieu,[2] et cette constatation devrait entrer en ligne de compte quand on traite des origines du premier évangile. Et si l'on cherche la raison pour laquelle Matthieu parle de la Parousie du Fils de l'homme, l'on est amené à songer, non pas à Paul, qui loin d'avoir introduit ce mot

[1] Dom J. Dupont, ΣΥΝ ΧΡΙΣΤΩΙ, *L'union avec le Christ suivant Saint Paul*, 1ère partie, *Avec le Christ dans la vie future* (Louvain–Paris, 1952), pp. 51–2.

[2] Cf. J. B. Orchard, 'Thessalonians and the Synoptic Gospels', *Biblica* (1938), pp. 19–42.

dans la langue chrétienne semble s'être simplement conformé à un usage déjà établi, mais bien plutôt au texte de Dan. vii. 13 où deux fois les LXX emploient le verbe πάρειμι: ὡς υἱὸς ἀνθρώπου ἤρχετο καὶ ὡς παλαιὸς ἡμερῶν παρῆν, καὶ οἱ παρεστηκότες παρῆσαν αὐτῷ. Or, notons le en passant, en ce passage-source sur le Fils de l'homme, sa venue sur les nuées n'est autre chose que l'établissement du règne messianique.

En fait l'étude objective du texte de Matthieu prouve qu'il entend le mot Parousie en un sens différent de celui qu'on lui attribue d'ordinaire. C'est ce que nous voudrions démontrer dans les pages qui suivent. Dans une première partie, nous chercherons quelle acception suggère pour le mot Parousie le contexte du premier évangile. Dans une seconde partie, nous verrons que l'Epitre de Saint Jacques apporte un précieux confirmatur à notre interprétation.

I. LA PAROUSIE DANS LE CONTEXTE DE MATTHIEU

Matthieu n'emploie qu'en trois passages le mot 'Parousie' (xxiv. 3, 27, 37–9), et ces trois textes appartiennent au grand discours eschatologique du chapitre xxiv. Nous partirons de la question des disciples qui sert d'introduction à tout le discours: τί τὸ σημεῖον τῆς σῆς παρουσίας καὶ συντελείας τοῦ αἰῶνος (v. 3).

Au premier abord il semble bien difficile d'échapper à l'impression que la Parousie dont il est ici question est le jugement final de l'humanité, puisqu'aussitôt après il est question de 'consommation du siècle' (συντέλεια τοῦ αἰῶνος), expression que parmi les évangélistes Matthieu est seul à employer, et qui ailleurs chez lui paraît toujours désigner la fin du monde au sens strict: cf. xiii. 39, 40, 49; xxviii. 20.

En réalité cette exégèse ne s'impose nullement. A priori elle est peu vraisemblable, surtout si on admet que l'évangile de Matthieu tel qu'il se présente à nous aujourd'hui n'a été définitivement rédigé qu'après la ruine de Jérusalem (comme pourraient le faire croire certains textes, par ex. xxii. 7: la ville des invités récalcitrants est brûlée, allusion à la ruine de la cité sainte qui est peut-être déjà un fait accompli). Dans ces conditions, comment l'auteur aurait-il osé rapporter une prédiction de Jésus si manifestement démentie par les faits, puisqu'elle confondait dans une même perspective destruction de Jérusalem et fin du monde? Non seulement il aurait sur ce point suivi la trace de ses prédécesseurs, mais il aurait beaucoup plus clairement qu'eux prêté cette erreur à Jésus; c'est tout le contraire qu'on attendrait. En fait les expressions 'Parousie' et 'consommation du siècle' n'imposent pas cette conclusion. Expliquons d'abord le vocable Parousie.

(*a*) *La Parousie*

Ce mot, qui dans le grec classique signifie présence, mais qui dans les papyri (à partir du IIIe siècle avant le Christ) revêt le sens de visite solennelle, joyeuse entrée d'un prince (roi empereur, magistrat)[1] est appliqué ici à la venue glorieuse du Christ, mais rien ne nous oblige à croire qu'il s'agit de son ultime venue. Dans Philadel. ix. 2, Ignace d'Antioche appelle Parousie le premier avènement du Christ, prélude de sa passion et de sa résurrection: τὴν παρουσίαν τοῦ σωτῆρος, κυρίου ἡμῶν 'Ιησοῦ Χριστοῦ, τό πάθος αὐτοῦ καί τὴν ἀνάστασιν. Les deux autres passages du même discours eschatologique de Matthieu où se rencontre le mot Parousie la montrent étroitement liée à l'annonce du châtiment du peuple juif incrédule. En xxiv. 27, la Parousie du Fils de l'homme est inséparable de l'abomination de la désolation établie dans le lieu saint. Quel que soit dans le premier évangile le caractère composite du discours eschatologique qui fond en un seul développement les deux traditions de Marc xiii et de Luc xvii. 22–37, il est clair que chez Matthieu tout comme chez ses prédécesseurs le drame comporte trois phases: les signes précurseurs de la fin, la fin (de Jérusalem), la venue du Fils de l'homme sur les nuées. Or c'est un fait très remarquable que Matthieu a situé la Parousie du Fils de l'homme antérieurement à sa venue sur les nuées et l'a identifiée, non avec la troisième phase, mais avec la seconde. Il écrit en effet 'Comme l'éclair part de l'orient et apparaît jusqu'à l'occident, ainsi en sera-t-il de la Parousie du Fils de l'homme. Où que soit le cadavre, là se rassembleront les vautours' (xxiv. 27–8). Et il ajoute: 'aussitôt après la tribulation de ces jours...'

[1] Il n'est pas du tout certain que Matthieu et même Paul, en employant le mot Parousie, veuillent faire allusion à ces joyeuses entrées. A l'encontre de L. Cerfaux, *Le Christ dans la théologie de Saint Paul* (Paris, 1951), pp. 35 ss., Dom Dupont estime que si le choix du mot παρουσία a pu être influencé par l'usage qu'on en faisait dans les milieux hellénistiques, les auteurs du Nouveau Testament lui donnent une signification qui nous renvoie exclusivement aux idées eschatologiques du judaïsme et au monde chrétien (ΣΥΝ ΧΡΙΣΤΩΙ, 1ère partie, pp. 49 ss.).

(v. 29). Ou bien Matthieu, qui passe pour posséder à un degré rare l'art de la composition, s'est ici montré d'une maladresse insigne, ou bien il faut admettre que la Parousie qu'il a en vue se confond avec 'la tribulation de ces jours', c'est à dire avec le châtiment final du peuple juif et de la ville sainte dont il est question depuis le verset 16. Et en faveur de ce dernier sens on peut rappeler les nombreux textes des Evangiles où le jugement des Juifs est prédit et présenté comme une venue du Fils de l'homme (Matth. x. 23; xxiii. 38–9, et aussi, croyons-nous, xvi. 28); comme l'a noté avec profondeur J. Schniewind,[1] à la mise en relief du privilège qu'a le peuple choisi d'entendre la parole de Jésus avant tous les autres hommes (cf. Matth. x. 5 et xv. 24) correspond l'affirmation d'un jugement spécial d'Israël: outre les passages que nous venons de citer, cf. encore Matth. xxi. 40–4; xxii. 7; xxvii. 25.

L'examen interne de notre verset confirme cette interprétation. Que veut dire la comparaison de la Parousie avec l'éclair? Elle pourrait signifier, comme on le soutient souvent, que le Messie sera visible pour tous: Jésus prendrait alors le contrepied de l'idée juive selon laquelle le Messie devait demeurer caché jusqu'au jour de son apparition (cf. Jo. vii. 27). Il nous semble cependant que l'image de l'éclair veut moins traduire la visibilité que la soudaineté et l'universalité de la venue. Schniewind fait remarquer avec raison[2] que déjà pendant sa vie terrestre Jésus est une incarnation *visible* du Règne de Dieu; si donc la Parousie du Christ doit apporter quelque chose de nouveau, ce doit être du fait que sa présence ne sera plus localisée en un coin de l'espace. Il ne faut pas oublier par ailleurs que les éclairs et le tonnerre sont dans l'Ancient Testament un véritable cliché dans la description des jugements divins historiques (cf. Isaïe, xxix. 6; xxx. 27–30–33; Zach. ix. 14; Ps. xviii. 14–15; xcvii. 4).

Le troisième passage où Matthieu parle de la Parousie nous oriente tout à fait dans la même direction; il fait partie de la série des instructions qui suivent le discours: 'Tels furent les jours de Noë, telle sera la Parousie du Fils de l'homme. En ces jours d'avant le déluge, les gens mangeaient et buvaient, prenaient femme et mari, jusqu'au jour où Noë entra dans l'arche; et ils ne se rendirent compte de rien jusqu'à ce que vint le déluge, qui les emporta tous; ainsi en sera-t-il de la

[1] *Das Evangelium nach Matthäus* (Göttingen, 1950), p. 246.
[2] *Ibid.* pp. 243–4.

Parousie du Fils de l'homme. Alors il y en aura deux dans un champ, l'un sera pris, l'autre laissé; il y en aura deux en train de moudre à une meule, l'une sera prise, l'autre laissée' (xxiv. 37–41). Nous sommes persuadé qu'il faut renoncer définitivement à l'exégèse courante qui entend 'être pris' au sens d'être emporté par les anges lors de l'apparition du Fils de l'homme sur les nuées. Le verset 31 qui parle de rassemblement (ἐπισυνάξουσιν) des élus par les anges est beaucoup trop loin pour qu'on puisse expliquer ainsi παραλαμβάνεται par ἐπισυνάξουσιν. Il y a plus: s'il s'agissait d'un transport dans les airs au sens de I Thess. iv. 17, Matthieu aurait dû écrire ἀναλαμβάνεται.[1] Enfin Paul, qui s'inspire de notre péricope, nous montre comment nous devons l'entendre: en I Thess. v. 2 ss. il décrit le jour du Seigneur faisant soudain irruption sur les coupables qui se croient en sécurité en ne leur laissant aucune possibilité de fuir (καὶ οὐ μὴ ἐκφύγωσιν). Et il ajoute à l'adresse des chrétiens fidèles: ὑμεῖς δὲ ἀδελφοί οὐκ ἐστὲ ἐν σκότει, ἵνα ἡ ἡμέρα ὑμᾶς ὡς κλέπτης καταλάβῃ. Le jour du Seigneur saisit les coupables et les emporte comme un voleur, telle est l'idée de l'Apôtre; telle est également celle de Matthieu qui à la comparaison du déluge joint celle du voleur: dans l'un et l'autre cas il n'est question que d'un châtiment qui atteint les uns et épargne les autres, et le παραλαμβάνεται du premier évangile équivaut pratiquement au καταλάβῃ de l'Apôtre. Le verbe ἀφίημι, qui signifie originairement lâcher, laisser aller, peut fort bien être compris au sens d'épargner: Moulton-Milligan cite Oxyrhynchus Papyri, IV, 744, 10, où l'on demande de n'épargner le nouveau-né que si c'est un garçon: ἐὰν...τέκῃς, ἐὰν ᾖν ἄρσενον ἄφες, ἐὰν ᾖν θήλεα ἔκβαλε.[2]

Si ce que nous venons de dire est exact, la Parousie du Fils de l'homme dont parle Matthieu est parfaitement distincte de sa venue sur les nuées à laquelle elle sert de prélude, comme chez les prophètes le jour de Yahvé, jour de ténèbres et de malheur, est le prélude du salut, de la belle lumière du jour (cf. par ex. Isa. viii. 21 à ix. 6). Mais il faut ajouter que la venue sur les nuées du Fils de l'homme n'a pas elle non plus le sens précis de conclusion de l'histoire du monde qu'on veut presque toujours lui conférer. Devant les Sanhédrites,

[1] Ces remarques ont déjà été faites par B. Weiss, *Das Matthäus-Evangelium* (Göttingen, 1890), p. 418.

[2] *The Vocabulary of the Greek Testament* (London, 1942), p. 97.

sur le point d'être mis à mort, Jésus affirme solennellement que sa venue sur les nuées suivra immédiatement sa disparition et qu'elle sera d'ailleurs un fait permanent; on a en outre l'impression très forte, pour ne pas dire l'évidence, que cette vision qu'il promet à ses juges n'est pas à entendre d'une vision corporelle: l'évangéliste qui rapporte cette déclaration savait fort bien en effet que les Sanhédrites n'avaient pas joui d'une telle faveur. Ce que par contre ils ont pu déjà constater à l'époque où il écrit, c'est la victoire progressive de la cause du Christ, et c'est donc cette portée que Matthieu doit attribuer aux paroles qu'il met sur les lèvres du divin condamné: 'A partir de maintenant (ἀπ' ἄρτι) vous verrez le Fils de l'homme assis à la droite de la Puissance et venant sur les nuées du ciel' (xxvi. 64). Comme l'écrit excellemment V. Taylor:[1] 'La phrase ὄψεσθε κ.τ.λ. ne décrit pas nécessairement un prodige visible, mais plus probablement se réfère à des évènements et à des circonstances qui prouveront que le Ps. cx. 1 et Dan. vii. 13 ont reçu leur accomplissement en la personne et en l'œuvre de Jésus.... Sans parler du fait que Dan. vii. 13 ne décrit pas une descente, mais une venue du Fils de l'homme vers l'Ancien des jours..., l'association du Ps. cx et de Dan. vii. 13 montre que Jésus n'a pas en vue une descente spectaculaire. Ce qu'il annonce, c'est qu'on verra réalisée en lui la destinée glorieuse réservée au Messie et décrite de diverses façons par le psalmiste et par le prophète.'[2]

Nous avons tout lieu de croire que la venue du Fils de l'homme de Matth. xxiv. 30 a exactement le même sens que celle de xxvi. 64: loin de s'identifier avec le jugement ultime du monde, elle n'est que la contrepartie glorieuse du jugement divin du peuple juif que Matthieu appelle Parousie, comme dans le récit de la Passion la même venue du Fils de l'homme sur les nuées est la contrepartie glorieuse de la mort du Christ.

A ce propos on a fait remarquer récemment[3] que presque tous les traits de l'apocalypse synoptique reçoivent une première réalisa-

[1] *The Gospel according to St Mark* (London, 1952), pp. 568–9.

[2] Ces remarques de Taylor font bonne justice des objections soulevées par Dom Dupont (ΣΥΝ ΧΡΙΣΤΩΙ, 1ère partie, p. 51 n. 1) contre mon interprétation de l'eschatologie des Evangiles Synoptiques et en particulier de la venue du Fils de l'homme sur les nuées.

[3] R. H. Lightfoot, *The Gospel Message of St Mark* (Oxford, 1950), ch. IV, 'The connexion of chapter thirteen with the Passion narrative', pp. 48–59. Dans les lignes qui suivent, nous nous inspirons de ce beau chapitre tout en modifiant

tion dans le drame de la Passion tel que l'ont compris les évangélistes, ce qui fait apercevoir de manière saisissante dans la vie de l'Eglise comme un prolongement du destin de son fondateur. La correspondance est surtout visible dans Marc, mais on la note également chez les deux autres synoptiques qui dépendent de lui. Jésus avait prédit à ses disciples qu'ils seraient battus dans les synagogues et qu'ils comparaîtraient devant des gouverneurs et des rois, il leur avait annoncé encore qu'ils seraient livrés: παραδώσουσιν ὑμᾶς...; ὅταν ἄγωσιν ὑμᾶς παραδιδόντες...; παραδώσει ἀδελφὸς ἀδελφὸν εἰς θάνατον: Marc xiii. 9–12. Or Jésus comparaît à la fois devant le Sanhédrin et devant le gouverneur romain des juifs, Ponce-Pilate (xiv. 53 à xv. 15); il est flagellé (xv. 15) et le verbe παραδίδωμι est constamment usité pour exprimer sa destinée tragique (xiv. 10, 11, 18, 21, 41, 42, 44; xv. 1, 10, 15). En Marc xiii. 22–3, Jésus avait prévenu ses disciples qu'il surgirait des faux prophètes, capables de séduire, s'il se pouvait, même les élus, et il leur avait demandé de se tenir sur leurs gardes, et aussi de veiller pour n'être pas surpris par son retour (xiii. 33–7); au chapitre xiv, Jésus s'en allant au Mont des Oliviers prophétise aux siens qu'ils vont trébucher et à Pierre qu'il va le renier (*vv.* 26–31); à Gethsémani, il demande à Pierre, Jacques et Jean de veiller et de prier, et quand il vient vers les trois apôtres et qu'il les trouve endormis, Abbott n'a pas tort de voir dans cette scène comme une sorte de *Parousie anticipée* et de comparer le ἔρχεται καὶ εὑρίσκει αὐτοὺς καθεύδοντας de xiv. 37 à la venue eschatologique du maître de la parabole qui trouve ses serviteurs endormis en xiii. 36: μὴ ἐλθὼν ἐξαίφνης εὕρῃ ὑμᾶς καθεύδοντας.[1] En outre est-ce pure coïncidence si les divers moments où l'homme de la parabole (xiii. 33–7) est censé pouvoir revenir: le soir (ὀψέ), à minuit (μεσονύκτιον), au chant du coq (ἀλεκτροφωνιάς), le matin (πρωΐ) semblent annoncer les grandes divisions chronologiques de la Passion: le soir (ὀψίας γενομένης: xiv. 17) où est instituée la Sainte Eucharistie, la nuit pendant laquelle a lieu l'arrestation (Matth. xxvi. 31: ἐν τῇ νυκτὶ ταύτῃ; cf. Marc xiv. 27), le chant du coq qui est l'heure

certaines données. Il est à peine besoin de faire remarquer qu'une telle constatation n'est pas en faveur de la théorie communément admise parmi les critiques qui cherche à la base de l'apocalypse synoptique une apocalypse juive remaniée, ce qui revient à en nier partiellement l'authenticité.

[1] *Johannine Vocabulary* (London, 1905), pp. 128–9.

du reniement de Pierre, le matin (πρωΐ, Marc xv. 1) qui est le moment de la condamnation définitive de Jésus à mort?

Cette mort de Jésus est d'ailleurs en rapports étroits avec la ruine du temple, c'est à dire avec l'évènement qui est pareillement au point de départ du discours eschatologique: d'une part le prophétie de la destruction du sanctuaire est une des accusations majeures portées contre Jésus (xiv. 57–8); d'autre part quand le Christ expire, le voile du temple se déchire (xv. 38). Il est prédit en xiii. 24 que la ruine de la ville sainte et de la maison de Dieu s'accompagnera de l'obscurcissement du soleil et de la lune; en xv. 33 tandis que Jésus agonise, des ténèbres couvrent la terre entière. La venue du Fils de l'homme sur les nuées, qui au chap. xiii suit sans transition aucune la grande tribulation (verset 24: ἐν ἐκείναις ταῖς ἡμέραις μετὰ τὴν θλῖψιν ἐκείνην), est donnée au chap. xiv comme la contrepartie nécessaire et immédiate de la mort de Jésus. Si tout ce qu'on vient de dire est exact, l'auteur du Quatrième Evangile n'aurait donc rien inventé en présentant la Passion du Sauveur comme le jugement du monde mauvais et du 'prince de ce monde' et en même temps et indivisiblement comme l'heure de la glorification du Fils de l'homme.

Même si tel ou tel des rapprochements que nous venons d'opérer apparaît problématique, une chose demeure hors de doute: ainsi que l'a souligné depuis longtemps A. Brown,[1] la venue eschatologique du Fils de l'homme est loin d'avoir dans les évangiles le sens univoque qu'on veut lui imposer. On n'est donc nullement obligé de voir dans la Parousie dont parle Matth. xxiv la venue ultime du Christ glorieux en vue du jugement général de l'univers.

Il convient d'autant moins de le faire que dans les passages obscurs, les Synoptiques doivent être éclairés les uns par les autres, car ils sont en rapports étroits et il est impossible qu'ils aient voulu se contredire positivement. Or, dans les textes de Marc et de Luc parallèles à Matth. xxiv. 3, il est incontestable que la question des apôtres ne renferme aucune allusion à un objet distinct de la ruine de Jérusalem: ils demandent seulement quand aura lieu cette catastrophe et quel en sera le signe précurseur. Marc: 'Dis nous quand ces choses arriveront et quel sera le signe que tout cela sera sur le point de s'accomplir' (xiii. 4). Et plus clairement encore Luc: 'Maître, quand ces choses arriveront-elles et quel sera le signe que ces choses

[1] Art. 'Parousia', dans Hastings, *Dictionary of the Bible*, vol. III, pp. 674–5.

seront près d'avoir lieu?' (xxi. 7: les simples mots ταῦτα γίνεσθαι remplacent le ταῦτα συντελεῖσθαι πάντα de Marc, qu'on eût pu prendre à tort par une allusion à la fin du monde). On est donc autorisé à croire que chez Matthieu pareillement Jésus ne traite que d'un seul sujet: la destruction de la ville sainte et du sanctuaire, et que la Parousie se rattache à cet évènement.

(*b*) *La Consommation du Siècle*

Mais le premier Evangile parle également dans ce même passage, de 'consommation du siècle', et aux yeux de l'ensemble des exégètes c'est presque une évidence qu'il est impossible d'entendre cette formule d'autre chose que de la fin du monde au sens strict; elle serait donc décisive pour la fixation de la signification du mot 'Parousie' qui lui est étroitement associé; régis par un même article, les deux termes doivent se référer au même évènement. Il vaut la peine d'examiner de près cette difficulté.

L'expression συντέλεια τοῦ αἰῶνος, qui dans le Nouveau Testament ne se rencontre que dans Matthieu et en Hebr. ix. 26 est tout à fait juive et apparaît sous diverses formes dans les Apocalypses et les Targums. Elle correspond assez bien à la formule si fréquente dans l'Ancien Testament: בְּאַחֲרִית הַיָּמִים. Mais ce qu'il importe le plus de peser ici, se sont les réalités exprimées.

Aux yeux des prophètes de l'ancienne alliance, l'histoire du monde se divise en deux grandes parties: avant et après la venue du Messie; le Messie apparaît à la fin des temps, et il inaugure un monde nouveau. Dans l'ancienne littérature rabbinique, et aussi, selon l'opinion de Schürer,[1] dans les Paraboles d'Hénoch (cf. xlv. 4–5; xci. 16), l'équivalence est maintenue entre le siècle futur et l'ère messianique: celle-ci comme celui-là sont considérés comme le temps du salut définitif. Il n'en va pas de même dans la théologie rabbinique tardive, dans les apocalypses d'Esdras et de Baruch: alors l'ère messianique est soigneusement distinguée de la béatitude éternelle et passe au second plan simplement comme un stade intermédiaire.[2]

[1] *Geschichte des Jüdischen Volkes im Zeitalter Jesu Christi*, vol. II (Leipzig, 1898), pp. 544 ss.

[2] Cf. sur tous ces points P. Volz, *Die Eschatologie der jüdischen Gemeinde* (Tübingen, 1934), pp. 71 ss., H. L. Strack et P. Billerbeck, *Kommentar Zum Neuen Testament aus Talmud und Midrasch*, vol. IV (München, 1928), pp. 815 ss.

Dans le Nouveau Testament, qu'en est-il? Il nous paraît incontestable, quoi qu'en dise Spadafora,[1] qu'en Matth. xiii. 39, 40, 49 et xxviii. 20 la consommation de siècle signifie la fin du monde au sens strict. Nous pensons également que, dans plusieurs passages du Nouveau Testament 'le siècle futur' désigne la béatitude céleste: Marc x. 30; Matth. xii. 32; Luc xviii. 30; Eph. i. 21. En ce sens le siècle ou le monde présent est maintes fois opposé au monde futur: Rom. xii. 2; I Cor. i. 20; ii. 6–8; iii. 18; Gal. i. 4.

Mais si grandes que soient les affinités du Nouveau Testament avec l'apocalyptique juive de l'époque, on ne doit pas oublier qu'il a son point de vue propre. Ainsi que l'a montré si fortement C. H. Dodd,[2] les écrivains du Nouveau Testament sont persuadés qu'en venant en ce monde Jésus a déjà apporté avec lui le siècle futur; ils croient en particulier que sa résurrection est le commencement de la résurrection générale des morts (I Cor. xv. 20–3).[3] En conséquence déjà les fidèles sont arrachés au siècle présent (Gal. i. 4); déjà ils expérimentent les merveilles du monde à venir (Hebr. vi. 5). Quoi d'étonnant dès lors si l'Epitre aux Hébreux place 'la consommation du siècle', non pas à la fin de l'ère messianique lors de la résurrection et du jugement général, mais à la fin de l'ancienne alliance, ce qui est tout simplement revenir à la conception des prophètes. 'Il s'est manifesté maintenant, à la consommation des siècles (ἐπὶ συντελείᾳ τῶν αἰώνων) une seule et unique fois, pour abolir le péché par le sacrifice de lui-même' (ix. 26).

Il faut tenir compte de toutes ces données pour interpréter la consommation du siècle de Matth. xxiv. 3. De même que selon le récit de la Passion (xxvi. 64), le retour du Fils de l'homme s'inaugure dès le premier instant de sa glorification, de même la consommation du siècle s'inaugure dès la mort de Jésus. Matthieu a même souligné ce point plus fortement que ses devanciers. En effet, non seulement il raconte comme eux comment, au moment de la mort de Jésus, le voile du temple se déchire et des ténèbres se répandent sur la terre, ce qui veut dire qu'avec Jésus le monde ancien est en train de mourir, mais il est seul à nous montrer l'empire de la mort brisé à l'instant

[1] *Gesù e la fine di Gerusalemme* (Rovigo, 1950), pp. 31–7.

[2] Surtout dans son beau livre, *The Parables of the Kingdom* (Cambridge, 1946).

[3] Cf. *Theologisches Wörterbuch zum Neuen Testament* de Kittel, vol. I, art. αἰῶν (Sasse), p. 207.

même où Jésus rend le dernier souffle. Il nous dit en effet qu'alors 'les tombeaux s'ouvrirent, et beaucoup de Saints dont les corps y reposaient ressuscitèrent et, sortis des tombeaux après sa résurrection, ils entrèrent dans la ville sainte et apparurent à plusieurs' (xxvii. 52–4): c'est donc bien le siècle futur, celui de la résurrection, qui fait ici son entrée. Et de même qu'après ce tournant décisif dans l'histoire du monde l'Evangile regarde encore comme une venue glorieuse du Fils de l'homme plus spécialement son intervention contre le peuple juif coupable (cf. Matth. x. 23; xvi. 28), de même il est tout naturel que ce jugement de la nation choisie soit censé mettre fin à l'ordre ancien et inaugurer un ordre nouveau.

Quand on comprend ainsi les choses, le texte de Matthieu s'éclaire immédiatement. Le mot τέλος, étant en soi synonyme de συντέλεια, le τὸ τέλος de xxiv. 14 (καὶ τότε ἥξει τὸ τέλος), qui sert à introduire la longue description de la catastrophe de Jérusalem (versets 15–28) ne peut que renvoyer à la συντέλεια sur laquelle les apôtres ont questionné le Maître.[1] Il est facile en outre d'harmoniser la donnée de Matthieu avec celles de Marc et de Luc. La 'consommation du siècle' du premier évangile sur laquelle les disciples interrogent le Sauveur ne signifie pas autre chose que le ταῦτα συντελεῖσθαι πάντα de Marc et le ταῦτα γίνεσθαι de Luc: dans les trois cas c'est avec la ruine du temple que coïncide la fin du monde ancien, cette fin expressément mentionnée d'ailleurs même par Marc et Luc. Il est clair en effet que le τέλος de Marc xiii. 7 (οὔπω τὸ τέλος) commence au *v.* 14: 'Quand vous verrez l'abomination de la désolation'; de même en Luc xxi. 9, οὐκ εὐθέως τὸ τέλος est une annonce du verset 20.

Cette consommation du siècle et cette ère nouvelle, on les comprend mieux encore quand on se souvient que Jésus a repris pour son compte l'antique espérance d'un sanctuaire eschatologique et qu'il l'a liée à l'annonce du châtiment des Juifs et de la destruction du temple matériel de Jérusalem. Michée (iii. 12) et Jérémie (xxvi. 18) avaient prophétisé la ruine du sanctuaire, prédiction qui dans le judaïsme tardif avait été à peu près complètement oubliée, on ne s'en souvint guère qu'au temps de la guerre juive.[2] Le Christ renouvelle cette annonce, mais, conformément au caractère de sa

[1] Cf. M. Brunec, *Sermo eschatologicus, Verbum Domini* (1952), p. 265.

[2] Cf. Josèphe, *Guerre Juive*, VI, 5, 3.

prédication qui joint toujours aux menaces de châtiment des perspectives de salut, il accompagne sa terrible prophétie d'une promesse consolante; c'est ce que prouve l'accusation portée contre lui devant le Sanhédrin d'avoir voulu détruire le temple fait de main d'homme pour le remplacer par un autre non fait de main d'homme (Marc xiv. 58; Jo. ii. 19). Selon nombre d'exégètes,[1] même dans les Synoptiques, la purification du temple a une portée messianique et est en rapport avec l'espérance d'un nouveau sanctuaire. Dès lors n'est-il pas tout naturel que cette double perspective menaçante et consolante se retrouve dans le grand discours eschatologique qui prédit la destruction du temple?

2. CONFIRMATION DE CETTE INTERPRÉTATION: LA PAROUSIE DANS JAC. V, I–II

Même si Matthieu était le seul auteur du Nouveau Testament à employer le mot Parousie avec l'acception que nous venons de définir, il faudrait sans hésiter accepter cette interprétation si elle est commandée par le texte. Il est clair toutefois qu'elle paraîtra plus solidement fondée encore, si d'autres passages du Nouveau Testament entendent de la même façon la Parousie du Christ. Nous croyons que c'est précisément le cas pour Jac. v. 1–11. Un certain nombre d'indices orientent en effet la pensée dans cette direction. Nous examinerons d'abord qui sont ces riches que Jacques menace de châtiment, et en second lieu qu'elles sont les caractéristiques de l'évènement eschatologique qu'il nous faut entrevoir.

(a) *L'identification des riches menacés*

On a beaucoup discuté sur les destinataires ainsi que sur la date et l'origine de la lettre de Jacques. L'opinion la plus commune est qu'elle est adressée à des Juifs convertis: c'est ce qui résulte de son contenu. S'il en est ainsi, les douze tribus de la dispersion dont parle la salutation initiale doivent s'entendre au sens figuré: les chrétiens, et tout particulièrement les judéo-chrétiens, se considéraient comme les héritiers du peuple de Dieu de l'Ancien Testament: de même qu'autrefois les Juifs avaient été dispersés parmi les Gentils, ainsi

[1] Cf., par exemple, J. Schniewind, *Das Evangelium nach Markus* (Göttingen, 1952), pp. 150–1.

maintenant les judéo-chrétiens sont dispersés parmi les incroyants. On le voit, le mot 'dispersion' compris de la sorte n'empêche nullement de croire que l'auteur s'adresse en premier lieu à des Juifs convertis de Palestine, voire de Jérusalem. Et même si l'auteur de la lettre est Jacques de Jérusalem, il est assez naturel qu'il vise d'abord la communauté qui lui est confiée, les membres de son troupeau que sa parole ne peut atteindre.

En tout cas la communauté chrétienne qu'il a en vue se compose d'une grande majorité de pauvres, mais aussi d'une minorité de riches. C'est ce qui ressort de i. 9–11 où il semble bien qu'il y ait antithèse entre deux chrétiens dont l'un est pauvre et l'autre riche. C'est encore ce que permet de conclure la petite parabole (ii. 1–4) du riche et pauvre pénétrant dans la même assemblée si toutefois ces visiteurs sont des chrétiens, ou encore l'avertissement donné aux commerçants en iv. 13–17, à la condition que là encore on soit en présence de marchands chrétiens.

Capitale est pour nous la question de savoir si les riches menacés en v. 1–6, sont eux aussi des chrétiens. Zahn,[1] Chaine,[2] Charue,[3] etc. . . . le pensent. Par contre Ropes,[4] Dibelius,[5] Meinertz,[6] sont d'un avis contraire. Pour notre part, nous croyons pareillement que ces riches sont des non-chrétiens, et plus précisément encore des non-chrétiens Juifs.

Ce sont des non-chrétiens. C'est ce qui résulte du contraste très fort établi entre les deux volets de dyptique: d'un côté les riches (v. 1) de l'autre côté les frères (v. 7): les uns menacés, les autres encouragés. Que ce contraste soit voulu, cela est clair, car l'unité du passage vient de ce qu'il annonce d'un bout à l'autre l'avènement du Seigneur. Aussi bien la dureté de l'invective serait-elle autrement difficilement compréhensible: nous avons là une pure annonce du châtiment; quand Jacques s'adresse à des frères, il les exhorte à la conversion.

Nous croyons que ces non-chrétiens sont par surcroît des Juifs. Pour prouver qu'il peut s'agir d'ennemis de nom chrétien, Windisch

[1] *Einleitung in das Neue Testament*[3] (Leipzig, 1907), vol. I, pp. 61 ss.

[2] *L'Epitre de Saint Jacques*[2] (Paris, 1927), pp. 112–13.

[3] *Les Epitres Catholiques, dans la Sainte Bible de Pirot*, t. XII (Paris, 1938), p. 426.

[4] *A Critical and Exegetical Commentary on the Epistle of St James* (Edinburgh, 1916), p. 282.

[5] *Der Brief des Jacobus* (Göttingen, 1921), pp. 217 ss.

[6] *Die Katholischen Briefe* (Bonn, 1932), pp. 47 ss.

renvoie à ii. 6–7.[1] Ce rapprochement est très heureux. Dans ce passage, l'auteur après avoir montré aux chrétiens combien serait à réprouver leur mépris des pauvres que Dieu lui-même a choisi comme héritiers du royaume (versets 5–6a) souligne l'inconséquence de leur conduite: en effet ne sont-ce pas précisément les riches qui font du mal aux chrétiens? 'Est-ce que ce ne sont pas les riches qui vous oppriment et qui vous traînent devant les tribunaux? Ne sont-ce pas eux qui blasphèment le beau nom qui est invoqué sur vous?' Dans une lettre chrétienne comme celle-ci, le 'beau nom' que les riches outragent a toutes chances d'être celui de Jésus, et l'action devant les tribunaux ne peut-être simplement une forme d'oppression sociale: il doit s'agir d'une persécution religieuse; cf. Matth. x. 17–18; xxiv. 9; Luc xxi. 12–18; Jo. xvi. 2...; 'Dans les Actes les exemples sont nombreux: on pense à Saul qui pénétrait dans les maisons pour arracher les hommes et les femmes et les faire jeter en prison: viii. 3; cf. iv. 3; vi. 12; xxvi. 11'.[2]

Dans la péricope même que nous étudions, nous avons un argument très fort en faveur de l'identification des riches avec les Juifs ennemis du Christ. On lit en effet au verset 6: κατεδικάσατε, ἐφονεύσατε τὸν δίκαιον· οὐκ ἀντιτάσσεται ὑμῖν. Remarquons d'abord, quel que soit le sens précis de la phrase, la gravité de cette accusation: les riches ont condamné et tué le juste; vraiment est-il possible que des chrétiens soient l'objet de pareils griefs? On ne peut que donner raison à Dibelius quand il déclare que les riches qui commettent de tels crimes sont à chercher dans le monde des impies.

Mais quel est donc ce juste qu'ils ont tué? La plupart des auteurs estiment que ce passage ne vise pas un cas précis et que ὁ δίκαιος est un nom collectif. Ils allèguent que l'Epitre de Jacques se rattache à la littérature des Pauvres de l'Ancien Testament (Prophètes et Sapientiaux) où la persécution du pauvre par le riche est un lieu commun: Amos v. 12; vi. 12; Michée iii. 1–3, 9–10; Ps. xxxvii. 32; Prov. I. 10, 14; Sap. ii. 10–20.... Plusieurs exégètes ajoutent que le meurtre dont il est question ici peut très bien n'être que métaphorique, étant donné le vocabulaire habituel en ce genre de littérature: on cite par ex. Eccli. xxxiv. 21–2; Hénoch xcix. 15, où commettre l'injustice et égorger semblent être des expressions synonymes.

[1] *Die Katholischen Briefe* (Tübingen, 1930), p. 30.

[2] *L'Epitre de Saint Jacques*, p. 48.

Contre ces explications, on peut faire valoir les arguments suivants. Quoique le mot 'pauvre' ait pris de plus en plus dans l'Ancien Testament une coloration morale et religieuse, il n'est pas synonyme de 'juste'; or ici il s'agit du meurtre, non d'un pauvre, mais d'un juste. Cette remarque montre également que ce meurtre n'est pas symbolique comme celui que l'on commet en privant de nourriture des indigents. Il est fort possible, comme beaucoup d'auteurs l'ont pensé, par ex. Dibelius, Moffatt,[1] qu'en ecrivant κατεδικάσατε, ἐφονεύσατε τὸν δίκαιον Jacques ait voulu faire allusion à la description des souffrances du juste de Sap. ii. 12–20 (tableau qui lui même rappelle Isaïe liii et le Ps. xxii). Cf. en particulier les versets 12 et 20: ἐνεδρεύσωμεν τὸν δίκαιον...θανάτῳ ἀσχήμονι καταδικάσωμεν αὐτόν. Si l'Epitre se réfère à ce passage, elle doit parler d'un meurtre réel du Juste par excellence. Au reste dans l'interprétation courante, on est très embarrassé pour expliquer οὐκ ἀντιτάσσεται, et cela quelle que soit la traduction adoptée: 'le juste ne vous résiste point' (Charue, Meinertz, Dibelius, Windisch); 'le juste n'est pas votre adversaire' (Chaine). D'abord on est étonné de ce présent faisant suite à deux aoristes: aussi Calmes traduit-il, mais en s'éloignant du texte: 'vous avez tué le juste qui ne vous a pas résisté'.[2] Autre difficulté: l'asyndeton surprend et plusieurs témoins ont cherché à le supprimer, soit en mettant καὶ devant οὐκ ἀντιτάσσεται, soit en changeant cette forme verbale en ἀντιτάσσοντα ou ἀντιτασσόμενοι.[3] Mais ces corrections ne jouissent d'aucune autorité. On peut noter encore que, depuis le début de l'invective, tous les versets se terminent par la perspective du châtiment final: *v.* 1: les malheurs qui arrivent; *v.* 2: les vêtements rongés; *v.* 3: les chairs rongées, les derniers jours; *v.* 4: les cris parvenus aux oreilles du Seigneur; *v.* 5: le jour de l'égorgement. On attend donc ici l'indication du châtiment du meurtre du juste, cela d'autant plus que l'on est arrivé à la fin du premier développement. Par contre, comme le note Ropes, la mise en relief de la non résistance du juste et de sa soumission jure avec tout le contexte destiné à inculper la revanche prochaine du juste sur le riche.

A la suite de Oecumenius, Bède, Mayor,[4] nous pensons que ce

[1] *The General Epistles* (London, 1947), pp. 70–1.
[2] *Épitres Catholiques* (Paris, 1905), in h.l.
[3] Cf. Dibelius, *Der Brief des Jacobus*, p. 221 n. 2.
[4] *The Epistle of St James* (London, 1904), in h.l.

verset s'applique au Christ, et avec l'édition du Nouveau Testament de Westcott et Hort, nous mettons un point d'interrogation à la fin de la phrase, ce qui permet de la traduire ainsi: 'Vous avez condamné, vous avez tué le juste, n'entre-t-il pas en lutte avec vous (par le jugement)?' Cette exégèse nous paraît solidement fondée. Le verbe ἀντιτάσσομαι exprime plus qu'une attitude hostile, une résistance active: cf. son emploi en Esther iii. 4; Prov. iii. 15; IV Macch. xvi. 23 (cod. א). Dans le Nouveau Testament le Christ est souvent appelé 'le juste': Matth. xxvii. 19; Act. iii. 14; vii. 52; xxii. 14; I Petr. iii. 18; I Jo. ii. 1; cf. Matth. xxvii. 4 (αἷμα ἀθῷον). C'est là une désignation messianique empruntée à l'Ancien Testament, en particulier, croyons-nous (le contexte des Actes le suggère) aux poèmes du Serviteur de Jahvé (cf. Isa. liii. 11 b). Pierre et Etienne reprochent aux Juifs d'avoir renié et tué le juste, après avoir persécuté et mis à mort ceux qui prédisaient sa venue: Act. iii. 14-15; vii. 52. Au reste, si la lettre a pour auteur Jacques de Jérusalem et s'il est vrai qu'il s'adresse ici à des Juifs incrédules, n'est-il pas naturel a priori qu'il leur rappelle leur grand crime? Quant au sens que nous prêtons à ἀντιτάσσομαι, outre qu'il correspond à l'emploi du même verbe en iv. 6 (Dieu résiste aux orgueilleux: ἀντιτάσσεται), il s'accorde à merveille, soit avec le contexte antécédent, soit avec le contexte subséquent: avec le contexte antécédent, car, ainsi qu'on l'a vu, on s'attend à trouver exprimée ici l'idée de la punition des riches;[1] avec le contexte subséquent: en effet aux versets 7-8, il sera question de la Parousie du Seigneur; le Seigneur est ici Jésus, mais on ne saurait le deviner, ni par ce qui précède, ni par ce qui suit où Κύριος désigne toujours Dieu (cf. i. 7; iv. 10-15; v. 10-11). Tout devient clair si le verset 6 annonce déjà l'intervention vengeresse du 'Juste' par excellence, le Christ.

[1] Cette idée d'une revanche du juste est tellement celle qu'on attend que nombre d'exégètes l'introduisent ici, tout en pensant qu'il s'agit du juste en général. Certains traduisent comme nous par une interrogation en suppléant Θέος comme sujet de ἀντιτάσσεται: on sait que dans le judaïsme tardif on évitait par respect de prononcer le nom de Dieu; toutefois ici ce sous-entendu est peu naturel. Ropes, qui suppose lui aussi que la phrase est interrogative, veut que la résistance active exprimée par ἀντιτάσσεται soit celle des justes au jour du jugement, mais dans la Bible la revanche eschatologique n'est pas l'œuvre des hommes, mais celle du juge divin.

(*b*) *Les Caractères du jugement annoncé par Jacques*

Les considérations qui précèdent prouvent ou en tout cas suggèrent que les riches invectivés par Jacques en *v.* 1 ss. sont des Juifs meurtriers du Christ et ennemis du nom chrétien. Nous pouvons ajouter maintenant que les caractères du jugement annoncé par Jacques font penser au jugement historique de l'incrédulité juive. La première partie de la description (v. 1–6) où l'auteur invite les riches à pousser des hurlements de douleur, rappelle tout à fait par son style les annonces par les prophètes des catastrophes historiques. Surtout, au verset 5 le jugement des riches est appelé 'le jour de l'égorgement'; c'est de cette manière que s'expriment les prophètes quand ils décrivent la punition des nations ou de Jérusalem; ils songent en effet à une guerre ou à un carnage; cf. Ez. xxi. 15; Jer. xxv. 34; i. 27; Soph. i. 7, 14–17; Isa. xxxiv. 2–4. Cette expression convient mal par contre au jugement général de l'humanité tel que le Christ le décrit, car jamais il ne présente les sanctions de l'au-delà comme un massacre; elle n'a d'autre correspondant dans son message que les predictions du châtiment temporel de la nation juive: Matth. xxii. 7; xxi. 41; Luc xiii. 1–9.... Aussi bien ce 'jour de l'égorgement' paraît-il déjà inauguré. En effet, littéralement traduit, le verset 5 veut dire que les riches 'ont vécu sur la terre dans la mollesse et les délices et qu'ils ont nourri leur cœur *en un jour d'égorgement* (ἐν ἡμέρα σφαγῆς)'. Chaine comprend 'pour le jour de l'égorgement', mais rien ne justifie ici cette assimilation de ἐν avec le datif à εἰς avec l'accusatif. Soden adopte la leçon de quelques manuscrits: ὡς ἐν ἡμέρα σφαγῆς, ce qui nous met en présence d'une comparaison: vous vous êtes repus comme des animaux qui s'engraisseraient le jour même de leur égorgement. Toutefois cette lecture plus facile est par le fait même suspecte. Dibelius interprète: vous vous êtes repus en un jour où les justes étaient égorgés. Mais tout le contexte antécédent et en particulier le ἐν ἐσχάταις ἡμέραις du verset 3 imposent d'attribuer à ἐν ἡμέρα σφαγῆς une portée eschatologique. Cette perspective d'un châtiment qui vient subitement atteindre les hommes au beau milieu de leurs réjouissances fait songer à Matth. xxiv. 37–8 que nous avons étudié plus haut.

La seconde partie de la description (versets 7–11), qui renferme nombre de coïncidences littéraires remarquables avec le discours eschatologique de Jésus, rappelle tout à fait du point de vue des idées les conseils de patience donnés par le Christ à ses disciples, le châtiment prochain de la ville sainte coupable devant être pour eux le signal de la délivrance. Quand on lit le verset 8: 'Ayez patience vous aussi, fortifiez vos cœurs, car l'avènement du Seigneur est proche', n'est-il pas vrai qu'on se souvient spontanément de Luc xxi. 28: 'Quand ces choses commenceront à arriver, redressez-vous et relevez la tête, parce que votre délivrance est proche.' Par ailleurs le juge qui se tient aux portes (πρὸ τῶν θυρῶν, *v.* 9) fait songer au Fils de l'homme qui est aux portes (ἐπὶ θύραις, Matth. xxiv. 33; Marc xiii. 29; cette expression est absente de Luc). La recommandation d'endurance (μακαρίζομεν τοὺς ὑπομείναντας), l'endurance de Job (τὴν ὑπομονὴν 'Ιὼβ) et la fin (τὸ τέλος) que le Seigneur lui a donnée (*v.* 11), tout cela rappelle: 'Celui qui aura enduré jusqu'à la fin (ὁ δέ ὑπομείνας εἰς τέλος)' de Matth. xxiv. 13 et Marc xiii. 12. On remarquera encore que le ἵνα μὴ κριθῆτε de 9a montre qu'en 9b ὁ κριτής est pris au sens péjoratif: il s'agit d'un juge qui vient non pas récompenser les bons et châtier les méchants, mais seulement punir. Le grand motif de consolation proposé par Jacques aux 'Frères', le motif de la patience qu'il leur recommande avec tant d'insistance, c'est la prochaine intervention du juge divin contre les riches. Or la promesse d'une prompte vengeance (ποιήσει τὴν ἐκδίκησιν αὐτῶν ἐν τάχει), n'est-ce pas là précisément le thème de la parabole du juge et de la veuve (Luc xviii. 1–8) morceau dont nous avons montré ailleurs[1] le lien avec l'annonce du châtiment des Juifs? On remarquera le verbe μακροθυμεῖν commun aux deux passages: Luc xviii. 7 et Jac. v. 7 (deux fois), 8; au verset 10, on a μακροθυμία.

3. CONCLUSION

La conclusion que nous croyons pouvoir dégager de cette étude, c'est que Matth. xxiv et Jac. v. 1–11 entendent la Parousie du Seigneur au sens du jugement historique du peuple juif, à la différence des autres écrits du Nouveau Testament qui appellent Parousie la manifestation suprême du Christ à la fin de l'histoire du

[1] *Recherches de Science religieuse* (1948), pp. 560–5.

monde.[1] Cette particularité propre à Matthieu et à Jacques s'explique dans les deux cas de la même façon: nous sommes là en présence d'une manière de parler archaïque antérieure à l'époque où la prédication paulinienne devait imposer au mot Parousie le sens technique qu'il gardera par la suite.

Pour la lettre de Jacques, cette explication devrait trouver aisément crédit auprès des critiques qui, à l'exemple de Mayor, Michaelis, Kittel, regardent cet écrit comme étant le plus ancien ou l'un des plus anciens du Nouveau Testament.[2] En ce qui regarde le premier Evangile, la question est plus complexe, car il est certain que notre Matthieu actuel est postérieur à Marc, dont il semble même dépendre fréquemment, soit pour l'ordonnance des récits, soit pour le style. Mais nous sommes persuadé avec plusieurs critiques (Vaganay, Cerfaux, Benoit) que Matthieu grec dépend du Matthieu araméen dont parle Papias, le premier de tous les Evangiles, et qu'il en a conservé, sous son vêtement grec, les principales caractéristiques; ainsi s'explique la couleur sémitique si accentuée de son vocabulaire et de son style.[3] Nous pensons en outre avec M. Vaganay[4] et conformément au texte de Papias[5] qu'il a existé plusieurs traductions grecques de l'original araméen de Matthieu et que notre premier évangile actuel en est tributaire. Dans ces conditions on peut très bien admettre que le mot παρουσία du chap. xxiv de Matthieu vient d'une traduction grecque de Matthieu araméen antérieure au temps où la Parousie avait revêtu un sens technique. Se souvenant de la prédication de Paul, Marc composé plus tard aura évité ce mot pour ne pas induire ses lecteurs en erreur, et Luc pour le même motif

[1] Nous faisons expressément abstraction ici de la Parousie mentionnée en II Thess. ii. 8; A. Sabatier (*L'Apôtre Paul*[2] (Paris, 1881), pp. 98–100) a vu dans ce passage une annonce du châtiment des Juifs. Nous croyons que le dernier mot est loin d'être dit sur l'eschatologie des Epitres aux Thessaloniciens, et même des Epitres pauliniennes en général.

[2] Cf. Mayor, *The Epistle to St James*, pp. cxxi–cliii; Michaelis, *Einleitung in das Alte Testament* (Bern, 1946), pp. 284 ss.; G. Kittel, *Zeitschrift für die neutestamentliche Wissenschaft* (1942), pp. 71–105.

[3] Cf. L. Vaganay, *La Question synoptique* (Ephemerides Theologicae Lovanienses, 1952), pp. 238–56; L. Cerfaux, *La voix vivante de l'Evangile au début de l'Eglise* (Tournai–Paris, 1946), pp. 42 ss.; P. Benoit, *L'Evangile selon Saint Matthieu* (Paris, 1950), pp. 12 ss.

[4] *La Question synoptique*, pp. 246–7.

[5] 'Matthieu dans le dialecte hébraïque (araméen) a mis en ordre les enseignements (τὰ λόγια) du Seigneur, et chacun les traduisit comme il le pouvait' (Fragm. II, 26).

l'aura remplacé par l'expression 'le jour (ou les jours) du Fils de l'homme' (xvii. 22, 24, 26, 30).

Il ne faudrait pas croire d'ailleurs que Matthieu et Jacques soient les seuls auteurs à parler du jugement historique imminent du peuple juif, alors que cette idée se retrouve un peu partout dans le Nouveau Testament. Nous croyons que l'étude de l'eschatologie du Nouveau Testament est à reprendre sur des bases partiellement nouvelles en tenant compte davantage de cette perspective. Dans une étude suggestive, quoique gâtée à notre sens par l'esprit de système,[1] S. G. F. Brandon a souligné l'importance historique considérable, et malheureusement trop peu soulignée par les historiens, de la ruine de Jérusalem: cet évènement, dit-il avec raison, marqua une véritable renaissance du christianisme, et, après les expériences de la Résurrection, il n'en fut pas de plus crucial ni de plus décisif. Jusqu'à cette date en effet, en dépit de la prédication de Paul, l'Eglise judéo-chrétienne de Jérusalem était demeurée le centre de la nouvelle religion et s'était efforcée de garder le vin nouveau du christianisme dans les vieilles outres de la foi ethnique d'Israël; au contraire, à partir de 70, le message du Christ, désormais parfaitement distinct du judaïsme, put se répandre librement sans être entravé auprès des Gentils par des questions de race et de nationalité; ce fut donc bien alors, selon la vue prophétique de Jésus. la fin d'un monde et le commencement d'un monde nouveau.[2] Assurément l'on n'a pas manqué de soutenir que tous les passages évangéliques où Jésus prédit clairement la ruine de la cité sainte châtiée à cause de son rejet du Messie ne sont autre chose que des *vaticinia ex eventu*, mais il est impossible de fournir la preuve de cette assertion.

[1] *The Fall of Jerusalem and the Christian Church* (London, 1951).

[2] Ces considérations réduisent à néant l'objection faite par T. W. Manson à ceux qui voient dans la ruine de Jérusalem la catastrophe prédite par Jésus: 'La répression impitoyable par un grand empire militaire d'une rébellion insensée dans une partie limitrophe de son territoire a autant — ou aussi peu — de rapports avec la venue en puissance du Règne de Dieu que la suppression de la révolte dans les Indes' (*The Teaching of Jesus* (Cambridge, 1951), p. 281).

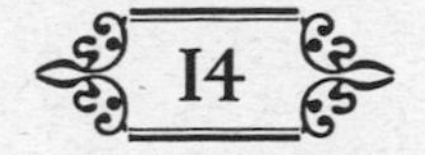

AGNOSTOS CHRISTOS

JOH. ii. 24 UND DIE ESCHATOLOGIE DES VIERTEN EVANGELIUMS

E. STAUFFER

SEIT Johannes Weiss und Albert Schweitzer gilt die Erwartung des nahen Weltendes weithin als die Grundvoraussetzung der Botschaft Jesu. Martin Werner hat diesen Gedanken weiter ausgeführt und das Ausbleiben der Naherwartung als die große Krise der Urkirche verstanden, aus der das Christusdogma erwachsen sei. Aber die Forschungen der letzten fünfzig Jahre haben uns die Augen dafür geöffnet, wie hochgespannt allenthalben im Palästinajudentum des Neutestamentlichen Zeitalters die Enderwartung gewesen ist. Jesus wäre demnach nur einer von vielen Apokalyptikern seiner Zeit, die den großen Wandel aller Dinge für die nächste Zukunft vorausgesagt haben, und es wäre nicht recht einzusehen, warum gerade Jesus mit dieser Zukunftsbotschaft so starken Widerhall gefunden hat.

Wenn aber die Naherwartung im damaligen Palästinajudentum so vulgär war, dann war auch das Ausbleiben der Naherwartung in jenen Kreisen ein alltägliches Problem und keineswegs die spezielle Aporie der christlichen Urkirche, wie Martin Werner voraussetzt. Tatsächlich stoßen wir allenthalben auf dies Problem und können leicht feststellen, daß die Zeitgenossen das Ausbleiben des Weltendes keineswegs so problematisch nahmen, wie die moderne Forschung es zu nehmen geneigt ist. Die meisten Propheten des Alten Testaments haben den nahen Anbruch des Gottesreiches verkündet. Ihre Erwartung blieb unerfüllt. Aber die Geltung und schließlich die kanonische Autorität ihrer Verkündigung wurde dadurch nicht erschüttert. Die Ordensleute von Jericho und Damaskus haben generationenlang auf das Kommen des Messias aus Aaron und Israel gewartet, und wenn er zu dem angesetzten Termin nicht erschien, so haben sie einen neuen Adventstermin errechnet. Aber die Eschatologie blieb lebendig, von einem Ultimotermin zum anderen. Anno 116 verkündigte der Prophet Elchasai am Toten Meer: Wenn wiederum drei Jahre des Kaisers Trajan erfüllt sind, wird das Weltende eintreten (Hippolyt 9, 16, 4). Aber Trajan starb schon 117, und das Dritte Jahr (119) ging vorüber ohne Weltkatastrophe. Doch die Gemeinde Elchasais überlebte alle diese Enttäuschungen. Um 220 wirkte Alkibiades in Rom als Apostel des Propheten vom Toten Meer. Um 400 lebten noch zwei Schwestern aus dem Hause Elchasais, die göttlich verehrt wurden (Epiph. Haer. 19, 1. 2; 53, 1. 2). Und noch um 900 gab es am Toten Meer elchesaitische Gemeinden. Das scheint nach dem Fiasko der Naherwartung zunächst schwer begreiflich. Aber wer den modernen Pietismus kennt, der weiß, daß es auch heute noch Kreise genug gibt, die ihre selbsterrechneten Endzeittermine unbeirrt überleben.

Die Forschung der letzten hundert Jahre hat sich weithin angewöhnt, das synoptische Jesusbild im Gegensatz zum johanneischen als das historische Jesusbild zu behandeln und unter den synoptischen Jesusworten wiederum die Worte vom nahen Gottesreich als die echtesten Jesuslogien zu betrachten. Bultmanns Jesusbuch ist ein charakteristisches Beispiel für dieses Selektionsverfahren, das den Einfluß von Johannes Weiß und Albert Schweitzer nicht verleugnet. Die Urgemeinde, so deduziert man dann weiter, hat noch einige Zeit auf die Erfüllung dieser Endworte gewartet. Dann hat sie behutsam begonnen, sie zu verklausulieren oder umzudeuten. Aber vielleicht ist es umgekehrt? Vielleicht war Jesus, der historische Jesus, gar kein Apokalyptiker im hocheschatologischen Sinne, vielleicht haben nur die Zeitgenossen ihn so apokalyptisch verstanden, vielleicht hat erst die Jüngergemeinde nach Ostern ihm die hocheschatologischen Zukunftsworte in den Mund gelegt, die heute vielfach als die echtesten Jesusworte gelten. Es gibt mancherlei Zeugnisse, die für diese umgekehrte Traditionsfolge sprechen. Drei nur seien hier herausgegriffen: Mk. viii. 27ff., Lk. xix. 11 und Ag. i. 6.

In Mk. viii. 27ff. stellt Jesus die bekannte Frage: 'Wer sagen die Leute, daß ich sei?' Die Jünger referieren über die verschiedenen Volksmeinungen: der Täufer, Elia oder sonst ein Prophet. Das ist ein religionsgeschichtlich unschätzbares Referat. Denn in einem Punkt treffen diese gegensätzlichen Jesusdeutungen zusammen — in der Grundvoraussetzung, daß die Gottesmänner der Vergangenheit ihren geschichtlichen Auftrag noch nicht vollendet haben, daß sie vielmehr seit dem Tage ihres Todes, ihrer Entrückung, irgendwo auf ihre zweite und endgültige Epiphanie oder Inkarnation warten. Wir werden auf dieses Theologumenon noch zurückkommen. Jesus wiederholt seine Frage mit persönlicher Zuspitzung: 'Ihr aber, wer saget ihr, daß ich sei?' Petrus antwortet wie einer, der längst schon die Frage erwartet, längst schon die Antwort bereit hat: 'Du bist der Messias!' Das ist kein Bekenntnis, das ist ein Appell, Petrus ruft den Messias zur Tat.[1]

Jesus aber weist diesen Appell zurück, er verbietet jede Messiasproklamation und verwirft den Messiasbegriff des Petrus, um ihm das Selbstzeugnis vom Menschensohn entgegenzustellen. Das ist der historische Sinn und Verlauf des Dialogs von Caesarea Philippi nach Markus, der noch deutlicher ans Licht treten würde, könnten wir hier das Ringen zwischen Messianologie und Menschensohntheologie in der jüdischen Apokalyptik jener Zeit studieren, das in konkreter Aktualisierung sich wiederholt in dem Ringen zwischen dem Menschensohnzeugnis Jesu und der Messiasdogmatik seiner Jünger. Lukas stellt den Zusammenstoß in Caesarea Philippi nicht ganz so schroff, aber sachlich im wesentlichen ebenso dar wie Markus (Lk. ix. 18–22). Matthäus hat die Geschichte völlig umgeformt und ihr dadurch einen ganz neuen Sinn gegeben (Matth. xvi. 13ff.). Hier ist der Gegensatz zwischen Menschensohnbegriff und Messiasdogma schon im Ansatz verwischt (xvi. 13), aus dem messianischen Appell ist das liturgisch erweiterte Messiasbekenntnis geworden, das Jesus als göttliche Offenbarung begrüßt und zum Anlaß für die Schlüsselverleihung nimmt (Matth. xvi. 16ff.), deren historischer Ort vermutlich an einer späteren Stelle der Geschichte Jesu zu suchen ist (vgl. *Z. f. Kircheng.* LXII (1943), S. 16ff.). Das Verbot der Messiasproklamation erhält dadurch einen veränderten und künstlichen Sinn (xvi. 20), und erst in xvi. 22f. hören wir etwas von einem ernsten Konflikt, der

[1] Der Messias ist erschienen und wandert durch Palästina in der unscheinbaren Gestalt Jesu von Nazareth. Die führenden Männer lehnen ihn ab, das Volk schwankt. Aber Petrus hat ihn erkannt und ruft ihn auf, seine Macht und Herrlichkeit nunmehr vor aller Augen zu offenbaren.

nun aber ganz unvorbereitet erscheint. Der kritische Historiker wird gerade durch diese sekundären Umdeutungsversuche darauf aufmerksam, daß es sich hier um einen grundsätzlichen und durchgehenden Gegensatz handelt, über dessen Ausbruch Markus und Lukas freimütig berichten, während Matthäus nach Kräften mildert. Aber selbst bei Matthäus ist es noch erkennbar, daß die Jünger eine fertige Messiasdogmatik und Eschatologie an Jesus herantragen, die Jesus schroff ablehnt.

In Lk. xix. 11 lesen wir: 'Während sie noch zuhörten, fuhr er fort und erzählte ein Gleichnis, darum, daß er nahe bei Jerusalem war und sie meinten, das Reich Gottes werde nun alsbald in Erscheinung treten.' Der Ort der Handlung ist Jericho, der Zeitpunkt unmittelbar vor dem Aufbruch zur letzten Wegstrecke nach Jerusalem. Das Gleichnis ist die Parabel von den anvertrauten Pfunden, die aus der Logienquelle stammt und bei Matthäus in der dort üblichen Sachgruppierung mit fünf anderen Wiederkunftsgleichnissen zusammen am Schluße der Synoptischen Apokalypse erscheint (Matth. xxv. 14ff.). Nur Lukas bringt das Gleichnis von den anvertrauten Pfunden in einem konkreten historischen Rahmen, und seine Situationsbestimmung verrät mehr orts- und zeitgeschichtliche Sachkenntnis, als man dem hellenistischen Autor zutrauen möchte, dürfte demnach auf vorlukanischer Tradition fussen.

Jericho war ein heißer Boden. Der Lukastext nimmt in der besonderen Fassung des Gleichnisses von den anvertrauten Pfunden Bezug auf die stürmischen Monate nach dem Tode Herodes des Großen (4 ante), die gerade in Jericho gewiß noch lange unvergessen waren. Damals hatte der Sklavenkönig Simon ein spartakistisches Zukunftsreich proklamiert und den Königspalast in Jericho samt den Lustschlössern der Reichen in Asche gelegt (Jos. *Bellum* 2, 5, 2). Südlich von Jericho liegen die berühmten Orte, wo die Jericholeute, die Essener und verwandte Gruppen ihre Niederlassungen oder Depots hatten, Ain Fescha, Kumran, Murabaat, Engedi. Dort hat wahrscheinlich Johannes der Täufer seine Wüstenjahre zugebracht (Lk. i. 80). Im Raum der Jordanmündung und des Toten Meeres hat die Täuferbewegung ihren Ursprung, dort haben die ältesten Täufergemeinden ihren Sitz. Alle diese Gruppen und Gemeinden warteten damals mit Hochspannung auf das Reich Gottes und verfolgten jedes Wort und Zeichen Jesu mit fieberhafter Erwartung.

Im Herbst 31, kurz nach dem Konflikt von Caesarea Philippi, hatte Jesus Galilaea verlassen und sein 'Antlitz gen Jerusalem gerichtet' (Lk. ix. 51). Alle großen Entscheidungen müssen in Jerusalem fallen (Lk. xiii. 33; vgl. Joh. vii. 3 f.; xi. 16). Im März 32 zog er auf dem Pilgerweg durch das Jordantal seinen Jüngern voraus, geheimnisvoll und unheimlich zugleich (Mk. x. 32). Die Naherwartung der Jünger steigert sich. Man streitet sich bereits um die Ehrenplätze in nahen Messiasreich (Mk. x. 35 ff.). Der Einzug in Jericho erfolgt mit ungeheurem Zulauf. Man darf wohl annehmen, daß auch zahlreiche Männer aus den apokalyptischen Sondergemeinden rings um Jericho unter der Menge sind, die entweder Jesus sehen oder nach Jerusalem pilgern oder beides miteinander verbinden wollen. Begreiflich, daß diese Männer die eschatologische Spannung im Volke noch vermehren. Das Passahfest steht bevor, immer ein Höhepunkt der apokalyptischen Fieberkurve (vgl. Lk. xiii. 1). Denn an einem Passahfest soll der Messias erscheinen.

Jesus ist auf dem Wege nach Jerusalem, auf dem Wege zur Passahfeier. Die Festpilger und Jericholeute sammeln sich zum messianischen Marsch auf Jerusalem. Das ist die Situation von Lk. xix. 11: Man ist nahe bei Jerusalem und meint, das Reich Gottes werde alsbald in Erscheinung treten. Aus dieser Situation ergibt sich fast zwangsläufig die Adventskundgebung beim Einzug in Jerusalem (Lk. xix. 28 ff.), die eschatologische Terminfrage der Jünger (Mk. xiii. 4), die Salbung in Bethanien (Mk. xiv. 3 ff.), die Enttäuschung des Judas (Mk. xiv. 10 ff.), die Anklage vor Pilatus (Lk. xxiii. 2 ff.), die Verspottung durch Herodes (Lk. xxiii. 11), die Kreuzesinschrift (Mk. xv. 26). Das ist die apokalyptische Atmosphäre, von der Jesus auf Schritt und Tritt umgeben war. Ob er wollte oder nicht, man betrachtete ihn als eschatologische Gestalt. Die Streitfrage war zuletzt nur noch die, ob er der Messias sei oder ein Pseudomessias. So festgefahren war das Palästinajudentum der Zeit Jesu im eschatologischen Denken.

Jesus starb, ohne vom Kreuz zu steigen, ohne 'Israel zu erlösen' (Mk. xv. 32; Lk. xxiv. 21). Aber am Ostermorgen war sein Grab leer, und alsbald erfolgten die ersten Epiphanien des Auferstandenen, noch in der Passahwoche, noch in der messianischen Adventszeit! Da verkündeten die Apostel: Die Auferstehung der Toten hat begonnen! Und schon regten sich wieder die verdrängten End-hoffnungen, nun in einer neuen Form: 'Herr, wirst du in dieser Zeit das Reich Israel wiederaufrichten?' So fragen die Jünger in Ag. i. 6 den Auferstandenen. Die Frage zeigt, wie fruchtlos alle Gegenerklärungen Jesu geblieben sind gegen die zeitgenössischen Enderwartungen, die man mit seiner Person, Botschaft und Wirksamkeit in Verbindung gebracht hat. Nun erzeugten die Osterereignisse ein apokalyptisches Fieber wie nie zuvor. Wieviele Endzeitworte der Evangelien, die heute als urjesuanisch gelten, mögen in dieser Situation entstanden sein? Man weiß aus den Paulusbriefen, wie lange diese enthusiastische Naherwartung anhielt, die nicht nur die Gemeinden ergriffen hat, sondern weithin auch den Apostel Paulus selbst.

Das Johannesevangelium, so scheint uns, ist der Protest des letzten Apostels gegen die Mißdeutung und Verzeichnung Jesu, die in jener Epoche des apokalyptischen Enthusiasmus das Feld beherrschte. Der Vierte Evangelist korrigiert die Synoptiker mit dem Anspruch des Augenzeugen, der Jesus und seine Geschichte besser kennt als die älteren Evangelisten, die aus zweiter Hand schöpfen mußten. Er korrigiert Kleinigkeiten wie die Behauptung des Markusevangeliums, alle Jünger außer Petrus seien bei der Gefangennahme Jesu geflohen (Mk. xiv. 50ff.; dagegen Joh. xviii. 15), oder die Meinung, Jesus sei nach der Verhaftung sogleich dem Hochpriester Kaiphas vorgeführt worden (Matth. xxvi. 57; dagegen Joh. xviii. 13). Er korrigiert die gesamte Chronologie der Synoptiker (Joh. iii. 24; xviii. 28). So korrigiert er auch die Messiaseschatologie der Synoptiker, und diese Korrektur ist ihm offenbar ein besonders ernstes Anliegen. In Chronologicis ist der Vierte Evangelist zweifellos besser unterrichtet als die Synoptiker. Wir müssen deshalb a priori mit der Möglichkeit rechnen, daß Johannes auch in Eschatologicis die Gestalt und Botschaft Jesu richtiger gezeichnet hat als seine Vorgänger. Mit dem Problem der johanneischen Eschatologie ist darum die Frage der 'eschatologischen' Haltung und Bedeutung Jesu selbst unlöslich verknüpft.

Die Eigenart der johanneischen Eschatologie tritt uns fast auf jeder Seite des Vierten Evangeliums direkt oder indirekt entgegen und ist oft behandelt worden. Wir wollen sie hier lediglich an einem Paradigma studieren, das in den Kommentaren üblicherweise nur ganz kurz besprochen wird und in den bisherigen Verhandlungen über die Eschatologie des Johannesevangeliums so gut wie völlig außer Acht geblieben ist. 'Jesus selbst aber vertraute sich ihnen nicht an; denn er kannte sie alle und hatte es nicht nötig, daß jemand Zeugnis gab vom Menschen. Denn er wußte von sich aus, was im Menschen war' (Joh. ii. 24f.).

In der spätjüdischen Messiaserwartung spielt die Vorstellung eine große Rolle, daß der Messias eine zeitlang im Verborgenen bleibt, bevor er seine Wirksamkeit vor den Augen Israels und aller Welt eröffnet. Diese Vorstellung liegt schon der apokalyptischen Terminologie vom Hervortreten, Erscheinen, Offenbarwerden des Messias zugrunde, die uns bereits im vorchristlichen Palästinajudentum bezeugt ist.[1] Der Damaskustext scheint damit zu rechnen, daß der verstorbene oder umgebrachte Lehrer der Gerechtigkeit demnächst mit messianischer Macht und Herrlichkeit wiederkehren werde (Dmt. xx. 1 und öfter). Auch in der Zeit und Umwelt Jesu waren derartige Vorstellungen in mannigfachen Abwandlungen lebendig. Das ergibt sich aus den Berichten des Markusevangeliums von den anfänglichen Volksmeinungen über Jesus.[2] Einer der ältesten rabbinischen Originaltexte zur Messiasfrage findet sich in einem tannaitischen Traditionsstück des Jerusalemer Talmud über Rabbi Jochanan ben Zakkai, der um 78/80 in hohem Alter gestorben ist. רבן יוחנן בן זכאי מי דמיך פקיד ואמר פנו חצר מפני הטומאה והתקינו כסא לחזקיה מלך יהודה. 'Als Rabban Jochanan ben Zakkai entschlief, ordnete er an: Räumet den Hof auf wegen der Unreinheit und stellet einen Thronsessel bereit für Hiskia, den König Judas.'[3] Der Ausspruch

[1] Der hebräische Grundbegriff ist גלה (aram. גלא) und bezeichnet die Enthüllung verborgener Wirklichkeiten oder Wahrheiten, z.B. Dan. ii. 19, 22, 28f., 30, 47; *Dead Sea Manual* i. 9; viii. 1, 15; ix. 13, 19; xi. 1. גלה von der Offenbarung Gottes in Gen. liii. 7; Jes. xl. 5; liii. 1. Entsprechend ist in II Makk. ii. 7f. vom Offenbarwerden eines verborgenen Ortes, in II Makk. iii. 28ff.; III Makk. vi. 9; Test Juda xxii. 2 von der Epiphanie oder Parusie Gottes, in Ass. Mos. x. 1 vom Erscheinen des Gottesreichs, in Test. Levi viii. 15 von der Parusie des Enderlösers die Rede.

[2] Mk. vi. 14ff.; viii. 28. Vgl. V. Taylor, *The Gospel according to St Mark* (London, 1952), pp. 308f., 376.

[3] j Sota ix. 16 a.E. Ähnlich Aboth RN 25 (76) und die Baraitha in Ber 28b, die jedoch am Schlusse hinzusetzt 'wenn er kommt' (שבא) und dadurch der Naherwartung Jochanans ihre Aktualität nimmt. Über das Messiasamt Hiskias s. Strack-Billerbeck, II, S. 332 u.ö. M. Schwab denkt in j Sota ix. 16 an einen Thron im Garten Eden (s. *Le Talmud de Jérusalem*, VII, p. 344). Aber Jochanan denkt doch wohl an einen Thron auf Erden, denn nur auf Erden gibt es Unreinheit, die beseitigt werden muß. Über Jenseitsvisionen Jochanans s. W. Bacher, *Die Agada der Tannaiten*, I² (1903), p. 40f.

ist zunächst ein bedeutsames Zeugnis für die hochgespannte Enderwartung der Rabbinen nach der Tempelzerstörung des Jahres 70. Sodann beweist er, wie geläufig im Rabbinat jener Zeit die Vorstellung von der messianischen Wiederkehr eines Gottesmannes der Vorzeit war. Und endlich führt er uns anschaulich vor Augen, wie das Spätjudentum die Theorie von der Davidssohnschaft des Messias (Ps. Sal. xvii. 21, Schemone Esre und öfter) mit dem Bilde des Messias absconditus et revelatus zu vereinigen wußte: Der sterbende Rabbi Jochanan schaut den Davididen Hiskia in der Himmelswelt, wie er sich bereit macht, den Messiasthron in Jerusalem zu besteigen.

Etwa zehn Jahre vor dem Johannesevangelium ist das Vierte Esrabuch entstanden. Hier erscheint die Idee von der Verborgenheit und anschließenden Offenbarung bereits als ein fester Schematismus, der unterschiedslos auf die beiden konkurrierenden Endgestalten übertragen wird, auf den Messias sowohl als auf den Menschensohn. So sagt Gott in IV Esra vii. 28f. vom Messias: 'Revelabitur enim filius meus Christus cum his qui cum eo (in caelis!) sunt...et erit post annos hos et morietur filius meus Christus.' In xiii. 52 sagt Gott wiederum vom Menschensohn: 'Non poterit quisque super terram videre filium meum...nisi in tempore diei.' Beidemale wird die Endgestalt ausdrücklich als Filius Dei bezeichnet, der Christus sowohl, als auch der Menschensohn. Aber der Christus stirbt nach einer vierhundertjährigen Zeit der Macht- und Herrlichkeitsoffenbarung. Dann kehrt die Schöpfung für sieben Tage zum Schweigen der Urzeit zurück. Dann erst erfolgt die Auferstehung der Toten, die Erscheinung des Menschensohnes, der Beginn der Neuen Äons. Man musste einmal der Frage nachgehen, ob der Menschensohn des Vierten Esrabuches die neue und endgültige Epiphanie des Filius Dei ist, der zuvor in der vorläufigen und todverfallenen Gestalt des Messias erschienen war. Wo harrt der Filius Dei auf den Tag seiner Revelatio? In der Himmelswelt, im Kreise seiner heiligen Engel. Dorthin wird auch Daniel nach seinem Tode entrückt, um in Gemeinschaft mit dem Sohne Gottes auf das Ende der Zeiten zu warten (IV Esra xiv. 9). Der Zeitpunkt der Entrückung Daniels liegt weit vor der Epiphanie des Messias und vollends vor der Endoffenbarung des Menschensohns. Dennoch findet Daniel in der Himmelswelt nicht etwa zwei praeexistente Endgestalten vor, den

Messias und den Menschensohn, sondern nur den Einen Filius Dei. Auch das spricht (*wenn* man die verschiedenen Traditionen und Enderwartungen des Vierten Esrabuches überhaupt auf eine und dieselbe Bildfläche auftragen darf) dafür, daß Messias und Menschensohn im Sinne des IV Esra zwei verschiedenartige und zu verschiedenen Zeiten vorgesehene Epiphanien desselben Filius Dei sind. Bei alledem hat man aber auch die Theorie von der Davidssohnschaft des Messias nicht aufgegeben. Das zeigt sich in IV Esra xif. Dort hören wir von dem Löwen aus Juda, der plötzlich aus dem Walde hervorbrechen und den römischen Adler, speziell die letzten Flavier überwinden wird. Der siegreiche Löwe ist der Messias aus dem Stamme Davids. Der Wald aber ist das Bild der Verborgenheit, in der der Messias auf seine Stunde wartet. So sagt IV Esra xii. 30f.: 'Et leonem, quem vidisti de silva evigilantem...hic est Unctus, quem reservavit (s.o. גלה) Altissimus in finem dierum, qui orietur ex semine David.'[1] Man sieht, wir haben hier dieselbe Ideenverbindung vor uns wie in dem Wort Jochanan ben Zakkais vom Davididen Hiskia, der in der Himmelswelt zum Losschlagen bereitsteht.

Im zweiten Jahrhundert bezeugt Justin in seinem Dialogus cum Tryphone Judaeo die weitverbreitete Geltung der Vorstellungen vom Christus absconditus in der jüdischen Apokalyptik. In Dialogus 109f. zitiert der Kirchenvater Micha iv. 1ff. und sagt im Anschluß daran zu den Juden: Καὶ ὅτι οἱ διδάσκαλοι ὑμῶν, ὦ ἄνδρες, τοὺς πάντας λόγους τῆς περικοπῆς ταύτης εἰς τὸν Χριστὸν ὁμολογοῦσιν εἰρῆσθαι, ἐπίσταμαι, καὶ αὐτὸν ὅτι οὐδέπω φασὶν ἐληλοθέναι, καὶ τοῦτο γινώσκω· εἰ δὲ καὶ ἐληλυθέναι λέγουσιν, οὐ γινώσκεται ὅς ἐστιν, ἀλλ' ὅταν ἐμφανὴς καὶ ἔνδοξος γένηται, τότε γνωσθήσεται ὅς ἐστι, φασί. Καὶ τότε τὰ εἰρημένα ἐν τῇ περικοπῇ ταύτῃ φασὶν ἀποβήσεσθαι (Dial. 110, 1). Hier ist die Tradition vom Messias absconditus, der an einem verborgenen Ort auf seine Epiphanie wartet, spezialisiert zur Theorie vom Agnostos Christos, der sich incognito mitten unter den Menschen bewegt, bis die Stunde seiner Herrlichkeitsoffenbarung gekommen ist. Noch weiter zugespitzt erscheint diese Theorie in Dialogus 8, 4: Χριστὸς δέ, εἰ καὶ γεγένηται καὶ ἔστι που,[2] ἄγνωστός ἐστι καὶ οὐδὲ αὐτός πω ἑαυτὸν ἐπίσταται οὐδὲ ἔχει

[1] Siehe L. Gry, *Les Dires Prophétiques d'Esdras*, II (Paris, 1938), pp. 354f.

[2] Hier wirkt die Theorie vom Messias absconditus nach, vgl. unten Rom!

δύναμίν τινα, μέχρις ἂν ἐλθὼν Ἠλίας χρίσῃ αὐτὸν καὶ φανερὸν πᾶσι ποιήσῃ. Hier dürfte eine jüngere und hellenisierte Form der Idee vom Messias incognitus vorliegen. Denn hier scheint eine im Jahrhundert Justins weitverbreitete gnostische Idee eingewirkt zu haben, die Idee vom himmlischen Erlöser, der in der Erdenwelt seine jenseitige Herkunft und Würde vergißt, bis er durch eine himmlische Botschaft zur Besinnung gebracht wird.[1]

Beide Vorstellungen, die Idee des Messias absconditus und die Theorie des Messias incognitus, leben in der Amoräerzeit weiter und verbinden sich z.B. in den Spekulationen über den Messias, der bereits auf Erden erschienen ist, aber zur Zeit noch in einem verborgenen Winkel Roms unscheinbar und unerkannt ein elendes Dasein fristet (Sanh. 98 a.b.; vgl. Pesikta R. 31 ff. und öfter). Aber auch andere Stätten werden als geheime Aufenthaltsorte des Messias genannt: der ferne Norden, das irdische Paradies, die Himmelswelt. Die einschlägigen Texte sind oft gesammelt worden.[2]

Dagegen hat das Targum Jonathan zu Micha iv. 8 mehr Beachtung verdient, als ihm gemeinhin zuteil wird: ואת משיחא דישראל דטמיר מן קדם חובי כנשתא דציון לך עתידא מלכותא· 'Und du, Messias Israels, der wegen der Sünde der Gemeinde Zion verborgen gehalten wird, in deine Hand wird die Königsherrschaft kommen.' Das Targum des Jonathan ben Uzziel ist erst in amoräischer Zeit zum Abschluß gekommen. Aber seine Anfänge reichen bis in die Hasmonäerzeit zurück.[3] Wann ist unsere Auslegung zu Micha iv. 8 entstanden? Einen terminus ante quem bietet zunächst Justins Dialog 110, 1. Hier wie dort handelt es sich um die Deutung von Micha iv, hier wie dort um des Messiasgeheimnis. Die jüdische Theorie vom Messias absconditus war demnach schon um 135/150 mit der haggadischen Exegese von Micha iv fest verbunden. Mit dieser Synchronisierung gewinnen wir aber auch eine willkommene Hilfe für die Interpretation des Targumtextes. Der Ausdruck דִּטְמִיר ist vieldeutig. Denn der aramäische Terminus טְמַר bedeutet zwar in erster Linie 'versteckt halten', kann aber auch 'verheim-

[1] Vgl. z.B. Oden Salomos 23 und Acta Thomae 109 ff.

[2] Z.B. *Strack-Billerbeck*, I, 481; II, 339 f.; IV, 766 u.ö.

[3] Über Spuren des Targum Jonathan in den Synoptikern und im IV Esrabuch s. J. J. Brierre-Narbonne, *Exégèse Targumique des Prophéties Messianiques* (Paris, 1936), p. 3.

lichen' heißen.[1] Im ersteren Falle wäre an den Messias absconditus, im letzteren Falle an den Messias incognitus zu denken. Was ist gemeint? Die rabbinischen Michaexegeten in Dialogus 110, 1 unterscheiden anscheinend drei Stufen der Messiasoffenbarung: Zunächst den Messias absonditus (verborgen in der Himmelswelt), sodann den Messias incognitus (unerkannt inmitten der Menschenwelt), zuletzt den Messias revelatus (in Macht und Herrlichkeit in der Menschenwelt). Dieselbe Vorstellung liegt wohl auch dem Targumtext zugrunde. Dieselbe Theorie dürfte aber schon in Mk. viii. 29, Lk. xix. 11 und xxiv. 21 vorausgesetzt und in Ag. i. 6 im Sinne der Erwartung von der machtvollen Wiederkehr des entrückten oder ermordeten Gottesmannes abgewandelt sein. Wenn das richtig ist, dann dürfen wir den Schluß ziehen, daß die Theorie vom Messias incognitus, die uns bei den Thoralehrern Justins begegnet, schon im vorchristlichen Palästinajudentum aufgekommen ist.[2]

Jedenfalls aber knüpft der Vierte Evangelist an diese Theorie an, wenn er den Täufer in Joh. i. 26 sagen läßt: 'Mitten unter euch steht Er, den ihr nicht kennt, der nach mir kommt, dem ich nicht wert bin die Schuhriemen zu lösen.' Jesus ist der Agnostos Christos. Der Elias aber, der ihn erkennt und vor aller Welt proklamiert, ist der Täufer: 'Auch ich kannte ihn nicht. Aber der mich gesandt hat, mit Wasser zu taufen, er sagte zu mir: Der, auf dem du den Geist sich herablassen und bleiben siehst, der ist es, der da tauft mit heiligem Geist. Und ich habe gesehen und habe bezeugt, daß dieser ist der Sohn Gottes' (Joh. i. 33 f.).

Das Vierte Evangelium liebt den Gedanken des Messias incognitus und bringt ihn in mannigfachen Abwandlungen zur Geltung (Joh. vi. 42; vii. 27; xiv. 7 und öfter). Offenbar hat diese Theorie in den Auseinandersetzungen mit der Täufertheologie eine besondere Rolle gespielt. Denn wir hören an einer wenig beachteten Stelle der pseudoklementinischen Recognitionen von den puristischen Täuferjüngern, daß sie lehrten, ihr Meister weile gewissermaßen in der Verborgenheit: Οἱ δὲ καθαροὶ Ἰωάννου μαθηταὶ πολὺ τοῦ λαοῦ διαφέροντες τὸν διδάσκαλον αὐτῶν ὡς ἐν ἀποκρύφῳ εἶναι ἔλεγον (Ps. Clem. Rec. 1, 54, 8 Frankenberg). Das Stück stammt nach der

[1] Siehe J. Levy, *Targumwörterbuch*, I (1881), S. 308 f.; *Talmudwörterbuch*, II (1924), S. 167; Jastrow (1950), p. 540.

[2] Auch Paulus scheint eine ähnliche Theorie zu kennen, s. I Kor. ii. 8.

Waitzschen Quellentheorie aus den judenchristlichen Kerygmata Petri, die (nach Waitz) um 138 in Caesarea Palaestinae entstanden sind, dürfte jedenfalls zu den ältesten Traditionselementen der Pseudoklementinen gehören.[1] Auch hier stoßen wir wieder auf die Theorie vom Messias absconditus, hier aber ist sie auf den Täufer übertragen (vgl. Mk. vi. 14ff.). Wir wissen, daß die Täuferjünger in den Tagen des Paulus in Ephesus eine Gemeinde hatten und Mission trieben, und erkennen aus Joh. i. 1ff., daß sie dort noch im spätapostolischen Zeitalter eine offenbar nicht unbedeutende Rolle spielten. Es kann darum kaum zweifelhaft sein, daß der Vierte Evangelist der täufertheologischen Theorie vom Messias absconditus (=Johannes d. Täufer) in Joh. i. 26ff. die christologische Theorie vom Messias incognitus (=Jesus Christus) polemisch und propagandistisch entgegenstellt.

In Joh. ii. 24 erfährt diese These ihre letzte Vertiefung und Entfaltung. Die grundlegende revelatio des Christus incognitus ist erfolgt (Joh. i. 34ff.; ii. 11). Er tut Wunder und Zeichen und findet Glauben (Joh. ii. 23). Aber er vertraut sich keinem Menschen an. Er ist immer noch ein incognitus, auch nach und trotz aller revelatio. Joh. ii. 24 steht im Rahmen des johanneischen Berichtes von der täuferzeitlichen Wirksamkeit Jesu und ist charakteristisch für jene Frühperiode, in der Jesus nur kurz und halb aus seinem Incognito heraustritt (Joh. ii. 9!), im übrigen aber im Schatten des Täufers bleibt (Joh. iv. 1–3) — so bewußt und betont, daß die Synoptiker jene Frühzeit ganz übergehen. Dies Schweigen will der Vierte Evangelist in ii. 24 zugleich erklären und in seiner Weise berichtigen. Aber auch in der Hochperiode der Wirksamkeit Jesu schwindet jenes Incognito nie ganz, bis zuletzt (Joh. xiv. 9; xvi. 12ff. und öfter). Man tötet den Messias, weil man ihn nicht erkennt (Joh. i. 5, 10f.). Nur Einer kennt den Sohn — der Vater selbst (Joh. x. 15). Er gibt Zeugnis von Jesus, und dieses Zeugnis ist die Grundlage aller legitimen Kenntnis Jesu (Joh. v. 32, 37; viii. 18; xii. 28).

Kein Mensch kennt Jesus. Er aber kennt sie alle und kennt sie von sich aus, nicht durch fremdes Zeugnis (Joh. ii. 24f.). Er kennt

[1] Zur neueren Debatte s. H. J. Schoeps, *Theologie und Geschichte des Judenchristentums* (1949), S. 399 und die Quellenanalysen Bernhard Rehms in *ZNW* XXXVII (1938), S. 155ff., die jedoch unseren Text nicht unmittelbar berühren. Zur Motivgeschichte s. 4 Esra vi. 26; Ginza I. 201f. (s. M. Lidzbarski (1925), p. 30).

Petrus, Nathanael, die Samariterin, Judas, von Anfang an (Joh. i. 47ff.; iv. 39; vi. 70f. und öfter). Das ist die erste Erfahrung, die die Menschen mit Jesus machen, daß sie sich von Jesus erkannt sehen bis ins letzte. Er kennt sie besser, als sie sich selber kennen. So kennt nur Gott den Menschen (Ps. cxxxix und öfter). Man muß diese immer wiederkehrenden Begegnungen zwischen dem Christus incognitus und dem zutiefst bloßgestellten Menschen im Lichte des jüdischen Axioms verstehen: Gott sieht und wird selbst nicht gesehen,[1] Gott ist unsichtbar, Jesus ist sichtbar. Und dennoch gilt der Satz: Jesus sieht und wird selbst nicht gesehen. Ecce Deus!

Im übrigen hat Joh. ii. 24 einen sehr resignierten Grundton. Niemand kennt Jesus — er ist völlig allein mitten unter den Menschen, unter Verwandten, Freunden und Schülern. Er kennt den Menschen, kennt alle, die um ihn herum sind. Wer aber weiß, was im Menschen ist, der weiß nichts Erfreuliches. Darum vertraut Jesus sich niemandem an, letztlich auch dem Lieblingsjünger nicht.

Es gehört zum Wesen und Schicksal des Agnostos Christos, daß sein Tun und Reden nicht verstanden wird. Er ist von Mißverständnissen umgeben. Der Kosmos versteht ihn nicht (Joh. ii. 20; iii. 4, 10ff.; iv. 10f.; vi. 52; xii. 28f.). Aber auch die Jünger und Anhänger begreifen ihn nicht (Joh. vi. 61f.; xi. 12; xiii. 28f.; xvi. 12ff.). Darum kann es garnicht ausbleiben, daß auch die eschatologische Botschaft, Haltung und Bedeutung Jesu mißverstanden wird (Joh. vi. 26f., 34f.; vii. 3f., 33ff.; viii. 21f.; xiv. 3ff., 22). Jesus sagt zur Samariterin: ἔρχεται ὥρα καὶ νῦν ἐστιν.[2] Die Samariterin versteht nur das ἔρχεται und bekräftigt den ersten Satz ganz im Sinne der traditionellen Messiasdogmatik: οἶδα ὅτι Μεσσίας ἔρχεται. Jesus aber unterstreicht den zweiten Satz: ἐγώ εἰμι ὁ λαλῶν σοι (Joh. iv. 23ff.). Jesus sagt zu Martha: 'Dein Bruder wird auferstehen.' Martha antwortet mit einer Katechismusformel, ganz ähnlich wie die Samariterin: 'Ich weiß, daß er auferstehen wird bei der Auferstehung am Jüngsten Tage.' Da sagt ihr Jesus, daß in seiner Epiphanie Futurum und Praesens ineins fallen: 'Ich bin die Auferstehung und

[1] Gott heißt im Rabbinischen ganz formelhaft: 'Er, der sieht und nicht gesehen wird', s. z.B. Chag. 5b; Lev. r 4.

[2] Joh. iv. 23. Dieselbe Formel in Joh. v. 25, charakteristisch für die johanneische Eschatologie, anscheinend ohne Parallele in der zeitgenössischen Umwelt. Zur Sache s. C. H. Dodd, *The Interpretation of the Fourth Gospel* (Cambridge, 1953), pp. 148, 364ff.

das Leben. Wer an mich glaubt, der wird leben, ob er gleich stürbe. Und ein jeder, der lebt und glaubt an mich, der wird nicht sterben in Ewigkeit' (Joh. xi. 24ff.). Man kann den beinahe hoffnungslosen Kampf Jesu mit der vulgären Eschatologie nicht drastischer darstellen, als es in Joh. iv. 23ff. und xi. 23ff. geschieht.

Jesus steht in Joh. xi bereits dicht vor dem Endpunkt seiner geschichtlichen Wirksamkeit. Er weiß es und erlebt es täglich, daß auch die engsten Freunde ihn mißverstehen. Aber er verheißt seinen Jüngern, daß sie ihn nach seinem Tode verstehen werden. Wenn der Gott des Alten Testaments vorüberzieht, dann ist der Mensch wie betäubt. Aber wenn der Mensch ihm nachschaut, dann begreift er, wer hier vorübergegangen ist (Ex. xxxiii. 22f.). Auch Jesu Epiphanie ist nur ein Zelten (Joh. i. 14), nur ein Vorübergehen,[1] dessen einmalige Herrlichkeit den Augenzeugen erst in der Rückschau voll bewußt wird. Langsam und mehr und mehr wird den Jüngern die ewige Tragweite der allgeschichtlichen Stunde aufgehen, durch die sie wie geblendet hindurchgetaumelt sind. In diesem Sinne sagt Jesus zu Petrus: 'Was ich tue, das weißt du jetzt noch nicht, du wirst es aber später begreifen' (Joh. xiii. 7). Und in Joh. xvi. 12ff. spricht Jesus: 'Ich hätte euch noch viel zu sagen. Aber ihr könnt es jetzt nicht tragen. Wenn er aber kommt, der Geist der Wahrheit, so wird er euch hineinführen in die ganze Wahrheit. Denn er wird nicht von sich selbst aus reden, sondern was er hört, das wird er aussprechen, und das Kommende wird er euch verkündigen.' Unter den Jüngern, zu denen Jesus hier spricht, befindet sich auch der Lieblingsjünger, der in Joh. xxi. 24 als Autor des Vierten Evangeliums erscheint. Der Evangelist zählt sich demnach selber zu denen, die die eschatologische Bedeutsamkeit, Haltung und Botschaft Jesu nicht sogleich, sondern erst nach dem Tode Jesu begriffen haben (vgl. Lk. ix. 54; Mk. x. 35ff.).

In Joh. ii. 24 spricht der Vierte Evangelist. Spricht er im Sinne des historischen Jesus oder im Sinne einer gnostischen Gemeindetheologie? Die neueren Kommentare, die zur religionsgeschichtlichen Erklärung des Johannesevangeliums so überreiches Vergleichsmaterial aus der Gnosis gesammelt haben, bieten zu unserer Stelle

[1] Vgl. E. Lohmeyer, 'Und Jesus ging vorüber', *Nieuw Theol. Tijdschrift*, 1934, pp. 206ff.

keinerlei gnostische Parallelen.[1] Dagegen konnten wir einige jüdische und täufertheologische Zeugnisse aus dem palästinischen Raume beibringen, die die Messianologie von Joh. ii. 24f. als eine höchst individuelle Umprägung der palästinajüdischen Anschauungen vom Messias absconditus und speziell vom Agnostos Christos erscheinen lassen. Demzufolge muß der jesuanische Ursprung der Christologie von Joh. ii. 24f. zumindest als möglich gelten. Aber wir dürfen wohl noch einen Schritt weiter gehen. Die synoptische Tradition enthält, eingesprengt in die Fülle vulgärapokalyptischer Logien, eine ganze Anzahl von Jesusworten, die eng mit Joh. ii. 24f. verwandt sind. An der Spitze ist hier das Wort vom Filius incognitus zu nennen (Lk. x. 22/Matth. xi. 27), das aus der Logienquelle stammt und demnach auf jeden Fall einige Jahrzehnte früher zu literarischen Fixierung gekommen ist als das Johannesevangelium. 'Niemand erkennt, wer der Sohn ist, als nur der Vater.' Das ist derselbe Grundgedanke wie Joh. ii. 24 in anderer Formulierung. Und auch die sonstigen Denkmotive des synoptischen Logions berühren sich, wie man längst beobachtet hat, aufs engste mit den Worten des johanneischen Christus in Joh. iii. 35; vii. 29; x. 15; xvi. 15 und öfter. Man hat das Logion darum vielfach als 'johanneisch', gnostisch, hellenistisch, jedenfalls als unjesuanisch abtun wollen. Aber schon in den Jerichotexten finden sich verwandte Sätze. Der Würdename 'Der Sohn' erinnert an die Terminologie des Vierten Esrabuches (Filius absconditus = Messias = Menschensohn), die lukanische Traditionsform γινώσκειν τίς ἐστιν ὁ υἱός stimmt fast wörtlich zusammen mit der jüdischen Formulierung in Justins *Dialogus* 110, 1 (γινώσκεται ὅς ἐστιν, γνωσθήσεται ὅς ἐστιν). Zur Traditionsgeschichte des Herrenworts ist zu beachten, daß die Logienquelle, Matth. und Lk. keineswegs die einzigen urchristlichen Jesusbücher waren, die das Wort vom unerkannten Gottessohn überliefert haben. In der patristischen Literatur lief das Logion vom Filius incognitus in mancherlei Formen um, die auf außerkanonische Traditionen oder Quellen zurückweisen. Vor allem scheint das Nazaräerevangelium dieses Jesuswort enthalten zu haben, neben vielen anderen Ichworten Jesu, die einen

[1] Das gilt auch von H. Odeberg, *The Fourth Gospel* (Uppsala, 1929), der pp. 44ff. zum Thema γινώσκειν in Joh. ii. 24b/25 eine Fülle wichtigen Vergleichsmaterials aus Mechiltha, Hebr. Henoch u.a. bietet, nicht aber zum Problem des Messiasgeheimnisses in Joh. ii. 24a.

ähnlich 'johanneischen' Klang haben. In summa: Nichts spricht dagegen, vieles spricht dafür, daß das Logion vom unerkannten Gottessohn ein echtes Jesuswort ist.[1]

Andere synoptische Herrenworte verraten den gleichen Geist. Wir zählen nur einige auf: Lk. xvii. 21; xi. 20; x. 18; x. 42; Lk. vii. 22f./Matth. xi. 4ff.; Lk. x. 23f./Matth. xiii. 16f. u.a.m. Die meisten Logien, die wir hier genannt haben, stammen aus dem lukanischen Sondergut, die übrigen hat Lukas aus der Spruchquelle entnommen. Es ist wohl kein Zufall, daß derselbe Autor, der den Kampf Jesu mit der vulgären Eschatologie so stark betont (s.o. zu Lk. xix. 11 und Ag. i. 6), zugleich eine besondere Vorliebe für die Jesusworte von der apokalyptischen Gegenwart an den Tag legt.

Es hieße Eulen nach Athen tragen, wollten wir uns hier über die Gleichnisse Jesu verbreiten. Hat doch der Forscher, dem diese Zeilen gewidmet sind, seine These von der Realized Eschatology gerade auf der Gleichnisanalyse aufgebaut und damit die längst fällige Gegenbewegung gegen Albert Schweitzers radikal eschatologische Interpretation der Gleichnisse eingeleitet.[2] Joachim Jeremias schließt seine Exegese der Gleichnisreden mit den Sätzen: 'Die Stunde der Erfüllung ist da, das ist ihr Grundton....Denn erschienen ist der, dessen verborgene Herrlichkeit hinter jedem Wort und jedem Gleichnis aufleuchtet.'[3] Und Gustav Stählin hat sich über die Gleichnishandlungen Jesu soeben in grundsätzlich gleichem Sinne geäußert.[4]

Vor mehr als fünfzig Jahren hat William Wrede in seinem genialen Buch über *Das Messiasgeheimnis in den Evangelien* (Göttingen, 1901) etwa folgende Leitgedanken entwickelt: Jesus hat sich nicht als Messias betrachtet. Erst die Urgemeinde hat ihn zum Messias erklärt und diese ihre Messiasproklamation in das Selbstzeugnis Jesu retro-

[1] In Matth. xi. 25 ff./Lk. x. 21 f. ist vom Filius incognitus die Rede, nicht vom Messias incognitus. Auch das spricht fur die Echtheit dieses Logions. Denn Jesus hat den Messiasbegriff nicht geliebt.

[2] C. H. Dodd, *The Parables of the Kingdom* (1938), u.ö.

[3] J. Jeremias, *Die Gleichnisse Jesu* (2. Aufl. 1952), S. 162. Vgl. ferner V. Taylor, *St Mark* (1952), pp. 114f., 256ff.; W. Eltester in *ZNW* XLIV (1952/3), S. 267.

[4] G. Stählin, 'Die Gleichnishandlungen Jesu', in *Kosmos und Ekklesia, Festschrift für W. Stählin* (1953). Vgl. schon G. Stählin, 'Zur Eschatologie des Vierten Evangeliums', *ZNW* XXX (1934), S. 225ff.

jiziert — mit der Klausel: Jesus habe sich zwar als Messias gewußt, aber er habe seine Messianität als Geheimnis behandelt und ihr Bekanntwerden nach Kräften verhindert. So ist das 'Messiasgeheimnis' um Jesus nach Wrede nur eine sekundäre Hilfskonstruktion der Urgemeinde, um die historische Überlieferung vom unmessianischen Jesus mit dem dogmatischen Postulat vom messianischen Selbstbewußtsein Jesu auszugleichen. Wredes Buch ist das Opus classicum der 'gemeindetheologischen' Forschung geworden und aus der Wissenschaftsgeschichte unseres Jahrhunderts nicht wegzudenken. Dem kritischen Leser aber müssen in dem Buche drei Dinge auffallen.

Erstens nimmt Wrede das religionsgeschichtliche Problem nicht ernst genug. Er begnügt sich im Anschluß an Schürer u.a. mit einem Hinweis auf Justins Dialogus und der Feststellung, 'daß die Verborgenheit hier und dort etwas ganz Verschiedenes bedeutet' (a.a.O. S. 212f.). Weder die Variationsbreite der jüdischen Idee vom verborgenen Messias wird hier berücksichtigt, noch das Gesetz der Umformung, das bei jeder religionsgeschichtlichen Übernahme und Weiterbildung wirksam, in der Frage nach der Praeformation jesuanischer Gedanken aber von allergrößter Tragweite ist. Zweitens gleitet Wrede über das synoptische Logion vom Filius incognitus (Lk. x. 22/Matth. xi. 27), dem für die Thematik seines Buches gewißlich zentrale Bedeutung zukommt, mit einigen peripherischen Bemerkungen hinweg (a.a.O. S. 150f.). Drittens aber, und das ist das Erstaunlichste, behandelt er das Wort vom Agnostos Christos in Joh. ii. 24f. überhaupt nicht.[1]

Wenn man das nachzuholen versucht, es konnte hier nur sehr skizzenhaft geschehen, so ändert sich das Bild radikal.

Das vorchristliche Palästinajudentum hat aus der Erwartung des Messias absconditus, zumindest ansatzweise, die Idee des Messias incognitus entwickelt, der unerkannt unter den Menschen lebt, bis er durch den wiederkehrenden Elias erkannt und bekannt gemacht wird. Auf dieser Idee fußt das Logion Lk. x. 22. Die Formulierung zeigt engste Verwandtschaft mit der jüdischen Tradition. In re aber liegt hier ein Novum vor. Denn das Incognito des jüdischen Messias endet mit der Salbung durch Elias; von nun an ist er aller Welt

[1] Dieselben drei kritischen Feststellunge gelten mutatis mutandis auch für die zahlreichen Arbeiten pro oder contra Wrede, die seit 1901 erschienen sind, z.B. für C. K. Barrett, *The Holy Spirit and the Gospel Tradition* (London, 1947), pp. 88, 119f.

bekannt. Aber das Incognito Jesu Christi hört nicht auf. Auch nach der Taufoffenbarung wird er nicht aller Welt offenbar, am allerwenigsten den Weisen und Klugen, sondern allenfalls den Unmündigen und Unmaßgeblichen.

Jesus bleibt letzten Endes der Filius incognitus bis in den Tod. Seine Jünger aber, seine Anhänger und alle, die etwas vom Messiasgeheimnis ahnen, warten von Tag zu Tag auf die Stunde der Offenbarung und Machtergreifung, auf den Beginn der Endereignisse im Sinne der jüdischen Vorstellung vom Messias incognitus et revelatus (Lk. xxiv. 21). Dagegen kämpft Jesus in Mk. viii. 30ff., in Lk. xix. 11 und öfter. Das ist das Skandalon, das gerade den Freunden Jesu zu schaffen macht (Lk. vii. 23 und öfter).

Die Osterereignisse entfachen die alte Hoffung mit neuer Gewalt (Ag. i. 6): jetzt endlich wird die längst erwartete revelatio des Messias incognitus erfolgen, die Offenbarung Jesu Christi in Macht und Herrlichkeit. Nun geht der große Einbruch der jüdischen Messiasdogmatik und Vulgärapokalyptik in die Urgemeinde und ihre Evangelientradition vor sich. Alle diese eigenmächtigen Hoffnungen und Pseudoverheißungen haben sich nicht erfüllt. Die Menschen sterben, die Apostel gehen dahin, einer nach dem anderen, und der Wandel aller Dinge kommt nicht. Am Ende des apostolischen Zeitalters tritt die große Ernüchterung ein, die Neubesinnung auf die Ursprünge, der Rückgriff über die enthusiastische Vulgärapokalyptik der Urgemeinde auf die eschatologische Botschaft, Haltung und Bedeutsamkeit Jesu von Nazareth — wahrhaft eine reformatio. In diesem Sinne ist Johannes der Reformator unter den Aposteln und Evangelisten.

Die Synoptiker schreiben von der geschichtlichen Unscheinbarkeit und eschatologischen Herrlichkeit Jesu Christi. Das Johannesevangelium aber ist das Evangelium von der geheimen Herrlichkeit des historischen Jesus, deren Fülle dem Glauben erst jetzt faßlich wird und noch immer tiefer und größer offenbar werden soll. Johannes gibt deshalb die Zukunftserwartung nicht preis. Das bezeugt allein schon die johanneische Apokalypse, gleichviel, ob sie nun auf den Apostel und Evangelisten Johannes selber oder auf seine Schule zurückgehen mag. Aber die Zukunft, die Johannes erwartet, ist nur die sichtbare Entfaltung der geheimen Herrlichkeit, die in dem historischen Jesus erschienen ist.

Wo Jesus ist, da ist Gott (Joh. ii. 25; xiv. 9). Da ist der Gegensatz zwischen Diesseits und Jenseits aufgehoben (Joh. i. 14, 18, 51). Auch der Gegensatz zwischen Tod und Leben (Joh. v. 24; xi. 25), zwischen Zeit und Ewigkeit, zwischen Gegenwart, Vergangenheit und Zukunft (Joh. i. 5; viii. 58; xii. 31; xvi. 11) ist relativiert. Selbst das Grundgesetz unserer physikalischen Welt, das Gesetz der Schwere, ist eingeklammert (Joh. vi. 19). In der Epiphanie Jesu Christi, in der Begegnung mit ihm erschließt sich eine Dimension sui generis, die dem Menschen ohne die Begegnung mit Jesus Christus verschlossen bleibt. Darum wird durch diese Epiphanie ein neuer Gegensatz akut, der über alle anderen Gegensätze hinweggreift. Es ist der Gegensatz zwischen Offenbarung und Verhüllung. Darum schreibt Johannes in der Rückschau auf die Anfänge der Christusoffenbarung das Wort vom Agnostos Christos: 'Er vertraute sich niemandem an.' Am Ende der Christusbegegnung aber steht das Bekenntnis des letzten Apostels: 'Wir sahen seine Herrlichkeit.'

ACTS AND ESCHATOLOGY

HENRY J. CADBURY

It is usually believed that religious experience precedes expression and hence that theology is the interpretation of prior occurrences. But there is some influence in the reverse direction. Expectation, preconceived notions often affect experience or at least condition the reporting of it. I am not quite sure what is meant by the term historical theology, though I am a member of a society that bears that name. If it means the theology that is based on history, then we do well to remind ourselves that there is also a theological history, namely a proclamation of events based on theology. And the problem is often to conjecture the relation of the two and the sequence of the different factors.

This problem is well illustrated in the beginnings of the Christian belief as reflected in the New Testament, and in particular in the opening chapters of Acts. The writings are part of the interpretative process as well as of the recording process, but they are only a part since they were preceded by years of thought by sundry other Christians. To analyse the factors and the directions of this development is a fascinating problem. It is easier to ask questions or present alternatives than to give answers or make choices.

The Book of Acts suggests that the early Church had side by side three noteworthy convictions.

A. Jesus of Nazareth had risen from the dead.

B. He would return from heaven.

C. His followers had received the Holy Spirit.

There is no reason to doubt the primitive, not to say primary character of these beliefs—the resurrection, the *parousia*, and the Spirit. Important results followed from them, as, for example, assurance of Christ's messiahship, unless it is supposed that belief in his messiahship led to belief in his resurrection and not vice versa as in Rom. i. 4. But if we may start when all were there already existing side by side we shall find that they provide materials for inquiry such as we have indicated. The letters of Paul, our earliest Christian literature, already include all three as cardinal beliefs. Though they pertain to different times, the past, the future and the present, they were beliefs charged with emotion and impulse. It would be difficult to disentangle or to compare the enthusiasm which each separately generated. For the author of John's Gospel they appear to be almost interchangeable. There Jesus is represented as promising to return himself or to send the Comforter in his place. And his own return is referred to in terms that vary between resurrection and *parousia*, or at least are ambiguous enough to refer to either.

What is the connection, if any, between these three beliefs? Luke certainly finds a relation between them. Like John[1] he implies that the Spirit would only come after Jesus had died and risen or ascended. The disciples were to wait for it. On the other side the Spirit was connected with the *parousia*. It was a characteristic of 'the last days'—a phrase added by Luke to Joel. Paul calls it an earnest or first-fruits. It was even in the present an apocalyptic phenomenon. Passages in the Synoptic Gospels suggest the same connection, though references to the Spirit there are notably few.[2] Of the connection of resurrection with *parousia* the traces are obscured by the separation of the former into two stages in Luke's presentation. Probably in other early Christian thought it was more evident, as it is in John. It can be taken for granted that for Jesus to return from heaven he must have risen to heaven, and the similarity of the two transits is explicitly stated in Acts i. 11.

It is necessary at this point to inquire at more length into the history of the resurrection belief, and its evidences. In our gospels we have no account of the resurrection itself. That is described only in the Gospel of Peter. What we do have is accounts of appearances of the risen Jesus and the notice of the empty grave. One can hardly regard these as three unconnected beliefs. What was the connection between them? Was the resurrection inferred from the appearances? or from

[1] This is found in the farewell passages in John xiv–xvi. Cf. also vii. 39 where 'glorified' seems to mean ascension rather than death, as does 'lifted up' at iii. 14.

[2] Matt. xii. 28; Luke iv. 18; and the variant in Luke's version of the Lord's Prayer in which the petition for the coming of the Kingdom becomes one for the cleansing by the Spirit.

the empty grave? Or one of these latter from the other? Certainly both the appearances and the empty grave are reported to us in terms so plainly apologetic that it is easy to suppose that sometimes or at some time the belief in the resurrection itself was primary.

Even that belief may well have been sometimes in a somewhat different form. It has been argued that parallel, perhaps prior, to the gospel accounts, there was a belief that Jesus had risen directly from death to heaven.[1] This is the exaltation to which the Old Testament looked forward. It was in heaven that he belonged, and it was not necessary that he should sojourn either under the earth or on the earth. If he was indeed risen he could appear quite as well from his heavenly abode. It was there that Stephen saw him later. It was there he promised the thief on the cross to be 'today'. Neither in Paul's list nor in the several gospel accounts is the possibility excluded that the risen Jesus was a heavenly apparition. As such it was again later that he appeared to Paul.

Beliefs in heavenly apparitions were congenial enough in the ancient world. That would be one natural form for 'evidences' of the risen Jesus to take. But they would not satisfy all believers, not to mention unbelievers, for example those to whom Paul makes answer in I Cor. xv. Apparently to meet these doubts the stories in our gospels are presented—that on the third day (Sunday) and afterwards the grave was found to be empty and that the risen Jesus had sundry encounters with his disciples. These stories circulated in terms that were appropriate to their purpose and to the presuppositions of the time. They were calculated to meet unbelief rather than to fill out an outline of factual events. Minor discrepancies are to be expected. Their abundance is partly due to the large number of our authorities. For we have here no less than eleven different writings, some of them incomplete, from at least nine writers.[2] Nowhere else do we have such 'riches' and they are truly an 'embarrassment'. The process of development cannot be traced, even in matters where the accounts agree or overlap.

[1] G. Bertram, 'Die Himmelfahrt Jesu vom Kreuz aus und der Glaube an seine Auferstehung', *Festgabe für Adolf Deissman* (Tübingen, 1927), pp. 187–217.

[2] I Cor. xv. 5–8; Mark xvi. 1–8 (incomplete); Matt. xxviii; Luke xxiv; Acts i. 1–11 (from the same writer); John xx; John xxi (perhaps from the same writer); Mark xvi. 9–20; Mark xvi. 8 (shorter variant ending); Gospel of Peter (incomplete); Gospel according to the Hebrews (incomplete).

Let us take for example 'the third day'. Since none of our sources except one of the latest (the Gospel of Peter) reports as a witnessed event the actual resurrection from the tomb it is not unfair to suppose that this dating was an inference. But from what? The unreflecting Bible reader is probably willing to infer the date of the resurrection from the date at which Jesus is seen alive and the tomb is found empty, but at most these suggest the time *ante quem*. Paul and the evangelists connect the rising, or perhaps the rising on the third day, with scriptures. But what scriptures? We are not told. Jesus is reported also as predicting a resurrection on the third day. There is another possibility of a reason for a third day *ante quem*. There is some evidence that it was believed that the body decomposed on the fourth day. On the third day the soul and the body were still able to be reunited. Or, finally, is the official date due merely to the literal understanding of the phrase 'the third day' used in the frequent but inexact sense of 'soon'?

Returning now to the specifically Lucan version of these early Christian beliefs, we naturally inquire how far his account as elaborated by his predecessors, who gave him his accounts in oral or written form, and his own editorial work are based on such ingredients as we have mentioned. Inference, whether from scripture, folklore or logic, almost certainly tended to supplement any data that the transmitters accepted as factual.

Luke himself had apparently an orderly mind and a strong belief in objective reality. This shows itself in his attitude to the three aforementioned enthusiastic beliefs of the early Christians. We would do an injustice to the evangelist if we attributed to him any notion of merely natural and subjective convictions as characteristic of the early Church. He would not understand if told that the supernatural is often merely a way of representing the subconscious. The resurrection, the Spirit, and the *parousia* were not for him to be transferred to events of mere imagination, or to be regarded as poetical expressions not to be understood quite literally. Particularly in the case of the Holy Spirit we moderns find it easy to understand the phenomena as a release from inhibitions, a heightening of the inner resources, an integrating of the personality, a consciousness of new power, an assurance. No doubt all these and similar psychological features occurred, but they were not the whole experience as understood by an early Christian like Luke. Its mystery was due to its supernatural not to its wholly inward character. It had outward signs but they were not merely symbols of an inward and spiritual grace.

This feature of Luke's doctrine of the Spirit is generally recognized. It occurs throughout his references in Acts and even in the Gospel where, unlike his parallels, he describes the descent of the Spirit like a dove explicitly as 'in bodily form' (iii. 22). In the story of Pentecost the tongues of fire are equally *massif*, perceptible to the senses as much as the speaking is intelligible to the foreigner's understanding. John's baptism with water is no more objective than is the Christian baptism with fire or the Holy Spirit. They are two parallel but distinct experiences. The Spirit remains a physical element; it is no mere figure of speech. Luke thinks of its coming to the individual at a definite time and place accompanied before or after with such perceptible phenomena as laying on of hands, water baptism, speaking with tongues.

The story of Pentecost is only a particularly full revelation of this way of thinking. The concreteness of the experience is attributed to an initial occasion with appropriate circumstantiality. Undoubtedly it has some historical roots, but these have been presented in characteristic manner. The kind of speaking with tongues mentioned in I Corinthians probably lies behind it. But the term is given a philological as well as a physical meaning in Acts. The author is interested in the phenomena of human languages. He is also interested in the extension of Christianity across the many cultural frontiers. It is perhaps no accident that Jewish tradition believed that the Law was first proclaimed simultaneously to all peoples in their own tongues and that the proclamation occurred on Pentecost. Elsewhere in Acts the influence of non-Biblical Jewish tradition has apparently affected the author or his sources.

Luke's accounts of the risen Jesus also illustrate his concreteness of presentation. In this he is like the other gospels but is also independent of them in some respects. One suspects that both in his views of the Spirit and in his thought of the risen Jesus Paul would stand somewhat in contrast to Luke. In Luke one notes that the risen Jesus has flesh and bones (xxiv. 39). In the same kind of connection Paul asserts that flesh and blood cannot inherit the Kingdom of God

(I Cor. xv. 50). In Luke also Jesus demonstrates his capacity to eat—a piece of broiled fish, and perhaps some comb honey.[1] While both these are given as satisfactory evidence that Jesus was really risen and not a mere phantom, their special purpose has not carried this evangelist to an extreme of defence uncongenial to him. Perhaps the other evangelists were prepared to go as far. It may be Luke's distinction that he tackled more realistically some of the consequences of the common apologetic.

Reference has already been made to the possibility of the existence in early Christianity of two views of Jesus' resurrection. One was connected with his death, the other with his return. In the first the important thing was to show by terrestrial evidence that death had not held him, in the second to assure him the celestial position from which the *parousia* was to be expected. It was possible to combine the two by placing the exaltation to heaven prior to the appearances on earth. How far other early Christians explicitly recognized this as a solution is not clear. Perhaps the Gospel of Peter is again in this instance the most fully developed. Luke at least is clear and has a different solution. The exaltation follows a sufficient series of earthly appearances. It is a separate event, or at least it occurs in two stages, the resurrection from the grave to earth, the ascension from earth to heaven. Luke's main narrative is here quite shipshape. It can be charted as follows:

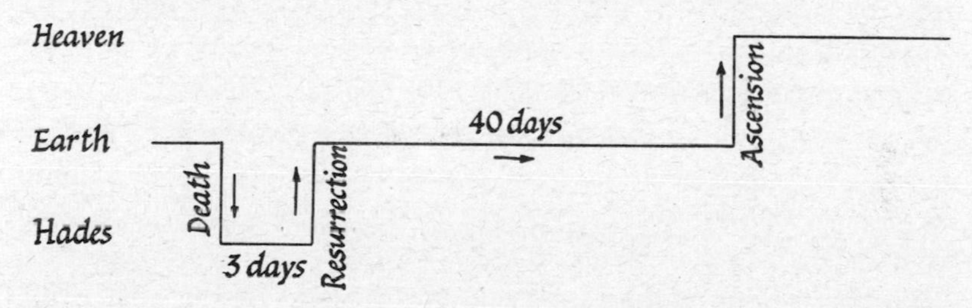

To satisfy this itinerary and chronology Luke must imply that belated appearances of Jesus are either in heaven (Stephen) or from heaven (Paul). He of course expects his final *parousia* from heaven.

There are, however, in Luke–Acts hints of a different or at least a less systematic programme. The Gospel ends with a less formal separation (even in the longer text which adds to 'was parted from

[1] Luke xxiv. 41–3. Cf. 30, 35 and Acts x. 41.

them' in xxiv. 51 'and was carried up into heaven') after an unspecified interval. Beside the 'today' of Luke xxiii. 43, there are other passages which do not indicate any interval between death and entering into glory (xxiv. 26). In fact it is often difficult to tell whether the verbs cited from the Old Testament are being applied to the ascension, the resurrection or merely to the advent of Jesus.[1] That the ascension was no mere insertion or afterthought of Luke is probably attested by the use of that word in Luke ix. 51. In this editorial introduction to a major section of his gospel the writer points to the climax to which he is leading in a word which could conceivably mean death or resurrection but which more naturally is understood of the ascension as concluding or including the three items.[2]

In the full ascension story as in the Pentecost story one sees the characteristic thinking of Luke. These two scenes represent in his second volume as elaborate a bit of frontispiecing as we find in the first volume. Each is dated with considerable definiteness but in such a way as to make the bestowal of the Spirit definitely later than Jesus' period of intercourse with his disciples but 'not many days after' (Acts i. 5). Each is also kept in a quite restricted geographical setting, for beside the consistency of cosmic topography of Luke's outline there is consistency of terrestrial topography as well. He is quite insistent that this part of the story in spite of its promise of later wide expansion (Luke xxiv. 47; Acts i. 8) is kept in Jerusalem and its environs. The only references to distances in the whole work, in spite of the itinerating character of much of both volumes, are to the proximity to Jerusalem of two scenes in this brief period. Emmaus was within sixty stades (7½ miles, Luke xxiv. 13), the Mount of Olives within a Sabbath day's journey (three-fifths of a mile, Acts i. 12). From both places the return to the city was short and immediate. The command not to depart from Jerusalem but to tarry in the city was strictly observed, and even after the gift there promised was received, and a persecution arose against the Church there, the Apostles are said not to have joined in the general Christian exodus (Acts viii. 1). This pointed geographical emphasis in Luke–Acts has

[1] For example the verb 'raise up'. Similarly the allusion of the words 'His life is taken up from the earth' (Acts viii. 33 from Isa. liii) is very obscure.

[2] Cf. L. Girard, *L'Évangile des Voyages de Jésus* (Paris, 1951), p. 23 n. 1.

long raised questions, for it cannot be taken for granted. The writer 'protests too much'. Even without any alternative tradition of appearances of the risen Jesus in Galilee such as are implied or recorded in all the other gospels—the Gospels of Mark and Peter in their extant text only imply them—the Jerusalem locale of Luke's *post mortem* scenes of Jesus demanded some inquiry. The change of Mark xvi. 7 'you will see him in Galilee' to Luke xxiv. 6 'he told you while he was still in Galilee' looks deliberate. Was he consciously refuting the Galilean claim? And if so was it because of a counter-tradition, or was it because either he or the tradition had reason for doing so? Of course the old tradition of the empty grave could have relied only on witnesses based at Jerusalem. Did Luke have reason to think it appropriate for Jesus himself as well as for the disciples to tarry there, the latter for the Holy Spirit, the former for an ascension to heaven. The problem is better stated not, Where was the risen Jesus? but, Where were the disciples when they saw him? The former could certainly have mobility, as Luke also implies.

It has been suggested in recent years that the whole Galilean version is based on a theological assumption and refers to the *parousia* and not to the resurrection at all. Mark and his circle expected the risen and ascended Jesus to return while some of his contemporaries were still living (Mark ix. 1). It was natural that this should be in the scene of his former successes. According to this view that gospel originally ended with a reminder by some angels at the tomb (xvi. 7) of Jesus' promise (xiv. 28) to that effect. To understand it otherwise would be only another example of the easy interchange already mentioned between resurrection appearance and *parousia*.

If the Galilean tradition is suspect as theologically motivated that does not in itself decide in favour of the Judean. Sometimes our choice is between alternatives, both of which may be accounted for on non-factual grounds. The two dates for the Last Supper may illustrate this dilemma. Was it fixed for the night of the Passover meal in order to coincide with that festival, or was it fixed for the night before in order that the actual death of Jesus might coincide with the killing of the paschal lamb? The motives are not quite the same but either liturgical or figurative—in the interest of Christian calendar and Christian typology respectively. In like manner it may be suggested that Luke's Judean emphasis may have some hidden basis. Did it seem to his orderly mind more suitable for the Christian movement to fan out from an established centre? Is it possible that he or his predecessors also had a preconceived view of the place of the Lord's return, but not in Galilee but Judea? Zech. xiv. 4 could have localized that hope in the first century at the Mount of Olives as it has for many Jews in the centuries since. Or does Luke retain an early Christian feeling of the centrality of Jerusalem, which even Paul had shared (Gal. i, ii; II Cor. viii, ix; Rom. xv. 19, etc.)?

If it is granted that the *parousia* required the exaltation of Christ to heaven and that both of these were established Christian tenets, and that the resurrection to earth became also a settled belief, it is obvious that to complete the itinerary in orderly fashion there was a logical necessity for a journey of the risen Jesus from earth to heaven. Thus it would be possible to combine all these elements. Though Luke alone gives us a definite record of it, such a view plainly underlies Jesus' words in John xx. 17 to Mary Magdalene: 'Do not hold me, for I have not yet ascended to the Father; but go to my brethren and say to them, I am ascending', etc. This is true even though this evangelist and the others may be contemplating appearances of the risen Jesus from heaven. Luke's itinerary is consistent and clear.

Now the assumption of living persons to heaven was not an unfamiliar item in contemporary folklore and tradition, either Jewish or pagan. Undoubtedly the Jewish heritage was adequate to account for any influence of this kind on the story in Acts, but the author shows awareness of some non-Jewish motifs in other contexts.[1] In the Old Testament Elijah, Enoch and, in later thought Moses, were examples. The apocalyptic literature had for understandable reasons fixed on these figures for its own purposes. The literature surviving under their names is not of equal extent but is sufficient to indicate their availability as names and, I believe, more because of their exemption from death than for any credentials of their earlier life. They became by it more available as revealers of secrets and indeed more available for return to earth. In Christian story Moses and Elijah appear on the Mount of Transfiguration. It is Luke alone

[1] With the availability of Jewish precedents for ascension scenes may be contrasted the unavailability of such precedents for resurrection scenes. See the thesis of Johannes Müller-Bardorff as summarized by J. Leipoldt in *Theologische Literaturzeitung* (1948), cols. 737–42.

(ix. 31) who tells us that they discussed with Jesus his departure which he was to accomplish at Jerusalem. Can this mean anything different from their own assumption experiences? In Rev. xi. 3–12 their reappearance, death and a second assumption from earth to heaven are contemplated.

It is impossible to indicate just what ingredients formed the ascension story in Acts. It was as natural that the author should present it with the motifs belonging to such scenes as that he should use current Greek words to express it. Among the former would be the reference to eyewitnesses, the interpreting angels, the site precisely at the Mount of Olives. While the author does not say that this site is to be the site of the *parousia*, he does say that the manner of assumption is to be the manner of return. The use of ὃν τρόπον is hardly to be taken in the more general sense sometimes implied by the simpler words ὡς, καθώς. Conditions are to be similar—actual transit, visible to spectators, and probably accompanied with angels and a cloud. Possibly in the tradition, not only the place but the manner of the expected return supplied features for the manner of his going. For the return also was to be visible and actually seen. Note the frequent emphasis on its conspicuousness: 'ye (they, many) shall see'. Also from the time of Dan. vii. 13 'on (with) the cloud (clouds)' was a constant feature of the coming. It was evidently a natural accompaniment of the going. A writer contemporary with Acts, Flavius Josephus, in rehearsing the Old Testament story of Moses' end, quite naturally adds this feature of a cloud. Another coincidence may be noted between Acts and contemporary Jewish writing. The two apocalypses of Esdras (IV Ezra) and Baruch are not quite independent literary pieces, though their exact connection is not known. It is therefore not remarkable that they coincide in the number of seven visions and in the separation between the visions and in a final scene after an identical number of days. But it is noteworthy that that number of days is forty, the same as is noted in Acts as preceding the final farewell of Jesus.

We turn finally to the treatment of the *parousia* and associated items in Luke–Acts. They did not lend themselves to creative logic quite as the resurrection-ascension and Pentecost stories did for the simple reason that they could not be reported as events already experienced. For Luke, as for the tradition behind him, they were still future. A certain indefiniteness was therefore inevitable. Here, as in other *theologoumena*, the Christians could and did draw on Jewish expectation found in what are for us canonical scriptures and also outside of them. We can compare with Luke–Acts not only the New Testament epistles but also the abundant apocalyptic material in the gospels, with parts of which Luke is in literary interdependence. There is no reason to suppose that Luke would not objectify this subject in the same way in which he did the other matters, at least as far as circumstances permitted. Geographically and chronologically it could be as definite as the other supernatural events, except that its time and place would not be known in advance. Jesus would remain in the heaven to which the ascension had raised him. He would stay there for a determined length of time. There would be no vague or partial return. Luke is particularly definite that events of this sort, the ascension (Luke ix. 51), the day of Pentecost (Acts ii. 2), the periods of the Gentiles (Luke xxi. 24) occur when such determined lengths of time expire. Note the verb fulfil (πληρόω). The same God and the same Jesus will be the actors in the future scene as in the past. The resurrection of Jesus is a credential of the coming judgment by Jesus (Acts iv. 10–12; xvii. 31). This is one of the purposes of the ambiguous term used, God's 'raising up' of Jesus. The time indeed is not known to men, nor to be known to them, but the certainty of the event is attested not only by the resurrection but by the ascension and the gift of the Holy Spirit (Acts i. 6 and 8; ii. 17–20, 32).

The eschatological element in the Book of Acts taken by itself is often thought to be slight. That is of course partly because the book is mainly narrative. For this or indeed for any branch of theology in Acts we are mainly dependent on the missionary addresses, though we may legitimately add the conversations and other briefer spoken parts. What eschatology there is is tersely given—much of it merely in rubrics. This means that it is taken for granted rather than that it is slighted. The writer deals at length more with other aspects of the message. He had perhaps no reason to answer such questions as were the occasion for the extended treatment of II Thess. ii, I Cor. xv, or even of Mark xiii and parallels. What he does say on the subject is therefore all the more natural and spontaneous and perhaps more revealing than if it were specially motivated.

It includes many of the familiar elements in New Testament eschatology. The preachers preach the Kingdom of God or the things about it (i. 3, viii. 12, xix. 8, xx. 25, xxviii. 23, 31). This term appears from almost the first verse to the last verse in the book. As object of sundry verbs of speaking it constitutes a formula apparently parallel to the writer's more characteristic single verb 'evangelize'. Nothing obviously distinguishes the term Kingdom of God in Acts from such apocalyptic use as it has in the Synoptic Gospels. For example, one enters into it (xiv. 22) through much tribulation. The other term that one associates with this one is Son of Man. Its rarity outside the gospels is notorious and even in them it is confined to Jesus as a speaker. Jesus is rarely speaker in other New Testament books. Hence this self-designation is not be to expected. Of two early instances of its application to Jesus, one is on the lips of his brother James in the Gospel according to the Hebrews, the other is in Acts on the lips of Stephen (vii. 56). Its association with Dan. vii. 13 is as obvious here and in some gospel passages as it is in Rev. i. 13; xiv. 14. The Book of Acts does not often say explicitly that Jesus is to return, as it does in i. 11, but this is implied by the temporariness of his being in heaven (iii. 21). At the end of this period the Lord will send the Christ appointed for you, even Jesus (iii. 20). Possibly the blotting out of sins and the times of refreshing (iii. 19) belong to this terminus rather than earlier, though this is uncertain.

The terminus of that interval is also described in this context as 'the establishment of all things that God spoke by the mouth of his holy prophets from the beginning of time'. The same word 'establish'—not, I think, re-establish or restore—occurs in the disciples' question to Jesus (i. 6): 'Do you at this time establish the kingdom for Israel?'

Other features of the last times are the resurrection and the day of judgment. These are appropriately mentioned in speeches in Acts as matters that the reader will understand without the speakers' explaining them. After all, the speeches are reported for the reader, not for the original audience. For that audience sometimes more explanation would be expected. The resurrection of Jesus is of course not future but past, but the resurrection of others implied from it is mentioned at iv. 2; xvii. 18, 32; xxiii. 6; xxiv. 15, 21; xxvi. 8, 23.

The plural 'dead persons' is used as elsewhere in both usual forms, resurrection *of* the dead and resurrection *from* the dead. In xxiv. 15 we have one of the few passages in the New Testament which answer the question whether the good only rise or whether both the good and evil. Paul is here quoted as having a faith in God that there is to be resurrection of both the just and the unjust. The context suggests that this view is what accords with the law and with what is written in the prophets, and also that it was the expectation of his Jewish accusers themselves.

References to the future judgment occur less often, but they are clear at x. 42; xvii. 31 and xxiv. 25. In two of these passages the verb μέλλω occurs, as it does of the future wrath in Luke iii. 7 and of the resurrection of the just and unjust in the passage of Acts just quoted. Cf. also xxvi. 23. The judge when identified in these passages is Christ not God, a matter on which the Christian writers have not unanimity.[1] In x. 42 it is explicit that the judgment will be for both living and dead. This reminds us of the distinction Paul makes between the living and the dead (I Thess. iv. 15; I Cor. xv. 52) in connection with the *parousia*. It implies that for the author of Acts also those living at the time of the end would have experience parallel to that of those already dead.

There may be other passages in Acts which should be included in a summary of its eschatology, for example, some of the verses which contain the words 'save', 'salvation' and 'life'. The passages already cited are sufficient to indicate that the author has no ignorance of its doctrines as a welcome part of early Christian belief. Perhaps the Book of Acts ought not to be treated as a unity. We do not know whether the speeches rest any or all of them on sources written or oral. As far as the eschatology is concerned it is consistent enough to have been acceptable to the single mind of the writer. It is also consistent enough with the eschatology of his other volume, the Gospel of Luke. There written sources were almost certainly used. But neither the influence of sources, nor the author's own adjustment of material to avoid anachronism, nor any effort he may have made to vary what the several speakers say to suit their several times or roles, has seriously disturbed a reasonably coherent view of the last

[1] The judgment seat before which we must appear or be presented is in II Cor. v. 10 that of Christ, in Rom. xiv. 10 that of God.

things. There are reasons to believe that Luke did not always think through his conceptions. Behind any diversity of Christian sources the Jewish apocalyptic hope, based as it was in part on unconnected passages in more than one book of Scripture, provided reason for vagueness.

It would seem appropriate on the present occasion to try to relate these comments on Acts and eschatology with two analyses of Christian beginnings which are associated with the name of Professor C. H. Dodd. His theses recommend themselves to many scholars, at least in the English-speaking world, and not only because of his recognized competence in the field of New Testament study and his persuasive way of presenting them. They also concur very comfortably with certain current theological interests. They have the great advantage of being christened with definite names. One of them has a Greek name, and when a term from a foreign language is employed in such matters it often seems to the simple-minded to give to the concept a validity even greater than if plain English was used. The Greek word is *kerygma* (κήρυγμα). It means 'preaching' or better 'proclamation'. In the New Testament it means primarily the act or function of proclaiming, but in contemporary theology it appears to be used or misused of the content—the apostolic message, for which content the New Testament has words such as 'the gospel' and sometimes simply 'the word'. The other term is 'realized eschatology'. No Greek name is given to it. Indeed I hardly know how it would be expressed in Greek. Those who deal with it often affect another Greek term in this connection, 'the *eschaton*'.

It is unnecessary to repeat in detail Professor Dodd's argument about these matters.[1] Using the Epistles of Paul and the addresses in the early part of Acts, he undertakes to construct a list of items that were prominent in the preaching of the Apostles. He finds the two sources in substantial agreement on some seven affirmations. They

[1] See his *The Apostolic Preaching and Its Developments* (London, 1936, Chicago, 1937; new ed. London, 1944). References here are to the last. The term and the sketch of the contents could have been derived from part of the second chapter of Martin Dibelius' *Die Formgeschichte des Evangeliums* (1919; second ed. 1933; Eng. trans. 1935), as indeed Dodd himself suggests in the *Expository Times*, vol. XLIII (1932), p. 399, reprinted in *New Testament Studies* (Manchester, 1953), p. 9. Dodd's views on realized eschatology are not available so conveniently but were propounded in *The Parables of the Kingdom* (London, 3rd edition, 1936).

are mainly in the past but Professor Dodd feels that they are so suffused with eschatological implications that they secure a kind of eschatological significance. In other words, what has happened and is happening for the first Christians seemed to be of the quality of the end. In them eschatology has been 'realized'. To use the three items mentioned at the beginning of this essay, the resurrection of Jesus and the presence of Jesus are of a piece with the supernatural dénouement still to be expected and in fact anticipate in experience what was expected. This Dodd regards as the primitive stage of apostolic message. He speaks of it as coeval with the Church, as original.

While the headings of the *kerygma* continue in later times, its 'development' hinges largely upon changed views of eschatology. The recent past and present by their supernatural character had seemed to be very near the consummation. But as the consummation tarried, its character was construed in more apocalyptic terms at least in some quarters. It becomes futurist rather than realized. This development Dodd finds in II Thess. ii, Mark xiii and in Revelation. But the true continuation of the realized eschatology of the primitive period he finds most fully expressed in other parts of Paul's teaching, such as his Christ-mysticism of the believer and the embodiment of the future in the Church, and especially in the Fourth Gospel. 'The work of Paul and John represents the most significant and far-reaching developments of the apostolic Preaching in the New Testament.'[1]

How does Acts fit into this scheme of doctrinal evolution? According to Dodd its early speeches represent pretty faithfully as the Jerusalem *kerygma* the first stage when the expectation of the end becomes relatively unimportant because of the assurance and importance of its past and present realization. The position is earlier than the apocalyptic emphasis. But what sign is there of realized eschatology either primitive or late in this volume? Certainly recent historical events are premonitions of the later stages. The gift of the Spirit is assurance of the last days for which it was promised. The resurrection of Jesus is in Acts assurance of the coming resurrection of Christians. It is noticeable that in Paul these anticipatory data are both described by the same figure of speech—the firstfruits (Rom. viii. 23; I Cor. xv. 20, 23). The resurrection of Jesus is in Acts also an assurance (πίστις, xvii. 31) of the coming judgment. Possibly

[1] *The Apostolic Preaching*, p. 73.

the healing by Jesus of those overpowered by the devil is mentioned in Acts x. 38 as a foretaste of the final victory of God over the devil. Something of the sort underlies the exorcisms and other cures in the gospels. In fact realized eschatology in the Lucan writings nowhere comes so near to a single definite expression as it does in the Q saying, 'If I by the finger of God cast out demons, then the kingdom of God has come upon you (ἔφθασεν) ahead of time' (Luke xi. 20). The Greek verb here is not the usual verb 'to come' nor even 'to draw near'. The latter occurs in the perfect tense (ἤγγικεν), but it has not the same meaning of the future realized but rather of the future imminent, whereas the verb 'to come' even in the present tense means future. Thus, when in Luke xvii. 20, 21 Jesus is asked by the Pharisees, 'When does the kingdom of God come?', the verb means 'will come' or, as we say futuristically in English also, 'is coming'. The answer, whatever the phrase ἐντὸς ὑμῶν means, is not an emphatic change of time from future to present. The tense of the Pharisees is not what Jesus corrects, but the reliance on 'observation'. So also in Acts i. 6 the question, 'Do you at this time establish the kingdom for Israel?' is not corrected by any hint of present partial realization, as it is not by any hint of a less nationalistic character.

There are many forms of anticipation that do not alter the ultimate character of the later event. The death and resurrection of Christ were believed to be predicted in the Scriptures, but that did not reduce the objective reality of the events themselves. They came true only at their appointed time. It has been argued that the Holy Spirit is inconspicuous in the synoptic record because the presence of Christ himself was an equally numinous experience,[1] but for the first Christians the Spirit's contemporary presence was no less in full measure because of the events that preceded the experience which Acts dates at Pentecost. They expected still other experiences promised in the past scriptures and renewedly promised by what had happened recently. Luke on the whole has more to say about recent or present fulfilment of past prophecy than about present adumbrations of future expectations.

The Book of Acts does not spiritualize away the concrete eschatological hopes of Christianity nor on the other hand does it emphasize their imminence and urgency with vivid details of apocalyptic.

[1] C. K. Barrett, *The Holy Spirit and the Gospel Tradition* (1947).

It retains, I am persuaded, the old and literal expectation but is satisfied to leave the time to God's ordering. It is true to the fundamental Jewish-Christian conception of religion as events in time sequence. To remind us of this characteristic is the great service of Oscar Cullmann's *Christ and Time*, whatever one may think of some other features of his book.

The two aspects of the *parousia* discussed in the New Testament are its reality and its degree of nearness. They are not entirely dissociated, but suffice it to say that the attitude of Luke in the Gospel is one of discouraging too early expectation. This I have sufficiently argued elsewhere.[1] Nothing in the speeches of Acts contradicts that emphasis. Nor does this emphasis mean that the event when it came would be any less definite and literal, or that it was to be anticipated in any partial way and was therefore less important. We can prepare for it now, and should urgently do so. We can receive now the Spirit which is its earnest. But the thing itself is a separate event, sudden and universal (Luke xxi. 34–36). In the light of Luke's whole treatment of the other phenomena mentioned at the beginning of this essay there is little reason to suppose that he would blur the concreteness of the other events or series of events to which Jews and Christians looked forward. Neither did the earthly life of Jesus fulfil the ultimate hopes of Luke's canticles, nor did the experience of the Church reduce at all the unfinished purposes of God in Christ. Whatever evidence may be found in the Gospel of John or even in the synoptic material of what has come to be called realized eschatology, Luke's own emphasis and contribution does not seem to have lain in that direction. It would be quite contrary to the practice of giving precision of time and place and manner to the divine intervention in history as Luke conceived it. If other Christians ancient or modern have found the primitive emphasis on such a literal future event embarrassing, Luke gives no real countenance to any of their ways of avoiding it.

The idea of the *kerygma* as a primitive collection of common Christian beliefs is also an attractive one, especially in an age when the Church is seeking for authority which will have the sanction of history and which thus will render a service towards providing

[1] *The Making of Luke–Acts* (1927), pp. 284–96, esp. pp. 292 ff.

a norm for modern interdenominational unity. No one will challenge the fact that our New Testament sources display considerable overlapping in what their authors believed as a Christian message. Chronologically Paul's letters are the earliest documents, and the speeches by Peter and others in Acts, in so far as they are true to the time assigned them, are no later in date. Yet according to Professor Dodd himself parts of Paul's letters are development rather than early *kerygma*. The speeches also have to be handled somewhat cautiously and selectively. It is unfortunate that the suspicion can never be banished that the speeches of Peter, even those with apparent Aramaic colouring, are not more than a skilful writer's conception of what seemed to one Christian of later date appropriate for an earlier one.

Yet even if we had several Christian documents of undoubted primitiveness, variety of authorship, and complete independence, would their area of coincidence in beliefs be of convincing historical and present-day significance? In such matters there is always the factor of statistical accident. Are affirmations mentioned only in one source, or mentioned perhaps not at all, less characteristic of the early faith than those which recur? Professor Dodd has indicated that some points in the Pauline *kerygma* do not appear in the Jerusalem *kerygma* of Acts and vice versa.[1] This is only to be expected, and it suggests that the rule of two witnesses cannot be used to exclude the testimony of only one. The contents of Paul's letters are obviously based on what humanly speaking must be called the accident of practical demands. They may not even represent at all adequately his missionary preaching, since their purpose was rather pastoral. The author of Acts for all his skilful variety may well regard his speeches as mutually supplementary. If the later creeds were influenced by contemporary controversy, may that not also have been true, even if less obviously, of the credal elements in the earlier Christian literature?

Harnack calls attention to one absence from the usual creeds which will illustrate this point. He says:

> The choice and sending out of the Apostles (after the resurrection) found its way even into the Rules of Faith, and we may say that simply by an accident of history it did not find a place in the ancient Roman Symbol. Passages from prophecy are alleged as foretelling it just as in

[1] *The Apostolic Preaching*, pp. 25ff.

the case of the main incidents in the life of Jesus himself. Writers in Asia Minor, Rome, and Egypt (before A.D. 160) unite in their testimony on this point, and even the Gnostics shared in part this conception.[1]

Though the *kerygma* is conceived as a body of beliefs a full century earlier, reconstructions of it can easily have as striking omissions. Indeed it is hard to believe that precisely the command to preach was not reported in the preaching. As good a case for this clause could be made from the same sources as confirm the usual items in aspostolic preaching. The Muratorian Canon's summary of the four-fold Gospel is taken by Dodd as 'an expression of the original apostolic Preaching'.[2] It lists Christ's nativity, passion, the resurrection, his converse with the disciples and his two advents. One suspects that here his converse with the disciples means his post-resurrection commission.

One source for the reconstruction of the apostolic preaching is the Gospels themselves. Cannot the words of Jesus be used as legitimately as the speeches of others in Acts to reconstruct the *kerygma*? Two well-known books on the apostolic age of an earlier generation (Weizsäcker and Ropes) started precisely with the gospel records of the commission of the disciples. Also the following sounds very much like the apostolic message though the risen Jesus is the speaker: 'Thus it is written, that the Christ should suffer and on the third day should rise from the dead, and that repentance and forgiveness of sins should be preached in his name to all nations' (Luke xxiv. 46, 47). The last phrase implies the universalism of the preaching and that is a constant feature of this clause of *kerygma*. It is not only in the Pauline Epistles as one would expect it to be but is explicit or implicit in some of the speeches in Acts.[3]

The formulation of the *kerygma* is, I believe, defective in another way. It ignores the unequal age and origin of its several parts. When one presents a body of beliefs as a summary of Christian faith at an

[1] *The Origin of the New Testament* (1925), p. 48.

[2] *The Apostolic Preaching*, p. 55.

[3] Since this essay was written criticisms have been made of the selection of items in the *kerygma* by Donald J. Selby, 'The Pre-literary Development of the *Kerygma*' (unpublished Ph.D. thesis, Boston University, 1954), and T. F. Glasson, 'The Kerygma: Is Our Version Correct?' *Hibbert Journal*, LI (1953), pp. 129–32. Glasson thinks one article should be added—the apostles as witnesses, and one subtracted—the return of Christ in glory to judge the world.

early time and then speaks of a subsequent development there is a suggestion that the clauses are coeval and in a sense original. I think A. M. Hunter is responsible for the clever parody: 'In the beginning was the *kerygma*.'[1] And to the temper of some modern Christians what was 'in the beginning' is also ultimate, normative and final—'the faith once for all delivered to the saints'.

If, however, what was said at the beginning of this paper has any historical validity we must think of the great affirmations of early Christianity as having themselves not an original givenness but a genetic character. Catch the apostolic preaching as early as you can, but you must still admit that development preceded as well as followed that date. The early beliefs are a result of the kinds of development that we can trace later in the canonical records. No matter how much the records coincide, there was apparently much freedom and variety. Canonization may have eliminated expressions that lost 'heretical' documents would have given us. Even as it is, we know from the canonical records that for such matter for reflection as the origins of Jesus, sundry lines of thought were active. Beside the Davidic ancestry and descent, there was pre-existence and incarnation, original deity and kenosis, original humility and divine adoption, supernatural generation, etc.

In this pre-*kerygma* development various forces were at work. Logical inference was probably one of them, but in the end the inference gets listed parallel to the datum from which it is inferred, as though they were of equal standing. The Old Testament scriptures played an important part in confirming the beliefs. That is happily recognized by modern scholars, but one cannot rule out the possible influence of Scripture in creating beliefs. Confirmation and suggestion are psychologically too close together to permit always of easy discrimination. The contribution of the Old Testament to narrative details in the Gospels is only more evident and concrete than its influence on the larger units of the faith. Experience too had its effect all along the line. 'Experience worketh' in a sense not intended in the Greek of Rom. v. 4. In the area of apocalyptic, with which we have been here concerned, the different viewpoints are, I believe, not so much due to changing perspectives of a delayed

[1] *The Unity of the New Testament* (London, 1943), p. 22; reprinted as *The Message of the New Testament* (Philadelphia, 1944), p. 26.

parousia as to the practical considerations of the Christian teachers. Indeed, from the start the apocalyptic forecasts had been based very largely on moral considerations. They were not so much inferences from external and political conditions as from the demands which the conduct of men forced upon a moral God who controls history.

Even after this kind of forecasting had been established Christian teachers used it to bring pressure to bear upon the conduct of men. Their variations are within this pattern, for sometimes it seems most useful to press both the certainty and the nearness of the event. At other times, when this approach had succeeded only too well and converts had become so expectant as to be in danger of disillusion by delay, the Christian teachers felt it incumbent upon them to emphasize that it was not so imminent. Certain other things 'must needs happen *first*', including the preaching of the gospel to all nations, and the kind of ominous experiences a persecuted Church and a perplexed society were already suffering, only more of them and worse. If such were the motives and factors that influenced the author of Luke–Acts, we cannot take his apocalyptic as either more or less standard and normative than that of other factors or influences. Neither represents what is intrinsically prior, or continuously fundamental. Neither in his day nor previously is the content of the apostolic preaching static or monolithic. It is a message in process—what in another connection Paul called 'the progression of the gospel'.

The study of eschatology in Luke–Acts leads to some general conclusions that may here be summarized. In spite of the diverse and vague character of the apocalyptic hope that writer has his own distinctive way of dealing with it. He is required by practical conditions to correct the over-expectant attitude by emphasizing the delay that was to be expected. His editorial method, as it has been studied by Hans Conzelmann, shows a consistent interpretation of history in the light of that delay. Attention may be called to this fact, but I defer elaboration until Conzelmann's fuller study is available.[1]

[1] I am indebted to him for a brief outline of his study as it affects eschatology. The only printed material available about it is his article 'Zur Lukanalyse' in *Zeitschrift für Theologie und Kirche*, vol. XLIX (1952), pp. 16–33. It is possible in correcting proof to name the fuller work since published: Hans Conzelmann, *Die Mitte der Zeit: Studien zur Theologie des Lukas* (Beiträge zur Historischen Theologie 17. Tübingen, 1954).

The assurance of the final events of history is strengthened rather than weakened by Luke's acceptance of this delay. Not only the career of Jesus but the history of the early Church with which he supplements his Gospel are legitimate parts of the kind of assurance that is implied in the other gospels. But the present and past do not reduce the importance of the future, or much alter the nature of its expected fulfilment. The *eschaton* remains intact in the future.

Any distinctiveness which there is in the eschatology of Luke–Acts enriches our appreciation of the variety in early Christianity and warns us from thinking of its message as either a contemporary unity or a rectilinear development. In different persons or circumstances Christian thought fluctuated one way or another. It was no one-way street. The word development must not be used to imply that priority or direction can be accepted by us as in accord with anything but our own arbitrary standard. Development preceded as well as followed any stage of evolving doctrine that one may select.

The unity in early Christian preaching is in part due to the common Jewish background, in part to the facts of Jesus' career, in part to the operation of like processes of inference and conclusion. But the several coincident items in the several sources do not form a logical unity or a uniform weight of emphasis so much as an uneven set of beliefs of quite varied origin.

The genetic character of these beliefs is suggested by some features of Luke's report of early Christianity. Beside the interpretation of factual experience various factors were operative and not merely in a single creative chain but continuously. They include combination and logical conclusions, the Old Testament scriptures as formative as well as confirmatory, inference from contemporary *Weltanschauung* or folklore, controversy within and without the Christian community on subjects of theology, and the practical demands of basing ethical exhortation upon some doctrinal affirmation. The prior premise and the subsequent deductions, though they come to stand in our records side by side, have nevertheless quite diverse origins. To that extent any collection of early Christian affirmations has an illusory homogeneity.

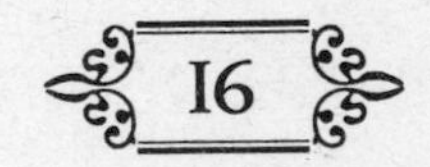

LE CARACTÈRE, À LA FOIS ACTUEL ET FUTUR, DU SALUT DANS LA THÉOLOGIE PAULINIENNE

MAURICE GOGUEL

La religion est, dans la vie, aussi bien individuelle que collective, des croyants, un principe d'organisation et d'unification. Cela rend nécessaire de ne pas isoler les problèmes mais de les considérer dans leurs connexions.

Avant d'aborder la question sur laquelle nous voudrions présenter quelques observations, il faut préciser le sens des termes d'eschatologie et d'apocalyptique, considérés, à tort parfois, comme étant synonymes ou à peu près synonymes. Eschatologie signifie doctrine des choses finales. Toute religion est eschatologique parce qu'elle se présente à l'homme comme un moyen de se dépasser lui-même et de réaliser ainsi la destinée à laquelle il aspire et dont il a le sentiment, plus ou moins confus, qu'elle est sa véritable destinée, bien qu'il ait le sentiment aussi qu'elle ne puisse être réalisée ni par ses propres efforts, ni par le jeu naturel des évènements. Mais, pratiquement, dans le langage habituel de l'histoire des religions, le terme d'eschatologie est, le plus souvent, employé pour désigner une conception d'après laquelle le monde nouveau dans lequel la destinée de l'homme pourra se réaliser, s'établira pour tous les hommes à la fois, dans un monde nouveau établi par la puissance souveraine de Dieu. De cette attente, parfois fiévreuse, on peut, par un glissement psychologiquement fort explicable, passer à l'idée qu'il est possible de se représenter la manière dont se fera le passage du monde présent au monde futur. Dans le judaïsme du temps de Jésus, une apocalyptique complexe et touffue s'était développée dont le christianisme a recueilli l'héritage.

Toute apocalyptique implique une eschatologie mais toute eschatologie n'est pas nécessairement apocalyptique. C'est ainsi que la pensée de Jésus a été nettement eschatologique mais qu'elle n'a pas été apocalyptique. Il est vrai que les Evangiles synoptiques ont mis dans la bouche de Jésus une petite apocalypse (Marc xiii et par.). Mais ce morceau porte nettement la date de sa rédaction. Il est du printemps de 70, du moment où les préparatifs du siège de Jérusalem par Titus étaient commencés mais pas encore assez avancés pour qu'il ne fût plus possible de quitter Jérusalem. Il est possible que ce morceau soit la révélation d'un prophète à la suite de laquelle, d'après Eusèbe (*H.E.* iii, 5, 3), la communauté chrétienne de Jérusalem quitta la ville pour se réfugier à Pella.[1]

Il y a eu un temps où les déclarations messianiques, eschatologiques et apocalyptiques attribuées à Jésus étaient interprétées allégoriquement ou déclarées inauthentiques.[2] Cette position est maintenant dépassée et, depuis une soixantaine d'années, le caractère eschatologique de la pensée de Jésus a été reconnu et on en a donné une interprétation réaliste. Mais, si on compare entre elles les diverses déclarations eschatologiques de Jésus, si on cherche à les situer dans son ministère, on constate que sa pensée a évolué dans le sens d'un recul ou plutôt d'une indétermination du moment de la fin. Quand Jésus a envoyé ses disciples en mission,[3] à la fin de la première partie du ministère galiléen avant que n'ait éclaté une crise, il leur a donné pour la mission qu'il leur confiait des instructions qui vont toutes dans le même sens: donner à leur mission le maximum de rapidité; il leur a déclaré que, même en se hâtant, ils n'auraient pas achevé de parcourir les villes d'Israël avant que le Fils de l'Homme ne vienne (Matt. x. 23).

Un peu plus tard, après la crise galiléenne,[4] quand la perspective des souffrances et de la mort possible a commencé à se dessiner à l'horizon, après avoir parlé à ses disciples des souffrances qui les attendent, eux aussi, Jésus leur dit: 'Je vous le dis, il y en a, parmi ceux qui sont ici présents qui ne goûteront pas la mort, avant d'avoir vu le Royaume de Dieu venir avec puissance' (Marc ix. 1 et par.). Enfin, dans l'apocalypse synoptique, on trouve chez Marc (xiii. 32) et chez Matthieu (xxiv. 36) une déclaration qui marque un recul, ou

[1] Voir la dessus notre livre, *Jésus*[2] (Paris, 1950), pp. 338 ss.

[2] Voir, par exemple, Colani, *Jésus et les croyances messianiques de son temps* (Strasbourg, 1864).

[3] L'historicité de cette mission a été contestée, à tort selon nous. Voir notre *Jésus*, pp. 276 ss.

[4] *Jésus*, pp. 281 ss.

plus exactement une indétermination du moment de la fin: 'Quant à ce jour et à cette heure,[1] nul ne les connaît, ni les anges dans le ciel, ni le Fils, personne, si ce n'est le Père.'

Ce logion ne peut pas avoir fait partie de l'Apocalypse synoptique sous sa forme originale car il est en contradiction avec le principe même de l'apocalyptique. C'est une parole authentique de Jésus. La tradition ne peut avoir imaginé cette parole pour calmer la fièvre eschatologique qui se serait emparée des fidèles, car un logion affirmant l'ignorance de Jésus sur un point essentiel, ne peut avoir été créé par la tradition dont la tendance a été d'affirmer toujours plus nettement la toute-science de Jésus. L'évolution de la pensée de Jésus a donc été caractérisée par un recul toujours plus marqué de la perspective de la fin du monde et même par l'idée qu'il est impossible d'en préciser le moment.

Ce mouvement s'est poursuivi à travers toute l'histoire de l'Eglise qui a été marquée par un recul toujours plus net du moment fixé pour la fin du monde et le retour du Christ et cela malgré la domination du littéralisme biblique. Sans que ces idées aient jamais été théoriquement niées, elles ont pris un caractère théorique et n'ont plus guère eu d'influence sur le comportement spirituel et pratique des croyants. L'Eglise d'aujourd'hui confesse encore, dans le symbole apostolique, la foi au retour du Christ et au jugement dernier, mais quelle est la proportion des Chrétiens pour qui ces formules représentent encore ce qu'elles représentaient au temps où elles se sont fixées? Ce qui en reste, c'est, tout au plus, le sentiment que la foi est orientée vers une réalité toute autre que la réalité présente et dans laquelle seulement sa véritable destinée pourra être réalisée.

Ce mouvement qui a tendu sinon à l'élimination, du moins à la spiritualisation et à l'actualisation de l'eschatologie a eu des causes diverses. Ces causes ont-elles été internes ou externes et si, comme il est vraisemblable, il y a eu, à la fois, des causes internes et des causes externes, quel a été le rôle des unes et des autres?

La cause externe à laquelle il faut tout d'abord penser est la suivante: le christianisme est né en milieu sémitique, c'est-à-dire dans un milieu dominé par un dualisme temporel qui oppose le monde futur au monde présent, mais il s'est réalisé dans le monde hellénique dominé

[1] Ceux de la parousie.

par un dualisme d'un tout autre type, un dualisme ontologique, à expression spatiale, qui oppose le monde matériel au monde spirituel, le monde d'en bas à celui d'en haut. Dans la première génération, le centre de gravité géographique de l'Eglise s'est déplacé pour se fixer dans le monde grec et c'est là seulement que le christianisme s'est développé alors que, dans le monde juif, il n'a abouti à rien de durable. Que cette circonstance ait joué un rôle dans ce qu'on peut appeler la déseschatologisation du christianisme, ne peut être mis en doute, mais l'actualisation et la spiritualisation de l'eschatologie a été tout autre chose qu'un aspect ou qu'une conséquence de son hellénisation. L'apôtre Paul qui a très puissament contribué à cette actualisation n'a été que très peu et très superficiellement touché par l'hellénisme.[1]

On comprendrait mal le paulinisme si on voulait y voir avant tout un système théologique. Certes, Paul a été un grand et puissant théologien, mais ses préoccupations dominantes ont été non d'ordre spéculatif mais d'ordre pratique. Il s'agissait de conquérir des âmes au Christ, d'édifier l'Eglise et, pour cela, il pensait ne disposer que d'un temps très court.

Dans la mesure où il y a eu une théologie paulinienne, que l'apôtre n'a d'ailleurs jamais pris le temps ni éprouvé le besoin d'exposer systématiquement, cette théologie a été non pas celle d'un état mais celle d'un mouvement. Il y a certainement chez Paul des idées théoriques sur Dieu, sur la création, sur l'homme et sa position dans le monde et devant Dieu, mais, si important que cela soit, ce sont des idées qui sont plutôt les présuppositions du paulinisme que le paulinisme lui-même dont l'objet principal n'est pas ce que Dieu est, mais ce qu'il veut et ce qu'il fait.

Le cadre de la théologie paulinienne est vaste puisqu'il va de l'état intemporel antérieur à la création à un τέλος, état intemporel, lui aussi, qui est caractérisé par la formule: 'Dieu tout en tous', c'est-à-dire non plus Dieu seul, mais Dieu recevant l'hommage de l'obéissance et de l'adoration de la création. C'est entre ces deux moments que s'encadre toute l'œuvre de Dieu. Pour Paul, Dieu est celui qui a droit et qui, seul, a droit à l'adoration et à l'obéissance, sans lesquelles, peut-on-dire, il ne serait pas pleinement Dieu. C'est pour se procurer cette

[1] Il suffit de rappeler que, dans I Cor. xv, Paul se montre incapable de comprendre l'idée grecque de l'immortalité de l'âme et qu'il voit dans la négation de la résurrection des corps, la négation de toute vie d'outre-tombe.

obéissance et cette adoration qu'il a entrepris l'œuvre de la création, puis, celle-ci ayant échoué par suite du mauvais usage fait par l'homme de sa liberté,[1] l'œuvre de la rédemption. On peut ainsi dire que le Dieu paulinien est un dieu en expansion.

Mais il y a aussi dans cette théologie des éléments rationnels, notamment une certaine conception anthropologique qui est plus sémitique qu'hellénique. Paul emploie le terme de σάρξ dans deux sens différents. C'est, d'une part, l'état dans lequel l'homme a été créé, neutre à l'égard du péché, c'est à dire susceptible de pécher mais non nécessairement contrainte à pécher. C'est la chair intègre. Mais ce même mot de chair désigne aussi chez Paul, la chair corrompue et devenue siège et cause du péché.[2]

Même sans la chute, ce plan de Dieu n'aurait pas pu aboutir sans une nouvelle intervention de sa part pour réaliser la seconde étape de la création. Ce n'est pas seulement à la chair corrompue et devenue siège et cause du péché mais à la chair, en général, que s'applique le principe énoncé dans I Cor. xv. 50: 'Je vous le dis, frères, la chair et le sang ne peuvent pas hériter du Royaume de Dieu ni ce qui est corruptible de l'incorruptibilité.' Dans ce qui précède immédiatement, Paul avait esquissé la théorie de deux Adams (le second étant le Christ). Le premier était ψυχή ζῶσα,[3] le second πνεῦμα ζωοποιοῦν.[4] Paul insiste sur cette consécution chair-esprit. 'Ce qui vient d'abord,' dit-il, 'ce n'est pas ce qui est pneumatique mais ce qui est psychique, ensuite vient ce qui est pneumatique.'[5]

La pensée paulinienne implique donc l'idée d'une création en deux étapes, au point de départ de chacune d'elles, il y a l'action du Christ. S'il n'y a pas, en effet, chez Paul, une doctrine du rôle créateur du

[1] Liberté que Dieu avait laissée à l'homme parce que seules une adoration et une obéissance libres peuvent avoir de la valeur. Voir à ce sujet notre étude: 'Le paulinisme théol. de la liberté', *Rev. de Théol. et de Philos.* (1951), pp. 93–104, 175–83.

[2] Dans Rom. vii. 7, Paul dit que le commandement a provoqué le péché en sorte que ce qui était 'pour la vie' a provoqué la mort. Ce texte n'est intelligible que si on admet que la promulgation de la Loi appartient au plan de la création qui a continué à se développer même après que la chute l'a rendu irréalisable.

[3] C'est-à-dire possédant la vie comme un souffle que Dieu avait mis en lui et qu'il pouvait aussi bien lui laisser que lui retirer.

[4] C'est à dire possédant la vie d'une manière telle qu'il peut la donner.

[5] Il est possible que Paul vise ici quelque théorie gnostique qui explique le péché par une chute de l'esprit dans la matière.

logos aussi précisément exposée que dans le prologue du Quatrième Evangile ou dans le premier développement de l'épître aux Hébreux, ce rôle cependant apparaît nettement dans I Cor. viii. 6 où Paul dit: 'Il y a un seul Seigneur, Jésus Christ par qui sont toutes choses et nous sommes par lui.' C'est donc lui qui est l'organe de la première comme de la seconde étape de la création.

L'œuvre du Christ dans la rédemption apparaît donc comme étant double, ayant un caractère à la fois négatif et positif. Les formules pauliniennes de la rédemption sont, en apparence, déséquilibrées; le rôle de la rédemption étant à la fois négatif et positif. L'humanité est tombée sous le joug du péché et par là sous le coup d'une condamnation qui le voue à la mort.[1] Quand Paul dit: 'Le Christ nous a rachetés de la malédiction en devenant malédiction à notre place' (Gal. iii. 13) cela signifie 'il vous a rachetés de la malédiction et vous a libérés du poids du péché'. On s'attendrait à ce qu'il continue sur la même ligne en disant: 'Vous êtes rétablis dans une chair intègre; veillez donc à ne pas retomber sous le joug du péché.' Pourtant ce n'est pas là ce qu'il dit, mais: 'Vous êtes devenus spirituels, vous êtes morts au péché, ne retombez pas dans le péché.' C'est qu'il y a un double élément dans l'œuvre du Christ, l'un négatif, l'autre positif. L'élément négatif, c'est la justification rendue possible par l'expiation du péché sur la croix du Christ. L'élément positif, c'est le passage de la vie du justifié du plan de la chair à celui de l'esprit.

Si le chrétien justifié est devenu spirituel, ce n'est pas encore totalement. Il continue à vivre dans la chair et à subir sa pression qui le pousse au péché. Il n'est pas devenu incapable de pécher. Il n'a reçu que les gages de l'Esprit et d'une manière telle que s'il manque de vigilance il retombera dans la vie de la chair. Telle est la raison de la tension qu'il y a dans la vie du chrétien telle que Paul la conçoit.

Quelle est pour Paul, l'assurance que le chrétien peut avoir de son salut?[2] Théoriquement il ne devrait en avoir aucune. Comment pourrait-il être certain de ne jamais retomber dans le péché? Il

[1] Etant donnée la question qui nous occupe nous ne tiendrons compte que de la ligne juridique de la sotériologie paulinienne, mais il ne faut pas oublier que, comme l'a bien mis en lumière le théologien suédois Aulen (*Christus Victor*, trad. G. Hoffmann, Paris, 1949), il y a une autre ligne qui se développe sur la plan de la puissance.

[2] Voir notre étude, 'Les fondements de l'assurance du salut chez l'apôtre Paul', *Rev. d'Hist. et de Philos. rel.* vol. XVII, pp. 105–44.

y a cependant dans les épîtres pauliniennes de magnifiques et triomphantes affirmations de la certitude du salut, en face desquelles on peut, tout au plus, mettre deux passages ou s'exprime un léger doute, surtout théorique, sur l'achèvement du salut. C'est d'abord I Cor. ix. 27: 'Je traite durement mon corps et je l'asservis de peur qu'après avoir prêché aux autres, je ne sois moi-même rejeté.' Et c'est Phil. iii. 1, ces mots par lesquels Paul définit le but de son effort: 'pour parvenir, si je puis (εἴ πως) à la résurrection d'entre les morts.' La disproportion est flagrante entre les affirmations de la certitude du salut et le doute sur sa réalisation.

La certitude paulinienne du salut n'est fondée que sur le sentiment de la puissance et de la bonté de Dieu qui ne laissera pas inachevée l'œuvre qu'il a entreprise.

La christologie paulinienne ne peut être vraiment comprise que par une comparaison avec deux autres types de christologie que nous rencontrons dans le Nouveau Testament. La plus simple est celle que l'on rencontre dans les discours de Pierre au début du livre des Actes:[1] Jésus est un prophète envoyé par Dieu. Les Juifs n'ont pas accueilli sa prédication et l'ont fait mourir. Mais Dieu l'a ressuscité et l'a élevé à sa droite en qualité de Messie. Cette christologie pourrait être graphiquement représentée de la manière suivante ⟋. Pour Paul Jésus préexiste en qualité de Messie et de Fils de Dieu. Les Juifs l'ont fait mourir mais Dieu l'a ressuscité et l'a élevé au rang de Kurios, ce qui pourrait être présenté par le schéma suivant ¬√. Enfin la conception johannique présente le Christ reprenant après sa résurrection la gloire qu'il avait de toute éternité avant la création du monde, ce qui peut être représenté par le schéma suivant ‾\/‾.

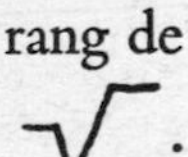

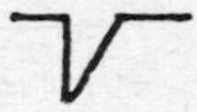

Le paulinisme est une eschatologie,[2] non seulement parce que les deux épîtres aux Thessaloniciens et la première aux Corinthiens contiennent des tableaux apocalyptiques, mais surtout parce que son objet, c'est une action que Dieu poursuit en vue d'une certaine fin

[1] Il n'est pas certain que ces discours soient de Pierre, mais l'essentiel est qu'ils expriment une forme très archaïque de la pensée chrétienne.

[2] Dans une certaine mesure aussi une apocalyptique.

qui ne sera pleinement réalisée que dans un au delà. Mais entre cette apocalyptique paulinienne et l'apocalyptique juive, il y a une différence essentielle. L'apocalyptique juive comporte un schéma à deux termes. Monde nouveau et monde ancien se succèdent directement, étant séparés l'un de l'autre par l'apparition du Messie et par un jugement qui opèrera une discrimination entre ceux qui seront admis dans le monde nouveau et ceux qui en seront exclus.

A ce schéma à deux termes, Paul a substitué un schéma à trois termes, en intercalant entre le monde ancien et le monde nouveau une période intérimaire pendant laquelle les deux mondes coexistent, chevauchant l'un sur l'autre. Paul s'est représenté cette période comme devant être courte. A un certain moment de sa vie,[1] il a eu le sentiment qu'elle se terminerait encore de son vivant. (Cf. I Thess. v. 5; I Cor. xv. 52.) Dans la suite pourtant, le moment de la parousie a reculé dans la pensée de Paul et la possibilité, voire même la quasi-certitude de sa mort avant le moment où elle se produirait s'est imposée à son esprit.[2] La période intérimaire de la coexistence des deux mondes doit durer depuis la résurrection jusqu'à la parousie du Seigneur. Le monde nouveau, celui de l'Esprit et non plus de la chair, est devenu une réalité actuelle depuis que le Christ a été élevé au rang de κύριος. Il ne l'est pas seulement pour lui, mais aussi d'une manière réelle mais encore inachevée pour ceux qui, unis à lui par la foi, ont reçu le gage de l'Esprit bien qu'ils n'en aient pas encore la pleine possession. Le monde nouveau n'est pas encore la seule réalité. A côté de lui — et en lutte avec lui — le monde ancien subsiste, soumis à Satan dont l'action s'exerce même sur les élus qu'il cherche à faire retomber dans le péché. De là vient cette tension

[1] Au moment où il a écrit les deux épîtres aux Thessaloniciens et la première aux Corinthiens.

[2] A. Sabatier ('Comment la foi chrétienne de l'apôtre Paul a triomphé de la crainte de la mort', *Rev. chrétienne* vol. I (1894), pp. I ss.) a fait remarquer qu'entre la rédaction de la première et de la seconde épître aux Corinthiens, Paul s'est trouvé dans une situation si critique qu'il a désespéré de la vie. Il y fait allusion dans II Cor. i. 8–11 en des termes qui étaient clairs pour les Corinthiens qui savaient à quoi il faisait allusion et qui ne le sont pas pour nous. Ce serait alors que Paul aurait compris que la mort même ne pourrait pas interrompre, ne serait-ce que provisoirement, sa communion avec le Christ. Sur les raisons qui ne nous permettent pas d'accepter cette explication des deux aspects de l'eschatologie paulinienne voir notre étude, 'Parousie et Résurrection', dans *Trois études sur la pensée religieuse du christianisme primitif* (Paris, 1931), pp. 9 ss.

dans la situation du chrétien dont nous avons déja parlé. Le croyant est justifié, mais il n'est pas sauvé, du moins ne l'est-il qu'en espérance (Rom. viii. 24) et si cela signifie beaucoup plus qu'avoir l'espérance du salut, cela signifie aussi beaucoup moins que posséder le salut. Le chrétien n'est pas devenu incapable de pécher et, par conséquent, il reste toujours susceptible d'être rejeté. Pourtant il y a pour Paul une possession actuelle du salut, par anticipation, si on veut, mais dont l'Esprit est le gage, cet Esprit pourtant, qui est un don qui n'est pas inamissible puisque Paul écrit 'N'éteignez pas l'Esprit' (I Thess. v. 19).

Aucune doctrine n'est plus étrangère à la pensée de Paul que le synergisme, c'est à dire que l'idée d'un salut devant être réalisé par une collaboration de Dieu et de l'homme. Le salut est l'œuvre exclusive de Dieu mais, en raison de son caractère spirituel, il ne peut pas être réalisé en l'homme sans une acceptation active de sa part. Dans I Cor. xv. 10, Paul dit que la grâce de Dieu n'a pas été vaine en lui, ce qui indique qu'elle aurait pu l'être. L'homme garde la faculté d'accepter et de refuser la grâce.

Sans entrer dans la discussion d'une question controversée, nous observerons que dans le fameux passage de Rom. ix. 19 sur le potier qui, de la même pâte, peut modeler des vases destinés à un usage noble et d'autres à un usage vil, sans que personne puisse être fondé à lui demander des comptes, Paul est surtout préoccupé d'écraser l'homme devant Dieu et, s'il dit que Dieu peut prédestiner les uns au salut et les autres à la perdition, il ne dit pas, pour autant, qu'il le fasse ou qu'il le fasse toujours.

La foi est conçue par Paul comme une mort et une résurrection. Dans Phil. iii. 11, Paul définit le salut, objet de son espérance, par la formule: 'parvenir, si je puis, à la résurrection d'entre les morts' (iii. 11). Le monde présent est entaché de faiblesse, de souffrance et de péché. Le monde futur, le règne de Dieu, sera, lui, glorieux et saint. On y entrera par la résurrection d'entre les morts.[1]

Ici se pose une question délicate sur laquelle les interprètes du paulinisme ne sont pas d'accord, celle du jugement.[2]

[1] Ou, pour ceux qui seront encore en vie au moment de la parousie, par une transformation qui fera passer les élus de l'état charnel à l'état spirituel (cf. I Cor. xv. 51–2).

[2] Voir sur ce point notre étude, 'Le jugement dans le Nouveau Testament', *Bull. Fac. de théol. prot. de Paris* (1942), pp. 5–20.

L'idée du jugement occupait dans la pensée apocalyptique juive une place centrale, c'était le point culminant du drame final. Par lui devait être réalisée la discrimination entre ceux qui seraient admis dans le monde futur et ceux qui en seraient exclus.

Au seuil de l'Evangile, se dresse la figure de Jean-Baptiste avec l'annonce d'un jugement rendu suivant la stricte justice et dans lequel le fait de descendre d'Abraham n'aura aucun rôle.

Plusieurs lignes s'entre-croisent dans la pensée de Jésus sur le jugement. En définissant sa position vis à vis de la Loi et des Prophètes (Matt. v. 17–19), Jésus paraît rester fidèle au principe du nomisme: le sort de chacun sera fixé par un jugement sur la manière dont il aura observé les commandements de Dieu, mais, par la manière dont il comprend l'obéissance à la Loi, Jésus rend infiniment plus rigoureuses les conditions que l'homme devrait remplir pour avoir droit au salut et échapper à la condamnation.

Le tableau du jugement dans Matt. xxv. 31–46 montre qu'il ne suffit pas de ne pas violer la Loi. La notion du jugement est dépassée. Elle l'est aussi par cette déclaration de Jésus à ses auditeurs que si leur justice ne dépasse pas celle des scribes et des pharisiens, ils n'entreront pas dans le Royaume de Dieu (Matt. v. 20). Si les rapports de l'homme avec Dieu étaient règlés par le seul principe de la justice distributive, aucun homme n'échapperait à la condamnation.

Mais le plan de Dieu pour la réalisation de son Royaume ne peut être tenu en échec par le péché des hommes. L'entrée dans le Royaume de Dieu doit être rendue possible par autre chose que par la réalisation du programme de justice tracé par la Loi.

Il y a des paroles de Jésus qui semblent présenter le salut comme la récompense de certains actes, la compensation de certains sacrifices, la réparation de certaines injustices. Jésus cependant entend ces notions tout autrement que ses contemporains, comme le montre la parabole des ouvriers, loués à diverses heures et qui, le soir venu, reçoivent tous le salaire normal d'une journée de travail (Matt. xx. 1–16). Deux ordres se superposent, celui de la justice et celui de la grâce, le second n'abolissant pas le premier, du moins en principe. En réalité la pensée de Jésus dépasse les notions de mérite et de salaire.

L'épisode du danger des richesses (Marc x. 17–31 et par.) est délicat à interprèter, les éléments qui le constituent n'ont pas tous la même signification et un élément important de rédaction paraît être intervenu dans le texte que nous avons. Même sans les réserves d'ordre critique qu'il appelle, le texte de Matthieu ne justifierait pas l'idée que l'acceptation de certains sacrifices permettrait de gagner le salut, de mériter l'entrée dans le Royaume de Dieu. Jésus déclare qu'il est plus difficile à un riche d'entrer dans le Royaume de Dieu qu'à un chameau de passer par le trou d'une aiguille. Et, comme ses disciples s'étonnent de ce qu'il vient de dire, il aggrave encore sa déclaration en répondant à la question: Qui peut donc être sauvé? 'Aux hommes, c'est impossible, mais tout est possible à Dieu.'

Jésus paraît insister sur le côté négatif de l'idée de jugement, comme si son rôle était seulement d'exclure ceux qui ne sont pas dignes d'entrer dans le Royaume de Dieu. C'est ce qu'exprime la conclusion de la parabole de l'ivraie dans le champ (Matt. xiii. 36–43). L'idée d'un pardon dont la source est l'amour miséricordieux de Dieu occupe dans la pensée de Jésus une place sur laquelle il est inutile d'insister. Cette idée suppose une conception juridique qui fait l'homme responsable de ses actes et devant en rendre compte devant une autorité qui fixera son sort, la miséricorde divine n'intervenant que pour assurer à certains hommes un sort différent de celui qu'ils ont mérité. Le pardon tel que Jésus le conçoit, n'est ni général ni mécanique. C'est un acte tout à fait individuel.

Au cours de son ministère, à des hommes et à des femmes, Jésus a accordé un pardon qui était à la fois l'annulation de leurs péchés et de leurs conséquences et une délivrance matérielle.[1] Au paralytique Jésus dit: 'Tes péchés te sont pardonnés' et il lui donne cet ordre: 'Lève-toi, prends ton lit et marche' (Marc ii. 1–12). Ces deux expressions sont équivalentes. Il ne s'agit pas d'une promesse pour un avenir plus ou moins lointain ou subordonnée à quelque condition mais d'une réalité actuelle. De même, à la femme à la perte de sang Jésus dit: 'Ma fille, ta foi t'a sauvée, va en paix et sois guérie de ta maladie' (Marc v. 34). Dans de tels cas la notion du jugement est nettement dépassée, d'abord en ce que la décision de Jésus n'est pas déterminée par ce qu'ont pu faire ceux qui en bénéficient mais par la considération de leur foi. Il s'agit d'un acte de la toute puissance de Dieu qui n'a

[1] Tel est le sens des guérisons et des expulsions de démons rapportées dans les Evangiles.

pas d'autre justification que lui même. Il ne se place pas à la fin des temps mais au moment où Jésus parle. Ce n'est pas une promesse, c'est un don, mais un don qui peut être perdu si l'homme retombe sous le joug de Satan. L'accent n'est pas mis sur l'action de l'homme mais sur celle de Dieu. Ce qui est demandé à l'homme c'est une acceptation qui l'engage et qui l'engage non seulement à l'égard de Dieu mais encore à l'égard de Jésus. 'Celui qui aura eu honte de moi et de mes paroles', dit Jésus, 'dans cette génération adultère et perverse, le Fils de l'Homme aura honte de lui quant il viendra dans la gloire de Dieu avec les saints anges' (Marc viii. 38). Renier ou confesser Jésus, ne sont pas des actes liés à un certain moment du temps. Ils ne valent, en bien et en mal, que par leur continuité. Il s'agit d'une attitude sur laquelle seul un jugement d'ensemble peut être porté et seulement sur une vie achevée. Ces idées ne peuvent pas être coordonnées en un système tout à fait logique car elles ne sont pas le produit d'une élaboration spéculative. Leur caractère est tout intuitif. Jésus n'est pas asservi aux conceptions traditionnelles. Il les domine et leur donne un contenu et un sens nouveaux.

Comme dans la pensée de Jésus, il y a dans celle de Paul un entre-croisement de lignes qui ne peuvent être réduites à un système cohérent. Le paulinisme cependant présente une réelle unité spirituelle. Bien qu'il soit né dans la diaspora, Paul est resté dans la ligne de la pensée juive. Le problème du salut est resté pour lui celui de la justification, entendu dans un sens forensique, une décision de Dieu, le juge suprême, devant fixer la destinée éternelle de chaque homme.

Dans II Cor. v. 12, Paul dit: 'Il faut que tous nous comparaissions devant le tribunal du Christ afin que chacun reçoive (son salaire) d'après ce qu'il aura fait en bien et en mal, étant dans son corps.'[1] Il est pourtant typique que dans les tableaux de I Thess. iv. 13 et de I Cor. xv. 22 ss., il ne soit pas question du jugement. A propos de I Cor. xv, il se pose une question sur laquelle les exégètes ne sont pas d'accord: La résurrection dont il est question dans ce texte sera-t-elle universelle ou seuls les élus en bénéficieront-ils? Certains

[1] Cette déclaration est particulièrement importante du fait quelle sert de conclusion à un développement qui implique une eschatologie toute différente de celle du jugement, celle de la croissance de l'homme intérieur qui arrivera à son plein épanouissement au terme de sa vie terrestre.

interprètes, notamment Jean Héring,[1] contestent que Paul ait admis l'idée d'une résurrection universelle. Il y a deux raisons pour lesquelles ils excluent la résurrection des non-élus. La première est que après avoir dit que la résurrection ne se produira pas d'un seul coup, mais que chacun ressuscitera à son rang (τάγμα), Paul ne mentionne que la résurrection du Christ qui déja appartient au passé et celle de ceux qui lui appartiennent et qui se produira au moment de la parousie, et ne mentionne pas celle des non-élus. Héring ajoute que la résurrection des non-élus ne servirait à rien puisqu'ils seraient voués à l'anéantissement et que la discrimination entre élus et non-élus, qui serait la seule raison d'être de leur résurrection, est déja réalisée par le fait qu'ils ne ressuscitent pas au même moment. Ces deux observations sont justes, mais elles ne sont pas décisives. Il arrive à Paul de commencer une énumeration et de ne pas la poursuivre.[2] Par ailleurs le paulinisme n'est pas un système strictement logique. Mais ce qui est décisif c'est que dans I Cor. xv. 21–2, Paul s'exprime ainsi: 'Comme par un homme (la mort est entrée dans le monde), ainsi en sera-t-il de la résurrection des morts. Comme du fait d'Adam, tous meurent, ainsi du fait du Christ, tous seront faits vivants.' Il résulte de là que, pour Paul, la résurrection doit avoir la même extension que la mort. Si la résurrection des non-élus est maintenue alors que, pratiquement, elle ne sert à rien, c'est qu'une conception religieuse conserve souvent, à titre de survivance, des éléments traditionnels qui ne jouent pour elle aucun rôle. Il en est ainsi du jugement dernier chez Paul, jugement qui ne peut, en tout cas, pas faire plus que manifester une discrimination qui existe déja. Paul ne déclare-t-il pas, par ailleurs, que, pour ceux qui sont en Christ, il n'y a plus de condamnation possible (Rom. viii. 1)? Qu'est-ce qu'un jugement qui ne comporte pas la possibilité d'une condamnation?

Si les croyants échappent à la condamnation, c'est que, par la communion avec le Christ, ils sont devenus de nouvelles créatures qui sont esprit et non plus chair.

[1] Jean Héring, *Le Royaume de Dieu et sa venue d'après Jésus et d'après l'apôtre Paul* (Paris, 1937). Sur ce livre voir notre article, 'Quelques remarques sur les origines de la christologie. A propos d'un livre récent', *Rev. de l'hist. des rel.* vol. CXIX (1939), pp. 5–52.

[2] Voir par exemple Rom. iii. 2.

En dehors du Christ, l'homme est voué à l'anéantissement par sa chair corrompue et devenue siège et cause de péché et cela fait de lui l'objet de la colère de Dieu. Il l'est aussi par le fait que, comme Paul le déclare, dans I Cor. xv. 50, 'La chair et le sang[1] ne peuvent hériter du Royaume de Dieu ni ce qui est corruptible de l'incorruptibilité'. Même si le péché n'était pas intervenu la création ne pouvait aboutir à son but qui est la gloire de Dieu, que par la venue du second Adam qui, d'une humanité psychique, charnelle et terrestre peut faire une humanité spirituelle et céleste portant son image[2] après avoir porté celle du premier Adam.

Cet achèvement de la création n'a pas pu se produire à cause du péché. Mais Dieu ne s'est pas résigné à l'avortement de son œuvre,[3] il a superposé au plan de la création un plan de rédemption. Ainsi le rôle du Christ est double, à la fois négatif et positif: négatif, par la destruction du péché et de ses conséquences, positif en ce qu'il fait passer les élus justifiés du plan de la chair à celui de l'esprit, en principe, au moins, car cette transformation ne peut être totale aussi longtemps que dure la vie dans la chair. Car ce qui est réalisé par la mort et la résurrection de Jésus ne l'est qu'en principe et en théorie mais doit encore être réalisé en fait dans la vie de chaque croyant. Cela se fait par une double voie, la foi et les sacrements.[4]

La situation du croyant, telle que Paul la conçoit, est paradoxale. Elle est dans le devenir et comporte un élément d'incertitude. C'est ici que se place la notion centrale pour Paul de la sanctification. Aussi longtemps que l'homme vit dans la chair, elle le pousse au péché alors que l'homme intérieur (la nouvelle créature) voudrait obéir à la loi de Dieu. La sanctification — c'est là un des paradoxes de la pensée paulinienne — est, à la fois, un effort demandé à l'homme et duquel dépend l'achèvement de son salut et, en même temps, une œuvre du Saint Esprit en lui, suite et conséquence de la justification. Par la parénèse, dont on sait quelle place elle occupe dans ses épîtres, Paul demande aux chrétiens de s'efforcer de devenir en fait ce qu'ils

[1] Il s'agit de la chair intègre, non de la chair corrompue par le péché.

[2] La ressemblance dans la pensée du Nouveau Testament implique la participation.

[3] De même qu'il ne s'est pas résigné à anéantir la création pour renouveler sa tentative jusqu'à ce qu'elle aboutisse.

[4] Nous ne parlerons d'abord que de la foi pour revenir ensuite sur la question des sacrements.

sont en principe. Le salut est ainsi, à la fois, une réalité acquise et un but vers lequel il faut tendre en y travaillant avec crainte et tremblement (Phil. ii. 12).

Comment expliquer cette apparente contradiction du paulinisme? C'est, pour une part, qu'il a été une pensée toujours en mouvement. L'intense activité missionnaire de l'apôtre ne lui a laissé ni le temps ni la tranquillité d'esprit nécessaires pour donner à sa pensée une forme équilibrée. Le fait, cependant, a des raisons plus profondes qui apparaissent si on considère les deux courants eschatologiques de la pensée paulinienne, représentés, l'un, par l'eschatologie des épîtres aux Thessaloniciens et de la première aux Corinthiens (ce que l'on pourrait appeler l'eschatologie collective de la résurrection), l'autre par celle de l'épître aux Philippiens et de la IIe épître aux Corinthiens (ce que l'on peut appeler l'eschatologie individuelle de l'épanouissement de la vie en Christ).

Si, comme Paul le dit dans Phil. i. 24, mourir c'est aller avec le Christ, ce ne peut être en même temps entrer dans un état de sommeil ou d'anéantissement provisoires dont on sortira par la résurrection au moment de la parousie du Seigneur. Ces deux eschatologies n'ont pas la même origine. La première est l'héritage de l'apocalyptique juive. L'autre dérive de l'expérience chrétienne de l'apôtre. S'il a gardé quelque chose de l'apocalyptique juive, ce n'est pas seulement parce qu'il ne serait pas arrivé à se complètement détacher de la tradition, c'est aussi et surtout parce que cette eschatologie collective exprime quelque chose qui est essentiel pour lui, à savoir que le but de l'œuvre du Christ a été de créer un peuple d'adorateurs, sur lequel Dieu règnera et qui lui rendra l'hommage d'adoration et d'obéissance qui lui est dû. C'est l'édification de l'Eglise, corps du Christ qui est le τέλος vers lequel tend l'œuvre de Dieu.

Ce n'est pas faire un rapprochement artificiel que de considérer les sacrements du point de vue de l'eschatologie. Le temps n'est pas très éloigné où certains interprètes du paulinisme considéraient la doctrine des sacrements comme y étant une sorte de corps étranger. Il est maintenant généralement admis — et, nous semble-t-il, avec raison — qu'elle en est un élément essentiel. Or la doctrine sacramentaire de l'Eglise primitive a un caractère nettement eschatologique.

Les origines du baptême chrétien ne sont pas parfaitement claires. Il ne semble pas que Jésus ait lui-même pratiqué le baptême.[1] Le rite s'est cependant introduit de bonne heure puisque Paul a été baptisé et qu'on ne voit pas quand il aurait pu l'être sinon tout au début de sa vie chrétienne (Rom. vi. 3). Ce qui est certain aussi, c'est qu'il y a un rapport entre le baptême et le précurseur.

Les évangiles déjà font du baptême de Jean une prophétie et une préfiguration du baptême chrétien. Jean aurait annoncé qu'après lui viendrait le plus grand que lui qui donnerait non le baptême d'eau mais le baptême d'esprit (Marc i. 7–8). Mais Matthieu (iii. 11–12) et Luc (iii. 16–17) ont ici un texte plus long mais qui ne peut pas être compris comme étant un simple développement littéraire de Marc: 'Il vous baptisera d'esprit.'[2] Ils ajoutent 'et de feu. Il a son van dans sa main; il nettoiera son aire, le grain, il l'amassera dans son grenier; la balle, il la brûlera au feu qui ne s'éteint pas'. Ce texte permet de reconnaître en Jean-Baptiste, non un prophète qui annonce et préfigure le baptême chrétien, mais le prophète du Messie et du jugement eschatologique présenté sous la forme d'une ordalie par le vent et par le feu qui séparera ceux qui seront exclus du monde nouveau de ceux qui y seront admis. Il a été, d'autre part, le rite par lequel on entrait dans le groupe — dans la confrérie, pourrait-on dire — de ceux qui entendaient se préparer par la pénitence à la venue du Messie et du jugement.

Il serait surprenant que rien de cette orientation eschatologique du baptême de Jean-Baptiste n'ait passé dans le baptême chrétien. Reportons nous d'ailleurs à l'instruction de Rom. vi sur le baptême. Le baptême qui était donné par immersion, comportait deux moments: la descente dans l'eau et la sortie de l'eau. Ces deux gestes représentent pour Paul une mise au tombeau et une sortie du tombeau par la résurrection. Il est donc participation au drame de la mort et de la résurrection du Christ: 'Nous tous, écrit Paul, qui avons été baptisés[3]

[1] Un seul témoignage va en sens inverse, c'est Jean iii. 22 ss., mais il se rapporte à un moment où Jésus était encore un disciple et un collaborateur de Jean Baptiste et avant qu'il ait commencé son ministère propre. Voir notre *Jésus*, pp. 210 ss.

[2] Ou 'de vent', cf. Jean iii. 8. Il y a lieu de penser que Matthieu et Luc ont utilisé ici les Logia et que ceux-ci ont recueilli des traditions qui venaient du milieu baptiste.

[3] Il serait plus exact de dire 'noyés'. Tel est, en effet, le sens du grec βάπτειν. Cf. Oepke, art. βάπτω dans le *Dictionnaire* de Kittel, vol. I, p. 526.

nous avons été baptisés dans sa mort. Nous avons été ensevelis avec lui par le baptème (c'est à dire par l'immersion) dans sa mort.' Le second moment, la sortie de l'eau est orienté vers l'avenir, c'est l'association à la résurrection du Christ: 'Si nous avons été unis à lui[1] par la ressemblance[2] de sa mort, nous le serons aussi à sa résurrection' et, un peu plus loin, au *v.* 8, il dit: 'Si nous mourons avec le Christ, nous croyons que nous vivrons aussi avec lui.'

Passons maintenant à l'eucharistie.[3] Le récit du dernier repas de Jésus qui mérite le plus de confiance est celui de Luc (xxii. 15–20). Nous tenons pour primitif le texte long donné par les manuscrits orientaux et non le texte court (*vv.* 15–19^{a}).[4] On y voit que, contrairement à ce qui a été le cas dans la suite, les deux éléments de la cène, le pain et la coupe, ne sont pas parallèles et équivalents[5] mais complémentaires. Mais si le texte oriental nous paraît devoir être tenu pour primitif, il n'en résulte pas qu'il soit homogène. Les *vv.* 19^{b}–20 viennent d'une autre source que 15–19^{a}. Ce texte commence par une déclaration eschatologique. Jésus déclare que, contrairement à ce qu'il avait désiré, il ne mangera plus la pâque avec ses disciples[6] et qu'il n'en mangera plus avant qu'elle soit accomplie dans le Royaume de Dieu.

La première coupe dont parle Luc n'est pas, ce qu'elle deviendra dans la suite, une coupe d'alliance, c'est une coupe de rendez-vous ou une coupe eschatologique. Il en est autrement chez Paul, où la

[1] On est obligé de transposer l'image employée par Paul. Littéralement: 'Si nous sommes devenus une même plante avec lui.'

[2] C'est-à-dire 'par la participation à sa mort'.

[3] Pour la justification de ce que nous avançons ici voir nos livres *L'eucharistie des origines à Justin Martyr* (Paris, 1910) et *l'Eglise primitive* (Paris, 1947).

[4] Texte de D et de quelqus manuscrits de la vieille version latine, de la Syriaque du Sinaï, de celle de Cureton, de la Peschitto et de Marcion. Nous avons donné un tableau synoptique de ces textes dans *l'Eucharisti*, pp. 110–11. On en trouvera un autre, établi par Kenyon et Legg, 'The textual data' dans *The Ministry and the Sacraments. Report of the Commission appointed by the Continuation Committee of the Faith and Order Movement* (under the Chairmanship of the Right Rev. A. C. Headlam), edited by R. Dunkerly (London, 1937), pp. 271–86.

[5] A la manière des doubles paraboles comme celles de la brebis et de la drachme perdues.

[6] Il y a là une indication précise qui montre que le dernier repas de Jésus n'a pas été un repas pascal mais qu'il a été pris à une date antérieure au 14 Nisan. Il n'est pas impossible que l'indication donnée dans Jean xii. 1, 'six jours avant la Pâque', se rapporte au dernier repas.

coupe est seulement coupe d'alliance, l'élément eschatologique n'étant plus représenté que dans le commentaire qui accompagne le récit: 'Ainsi chaque fois que vous mangez ce pain et que vous buvez cette coupe vous annoncez[1] la mort du Seigneur jusqu'à ce qu'il vienne' (I Cor. xi. 26).

Dans I Cor. x. 18 ss., Paul établit un parallèle entre le repas du Seigneur et le repas sacrificiel païen: 'Je ne veux pas, écrit-il, que vous soyez en communion avec les démons. Vous ne pouvez boire la coupe du Seigneur et la coupe des démons, participer à la table du Seigneur et à la table des démons.'

Pour Paul les dieux païens ne sont pas des êtres irréels n'existant que dans l'imagination déréglée des hommes, ce sont des démons, c'est à dire des êtres celestes qui ont suivi Satan dans sa révolte contre Dieu et qui ont réclamé pour eux l'adoration due à Dieu seul.[2]

C'est notamment par le sacrifice et le repas sacrificiel que l'on supposait qu'un rapport s'établissait entre la divinité (les démons) et ses adorateurs. De la viande de la victime immolée, une partie brûlée sur l'autel était censée absorbée par la divinité à laquelle le sacrifice était offert. Du reste, deux parts étaient faites. L'une revenait au Temple et servait à nourrir son nombreux personnel.[3] Avec la troisième partie, le sacrifiant donnait un banquet qui avait lieu dans le Temple et auquel il convoquait ses amis;[4] Paul blâme l'attitude de certains chrétiens de Corinthe qui se croyaient libres de participer à de tels repas.

Semblablement, pour Paul, la participation au repas du Seigneur met en communion avec lui. 'La coupe de bénédiction que nous bénissons, n'est-elle pas communion au sang du Christ? Le pain que nous rompons n'est-il pas communion au corps du Christ?'[5] L'expression 'communion au corps du Christ' est aisée à interprèter. Le corps du Christ c'est l'Eglise. La participation à l'eucharistie

[1] Ou bien 'annoncez', καταγγέλλετε, peut être aussi bien un impératif qu'un indicatif.

[2] D'après Rom. i. 18 ss, l'idolâtrie est le premier péché, source de tous les autres.

[3] L'excédent, s'il y en avait, était vendu au marché. Certains chrétiens scrupuleux se demandaient s'ils pouvaient manger de la viande achetée au marché sans s'être enquis de son origine (cf. I Cor. x. 25).

[4] Des papyrus ont conservé des invitations à de semblables repas. Cf. Lietzmann, *An die Korinther*[2] (Tübingen, 1949), pp. 49 ss.

[5] Accessoirement Paul note (x. 17) que le fait de manger le même pain réalise et manifeste l'unité de l'Eglise.

assure et maintient l'intégration du croyant dans l'Eglise. Mais il est plus difficile de comprendre l'expression 'communion au sang du Christ', alors que Paul déclare que la chair et le sang ne peuvent hériter du Royaume de Dieu. Il faut entendre ici sang au sens figuré comme une désignation de la mort et cela évoque l'idée de l'association à la mort du Christ comme condition de la participation à sa résurrection. 'Si nous souffrons avec lui', dit Paul, dans Rom. viii. 17, 'nous serons glorifiés avec lui.' On retrouve ici le caractère eschatologique de la Cène.[1]

Toute une série de déclarations pauliniennes vont dans le même sens. Il suffira d'en rappeler une ici, celle de II Cor. iv. 14 où Paul écrit: 'Nous savons que celui qui a ressuscité le Seigneur Jésus nous ressuscitera avec lui.' Dans Col. iii. 3, Paul dit: 'Vous êtes morts et votre vie est cachée avec le Christ en Dieu. Et quand le Christ, votre vie, sera manifesté,[2] vous serez manifestés avec lui dans la gloire' (cf. ii. 12).

Le mouvement qui s'amorce dans le paulinisme s'est poursuivi dans la suite, d'abord dans le johannisme dans lequel plus encore que chez Paul, on constate une actualisation et une spiritualisation de l'eschatologie. Mais le phénomène est ici plus complexe car aux raisons internes qui ont agi dans le paulinisme s'ajoute un facteur qui a agi encore plus fortement dans la suite. Il s'agit du dualisme héllénique qui, dans le johannisme, s'est substitué au dualisme sémitique.

Ce mouvement que l'on peut appeler de déseschatologisation s'est développé dans la suite non seulement pour les raisons que nous avons tenté d'indiquer mais pour d'autres encore.

Le développement du christianisme n'a pas été seulement celui d'une certaine manière de penser, de sentir ou d'agir, mais celui d'une société religieuse, d'une Eglise.

La notion d'Eglise présente un double caractère. Par un côté, l'Eglise est une société comme les autres, et qui, pour pouvoir subsister, doit remplir les conditions qu'il y a à l'existence et à la permanence de toute société. Mais elle a aussi un caractère qui lui est propre, c'est que son principe et ses fins sont non pas immanents

[1] Il y a eu ainsi toute une théologie du sang qui s'est développée à propos d'une mort qui n'avait pas été une mort sanglante.

[2] C'est à dire à la parousie.

mais transcendants et que ses principes et ses fins sont considérés comme ayant une valeur absolue. La religion est donc essentiellement traditionaliste car le traditionalisme n'est, dans son essence, que l'expression du sentiment qu'a la religion de rester identique à elle-même à travers le temps et en dépit des changements qu'il apporte en toutes choses. Il peut y avoir du relativisme en tout et jusque dans le domaine de la pensée religieuse et théologique, il ne saurait y en avoir dans la religion elle-même.

Ceci n'est vrai que de la religion mais, par un glissement naturel et quasiment inévitable, cette absoluté est transférée de la religion à son expression sur le plan intellectuel. C'est pour cela que les formules anciennes se maintiennent — et que, dans un certain sens au moins, il faut estimer qu'il est naturel et légitime qu'elles se maintiennent — bien qu'elles aient pris un tout autre sens que leur sens original.

BREVES REMARQUES SUR LA NOTION DE ΣΩΜΑ ΠΝΕΥΜΑΤΙΚΟΝ

H. CLAVIER

TOUT n'a-t-il pas été dit sur ce thème rebattu de σῶμα πνευματικόν? Est-il même possible de le dire autrement?

Σῶμα πνευματικόν ne se rencontre expressément, que dans un seul verset biblique, I Cor. xv. 44: σπείρεται σῶμα ψυχικόν, ἐγείρεται σῶμα πνευματικόν. Εἰ ἔστιν σῶμα ψυχικόν, ἔστιν καὶ πνευματικόν. 'Ce qui est semé "corps psychique" se réveille *corps pneumatique*; s'il est un corps psychique, il en est aussi un pneumatique.' Exclusivement paulinienne, cette expression est donc un hapax.

Ce maximum de sobriété dans l'usage biblique n'a pas empêché la méditation religieuse et la réflexion théologique de s'attacher, de bonne heure, à une locution qui suscitait des intérêts variés, dans un domaine où il est difficile de refréner l'imagination et le sentiment.[1]

[1] Ce serait une bien curieuse histoire à retracer que celle des interprétations de cet *hapax*. De la patristique à la scolastique, on y verrait des théologiens s'affronter sur d'étranges détails, et l'on constaterait que les plus sévères logiciens ne sont pas toujours les moins indulgents pour la fantaisie. Si l'exubérance alexandrine est allée peut-être (du moins, on le lui a reproché) jusqu'à attribuer au 'corps pneumatique' la forme idéale d'une sphère, il est piquant de constater quelle importance et quelle place Thomas d'Aquin donne à de graves problèmes comme ceux des divers organes et de leurs fonctions, sans oublier les ongles et les cheveux, du corps ressuscité, le même intégralement, numériquement, que le corps actuel: 'Et ita in partibus corporis animati quaedam ordinantur ad operationes animae exequendas, sicut cor, hepar, manus et pes; quaedam autem ad conservationem aliarum partium, sicut folia sunt ad cooperturam fructuum; ita capilli et ungues sunt in homine ad custodiam aliarum partium....Et quia homo resurget in omni perfectione suae naturae, propter hoc oportet ut capilli et ungues resurgant in ipso.' (*Summa*, P. III, Suppl., Qu. LXXX, art. II, éd. Migne (Paris, 1864), Tome IV, p. 1298.) Et l'ange de l'école a médité sur tous les détails, jusqu'à la pousse des cheveux ou aux fonctions intestinales des corps ressuscités.

Il serait facile de relever chez des auteurs plus récents des préoccupations analogues, et tout autant dans l'Eglise romaine que dans certaines sectes (cf. par exemple, Mgr. de la Bouillerie, *L'Homme, sa nature, son âme, ses facultés, sa fin*... (Paris 1879), pp. 254 ss.). Néanmoins, du côté protestant, la fantaisie s'oriente plutôt

Tout le problème de la nature et de la forme de la résurrection y était accroché, et l'on comprend que l'Eglise soit intervenue souvent pour en fixer la doctrine.[1] On ne peut pas dire que ce fut toujours heureusement, ni qu'elle ait pratiqué, en toute occasion, un 'ne quid nimis' aussi biblique, en l'occurrence, que classique.[2] Les intrusions d'un dogmatisme préconçu, même de défense contre la fantaisie, ou contre un autre dogmatisme,[3] ne sont pas tolérables. Ce qui

vers des spéculations analogues à celles de la théosophie ou du spiritisme: le corps spirituel se constituerait dans le corps actuel, dont il serait une sorte de double éthéré, en matière subtile et de plus en plus sublimée. On parle aussi de corps nerveux, lumineux, glorieux; mais il est rare que l'on revendique l'intégrité physique et numérique du corps présent (cf. F. Thomas, *Notre corps et ses destinées* (Genève, 1905), pp. 281 ss.; J. Gindraux, *L'existence dans l'au-delà* (Genève, 1914), pp. 150 ss.). Il arrive aussi que ce corps pneumatique soit considéré comme une sorte d'organisme invisible et permanent que revêt l'âme à la mort, dans un état intermédiaire, jusqu'à la résurrection du corps qui s'endosse comme un pardessus, mais très différent du corps actuel (cf. F. Splittgerber, *Après la mort* (Paris, 1879), pp. 60 ss., 186; A. Porret, *Au-delà* (Neuchâtel, 1918), pp. 30 ss. Sur les opinions des Pères, cf. *Enchiridion Patristicum* (11e éd., Fribourg, 1937), sous la rubrique Corpora Beatorum, p. 784, et notamment, les citations d'Athénagoras, Irénée, Hippolyte, Origène, Augustin, pp. 67, 98 ss., 142, 171, 583 ss. Sur les Pères et les Scolastiques, cf. A. Chollet, art. 'Corps glorieux', in *Dic. Théol. Cathol.*, Tome III, 2, pp. 1879–1906).

On observera qu'en cette matière, les *Réformateurs* ont retrouvé quelque chose de la sobriété biblique. Ce n'est pas eux qui nous convieraient, comme tel érudit sans malice, que nous avons connu, à exercer un jour, en patinant sur la mer de verre de l'Apocalypse, l'une des qualités reconnues du corps pneumatique: l'agilité. Le commentaire le plus copieux et le plus grave sur cette agilité est celui de Thomas d'Aquin (*ibid.* Qu. LXXXIV, pp. 1327–34); mais l'érudit était protestant.

Cf. critique de ces fantaisies dans H. Clavier, *L'Expérience de la Vie Eternelle* (Paris, 1923), *passim*.

[1] Ainsi dans la *Querelle Origéniste*: 'Si quis dicit aut sentit, in resurrectione corpora hominum orbiculata suscitari, nec confitetur nos suscitari rectos, anathema sit.' Cf. *Enchiridion Symbolorum* (26e éd., Fribourg, 1947), p. 96, et, sous la rubrique: Resurrectio mortuorum cum propriis corporibus, in Index Systematicus, p. 55. Aucun passage d'Origène sur la sphéricité du corps spirituel n'a été jusqu'ici retrouvé; il est vrai que son traité *De la Résurrection* a été perdu. Ce qui paraît certain, c'est que le grand Alexandrin admet la coexistence actuelle avec le corps mortel, d'un second corps, plus délié, d'où procèdera, comme d'un λόγος σπερματικός, le corps spirituel.

[2] Ainsi, quand elle spécifie que la résurrection est *de la chair*, et que c'est le corps actuel qui ressuscite. Cf. *Enchiridion Symbolorum*, pp. 2, 6, 7, 18, 170, 200, 230 ('credo etiam veram resurrectionem eiusdem carnis, quam nunc gesto...omnes cum suis propriis resurgent corporibus, quae nunc gestant' (Symboles de Léon IX et du 4e Concile de Latran)).

[3] Ainsi du dogmatisme ecclésiastique se raidissant contre l'hérésie, et allant jusqu'à plier les textes à des fins polémiques.

importe ici, c'est de savoir ce que l'apôtre a voulu dire. Il faut le lui demander en étudiant sereinement son texte dans le contexte littéraire et dans le contexte historique, plutôt que dans l'harmonie préétablie d'une doctrine ecclésiastique, théosophique, philosophique ou scientifique.[1] Cette tâche est difficile, et n'a été facilitée que depuis un temps relativement court, par une connaissance croissante du milieu complexe où Paul vivait et pensait.[2] Au temps où les pionniers de l'école historique ont commencé à élargir cette connaissance, le pli du dogmatisme était si fort qu'eux-mêmes ont eu le leur, comme tout le monde avait le sien.[3] Mais leur effort n'a pas été inutile, puisque les faits qu'ils ont découverts ou mis en lumière, sont maintenant entrés dans le patrimoine scientifique, et qu'il est loisible à chacun de les reprendre, tels qu'ils sont, et de les utiliser, en faisant, autant que possible, table rase de ses préjugés. S'il ne le peut entièrement, du moins doit-il les réduire à l'état d'hypothèses, toujours révisables quand les faits ont parlé. Mais ici, le premier fait, c'est le texte.

I. LE TEXTE

I Cor. xv. 44 ne présente aucune variante. Le texte peut donc être considéré comme très sûr. Les verbes σπείρεται, ἐγείρεται sont-ils ici impersonnels, ou bien σῶμα est-il sujet sous-entendu? Convient-il de traduire: il est semé, on sème; il est levé, on lève, — ou plutôt: le corps est semé, se sème; le corps est relevé, ressuscite? Ce problème est mineur; il n'engage pas le fond, et doit être réglé dans le contexte rythmé dont le verset 44 est le couronnement.[4] Ce qui importe

[1] Pas plus qu'aux décisions conciliaires ou aux décrets pontificaux, on ne saurait accommoder les textes aux théories philosophiques ou scientifiques. L'interprétation de la locution paulinienne à la lumière des découvertes atomiques est aussi dérisoire qu'en fonction d'un rescrit ou d'une encyclique. On ne saurait juger des textes au nom d'un critère externe. La seule exégèse qui compte est intrinsèque et congéniale à son objet.

[2] Cette connaissance était encore élémentaire il y a un siècle.

[3] Au temps où nous abordions pour la première fois ce thème eschatologique, il y a une trentaine d'années, le dogmatisme historique était à la mode, sous ses formes hégéliennes ou comtiennes. Posant en axiome une conception discutable du déterminisme historique, beaucoup de savants, et non des moindres, s'exerçaient à forcer tout élément nouveau dans un système préconcu. Mais les faits ne sont pas malléables à volonté. Les résidus irréductibles et incoordonnables viennent à bout des théories.

[4] Cf. *infra*, p. 347, où la forme impersonnelle est adoptée.

réellement, c'est de savoir quel est ici le sens du substantif σῶμα et de ses deux épithètes successives: ψυχικόν, πνευματικόν.

(i) Σῶμα. La signification habituelle de σῶμα, c'est: le corps en tant qu'organisme physique. Ses acceptions multiples, en tant qu'objet, ensemble, groupe, masse, matière ou forme, sont dérivées. Il est intéressant de noter que σῶμα est un terme spécifiquement grec, et qui n'a pas d'équivalent adéquat dans l'Ancien Testament. Σῶμα, dans les LXX, traduit souvent בָּשָׂר, mais bien plus souvent encore בָּשָׂר est rendu par σάρξ, dans son acception la plus neutre de substance carnée du corps, de chair sans indice éthique. Σάρξ a donné deux adjectifs qui en viennent à être pris parfois l'un pour l'autre,[1] mais dont le sens originel et habituel est différent: σάρκινος et σαρκικός. Σάρκινος veut dire: fait de chair, en chair, et peut être synonyme de corporel.[2] Σαρκικός désigne non pas une composition ou une constitution, mais une appartenance ou une orientation, un genre ou une qualité. Cette nuance deviendra importante en style chrétien, pour signaler et pour flétrir 'le charnel' en tant qu'opposé à l'Esprit.[3] Une distinction correspondante existe entre les expressions κατὰ σάρκα, selon la chair, avec le sens éthique et péjoratif de σαρκικός, charnel, et ἐν σαρκί, dans une chair, en chair, sans connotation éthique, et presque synonyme de ἐν σώματι, comme de σάρκινος. 'Εν σαρκί est employé notamment à propos de l'incarnation de Jésus-Christ.[4] Etre ἐν σαρκί, ἐν σώματι, c'est être σάρκινος. Si donc notre verset portait σπείρεται σῶμα σάρκινον, on sème un corps de chair, cela ne surprendrait pas; mais c'est un corps psychique, σῶμα ψυχικόν, que nous lisons.

(ii) Ψυχικόν. La désinence 'κόν', la même que dans σαρκικόν, semble indiquer que cette épithète ne désigne pas une composition, une formation psychique, en ψυχή,[5] mais une dépendance ou une direction. Une nuance péjorative y est-elle également attachée?

[1] Chez les Pères, cette confusion va jusqu'à appliquer σαρκικός à Jésus-Christ, σαρκικός τε καὶ πνευματικός (Ign., I Eph. vii. 2; comp. I Smyrn. iii. 3); jamais dans le N.T.; mais le sens, néanmoins, peut y être flottant; cf. I Cor. iii. 1, où σάρκινος est opposé à πνευματικός (comp. Rom. vii. 14).

[2] Comp. in Did. i. 4, αἱ σαρκικαὶ καὶ σωματικαὶ ἐπιθυμίαι.

[3] Cf. R. C. Trench, *Synonyms of the N.T.* nos. lxxi, lxxii (8e éd., London, 1876).

[4] Cf. I Jean iv. 2, 3; I Tim. iii. 16; II Jean vii.

[5] Cf. Trench, *op. cit.* no. lxxi; sur la ψυχή plus matérielle que spirituelle, cf. Clavier, *op. cit.* pp. 15 ss.

Il faudrait, dans ce cas, que 'psychique' eût pris un sens éthique analogue à celui de 'charnel', et opposé à 'pneumatique'. Qu'il y ait une antithèse dans notre texte, cela paraît évident; mais il n'est pas certain qu'elle se ramène à l'antagonisme de σάρξ et de πνεῦμα dans κατὰ σάρκα—κατὰ πνεῦμα, ou dans σαρκικός—πνευματικός. Il serait imprudent de se prononcer sans autre témoin.

(iii) <u>Πνευματικόν</u>. La même désinence 'κόν', dont le sens général a été déjà précisé, semble écarter, à première vue, la notion d'une substance 'pneumatique', dont serait constitué le nouveau corps.[1] Il s'agirait plutôt d'une orientation différente, d'une direction, d'une inspiration. L'antithèse très nette σῶμα ψυχικόν—σῶμα πνευματικόν se réduit-elle ainsi à celle de deux tendances, de deux forces qui régiraient successivement le même corps?[2] Ou bien 'l'identité numérique'[3] du corps est-elle nécessairement perdue dans ce processus? Ne serait-ce pas enfin, la même opposition qui s'exprimerait sous une forme plus claire au verset suivant: âme vivante — esprit vivifiant, ψυχὴ ζῶσα—πνεῦμα ζωοποιοῦν?[4] Il faut avoir recours au contexte immédiat.

2. LE VERSET 44 DANS LE CHAPITRE XV

Le long développement où figure la locution σῶμα πνευματικόν a pour objet d'affirmer la résurrection, soit du Christ en vue du chrétien, soit du chrétien en fonction du Christ.[5] Toutefois, le contexte immédiat peut se réduire à une incidente amorcée par cette question du verset 35: 'Comment les morts ressuscitent-ils? Avec quel corps, ou dans quel corps vont-ils?'[6] En s'efforçant d'élucider ce point important, l'apôtre ne s'égare point à la périphérie, mais revient au cœur du problème.

[1] Cf. pourtant, Eph. vi. 12 et Ign. I Eph. vii. 2. Dans les conceptions populaires, la matière sublimée dont sont constitués les esprits ou les doubles, est, indifférem-ment, psychique ou pneumatique. Le spiritisme en a hérité; cf. Clavier, *op. cit.* pp. 12–22. Cf. Luc. xxiv. 37, 39.

[2] Cf. Trench, *op. cit.* no. lxxi.

[3] Cf. Thomas d'Aquin, *supra*, p. 342 n. 1.

[4] ἐγένετο ὁ πρῶτος Ἀδὰμ εἰς ψυχὴν ζῶσαν· ὁ ἔσχατος Ἀδὰμ εἰς πνεῦμα ζωοποιοῦν. I Cor. xv. 45; comp. in Gen. ii. 7, נִשְׁמַת חַיִּים et נֶפֶשׁ חַיָּה.

[5] À partir du *v.* 12.

[6] Ἀλλὰ ἐρεῖ τις· πῶς ἐγείρονται οἱ νεκροί; ποίῳ δὲ σώματι ἔρχονται;

Dès le début d'une dialectique dont la rigueur a été contestée,[1] Paul fait appel aux métamorphoses de la nature vivante, en termes qui évoquent d'abord le parallèle johannique: 'Si le grain de blé ne meurt....'[2] La comparaison qu'il esquisse au verset 36, et qu'il oriente, dès le verset 37, vers le problème de la constitution des corps, est reprise dans la strophe rythmée qui commence au verset 42 et qui s'achève au verset 44:

Semailles dans la corruption	Résurrection dans l'incorruptibilité;
Semailles dans l'indignité	Résurrection dans la gloire;
Semailles d'un 'corps psychique'	Résurrection d'un 'corps spirituel'.[3]

A en juger d'après l'analogie ainsi répétée et amplifiée, le corps pneumatique serait au corps psychique ce que la plante dans sa croissance, ou même la fleur dans son épanouissement, seraient à la semence. Le corps psychique est comparé au grain sans apparence, infime et sans beauté, qui meurt et se décompose dans la terre. Le corps pneumatique ressemblerait à l'arbre dans la gloire de sa floraison ou dans sa force fructifiante. Il y aurait entre eux continuité, mais pas identité numérique.[4] Ce ne serait pas, il s'en faut de beaucoup, le même corps ayant seulement changé d'orientation, et désormais guidé par l'Esprit, mais un autre corps, de genre différent, comme de direction nouvelle.[5]

Ce changement d'organisme et de constitution au cours du processus était annoncé dès le verset 37.[6] Il est illustré par une série de comparaisons prises dans la nature, suivant les conceptions du temps, jusqu'au verset 41. L'ordonnance et la rigueur dialectique du

[1] Ainsi, Lietzmann, *Hdb. z. N.T.* vol. III (Tübingen, 1906), pp. 149, 153, 156.

[2] ἐὰν μὴ ὁ κόκκος τοῦ σίτου πεσὼν εἰς τὴν γῆν ἀποθάνῃ.... Jean xii. 24.

[3] σπείρεται ἐν φθορᾷ...ἀτιμίᾳ...ἀσθενείᾳ...—σῶμα ψυχικόν—ἐγείρεται ἐν ἀφθαρσίᾳ...δόξῃ...δυνάμει...=σῶμα πνευματικόν.

[4] Cf. *supra*, p. 346 n. 3 et p. 342 n. 1. Une interprétation de la pensée paulinienne sur ce point, à la lumière des découvertes ou des théories atomiques, peut ne pas manquer d'intérêt, mais reste inadéquate. Cf. J. W. Cobb, 'The Nature of the Resurrection Body', art. dans *The Review and Expositor* (Oct. 1952), pp. 435 ss., Louisville, U.S.A. Les arguments d'ordre purement exégétique suffisent, dans cet article, à établir la différence que les auteurs du N.T. font entre le corps du Christ avant et après la résurrection, et, de même, pour les fidèles, bien qu'il s'agisse de notions parfois confuses (*ibid.* pp. 438, 442).

[5] *Idem*, et *supra*, p. 342 n. 1.

[6] Καὶ ὃ σπείρεις, οὐ τὸ σῶμα τὸ γενησόμενον σπείρεις... I Cor. xv. 37.

raisonnement amorcé au verset 36 en sont compromises; mais cette digression n'est pas inutile comme on s'en aperçoit à la reprise de l'argumentation, au verset 42.

Si l'on examine de plus près ce qui paraît une incidente, on note que le verset 38 fait intervenir la volonté de Dieu dans le processus naturel.[1] Continuité et nouveauté ne se contredisent pas, mais se combinent harmonieusement, suivant le plan de Dieu.[2] Les versets 39 à 41 introduisent ici la notion d'une substance du corps.[3] Cette substance est σάρξ pour les êtres vivants de la terre, et δόξα pour ceux du ciel.[4] Mais de même que la substance carnée diffère suivant les espèces animales, de même la substance lumineuse, glorieuse, diffère suivant les corps célestes, conçus également comme vivants.[5] Néanmoins, au verset 40, nous apprenons qu'il y a aussi une δόξα des corps terrestres, bien que différente de celle des corps célestes.[6] Ce trait d'union inattendu entre la terre et le ciel n'est peut-être pas l'effet d'une simple maladresse d'expression, comme on l'a supposé.[7] Ne trahirait-il pas aussi bien le souci de continuité déjà signalé,[8] et que l'on retrouverait sous diverses formes, notamment dans l'impératif du verset 49: 'portons aussi l'image du céleste.'[9]

Au point où nous en sommes, il semble que le corps pneumatique, en continuité avec le corps psychique, doive, pourtant, se distinguer de lui, non seulement par son orientation ou son inspiration, mais par sa constitution même. Cette impression très nette se trouve confirmée par la déclaration catégorique et solennelle du verset 50:

[1] Ὁ δὲ Θεὸς δίδωσιν αὐτῷ σῶμα καθὼς ἠθέλησεν... I Cor. xv. 38.

[2] De même, par exemple, dans la parabole de la semence, en Marc iv. 26–9, où le miracle de la germination et de la croissance n'exclut pas la notion d'un développement naturel qui n'est, évidemment, pas moulé dans la catégorie du déterminisme naturel.

[3] Οὐ πᾶσα σὰρξ ἡ αὐτὴ σάρξ... κ.τ.λ.

[4] Cf. M. Dibelius, *Die Geisterwelt im Glauben des Paulus* (Göttingen, 1909), pp. 85 ss., et, à l'opposé, l'opinion traditionnelle maintenue par E. B. Allo, *St Paul, 1e ép. aux Cor.* (2e éd., Paris, 1935), pp. 422 ss. Comp. G. Kittel, art. δόξα, in *Theol. Wörterb. z. N.T.* (Stuttgart, 1934).

[5] *Ibid.*, et O. Everling, *Die paulinische Angelologie und Dämonologie* (Göttingen, 1888), pp. 40 ss., 46, 48; Th. Simon, *Die Psychologie des Apostels Paulus* (Göttingen, 1897), pp. 18, 21, 35, 99.

[6] ἀλλὰ ἑτέρα μὲν ἡ τῶν ἐπουρανίων δόξα, ἑτέρα δὲ ἡ τῶν ἐπιγείων. I Cor. xv. 40.

[7] Cf. M. Dibelius, *op. cit.* p. 86; H. Lietzmann, *op. cit.* p. 154.

[8] Cf. *supra*, p. 348 n. 2.

[9] La leçon φορέσωμεν, plus difficile et mieux attestée, nous semble la meilleure.

'Ce que j'affirme, frères, c'est que la chair et le sang ne peuvent hériter le royaume de Dieu, pas plus que la corruption n'hérite l'incorruptibilité.'[1]

Ainsi, le corps pneumatique, corps glorieux, surnaturel, céleste, exclut le sang comme la substance carnée. Malgré une opinion curieuse qui voudrait maintenir le squelette, sous prétexte que les pharisiens en faisaient procéder la résurrection,[2] on pourrait ajouter ὀστέα, les os.[3] Que reste-t-il du corps dans ces conditions, et que penser de l'identité numérique chère encore à Thomas d'Aquin, dans la Somme, et de ses essais d'anatomie et de physiologie eschatologiques, allant jusqu'aux ongles et aux cheveux?[4]

Mais aussitôt après la revendication spirituelle du verset 50, avec sa solennité péremptoire, Paul réintroduit une notion perturbatrice qui semblait moins le préoccuper que lorsqu'il écrivait aux Thessaloniciens: celle de la parousie prochaine imaginée comme un retour matériel et visible du Seigneur. L'apôtre change brusquement de ton; il se met à vaticiner;[5] il brosse, en deux versets,[6] une scène

[1] Τοῦτο δέ φημι, ἀδελφοί, ὅτι σὰρξ καὶ αἷμα βασιλείαν Θεοῦ κληρονομῆσαι οὐ δύναται, οὐδὲ ἡ φθορὰ τὴν ἀφθαρσίαν κληρονομεῖ. I Cor. xv. 50.

[2] Les pharisiens sont allés jusqu'à se demander à partir de quelle portion du corps commence la résurrection. On connaît la réponse de R. Joshuah, fils de Hananiah, à l'empereur Hadrien: 'la résurrection commence par l'épine du dos' (Midrash Rabba, Gen. xxviii. 2; Lev. xviii. 1).

[3] Sur l'importance des os dans les conceptions archaïques, cf. H. W. Robinson, art. 'Bones', in Hastings, *Encycl. of Relig. and Ethics*, vol. II (Edinburgh, 1930), pp. 791 ss.; en Théol. Bibl., cf. H. Lesètre, art. 'Os', in Vigouroux, *Dic. de la Bible*, vol. IV, 2 (Paris 1908), pp. 1902–4. Sur l'os de la résurrection, cf. J. Bonsirven, *Le Judaïsme palestinien au temps de J.C.* tome I (Paris, 1934), p. 484; Bornhäuser, *Die Gebeine der Toten* (1921), pp. 37 ss.

[4] Cf. *supra*, p. 342 n. 1. Néanmoins, Thomas d'Aquin, tout en affirmant que c'est la matière, et donc le corps physique, qui est le facteur et le lieu de l'individuation, admet sans discussion, et sans flairer la contradiction, que les adaptations et proportionnalités des âmes unies aux corps, demeurent en elles, même quand les corps se dissolvent, si bien qu'elles subsistent comme si elles ne dépendaient pas des corps; 'Haec enim anima est commensurata huic corpori et non illi, illa autem alii, et sic de omnibus. Hujusmodi autem commensurationes remanent in animabus, etiam pereuntibus corporibus, sicut et ipsae earum substantiae manent, quasi a corporibus secundum esse non dependentes' (Thomas d'Aquin, *Summa contra Gentiles*, II, LXXXI, d'après *Œuvres de Laberthonnière*, par L. Canet (Paris, 1942), p. 176. Comp. Platon, *Gorgias*, 524D (éd. Belles-Lettres, Paris, 1949)).

[5] ἰδοὺ μυστήριον ὑμῖν λέγω· κ.τ.λ. I Cor. xv. 51.

[6] ...πάντες οὐ κοιμηθησόμεθα, πάντες δὲ ἀλλαγησόμεθα, ἐν ἀτόμῳ, ἐν ῥιπῇ ὀφθαλμοῦ, ἐν τῇ ἐσχάτῃ σάλπιγγι, κ.τ.λ. I Cor. xv. 51 ss.

d'apocalypse qui présuppose des données étrangères à celles qui viennent d'être signalées: transformation soudaine des fidèles encore vivants; résurrection des morts qui se trouvaient, par conséquent, dans un état intermédiaire non défini;[1] revêtement, et non métamorphose intime et spirituelle, du corps présent, par deux qualités abstraites qui appartiennent proprement au seul corps pneumatique:[2] ἀφθαρσία et ἀθανασία.

Le cri qui résonne maintenant comme la trompette de la victoire après celle de la résurrection,[3] 'O mort, où est ton aiguillon, ô Hadès, où est ta victoire?' ne peut faire passer une incohérence dont l'explication est ailleurs.

3. LE CONTEXTE PAULINIEN

Si l'on étend à l'ensemble des écrits pauliniens, voire deutéro-pauliniens, le contexte de σῶμα πνευματικόν, on sent se renforcer l'impression d'une dualité difficilement réductible, et l'on a quelquefois de la peine à trouver la ligne de force d'une pensée vigoureuse entre des tendances opposées. Elle existe pourtant, mais non sans oscillations, quand on en vient à un thème aussi délicat et aussi mystérieux que celui de la nature de la résurrection. Comment en être surpris, si l'on se rappelle que le Nouveau Testament tout entier, s'il manque de précisions sur la constitution future de l'homme, n'est guère plus explicite sur sa constitution présente.

La formule tripartite πνεῦμα, ψυχή, σῶμα, que Paul utilise en I Thess. v. 23, n'a pas la rigueur trichotomique du platonisme.[4] On y trouvera, cependant, une indication, confirmée par beaucoup d'autres textes, sur la place et les fonctions de ψυχή. Ainsi pourrait être

[1] Sur cet état intermédiaire, contre lequel protestait Calvin, dans une *Psychopannychia* juvénile, cf. entre autres, A. Berthoud, *L'état des morts d'après la Bible* (Lausanne, 1913); H. Clavier, *op. cit.* pp. 210 ss. Sur les conceptions rabbiniques de cet état, cf. J. Bonsirven, *op. cit.* tome I, pp. 322 ss. Sur ce que Paul en pense, cf. A. Schweitzer, *Die Mystik des Apostels Paulus* (Tübingen, 1930), pp. 90 ss., et les points de vue différents, soit de F. Prat, *La Théologie de St Paul*, vol. II (Paris, 1937), pp. 434 ss., ou de W. D. Davies, *Paul and Rabbinic Judaism* (London, 1948), pp. 285 ss.

[2] Ὅταν δὲ τὸ φθαρτὸν τοῦτο ἐνδύσηται ἀφθαρσίαν καὶ τὸ θνητὸν τοῦτο ἐνδύσηται ἀθανασίαν... κ.τ.λ. I Cor. xv. 54.

[3] Ποῦ σου, θάνατε, τὸ κέντρον; ποῦ σου ᾅδη, τὸ νῖκος; I Cor. xv. 55.

[4] La trichotomie de Platon se prolonge dans l'âme elle-même, qui est partagée en trois. Cf. Platon, *Timée*, 35, 69–70 (éd. B.-L. Paris).

éclairée la relation entre le 'psychique', le 'somatique', le 'charnel', et leur opposition au 'pneumatique'. ψυχή n'a pas de frontières précises et strictement délimitées. Elle s'étend, avec des chevauchements, de σάρξ jusqu'à πνεῦμα, et des états conscients de καρδία jusqu'aux profondeurs subconscientes, dans ces zones indistinctes où il ne reste plus qu'individualité sans personnalité, et, finalement, physiologie plus que psychologie. ψυχή offre donc la vision la plus large et la plus floue de l'homme, au point de signifier, éventuellement, tous ses autres aspects.[1]

Toutefois, si ψυχή, à son point culminant, peut remplir les fonctions, même du πνεῦμα de l'homme,[2] l'adjectif ψυχικός, employé six fois dans le Nouveau Testament, dont quatre chez Paul, une en Jacques, une en Jude, y a toujours un sens péjoratif.[3] Le 'psychique', ainsi entendu, serait un homme dont la ψυχή est en descente spirituelle; elle a perdu contact avec le πνεῦμα; elle est en train de rentrer dans la σάρξ. Le corps psychique, participant de cette dégradation, n'est plus seulement corps vivant, mais corps déchu, comme le souligne la strophe rythmée de I Cor. xv. 42–4, en lui associant faiblesse, indignité et corruption.[4] C'est à ce psychique là qu'est opposé le pneumatique, celui du σῶμα πνευματικόν. Comme on l'a constaté, il ne s'agit pas d'une même constitution physique autrement orientée, mais d'une organisation totalement différente, adéquate à l'Esprit qui la règle et qui la commande.[5]

Ne pourrait-on trouver dans le contexte paulinien, la solution des difficultés signalées, ou, tout au moins, leur réduction partielle? Une étude attentive de l'eschatologie de Paul ne permettrait-elle pas,

[1] Cf. E. Rohde, *Psyché* (éd. franç. Paris, 1928), *passim*; Th. Simon, *op. cit.* pp. 35 ss.; W. Gutbrod, *Die paulin. Anthropologie* (Stuttgart, 1934); W. G. Kümmel, *Das Bild des Menschen im N.T.* (Zürich, 1948); H. Clavier, *L'Accès au Royaume de Dieu* (Paris, 1944), pp. 38 ss.

[2] ψυχή et πνεῦμα peuvent être synonymes dans les domaines du sentiment, de l'intelligence ou de la volonté. Cf. Matt. xi. 29; I Cor. xvi. 18; Luc i. 47; Jean xii. 27; xiii. 21; I Cor. ii. 11, Actes xix. 21; Matt. xxvi. 41.

[3] Cette nuance péjorative va de la misère, de la faiblesse du 'corps psychique' (I Cor. xv. 44 (bis), 46), jusqu'à l'opposition totale, et même démoniaque, du 'psychique' à l'Esprit (I Cor. ii. 14; Jacques iii. 15; Jude 19). Ainsi, tandis que, dans la psychologie classique, le 'psychique' est opposé au 'corporel' ou au 'charnel', dans le N.T., il leur est presque assimilé. Trench, *op. cit.* no. lxxi, cherche à déceler ce qui les distingue encore.

[4] Cf. *supra*, p. 347 n. 3. [5] Cf. *supra*, p. 347 nn. 4, 5 et p. 348 n. 2.

comme le faisait Auguste Sabatier,[1] de retracer l'évolution d'un point de vue à l'autre, soit, en gros, du matérialisme au spiritualisme, de l'apocalyptique à la vie ἐν Χριστῷ, ou de la parousie au Χριστὸς ἐν ὑμῖν? Les choses n'apparaissent pas si simples dans la réalité des faits, c'est à dire, ici, des textes. Si, par exemple, l'épître aux Philippiens date, comme le croient la plupart des auteurs, de la captivité romaine,[2] iii. 20 s. marquerait un singulier retour de flamme, de la flamme apocalyptique, vers la fin de la carrière de l'apôtre: 'Nous sommes citoyens des cieux, et c'est de là que nous attendons Notre Seigncur Jésus Christ, qui transformera notre corps misérable, pour le rendre conforme à son corps glorieux, par le pouvoir qu'il a de s'assujettir toutes choses.'[3]

Toutefois, il semble bien que la tendance intime, et proprement spirituelle, ait gagné du terrain, déjà des Thessaloniciens à I Corinthiens et surtout à partir de II Corinthiens, dont le locus classicus est ici v. 1–5, mais doit être étendu au contexte iv. 7 à v. 10. La perplexité de Paul semble s'être accrue entre I et II Corinthiens, à la suite d'épreuves auxquelles il fait allusion,[4] et qui l'ont conduit à envisager personnellement la mort. Sa foi en la résurrection n'en est pas atteinte;[5] mais elle fait ressortir un motif seulement entrevu jusqu'ici: Paul mentionne pour la première fois, explicitement, l'homme intérieur (ὁ ἔσω ἡμῶν (ou 'ἔσωθεν') ἄνθρωπος)[6] qui se renouvelle de manière continue, de jour en jour (ἀνακαινοῦται ἡμέρᾳ καὶ ἡμέρᾳ), tandis que l'homme extérieur (ὁ ἔξω ἄνθρωπος) se détruit (II Cor. iv. 16). Si l'on reprenait maintenant la comparaison de I Cor. xv sur la germination et la croissance, on dirait que ἔσω ἄνθρωπος est à ἔξω ἄνθρωπος ce que le germe vivant du grain est à l'enveloppe qui disparaît, comme pourrait l'être σῶμα πνευματικόν à σῶμα ψυχικόν, et l'on conclurait normalement sur la déclaration qui suit,

[1] Cf. A. Sabatier, *L'Apôtre Paul, esquisse d'une histoire de sa pensée* (Paris, 1896), pp. 180s.

[2] Il faut cependant constater le succès relatif de l'hypothèse d'une composition éphésienne, dont l'admission modifierait les données du problème.

[3] Ἡμῶν γὰρ τὸ πολίτευμα ἐν οὐρανοῖς ὑπάρχει, ἐξ οὗ καὶ σωτῆρα ἀπεκδεχόμεθα κύριον Ἰησοῦν Χριστόν, ὃς μετασχηματίσει τὸ σῶμα τῆς ταπεινώσεως ἡμῶν σύμμορφον τῷ σώματι τῆς δόξης αὐτοῦ...κ.τ.λ. Phil. iii. 20 ss.

[4] Cf. II Cor. i. 8–10; iv. 7 ss.

[5] Cf. II Cor. iv. 14.

[6] Cf. Behm, art. 'ἔσω' in *Theol. Wörterb. z. N.T.* (Stuttgart, 1935); H. Windisch, *Der 2te Korinth.* (Göttingen, 1924), pp. 152 ss.; E. B. Allo, *St Paul, 2de ép. aux Cor.* Exc. VIII (Paris, 1937), pp. 134–7.

dans sa haute et décisive spiritualité (II Cor. iv. 18): 'Nous ne regardons pas aux choses visibles, mais aux invisibles; car les choses visibles ne sont que pour un temps, tandis que les invisibles sont éternelles.'[1]

Mais voici qu'aussitôt après, au chap. v, l'élément perturbateur déjà signalé en I Cor. xv. 51 s.[2], semble réapparaître, pour embrouiller de nouveau le problème. Le développement, que l'on suivait sans peine, se complique d'un motif nouveau qui rompt ou compromet sérieusement la continuité suggérée: celui de la demeure céleste qui nous attend là-haut, au jour où nous délogerons. Constatons sur le texte[3] que l'image exaltante de cette οἰκοδομὴ ἐκ θεοῦ s'applique moins à une sorte de construction extérieure, d'édifice, de maison, qu'à une enveloppe à revêtir, c'est à dire à une espèce de corps.[4] Peut-on l'identifier avec σῶμα πνευματικόν? Dans ce cas, comment maintenir la continuité avec ὁ ἔσω ἄνθρωπος? Faut-il tenir τὸ οἰκητήριον ἡμῶν τὸ ἐξ οὐρανοῦ pour un revêtement nouveau à 'survêtir' (ἐπενδύσασθαι) par-dessus un σῶμα πνευματικόν en relation avec ὁ ἔσω ἄνθρωπος, et dont nous serions déjà revêtus, puisqu'il faut que nous soyons trouvés vêtus, et non pas nus?[5] Cela ferait un étrange compromis, et un imbroglio, entre la vie intérieure, le sens de la continuité, et l'attente apocalyptique. L'admission de la variante ἐκδυσάμενοι, au *v.* 3, ne changerait rien à l'affaire,[6] car le *v.* 4 insiste: 'nous ne voulons pas être dévêtus, mais "survêtus".'[7] De toutes façons, le présent corps est sacrifié, comme l'affirment explicitement les *vv.* 6–8, dans l'attente du départ ἐκ τοῦ σώματος pour le rapatriement auprès du Kyrios.[8] L'apôtre marche ici, non par la vue, mais par la foi (*v.* 7), ce qui ramène aux réalités invisibles de iv. 18.

[1] Μὴ σκοπούντων ἡμῶν τὰ βλεπόμενα ἀλλὰ τὰ μὴ βλεπόμενα· τὰ γὰρ βλεπόμενα πρόσκαιρα, τὰ δὲ μὴ βλεπόμενα αἰώνια. II Cor. iv. 18.

[2] Cf. *supra*, p. 349 nn. 5, 6.

[3] II Cor. v. 1–10.

[4] Cf. H. Windisch, *op. cit.* pp. 159 ss., 164 s.; E. B. Allo, *op. cit.* pp. 121 ss.

[5] ...εἴ γε καὶ ἐνδυσάμενοι οὐ γυμνοὶ εὑρεθησόμεθα. II Cor. v. 3. Sur l'aversion juive pour la nudité, cf. Bonsirven, *op. cit.* tome I, p. 485; comp. le point de vue classique grec chez Platon, *Gorgias* (éd. cit.), 523 C, D, E; 524 A, B, C, D; *Cratyle*, 400 C; 403 D.

[6] Cette leçon, dont les témoins sont rares, n'est guère défendable, et rend confuse une argumentation déjà embarrassée.

[7] ...οὐ θέλομεν ἐκδύσασθαι ἀλλ' ἐπενδύσασθαι. II Cor. v. 4. Sur le vêtement céleste à revêtir ou 'survêtir', cf. Windisch, *op. cit.* Exc. pp. 164 s.; Asc. Es. ix. 17–26, in Hennecke, *Neutest. Apokryph.* (Tübingen, 1924), p. 311.

[8] ...ἐνδημῆσαι πρὸς τὸν κύριον. II Cor. v. 8.

C'est la foi qui le tient au-dessus des difficultés logiques et des écarts d'une dialectique tiraillée dans divers sens, et qui perd pied dans le mystère de l'Au-delà. Demeurer ou déloger, toute image et tout argument, dont Paul semble éprouver les lacunes,[1] rien ne modifie la seule chose nécessaire: plaire au Seigneur;[2] car c'est à ce critère d'amour que se règlera le sort final de chacun, suivant le bien ou le mal qu'il aura fait διὰ τοῦ σώματος.[3]

Si l'on reprend la notion d'homme intérieur dans cette connexion, on s'aperçoit que les deux autres textes pauliniens où cette expression se retrouve[4] appuient la suggestion d'un lien et d'une continuité entre σῶμα πνευματικόν et ἔσω ἄνθρωπος. En Rom. vii. 22, l'homme intérieur prend plaisir à la loi de Dieu, et s'oppose violemment à ce corps de mort, dont Paul aspire à être délivré.[5] N'est-il donc pas licite d'interpréter à cette lumière la délivrance ou rédemption du corps dont il est question aux chapitre suivant (Rom. viii. 23)?[6] En Ephés. iii. 16, un courant de force est établi entre ἔσω ἄνθρωπος et πνεῦμα, pour rendre possible une habitation: celle du Christ dans les cœurs, par la foi.[7] Et si l'on pense de nouveau à Phil. iii. 20–1, où la parousie du Christ doit marquer la métamorphose de ce corps de misère en corps de gloire,[8] on saisit sur le vif le partage d'intérêts, le conflit de tendances dont Saint Paul était tourmenté. Mais, sous la parenthèse de sa foi, les contrastes et les tiraillements de cet homme de deux mondes trouvent une ligne de force, et contribuent, avec puissance, à la richesse et au rayonnement de son génie.[9]

Les problèmes de l'apôtre ne sont pas résolus sur le plan rationnel; mais ses perplexités trouvent des apaisements sur celui de la foi. Ce sera dans la vie intérieure de l'ἔσω ἄνθρωπος, mais aussi dans

[1] Les *vv.* 9 et 10 coupent court à une argumentation qui s'alourdit.

[2] εὐάρεστοι αὐτῷ εἶναι. II Cor. v. 9.

[3] ἵνα κομίσηται ἕκαστος τὰ διὰ τοῦ σώματος πρὸς ἃ ἔπραξεν, εἴτε ἀγαθὸν εἴτε φαῦλον. II Cor. v. 10.

[4] Rom. vii. 22 et Eph. iii. 16.

[5] Τίς με ῥύσεται ἐκ τοῦ σώματος τοῦ θανάτου τούτου; Rom. vii. 24.

[6] ...αὐτοὶ ἐν ἑαυτοῖς στενάζομεν υἱοθεσίαν ἀπεκδεχόμενοι, τὴν ἀπολύτρωσιν τοῦ σώματος ἡμῶν. Rom. viii. 23.

[7] ...ἵνα δῷ ὑμῖν κατὰ τὸ πλοῦτος τῆς δόξης αὐτοῦ δυνάμει κραταιωθῆναι διὰ τοῦ πνεύματος αὐτοῦ εἰς τὸν ἔσω ἄνθρωπον, κατοικῆσαι τὸν Χριστὸν διὰ τῆς πίστεως ἐν ταῖς καρδίαις ὑμῶν. Eph. iii. 16s.

[8] Cf. *supra*, p. 352 nn. 2, 3.

[9] Cf. H. Clavier, 'La Personnalité de Paul', dans *Paulus, Hellas, Oikumene, An ecumenical Symposium* (Athènes, 1951), pp. 44 ss.

l'obéissance concrète διὰ τοῦ σώματος,[1] qui établit déjà une relation entre ce corps de chair et la δόξα de Dieu (I Cor. vi. 20);[2] car c'est bien ce corps qu'il faut offrir 'en sacrifice vivant, saint, agréable à Dieu' (Rom. xii. 1).[3] Il y a encore les états mystiques, l'extase où Paul ne sait plus s'il est absent ou présent dans son corps,[4] quand il goûte la communion paradisiaque (II Cor. xii. 1–4); mais quel qu'en soit le privilège, il ne les cultive pas et ne les recommande pas.[5] Présence, absence, même sans le corps: Paul envisage donc la possibilité d'une vie personnelle, et la plus haute, dans un état anticipé de désincarnation. N'est-ce pas dans le même sens qu'il convient d'interpréter I Cor. v. 3, 4,[6] où il semble que le πνεῦμα de Paul, détaché de son corps, tienne conseil avec les Corinthiens, pour condamner l'incestueux?[7] Si telle est bien la conviction de Paul dans ses expériences extatiques et télépathiques, n'y a-t-il pas là de nouveaux éléments suceptibles d'embrouiller, ou d'éclairer notre difficile problème: celui de la pensée de l'apôtre sur le σῶμα πνευματικόν, dont la formule occasionnelle ne revient plus, sans doute parce qu'elle ne l'a pas satisfait entièrement?

Toujours est-il que cet apport nouveau s'ajoute aux observations précédentes pour nous pousser à consulter le contexte historique, celui du milieu où Paul a vécu, et dont il a emprunté, pour des usages nouveaux, la terminologie, les formes et les catégories. Cette démarche utile n'implique nullement une adhésion au déterminisme historique, dans un sens hégélien ou autre. Le résultat des parallèles peut être aussi bien de dégager l'originalité que d'établir une filiation ou une servile dépendance.

[1] II Cor. v. 10; cf. *supra*, p. 354 n. 3.

[2] ...δοξάσατε δὴ τὸν Θεὸν ἐν τῷ σωματι ὑμῶν. II Cor. vi. 20.

[3] ...παραστῆσαι τὰ σώματα ὑμῶν θυσίαν ζῶσαν ἁγίαν τῷ Θεῷ εὐάρεστον. Rom. xii. 1.

[4] ...εἴτε ἐν σώματι οὐκ οἶδα, εἴτε ἐκτὸς τοῦ σώματος οὐκ οἶδα, ὁ θεὸς οἶδεν. II Cor. xii. 2, 3.

[5] Il déconseille même l'extase glossolalique, bien qu'il l'ait éprouvée, et ne la réprouve pas. Cf. I Cor. xiv. 6 ss., 18 s.

[6] ...ἐγὼ μὲν γάρ, ἀπὼν τῷ σώματι, παρὼν δὲ τῷ πνεύματι, ἤδη κέκρικα ὡς παρὼν τὸν...συναχθέντων ὑμῶν καὶ τοῦ ἐμοῦ πνεύματος...κ.τ.λ. I Cor. v. 3 s.

[7] Telle est l'interprétation de M. Dibelius, *op. cit.* pp. 38 ss.

4. LE MILIEU HISTORIQUE

Le milieu historique de Paul est maintenant bien connu: c'est celui de l'Hellénisme, où le Judaïsme lui-même est plus ou moins encadré ou fondu.[1] La Palestine, bien que plus réfractaire qu'aucune autre région, n'a pu éviter les infiltrations.[2] L'un des meilleurs exemples rentre dans notre cadre, puisqu'il concerne les croyances ou les doutes sur la résurrection. Or ici, justement, le Nouveau Testament nous apporte un témoignage très important. Il s'agit du texte qui relate, dans les trois Synoptiques, le débat de Jésus et des Sadducéens sur la nature de la résurrection, c'est à dire, en somme, sur la constitution de l'homme ressuscité.[3] Un parallèle peut être esquissé, d'après ce texte, entre trois conceptions différentes: celle des Pharisiens, à laquelle s'oppose celle des Sadducéens, et celle de Jésus qui se meut sur un autre plan. Les Pharisiens, qui cultivaient la tradition, pensant, par elle, prolonger l'Ecriture, y avaient laissé pénétrer, sans s'en rendre compte, ou sans se l'avouer, bien des éléments étrangers.[4] Comme on sait, leur conception de la résurrection corporelle se faisait remarquer par un réalisme parfois grossier.[5] Les Sadducéens, plus perméables, dans d'autres domaines, aux infiltrations du dehors, pouvaient ici se donner l'apparence d'une fidélité scripturaire plus grande. Ce n'était pas le cas, en réalité, comme Jésus le leur montrera, en s'attachant non à la lettre, mais à l'esprit.[6] Pensant embarrasser Jésus, comme leurs adversaires pharisiens, parmi lesquels ils paraissent le ranger, les Sadducéens lui posent la question captieuse de la femme aux sept maris: de qui sera-t-elle l'épouse à la résurrection? La réponse de Jésus est, en substance, la même dans les trois Synoptiques, et fixe sa position, parallèlement aux deux autres. Contre le matérialisme des Pharisiens, il affirme qu'on ne se marie pas à la

[1] Cf. Ch. Guignebert, *Le Monde juif vers le temps de Jésus* (Paris, 1935), *passim* et notamment liv. II et IV. Sur l'apport considérable du Judaïsme à l'Hellénisme, cf. notamment C. H. Dodd, *The Bible and the Greeks* (London, 1935), pp. xi ss., 243 ss. Sur Paul et l'Héllénisme, H. Clavier, ''Η Συνείδησις, Une pierre de touche de l'Hellénisme paulinien', *Symposion* (Athènes, 1953).

[2] Sur les infiltrations étrangères en plein Judaïsme palestinien, cf. W. Bousset, *Die Religion des Judentums in neutestamentlichen Zeitalter* (3e éd. Tübingen, 1926), *passim*; Ch. Guignebert, *op. cit.* pp. 112 ss. et *passim*; J. Bonsirven, *op. cit.* tome I, pp. 35 ss., 38 ss.; tome II, p. 187; W. D. Davies, *op. cit.* pp. 5 ss.

[3] Cf. Marc xii. 18–27 et parall.

[4] Cf. *supra*, p. 356 n. 2.

[5] Cf. *supra*, p. 349 nn. 2, 3.

[6] Cf. Marc xii. 26 et parall.

résurrection, et que les ressuscités sont comme des anges dans les cieux. Contre la légèreté ou l'incrédulité sadducéennes touchant le fond même du problème de l'avenir humain, de l'avenir des fidèles, il fait valoir un texte de l'Exode,[1] qu'il interprète ainsi: 'Dieu n'est pas le Dieu des morts, mais des vivants', avec la conclusion implicite, déjà suggérée dans quelques passages de l'Ancien Testament: 'Il a pour la mort même des portes d'issue' (Ps. lxviii. 21); 'Tu ne permettras pas que celui qui t'aime (ton fidèle, חֲסִידְךָ) voie la corruption (ou le fond du Sheôl, שַׁחַת); Tu me feras connaître le chemin de la Vie' (Ps. xvi. 10, 11). C'est cette déclaration de principe qui importe dans la pensée de Jésus, et il n'est pas acquis qu'en parlant des anges, dans le même contexte, il ait pris à son compte les croyances populaires, d'ailleurs diffuses et flottantes, sur les corps angéliques.[2] De même en ce qui concerne les fantômes ou les doubles, qu'admettaient ses disciples.[3]

Les superstitions populaires, à base d'animisme, sont extrêmement tenaces; on en trouve, encore aujourd'hui, des vestiges nombreux dans le cadre des civilisations et des religions supérieures. Il en était de même, *a fortiori*, au temps de Paul. Les distinctions trop nettes que l'on veut établir entre l'hellénisme de l'immortalité de l'âme et le judaïsme de la résurrection des corps ne valent pas en milieu populaire, et, même au degré supérieur, elles paraissent outrées. Jusqu'à un certain niveau, celui d'une élite intellectuelle, le même fond animiste remonte, de part et d'autre, dans ce domaine très spécialement: celui des notions sur l'outre-tombe. Mais des hommes aussi cultivés que Plutarque sont loin d'en être exempts,[4] et il semble que Platon lui-même y ait apporté son tribut, en marge d'un idéalisme qui ne s'y accorde guère.[5] Avec des variations nombreuses,

[1] Exode iii. 6. Sur l'utilisation du texte biblique et son interprétation dans ce sens, cf. E. Lohmeyer, 'Das Evang. d. Markus', in. Meyer's *Komm. z. N.T.* (Göttingen, 1937), pp. 256 s.; M. J. Lagrange, *Evang. selon St Marc* (5e éd. Paris, 1929), pp. 319 s.

[2] Cf. Marc xii. 25, et *supra*, p. 348 nn. 4, 5. Cf. Actes xii. 15; xxiii. 9.

[3] *Idem* et comp. Marc vi. 49 et parall.; Luc xxiv. 37, 39; Marc ix. 17, 25, etc.

[4] Cf. Plutarque, *Brutus* 36; *de def. Ord.* 10. Comp. Dibelius, *op. cit.* pp. 194 ss.; A. C. Pearson, art. 'Demons and Spirits (Greek)', dans Hastings, *Encycl. of Relig. and Ethics* vol. IV (Edinburgh, 1935), pp. 590–4; G. A. Barton, 'Demons and Spirits (Hebrew)', *ibid.* pp. 594–601.

[5] Cf. Platon, *Phédon* 107D (éd. Belles-Lettres, Paris, 1949); *Cratyle* 398B; *République* 617D; comp. *Timée* 90A et *Epinom.* 984E.

et des nuances indéfinies, les vieilles superstitions demeurent: le Hadès homérique, le Sheôl sémitique, les ombres, les fantômes, les esprits, tout cela au premier plan chez les plus frustes, à l'arrière-plan, ou larvé, chez de plus raffinés, mais toujours prêt à revenir.[1] En pareille matière, la supériorité du Juif, même le plus inculte, réside surtout dans sa notion de Dieu et dans la relation qu'il cherche à établir, plus ou moins heureusement, entre l'Unique, le Tout-Puissant, le Saint, et les aberrances d'une antique tradition persistant sous diverses formes et à plusieurs niveaux.[2]

Or, il faut bien se dire que Paul s'adressait à des simples. C'est justement dans I Corinthiens qu'il le souligne le plus fortement: parmi ses lecteurs, il n'y a pas beaucoup de σοφοὶ κατὰ σάρκα, de δυνατοί ou d'εὐγενεῖς (I Cor. i. 26). Si donc il peut, à l'occasion, affronter, non sans érudition, des sophistes, comme à Athènes,[3] il ne semble pas qu'il argumente ainsi devant les Corinthiens, ni dans aucune de ses lettres adressées à des communautés analogues. Aussi, dans les textes qui nous ont retenus, il s'agit moins pour lui de caractériser l'espérance chrétienne par rapport à l'Académie, au Lycée ou au Portique, même syncrétisés ou vulgarisés dans la Diatribe, que de la dresser face aux superstitions populaires confuses, mais tenaces, où le vieux Sheôl-Hadès, les mânes, les âmes, les ombres, les esprits traînent encore leur vie misérable, qui n'en est pas une.[4] L'écho de ces croyances est souvent perceptible dans le Nouveau Testament, sans qu'il soit toujours possible de dire si elles sont tenues pour sans fondement ou si elles sont seulement dépassées par la foi nouvelle.[5] On peut en dire autant d'autres échos qui se rapportent aussi à la constitution future de l'homme, dans l'Au-delà ou dans l'éon nouveau. Il y a les analogies, probables ou certaines, de l'angélologie et de la démonologie courantes, avec leurs syncrétismes où Juifs et païens se rencontrent encore;[6] peut-être, incidemment, la notion, qui semble

[1] Cf. *supra*, p. 357 nn. 4, 5. *Add. al. cap.* in art. 'Demons and Spirits', *loc. cit.*

[2] Il y a des incompatibilités qui ne sont pas aperçues, ni soupçonnées, suivant les niveaux culturels, et surtout spirituels, qui ne coïncident pas. Cf. W. Hatch, 'St Paul's view of the future life', in *Symposium* (1951), *op. cit.*

[3] Cf. Actes xvii. 18 ss.

[4] Sur la similitude et la ténacité de ces croyances chez divers peuples, et à divers degrés, cf. Hastings, *E.R.E.* art. 'State of the Dead'.

[5] Cf. notamment, I Cor. viii. 4, 5; x. 20, 21, etc.

[6] Cf. *supra*, p. 357 n. 4 et p. 358 nn. 1, 4; Bonsirven, *op. cit.* tome 1, pp. 222 ss.

d'origine iranienne, d'une âme céleste, sorte de double plus pur et plus beau de l'homme terrestre, qui vient à la rencontre du juste quand il meurt,[1] ou qui le revêt comme un vêtement;[2] il y a les pouvoirs cosmiques et les esprits correspondant aux étages du monde;[3] il y a les corps célestes, glorieux et vivants, suivant l'astrologie du temps.[4]

Paul qui, des auteurs du Nouveau Testament, connaît le mieux, sans doute, cet ensemble confus, y puise à l'occasion, comme dans un arsenal, très disparate, ce qu'à tort ou à raison, il juge être une arme utilisable. Cela n'implique pas toujours une adhésion formelle à ce qui pourrait lui servir simplement de motif;[5] mais cela engage à être prudent lorsqu'on veut préciser les nuances de sa pensée, notamment en ce qui concerne τὸ σῶμα πνευματικόν.

Quand Paul emprunte à la Diatribe ou à la Gnose hellénistique tel terme ou telle notion (l'antithèse ἔξω ἄνθρωπος—ἔσω ἄνθρωπος, par exemple), cela ne veut pas dire nécessairement qu'il en ait adopté le sens technique;[6] ce pourrait être une arme pour établir plus sûrement et faire prévaloir le sens chrétien. De toutes façons, on peut être certain que l'emprunt n'est jamais servile et qu'il y aura toujours quelque nuance distinctive. Ainsi se justifie, dans ce domaine aussi, la parole de l'apôtre: 'Les choses vieilles sont passées; toutes choses sont devenues nouvelles.'[7] Après la découverte des parallèles, et l'engouement irréfléchi pour l'assimilation hâtive, on en revient à cette formule d'un sage comparatisme, posée au cinquième siècle par l'évêque Théodoret: 'Par la comparaison montrer la différence, et par le parallèle saisir ce qui distingue.'[8]

[1] Cf. Yasht xxii. 1–36. Ce thème est développé dans les écrits mandéens et manichéens. On trouve encore de nombreux parallèles dans la littérature gnostique. Dibelius en voit un jusque dans Actes xii. 15 (cf. *supra*, p. 357 nn. 2–4, et Martin Dibelius, 'Le N.T. et l'Hist. des Relig.', art. dans *Etudes Théol. et Relig.* (Montpellier, 1930), pp. 305 ss.).

[2] Cf. *supra*, p. 353 n. 7.

[3] Cf. I Cor. viii. 5; Rom. viii. 38 s.; Col. i. 16; ii. 10, 15; Eph. i. 21; iii. 10; Phil. ii. 10. Cf. *Ascens. Es.* in Hennecke, *op. cit.* pp. 311 ss.; M. Dibelius, *Die Geisterwelt...*, *op. cit.* pp. 93 s., 106 ss., 234 ss.

[4] *Idem.* Cf. encore: I Cor. xv. 40 s., 47 s., et *supra*, p. 348 nn. 4, 5.

[5] Ainsi, peut-être, en ce qui concerne le baptême pour les morts (I Cor. xv. 29).

[6] Cf. *supra*, p. 352 n. 6, p. 353 n. 1 et p. 354 nn. 4–7.

[7] II Cor. v. 17: εἴ τις ἐν Χριστῷ, καινὴ κτίσις· τὰ ἀρχαῖα παρῆλθεν, ἰδοὺ γέγονεν καινά (τὰ πάντα).

[8] Théodoret, 'Ελληνικῶν θεραπευτικὴ παθημάτων, κ.τ.λ. (*P.G.* vol. LXXXIII): δεῖξαι ἐκ συγκρίσεως τὸ διάφορον, ἐκ παραλλήλου θεώμενος τὸ διάφορον.

5. CONCLUSION

Avec cet élargissement progressif du champ d'investigation, il peut sembler que l'on soit moins en mesure que jamais de faire le point de la notion complexe de σῶμα πνευματικόν. Du moins sera-t-on à l'abri des conclusions hâtives.

La connaissance du contexte historique a fait comprendre dans quel imbroglio d'idées, de tendances, de craintes et d'espoirs, d'aspirations variées, convergentes ou divergentes, Paul se trouvait, de par ses origines et son éducation, son milieu et son temps. Il a été l'homme des dualités;[1] son caractère y prêtait déjà, son expérience humaine a fait le reste. Si ces dualités sont pratiquement vaincues par la foi, elles n'en laissent pas moins subsister des problèmes théoriques.

Σῶμα πνευματικόν est une association de mots qui peut sembler contradictoire en soi, sur le plan d'une certaine logique. Elle est réduite au terme matériel dans la conception courante, où l'esprit n'est qu'une substance raréfiée ou sublimée. On ne peut pas dire que Paul se soit absolument dégagé de cette manière de voir, si répandue de son temps, si vivace, même de notre temps.[2] Mais ce que l'on peut affirmer, c'est que guidé par sa foi (*fides quaerens intellectum*),[3] l'apôtre est tendu vers une intuition plus spirituelle de l'esprit, et, du même coup, du 'corps spirituel'.

Σῶμα πνευματικόν est encore une formule de combat, qui vise une objection particulière, dans une situation particulière, et qui n'a pas été reprise telle quelle par l'apôtre en d'autres circonstances. La négation de la résurrection par certains membres de la communauté corinthienne[4] n'équivalait nullement à une négation pure et simple de toute survie. Il n'est pas impossible que l'idéalisme platonicien ait exercé sur quelques-uns une influence directe ou indirecte, avec sa thèse classique de l'immortalité d'une âme libérée de tout organe physique. Mais, en milieu aussi populaire, il est probable que le vieil animisme et le Sheôl-Hadès, communs aux Juifs et aux Grecs,

[1] Cf. *supra*, p. 354 n. 9.

[2] Cf. *supra*, p. 342 n. 1, p. 346 n. 1 et p. 358 nn. 1, 2. Cf. E. Westermarck, *Survivances païennes dans la civilisation mahométane* (trad. de l'anglais par R. Godet, Paris, 1935), pp. 11 ss.

[3] Belle et célèbre devise d'*Anselme de Canterbury*.

[4] Cf. I Cor. xv. 12.

étaient encore le principal ennemi. Aussi, la leçon ποῦ σου, Ἅδη, τὸ νῖκος;, dans le chant triomphal du *v.* 55, semble-t-elle préférable, en même temps que plus conforme au texte d'Osée xiii. 14.[1] Au temps des grands MSS., les notions de Hadès, d'ombres, de mânes, étaient périmées, d'où la correction de ᾅδη en θάνατε, sauf chez quelques témoins qui, bien que plus récents, ont pu connaître et copier un texte plus ancien.

Qu'il y ait des esprits, tels que les figure l'imagination populaire, Paul ne semble pas l'avoir expressément nié par la formule σῶμα πνευματικόν. Plusieurs autres textes suggèrent qu'il y croit;[2] mais cette croyance ne tient aucune place dans sa vie religieuse. Son expérience chrétienne est diamétralement opposée aux perspectives d'une existence fantomatique, triomphe de Hadès et de Thanatos. Elle luttera encore, de toute son intimité spirituelle, contre l'attente apocalyptique et les matérialisations de la parousie, dont, spécialement, celle des organes ressuscités, mais avec un succès moindre. Elle cherchera dans l'Eglise, corps du Christ, une formule à la fois pratique et mystique où les difficultés d'un organisme individuel et spirituel pourraient trouver une solution d'ensemble.[3] Mais le danger de noyer la personne, la personnalité chrétienne, dans un plérôme panthéistique a toujours été surmonté.

Si l'on reprend ici la formule de Théodoret: 'par la comparaison, saisir ce qui distingue', on peut assurer que la caractéristique essentielle du σῶμα πνευματικόν selon Paul, n'est pas d'être ou non un corps en esprit, mais un organe de l'esprit, commandé par l'Esprit, par le Saint-Esprit.

En résumé, une exégèse purement philologique, et limitée aux deux termes de l'expression σῶμα πνευματικόν pourrait faire croire, avec une grande partie de la tradition, que le 'corps pneumatique' est, en substance, le même corps, ce corps de chair, mais contrôlé par l'esprit, comme le fut le corps de Jésus-Christ. Certains des problèmes de l'incarnation se poseraient alors sous l'angle eschatologique. L'analogie avec le corps de Jésus-Christ devrait être poussée jusqu'au bout, sans oublier la leçon de cette parole: 'Il vous est

[1] אֱהִי דְבָרֶיךָ מָוֶת אֱהִי קָטָבְךָ שְׁאוֹל. Osée xiii. 14.

[2] Cf. *supra*, p. 348 nn. 4, 5, p. 358 n. 2 et p. 359 n. 3.

[3] Eph. i. 23; ii. 16; iv. 4, 12. Comp. Col. i. 18; ii. 17, 19; I Cor. xii. 13, 20, 27; Rom. xii. 5.

avantageux que je m'en aille' (Jean xvi. 7).[1] Toutefois, restreinte à l'examen de deux mots, dont le sens habituel n'est pas exclusif, la philologie pure ne peut donner que des indications sommaires, à éprouver dans le contexte.

Le contexte littéraire a révélé que le problème de la direction du corps n'était pas le seul à préoccuper l'apôtre Paul, mais que celui de la constitution du corps ressuscité s'y mêlait étroitement. De toutes façons, pour lui, le 'corps pneumatique' ne sera pas ce corps matériel. 'Résurrection de la chair': cette formule qui a prévalu dans la plupart des églises, et qui regagne du terrain dans certaines, peut trouver dans l'histoire des explications ou des circonstances atténuantes; mais c'est une faute, contraire à la lettre du paulinisme comme à son esprit.[2] Néanmoins, la question: 'Comment les morts ressuscitent-ils, avec quel corps reviennent-ils?' (I Cor. xv. 35) oscille entre un problème d'énergie dominante, de force directrice, et un problème de constitution, qui dévie aisément vers celui d'une substance, avec ses implications et ses associations.[3]

L'extension de l'étude au contexte historique a montré combien ces associations ont pu être nombreuses et embrouillées. Enfin, un autre problème est venu accroître la confusion: celui de la parousie qui, dans la mesure où elle est conçue et imaginée comme matérielle, vient accentuer naturellement la déviation substantielle d'un problème de constitution.

Ainsi, des lignes nombreuses et variées viennent se croiser sur cette 'crux interpretum': σῶμα πνευματικόν. S'il est utile de les identifier, la tâche principale était d'en dégager la directive ou la ligne de force. Les expériences fondamentales et les élans décisifs de l'apôtre convergent tous vers ce témoignage de II Tim. i. 10: 'Jésus-Christ est venu; Il a réduit la mort à l'impuissance; Il a mis en lumière la Vie et l'Immortalité par l'Evangile.'[4]

[1] συμφέρει ὑμῖν ἵνα ἐγὼ ἀπέλθω, κ.τ.λ. Jean xvi. 7.

[2] Cf. *supra*, p. 349 nn. 1–3.

[3] Cf. *supra*, p. 349 nn. 1–6 et p. 350 nn. 1, 2.

[4] φανερωθεῖσαν δὲ νῦν διὰ τῆς ἐπιφανείας τοῦ σωτῆρος ἡμῶν Χριστοῦ Ἰησοῦ, καταργήσαντος μὲν τὸν θάνατον φωτίσαντος δὲ ζωὴν καὶ ἀφθαρσίαν διὰ τοῦ εὐαγγελίου. II Tim. i. 10.

18

THE ESCHATOLOGY OF THE EPISTLE TO THE HEBREWS

C. K. BARRETT

I. INTRODUCTION

THE author of Hebrews, profound theologian as he was, stood perhaps nearer to the main stream of Christian tradition, and drew more upon that stream and less upon extraneous sources, than is sometimes allowed. The Epistle is fundamentally a practical sermon, a λόγος παρακλήσεως (xiii. 22).[1] The readers to whom Hebrews was addressed were Christians of some standing (x. 32) who had failed to reveal the Christian maturity which lapse of time should have brought (v. 12). Repeated warnings (ii. 1; iii. 6, 12–14; iv. 11; v. 11; vi. 4–12; x. 23, 29, 32–9; xii. 4–17, 25–9) show that there was serious danger lest slackness, carelessness, sloth, cowardice and the like should lead to final and irretrievable apostasy. Even elementary Christian virtues such as fidelity in marriage, hospitality, practical sympathy, respect for teachers and freedom from avarice were in danger (see especially xiii. 1–5, 7, 17, 24). It is about these things that the author is concerned; above all he seeks to quicken an active, lively faith, a dread of sin, and moral and spiritual earnestness (especially ch. xii).[2]

The moral earnestness of Hebrews is reinforced by eschatological considerations, outspoken, and often quite primitive in form. For example, the readers must not neglect their assemblies because 'the day', clearly, the day of judgment, is drawing near (x. 25). The theme of judgment belongs to elementary but essential Christian

[1] 'Es geht im Heb. letztlich doch um den Anspruch Gottes an eine Gemeinde, nicht um christologische Geheimnisse, um Glauben, und nicht um Gnosis' (O. Michel, *Der Hebräerbrief*, 2nd ed. 1949, p. 22).

[2] These exhortations seem to me much too general to permit us to locate the persons to whom the Epistle was addressed, or to determine its date. On the whole, a setting in the Gentile Christianity of the end of the first century seems plausible, but attempts at greater precision are not convincing.

doctrine (vi. 2). What judgment day means is unmistakably clear. From condemnation there is no escape for those who neglect the salvation proffered in the Gospel (ii. 3). To commit apostasy is to incur the same fate, or indeed worse (x. 26f.). Wilful sinners can look forward to nothing but destruction (x. 39) in consuming fire (x. 27; cf. xii. 29). It is a fearful thing to fall into the hands of the living God (x. 31). The last day will be ushered in by the shaking and removal of heaven and earth (xii. 27). In this cataclysm, however, Christians will have nothing to fear. They receive a kingdom which cannot be shaken (xii. 28). God rewards those who seek him (xi. 6, 26), and will not forget the works of mercy which his people perform (vi. 10). At the last day Jesus will appear a second time[1] to those who await him, to bring them salvation.[2] Christians will thus be saved at the last day; but not automatically. They must show that piety and godly fear which the imminent judgment demands (xii. 28), remembering on the one hand that God will judge immoral persons (xiii. 4), and on the other that he will not fail or forsake those who trust him (xiii. 5f.). The rulers of the community watch over the souls entrusted to them, and will have to give an account concerning them (xiii. 17); neither they nor their charges may for a moment relax their vigilance.

In all this there is nothing specifically Christian apart from the belief that at the last day no unknown Messiah will appear but the Jesus who has already lived a human life (ix. 28), and that those who will be saved are those who now are Christians and persevere in their faith to the end. The characteristically Christian conviction, however, that eschatological events have already taken place (though others remain in the future as objects of hope), is found as clearly in Hebrews as in any part of the N.T. The first coming of Jesus was of course such an event, and indeed the primary eschatological event. God, who in the past had spoken to the fathers by the prophets, spoke to us in his Son 'at the end of these days' (i. 2). A variant, not strongly attested, runs 'in these last days', and the better text has probably a similar meaning. The days in which the Church lived were the last days, ushered in by the incarnation, death and ascension

[1] ix. 28, ἐκ δευτέρου—perhaps the earliest specific mention of a second advent.

[2] εἰς σωτηρίαν. This word has nearly always an eschatological sense: i. 14; ii. 3, 10; v. 9; vi. 9; ix. 28. Cf. xi. 7.

of Jesus and shortly to be consummated by his return, when all his enemies should have been subjected to him (ii. 8f., x. 12f.). Indeed, the consummation of the ages has already been reached,[1] and the present moment is that on which the meaning of the O.T. turns (xi. 39f.). The present is the time in which men must take up a decisive attitude (ii. 1–4) to the salvation secured by Christ in his sacrificial death (ix. 12). By his blood he will cleanse our conscience and enable us to serve the living God (ix. 14). From this relation with God it follows that Christians, though living in this world, have already begun to experience the world to come.[2] In their baptism[3] they have tasted the heavenly gift, become partakers of the Holy Spirit, tasted the good word of God and the powers of the age to come (vi. 4f.); and they have approached (προσεληλύθατε) Mount Sion, the heavenly Jerusalem (xii. 22–4). Their life is one of hope and struggle, in which they are sustained by the fact that that for which they strive has already been achieved for them, and that they have already begun to enjoy it.

When these data are considered it becomes very difficult to deny the central place of eschatology in Hebrews.[4] It is almost equally difficult to accept the mediating position of Moffatt,[5] who recognizes fully the existence of many strongly eschatological passages, but believes that, in incorporating them, the author was inconsistent. The 'speculative theory of the eternal and material orders', which

[1] ix. 26. Matthew (xiii. 39f., 49; xxiv. 3; xxviii. 20) uses a similar expression to denote a future time.

[2] Hebrews speaks of the coming αἰών (vi. 5, and in the phrases εἰς τὸν αἰῶνα, τοὺς αἰῶνας), and the coming οἰκουμένη (ii. 5). The latter noun is, in this connection, unusual, but it is doubtful whether it is significant for the thought of the Epistle.

[3] Baptism seems to be implied by the word φωτισθέντας, as was already recognized by the Syriac translators. φωτίζειν is commonly applied to baptism from the time of Justin.

[4] As does M. Goguel, *La Naissance du Christianisme* (1946): 'L'attente eschatologique est très atténuée. Les formules qui s'y rapportent n'ont plus guère que le caractère de survivances' (p. 373). Contrast H. Windisch, *Der Hebräerbrief* (*Handbuch zum N.T.*, 1931), p. 86: 'Die eschatologische Bedingtheit der urchristlichen Geschichtsanschauung, Gegenwartsbetrachtung und Zukunftserwartung bezeugt auch Heb.' and O. Michel, *op. cit.* p. 17: 'Zunächst ist seine Verkündigung ganz eschatologisch.... Der Hellenismus hat den eschatologischen Glauben Philos entkräftet, den eschatologischen Glauben des Heb. gestärkt.'

[5] *The Epistle to the Hebrews* (I.C.C. 1924).

was the author's 'deeper thought', was incompatible with his eschatological language and convictions.[1]

The present essay proceeds upon the opposite belief, namely, that the thought of Hebrews is consistent, and that in it the eschatological is the determining element. Features which do not upon the surface appear to be eschatological show, on closer examination, traces of eschatological, even apocalyptic, origin, and the thought of the Epistle (exemplified in what follows by three of its fundamental conceptions) arises out of the eschatological faith of the primitive Church.

2. THE SAINTS' EVERLASTING REST

At ii. 17f. our author reaches for the first time the theme, which occupies his attention for so long, of Jesus as the true high priest. He repeats the word ἀρχιερεύς in iii. 1, and thereafter we hear no more of the priesthood of Christ until iv. 14, where the earlier reference is picked up and developed (ἔχοντες οὖν ἀρχιερέα...). This verse might follow immediately upon ii. 18 and the intervening passage must be regarded as a digression, complete in itself. It begins with a comparison, not suggested by the context but resting upon Num. xii. 7, between Jesus and Moses. Each of these great figures may be described as faithful, but Moses was faithful to God as a servant within God's household, Jesus as a son over God's household; that is, when God and his people are seen over against each other, Moses stands on the human, Jesus on the divine side. We (continues Hebrews) are the household of Jesus over which he is faithful if we hold fast to our confidence and hope. This condition gives rise to a characteristic exhortation; men must not waver or draw back but maintain their faith undaunted. This exhortation is given in the words of Ps. xcv. 7–11 (Heb. iii. 7b–11), where the Israelites in the wilderness are described as provoking God's anger and being refused admittance to his 'rest'. But the Psalm begins with the word 'Today' and today the readers of the epistle must give heed to the admonition. They will receive what is promised them only if they hold fast their initial confidence (iii. 14) and do not

[1] *Op. cit.* p. liv: 'The category of the Highpriesthood...could not be fitted in with his eschatology any more than the idea of the two worlds could be.' Cf. pp. xxxii, xxxiv.

draw back from God (iii. 12). The full relevance of the quotation from the Psalm is not seen until *vv.* 16–19. The vital point is that entrance to the Holy Land was refused to those who disbelieved the favourable report of Caleb (and Joshua) and by their hesitation and cowardice rebelled against God (Num. xiii f., especially xiv. 22 f.). And we see (concludes the author, iii. 19) that οὐκ ἠδυνήθησαν εἰσελθεῖν δι' ἀπιστίαν. It follows that a similar lack of faith will exclude Christians now from the promised κατάπαυσις. Hearing a message of good news is in itself no guarantee that the thing promised will be received; only faith (πίστις) can give effect to the word heard (ὁ λόγος τῆς ἀκοῆς, iv. 2). At this point the author assumes an important conclusion which he does not however demonstrate till iv. 8 f. It was shown at iii. 18 that God swore that οἱ ἀπειθήσαντες should not enter into his 'rest'; but this did not mean that no Israelites entered Canaan. Caleb and Joshua, and the 'little ones' of less than twenty years of age at the time of the apostasy, did in fact enter (Num. xiv. 29 f.), and thus reach the 'rest' that had been promised. We might therefore ask, What then is this 'rest' to Christians in the first century? But this would be to overlook the fact that the matter is taken up again by David in Ps. xcv. Not only does David reopen the issue (some hundreds of years after the entry into Canaan), thereby showing that though Joshua had led the people of God into Canaan he had not given them their true 'rest' (iv. 8); he introduces his address with the word 'Today', showing further that the rest remains still open to the faith of those who hear his words. There remains therefore a 'rest' for the people of God (iv. 9); but it is now described as a σαββατισμός. This is because the author has already explained what κατάπαυσις means. The word suggests the use of the cognate verb in Gen. ii. 2. On the seventh day God rested,[1] his works being therefore completed from the beginning of the world. Thus the 'rest' was the rest of the seventh day, the Sabbath; a rest always available since God had prepared it and himself entered upon it, but never in the days before Christ entered by men (as the Psalm proves); a rest of which the Sabbaths kept by the

[1] κατέπαυσεν. The middle would have been more appropriate. Philo (*Leg. Alleg.* I, 6) notes this, and takes the active literally—'God caused to rest'. In Heb. iv. 8 also the active is given its proper meaning, and it may be that the author understood Gen. ii. 2 similarly—'God prepared a rest for his people'.

Jews might be regarded as a type—though this is never stated in Hebrews.

After this brief sketch of the author's argument a few questions suggest themselves for discussion. In what does the 'rest' which remains for the people of God consist? When do they enter into it? What is the role of the O.T. in the argument developed in Hebrews?

It will help us to answer these questions if for a moment we turn from them to consider two writers who handle similar material and are frequently, and with justice, compared with the author of Hebrews.

In Philo we look in vain for any eschatological interpretation of the Sabbath rest. Reinterpretation of the seven-day narrative of Genesis we do find. Philo is unable to contemplate this as a chronological record of the creation of the world. 'He says that in six days the world was created, not that its Maker required a length of time for His work, for we must think of God as doing all things simultaneously....Six days are mentioned because for the things coming into existence there was need of order. Order involves number...' (*De Opif. Mundi* 13; cf. *Leg. Alleg.* i, 2). Philo does not in his philosophical exposition lose sight of the practical importance and value of the Sabbath (*De Spec. Leg.* ii, 60, *De Vit. Mos.* ii, 211). As a good Jew he assumes that it will be kept, and describes how, on the Sabbath, the synagogues are open in every land for instruction (*De Spec. Leg.* ii, 62). Regular relaxation refreshes the body and enables men to work better (*De Spec. Leg.* ii, 60); and in this period of bodily rest the soul may be active (*De Spec. Leg.* ii, 64). The same point is emphasized in *De Decal.* 101: 'Let us not then neglect this great archetype of the two best lives, the practical and the contemplative.' This distinction corresponds to the fact that God himself did not on the seventh day cease from all activity: this would be unthinkable. Rather, since he can never cease making, he then began to shape things more divine (θειότερα, *Leg Alleg.* i, 5). At times Philo uses what appears at first sight to be mystical language about the seventh day: 'He [Moses] found that she was in the first place motherless, exempt from female parentage, begotten by the Father alone, without begetting, brought to the birth, yet not carried in the womb...she was also ever virgin, neither born of a mother nor a mother herself, neither bred from corruption nor doomed to suffer corruption' (*De Vit. Mos.* ii, 210). These curious remarks are, however, derived from Pythagorean speculations about the number seven.[1] A little more to the point, perhaps, is the description of the Sabbath as the birthday of the world (ἡ τοῦ κόσμου γενέθλιος; *De Spec. Leg.* ii, 59, *De Opif. Mundi* 89, *De Vit. Mos.* i, 207), 'a feast celebrated by heaven, celebrated by earth and things on earth as they rejoice and exult in the full harmony of the sacred number' (*De Vit. Mos.* ii, 210); but this theme is never (I believe) elaborated.

In Philo we see a really Hellenistic, un-eschatological interpretation of the creation narrative with its division into days, and of the weekly Sabbath festival. Nothing could be more remote from Hebrews.

The Epistle of Barnabas stands, at first sight, much closer to Hebrews, and that not merely because it is a Christian document. It certainly reinterprets O.T. material about the Sabbath in an eschatological sense. But Barnabas' treatment of the subject (ch. xv), which is found in a series of anti-Jewish chapters, presents considerable difficulties, not least in its relation to the text of the O.T.[2]

Barnabas' exegesis is as follows. Scripture states that God completed his works in six days. What does that mean? We must understand that God will complete the universe in 6000 years. In this interpretation two points are involved: the expansion of 'days' into millennia, and the change of the past tense (συνετέλεσεν) into the future (συντελέσει). The latter change Barnabas makes no attempt to justify. Clearly he is applying a ready-made set of canons of interpretation. In making the former he gives no sign of being motivated by such philosophical objections as Philo felt, but justifies it by means of Ps. lxxxix. (xc.) 4. This piece of eschatological mathematics, though very serviceable to Christians perplexed by the delay of the *parousia*, seems to have been Jewish in origin. Most of

[1] Cf. *De Opif. Mundi* 100; *Leg. Alleg.* 1, 15; and Stobaeus, *Ecl.* 1, i, 10.

[2] The chapter begins with the quotation of three passages. The first combines a reference to Exod. xx. 8, Deut. v. 12 or Jer. xvii. 22 with Ps. xxiii (xxiv) 4. The second may be a free combination of Jer. xvii. 24ff. and Exod. xxxi. 13–17. The third is a fairly accurate quotation of Gen. ii. 2, though here Barnabas says that God completed his work on the seventh (not sixth) day. In this he differs from the LXX, but agrees with the Hebrew text, and with Philo, *De Vit. Mos.* 1, 207 (other passages in Philo differ). It seems not unlikely that Barnabas is here using a collection of testimonies; cf. J. R. Harris, *Testimonies*, vol. 1 (1916), pp. 33–8, for other testimony material in Barnabas.

the evidence for this is given in Strack-Billerbeck, vol. III, pp. 773 f. (on II Pet. iii. 8); the rabbinic evidence can be traced back to the first century, and supplemented by Jub. iv. 30, where, however, there is no explicit reference to Ps. xc. In this point also Barnabas rests on Jewish tradition.

The universe will thus be completed in 6000 years. Gen. ii. 2 continues that on the seventh day God rested (κατέπαυσεν). This aorist also is changed into a future. The seventh day rest will truly come when the Son of God puts an end (καταργήσει) to the season of the lawless one (τοῦ ἀνόμου), judges the ungodly and changes the sun, the moon and the stars. This 'seventh day' (presumably a seventh millennium) must come at the end of the 6000 years which are still in progress. When it comes men will at length be able to sanctify the Sabbath with pure hearts and hands (xv. 1, 6), for then, when lawlessness (ἀνομία) is done away and the Lord has brought new things to birth, they will be made righteous and holy (δικαιωθέντες...ἁγιασθέντες), having received the promise.

Here Barnabas might have been content to stop, but does not. Unfortunately his addition does much to obscure the paragraph. He quotes (xv. 8) Isa. i. 13, in almost exact agreement with the LXX. This verse proves that not τὰ νῦν σάββατα (those kept by the Jews) are acceptable to God, but the Sabbath he has made (ὃ πεποίηκα), 'in which, when I have brought all things to rest (καταπαύσας) I will make (ποιήσω) the beginning of the eighth day, that is, the beginning of another world (ἄλλου κόσμου)'. Hence (xv. 9) Christians keep with gladness the eighth day, the day of Jesus' resurrection and ascension. The only point that is really clear here is perhaps the only point that Barnabas really wished to make: the Jews with their Sabbaths are in the wrong, the Christians with their Sundays are in the right. But this leads him to include the explicit statement that the eighth day is the beginning of a new world,[1] and if by this he means the eighth millennium what he says here is inconsistent with what he says in xv. 5–7, where the Sabbatical millennium in which sin is overcome is the seventh.

Thus in all his calculations Barnabas has simply adopted and transposed Jewish methods and results. We have already seen that

[1] Cf. Philo's description of the seventh day as the birthday of the world; see above, p. 369.

the equation of one day with a thousand years was Jewish; so also was the connection between the Sabbath and the age to come.[1] Notwithstanding the confusion introduced by the substitution of Sunday for the Sabbath it is clear that Barnabas' real view was that he and his contemporaries stood within the 6000 years, still waiting for the Son of God to usher in the millennial period with heavenly signs and portents.

When we return to Hebrews we can see at once how far removed this book is from both the Hellenism of Philo and the millennialism (no less marked on account of his anti-Judaism) of Barnabas. For Philo, the 'rest' of the people of God consists in the exercise of the βίος θεωρητικός, the practice of philosophy. For Barnabas, it is the time when the Son of God shall change the sun, the moon and the stars, when sin is done away, new things come into being, and we receive the promise (xv. 5–7). Between Philo and Hebrews there is no resemblance at all. Barnabas stands somewhat closer to Hebrews, but even so his 'Sabbath' is determined by an apocalyptic calculation which is noticeably absent from Hebrews, whereas the decisive factor in the thought of Hebrews is wanting in Barnabas. By his eschatological transformation of aorists into futures Barnabas actually implies that God did not 'rest' at all at the close of the creation; even for him 'rest' is something still to come. But it is essential to the thought of Hebrews that God did rest from his works (iv. 10), and that our rest is to be analogous with his (ὥσπερ). 'The rest of man is the rest of God: we shall enter into his rest...God rested from his work; what was his rest? The only rest from true work, the only true rest from work, is to be sought and found in the completion and perfection of the work.'[2] That is, the rest into which believers enter is the complete fulfilment of God's work in

[1] The evidence is well known. See among other passages Tamid vii. 4: 'On the Sabbath they sang [in the Temple] *A Psalm: a Song for the Sabbath Day* [Ps. xcii]; a Psalm, a song for the time that is to come, for the day that shall be all Sabbath and rest in the life everlasting.' Gen. R. xvii. 7: 'There are three antitypes [נובלות; Dalman's "unvollkommenes Gegenbild" is here a better rendering than Jastrow's "inferior variety"]: the antitype of death is sleep, the antitype of prophecy is dream, the antitype of the age to come is the Sabbath.' Life of Adam and Eve li. 2: 'Man of God, mourn not for thy dead more than six days, for on the seventh day is the sign of the resurrection and the rest of the age to come; on the seventh day the Lord rested from all his works.'

[2] W. P. DuBose, *High Priesthood and Sacrifice* (1908), p. 63.

them, and of their work in God. As the next verse (iv. 11), resuming the argument, implies, to enter into God's 'rest' is the opposite of unbelief and disobedience; it means that man shares at length in the perfection of God's ultimate purpose for mankind. This purpose is, yet is to be, achieved. Of this Barnabas has indeed some inkling,[1] but he has combined it with much else, and subordinated it to the rigid timetable by which his eschatology is controlled.

When do the people of God enter into the promised 'rest'? Now, or at some future date? Philo appears to have no thought beyond the philosophical and spiritual advantage that may be derived from the weekly Sabbath, and the extension to the whole of life of the philosophic outlook suggested by the Sabbath. Barnabas, as we have seen is tied to a rigid time-scheme, which is only obscured, not liberated, by his reference to the 'eighth day'. There is no such rigid and straightforward scheme in Hebrews. In iv. 3 the present tense is used: εἰσερχόμεθα εἰς τὴν κατάπαυσιν. The verb, however, is translated in the Vulgate *ingrediemur*. This interpretation is accepted by Moffatt *ad loc.* ('"we do (we are sure to) enter", the futuristic present'), but not by Westcott *ad loc.* ('The verb εἰσερχόμεθα is not to be taken as a future...but as the expression of a present fact.') Both expositors are right. The present tense is to be taken seriously, and it finds some slight support in iv. 10 (ὁ γὰρ εἰσελθὼν εἰς τὴν κατάπαυσιν αὐτοῦ), though here the aorist participle introduces a general statement ('to have entered means to have rested'). It finds stronger support in the σήμερον of the Psalm. But the next verse (σπουδάσωμεν οὖν εἰσελθεῖν...) is addressed to men who (though they have tasted the powers of the age to come, vi. 5) have not yet entered into the 'rest'. The 'rest' is and remains a promise, which some of the readers of the Epistle may fail through disobedience to achieve (iv. 1) and all are exhorted to strive to enter. The 'rest', precisely because it is God's, is both present and future; men enter it, and must strive to enter it. This is paradoxical, but it is a paradox which Hebrews shares with all primitive Christian eschatology.[2]

[1] xv. 7, ...δικαιωθέντες...μηκέτι οὔσης τῆς ἀνομίας...ἁγιασθέντες.

[2] In other words, Richard Baxter was right in speaking of the Saints' Everlasting Rest as a blessing to come in the future beyond this life, and at the same time urging upon his readers 'the importance of leading a heavenly life upon earth'. For the paradox see *Scottish Journal of Theology*, vol. VI (1953), pp. 144–50, 231–6, 239–43.

When, finally, we ask what role is played by the O.T. in the argument in Hebrews, and what other factors may have influenced the author's thought, contrast with Philo and Barnabas is again evident. Philo uses the O.T., but the real basis of his thought lies elsewhere. His numerical speculations are Pythagorean, and his description of the practical life and the contemplative is Aristotelian. He is a Jew in that he goes to synagogue on the Sabbath, but the message he hears and preaches there is not Jewish. Barnabas also quotes the O.T., but the textual looseness of his quotations is an index of the fact that his thought is determined not by the O.T. itself but by Midrashic tradition. Over against both Philo and Barnabas, Hebrews shows a fresh approach to the O.T., whose only presupposition is that of primitive Christian eschatology. The notion of the messianic Sabbath, which in several parts of the N.T. is a living conception,[1] is stultified by Barnabas, who, failing to see that the Sabbath had dawned, forced the Christian view of history into the form of a time-table, thereby destroying its essential and characteristic paradox. For Hebrews, on the other hand, the eschatology is alive and determinative, and it was this which gave the author his creative understanding of the O.T. His sense of the promise in the O.T. was quickened by the conviction that it had been in part fulfilled. Other factors helped to mould his thought in this paragraph—the strife over the relative greatness of Jesus and Moses,[2] the problem of the Law, the anxiety caused by the delayed *parousia*; but these were all factors native, and not alien, to the Church. The doctrine of the Sabbath rest in Hebrews is neither Hellenistic nor Midrashic but Christian.

3. THE PILGRIM'S PROGRESS FROM THE CITY OF DESTRUCTION TO THE CELESTIAL CITY

The teaching of Hebrews about the Sabbath rest reveals clearly the characteristic pattern of N.T. eschatology: the 'rest' is, and is to be; and men must strive to enter it. The teaching about the heavenly city is analogous,[3] and leads to a consideration of the meaning of faith in Hebrews.

[1] See, for example, E. C. Hoskyns, in *Mysterium Christi* (1930), pp. 74–8.

[2] Cf. *Clem. Recog.* I, 59, and see H. J. Schoeps, *Theologie und Geschichte des Judenchristentums* (1949), pp. 111f.

[3] For the transition cf. Test. Dan, v. 12.

Jerusalem was not one of the first Israelite cities in Canaan,[1] but its geographical advantages, and still more its connection with David, gave it in the Bible and in Jewish thought unparalleled prestige.[2] The varying fortunes of the city, its central cultic significance and the patriotic devotion of the Hebrews combined to vest Jerusalem itself with an aura of religious associations, and a Jewish state without its capital, and the Temple which was the glory of the capital, became unthinkable. Accordingly a 'new Jerusalem' and a 'new Temple' became part of the Jewish national hope, and this hope appears in various forms from the time of the Exile.

The Rabbinic literature in general looks forward to a restored Jerusalem under earthly conditions. The new city is described in detail in terms which are often fantastic,[3] but the welter of imagination bestowed upon the subject does not alter the fact that what the Rabbis hoped for, and described as ירושלם של עולם הבא, 'the Jerusalem of the age to come', was essentially the material capital of a material state. The Rabbis, however, spoke not only of this future Jerusalem but also of a 'Jerusalem above', ירושלם של מעלה, and the same conception of a heavenly city occurs in some apocalyptic books. The evidence is succinctly presented in Strack-Billerbeck, vol. III, pp. 532, 573, and need not be given in detail here. Of the Rabbinic material it will suffice to cite Hagiga 12b.[4] Of the seven heavens (said R. Meir) the fourth is זבול (*z^e^bul*, literally 'dwelling'), 'in which are the (heavenly) Jerusalem, and the (heavenly) temple, and an altar is built, at which Michael the great prince stands and on which he offers sacrifice, as it is written, I have surely built thee an house of habitation (*z^e^bul*), a place for thee to dwell in for ever (I Kings viii. 13). And how do we know that it (*z^e^bul*) is called heaven? Because it is written, Look down from heaven, and behold from the habitation (*z^e^bul*) of thy holiness and of thy glory (Isa. lxiii. 15).' The Syriac Apocalypse of Baruch (II Baruch) speaks of a 'Jerusalem above' which is also the 'Jerusalem to come'. 'This

[1] II Sam. v. 5–9.

[2] See, for example, Stanley Cook, *An Introduction to the Bible* (1945), pp. 134–52.

[3] Thus R. Johanan said (Baba Bathra 75b) that Jerusalem would be made 3 parasangs (roughly 10 miles) high. The calculation is based on Zech. xiv. 10.

[4] A saying rightly ascribed by S.-B. to R. Meir, *c.* A.D. 150; there is no reason why the thought should not be even earlier.

building now built in your midst is not that which is revealed with me, that which was prepared beforehand here from the time when I took counsel to make Paradise, and showed it to Adam before he sinned, but when he transgressed the commandment it was removed from him, as also Paradise. And after these things I showed it to my servant Abraham....And again also I showed it to Moses....And now, behold, it is preserved with me, as also Paradise' (iv. 3–6; cf. xxxii. 4). In IV Ezra[1] this conception occurs frequently and clearly. See among other passages: vii. 26: 'Then shall the city that now is invisible appear'; viii. 52: 'For you is opened Paradise, planted the tree of life; the future age prepared, plenteousness made ready; a city builded, a rest appointed; good works established, wisdom preconstituted'; xiii. 36: 'Sion shall come and shall be made manifest to all men, prepared and builded.'

R. Meir and Baruch are both somewhat later than Hebrews; IV Ezra scarcely earlier. But that the notion of a heavenly Jerusalem is early is proved beyond doubt by Rev. iii. 12, xxi. 2, 10, and especially by Gal. iv. 26, where Paul introduces 'the Jerusalem that is above' with no explanation, assuming the thought to be completely familiar.

The relation between the heavenly city and temple, the earthly city and temple, and the city and temple of the age to come, is, as it was bound to be, obscure. The present Jerusalem (that is, before A.D. 70) was certainly a copy of the heavenly; this appears at once from Exod. xxv. 9, 40; xxvi. 30; xxvii. 8 and Ps. cxxii. 3, as interpreted by the Rabbis.[2] The future city will represent the heavenly even better, though it appears that the notion that the heavenly city will itself descend (as described in Rev. iii. 12, etc.) is almost unparalleled in Jewish sources.[3] Too much, however, should not be made of this silence, and we may without hesitation conclude that, according to Jewish thought, there exists a heavenly city, of which the present earthly Jerusalem is an inferior copy; and that in the future this heavenly city will in some way be manifested as the Jerusalem

[1] Cf. I Enoch xc. 29, and *Studia Paulina in honorem J. de Zwaan* (1953), pp. 10f.

[2] Jerusalem, which is built like the city which is its fellow (חברא).

[3] 'Das vom Himmel herniederkommende Jerusalem wird in den Pseudepigraphen selten, in der älteren rabbinischen Literatur gar nicht und in den jüngeren kleinen Midraschim auch nur einige Male erwähnt' (S.-B., vol. III, p. 796).

of the age to come. This complex dualism is characteristic of apocalyptic;[1] and it is precisely this dualism (and not a Platonic dualism) which appears in Hebrews.

It is plainly laid down that Christians in this life have no abiding city; they seek the city which is to come (xiii. 14). In this they resemble the believers of the O.T., for they too were expecting, and seeking, a city or fatherland (xi. 10, 14, 16). This search, made by saints both of the old covenant and the new, cannot ultimately be in vain, for God has prepared for them a city (xi. 16). The 'city to come' is also the city which has foundations, and God is its maker (xi. 10). It can also be said that Christians in their conversion[2] have come to this city (xii. 22, προσεληλύθατε...πόλει θεοῦ ζῶντος). Closely related to this theme of the City of God is another, which has already been hinted at. In their search for the eternal city, the men of faith are represented as pilgrims. This theme is so familiar to Englishmen, who have known Bunyan's Pilgrim from their childhood, that it is well to pause and observe that it is set forth (in the N.T.) only in this Epistle. Elsewhere, for example in I Pet. i. 1; ii. 11, Christians are said to be, in this world, aliens; but they are resident aliens, dwelling for a time in a foreign land while they hold their citizenship elsewhere.[3] It is clear, however, from the language and imagery of Hebrews that more than this is involved. Summarizing his first set of O.T. illustrations of faith, the author says (xi. 14), They that say such things (that is, declare themselves to be ξένοι καὶ παρεπίδημοι) make it manifest that they are seeking a fatherland (πατρίς). They had abundant opportunity of returning (xi. 15) to the land whence they set out; that they did not do so proves that they desired a better land; and that must mean a heavenly land. Christians also must run with patient endurance the race set before them (xii. 1). Like the patriarchs who sought (ἐπιζητοῦσιν, xi. 14) a fatherland, they seek (ἐπιζητοῦμεν, xiii. 14) the city which is to come. The people of God are well described in the title of Dr E. Käsemann's penetrating study of Hebrews: they are 'das *wandernde* Gottesvolk', a pilgrim people, like Israel in the wilderness.

[1] *S.J.T.* vol. VI (1953), pp. 138f.

[2] See Windisch on προσεληλύθατε, *ad loc.*

[3] In Phil. iii. 20 Paul's use of πολίτευμα implies the same metaphor; cf. James i. 1.

Whence is this conception derived?[1] The words used in Hebrews are certainly drawn from a number of O.T. passages, among which the following may be noted: Gen. xxiii. 4 (πάροικος καὶ παρεπίδημος); Gen. xlvii. 9 (παροικῶ); Ps. xxxix. (xxxviii.) 13 (πάροικος, παρεπίδημος). These passages, however, and others like them, do not afford a source from which the author of Hebrews can have drawn the substance of his thought. The passages in Genesis describe a real wandering (though xlvii. 9 tends in the direction of metaphor); and Ps. xxxix. 13 is quite differently conceived, since in it the time of sojourning is the time of man's life (as in Gen. xlvii. 9) and the end of it is not arrival at the city of God but death. Where the O.T. language is not literal, it is symbolic in a sense quite different from that of Hebrews.

Philo allegorizes the O.T. material about travelling and pilgrimage but the result is markedly different from Hebrews.[2] His exegesis is primarily ethical, with a metaphysical twist; that is, he reads out of the O.T. texts the moral idealism of the eclectic philosophy which forms the Hellenistic basis of his thought. He is most explicit in his discussion of the wanderings of Abraham and others in Genesis. Thus *Quaest. in Gen.* iii, 45: 'What is the meaning of [Gen. xvii. 8]? ...The mind of the virtuous man is a sojourner in its corporeal place rather than an inhabitant. For its fatherland is the ether and the heaven...'; compare *Q. in Gen.* iv, 178. There is a full treatment of the theme in *De Conf. Ling.* 75–82, where Gen. xi. 2 is expounded. The wicked dwell in the land of folly as their fatherland. Not so the wise. 'This is why all whom Moses calls wise are represented as sojourners. Their souls are never colonists leaving heaven for a new

[1] W. Manson (*The Epistle to the Hebrews*, 1951; cf. also H. J. Schoeps, *Theologie und Geschichte des Judenchristentums*, 1949, especially pp. 239f.) brings the thought of Hebrews into closer historical relation with the substance of Stephen's speech in Acts vii than I am able to do. Both authors rightly emphasize the place of Hebrews in what may be called the 'eschatological tradition'. In this essay I have as far as possible avoided ground traversed by Dr Manson.

[2] So also with the 'city of God'. Philo either does not allegorize at all (*De Praem. et Poen.* 162 72, especially 165: ...πρὸς ἕνα...τὸν ἀποδειχθέντα χῶρον, ξεναγούμενοι...), or does so with a psychological interest, e.g. *De Somn.* II, 250: 'Now the city of God is called in the Hebrew Jerusalem and its name when translated is "vision of peace" (ὅρασις εἰρήνης). Therefore do not seek for (ζήτει) the city of the Existent (τὴν τοῦ ὄντος πόλιν) among the regions of the earth... but in a soul, in which there is no warring (ψυχῇ ἀπολέμῳ), whose sight is keen (ὀξυδορκούσῃ), which has set before it as its aim to live in contemplation and peace.'

home. Their way is to visit earthly nature as men who travel abroad to see and learn' (77). After a while, 'they make their way back to the place from which they set out at the first. To them the heavenly region, where their citizenship lies (πολιτεύονται), is their native land (πατρίδα); the earthly region in which they became sojourners (παρῴκησαν) is a foreign country' (78). 'The wise man does but sojourn in this body which our senses know, as in a strange land, but dwells in and has for his fatherland the virtues known through the mind (νοηταῖς ἀρεταῖς)' (81). Compare also *Quis Heres* 280; *De Gigantibus* 61, 64; *De Cherubim* 120f.; *De Agric.* 64f.; *De Abrahamo* 62–88; *De Migrat. Ab.* 2 *et passim*.

Philo's allegorical pilgrimage of the soul can be paralleled in the philosophers, who also think of man as imprisoned for the space of his earthly life within conditions which are essentially alien to him;[1] the pilgrimage described in Hebrews is different. Expressed in O.T. language, it is in fact freshly drawn from a fresh understanding of the eschatological circumstances of the people of God. This has been admirably expressed by Dr Käsemann (*op. cit.* pp. 6f.): 'That man possesses the εὐαγγέλιον on earth only as ἐπαγγελία is for our text a fundamental presupposition. But it follows from this that the only form of existence in time proper to the man who receives the revelation must be that of pilgrimage (*die Wanderschaft*)....The existential necessity of pilgrimage for bearers of revelation means that Israel journeying through the wilderness can be used as an antitype of Christianity....' This observation will be confirmed by detailed examination of the essential passages in ch. xi.

The saints of old did not receive (μὴ κομισάμενοι, xi. 13; οὐκ ἐκομίσαντο, xi. 39) the promises (*v.* 13; *v.* 39, the promise), though (*v.* 13 only) they saw them and saluted them (ἀσπασάμενοι) from afar; that is, they did not get what was promised them. With this *v.* 17 (ἀναδεξάμενος) and *v.* 33 (ἐπέτυχον) are in only apparent disagreement; the latter refers to special promises which were actually received, and the former says only that Abraham welcomed the promise made to him—as a promise.[2] More difficulty is caused by vi. 12–17. The use of κληρονομεῖν, κληρονόμος (*vv.* 12, 17) is possibly not decisive, but *v.* 15 can only mean that Abraham in some sense

[1] It is sufficient to refer to the *Phaedrus* and *Phaedo* of Plato.

[2] Cf. vii. 6, where Abraham is τὸν ἔχοντα τὰς ἐπαγγελίας.

received (ἐπέτυχε) what was promised. Yet, if the passage is taken as a whole, it is clear that Abraham 'attained the promise' in only a limited degree, since the birth of his son Isaac was only a first step towards πληθύνων πληθυνῶ σε.[1] In this paragraph it is the author's intention to emphasize the certainty of salvation for those who believe: God confirmed his promise to Abraham by an oath—the promise was certain, as its partial fulfilment proves; God has confirmed his promise (of an eternal high priest) to us by an oath—the promise will be equally secure (*v.* 17, τὸ ἀμετάθετον τῆς βουλῆς αὐτοῦ). That the future is in mind throughout is shown by *v.* 18, τῆς προκειμένης ἐλπίδος.

The O.T. saints, then, looked forward with steadfast faith to the realization of promises which had not been fulfilled. The examples of faith given in xi. 3–12 tell us little of what these promises were. Promises are not in Scripture addressed to Abel, Cain and Enoch, and *v.* 3 (on creation) stands by itself. No doubt Noah's promise was of salvation from the waters of the flood. Certainly Abraham was promised a 'place which he was to receive as an inheritance' (*v.* 8). This place was, in the first instance, the land of Canaan, but is in *v.* 10 interpreted as 'the city which hath the foundations, whose builder and maker (τεχνίτης καὶ δημιουργός) is God'. This is undoubtedly the heavenly city.[2] The same picture of a people on pilgrimage towards their inheritance is drawn in the latter part of the chapter. Abraham (*vv.* 17–20) offered his son in faith, although the security of the promise appeared to rest upon the life of Isaac; and he blessed Isaac, Jacob and Esau with reference to their future destiny. Jacob and Joseph (*vv.* 21 f.) similarly acted and spoke with reference to the future. Moses (*vv.* 23–9) chose reproach rather than the apparently solid but in fact transient security of Egypt, and led his people toward the promised land. The entry into Canaan was marked (*vv.* 30f.) by the destruction of the old cities in preparation for the establishment of the new.

[1] Rom. iv is not, as some commentators suppose, an exact parallel, because Hebrews quotes explicitly not the prediction that a son should be born to the aged Abraham (a promise capable of speedy and exact fulfilment) but Gen. xxii. 16f. Moreover, ἐπέτυχεν does not say when Abraham attained the promise; cf. Gal. iii. 16, where the 'seed' of Abraham is Christ.

[2] For the 'foundations' cf. IV Ezra x. 27 (*de fundamentis magnis*), and Rev. xxi. 14, 19f.

The O.T. record has more, much more (*vv.* 32–8), to tell of the story of faith in the invisible God, but even so the story has, in the O.T., no end. At the close of the chapter the author reiterates his assertion that the O.T. believers did not receive that which had been promised; their pilgrimage remained unfinished, and their story was to find fulfilment only in 'us' and in the 'better thing' (κρεῖττόν τι) which God provided for us.

So far Dr Käsemann's remark (above, p. 378) is vindicated. Is it as true of the N.T. period as of the O.T.? Here two questions present themselves: (*a*) Granted that in Hebrews *promise* finds its correlative in *faith*,[1] just as *city* finds its correlative in *pilgrimage*: is faith always directed to the future? Can it bear no other meaning? (*b*) Does the position of Christians differ from that of those who lived under the old dispensation? If so, how does it differ? If not, can Hebrews be regarded as a satisfactory presentation of the Gospel?

(*a*) The following verses in ch. xi come under consideration: 1, 3, 6, 27, and perhaps 4. The material is meagre in quantity, but significant, for here faith is bound up with the invisible world. This appears in reference to creation—only by faith can man perceive the invisible ground and origin of the visible universe; and also in reference to the divine power which enabled Moses to dare the wrath of Pharaoh and deliver Israel from Egypt—he endured, as seeing him who is invisible. But it is particularly important to note that even in these passages faith still looks to the future. Thus from *v.* 27 we must look back to *v.* 26. The structure of the two verses is similar:

> Moses chose to suffer with the people of God—ἀπέβλεπε γὰρ εἰς τὴν μισθαποδοσίαν.
>
> Moses dared the king's wrath in leaving Egypt—τὸν γὰρ ἀόρατον ὡς ὁρῶν ἐκαρτέρησεν.

Seeing the invisible God is parallel to receiving a reward at his hands. Precisely the same connection is made explicitly in *v.* 6. When man approaches God he must believe, and in his faith two elements are conjoined: he believes that the God whom he cannot see really exists, and that there is a reward for seeking this invisible God.

[1] Cf. the connection of πιστός and ἐπαγγέλεσθαι, x. 23; xi. 11.

It is not possible to extract a future reference from the faith of *v.* 3, or any particular reference from the faith of *v.* 4. The word αἰῶνας is used not (as some older commentators supposed) with a temporal but with a spatial sense. The author, who is allegorizing the narratives of the Pentateuch, begins with the first and notes that the creation story can be accepted not on the evidence of the senses but only by faith. He speaks of Abel's faith probably because Abel was traditionally 'righteous',[1] and it was with him axiomatic that righteousness was 'by faith alone'; compare xi. 5–7.

We return finally to xi. 1. In this verse the meaning of ὑπόστασις and of ἔλεγχος is obscure, but it is clear that the invisible (πράγματα οὐ βλεπόμενα) and the future (ἐλπιζόμενα) are brought closely together. Faith means a confident reliance[2] upon the future, a conviction of the invisible. These are not various elements in, but aspects of, faith. There are not two faiths, one of which looks to the future and believes that in the future good will come from God—an apocalyptic faith; and another, which penetrates beyond the world of phenomena to that of timeless and ideal truth—a 'Platonic' faith. There is but one faith, an eschatological faith which is convinced of future good because it knows that the good for which it hopes already exists invisibly in God.

Question (*a*) is answered. Faith is not merely a waiting for the fulfilment of the promise; it means through the promise a present grasp upon invisible truth. But this second meaning grows out of the first, and is not in any way opposed to or contrasted with it.[3] From this point, and on this basis, we can proceed to answer Question (*b*).

(*b*) The record of O.T. faith in Heb. xi ends (*vv.* 39f.) with a clear reference forward to the new covenant. For 'us' God has planned 'something better' (κρεῖττόν τι), in order that apart from 'us'

[1] Cf. Matt. xxiii. 35; Josephus, *Antiquities* I, 53, δικαιοσύνης ἐπεμελεῖτο.

[2] For this rendering of ὑπόστασις see Windisch *ad loc.*

[3] Cf. what is said about the Sabbath rest, above: also p. 372. Cf. Käsemann *op. cit.*: 'Als Echo des objektiven göttlichen Wortes ist folglich der Glaube eine objektiv begründete und an Sicherheit alle irdischen Möglichkeiten überragende Gewissheit' (p. 22); 'Wie die ἐπαγγελία mehr ist als ein blosses Versprechen, so ist auch die παρρησία mehr als ein bloß subjektives Vertrauen, nämlich das freudige Eintreten für eine von Gott bereits in einem objektiven ἔλεγχος verbürgte Sache' (p. 23); 'So wird Glaube zur getrosten Wanderschaft' (p. 24).

the O.T. believers might not be perfected (τελειωθῶσιν). From this it might be inferred that perfection, the goal of all O.T. hopes, had now come. The religion of the O.T. is one of promise and pilgrimage; that of the N.T. one of achievement and fulfilment. This conclusion is, however, never reached. Christians have not yet attained their goal; they too must run their course (xii. 1). There is more to this effect. To Christians also the Gospel is presented as a promise. Their new covenant has been enacted ἐπὶ κρείττοσιν ἐπαγγελίαις (viii. 6)—better promises indeed, but still promises. They have need of endurance that they may do God's will and receive these promises (x. 36); this is the substance of their faith, and it will be confirmed by the speedy coming of the Coming One (ὁ ἐρχόμενος ἥξει καὶ οὐ χρονιεῖ, x. 37).

This representation of Christians as pilgrims who have not yet reached their home might at first sight appear a deficiency in the writer's theology. What advantage, it may be asked, has been gained through the coming of Christ, if Christians are still in the same position as O.T. believers? Is there no difference between the O.T. and the N.T.? The suggestion is evidently absurd, for there is in fact no writing in the N.T. which emphasizes more strongly than Hebrews the inadequacy of the O.T. and its institutions, and the discontinuity (as well as continuity) between the testaments. More will be said on this subject below; here it will perhaps be sufficient to note that Jesus became the mediator of a new and better covenant (viii. 6). This meant that, in its day, the old covenant was imperfect (viii. 7), and that now it has grown old and is near to vanishing (viii. 13).

It is true that, on this side of the catastrophe and consummation in which heaven and earth are to be shaken and every transient thing removed, all men must live by faith. But, as we have seen, faith is directed not simply towards the future (which is the same for Abraham as for Christians), but also towards the unseen truth which already exists though it will not be manifested till the consummation. This too is of course the same for Christians as for the O.T. believers, but at this point the advantage of the Christians over their predecessors becomes for the first time clearly visible. For them the unseen truth which God will one day enact is no longer entirely unseen; it has been manifested in Jesus. God has spoken to 'us' not in prophets but in his Son (i. 2). This conviction that the invisible God has been manifested, can be otherwise expressed, by saying that in Jesus the 'end', in which all believe and towards which all move, has been anticipated, and proleptically disclosed. Jesus is now both the ἀρχηγός, initiator, and τελειωτής, consummator, of faith. He himself is our forerunner (vi. 20), and it is precisely because he has passed through the veil (vi. 20; x. 20) and entered now into the holy place in the city of God that we can be confident (x. 22) that in due course we shall endure the time of shaking (xii. 26) and reach the city that is to come (xiii. 14).[1]

4. THE HOLY PLACE ABOVE

An inevitable feature of the Jewish hope for the 'Jerusalem of the age to come' was the belief that the city would contain a restored temple, in which a revived sacrificial service would be performed.[2] The temple service was one of Israel's most precious possessions, upon which (with the Law) not only its own life but also the continuing existence of the world depended;[3] in the age to come it would be glorified rather than dispensed with. The heavenly tabernacle in Hebrews is often supposed to rest upon 'Platonic' conceptions, but, since we have seen reason to believe that the city of God in Hebrews is a fundamentally eschatological theme, it is more natural to think that the tabernacle was similarly conceived. This view is confirmed by a review of the treatment of the subject in Hebrews and a comparison with similar material in other authors.

It is perhaps best to take our departure from ch. viii. The author has already[4] established that in Jesus we have a great high priest, fulfilling completely the requirements of the high priest's office.

[1] So Moses also shared the reproach of Christ and saw him who is invisible (xi. 26).

[2] See above, pp. 374f., and the articles in *T.W.N.T.* on τὸ ἱερόν (G. Schrenk, vol. III, pp. 230–47) and ναός (O. Michel, vol. IV, pp. 884–95). Rev. xxi. 22 proves the rule; according to the Christian Apocalypse 'the City possesses no Sanctuary, for it is itself a Holy of holies, as its cubic form suggests (*v.* 16)....The Eternal Presence (*v.* 3) renders the new Jerusalem one vast ναός' (H. B. Swete, *ad loc.*).

[3] Rom. ix. 4; P. Aboth i. 2: 'Simeon the Just...used to say: By three things is the world sustained: by the Law, by the Temple-service, and by deeds of loving-kindness.'

[4] ii. 5–18; see below, pp. 388ff.

He is high priest not by his own choice but by God's appointment (v. 4f.); he shares the humanity of those who would approach God, and therefore can deal sympathetically with them as their brother (v. 2; ii. 11). Nevertheless, he remains without sin, and therefore does not need to offer sacrifice on his own account (iv. 15; vii. 27). He is in fact a high priest after the order of Melchizedek (v. 6 *et al.*), greater than Abraham, greater than Aaron: a high priest not for a short human lifetime but for ever (vi. 20; vii. 23f., 28). Such a high priest (says the author, resuming his argument) we have (viii. 1). He is the mediator of a better covenant (viii. 6), which is a second covenant (viii. 7), a new covenant (viii. 8), which is in fact the covenant foretold by Jeremiah as about to be established by God in days to come (ἰδοὺ ἡμέραι ἔρχονται, Heb. viii. 8, quoting Jer. xxxviii. 31 LXX). The covenant inaugurated by Jesus' sacrifice of himself is the fulfilment of prophecy; that is to say, it is an eschatological covenant. Like the Sabbath rest, and the pilgrimage of faith to the city of God, it falls within the scope of the unique Christian eschatology, partly fulfilled and partly forward-looking.

A high priest without a sacrificial ministry to fulfil is unthinkable; but where is Jesus to fulfil his? Not upon earth (viii. 4), since there is there an appointed priesthood, and there was clearly no need to establish a second. The new high priest requires a new sanctuary. It is particularly important to observe how this is described. It is the true tabernacle, which God pitched, not man (viii. 2), of which the earthly tabernacle is a copy and shadow (ὑπόδειγμα, σκιά, viii. 5; on these words see below); but it is also the scene of a superior ministry (λειτουργία, viii. 6) enacted upon better promises in a second covenant. Thus the true tabernacle exists eternally in heaven, whither Jesus has ascended (viii. 1); but the ministry exercised within it took its origin in the fulfilment at the appointed time of O.T. prophecy, and its consequences are still in process of realization. In chs. ixf. this twofold fact is worked out in great detail. The first covenant[1] had a sanctuary belonging to this world (ἅγιον κοσμικόν), which contained a number of objects, all instructive to the Christian reader (ix. 2–5). In particular there was an inner shrine entered only once a year by the high priest alone, armed with atoning blood (ix. 6f.). The relation of this process, which took place on the day

[1] ix. 1. διαθήκη, not σκηνή, is to be supplied.

of Atonement,[1] to that which Christ has performed is brought out in the next verses (ix. 8–10). The levitical system is described not only as inferior (it could never cleanse the conscience, being concerned only with foods, drinks and washings), and not only as a parable of the true service; it is temporally related to the true ministry of Christ (μήπω πεφανερῶσθαι...ἔτι τῆς πρώτης...εἰς τὸν καιρὸν τὸν ἐνεστηκότα...μέχρι καιροῦ διορθώσεως). The heavenly tabernacle and its ministrations are from one point of view eternal archetypes, from another, they are eschatological events. This is a fact of cardinal importance in the interpretation of Hebrews.

The temporal relation of the earthly and heavenly tabernacles and liturgies is emphasized in ix. 11 where Christ is said to be the 'high priest of good things to come'.[2] He entered once (ἐφάπαξ, *v.* 12) into the holy place, through death, the necessity of which, and of bloodshedding, is brought out in a long argument (ix. 16–22) which need not be pursued here. It leads to further discussion of the relation between the two tabernacles in ix. 23–8. Heavenly realities are ἀληθινά; on earth are ὑποδείγματα and ἀντίτυπα. These words seem[3] to describe somewhat loosely a 'Platonic' relation, and so does the argument of ix. 23: the earthly sanctuary furniture must be cleansed by means of animal sacrifices; but the heavenly things themselves call for better sacrifices (κρείττοσι θυσίαις). This impression is not altogether erroneous. But even this 'Platonic' paragraph proceeds to emphasize that Christ does not 'frequently' offer himself. He entered (εἰσῆλθεν), now (νῦν) to appear before God; he has been manifested 'now, once, at the consummation of the ages' (νυνὶ δὲ ἅπαξ ἐπὶ συντελείᾳ τῶν αἰώνων). This 'once' refers to an eschatological event that has taken place, and is followed by the plainest assertion of an eschatological event yet to come—the return of Christ (ὀφθήσεται τοῖς αὐτὸν ἀπεκδεχομένοις).[4]

In ch. x there follows further criticism of the Law, which had only a shadow of good things to come (σκιὰν...τῶν μελλόντων ἀγαθῶν, x. 1; cf. viii. 5). The unique self-offering of Christ (in fulfilment of

[1] Lev. xvi; xxiii. 26–32; Num. xxix. 7–11.

[2] τῶν μελλόντων ἀγαθῶν; if the variant γενομένων be read the present argument is not affected.

[3] See below, p. 386 n. 1.

[4] On the day of Atonement the high priest, having executed his office in the Holy of holies in plain garments reappeared to the people in his own splendid robes (Lev. xvi. 23 f.).

Scripture) shows a new and effective way of bringing men to God; and ἀναιρεῖ τὸ πρῶτον ἵνα τὸ δεύτερον στήσῃ (x. 9). This succession implies time and movement; not 'Platonism' but eschatology. Men are sanctified not by intellectual illumination but by the once-for-all offering of the body of Christ (x. 10). Throughout the rest of the paragraph (*vv.* 11–18) the sufficiency of the one offering is emphasized, and brought into relation with the traditional eschatology in the statement (x. 13) that Christ, having sat down at the right hand of God, now waits till his enemies shall be put under his feet (Ps. cx. 1; also Ps. viii. 7, Heb. ii. 8 f.). The rest of the chapter exhorts Christians to avail themselves of, and to hold fast to, the benefits of Christ's passion. The exhortation is in part couched in apocalyptic terms and based on eschatological sanctions, but it appeals to Christians to take advantage of the present consequences of a historical act.

This review of the sacrifice offered in the heavenly tabernacle by Christ as high priest bears out, beyond reasonable doubt, the view that the framework of thought in Hebrews is eschatological. Apocalyptic supplies the notion of both a heavenly temple, and an eschatological temple;[1] these were normally combined in the belief that, in the age to come, the heavenly temple would be manifested and established on earth. In Hebrews a different kind of manifestation takes place. Jesus after his death on earth enters at once into the heavenly temple to appear before God and sit down at his right hand. In due course he will return, but in the meantime his self-offering, and his intercession with God, effect the beginning of the new age. Eternal redemption has already been wrought (ix. 12), but awaits complete application and fulfilment.

[1] The important words ἀντίτυπος, σκιά, and ὑπόδειγμα are quite consistent with this view. σκιά at x. 1 (cf. Col. ii. 17) is used to describe a *fore*shadowing of good things to come; this meaning is not absent from viii. 5, where σκιά also carries ὑπόδειγμα with it. The latter word at iv. 11 means simply 'example', and ὑποδείγματα (ix. 23) and ἀντίτυπα (ix. 24) look back to the τύπος of Exod. xxv. 40; moreover, this passage is concerned with a real movement of Christ into heaven, not with the contrast of phenomenal and ideal. Cf. H. Wenschkewitz, *Die Spiritualisierung der Kultusbegriffe Tempel, Priester und Opfer im N.T.* (Angelos-Beiheft 4, 1932): 'Sicher abhängig ist der Verfasser [of Hebrews]...von spätjüdischen apokalyptischen und rabbinischen Gedanken über das im Himmel befindliche Heiligtum und die im Himmel befindliche Stadt Gottes, während bei der allgemeinen Spiritualisierung des Opferbegriffes ihn ein Psalm beeinflußt hat. In der Mehrzahl der Stücke aber ist er als ein Glied in der Kette christlicher Tradition zu werten' (p. 149).

This conclusion is reinforced when for a moment we consider what really Hellenistic writers could make of the Jewish temple and its heavenly counterpart. As an example of Philo's exegesis we may take[1] *Quaest. in Ex.* ii, 82: 'What is the meaning of the words [Exod. xxv. 40]? Through the "pattern" he again indicates the incorporeal heaven, the archetype of the sense-perceptible, for it is a visible pattern and impression and measure. He testifies to these things by saying "See", (thereby) admonishing (us) to keep the vision of the soul sleepless and ever wakeful in order to see incorporeal forms, since, if it were (merely a question of) seeing the sense-perceptible with the eyes of the body, it is clear that no (divine) command would be needed for this.' Here Moses is simply 'Platonized'.

In Barnabas the principal references to the Christian temple are as follows. In iv. 11 Barnabas exhorts his readers 'Let us become spiritual, let us become a perfect temple to God' (γενώμεθα ναὸς τέλειος τῷ θεῷ). vi. 15 is similar, and so is ch. xvi, though it contains more details, some of which (notably in xvi. 3) are notoriously difficult to interpret. These, however, need not detain us. The temple of the Jews (urges Barnabas) is no true temple. The poor wretches set their hope upon the building and not upon their God who made them. Their temple worship thus becomes little better than idolatry, for which they are justly punished (xvi. 1–5). It accordingly becomes necessary to inquire whether there really is a temple of God. A passage of Scripture[2] proves that there is. 'How then shall it be built in the name of the Lord? Learn. Before we believed in God the dwelling-place of our heart was corrupt and weak, truly a temple made with hands, for it was full of idolatry....But it shall be built in the name of the Lord....How? Learn. When we received forgiveness of sins and put our hope in the name [of the Lord] we became new men, created again from the beginning (ἐξ ἀρχῆς); wherefore truly in our dwelling God dwells in us. How? His word of faith, his calling of promise, the wisdom of the ordinances, the commandments of the teaching—he himself prophesying in us, he himself dwelling in us, leads into the incorruptible temple (εἰσάγει εἰς τὸν

[1] Cf. also 52, 90; *Leg. Alleg.* III, 102; *De Vit. Mos.* II, 74.

[2] According to Windisch (*ad loc.*) a combination of I Enoch xci. 13, Tobit xiv. 5 and II Kdms. vii. 13; cf. Test. Benj. ix. 2. Others have thought of Dan. ix. 24–7.

ἄφθαρτον ναόν), us who have been enslaved to death, opening to us the door of the temple (ναός), which is the mouth, giving us repentance....This is the spiritual temple built to the Lord (πνευματικὸς ναὸς οἰκοδομούμενος τῷ κυρίῳ)' (xvi. 7–10). Barnabas here, in spite of his curious (but characteristic) use of the O.T. material, writes as a Hellenist. The temple of which he speaks is the dwelling-place of the human heart; God dwells in the heart of man as the Deity was believed to inhabit a holy place; man is the bearer of God, who speaks through him. This was a popular idea with the philosophers of the Roman period,[1] and bears no relation to the Jewish eschatological hope—or, it may be added, to the conception in Hebrews of an act objectively wrought by Christ in the heavenly sanctuary.

The difference between Hebrews on the one hand and Philo and Barnabas on the other is twofold. Hebrews insists upon an eschatological act, a thing done in time with objective and corporate consequences, whereas the other writers speak either of the timeless reality of heaven or of subjective religious experience. And the author of Hebrews insists, as neither Philo nor Barnabas does, that such an objective and universal act as he describes was necessary in order to take away the objective and universal guilt of mankind. For him, what lies between heaven and earth, God and man, is not the difference between the phenomena of sense-perception and pure being, but the difference between holiness and sin.

One further point remains to be considered in this section. We have already noted that the author of Hebrews introduces his presentation of Jesus as high priest before, and perhaps independently of, his discussion of the heavenly sanctuary. What were the sources, and what is the meaning, of this Christological image?[2] Moffatt (xlvii–xlix) noted three (or four) sources. '(*a*) Once the conception of a heavenly sanctuary became current, the notion of a heavenly ἀρχιερεύς would not be far-fetched for a writer like this.' '(*b*) Another factor was the speculations of Philo about the Logos as high

[1] E.g. Epictetus, *Disc.* II, viii, 9–14: 'You bear God about with you...'; Marcus Aurelius III, 5: ὁ ἐν σοὶ θεός.

[2] For a much fuller discussion of this point see E. Käsemann, *op. cit.* pp. 124–40. 'Auch hier bildet der Anthropos-Mythos die Basis für die Christologie des Briefes' (p. 140). I should perhaps lay more stress on the Son of man tradition in primitive Christianity.

priest.'[1] '(*c*) A third basis for the conception of Christ's priesthood lay in the combination of messianic and sacerdotal functions which is reflected in the 110th psalm.' Moffatt goes on to compare Test. Reuben vi. 8, Test. Levi xviii. He adds: 'There is a partial anticipation of all this in the Enochic conception of the Son of man.' There seems reason to emphasize the fourth point (which Moffatt mentions only to reject it almost completely), and to modify the first and second.

The sense of these modifications has already been given. The heavenly tabernacle in Hebrews is not the product of Platonic idealism, but the eschatological temple of apocalyptic Judaism, the temple which is in heaven primarily in order that it may be manifested on earth. It is true that Hebrews conceives its earthly manifestation in a new way: Christ dies on earth, ascends with his own blood to the heavenly sanctuary and there appears before God on our behalf, in order that we may have access to God and find grace to help us in every time of need. The decisive eschatological act—the death and ascension of Christ—is already past, and the normal pattern of eschatological belief is thereby disturbed; but Jesus is primarily (in Hebrews as elsewhere in the N.T.) an actor in the eschatological drama of redemption rather than a mediator standing between the real and phenomenal worlds;[2] rather a priest who makes atonement for the sin of mankind than a Gnostic mediator who procures their passage from the material world to the spiritual. Now in Christian, and some other, apocalyptic the chief actor is the Son of man, or Man. In this fact may be found the roots of the conception, in Hebrews, of the divine high priest.

Jesus is first described as high priest in ii. 17. The paragraph begins with the statement (ii. 5) that it is not to angels that God has subjected the world to come. Ps. viii. 5–7 is quoted. Understood according to its plain sense this Psalm means that God has subjected to man the whole natural universe,[3] but it had already received a messianic interpretation in Christian theology (I Cor. xv. 27; Eph. i. 22), and the statement 'Thou didst put all things in subjection

[1] Philo also thinks of the Logos as the archetypal Man, but apparently does not directly connect the idea of representative humanity with that of priesthood. See above, pp. 368 f.

[2] Cf. Philo, *De Somn.* II, 28, quoted by Moffatt, *op. cit.* p. xlviii.

[3] The Psalm continues: 'All sheep and oxen, Yea, and the beasts of the field', etc.

under his feet' inevitably invited comparison with Ps. cx, in which a person, afterwards addressed as 'a priest for ever after the order of Melchizedek' receives the promise that God will 'make thine enemies thy footstool'. The author of Hebrews, following the lead of Paul himself, united the messianic and 'anthropological' interpretations of Ps. viii. It is simply not true, he says, that all things are now in a state of subjection to man; but we do see Jesus the Man crowned after his humiliation with glory and honour. Not man but the Son of man, not man but Man, reigns already with God, awaiting the entire subjugation of his foes (x. 13). Thc rest of the paragraph emphasizes the solidarity between Jesus and the rest of mankind in him. He died ὑπὲρ παντός (ii. 9). He was the ἀρχηγός of salvation,[1] and 'he that sanctifies and they that are sanctified are all of one'; hence Christians are the brothers of Jesus (ii. 11). He is not a heavenly Man in such a sense that he is remote from the conditions of physical life; rather he has shared them to the full. It was necessary that he should be made like his brethren in all things—in order that he might be a faithful and merciful high priest, able to expiate the sins of his people.

Thus the Epistle develops the idea of representation by him who was at once the heavenly and the earthly Man till there appears the picture of the high priest who, on behalf of his people, sacrifices no victim but himself, and so represents them before the face of God and makes atonement for their sins. If it is true (as it seems to be) that the notion of representation and incorporation were present from the beginning in the Biblical figure of the Son of man, we see once more how the original and independent theology of Hebrews sprang out of the primitive tradition and the primitive preaching.

5. CONCLUSION

Hebrews, though, as has now been shown, it stands in close contact with the primitive theology, is a profound Christian book, which touches upon and illuminates some of the dark places of Christian thought. Among these are the following.

[1] On this word see especially W. Bauer, *Wörterbuch* (1952), col. 204; but I should put Heb. ii. 10 not in his third but in his second paragraph with the meaning, '*der Anfänger*, der als erster einer Reihe mit etwas beginnt und so den Anstoß dazu gibt'.

(*a*) *The Problem of Eschatology*[1]

The common pattern of N.T. eschatology is in Hebrews made uncommonly clear. God has begun to fulfil his ancient promises; the dawn of the new age has broken, though the full day has not yet come. The Church lives in the last days, but before the last day. This appears from many general and explicit indications, and also from the special themes which have been treated in this essay. The Sabbath rest of the people of God is still to come, but today they must strive to enter it, and in faith they may do so. The city of God is still before them—a promise, and like pilgrims they must live by faith; but when they go forth outside the camp they go out not merely into the wilderness but unto Jesus (xiii. 13), and though they share his reproach they are brought near by his blood and actually approach the heavenly Jerusalem (xii. 22). Precisely at this point the third theme, of the heavenly tabernacle and the high priestly ministry of Jesus, comes under consideration. The high priest *has* entered the holy place, and *has* made atonement for sin; the benefits of his sacrifice are available for those who come to God through him. They are released from the power of death and the devil (though these are manifestly still at large), have access to God, and await the return of their triumphant high priest.

The most significant contribution of Hebrews to the growing problem of N.T. eschatology lies in the author's use of philosophical and liturgical language. By means of this terminology it is possible to impress upon believers the nearness of the invisible world without insisting upon the nearness of the *parousia*. The author of Hebrews did believe that the *parousia* was near (x. 25), but lays no stress on this conviction.

(*b*) *The Fulfilment of the Old Testament*

Consciously or unconsciously, Paul posed the Christian problem of the O.T. Christ is the end of the Law, and to return to it is to fall under the sway of the weak and beggarly elements. Yet through faith we do not make void but rather establish the Law. Early Christian writers made many attempts to resolve this paradox; the contribution of Hebrews, as it has been brought out in these pages, is briefly as follows.

[1] See *S.J.T.* vol. VI (1953), pp. 235–43.

(i) What the prophets spoke to Israel of old was no other than the word of God, and the word (of the Law) communicated through angels (ii. 2) proved steadfast. The teaching of the O.T. remains true. Again, the institutions of Judaism were ordained of God, and had a positive, if limited, value in their own time. It is nowhere suggested that the Jews ought not to have observed them.[1]

(ii) Parts of the O.T. were simple predictive prophecy. Some of these have already been fulfilled (most significantly, Jeremiah's prophecy of a new covenant, Jer. xxxi. 31–4; Heb. viii. 8–12). Others remain and await fulfilment in the future (e.g. Hag. ii. 6; Heb. xii. 26). The fact that such prophecies exist is itself sufficient to show that the O.T. is an incomplete book, which demands a complement before it can be fully understood.

(iii) The truths contained in the O.T. not only pointed forward in time to their fulfilment in the future Christian dispensation; they pointed upward to truth as it existed, and exists eternally, in the mind of God. It was God who spoke through the prophets, and though he then spoke in various portions and manners he was the same God that now speaks in his Son. It was God moreover who established the levitical institutions, and ordered Moses to make the earthly tabernacle in accordance with a pattern shown him on the holy mountain. The earthly tabernacle therefore stood in a close relation, and bore a close resemblance, to the heavenly tabernacle, which God pitched, not man. It follows on the one hand that the earthly tabernacle could never bring perfection, but on the other that it was a parable of the true and perfect ministry. Further, it was a parable not in the sense of being merely an imperfect image of the eternal, but a parable for the present time (ix. 9)—a pointer to the manifestation of the eternal in time. The parable itself can be understood only in the light of that which it parabolically portrays; Christians are therefore the first to perceive the true meaning of the O.T. cultus which they have themselves abandoned: *vetus testamentum in novo patet*; or, more precisely, *vetus testamentum in Christo patet*. When that which is perfect is come, that which is in part is done away; but that which is in part may yet illuminate our understanding of that which is perfect.

[1] Contrast Acts vii. 47–50, where Stephen's meaning is often taken to be that Solomon ought not to have built the Temple.

(*c*) *Christianity and 'Platonism'*

How far is it legitimate to use philosophical terms to clarify the presentation of the Gospel? How far do they distort it? It has been urged in this essay that certain features of Hebrews which have often been held to have been derived from Alexandrian Platonism were in fact derived from apocalyptic symbolism. This is in itself an important conclusion, but it is not the whole truth. The author of Hebrews, whose Greek style is so different from that of most of the N.T., may well have read Plato and other philosophers, and must have known that his images and terminology were akin to theirs. He had seized upon the idealist element in apocalyptic, and he developed it in terms that Plato—or, better, Philo—could have understood. But his parables are parables for the present time—eschatological parables. The shadows in his cave are all shadows of an event that happened once for all, the death of Jesus; and the death of Jesus effected the cleansing of men's consciences from guilt, the inauguration of a new covenant and the dawn of the new age. In all this the eschatological imagery is primary, as it must always be in any Christian approach to philosophical discourse. If the eschatology, rough, crude and intractable as it may appear, is abandoned, there can be no guarantee that the unique act of God in the weakness, humility and agony of his Son will remain central, or that the conviction will be maintained that through this act all things were made new and the powers of the age to come were released. But, provided that this priority is maintained, Hebrews itself, as part of the N.T. canon, shows that the language of philosophy may be more serviceable in expressing Christian truth than some Biblical theologians are prepared to allow.

ESCHATOLOGY IN I PETER

E. G. SELWYN

If the eschatological element in I Peter is not to appear something of a torso, it is necessary to consider it in close connection with the rest of the Epistle; for there is no book in the New Testament where the eschatology is more closely integrated with the teaching of the document as a whole. It is eschatology thoroughly appropriated and digested both in the mind of the author and in the life and thought of the Christians whom he addresses. A similar appropriation meets us in the Johannine writings, but with this difference, that the Petrine teaching clearly belongs to an earlier stage in the tradition and is the product of a simpler outlook on the Christian faith: that is no small part of its importance. Free both from the controversial preoccupations of parts of St Paul's Epistles and from the philosophical interests of St John, the author of I Peter presents us with a singularly clear mirror of Christian faith and life as we may suppose it to have been in the sixties of the first century. The case is not greatly altered if we date the Epistle in the eighties.

The position is fully illustrated in i. 19–21, when the author speaks of redemption having been already effected 'by the precious blood of Christ...who was foreknown indeed before the foundation of the world, but was manifested at the end of the times for your sake, who through him are believers in God, who raised him from the dead and gave him glory'. The end, that is to say, has already supervened (iv. 7) in the advent of the predestined Messiah, in his death and resurrection and exaltation, and in the believing community now called into existence by this new revelation of God. This 'now' is an important feature of the Epistle (i. 6, 8, 12; ii. 10, 25; iii. 21), not to be confined to the moment of conversion or of baptism, but indicating a period and a situation when the new Israel comprising both Jew and Gentile had been brought into being and the tide of the universal Gospel was felt to be in full flood. In this way it presents an instructive parallel with Ephesians, and not the less instructive for being quite un-Pauline; and even if Ephesians be dated much later, I Peter could stand as by itself a striking witness to the emergence in the sixties of the first century of the messianic community which later became known as the Catholic Church.

The end, then, has already begun. The eschatological pattern, which was a specialized form of prophecy, has become flesh and blood in Jesus and his Church, whose life is depicted as 'in Christ'. Clearly the historical facts handed down in the Christian tradition are presupposed: Christ's manifestation, his ministry, his teaching, his example, his passion, death and resurrection are taken for granted by the readers of the Epistle, as much by those who never saw him as by those who did (i. 8); his very words are constantly echoed and in one case are perhaps quoted (iii. 9). We are dealing here with something more than κήρυγμα, for it is κήρυγμα combined with διδασκαλία, which corresponded to the Jewish *halakhah*. So closely fused are they that one may reasonably question whether they were ever separated; Christian worship indeed, as Dom Gregory Dix has pointed out,[1] would have required them both from the beginning. For this reason I sometimes wonder whether the term κήρυγμα has not been worked too hard, and whether the word μαρτυρία and its cognates would not describe better the primitive and indispensable core of the Christian message. At any rate, if we examine the comparative occurrences in the New Testament of the two sets of terms, we find that the occurrences of the verbs alone which speak of 'witness' considerably outnumber the occurrences of κηρύσσειν, while the occurrences of the noun μαρτυρία outnumber those of the noun κήρυγμα by more than six to one. There is nothing here which will make C. H. Dodd's *The Apostolic Preaching and its Developments* less important than it was when it first appeared. But there is room for another monograph on the Apostolic *testimony*.

The end, then, has supervened; the eschatological Messiah has entered history; the eschatological community has been called out of the Jewish and Gentile world and brought into being through

[1] *Jew and Greek* (Westminster, 1953), pp. 96ff.

conversion and baptism; what had been a hope has become an experience. Moreover, the experience has been decisive, even though not final. It has been decisive, because it has involved a decision, in face of the judgment of God long taught by the prophets, to turn away from darkness to light, from aimless bewilderment to the care and guidance of the Good Shepherd, from idolatry and riotous living to rectitude of life in obedience to God's will. Yet it has not been final, partly because, while earthly life lasts, sin and backsliding also last, partly because judgment must 'begin at the house of God' (iv. 17)—and indeed is already beginning in the persecutions which will test them. Christians therefore must pass the time of their sojourning here in fear (i. 17), that is in the sober reverence which restrains faith from over-confidence. They live in grace, but not yet in glory. True, this grace is of a piece with the crown of glory which Christians shall have at the end. It is not merely that they look forward now to this glory (i. 4, 5 and 10; iv. 13); the grace they enjoy is regarded as in a sense thrown backwards from the world to come (i. 13): it is a foretaste of the final revelation and the eternal glory. This idea is not an easy one to express, and it is not surprising that it leads to some grammatical complications. Thus, in i. 13, the author speaks of 'the grace which is being brought to you' at 'the revelation of Jesus Christ'; and the usage of the Epistle indicates that this last phrase is eschatological and could be translated by 'when Jesus Christ is revealed'. Again, it cannot, I think, be doubted that ἀγαλλιᾶσθε in i. 8, if it is the right reading (which is highly doubtful), must be regarded as a present tense with a future meaning, the exultation in adversity alluded to in i. 6 being an anticipation, as in iv. 13, of the exultation which is associated with the salvation and glory which will be the Christian's privilege at the end of all things. Riesenfeld[1] has noted the connection between the ecstatic joy which marked the Feast of Tabernacles in Judaism and the concept of the eschatological joy which was associated with the future salvation; and indeed he thinks that the latter was in large part derived from the former. Yet a third example occurs in v. 1, when the author describes himself as not only μάρτυς τῶν τοῦ Χριστοῦ παθημάτων but also τῆς μελλούσης ἀποκαλύπτεσθαι δόξης κοινωνός. Those who believe that the author is St Peter may well see in this last

[1] *Jésus Transfiguré* (Copenhagen, 1947), pp. 34f.

phrase an allusion to Christ's transfiguration; and they will also feel that G. H. Boobyer's[1] interpretation of the transfiguration (even if they do not go all the way with him) as an experience (in St Mark's view) of the eschatological glory tends to confirm this view. But in any case we are not entitled to interpret κοινωνός in a future sense; the context is against it and κοινωνήσων was readily available if that were what the author meant. The grammatical difficulty in itself is of a piece with those we have just discussed. St Paul was happy in having hit upon the word ἀρραβών to signify the combination of present and future which lies at the heart of the Church's experience of the Holy Spirit. But here, as throughout this Epistle, our author was no Pauline.

Our author, therefore, conceives of the end as organically linked with what has already occurred, in the case both of Christ and of the Church: it is not a matter of something wholly novel but of the culmination of something already experienced and known. His favourite terms when speaking of the end are salvation, revelation, and glory. *Parousia*, on the other hand, which is almost a technical term elsewhere in the N.T., does not occur in this Epistle; and, except probably in iv. 5, it is the Father rather than the Christ who is thought of as the Judge. Nevertheless, as Bengel observes (on I Pet. iv. 17) 'it is one and the same judgment from the time of the preaching of the Gospel by the apostles until the last judgment', a doctrine well illustrated in ii. 6–8. Moreover, no detail is suggested in regard to the state of the lost. This is not to say that wide deductions of an eschatological kind have not been drawn from iii. 19, 20 and iv. 5, 6. Thus, for example, R. H. Charles[2] claims that 'we have here a clear apostolic statement that the scope of redemption is not limited to this life in the case of certain individuals, human or angelic', and interprets the second passage as substantiating the doctrine of the first and enunciating the 'larger truth' that by the time of the last judgment the Gospel will at least have been preached to all; though Charles admits that there is no hint in the Petrine teaching as to the success or otherwise of this preaching. I have discussed the passages at great length in my commentary on the Epistle, and so too has

[1] *St Mark and the Transfiguration Story* (Edinburgh, 1942).
[2] *Eschatology*, pp. 434–6 (2nd ed.).

Bo Reicke in *The Disobedient Spirits and Christian Baptism*, which was published in the same year; and I am glad to think that on the earlier passage, iii. 19, we are in substantial agreement. In his view as in mine the context of the passage is baptismal rather than eschatological, and the 'spirits in prison' are to be identified with those spirit-powers of evil whose rebellion Jewish tradition associated with the age preceding the Flood (Gen. vi. 1–6), and who were regarded, by Jew and Christian alike, as the motive force behind the heathen kings, war-mongers and tyrants of every age (cf., for example, Enoch lxvii. 4–lxix. 1; Ephes. vi. 10ff.). That these principalities and powers and the aggravation of their activities have a place in the eschatological pattern of the N.T. is beyond doubt (II Thess. ii. 5–12); but this eschatological reference is not primary in I Pet. iii. 19, except in so far as the redemption, and Christian baptism which depends upon it, are eschatological facts.

The case is different, however, in I Pet. iv. 5, 6; for here the main reference is to the impending judgment, whether the Judge be thought of as God or as Christ. But I think that Bo Reicke is mistaken in linking these verses with iii. 19, though he is far more guarded in what he says than many. It is tempting to see in iv. 5, 6 a reference to the universality of Christ's judgment corresponding to the universality of his redemption 'proclaimed' in iii. 19. Yet the objections to this view are formidable. Linguistically, there is no necessary identity of meaning between ἐκήρυξεν in iii. 19 and εὐηγγελίσθη in iv. 6; Reicke's view that καὶ νεκροῖς means 'to the dead also as well as to the imprisoned spirits of evil' seems to me even less acceptable than Windisch's that 'the spirits in prison' comprised human dead as well as angelic beings; above all, the context from iv. 1 onwards has changed too much to allow us to suppose that the motif of iii. 19 runs on into the later passage. For iii. 19 leads on to the marked climax of iii. 22; iv. 1ff. is a new beginning, and the passage is addressed in great detail to the situation and practical needs of St Peter's readers; and the eschatological theme runs through it down to iv. 19. Moreover, the phrase 'quick and dead' in iv. 5, though quite general and almost indeed a cliché, is by its context given a special reference to past and present members of the Church and their persecutors, and recalls the teaching of II Thess. i. 6–12; while in iv. 6 the reference is still further narrowed to those only who have died in the Christian faith, as in I Thess. iv. 13–18. It is significant that Silvanus, the amanuensis of I Peter, was also probably the amanuensis of the Thessalonian Epistles; at any rate he knew well what was in them.

There is yet a further resemblance to be noted between the Thessalonian Epistles and I Peter, namely the close connection between persecution and the approaching final judgment (I Thess. iii. 3, 4; II Thess. i. 4; I Pet. iv. 17–19). In the prophetic writings the premonitory signs of the judgment are commonly political events (Ezek. xxxviii, xxxix; Zach. xiv; Joel iii), and our Lord's words in Matt. xvi. 3 were in this tradition. The apocalyptic writers added to those signs sundry portents and disturbances in the natural and social orders, and these messianic woes became a regular feature of Jewish eschatological expectation. The inclusion of persecution for the faith among the signs of the end must be regarded, however, as a distinctively *Christian* view, and one indeed which goes back to our Lord himself (cf. Matt. v. 11, 12; x. 16–26; Mark xiii. 9–13). The Apostles crystallized this belief into dogmatic form in the broad statement, διὰ πολλῶν θλίψεων δεῖ ἡμᾶς εἰσελθεῖν εἰς τὴν βασιλείαν τοῦ θεοῦ (Acts xiv. 22). Such, in outline, is the context of thought which appears to underlie St Peter's words in i. 5–9 and iv. 12–19. And on the basis of this philosophy of persecution and suffering he enjoins on his readers courage and joy, tranquillity of mind and persistence in well-doing.[1]

We may conclude this brief study of the eschatology of I Peter by saying that it stands in that central tradition of New Testament teaching for which eschatology is for the most part eschatology fulfilled; fulfilled in the historical fact of the advent of the Messiah and in the life of the Church which has been built upon him and has its whole existence within him (ἐν Χριστῷ). Jewish monotheism, Jewish messianism, Jewish eschatology—these, as Dom Gregory Dix has observed,[2] are the focal points of this tradition, and they are focal in this Epistle; and what has released them from their Jewish limitations and made the Christian and Catholic faith possible—and opened men's eyes to the presence here and now of the new life of the world to come is Christ's resurrection. True, not all is yet accomplished;

[1] Cf. Bo Reicke, *op. cit.* pp. 211ff. [2] *Jew and Greek*, p. 99.

'we see not yet all things put under him' (Heb. ii. 8); there is still a judgment to be accomplished. Our author has little to say of those who will be condemned in that day; there is no geography nor chronology of what follows the judgment such as meets us elsewhere in the New Testament, notably in the Apocalypse, and will find classical expression in the *Divine Comedy* of Dante; but the event is to be looked for with awe, by believers and unbelievers alike. The emphasis, however, in this Epistle is on the blessedness of the life to come for Christians; on the hope and joy with which even in suffering they should look forward to it; on the life in glory which will be the ultimate issue of their life in grace. H. G. Wood[1] has recently drawn attention to a remark of Maeterlinck's, that we should live as always on the threshold of great joy, and the phrase might be taken as a fair transcript of the Apostle's eschatology no less than of our Lord's. 'Heaviness may endure for a night: but joy cometh in the morning' (Ps. xxx. 5).

Finally, we may ask what contribution, if any, this Epistle makes towards understanding and interpreting New Testament eschatology as a whole. If what we have in mind is the translation of its strange imagery and language into conceptual terms more in keeping with modern thought, the answer must be that I Peter offers no suggestions towards that task. But this does not mean that there is no translation indicated. On the contrary, the Epistle indicates plainly what the Synoptic Gospels hint at covertly and what St John was to assert more fully, that the best and perhaps the only intelligible translation of Jewish and Jewish Christian eschatology is to be found not in concepts but in facts. The strange facts of the *Mysterium Christi*—the advent of the Messiah, the manifestation of the Kingdom of Heaven in his teaching and mighty works, the foundation of the Apostolate, the new life in forgiveness and grace experienced by believers through the Holy Spirit and inaugurated and sustained by the sacraments—these strange facts were the true translation of the strange language and imagery of Apocalyptic. It is these strange facts of history and experience, not the eschatological terms in which they were originally forecast, that admit of and call for conceptual description. Terms such as 'transcendent', 'supernatural', 'trans-

[1] Article in the *Hibbert Journal*, Jan. 1954.

subjective' have been used to describe the new order of being which the Gospel unveils and the new quality of experience which it has introduced; and though the scientific naturalist (who is not to be confused with the natural scientist) may boggle at them, they are indispensable. The decisive fact which enabled the disciples of Jesus to remember and to understand and so to call him 'Lord' was the resurrection; and it is still the risen and exalted Lord, in ever-living relationship with his Church, who is at the heart of the distinctively Christian experience. Or again, we may interpret eschatological language as that which has to do with what is ultimate; and if this line of thought be followed, the Christian claim is that Christ is the ultimate truth of things, the ultimate way of life for men, and the ultimate life, namely 'life eternal'. Moreover, of the residue of the eschatological expectation not yet fulfilled and realized, we may expect the same to be true; its only true and intelligible translation will be in the events of final judgment and of final death or life which will mark the consummation of all things. 'This is life eternal, that they should know thee the only true God, and him whom thou didst send, even Jesus Christ'—that must suffice us for our life here. But we are assured also that a fuller knowledge awaits us at the last, when we shall see God as he is, face to face, and know even as also we are known.

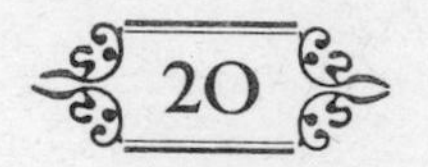

'THE BIBLE TO-DAY' UND DIE ESCHATOLOGIE

R. BULTMANN

Aus zahlreichen Büchern und Aufsätzen C. H. Dodd's habe ich reiche Anregung und Belehrung geschöpft. Meinen Dank dafür möchte ich heute dadurch zum Ausdruck bringen, daß ich einige Fragen an den verehrten Verfasser richte, die durch seine Schrift *The Bible To-day* in mir wachgerufen wurden, — eine Schrift, die für mich von ganz besonderem Interesse ist (1946, 1948[3]). Man darf wohl sagen, daß das eigentliche Thema dieser Schrift das erregende Problem *des Verhältnisses von Geschichte und Offenbarung* ist. Meine Hauptfrage ist die, wie weit es dem Verfasser gelungen ist, seine Absicht durchzuführen, nämlich zu zeigen, wie die Geschichte als Offenbarung verstanden werden muß; wie weit also seine Geschichtsbetrachtung eine *theologische* ist und ob sich nicht das theologische Verständnis der Geschichte mit einem *geschichtsphilosophischen* verbindet. Da dieses letztere die Geschichte von einer dem geschichtlichen Geschehen immanenten Idee aus versteht, das theologische Verständnis dagegen von dem der Geschichte im Christus-Geschehen gesetzten Ende aus, so möchte meine Frage zugleich ein Beitrag zur Diskussion des Themas der *Eschatologie* sein, dem so manche Ausführungen des verehrten Verfassers gewidmet sind.

Die theologische Intention des Verfassers spricht ja schon aus dem Titel *The Bible To-day*. Er fragt nicht nach dem Verhältnis von Offenbarung und Universalgeschichte, sondern nach dem Verhältnis der Offenbarung zu derjenigen Geschichte, von der die Bibel berichtet. Es ist die Geschichte, die von den Anfängen Israels bis zu Christus und der Kirche führt. Sie ist Offenbarungsgeschichte, weil in den Ereignissen dieser Geschichte die Hand Gottes unmittelbar wirkt. In den Ereignissen! Denn die Bibel läßt nicht nur eine Geschichte der Offenbarung erkennen in den Gedanken der biblischen Autoren über Gott, Mensch und Welt, sondern sie zeigt Geschichte als Offenbarung (S. 98f.). Sie lädt dazu ein, die Offenbarung Gottes im Geschehen der Geschichte zu erblicken (S. 58), in der geschichtlichen Bewegung, wie sie sich durch die Berufung Abrahams, den Exodus aus Aegypten, die Geschichte des Volkes bis zum Exil und zur Restauration abgespielt hat. Freilich, auch jene Gedanken gehören zu den Ereignissen; denn auch die Gedanken sind geschichtliche Faktoren.

Aber von wo aus wird nun diese Geschichte als Offenbarung erkennbar? Wer ist es, der sie als Offenbarung erkennt? Ich gestehe, daß mir die Gedanken des Verfassers hierüber nicht klar geworden sind.

Einerseits ist das Verständnis der Geschichte, von der die Bibel berichtet, abhängig von der Arbeit der Geschichtswissenschaft, die den Gang der Ereignisse und die Entwicklung der in ihr wirkenden Gedanken rekonstruiert. Der Verfasser geht so weit, zu sagen, daß die Aufgabe der chronologischen Ordnung der biblischen Schriften zum Studium der Offenbarung gehört (S. 28).

Andrerseits heißt es, daß der Zusammenhang der Geschichte nur vom Gesichtspunkt der Kirche aus sichtbar wird. Mit Recht protestiert der Verfasser dagegen, daß die Autorität der Bibel über die der Kirche gestellt wird. Denn nur in der Kirche hat die Bibel Autorität und wird durch ihre Verkündigung zum Wort Gottes, und zwar so, daß die Kirche ihre Autorität auf das Neue Testament (auf das in diesem bezeugte Christusgeschehen) gründet (S. 6–8). Von hier aus muß doch das Verständnis der Geschichte als ein theologisches bezeichnet werden. Aber wie verhält es sich zum historischen Verstehen?

Für den Verfasser scheint das Problem dadurch gelöst zu sein, daß die Kirche als die 'Erfüllung', als der End- und Höhepunkt der geschichtlichen Bewegung verstanden wird, von dem aus sich die Geschichte im Rückblick als Offenbarung deuten läßt. Aber wird damit nicht das theologische Verständnis zu einem geschichtsphilosophischen gemacht?

Das scheint mir auch aus Folgendem hervorzugehen. Nach der Ansicht des Verfaßers ist die Geschichte eine moralische Ordnung, in der sich das Gericht Gottes vollzieht (S. 61). Diese Ordnung kann aber auf der Ebene der uns bekannten Geschichte nicht festgestellt, sondern nur behauptet werden auf Grund der Annahme einer eschatologischen Vollendung. Die jüdische Apokalyptik erwartet, daß die Geschichte einmal ihren Höhepunkt erreichen wird, an dem Gottes Plan zur Vollendung kommt und sein letztes Wort gesprochen wird (S. 60f.). Das Neue Testament sieht diese Vollendung gekommen in Christus und der Kirche (S. 71).

Aber sind hier nicht theologische und geschichtsphilosophische Betrachtung eigentümlich vermischt? Ist nicht Gottes Plan zu einer geschichtsphilosophischen Idee gemacht? Ist die eschatologische Vollendung wirklich als eschatologische verstanden, wenn sie als der Höhepunkt der geschichtlichen Entwicklung und damit als ein Phänomen der Geschichte selbst verstanden wird? Daß der Verfasser sie so versteht, scheint mir daraus hervorzugehen, daß er die geschichtlichen Leistungen der Kirche als einen Beweis für die Richtigkeit der Behauptung ansieht, daß der Plan Gottes mit Christus und der Kirche zur Erfüllung gekommen sei (S. 77).

Nun ist die Kirche nach neutestamentlichem Verständnis gewiß das Ziel der Heilsgeschichte, aber doch nicht als der Höhepunkt einer geschichtlichen Entwicklung, — wie denn die Heilsgeschichte im Neuen Testament nicht unter dem Gesichtspunkt einer Entwicklung verstanden wird. Vielmehr ist nach dem Neuen Testament die Kirche eine eschatologische Größe in dem radikalen Sinne, daß sie kein weltliches Phänomen ist, und daß diejenigen, die zu ihr gehören, nicht mehr zur Welt gehören, sondern entweltlicht sind. Denn mit Christus hat die Geschichte der Welt ihr Ende erreicht.

Unterwirft der Verfasser nicht auch Christus der geschichtsphilosophischen Betrachtung, wenn er ihn in die Reihe der alttestamentlichen Propheten stellt als den, der den Ruf Gottes in vollkommenem Gehorsam beantwortet habe? Lassen sich von da aus die neutestamentlichen Aussagen über die Präexistenz und die Auferstehung Christi verstehen? Wohl redet das Neue Testament vom Gehorsam Christi. Aber indem er als der Präexistente gedacht wird, wird er gerade nicht als ein Mensch verstanden, der, wie die Propheten, den Ruf Gottes in einer konkreten geschichtlichen Situation vernommen und beantwortet hat. Im Unterschied von den Propheten erfaßt er ja nicht den gegenwärtigen Sinn der Volksgeschichte, sondern als der, der aus der Sphäre Gottes, von jenseits der Welt, gekommen ist, steht er jenseits der Geschichte, ist selbst der Ruf Gottes und ruft diejenigen, die ihn als den Herrn anerkennen, aus der

Welt und ihrer Geschichte heraus. So auch als der Auferstandene. Kann die Begegnung mit dem Auferstandenen unter die 'public facts' gerechnet werden (S. 102)? Ist er nicht der Auferstandene als der Herr, der, indem er den Geist, die eschatologische Gabe, gibt, die Seinen aus dem Tode ins Leben, aus der Welt und ihrer Geschichte in die göttliche Sphäre führt? Ist es nicht eine geschichtsphilosophische Betrachtung, wenn man sagt, daß an ihm Gottes Gericht und Gnade als das Gesetz der Geschichte anschaulich werden? Müßte theologisch nicht gesagt werden, daß er selbst das Gericht und die Gnade Gottes für die Menschen ist, je nachdem, ob sie im Glauben an seinem Kreuz und an seiner Auferstehung teilnehmen oder den Glauben verweigern?

Die Entweltlichung des Glaubenden ist allerdings eine paradoxe. Denn solange er noch 'im Fleisch' lebt, steht er, der Entweltlichte, doch zugleich in einer Geschichte und hat in seiner konkreten Situation jeweils den Ruf Gottes zu hören. Aber diesen 'Ruf' kann er neu verstehen, da er ihn verstehen soll im Gehorsam gegen Christus als den 'Ruf' Gottes, der ihn lehrt, den 'Ruf' der Situation im Lichte der Gnade Gottes zu verstehen. Er lehrt ihn aber nicht, retrospektiv die Geschichte als einen von Gott geleiteten Prozeß zu verstehen. Er lehrt ihn nicht so, daß die Einheit von Gericht und Gnade als das Gesetz des geschichtlichen Geschehens offenbart würde, sondern so, daß er je seinen Augenblick als eschatologischen verstehen kann.

Aber darin finde ich mich wieder mit dem zusammen, was der Verfasser S. 130ff. ausgeführt hat. Auch er will ja die Bedeutung der Christus-Offenbarung für die Zukunft deutlich machen und will nicht behaupten, daß das biblische Verständnis der Geschichte eine geschichtsphilosophische Theorie liefere. Auch er kommt doch darauf hinaus, daß die Offenbarung nicht das Gesetz des geschichtlichen Geschehens überhaupt erkennbar macht, sondern daß sie je die mir geltende Forderung als das Gesetz meines Handelns zeigt. Den eschatologischen Charakter der christlichen Existenz macht der Verfasser durch die entmythologisierende Interpretation der mythologischen Eschatologie deutlich, indem er sagt: 'By a characteristic "foreshortening", the End is always "round the corner". The *certainty* of the divine Event is translated into *imminence* in time' (S. 131).

In solchen Ausführungen scheint mir das theologische Verständnis der Geschichte zum Ausdruck zu kommen. Aber ist es wirklich rein durchgeführt und wird es nicht immer wieder durch geschichtsphilosophische Betrachtung verschleiert? Das scheint sich mir auch darin zu zeigen, daß der Begriff der Begegnung mit Gott (des Wortes Gottes) als eines Ereignisses nicht theologisch eindeutig bestimmt ist.

Von welchem Gesichtspunkt wird gesagt, daß der Sinn der in der Bibel erzählten Ereignisse die Begegnung mit Gott — die 'Gottes Wort' heißt — ist? Kann der Historiker mehr feststellen, als daß die Personen, die an den Ereignissen teilhatten, diesen Sinn in ihnen fanden? Der Verfasser möchte offenbar mehr sagen, nämlich daß sie diesen Sinn auch tatsächlich (objektiv) hatten. Denn wenn er sagt: die Wirkung der Propheten auf ihre Zeit spreche dafür, daß ihre Überzeugung von der Begegnung mit Gott keine Illusion gewesen sei (S. 102), so scheint er es doch für möglich zu halten, daß der Historiker, wenigstens indirekt, Begegnungen mit Gott in der Geschichte konstatieren kann. Ebenso, wenn er meint, daß das Werk des Paulus und die Entstehung der Kirche es unwahrscheinlich machen, daß das Bewußtsein, den auferstandenen Christus gesehen zu haben, eine Täuschung gewesen sei (S. 103).

Darf man so argumentieren? Bringt solche Argumentation nicht die Begegnung mit Gott, das 'Wort' Gottes, in den Bereich historischer Phänomene? Und ist das nicht auch der Fall, wenn der Verfasser sagt, die Offenbarung Gottes in der Geschichte sei vom Prinzip der Besonderung (*particularity*) bestimmt, denn das Wort Gottes komme zuerst zu einem einzelnen Volk, dann zu einem Rest und schließlich zu einer einzelnen Person (Jesus)? (S. 107–10.) Wenn wirklich das Wort Gottes der Sinn einer besonderen geschichtlichen Situation ist, der in ihr enthaltene Anruf Gottes, der in der Interpretation des Propheten erfaßt wird, dann ist wohl verständlich, daß sich der Ruf Gottes auf eine Situation des Volkes oder einer Gruppe beziehen kann, aber doch nicht, daß er zu einem Volk oder einer Gruppe kommen kann. Denn als Ereignis kann er doch nur vom Einzelnen erfaßt werden. Aber auch wenn man sagen wollte, daß die prophetische Interpretation der Situation als des Rufes Gottes vom Volk verstanden und angenommen werden kann, so ist dieser Ruf Gottes doch nicht mehr Ereignis für spätere Generationen und für uns heute. Denn wir stehen nicht mehr in jener Situation und können den Ruf Gottes, der ja eben der Sinn jener Situation ist, nicht mehr als an uns ergehenden Ruf hören.

Kann man vom Rufe Gottes als von einem Ereignis der Vergangenheit reden und nicht nur als von dem je an mich in meiner Situation gerichteten Rufe Gottes? Ja, ist nicht die Verkündigung der Kirche in echtem Sinne Gottes Wort nur als je an mich, den konkreten Menschen, in meiner konkreten Situation gerichtetes Wort? Wenn Gottes Wort Ereignis ist, dann doch immer nur als geschehendes, *in actu*. Es kann nicht Ereignis sein im Sinne eines in der Vergangenheit liegenden und konstatierbaren Faktums. Gottes Offenbarung ist nicht Offenbartheit.

Wer von der in der Bibel vorliegenden und für den Historiker wahrnehmbaren Offenbarung Gottes redet, ist entweder ein Fundamentalist, oder er macht die Offenbarung zu einer Idee, in deren Licht er die Geschichte interpretiert. Ich zweifle nicht, daß dem Verfasser diese Absicht fern liegt, aber ich möchte fragen, ob er dieser Gefahr ganz entgangen ist. Nun will ich nicht leugnen, daß in der kirchlichen Verkündigung auch das Alte Testament zum Worte Gottes werden kann, aber doch nur so, daß ein Wort des Alten Testaments *sub specie Christi* zum uns anredenden Worte wird, nicht aber so, daß wir konstatieren könnten, in der Geschichte Israels habe sich Gottes Wort ereignet.

Daß die Intention des Verfassers, die auf ein theologisches Geschichtsverständnis geht, sich mit einem geschichtsphilosophischen vermischt, scheint sich mir auch in einer für ihn entstehenden Schwierigkeit zu zeigen, nämlich in der Schwierigkeit, die objektive Offenbarung in der Geschichte, die er meint konstatieren zu können, zugleich als eine jeweils dem Individuum zuteil werdende verständlich zu machen (S. 144ff.). Er versucht diese Schwierigkeit dadurch zu überwinden, daß er zeigt, daß das Individuum nur innerhalb der Gemeinschaft existiert, so daß es dasjenige, das es als den Sinn der Geschichte wahrnimmt, zugleich als den Sinn seines eigenen Lebens versteht. Würde ein theologisches Geschichtsverständnis nicht eher das Umgekehrte sagen müssen? Muß nicht ein theologisches Verständnis der Geschichte vom Verständnis der Geschichtlichkeit (als zum Wesen menschlichen Seins gehörig) ausgehen, nicht aber vom Verständnis der Geschichte als des zusammenhängenden Ganges eines vergangenen Geschehens? Gerät der Verfasser nicht in geschichtsphilosophische Erwägungen, wenn er meint, dem Individuum solle seine Existenz innerhalb der Gemeinschaft dadurch zum Bewußtsein gebracht werden, daß es sich als Glied der Kirche als des universalen Leibes Christi versteht (S. 158f.)? Ist nicht die Gemeinschaft im Leibe Christi etwas grundsätzlich anderes als die Volks- und Menschheitsgemeinschaft innerhalb der Weltgeschichte? Denn als Leib Christi hat die Kirche gar keine Geschichte, sondern ist ein eschatologisches Phänomen. In der Kirche stehen, und in einer geschichtlichen Gemeinschaft stehen, ist zweierlei, und das Verhältnis zwischen beiden ist, wie schon gesagt, ein paradoxes.

Der Reichtum des Inhaltes von *The Bible To-day* ist in meinen Fragen nicht gewürdigt worden. Sie beanspruchen nicht mehr, als ein Diskussionsbeitrag und als solcher ein Zeichen des Dankes an den Verfasser zu sein.

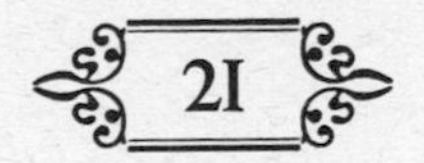

ESCHATOLOGY AND MISSIONS IN THE NEW TESTAMENT[1]

O. CULLMANN

DOES the expectation of the end paralyse the missionary impulse? Does it divert our attention from the task of preaching the Gospel here and now? It is sometimes said that this 'hope' has an inhibiting influence upon Christian action; is this true? To give an affirmative answer to these questions would mean that 'missions'—on the grand scale—would have been possible only because the eschatological hope had gradually faded. In point of fact, the missionary enterprise of the Church is often represented as a kind of 'second best'—something which has been substituted for the unrealized hope of the Kingdom of God. If this were true, then the Church has carried on its mission because it has been obliged to renounce eschatology.

Such ideas are due to a mistaken conception of early Christian eschatology. It is of course true that in the early Church there was a tendency to distort the Christian hope, which diverted the attention of Christian people from the sphere of present duty, as for instance at Thessalonica, in the time of Paul, and one hundred years later, in Asia Minor, in Montanism. But in the New Testament itself this tendency was explicitly rejected and condemned as heretical. The genuine primitive Christian hope does not paralyse Christian action in the world. On the contrary, the proclamation of the Christian Gospel in the missionary enterprise is a characteristic form of such action, since it expresses the belief that 'missions' are an essential element in the eschatological divine plan of salvation. The missionary work of the Church is the eschatological foretaste of the Kingdom of God, and the Biblical hope of the 'end' constitutes the keenest incentive to action.

[1] This essay was translated from German by Miss Olive Wyon, D.D., to whom the author and editors are greatly indebted.

It is the purpose of this article to show that this thought can be traced throughout the New Testament, and is deeply rooted in New Testament eschatology.

The close relation between Christian action and the expectation of the end comes out in two prominent characteristics of New Testament eschatology: (*a*) we do not know when the end will come; (*b*) although the end lies in the future, the present is already part of the period which begins with the death and resurrection of Christ.

(*a*) This first point is connected with the fact that the very heart of Biblical eschatology is its emphasis upon the divine omnipotence. Nowhere is this stressed more strongly than in the doctrine of creation and in the eschatological hope. Eschatology is the new creation. The last day will appear at God's command, uttered with the same divine authority as the primal word: 'Let there be light!' Both are the sovereign act of God. This means, however, that no human effort or knowledge will enable us to ascertain when the Kingdom of God will come.

We cannot achieve the coming of the Kingdom of God by our own action: *we* cannot 'bring in' the Kingdom of God. The whole witness of the New Testament is so clear on this point that no further proof is needed. Then does this mean that all that is required from us, in response to the eschatological hope, is a passive attitude? and not a stimulus to action? By no means! For it is only those who are firmly convinced that the Kingdom comes from God who are given the courage to work here and now, whether success or failure be their portion. If we believed that the coming of the Kingdom depended on us, when confronted by failure we would inevitably despair. But we can work joyfully and courageously, not in order to 'hasten' the coming of the Kingdom, but because we know that the Kingdom comes from God.

On the other hand, no human effort will enable us to know when the Kingdom of God will come. At this point, even Jesus himself, during his life on earth, had to confess: 'But of that day or that hour knoweth no one...neither the Son, but the Father' (Mark xiii. 32). It is very significant that the New Testament emphasizes this point: that the Son does not know when the Kingdom will come, when it lays so much stress on the fact that no one knows the Father 'save the Son...' (Matt. xi. 27). This ignorance of the 'day and the hour' is, however, a spur to Christian action, to 'watchfulness': 'Watch therefore: for ye know not on what day your Lord cometh' (Matt. xxiv. 42). We are in the position of the householder who does not know when the thief will come (Luke xii. 39), or in that of the bridesmaids who do not know when the bridegroom will come, and must therefore keep their lamps trimmed and burning all night long (Matt. xxv. 1 ff.). It is true, of course, that Jesus expects his death and resurrection to be of decisive significance for the fulfilment of God's purpose, for the end he has in view; and indeed, since the first Easter it has been a fundamental conviction of the Church that the end has already been 'introduced' by this fundamental saving event. But the Church is also aware that the 'new creation' has not yet been realized. Thus for the Church, seen in the light of the resurrection, it is true that 'the day of the Lord cometh as a thief in the night' (I Thess. v. 2); hence she too must 'watch' and 'not sleep, as do the rest'. Because the day of the Lord is always near, there should be no feverish agitation about its coming, as though the 'time' mattered to us; on the other hand, it is the duty of every Christian to 'watch', sustained by hope.

(*b*) This brings us to the second characteristic of New Testament eschatology, which is indeed the basis of Christian action. The end is not yet, it is true, but since the resurrection has taken place we know that the decisive event leading to the end has already happened. The end may seem to be delayed, but this should cause no disappointment, doubt, or despondency. When faith in the resurrection is strong, it breeds a firm conviction that the royal sovereignty of Christ has already begun, and that it will be exercised for a period of unknown length until Christ 'shall deliver up the Kingdom to God, even the Father' (I Cor. xv. 24). Thus it is a mistake to think that eschatology has nothing to do with the present day, and, therefore, that it has a paralysing effect upon Christian action. Indeed, it is rather the other way round, because the Kingdom of God has actually come nearer, with Christ, than would have been the case if all had been left to the usual course of events. From the chronological point of view, something has happened: the present 'age' has taken a great leap forward. We are reminded that God is lord of time. We have entered the final phase of this 'age', which will end with the return of Christ.

One eschatological element has, however, already been realized, which points clearly to the fact that we are already living in and from the end, although the end itself still has to come: the Holy Spirit. He belongs to the future, for God has given us 'the earnest of the Spirit in our hearts' (II Cor. i. 22); we have 'the firstfruits of the Spirit' (Rom. viii. 23). The miracle of Pentecost was rightly interpreted by Peter (Acts ii. 17ff.) when he appealed to the passage in the prophet Joel: 'And it shall be in the last days, saith God, I will pour forth my Spirit upon all flesh.' This, however, is more than a foretaste; the Spirit is already part of the fulfilment. The risen Lord himself points this out when his disciples ask him when the Kingdom will come. He says: 'Ye shall receive power...when the Holy Ghost is come upon you.' In his reply to their question he points out that it is not for them 'to know times or seasons, which the Father hath set within his own authority'. But they will now receive the Holy Ghost. This means that the end has already dawned, although this 'age' is still present. Within this period there is a stage—of undefined extent—which still forms part of 'this present age'. Thus our relation to eschatology is different from that of mankind at other periods in world history: 'Little children, it is the last hour', says the writer of the First Epistle of John (ii. 18).

We are living in an interim period, which already belongs to the end, and yet still forms part of 'this present age'. Thus, with A. Schweitzer, we may describe the ethic which belongs to this period as an 'interim ethic', but not in the sense that it was only valid for the first century A.D. For the 'interim period' is still going on. The future, it is true, still influences this ethic, but it is also influenced by that element of the future, which is partially realized in the present, namely, the Holy Spirit. The Holy Spirit, who guarantees that one day our sinful bodies and the whole material universe will be re-created by him, enables us here and now to take the old law seriously, with all that this involves, and to fulfil it. Under the impulse of the Holy Spirit the eschatological summons to action: 'Repent!' is seen in the right light. It is because the Kingdom has come nearer to us, and, in the Holy Spirit, is, in part, already here, that it is now possible for us to act in a Christian way.

It is the presence of the Holy Spirit which makes the action of the

Church, as such, eschatological. The Church itself is an eschatological phenomenon. It is in the centre of the present lordship of Christ. It was constituted by the Holy Spirit at Pentecost. That is why the task of the Church consists in the proclamation of the Gospel to the whole world. This is the very essence of the Holy Spirit's work, and the meaning of the miracle of Pentecost, when, quite suddenly, all present understood each other. Precisely in the period to which we belong—between the resurrection and the return of Christ—it is the duty of the Church to go out 'into all the world, and preach the Gospel to every creature', looking towards the end. That is why the disciples' question to the risen Lord: 'Dost thou at this time restore the Kingdom to Israel?' receives this answer: 'It is not for you to know times or seasons, which the Father hath set within his own authority. But ye shall receive power, when the Holy Ghost is come upon you: and ye shall be my witnesses both in Jerusalem, and in all Judaea and Samaria, and unto the uttermost part of the earth' (Acts i. 7–8).

The Holy Spirit, and the World-Mission: these are the 'signs' of the final phase, determined by the future, in which we stand. Does this mean, however, that the Kingdom of God will only come when all men have been converted? If that were so, then its coming would depend on man, and the divine omnipotence would be ignored. On the other hand, the conviction that evil will be intensified during the last days is part of Christian eschatology. All that matters, however, is the fact that the Gospel should be preached to all nations. Evidently, God means that everyone should have an opportunity of hearing the Christian message; therefore the call to repentance must be made to all. But the coming of the Kingdom does not depend upon men's acceptance of the call. This view contains the strongest incentive for human decision, and yet the divine sovereignty is not in the least impaired. The proclamation of the Gospel to all nations itself becomes a 'sign' of the end, an integral element in the eschatological divine plan of salvation.

We must examine these ideas more closely; first of all, we must investigate their origin in Judaism, in order that we may have a clearer grasp of the novelty and the theological significance of the New Testament conception.

Pre-Christian Judaism has a sense of 'mission', it is true, but not as the pre-condition of the messianic kingdom. But we also find another conception which prepares the way for the New Testament doctrine of the Church's mission as a 'sign' of the end, which is, at the same time, corrected by it. In Judaism there were constant efforts to calculate the 'date' of the messianic kingdom. We cannot here go into details about the various calculations and conclusions to which they led. Again and again these efforts proved abortive, for the Kingdom of God did not 'come' on the dates which had been calculated beforehand. During the New Testament period there arose a view, often expressed in the Talmud and in the apocryphal books, that the Kingdom of God would not come until Israel as a whole had repented. In this connection, this question often appears in the Talmud: 'Who is preventing the Messiah's appearing?' To estimate the New Testament conception of the mission aright, we note that it is significant that within Judaism, according to Rabbinical texts, there were two different schools of thought, which answered the question in different ways, and in so doing both broke away from the idea of the divine omnipotence, which, however, is the constitutive element in eschatology as a whole. The school of Eliezer gave up any attempt to calculate the date. It taught that the Messiah will come when all Israel has repented. This, however, makes the coming of the Kingdom dependent on the moral attitude of man, and this impairs the doctrine of divine sovereignty. The coming of the Kingdom is no longer a divine, sovereign act. The opposite school of thought insists upon fixing a date, namely, the year A.D. 240, when, apart from man, the end of the world will come. The leader of this school of thought does not answer the question: 'What prevents the Messiah's appearing?' by saying: 'Israel has not yet fully repented', but 'the time has not yet come'. This view, however, also impairs the idea of divine sovereignty, because it links the coming of the Messiah with this element of calculation which depends upon human effort.

In the New Testament eschatology, on the other hand, the divine sovereignty is fully maintained, in so far as neither by his action nor his knowledge can man know when the Kingdom will come. This is taken seriously in the particular conception of 'mission' which we are here examining, according to which the end will not come until the Gospel has been preached to all nations. Before I present the evidence for this view, I will indicate two other lines of thought within Judaism which more directly prepared the way for the Christian conception of 'mission' as the eschatological 'sign' (or 'promise'): (i) Elijah will preach repentance in the last days (Mal. iii. 1; Ecclus. xlviii. 10, 11); and (ii) there is the other view, according to which the Kingdom will come when the number of the elect has been completed (I Enoch xlvii. 4; II Baruch xxx. 2; IV Ezra).

Now we come to the New Testament textual evidence. We must begin with the two parallel passages in the Little Apocalypse, Mark xiii. 10: 'and the gospel must first be preached unto all the nations' (R.V.); and in Matt. xxiv. 14: 'and this gospel of the Kingdom shall be preached in the whole world for a testimony unto all the nations; and then shall the end come.' In both passages note particularly the clear chronological definition: in Mark 'first' (after this comes the passage about the appearance of Anti-Christ). In Matthew it is still clearer: 'then shall the end come'; and this 'end' is likewise ushered in by the appearance of Anti-Christ. In both passages the mission is mentioned as a divine 'sign', along with the eschatological woes: wars, famines, cosmic catastrophes, persecutions, etc., and the intensification of evil in men. Thus it appears that the coming of the Kingdom does not depend upon the success of this 'preaching', but only upon the fact of the proclamation itself.

We find further evidence for the same view in the Book of Revelation (vi. 1–8). In this passage it is clear what the second, third and fourth riders mean. In each instance the reference is to one of the characteristic eschatological 'plagues' which are personified by these mysterious figures. Their outward appearance corresponds with the destructive task which they fulfil upon earth. But what does the first rider mean? Many and varied interpretations have been suggested. First of all, we must note that the description of this first rider has no connection with the sinister aspect of the other three. On the contrary, he is a rather radiant figure; he is seated upon a white horse, and when we remember that white is always represented as a Heavenly quality, it makes us question the theory that this first rider, like the other three, also had to pour out an eschatological plague upon the earth. Even the crown with which he is adorned gives him rather the air of a force for good. Finally, it is said of him: 'He came forth conquering and to conquer.' But the verb 'to conquer' (in Revelation) does not carry with it the negative sense of 'conquering by violence', but, on the contrary, it describes the quality of God's action. Therefore it is very improbable that, as is usually said, this first rider must mean some military power, like Rome or Parthia. To me this seems out of the question, because this rider would then have the same task as the second rider who sits upon a red horse; of whom it is said explicitly: 'To him it was given to take peace from the earth, and that they should slay one another.'

Who then is this first rider? This becomes clear when we compare this passage with the similar passage in Rev. xix. 11 ff. in which a rider on a white horse also appears. There the explanation is given: 'Behold, a white horse, and he that sat thereon, called Faithful and True...and his name is called the Word of God.' In other words, it is his task to proclaim the Gospel to the world. This must also be the mission of the first rider, and indeed it fits in with his description. What then has the preaching of the Gospel in the world in common with the task of the other three riders? It also is a divine 'sign' (or 'promise') of the end, and, as a final offer of salvation, it runs parallel with all those horrors, which are indeed connected with the evil in man. Further, in other passages in this book the necessity for the summons to repentance before the end is emphasized. In xi. 3 the 'two witnesses' are mentioned (Elijah and Moses) who prophesy. In xiv. 6–7 is the picture of the angel with the 'eternal Gospel', who addresses a final appeal to repentance 'to every nation and tribe and tongue and people'.

The fact that the proclamation of the Gospel as an eschatological 'sign' is not a peripheral phenomenon, comes out very clearly in the passage in Acts i. 6–7 which has already been quoted. Here, the risen Lord tells his disciples: 'It is not for you to know times or seasons.' Why? 'Because the Father hath set (them) within his own authority'; hence we have no business to pry into his mysteries; the 'time' of the coming of the Kingdom is known to him alone, and is under 'his own authority'. But there is one thing the disciples can be sure of: that they must proclaim the Gospel to all the world, until that 'day' comes. This duty is laid upon them by the gift of the Spirit, which they have received. The period between the resurrection and the unknown 'day' of the Lord's return must be filled with the missionary preaching 'from Jerusalem...unto the uttermost part of the earth'. For this is the era of 'grace', granted to mankind: it is God's will that all men shall have the possibility of hearing the Gospel. Here, too, this allusion to the world-mission before the end comes is not stated primarily as an imperative but as an indicative, as an eschatological statement: 'Ye shall be my witnesses.' It is God who through his messengers gives us this 'sign', which offers the Gospel to the world. In all this the Apostles are only the instruments through whom the eschatological plan of salvation is carried out.

But this view is also expressed in a missionary command in the famous words at the end of Matthew's gospel: 'Go ye therefore and make disciples of all the nations' (R.V.). This command also applies to the final phase of this 'age', which, as we know, is strictly limited. This comes out very plainly in the promise which is linked with the command: 'I am with you alway, even unto the consummation of the age' (R.V. margin). This is not a vague chronological statement like 'always' (as we usually interpret it), but it is a clear reference to the eschatological character of the missionary enterprise, which must take place precisely in this form, before the end of the age, and itself gives its meaning to this age.

In Pauline thought the missionary motive, as the pre-condition of the coming of salvation, permeates the whole theology of the Apostle, and is intimately connected with his sense of missionary vocation. Paul's sense of vocation is clearly influenced by eschatological ideas; this comes out in his conviction, that he is an instrument of the eschatological plan of salvation. This is shown very clearly, first of all, in Romans, chs. ix–xi. These chapters are a very apt commentary on the words in Mark xiii. 10: 'And the gospel must first be preached unto all the nations.' In ch. x the Apostle emphasizes the fact that God is indeed carrying out his own plan, precisely as he intends, but that our human responsibility is equally clear. For all have the opportunity of hearing the Gospel (Rom. x. 14ff.). 'How then shall they call on him in whom they have not believed? ...and how shall they hear without a preacher?' Opportunity must be given to all to hear the Gospel. The Jews have already had it; 'but they did not all hearken to the glad tidings', hence the call now goes forth to the Gentiles before, finally, the Jews will enter the Kingdom. So the word of the Gospel, which must first of all be proclaimed to the Gentiles, has a particularly concrete meaning in Pauline terminology, in which the main emphasis is certainly upon the word 'Gentiles'. But the chronologically-eschatologically determined character of the 'missionary message' as a 'sign' of the 'end' is here also quite evident. Only Paul regards this 'sign' first of all, so to speak, from 'within', that is, from the angle of his apostolic vocation as an instrument of this plan (of salvation). When he speaks of the divine eschatological plan Paul continually emphasizes the fact that his calling is especially to the Gentiles. In Rom. xi, where he speaks of the 'mystery' of that divine plan, he mentions his own office: 'Inasmuch then as I am an apostle of the Gentiles, I glorify my ministry' (Rom. xi. 13).

In the Epistle to the Colossians, i. 22–9, he underlines the close connection between his personal 'office' and the divine plan of salvation (the 'dispensation of God', *v.* 25), which is related to 'this mystery among the Gentiles'. When we remember that Paul knows he has been 'integrated' into a divine plan, whose fulfilment depends upon the coming of this Kingdom, we understand better the 'necessity' (I Cor. ix. 16) laid upon him to 'preach the gospel', as a 'debtor' both to Gentiles and to barbarians (Rom. i. 14). He regards himself as 'Christ's prisoner' for the Gentiles (Eph. iii. 1). It is from this point of view that we understand more fully his eagerness to go to new places, where the Gospel has not been proclaimed, from Jerusalem to Illyria, and when his work is finished in that part of the world, he intends to turn towards Spain. The time is short: 'Woe is unto me, if I preach not the Gospel' (I Cor. ix. 16).

From all this it seems very probable that in the much disputed passage in II Thess. ii. 6ff., καὶ νῦν τὸ κατέχον οἴδατε—'you know the withholding thing...' with the following reference to the Anti-Christ, there is an allusion to the proclamation of the Gospel as a 'sign' of the end. When we consider that this conception of the missionary message can be traced right through the whole of the New Testament, as we have seen, this hypothesis is as probable as any hypothesis can be. Usually the passage is taken to refer to the Roman Empire. But we can find no other passage in support of the view that the State, the manifestation of the Anti-Christ, delays the end. On the contrary, both in Jewish and in Primitive Christian Apocalyptic the Anti-Christ is usually represented as some kind of Satanic empire. Precisely in II Thess. ii. 4 it is described in images taken from the Book of Daniel, which there certainly refer to Syria. Can it be that in the very passage where Paul alludes to the Anti-Christ in these 'images', at the same time he would have introduced the State as that which 'restrains' the Anti-Christ? If this is what he means, he would have brought strange confusion into the realm of eschatological ideas, since in the same passage he would have spoken of the State as the opponent of the Anti-Christ, and as a Satanic power.

On the other hand, a great deal could be said for the view, suggested first of all by Theodore of Mopsuestia and by Theodoret, and later on by Calvin, according to which 'the withholding thing' in II Thess. ii. 6 is the eschatological missionary message. At first the Greek verb for 'withholding' had a temporal meaning in the sense the 'retarding', 'delaying'. Here the allusion is to the 'time', or 'date' of the coming of the Kingdom of God. Nowhere, however, is there a relation of this kind between the State and the 'time' when the end is expected to come; we have, however, seen that there is (a relation) of this kind between the preaching of the Gospel to the nations and the question of the 'date' of the *parousia*. According to the Synoptic passages in Mark xiii. 10–14 and Matt. xxiv. 13–15 the Anti-Christ appears after the preaching of the Gospel to the Gentiles, just as in II Thess. ii. 6ff. he will appear after 'the withholding thing' has been removed.

Further, this assumption is directly connected with that Jewish Rabbinic question, 'Who is preventing the appearing of the Messiah?' which we have already mentioned. We have already seen that the most usual Jewish answer to that question was: 'the repentance of Israel which is not yet complete', and this answer points clearly towards the Christian view of the eschatological necessity for the proclamation of the Gospel to the 'heathen', and it is corrected by it, in so far as here the essential element is the call to repentance.

The whole context in which the passage (II Thess. ii) occurs also supports the idea of a relation with the preaching to the Gentiles, and shows why the Gospel must be preached to all nations before the appearance of Anti-Christ. In ii. 9–12 we read of those 'who received not the love of the truth, that they might be saved'; and in ii. 13–14 Paul sets—against those who reject the preaching of the Apostle—the readers themselves, and of them he says: 'God chose you from the beginning unto salvation...whereunto he called you through our gospel.' The whole of the preceding chapter, too (ch. i), deals with the relation between eschatological events and the acceptance or rejection of the Gospel which they have heard: 'We are bound to give thanks for you, brethren...for your faith...and love...which *is* a manifest token of the righteous judgment of God; to the end that ye may be counted worthy of the Kingdom of God, for which ye also suffer....at the revelation of the Lord Jesus from heaven with the angels of his power in flaming fire...rendering vengeance...to them that obey not the gospel of our Lord Jesus.' We could almost regard this as an allusion to the proclamation of the Gospel to the heathen, in this connection, if it were not included in the allusion to 'the withholding thing'.

In the same passage there is first the neuter (*v.* 6, '*that* which withholds'), then the masculine (*he who* withholds). If '*that* which withholds' is the missionary message, then it is probable that 'he who restrains or withholds' is the Apostle himself. This would fit in well with what we have said about St Paul's deep sense of missionary vocation, which indeed is influenced by that eschatological conviction that the Gospel must be offered to the non-Christian world. The question of Paul speaking of himself in this way in the third person should not cause any difficulty, since elsewhere he uses the third person in speaking of the grace granted to him (II Cor. xii. 2).

Even if this interpretation of II Thess. ii. 6ff.—which has a solid foundation, and could be further supported by passages from early Christian writers of the first and second centuries—should not be correct, there are other New Testament passages which would give sufficient evidence for the fundamental insight of faith that the missionary enterprise is the work of God, which his servants are carrying out during the final period of this age, in which we are living. For this final period is a time of grace, which God in his mercy has granted us for repentance. This view springs out of the nature of New Testament eschatology. It leaves the doctrine of divine omnipotence unimpaired, since it does not make the coming of the Kingdom of God dependent upon man, and excludes all human calculations. On the other hand, it greatly intensifies the responsibility of man in view of the eschatological period of grace, and finally gives the Church its peculiar commission, namely, in God's name to carry the Gospel to all nations. This is the eschatological saving work in the period between the resurrection and the return of Christ. From every point of view, this was, theologically speaking, a deep and fruitful conception, which, alas! was soon forgotten, and only sporadically reappears as a missionary motive.

Like all other 'signs', that of the missionary enterprise cannot be limited to this or that generation. For it is characteristic of this final period, in which we are living, that it forms a unity, and that as a whole it is characterized by 'signs'. But we can never say, 'this is the final hour' in which the 'sign' will appear. This means that the Reformers were wrong when they thought they could get rid of 'missions' by saying that the Gospel had already been proclaimed to all nations by the Apostles. Rather, it is of the essence of a 'sign' that to the very end it should appear in each generation which belongs to the present final phase of this 'age'. This means, however, that the missionary obligation covers the whole time which remains, right down to the unknown final end, and that each generation anew must proclaim the Gospel to the 'heathen' of their own day, without wondering whether their ancestors before 1900 had had an opportunity of hearing it. Hence, in every generation the Church must carry on the Apostles' work and proclaim the Gospel to all nations, so far as is humanly possible at any given time.

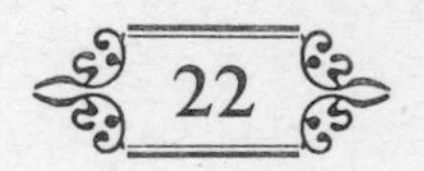

CHRIST, CREATION AND THE CHURCH

N. A. DAHL

THE rediscovery of the importance of eschatology within the New Testament has been one of the most outstanding achievements of historic theology. It is also one of the factors which has led to a new understanding of the New Testament Church; we have learned to see the Church as an 'eschatological community'. This does not only mean that the Church has an eschatological hope for the future, but also that the very existence of the Church is due to what Professor Dodd has called 'Realized Eschatology'. The Church exists in the interval between Christ's death, resurrection and heavenly enthronement and his final revelation as Lord, Judge and Saviour; and not only his *parousia* but also his birth, death and resurrection are seen as messianic, 'eschatological' events, happening 'when the fullness of time was come', 'in these last days'.

According to this view the Church is something new; it is seen not simply as a new religious society but rather as a new creation: 'the old has passed away, behold, the new has come' (II Cor. v. 17, R.S.V.). This complete, eschatological newness does not mean, however, that the Church stands without positive relations to the times before Christ. The 'new things' are the fulfilment of prophecy; the new covenant is bound up with the old one, and what happened in the Old Testament is a 'type' and prefiguration of the events of the last days. The Church is the eschatological community as being the 'people of God', redeemed by Christ; Gentiles are included, but the continuity with the old Israel is not broken.

As has eschatology in general, so has the realized eschatology of the New Testament a more universal outlook. What is given in Christ is not only a new covenant, but a new creation. Not only have the first covenant, the 'letter', the external descent from Abraham and the circumcision of the flesh, grown old, but also the whole of the present age, from which Christ delivers those who believe in him. This fact does not exclude the existence of a positive connection between salvation and creation, corresponding to the continuity between the old covenant and the new. The New Testament conception of the Church as the eschatological community has in this way a double consequence for its relation to the world: a contrast between the Church and 'this world' and a positive attitude to all things which God has created.

It is important that neither of these two aspects should be neglected. So far as I see, both protagonists and antagonists of 'consistent eschatology' have in general stressed the negative aspect in a too exclusive manner.[1] But already in Jewish eschatology the correlation of first and last things is hardly less emphasized than the contrast between this aeon and the coming one.[2] It is also worth while to observe that the positive correlation of 'eschatology' and 'protology' held a very firm position within the ancient Church.[3] This was partly due to anti-gnostic tendencies; Irenaeus developed his theory of 'recapitulation' and Origen taught the *apokatastasis* of all things. But the idea is not only a favourite theme of the anti-gnostic fathers, it belongs to the common tradition of the Church. The renewal at baptism is seen as a new creation, conforming to the patterns of the first one.[4] At the eucharist the fruits of the earth mediate the heavenly gifts, and God is praised for his creation through Christ

[1] Among scholars who have paid attention to the positive correlation I can mention: Joach. Jeremias, 'Jesus als Weltvollender', *Beiträge zur Förderung christlicher Theologie*, vol. XXX (Gütersloh, 1930), p. 4; L. Goppelt, 'Typos', *B.F. chr. Th.* series II, vol. XLIII (1939); J. Héring, 'Les bases bibliques de l'humanisme chrétien', *Revue d'hist. et de philos. rel.* vol. XXV (Strasbourg, 1945), pp. 17–40; W. D. Davies, *Paul and Rabbinic Judaism* (London 1948), esp. pp. 36–57, 147–76; G. Lindeskog, 'Studien zum neutestamentlichen Schöpfungsgedanken', *Uppsala Universitets Årsskrift 1952*, vol. XI (Uppsala/Wiesbaden, 1952).

[2] Cf. H. Gunkel, *Schöpfung und Chaos in Urzeit und Endzeit* (Göttingen, 1895). B. Murmelstein, 'Adam. Ein Beitrag zur Messiaslehre', *Wiener Zeitschr. für die Kunde des Morgenlandes* (1928), pp. 242–75; (1929), pp. 51–86. Rich collections of material are given by H. L. Strack und P. Billerbeck, *Kommentar zum Neuen Testament aus Talmud und Midrasch*, vols. I–IV (München, 1922–8); W. Staerk, *Die Erlösererwartung in den östlichen Religionen*, Soter II (Stuttgart/Berlin, 1938); and P. Volz, *Die Eschatologie der jüdischen Gemeinde* (2. ed. Tübingen, 1934).

[3] Cf., for example, J. Daniélou, *Sacramentum futuri* (Paris, 1950).

[4] Daniélou, *op. cit.* pp. 13 ff.; cf. N. A. Dahl, 'La terre où coulent le lait et le miel, selon Barnabé vi. 8–19', in [M. Goguel], *Aux sources de la tradition chrétienne* (Neuchatel/Paris, 1950), pp. 62–70.

as well as for salvation in him.[1] The idea that God will make 'the last things like the first things' (Barn. vi. 13) is used as a hermeneutical principle for the interpretation of Genesis.[2] In legendary traditions, especially popular in the East and partly bound up with local traditions of Jerusalem, the parallelism between Adam and Christ is carried through even in details.[3]

The purpose of the present article is to give a short survey of similar ideas within the New Testament, especially in the Epistles of Paul—a thorough investigation would require a whole book. I find it most convenient to start with the general patterns of eschatology, then to proceed to christology, and finally to point out the consequences for the doctrine of the Church and its relation to the created world. This last topic will also have an indirect bearing upon the present-day discussion about the relevance of Christian ethics for the orders of society, an ecumenical discussion in which Professor Dodd has taken a very prominent part.

When Gunkel in 1895 wrote his book *Schöpfung und Chaos in Urzeit und Endzeit*, he assumed that the myth of creation had been transposed into an eschatology that had already been accepted by the Babylonians. Later research has, as far as I know, not corroborated this hypothesis. The correlation of eschatology and protology in Israel has turned out to be at the same time more organic and more complex. Most important has been the discovery of the importance of the worship of the temple, especially the great festivals, as a common point of departure and coincidence. In the common worship the creation was commemorated and re-enacted, and the future renewal for which Israel hoped, was prefigured.[4]

Salvation is conceived not only as a counterpart to the beginnings of the world, but still more as a parallel to the primeval times of the

[1] Cf. the anaphora in *The Apostolic Tradition* of Hippolytus or in *The Apostolic Constitutions* VIII, 12. Further: Justin, *Dial.* XLI, 1, CXVII, 3; Irenaeus, *Adv. Haer.* IV, 17–18 and V, 2.

[2] Cf. my study on Barn. vi. 8–19 (*loc. cit.*), esp. p. 69.

[3] Most interesting are the legends in the Syriac 'Cave of Treasures', *Die Schatzhöhle*, ed. C. Bezold, 2 vols. (Leipzig, 1883–8). Cf. Joach. Jeremias, 'Golgotha und der heilige Felsen', in *Angelos*, vol. II (Leipzig, 1926), pp. 74–128.

[4] Cf. S. Mowinckel, 'Psalmenstudien II. Das Thronbesteigungsfest Jahväs und der Ursprung der Eschatologie', *Skrifter utgitt av Det Norske Videnskaps-Akademi i Kristiania (Oslo)*. II. Hist-Filos. Klasse, 1921, 6 (Kristiania, 1922); and more recently *Han som kommer* (Köbenhavn, 1951), esp. pp. 100f., and *Offersang og sangoffer* (Oslo, 1951), pp. 145ff., 183ff.

people, as a new Exodus. But as the first Exodus is already depicted as a divine act of creation, conforming to the creation of the world, eschatology and creation can be linked up with one another even in this way (e.g. Isa. xliii. 16ff.). At an early stage the narratives about Paradise can also more directly influence the prophecies concerning coming, happy days (e.g. Isa. xi. 6–8; Ezek. xxxiv. 25–7). In the learned theology of the Scribes the conceptions of Paradise, of the Mosaic times, and of the days of the Messiah still mutually influence one another.[1]

The hope for a return of a 'golden age' seems to be widespread, and can perhaps be found in every religion which has developed an eschatology. Both among the Greeks and the Babylonians we find also the theory of a periodical return of the end to the beginning in a cycle of successive world-ages. This idea may to a certain extent have influenced the more systematic elaboration of the correspondence between protology and eschatology in the Judaism of the Hellenistic and Roman age; but this does not justify the view that this doctrine of a cyclic return should be the root of the whole conception that the last things shall be like the first.[2]

It is further necessary to observe that the correlation between the first and the last things can be elaborated in several forms, between which we must differentiate, even if in practice they are often combined in various ways. The main types may be summarized in the following way:

First, we find *analogy* or parallelism; here we may mention the ideas of a new creation, a new heaven and a new earth, etc.[3] This

[1] Cf., for example, Wisd. xix. 6, and further, Strack-Billerbeck, *Kommentar*, vol. I, pp. 69f., 594–6; Murmelstein, *Wiener Zeitschr. für die Kunde des Morgenlandes* (1929), pp. 51–64.

[2] This view is held by Staerk, *Erlösererwartung*. Cf. also R. Bultmann, 'Ursprung und Sinn der Typologie als hermeneutischer Methode', in [G. van de Leeuw], *Pro Regno pro Sanctuario* (Nijkerk, 1950), pp. 89–100. For criticism of Staerk, see Mowinckel, *Han som kommer*, pp. 110, 323, etc. The influence of Greek terminology is manifest in places like Rom. xi. 36, I Cor. viii. 6, Col. i. 15–20.

[3] Isa. lxv. 17, lxvi. 22; Jubil. i. 29; I Enoch xci. 16; IV Ezra vii. 30ff.; Targ. Jer. xxiii. 23, etc.; Rev. xxi. 1, 5; II Pet. iii. 12f.; James i. 18 (?). Cf. Volz, *Eschatologie*, pp. 338f., 361; Strack-Billerbeck, *Kommentar*, vol. III, pp. 840–7; E. Sjöberg, 'Wiedergeburt und Neuschöpfung im palästinischen Judentum', *Studia Theologica cura Ordinum Theologicorum Scandinavorum edita*, vol. IV (Lund, 1950), pp. 44–85. C.-M. Edsman, 'Schöpfung und Wiedergeburt', in [K. Kundsin] *Spiritus et Veritas* (1953), pp. 43–55.

pattern is especially applied to the acts of God at the beginning and the end of the world; they are to conform to one another. But also the doctrine of the Saviour can come in under the same pattern. According to the similitudes of Enoch, the name of the Son of Man is named on the day of judgment as it was named before the creation (I Enoch xlviii. 2, 3).[1] The Pauline typology Adam-Christ also comes in here (Rom. v. 12–19; I Cor. xv. 22).[2]

Where the sin of Adam and its effects stand in the foreground, we find, on the other hand, the idea of a *contrast* (e.g. Rom. v. 18, 19, παρακοή—ὑπακοή).[3] The contrast is in general bound up with the idea of a *restitution* of creation, which has been laid under a curse. Rabbinic theologians speak about the glory and other things which were lost through the fall of Adam, but shall be brought back when the Messiah comes,[4] and Paul thinks in similar categories.[5]

The ideas of 'typological' analogy and of restitution may easily be combined. But the *superiority* of the new creation can also be stressed; it brings not only a restitution but also a *transformation* of

[1] Cf. E. Sjöberg, *Der Menschensohn im äthiopischen Henochbuch* (Lund, 1946), pp. 87ff.

[2] In Jewish lore there are many similarities between the figures of Adam and Messiah (Murmelstein, *Wiener Zeitschr. für die Kunde des Morgenlandes* (1928), and Staerk, *Erlösererwartung*, pp. 7–40). To a large extent they are, however, due to a general phenomenological kinship and a common origin in the ideology of 'divine kingship', not to any scheme of correspondence between 'Urzeit und Endzeit'. The relation between king, 'Urmensch', first created man, and Messiah is discussed by Mowinckel and Bentzen, *Stud. Theol.* vol. II (1948), pp. 71–89 and vol. III (1949), pp. 143–57. Cf. further E. Sjöberg in *Svensk Teologisk Kvartalskrift* (Lund, 1950), pp. 35–44 and I. Engnell, 'Människosonen', *Svenskt bibliskt Uppslagsverk* (ed. Engnell and Fridrichsen, 2 vols., Uppsala, 1948–52), vol. II, pp. 399–403, and review of Sjöberg, *Der Menschensohn* in *Bibliotheca Orientalis*, vol. VIII (Leyden, 1951), pp. 187–92.

[3] Some scholars hold this contrast to be the background also for Phil. ii. 5ff. Cf. esp. J. Héring, 'Kyrios Anthropos', *Revue d'hist. et de philos. rel.*, vol. XVI (Strasbourg, 1936), pp. 196–209.

[4] Gen. R. xii. 6 and par., cf. Test. Levi xviii. 10f.; Strack-Billerbeck, *Kommentar*, vol. I, p. 19; vol. IV, pp. 886ff.; Murmelstein, *Wiener Zeitschr. für die Kunde des Morgenlandes* (1928), pp. 254–7. For the general idea of restitution, cf. for example, Jubil. xxiii. 26ff., I Enoch xc. 37f., further Strack-Billerbeck, vol. III, pp. 247–55; Volz, *Eschatologie*, pp. 359ff., 383, 398; Staerk, *Erlösererwartung*, pp. 23f., 166, 178.

[5] Cf. his words about the 'glory of God' in Rom. iii. 24 and v. 2; C. H. Dodd, *The Epistle to the Romans* (London, 1932), pp. 50f., 73. For the idea of restitution cf. Rom. viii. 19ff.; Col. i. 15–20, etc.; Rev. xx. 13; xxi. 4. Also Matt. xix. 28?

the first one. The light of the heavenly bodies will be much stronger (Isa. xxx. 26)—or, there will be no need for them, as God himself (and the Lamb) will be the light (Isa. lx. 19f.; Rev. xxi. 23). The righteous will at the resurrection be transformed into glory and brightness (Dan. xii. 3).[1] By Paul the superiority of the coming glorious and incorruptible state of things is clearly emphasized.[2]

The idea of restitution can, on the other hand, also be combined with the other idea, that the very things which existed at the beginning will come back: Paradise, the tree of life, etc.[3] In this case we have an *identity* between the first and the last things. In certain Jewish-Christian circles even Adam and Christ are identified; this view is perhaps influenced by Gnostic ideas, which, however, in general distinguish between the primordial (heavenly) Man—sometimes identified with the Saviour—and the first created man.[4]

Another idea, which is less familiar to us, is that of a *reservation* of some of the first things for the end of the world. Thus, the light of the first day (Gen. i. 3) is said to be reserved for the righteous in the age to come,[5] and similar statements can be made concerning Leviathan and Behemoth.[6] These ideas are not found in the New Testament, but the conception of the sabbatical rest in the Epistle to the Hebrews belongs to the same type of thought. The 'works were finished from the creation of the world', but it still 'remains for some to enter into it' (iv. 3–6); the 'rest' is reserved for the people of God in the last days. According to this view, Christ is not thought to bring a new creation, restoring and transforming the first one, but to open the free entrance to that 'sabbatical rest',

[1] Cf. I Enoch xlv. 4–5; II Baruch li, etc.; Strack-Billerbeck, vol. IV, pp. 891 + 958ff., 887 + 941f.; Volz, *Eschatologie*, pp. 339f., 396–401. In later Judaism, especially among the Rabbis, there is a tendency to make the idea of transformation subordinate to the idea of restitution; cf. Sv. Aalen, *Die Begriffe 'Licht' und 'Finsternis' im Alten Testament, im Spätjudentum und im Rabbinismus. Skr. Norske Viden. Akad.*, 1951, I (Oslo, 1951), pp. 25ff., 162f., 181f., 261f., 319f.

[2] I Cor. xv. 35ff., etc.; cf. Mark xii. 25.

[3] I Enoch xxiv–xxv, etc.; Strack-Billerbeck, vol. IV, pp. 1144ff.; Rev. ii. 7; xxi. 1, 14, 17, 19.

[4] Cf., for example, H. J. Schoeps, *Theologie und Geschichte des Judenchristentums* (Tübingen, 1949), pp. 100ff.; Staerk, *Erlösererwartung*, pp. 125ff.

[5] Gen. R. iii. 6; bab. Ḥag. 12a, etc.; Strack-Billerbeck, vol. IV, pp. 961f.; Aalen, '*Licht*' *und* '*Finsternis*', pp. 265f.

[6] IV Ezra vi. 49f.; II Baruch xxix. 4; Strack-Billerbeck, vol. IV, pp. 1147, 1159ff.

the world to come, which since creation exists as a heavenly reality.[1]

The idea of reservation can be said to be based on the *inclusiveness* of creation; it includes also the world to come. In Rabbinic writings the proof of this is found in prepositions, conjunctions and the like in Gen. i, which are taken to signify that also the new heaven and the new earth are included.[2] A similar view is again found in Hebrews: 'the aeons' which are created in Christ seem to include the world to come (i. 3; cf. iv. 3); in ch. ii it is quite clear that 'all things' in Ps. viii is taken to include also the world to come (cf. *vv.* 5, 8 and 10).

This synthetic view is, in somewhat divergent forms, characteristic of the more speculative trends in Judaism. The 'new creation' is seen as the final establishment and perfection of the first one, rather than as an independent, parallel act. 'This world' is marked by the duality of light and darkness and of good and evil powers; even the darkness is created by God and has a necessary function in this present, preparatory world. What the new creation will bring is the *elimination* of the powers of darkness. This view is most clearly stated in the Dead Sea Manual of Discipline (D.S.D., cols. III–IV), but it seems to be predominant in Rabbinic sources too, even if the dualism is here still more modified.[3] In a somewhat similar way, the putting away of sin and the removal of the present earth and heaven is stressed in Hebrews (ix. 26; i. 11f. and xii. 27); but here there is a sharper contrast between this visible world and 'that which cannot be shaken', and we find no trace of the rationalizing view that the potentiality of sin is implied in creation.

Two other themes have still to be mentioned, the ideas of *pre-existence* and of *predestination*; the things which are to appear at the end of the world are thought to have existed since the beginning,

[1] For Jewish speculations cf. E. Käsemann, 'Das wandernde Gottesvolk im Hebräerbrief', *Forschungen zur Religion und Literatur des Alten und Neuen Testaments* (Göttingen, 1939), pp. 40–5; H. Riesenfeld, 'Jésus transfiguré', *Acta Seminarii Neotestamentici Upsaliensis*, vol. XVI (Köbenhavn, 1947), pp. 206–16; Strack-Billerbeck, vol. II, p. 77; vol. III, p. 687; Volz, *Eschatologie*, p. 384.

[2] Gen. R. i. 10 (the world created with ב); ix. 3 (*and* behold—, Gen. i. 31, R. Simeon b. Lakish); i. 13 (*the* new heavens—, Isa. lxvi. 22, R. Eliezer b. R. Jose).

[3] Cf. Aalen, '*Licht' und 'Finsternis*', esp. pp. 170–5, 269–71, 306–14; and, for criticism of some exaggerations in the book of Aalen, my remarks in *Norsk Teol. Tidsskrift* (Oslo, 1952), pp. 61–84.

as heavenly realities or in the mind and purpose of God.[1] The whole conception of the last things as mysteries which are to be revealed comes in here.[2] The distinction between 'real' and 'ideal' pre-existence is often fluid, and so is also the distinction between existence from the foundation of the world, pre-creational or eternal existence.

In general these various themes and patterns are combined, a systematic and consistent elaboration of one of them seems rather to be an exception. The main idea, which is common to the different forms of combining the last things with that which was at the beginning, is the idea that the end will bring the final realization of what from the beginning was the will of God the Creator, who is himself the first and the last (Isa. xliv. 6, xlviii. 12; Rev. i. 8, xxi. 6, etc.). Most of the themes and patterns can be found in Christian as well as in Jewish eschatology. But there is a rather clear difference of emphasis: the antithetic parallelism between creation and salvation is more marked in Christianity, whereas a synthetic view is more characteristic of Jewish cosmology and eschatology.

The difference can most clearly be illustrated by the interpretation of the first two chapters of Genesis. Paul, and the Fathers after him, give the words in Genesis an eschatological application according to the principle of analogy (typology), often combined with the idea of the superiority of the new creation. The statement in Gen. ii. 7 that (the first) man (Adam) was made a living soul is thus taken to imply that 'the last Adam' was made 'a life-giving spirit' (I Cor. xv. 45).[3] In Rabbinic writings too, the story of creation can be used to illustrate eschatology. But the fundamental idea is here not the conformity of the eschatological salvation with the original creation, but the idea that creation, as described in Genesis, prefigures the

[1] Matt. xxv. 34; Eph. i. 3ff.; I Pet. i. 2, 20; Rev. xvii. 8; xxi. 2, etc. Cf. IV Ezra iv. 36f.; vii. 70; Gen. R. i. 4; bab. Pes. 54a, etc.; Strack-Billerbeck, vol. I, pp. 974f., 981f.; vol. II, pp. 334f., 353. In Judaism also present things of central religious significance are thought to be pre-existent. The Christian idea of pre-existence seems to have its root in eschatology, but soon to have gained an independent importance; the christology of 'realized eschatology' was superseded by a christology of pre-existence. The whole theme requires a new, thorough investigation.

[2] Matt. xiii. 35; I Cor. ii. 6ff., etc. For Jewish conceptions cf. G. Bornkamm, *Theologisches Wörterbuch zum N.T.* ed. G. Kittel, vol. IV (Stuttgart, 1933ff.), pp. 821ff.; E. Sjöberg, *Der Menschensohn im äth. Henoch.*, pp. 102–15.

[3] Cf. I Cor. xv. 47–9; vi. 16; Eph. v. 31f.; II Cor. iv. 6; see also above p. 423 n. 4.

whole history of the world, including its eschatological fulfilment. This is the meaning when, for example, the Spirit of God moving upon the face of the waters is said to be the Messiah, or when the evening and the morning of the first day are taken to signify the evening for the godless and the morning (of salvation) for the righteous, and so on.[1] In this connection it may also be mentioned as highly symbolical that the Jews celebrate the Sabbath, pointing to the fulfilment of creation, whereas Christians celebrate the first day of the week, pointing to the beginning of the new creation by the resurrection of our Lord.[2]

This difference of emphasis corresponds to a different doctrine of sin; as the corruption of man and the world is thought to be more total, the newness of the new creation is stressed in the New Testament and especially by Paul, much more than is usual in Judaism. The deeper consciousness of sin is again bound up with the faith in Jesus as the crucified Christ, in whose name forgiveness of sins is offered; Christ, the Messiah, has already risen from the dead and is enthroned in heaven. This Christian faith, and not a divergence into eschatological themes and patterns, is the essential fact, which also gives the correlation of the first and the last things a new meaning and significance in Christianity. Eschatology is thought to be 'in process of realization'; the last things which correspond to the first are no longer merely future, they are also present, actual realities.

At this point it is, however, important that we should not forget that, even to Judaism, it is not only an eschatological hope but also an actual experience, that God the Creator deals with the world, man and Israel, in a similar way as at the creation of the world.

[1] Gen. R. ii. 4 (R. Simeon b. Lakish), ii. 3 (R. Judah i), ii. 5 (R. Abbahu, and R. Ḥiyya), iii. 8 (R. Yannai). A closer parallel to the Christian way of interpretation is perhaps to be found in Pesikta Rabbati 33 (ed. Friedmann), p. 152, a text which has not been accessible to me. According to Murmelstein, *Wiener Zeitschr. für die Kunde des Morgenlandes* (1928), p. 245 n. 2, and Staerk, *Erlösererwartung*, p. 21, Gen. i. 1f. is here applied to the creation of the new heaven and the new earth. It should be observed that in Jewish theology Gen. i can also be used to illustrate the revelation of the Law; R. Tanḥum b. Hanilai finds an hermeneutical justification for this in Isa. xlvi. 10: 'Declaring the end from the beginning', Gen. R. iv. 6. The analogy with, and difference from, Barn. vi. 13 is very remarkable. Cf. also Gen. R. iv. 2 (R. Abba b. Kahana), where the stories of creation and of lawgiving are said to elucidate each other mutually.

[2] Cf. esp. Ignatius, *Magn.* IX, and Barn. XV, Justin, *Dial.* 138.

We can here apply the notion of *creatio continua*, but can also speak of a *creatio actualis*: by liberating a man from disasters and bringing him into a new positive relation to himself, God makes him 'a new creation'. This actual experience does not need to have any relation to eschatology, but eschatological connotations easily come in.[1]

Especially is the cultus, even in later Judaism, related both to 'protology' and to 'eschatology'; this is true not only of the great festivals and the days of New Year and Atonement,[2] but also of the Sabbath, which corresponds both to the Sabbath of the creation week and to the final Sabbath in the world to come.[3] In the daily liturgy God is praised for renewing the work of creation every morning.[4]

In a more speculative way Sion, the temple and the 'stone of foundation' (*'æbæn š^etiyya*) are thought to be the cosmic centre, from which the world was created and at which the glory of God shall be revealed at the end of the world.[5] From a more historical point of view, Israel is seen as the centre; this world has come into being on account of the righteous, and it is only on their account that that which is to come shall do so (II Baruch xv. 7).[6] The first and the last things are also, to an increasing degree, bound together by the Torah, which as the expression of God's will contains not only his commands, but also his entire plan for the world, from its beginning to the end.[7]

In the New Testament, Christ has a central significance, which corresponds not only to that of the Jewish Messiah, but also to that of the temple and cultus and of the Torah and Wisdom. The Christian correlation of salvation and creation is not merely derived from the

[1] Cf. the acute investigation of Sjöberg in *Stud. Theol.* vol. IV referred to at p. 425 n. 3.

[2] For the interrelation of eschatology and cultus in Judaism, cf. Riesenfeld, *Jésus transfiguré*; Sjöberg in *Stud. Theol.* vol. IV pp. 56ff., 66f.; Aalen, '*Licht*' *und* '*Finsternis*', pp. 255–8.

[3] Cf. Gen. R. xvii. 5 (R. Ḥanina b. Isaac), bab. Ber. 57b; Strack-Billerbeck, vol. III, p. 672; vol. IV, pp. 839f., and above, p. 428 n. 1.

[4] Especially in the benediction *yoṣer 'or*; cf. Aalen, pp. 248–54.

[5] Cf. for example, Jubil. i. 27–9; viii. 19; bab. Yoma 54b; Aalen, pp. 263f., 290, 299; Jeremias, in *Angelos*, vol. II, pp. 94f.

[6] Cf. Gen. R. lxvi. 2; N. A. Dahl, 'Das Volk Gottes', *Skr. Norske Viden. Akad. 1941*, 2 (Oslo, 1941), pp. 77f., 88.

[7] Cf., for example, Gen. R. i. 1; Aboth iii. 19; Strack-Billerbeck, vol. II, pp. 174–6, 356f.; vol. I, pp. 245f.

eschatological idea that the end shall be like the beginning; it has also antecedents in applications of the creation-pattern to historic and actual experiences of God's dealing with man. What we find in the New Testament is due to a coincidence of eschatological doctrine and actual experience, where eschatology is 'realized', and 'reality', as given in Christ, is eschatologically interpreted. As in Judaism, both the actual facts of central religious significance and the last things are put in relation to creation, or thought to be predestined or pre-existent; but in the New Testament these two lines of thought fall together, as that which is already given in Christ is thought to be part of the last things.

We must now proceed from the survey of general motifs to sketch their more concrete application in the doctrine of Christ and the Church. Especially I will draw attention to some texts in which the analogy between the beginning of the world and the beginning of the Church is made manifest. I therefore only just mention the application of predicates of divine eternity to Christ: as God he is the first and the last.[1] Further, as Christ is pre-existent and elected from eternity, and is revealed in the last days, in him also the mystery of the whole divine plan of salvation is revealed.[2]

The accord between the work of salvation and the eternal purpose of God is made especially clear in Eph. i. 3–14.[3] To the actual 'blessing' in Christ, i. 3, corresponds the election in him before the foundation of the world, i. 4. The whole 'eulogy' develops this theme, showing how the eternal universal purpose of God is realized in Christ. That also Gentiles are given a share in Christ is part of the 'recapitulation of all things' in him.

In other texts it is directly said that Christ is the mediator of creation as well as of salvation; this corresponds to the Jewish ideas about wisdom and the Torah. In John i it is not quite clear how far the 'Urzeit-Endzeit'-scheme has had an essential importance for the formulation; but both in Heb. i and in I Cor. viii. 6 and Col. i it is manifest. In Heb. i the scheme seems to me to have even a greater

[1] Rev. i. 17; ii. 8; xxii. 13; Heb. xiii. 8.

[2] Col. i. 26f.; Eph. i. 9f.; iii. 4ff.; II Tim. i. 9f.; Tit. i. 2f.; I Pet. i. 20. Cf. above, p. 429 n. 2.

[3] For a closer analysis of this passage cf. N. A. Dahl, 'Adresse und Proömium des Epheserbriefes', *Theol. Zeitschr.* vol. VII (Basel, 1951), pp. 241–64.

importance for the whole structure than has been generally recognized. Clauses speaking about the eschatological appointment or enthronement of Christ alternate with predications of his eternal status, in a series of introverted parallelisms according to the scheme *abba ab*(*ba*):

...by (his) Son

a whom he hath appointed heir of all things

b by whom also he made the worlds;

b who being the brightness of his glory...
and upholding all things by the word of his power

a when he had...purged (our) sins
sat down on the right hand of the Majesty on high;

a being made so much better than the angels

b as he hath...obtained a more excellent name than they

b For unto which... Ps. ii. 7+II. Sam. vii. 14

a And again... Deut. xxxii. 43 (LXX).

The recognition of this formal structure[1] renders superfluous and unlikely the assumption that the names-giving, *vv.* 4–5, should be thought to take place at the enthronement of Christ, a view which can hardly be harmonized with the use of the title 'Son' already in *v.* 2. Much more, a reference to primeval time is an old feature of enthronement hymns (cf. Ps. cix. 3 LXX; I Enoch xlviii. 3).[2]

As the aeons were created through Christ, all things, and especially the world to come, are also put in subjection to him (Heb. i. 2; cf. ii. 5 ff.). Not only his enthronement is set in relation to the creation; also his identification with his 'brethren' through incarnation and passion is brought into correspondence with their common origin in God, 'for whom and by whom all things exist' (ii. 10–11). Through the sacerdotal purification which Christ has accomplished, the people of God is given access to the heavenly world, which is also the world to come (i. 3; cf. x. 19 ff., etc.). But in accordance with the whole eschatological outlook of Hebrews, the Church itself is not directly said to be a new creation.

At this point the Pauline idea is different. In I Cor. viii. 6 the creation of all things through Christ and the creation of the Church

[1] The same formal structure, a threefold introverted parallelism according to the scheme *ab ba ab*, is found also in the hymn, I Tim. iii. 16.

[2] References are given by the authors referred to at p. 426 nn. 1, 2.

through him are mentioned side by side. In Col. i. 15–20 this parallelism is worked out in detail: Christ is πρωτότοκος πάσης κτίσεως and πρωτότοκος ἐκ τῶν νεκρῶν; all things are created 'in him...through him and to him', and 'in him' the fullness was pleased to dwell, and 'through him' to reconcile all things 'to him'. In a very impressive way, the idea of universal restitution is here combined with the conception that the reconciliation is a parallel to the creation. Here also the Church is included in the protological-eschatological parallelism; it is the body of which Christ is the head, just as all things, the universe, are held together in him (cf. ii. 10, 19; Eph. i. 22f.). We have the right to say that in the Church the reconciliation and re-creation of the universe is already realized.

Parallels to the christological hymn in Col. i can be found in Gnosticism and in Hellenism in general, but it can hardly be denied that the Jewish ideas of the Law, Israel, the Temple, etc., must also be taken into account.[1] It is at least possible also to find an allusion to Gen. i. 1; 'In the beginning...' seems here to be interpreted as meaning 'in Christ', as in Rabbinic interpretation it is taken to mean 'by the Torah' (=Wisdom, Prov. viii. 22) or 'on account of Israel' (the beginning=the firstfruits, Jer. ii. 3).[2] More indisputable is the allusion to Gen. i. 26f. when Christ in Col. i. 15 is said to be 'the image of the invisible God'. As εἰκὼν τοῦ θεοῦ Christ is the representation and manifestation of God, both as the mediator of creation and in his work of atonement, when 'the fullness was pleased to dwell' in him. We may therefore safely assume that we have here traces of a 'christological' interpretation of Gen. i, with a double reference, both to creation and to salvation.

In II Cor. iv. 4 the idea is simply that Christ, as proclaimed in the Gospel, is the 'image of God', in whom God is revealed; the glory of Christ is, accordingly, 'the glory of God in the face of Christ'.

[1] Cf. the commentary of Dibelius (in Lietzmann, *Handbuch zum N.T.* vol. XII, 2nd ed.) and E. Käsemann, *Leib und Leib Christi* (Tübingen, 1933), and on the other hand the commentary of Lohmeyer (Meyer, *Kritisch-exegetischer Kommentar*, vol. IX, 8th ed. Göttingen, 1930) and Sv. Aalen, 'Begrepet πλήρωμα i Kolosser- og Efeserbrevet', *Tidsskrift for Teologi og Kirke* (Oslo, 1952), pp. 49–67. In such cases we should not assume that either the Jewish or the 'Hellenistic' parallels are alone relevant.

[2] Cf. W. D. Davies, *Paul and Rabbinic Judaism* (London, 1948), pp. 150ff., and C. F. Burney, 'Christ as the ΑΡΧΗ of Creation', *J. Theol. Stud.* vol. XXVII (1926), pp. 160–77; Strack-Billerbeck, vol. IV, p. 852.

But the allusion to Gen. i. 3 in iv. 6 makes it probable that here too, we have a vestige of an identification of the image of God in Genesis with Christ. Here, in II Cor. iv, the two notions εἰκών and δόξα are closely associated with one another. This combination reappears in I Cor. xi. 7, and also in some passages in which Paul speaks of the 'image' of Christ as the archetype, to which the faithful are to be made to conform in glory (Rom. viii. 29; I Cor. xv. 49; cf. Phil. iii. 21).[1]

In I Cor. xv. 44–9 the allusions to Genesis are clear. The point is the difference between the 'psychic body' of created man and the 'pneumatic body' of the resurrected. The archetypes are respectively the first man, Adam, who is a man of dust, and the 'second man', the resurrected Christ, who is from heaven: as we have borne the image of the man of dust (cf. Gen. v. 3), we shall also bear the image of the man from heaven. The superiority of the 'image of Christ' over that of Adam marks the superiority of resurrection over creation. It is quite clear that Christ as the 'last Adam' is here thought to bring something more than what was lost through the Fall. Yet Paul has probably found the intention of the Creator to make man conform with Christ as the archetype, to be contained in Gen. i. 26f. We may here compare Rom. iii. 23 and viii. 29f.: 'All have sinned and come short of the glory of God'—but justification leads to conformity with the image of Christ and thus to glory, in accordance with the predestination of God.

Without direct use of the noun 'image' the idea of Christ as Adam's antitype is also found in I Cor. xv. 22 and Rom. v. 12ff. Here the point is not correspondence on a higher level, as in I Cor. xv. 44ff., but analogy in contrast.[2] Resurrection and life stand

[1] On Christ as 'Image', cf. G. Kittel in *Theol. Wörterb. zum N.T.* pp. 394–6; H. Willms, *Eikon* (Münster i.W., 1935). It is worth while to remember also the sage remark of Ad. Schlatter: 'Der Gedanke "Bild Gottes" ließe sich leicht als Grundgedanke benützen, der alle christologische Sätze des Paulus umfaßt. Man darf aber bei der Darstellung der paulinischen Gedanken nicht konstruieren' (*Die Theologie der Apostel* (Stuttgart, 1922), p. 338 n. 1).

[2] As to the analogy in contrast, cf. IV Ezra iv. 30–2 and also the citation from Sifra on Leviticus by Raymundus Martini which is given by Jeremias in *Theol. Wörterb. zum N.T.* vol. v, p. 694. That the idea of Christ as the antitype of Adam is especially connected with his resurrection, may be explained by the general view that resurrection is a new act of creation (Rom. iv. 17; Sjöberg in *Stud. Theol.* vol. IV, pp. 60, 76f.). As Adam is the father of mankind, his resurrection has a special importance (Apoc. Mosis 28 and 41; cf. the late *Pirke Mashiaḥ*, Strack-Billerbeck, vol. III, p. 10).

against death, but the relation of the one and the many is the same in the realm of life as in the realm of death. In the fuller development of the theme in Rom. v the point is that the trespass of Adam, which brought sin into the world, also caused the death of all men; accordingly, the obedience of Christ and the grace of God in him, which has brought justification, will also bring life to all men, without difference. Salvation is as universal as sin; the Law has come in as an intermediate ordinance, which neither belongs to the first nor to the last things.[1]

A similar, yet different, conception is that of the 'new man' (Col. iii. 10; Eph. iv. 24; cf. ii. 15). The contrast here is not Adam as the prototype of humanity, but 'the old man', man under the domination of sin, conceived as a kind of 'corporate personality', and at the same time the individual, sinful self, mankind, and the totality of vices, the 'members which are upon the earth' (cf. especially Col. iii. 5ff., and also Rom. vi. 6). In a similar way, 'the new man' is not simply the converted individual, but an eschatological entity, personal, corporate and pneumatic, nearly identical with Christ himself, whom the baptized have put on and ever again are to put on (Gal. iii. 27; Rom. xiii. 14). By putting on this 'new man', men become what God at the creation intended that men should be; the new man is created 'after God' (Eph. iv. 24) and is 'renewed in knowledge after the image of him that created him' (Col. iii. 10).[2]

The corporate aspect, which is quite clear in Col. iii. 10f., is the main theme in Eph. ii. 15. The whole passage Eph. ii. 11–22 has a background—not necessarily the only background—in the terminology of Jewish proselytism. According to Jewish doctrine individual Gentiles were 'brought near', incorporated in Israel and given access to the holy sphere of worship, through (*a*) the 'blood of the covenant' at circumcision, (*b*) the proselyte baptism and (*c*) the expiating blood of the proselyte sacrifice. In analogy to this, the Gentiles are in Eph. ii said to have been brought near by the

[1] Cf. my notes on Rom. v in *Stud. Theol.* vol. v (1951), pp. 37–48; M. Black, 'The Pauline Doctrine of the Second Adam', *Scot. Journ. Theol.* vol. VII (1954), pp. 170–9.

[2] Cf. Davies, *Paul and Rabbinic Judaism*, pp. 120ff. and P. V. Hansen, 'Det nye Menneske', *Dansk Teol. Tidsskrift* (1950), pp. 193–202; also my article 'Gamla Människan' in *Svenskt bibliskt Uppslagsverk*, vol. I, p. 644f.

blood of Christ, and made, not only strangers and sojourners (*gerim*) but real fellow citizens, members of the household of God.[1] Eph. ii. 13–18 is a kind of 'midrash' on Isa. lvii. 19, a passage which in Judaism was referred to those Gentiles 'far off' who had become proselytes—or to the penitents—and the Israelites who were near; it is here applied to Gentiles and Jews in the Church, to whom Christ has brought peace through his work of reconciliation.[2] Whoever brought a Gentile near and made him a proselyte, was said to be as if he had created him;[3] but here Christ is said to create 'in himself one new man', reconciling Jew and Gentile to God in one body, his Church, and giving both access to the Father in one Spirit. The 'dividing wall' of enmity, which was caused by the Law but has been broken down by Christ, not only alienated the Gentiles from Israel, but also separated Gentiles and Israelites from God, in the time when both of them were 'in the flesh'.[4] The creation of the church as 'one new man' in Christ means at the same time the incorporation of Gentiles in the people of God and the coming of the new age of the Spirit. Reconciliation brings a new creation in the double sense of the conversion of the Gentiles and the realization of eschatology (cf. also Gal. vi. 15 and II Cor. v. 17).[5]

[1] H. Sahlin, 'Die Beschneidung Christi', *Symbolae Biblicae Upsalienses 12* (Lund, 1950), has given a stimulating, even if in details somewhat fantastic, interpretation of the passage in question. He assumes that the 'blood of Christ' is to be contrasted with the blood of circumcision. That also an analogy to the proselyte sacrifice may be intended, is a conclusion which can be drawn from the study of W. C. van Unnik, 'De Verlossing I Petrus i. 18–19 en het Problem van den Eersten Petrusbrief', *Mededeelingen der Nederlandsche Akademie van Wetenschappen, Afdeeling Letterkunde* (Nieuwe Reeks, vol. v, 1) (Amsterdam, 1942), esp. pp. 51–7, 69–87.

[2] Cf. Num. R. viii. 4 (149d): the proselytes; Targ. Isa. lvii. 19; S. Num. vi. 26, § 42; bab. Ber. 34b; Sanh. 99a: the penitents. Strack-Billerbeck, vol. I, pp. 167, 216, 603; vol. III, p. 586.

[3] Gen. R. xxxix. 14; Sjöberg in *Stud. Theol.* vol. IV, pp. 53f.

[4] The main theme of the passage is the idea that the Gentiles are in Christ rendered free approach to God, on equal terms with the Israelites; cf. Percy in *Zeitschr. f. d. neutest. Wiss.* vol. XLIII, pp. 187f. This approach to God is understood as approach to God in the temple (of the Church), ii. 20–2. I therefore adopt the view, that the 'middle wall of partition' alludes to the wall in the temple, dividing the court of the Gentiles from the inner yards, into which Gentiles were not allowed to enter, under penalty of death. But this does not exclude the possibility that the passage also contains vestiges of a cosmic symbolism, according to which the wall is the boundary which separates the divine world from this one. Cf. the notion of the veil in Heb. vi. 19; ix. 3ff.; x. 20; Num. R. xii. 13.

[5] Cf. Davies, *Paul and Rabbinic Judaism*, pp. 119ff.

The unity of Jews and Gentiles is to Paul an essential sign of the new creation or the 'new man'. This unity is of an eschatological character, but it is already a sacramental and social reality in the Church. In this world the differences between circumcised and uncircumcised, slave and free, remain, and are to remain, even if they are no more of any essential relevance (I Cor. vii. 17–24). But none the less, the unity within the Church is thought to be a restoration of the original unity of mankind and creation. Through the very existence of the Church, in which Jews and Gentiles are united, 'the manifold wisdom of God' is made known to the principalities and powers which constitute the universe, and the dispensation of the Creator to re-unify all things begins to be realized (Eph. iii. 10). And to the soteriological arguments for the equality of Jew and Greek in justification Paul can also add the more 'rational' argument, that God is not the God of Jews only, but also the God of Gentiles (Rom. iii. 29).[1]

The unity in Christ is also a unity of male and female (Gal. iii. 27f.). To Paul, this unity does not imply any social equality; the wife has to be subject to her husband. In this case the difference is not caused by the Law, but belongs to the original order of creation (I Cor. xi. 2ff.). But none the less, the Apostle finds that also the equal dignity and interdependence 'in the Lord' is foreshadowed in the order of creation and procreation. The eschatological unity corresponds to the common origin.[2] The subordination of women, of which their hair-dress and their silence is to be a sign, belongs to the order of creation, not to the order of salvation. But a decent order is to be respected also in the Church and especially there. This, and not any incapacity in women to represent Christ as his messengers, is the motivation for the Pauline ordinances in I Cor. xi. 2ff. and xiv. 34ff.[3]

[1] Cf. also the summary of the history of salvation in Rom. xi. 32–6. Stig Hansson, 'The Unity of the Church in the N.T.', *Acta Seminarii Neotestamentici Upsaliensis*, vol. XIV (Uppsala, 1946), has, with good reason, made the restoration of the original unity a main theme of his book.

[2] I Cor. xi. 11–12; cf. the similar words in Gen. R. xxii. 2 (R. Akiba) and viii. 9 (R. Simlai): 'Neither man without woman nor woman without man nor both of them without Shekinah.'

[3] This against H. Riesenfeld in *En bok om kyrkands ämbete*, ed. Hj. Lindroth (Uppsala, 1951), pp. 64ff. Some valuable remarks on the passage are made by R. Gyllenberg, 'Den välklädda kvinnan', *Acta Acad. Aboensis*, Humaniora 18 (Abo, 1949), pp. 143–55.

(The problem is whether merely the main idea, or also the conception of what is decent according to the order of creation, should be regarded as binding for the Church today.)

The idea of a Christian marriage is a very characteristic proof of the practical consequences of the correspondence between the first and the last things. In Eph. v. 21–33 the theme is the relation between husband and wife, which has its model in the relation of Christ to the Church. The exhortation is strengthened by a reference to Gen. ii. 24. According to the hermeneutical principle that the last things shall be like the first, this text is taken to point to Christ as the 'Man' and the Church as his wife. But this 'mysterious' interpretation does not exclude the literal one; it gives it a definite validity. The marriage which reflects the relation between Christ and the Church, is at the same time the marriage which corresponds to the will of the Creator.

In I Cor. vi. 16f. we find a similar application of Gen. ii. 24 in a more individualized form: 'He who is joined to the Lord becomes one spirit (with him).' The introduction of the word 'spirit' is due to the superiority of the eschatological antitype, as in I Cor. xv. 45. The idea is here that the union with Christ, which is the eschatological fulfilment of Gen. ii. 24, should make fornication impossible, whereas it sanctifies marriage (cf. I Cor. vii. 14). Marriage belongs to 'the form of this world' which is passing away (I Cor. vii. 25–31); and yet, the order of creation is not to be destroyed but rather to be restored in the 'eschatological community' of the Church.

We may at this point add some general remarks on Pauline ethics. Its basis can be said to be eschatological, christological and sacramental. But the concrete content of the exhortations is to a considerable extent ethical commonplace, well known also to Judaism and Hellenism. The 'great mystery' of Eph. v, for example, motivates rather traditional moral commands of a *Haustafel.* The somewhat sublime arguments of I Cor. xi. 2ff. are corroborated by a reference to what is decent and proper, according to common opinion and the teaching of nature (xi. 13–14). This and similar appeals to 'natural law' are not due to any lack of consistency; they are in full harmony with the Apostle's fundamental conviction, that what is realized in the Church, the new creation, is in harmony with the original will of God the Creator. Sin corrupts creation; deification of the creature in the end leads to unnaturalness (Rom. i). But in the Church all natural, human virtues should be in high esteem (Phil. iv. 8).[1]

Not only the personal relation between men is restored in Christ, but also the right relation to material things. The great christological hymn in Col. i implies an indirect polemic against the asceticism of the false teachers. Later in the Epistle Paul goes on to say that Christians, who are dead with Christ to the *stoicheia tou kosmou*, are therefore free to use what God has created, the things which 'perish when they are used' (Col. ii. 20–3; cf. Rom. xiv. 6, 14; I Tim. iv. 4). The paradoxical situation of the Church here becomes very clear; Christians are no longer living 'in the world', but just because of this they are free from 'ordinances' and free to make use of the material things, without discrimination. In a similar way, there is a clear inner unity between the theological statement in I Cor. viii. 6 and the practical rules given in x. 23 ff., to eat whatever is sold in the meat market. 'The earth and its fullness' belongs to the Lord, and in Christ men are made free to make the right use of it.

The doctrine of correspondence between the first and the last things has in this way very practical consequences. Christian ethics are more other-worldly than Jewish, but at the same time characterized by a free and thankful acceptance of all gifts of the Creator, without any legal restrictions. The inner unity between these two apparently divergent tendencies is given by the fundamental, eschatological conception. Where this has been lost, the other-worldliness has deviated into a dualistic asceticism or a pietistic *blosse Innerlichkeit*, and the positive attitude to the world has resulted in tendencies towards an ecclesiastical world-domination, or in a cultural optimism and evolutionism on a religious basis.

Against such deviations, it is important to reconsider the Biblical, and especially Pauline doctrine, that the purpose of the Creator is realized in the new creation, that is in Christ, who is both the mediator of creation and the first-born from the dead, the head of the Church. In the Church men are included in this new creation in Christ. The Gospel is itself a divine word of creation, like the first

[1] Cf. C. H. Dodd, 'Natural Law in the Bible', *Theology* (1946), pp. 130–3, 161–7. (On this subject Professor Dodd lectured in Oslo, when he received his honorary doctor's degree.)

'let light shine out of darkness' (II Cor. iv. 6). In baptism the 'old man' is put off and the 'new man' is put on.[1] The Gospel and the sacraments are the means by which the Church on earth is called into existence as the eschatological community, in which the will of the Creator is brought to realization.

The restoration of creation in Christ is not simply an empirical, visible fact; like the life of the Christians it can rather be said to be hidden with Christ in God (Col. iii. 3). Creation is in the present time not yet delivered from the futility to which it was subjected. It is still 'groaning', and even those who are in Christ and have received the Spirit as firstfruits, are groaning and waiting with patience. Until the day of redemption they have to endure sufferings; their relation to the course of events in the world is restored only in so far as they know that 'everything works for good with those who love God' (Rom. viii. 18–28).

Christians have to face sufferings, and they have also to face temptations. There exists a real danger, that the deception of Eve shall also find an analogy within the Church, a satanic travesty of the correspondence between the first and the last things (II Cor. xi. 3). But sufferings and temptations are not the only actual experiences of Christians; the renewal of the 'new man' in a life of Christian virtues is also part of their experience (Col. iii. 10ff.). The Spirit makes the transformation into the likeness of Christ, 'from glory to glory', beginning already here and now (II Cor. iii. 18). The Church is growing towards its eschatological perfection (Eph. iv. 13ff.).

That the life of the Church is, at the same time, marked by sufferings and temptations, and by renewal and growth, may seem to be paradoxical. But this paradox is only the reflection of the faith, that it is the crucified and resurrected Lord who is the beginning

[1] Nearly all the texts about the new creation seem in some way to have the renewal at baptism in view, however the relation between the creative act of God in Christ and the baptismal rite is to be defined. Cf. the studies of Hansen and Sahlin (above, pp. 436 n. 2, 437 n. 1), Lindeskog, *op. cit.* pp. 252ff. and also my article 'Dopet i Efesierbrevet', *Svensk Teol. Kvartalskrift* (1945), pp. 85–103. The hymnic texts, praising Christ as the mediator of creation and of salvation, like Col. i. 15–20 and Heb. i. 2ff., probably also have a liturgical background, perhaps especially in the eucharistic thanksgiving. Cf. p. 424 n. 1 above, and also my study 'Anamnesis', *Stud. Theol.* vol. 1 (1947), esp. pp. 86f.

and archetype of the new creation. The growth of the Church is growth towards him (Eph. iv. 15). The signature of the new creation is therefore conformity with Christ in sufferings and future glory (Rom. viii. 17ff.; Phil. iii. 8ff.), a glory which is already partly anticipated by the activity of the Spirit.

The Pauline idea of a restoration of creation in the Church is rightly understood only if the main emphasis is laid, not upon any moral and social ameliorations, but upon the participation in Christ through the Gospel and the sacraments, leading to conformity with him in life. Accordingly, the Church's conformity with creation is dependent upon its conformity with Christ.

Outside the Pauline corpus, the idea of correspondence between the first and the last things is not in the same direct way applied to the doctrine of Christ and the Church. The fundamental idea can, however, be expressed in a different terminology, where the eschatological conception differs from the Pauline pattern. Some incidental remarks on the Epistle to the Hebrews will have made this clear. In still another way also the Fourth Gospel stresses the intimate connection between the work of God in creation and in salvation: 'The gospel is a record of a life which expresses the eternal thought of God, the meaning of the universe', to put it in the words of C. H. Dodd.[1]

I would now only like to add a few remarks on the interpretation of the Synoptic Gospels. Here, too, we must take care not to elaborate with a false antithesis between eschatology and the work and will of God the Creator. The miracles of Jesus should, for instance, hardly be understood as *either* eschatological signs *or* deeds of mercy; they are one of these things in being the other. In a similar way, the moral teaching of Jesus insists upon the original will of the Creator, and just in this way it is the revelation of the will of God for the last days, in which the Kingdom of God is proclaimed on earth.[2] The freedom of Jesus with regard to Sabbath laws is derived from his messianic authority, and at the same time brings the purpose of the

[1] Here just before finishing the article, I can make use of the magistral work of C. H. Dodd, *The Interpretation of the Fourth Gospel* (Cambridge, 1953). The citation is taken from p. 284.

[2] Cf. Jeremias, *Jesus als Weltvollender*, p. 68; H. J. Schoeps, '*Restitutio principii*, as the basis of the *Nova Lex Jesu*', *Journ. Bibl. Lit.* (1947), pp. 453–64.

Creator to realization: 'The sabbath was made for man, not man for the sabbath' (Mark ii. 23–8).

Even other points might be mentioned. It is, however, impossible here to pursue the investigation any further. The intention of my article has not been to exhaust the material, but only to draw attention to an important aspect of the 'realized eschatology' of the New Testament, in the hope that I could also bring clarification at some points.

23

ESCHATOLOGIE BIBLIQUE ET IDÉALISME PLATONICIEN

J. HERING

I. INTRODUCTION

Il y a un quart de siècle parut un livre écrit avec un enthousiasme tout juvénil et portant ce titre: *Platonic Tradition in English Religious Thought.* Il avait pour auteur le Dean Inge, alors bientôt septuagénaire, et visait bien plus haut que l'élucidation de quelques problèmes historiques. Résumant les études et les réflexions d'une grande partie de sa vie, l'illustre Doyen de St Paul rompait une lance en faveur de la restauration d'un 'troisième type de christianisme' à côté du catholicisme et du protestantisme, à savoir le 'christianisme platonicien', qui aurait existé dès les premiers temps du christianisme.

Inge n'était évidemment pas le seul à porter à cette époque un jugement très positif sur les synthèses entre christianisme et platonisme, qui avaient souvent été élaborées par des chrétiens à tendance mystique. Des savants comme Bigg en Angleterre, comme De Faye en France et beaucoup d'autres, avaient au début de notre siècle étudié avec sympathie les théologiens Alexandrins qui furent les principaux fondateurs de cette 'troisième confession'. Et nombreux étaient aussi les intellectuels non théologiens, qui désiraient une nouvelle célébration du mariage entre christianisme et platonisme.[1] D'une manière générale on peut dire que le fameux problème appelé 'Christianisme et Humanisme' se ramenait presque toujours en dernière analyse à la question: 'Christianisme et Platonisme.'

Il est certain qu'un revirement s'est fait depuis lors. Les théologiens

[1] Rien n'est plus caractéristique à ce sujet que le jugement du philologue Edouard Schwartz, qui dans un compte-rendu très sympathique du livre de De Faye sur Clément n'hésitait pas à voir dans des passages particulièrement platonisants du grand Alexandrin 'quelque chose qui dépassait en beauté tout ce que les chrétiens ont écrit par ailleurs' (*Das Grossartigste was jemals ein Christ geschrieben hat*), *v. Hermes*, tome XXXVIII, pp. 75 suiv.

bibliques et les dogmaticiens notamment accusent de nos jours une attitude beaucoup plus réservée à l'égard de ce type de christianisme, et ce n'est pas dévoiler un mystère que de voir un des principaux motifs de ce renversement dans une appréciation plus positive de l'eschatologie du christianisme primitif, qu'une certaine théologie spiritualiste avait tendance à écarter comme appartenant à une forme périmée de la pensée — ou de l'imagination — chrétienne.

On ne voit pas bien, en effet, quelle place pouvait occuper par exemple l'espérance d'une résurrection et d'une création nouvelle dans une pensée religieuse pour laquelle la religion ne pouvait s'intéresser qu'à la vie de l'Esprit.[1]

Indubitablement on voyait alors dans l'eschatologie du Nouveau Testament une survivance malheureuse de l'apocalyptique juive, trop 'matérialiste' pour pouvoir être conservée. Si on employait encore le terme d'eschatologie, c'était pour exprimer la foi en un monde des esprits, débarrassé non seulement du péché, mais aussi de toutes les limitations d'un monde caractérisé par sa 'finitude'.

Emile Brunner, dans son étude *Erlebnis, Erkenntnis und Glaube* (2e et 3e éd. 1923), n'avait pas tort de parler d'une absence d'eschatologie chez les théologiens dits modernes (*Das eschatologische Loch*).

Il est vrai qu'Albert Schweitzer avait déjà au début de ce siècle entrepris de montrer la nécessité d'une interprétation eschatologique de l'Evangile, dans son étude magistrale *Von Reimarus bis Wrede*.[2] Mais affirmant la nécessité d'une évolution de la pensée chrétienne, il estimait que celle-ci pouvait se débarrasser de l'eschatologie évangélique, sans altérer l'essence de l'Evangile éternel. Ce n'est plus l'avis des eschatologues contemporains.

C'est encore un signe du temps que les études qui nous rappellent certaines particularités de la notion du *temps* présupposée par la Bible (et on pourrait ajouter: aussi par le Mazdéïsme) et opposée à celle

[1] Il est sans doute injuste de reprocher à des théologiens comme Auguste Sabatier (*Les Religions d'autorité et la religion de l'esprit*, Paris, 1903) d'avoir fait du Dieu chrétien une grandeur immanente à l'esprit humain. Mais les choses se passent comme si le Dieu transcendant ne pouvait agir que sur l'esprit des hommes. Dès lors les ponts entre Dieu et la Nature (y compris la nature humaine) sont pratiquement coupés. La Théologie s'intéresse 'à la vie de l'âme' seulement, le reste regarde les Facultés de Médecine et des Sciences exclusivement.

[2] 1906; 2ème éd. sous ce nom: *Geschichte der Leben-Jesu-Forschung* (1913). Traduction anglaise sous ce titre: *The Quest of the Historical Jesus* (1910).

de la philosophie grecque.[1] Tandis que celle-ci (la conception dite cyclique du temps), exclut toute possibilité de progrès et de nouveauté dans l'histoire humaine, celle-là (la conception dite linéaire) fait tendre le développement de la planète vers un but, qui permet de parler d'une histoire sacrée voulue par Dieu.

Il pourrait paraître superflu — *rebus sic stantibus* — d'apporter encore une contribution à la confrontation entre espérances chrétiennes (au sens biblique) et espérances platoniciennes. Mais il nous semble que les clous ne sont pas toujours enfoncés à la bonne place. Nulle part ailleurs peut-être, les malentendus et les confusions risquent d'être aussi nombreux que dans toute tentative de parler des idées chrétiennes de 'l'au-delà'. De plus, nous estimons que ni l'histoire ni la dogmatique ne peuvent se contenter d'envisager ces problèmes *in abstracto*. C'est pourquoi il nous a paru intéressant de souligner ce qu'on pourrait appeler, avec un terme en usage en géologie, les métamorphoses de contact qu'ont subies soit la pensée biblique soit la pensée platonicienne, chez des auteurs chrétiens des premiers siècles, dans l'esprit desquels les deux couches de tradition se sont rencontrées. Car ces phénomènes nous montrent sur des points précis, dans quelle mesure une véritable synthèse entre les deux courants est essentiellement possible ou non.

Comme il nous faut faire un choix, nous attirerons l'attention du lecteur surtout sur la théologie de l'Epître aux Hébreux d'une part, sur l'eschatologie d'Origène d'autre part, ce qui naturellement nous amènera aussi à jeter d'abord un coup d'œil sur le platonisme juif de Philon, qui est un peu le père du platonisme chrétien.

2. PHILON

L'interprétation de la doctrine du grand rabbin Alexandrin est souvent rendue ardue par le caractère touffu de son œuvre, ainsi que par sa terminologie flottante. Nous espérons néanmoins arriver à des résultats satisfaisants en la question qui nous intéresse ici.

Jetons d'abord un coup d'œil sur sa doctrine de la création. On peut la définir comme le résultat d'une rencontre entre le Timée et la Genèse. On sait que d'après le fameux traité platonicien, dont

[1] Oscar Cullmann, *Christ et le Temps* (1947); traduction angl. par F. Filson (S.C.M. Press, London, et Westminster Press, Philadelphia).

l'interprétation détaillée n'est pas toujours aisée, mais dont les grandes lignes se détachent assez bien, Dieu a créé d'abord les idées, puis les esprits, ensuite, par l'intermédiaire de divinités inférieures, le monde visible — celui-ci représentant quelque chose comme l'empreinte donnée, à l'aide des idées, à une ὕλη, entité amorphe, qui joue, par rapport aux idées, le rôle d'une matière première.

En ce qui concerne le monde invisible, cette cosmologie ne créait pas de difficultés particulières à Philon, lequel, à l'aide de la méthode allégorique, la retrouvait dans la Genèse,[1] et ceci d'autant plus facilement qu'il avait l'habitude d'identifier les idées avec les anges.

Mais que pensait-il de la préexistence d'une matière à la création visible? Certains historiens ont voulu lui prêter cette doctrine. C'est ainsi qu'Emile Bréhier, tout en recommandant une grande prudence dans l'utilisation du traité *De aeternitate mundi* (ou *De incorruptibilitate mundi*),[2] pensait que Philon — qui ne parle jamais autrement du Créateur qu'en employant les termes δημιουργός ou τεχνίτης ou d'autres expressions équivalentes — ne lui attribue en aucune manière la création d'une matière. 'Aussi, dit-il, la création se fait sur la matière, mais cette matière n'est pas l'objet d'une création. L'action divine reste toujours celle d'un démiurge.'[3] Une création *ex nihilo* ne serait admise par notre Alexandrin que pour le monde invisible.

Nous ne pouvons cependant pas nous ranger à l'avis de l'illustre historien. Comme l'ont montré récemment les recherches approfondies de Wolfson,[4] les textes décisifs du *De opificio mundi* ne laissent que peu de doute à ce sujet: Philon croyait non seulement à la création du monde, mais aussi à la création du 'chaos' par Dieu. Même le temps et l'espace sont l'œuvre du Créateur, ce qui exclut toute possibilité de leur faire jouer le rôle d'une ὕλη préexistante.

[1] Vide *De opificio mundi*, ch. 2, § 7 et suiv.; ch. 7, § 29; ch. 13, § 44; ch. 44, §§ 129–30.

[2] Bréhier croit à l'authenticité de ce traité. Mais il craint que l'auteur n'y résume des doctrines étrangères à la sienne propre. Vide *Les Idées philosophiques et religieuses de Philon d'Alexandrie* (1908), pp. 80 suiv. Le cas serait alors analogue à celui des *Excerpta e Theodoto* de Clément d'Alexandrie.

[3] Vide *ibidem*, p. 81. Edouard Herriot, dans son livre injustement oublié sur *Philon le Juif* (1898), avait déjà soutenu la même explication; vide p. 319: 'Bien qu'il ne se soit pas nettement expliqué sur ce point, il semble bien avoir admis antérieurement à la création une matière chaotique et informe.'

[4] H. A. Wolfson, *Philo*, 2 vols (Cambridge, Mass., 1947); vide surtout vol. I, pp. 306 suiv.

Et cependant — détail piquant que le savant livre américain ne semble pas avoir entrevu — la Genèse ne souffle mot de la création du Chaos (*tohou-va-bohou*). C'est donc ici ou nulle part que le philosophe alexandrin eût pu trouver un texte biblique en faveur de l'éternité de la matière, si vraiment il eût voulu l'enseigner. Mais avec le rabbinisme de son époque, il tient à la création *ex nihilo*.

Voici donc un point où l'union entre Platonisme et Judaïsme s'est révélée impossible. Philon a dû infliger une grave entorse à la cosmologie du 'Timée'. Et cette prise de position est devenue paradigmatique pour les théologiens chrétiens, qui d'ailleurs pouvaient s'appuyer, pour l'enseignement de la *creatio ex nihilo*, sur des textes bien plus probants que Genèse i (par exemple sur le Prologue johannique).

Mais ce qui est encore plus intéressant, c'est d'examiner les idées de notre rabbin sur la fin du monde. C'est ici qu'une surprise attend les lecteurs qui pourraient croire à une influence sérieuse de l'apocalyptique sur le Judaïsme de la Diaspora: L'idée même de la fin du monde est rejetée. Ce n'est pas que le Cosmos serait incorruptible par lui-même. Ce que Dieu a créé, il peut aussi le détruire. Mais les promesses faites à Noé après le déluge permettent d'espérer (!) la perdurance de la Création.[1] Le thème d'un éon corrompu réclamant son remplacement par un autre a tout aussi peu de place ici que l'enseignement stoïcien sur les catastrophes périodiques.

On peut toutefois se demander si Philon ne conserve pas quelque chose des espérances messianiques juives devant se réaliser dans *notre* monde. On ne s'étonnera pas de constater qu'il les a spiritualisées à l'aide de la méthode allégorique. Le règne messianique finit par se réduire au règne universel de la loi (interprêtée convenablement, cela va sans dire), qui un jour sera acceptée par tous les peuples.[2] L'idée messianique s'est donc modifiée, mais sans s'évanouir complètement. L'histoire humaine a un sens; car elle tend vers un but connu et voulu par Dieu. Nous sommes en présence de quelque chose comme la conception irréversible (*vulgo*: linéaire) du temps, manifestation de la sensibilité biblique de notre auteur.

On voit que la balance ne peut jamais rester en suspens: Nous venons de signaler deux cas où elle penche plus ou moins nettement en faveur du Judaïsme. Le cas inverse peut s'observer, si nous

[1] Vide la discussion de cette question chez Wolfson, vol. I, pp. 316–48.

[2] Vide *Vita Mosis*, I, ch. I, § 2; II, ch. 4, §§ 20–4; ch. 5, § 25; ch. 12. §§ 63–4.

interrogeons notre Alexandrin sur la résurrection corporelle. Après tout ce qui précède, on ne s'étonnera pas de voir disparaître ce théologoumène. Aucun de ses interprêtes n'en a retrouvé la moindre trace.[1] Bréhier ne se donne même pas la peine de signaler cette disparition. Le fait est que ni le fameux texte de Daniel (xii. 1–3) ni ceux du 2e livre des Macchabées (surtout vii. 9–14) — écrits canoniques à Alexandrie ! — ne semblent avoir impressioné notre platonicien juif. Il n'y voit que des témoignages en faveur de l'immortalité de l'âme, et c'est à cette croyance que se réduit la doctrine de la résurrection.[2] Dans les *Quaestiones in Genesin iii*, ch. xi, on nous explique que l'âme retourne 'à la métropole de sa patrie', d'où elle avait 'émigré' primitivement pour entrer dans un corps (cf. Wolfson, vol. I, p. 404).

Selon *Cherubin*, ch. 32, § 114, les âmes se dirigent vers une παλιγγενεσία, où elles vivront avec des êtres incorporels (μετὰ ἀσωμάτων).

Mais l'âme humaine est-elle immortelle par essence, comme dans le Phédon ? Ou bien subsiste-t-elle par une grâce accordée par la Divinité ? Sur ce point important, nous ne recevons guère de réponse claire. Dans certains textes, Philon insiste sur la 'mort' éternelle des âmes des méchants. Mais encore que Wolfson (vol. I, pp. 409–11) incline à prendre ces déclarations au sens littéral, on ne peut être sûr que le terme de 'mort' n'ait pas un sens purement religieux, signifiant quelque chose comme l'absence de la vision de Dieu ou simplement le rejet de l'âme par Dieu. Ailleurs il parle de l'âme comme si son immortalité allait de soi. Il est inutile d'étudier ici les textes, dont l'examen, de toute manière, se termine par un *non liquet*.

Mais revenons à la négation de la résurrection corporelle. Nous avons voulu rappeler qu'elle est rendue nécessaire par le platonisme de l'auteur.

Toutefois il ne faut pas oublier que Philon n'est pas le seul à prendre — à l'encontre du Rabbinisme palestinien — cette attitude. On sait que les Sadducéens, hostiles, pour d'autres motifs, à toute

[1] Vide E. R. Goodenough, *By Light, Light* (New Haven, 1935), pp. 79, 367 suiv. ; Wolfson, vol. I, pp. 404 suiv.

[2] Goodenough insiste sur les parallèles que présente sur ce point — comme sur d'autres — l'enseignement philonien avec celui de la Cabbale. Mais l'antiquité de celle-ci, telle que nous la connaissons, n'a pas encore pu être démontrée péremptoirement, tandis que l'influence du Platonisme sur Philon est patente.

apocalyptique, rejetaient également la doctrine de la résurrection. Et quant aux livres de la 'Sagesse', en grande partie d'origine alexandrine et se ressentant sans doute déjà d'une certaine influence grecque, ils semblent eux aussi l'ignorer.

Mais il va sans dire que pour les penseurs chrétiens la situation sera beaucoup plus dramatique, comme nous le verrons encore en détail. Car il est bien difficile de nier le rôle énorme joué dans le christianisme primitif par la doctrine des deux éons successifs et ses conséquences.

3. L'ÉPÎTRE AUX HÉBREUX

Le cas de l'auteur ad Hebraeos est encore plus curieux que celui de Philon. Lui aussi s'efforce d'intégrer sa théologie dans le cadre d'une cosmologie manifestement très apparentée au platonisme. Il est vrai qu'à y regarder de près, il s'agit d'un platonisme juif, très proche de celui de Philon. Mais ceci ne simplifie pas la question sur le point que nous avons à examiner, à savoir l'eschatologie. Car si l'opposition entre les deux éons joue un rôle relativement effacé dans l'A.T., si bien qu'on pouvait sans difficulté rester théologien juif en la niant, il en est autrement sur le terrain de l'Evangile, où elle est présupposée même lorsqu'elle n'est pas expressément développée.

Or, la cosmologie de l'auteur aux Hébreux est manifestement dominée par l'idée platonisante de deux mondes superposés et coëxistants, à savoir celui des 'noumènes' et celui des 'phénomènes'. C'est ce qui ressort par exemple de la célèbre affirmation de xi. 3: 'C'est par la foi que nous savons que les mondes sont ordonnés par la parole de Dieu, de sorte que le monde visible ne tire pas son origine des phénomènes (εἰς τὸ μὴ ἐκ φαινομένων τὸ βλεπόμενον γεγονέναι).' Ce qui intéresse l'auteur, c'est que le monde visible ne s'explique pas par lui-même. Mais l'emploi du terme φαινόμενα, introduit sans explication comme un terme familier, terme qui n'a pas de sens sans sa contrepartie, qui serait νοούμενα, est extrêmement caractéristique et trahit son origine platonicienne ou philonienne.[1]

Les longs développements très philonisants sur le vrai tabernacle,

[1] Sur les rapprochements de détails à faire entre l'exégèse de l'A.T. faite respectivement par Philon et par l'épître aux Hébreux, le *standard work* est toujours le livre magistral d'Eugène Ménégoz, *La Théologie de l'Épître aux Hébreux* (1894).

L'étude la plus récente, à notre connaissance, est celle du R. P. Spicq, 'Le Philonisme de l'Épître aux Hébreux' (*Revue Biblique*, octobre 1949 et avril 1950),

qui se trouve dans le monde invisible (dont le tabernacle de Moïse et d'Aaron n'était qu'une pâle copie) et en lequel le Grand Prêtre céleste célèbre un culte parfait, s'accordent très bien avec cette opposition entre le monde invisible et le monde matériel et imparfait. (Vide surtout chs. 8 et 9.)

Ce cadre idéaliste a lourdement pesé sur l'eschatologie de notre épître. Car tout aussi peu que chez Philon, on ne voit, pour signaler de suite l'essentiel, la place qu'y pourrait trouver la doctrine de la résurrection. Celle-ci, en effet, s'inscrit en faux contre la dévalorisation des choses visibles, le monde de la résurrection n'étant nullement dépourvu de corporéité. De plus, la résurrection suppose l'apparition d'un monde nouveau, qui est encore dans l'avenir, et inconnu des platoniciens. Le salut dans le cadre de la cosmologie platonicienne ne peut consister que dans le passage dans le monde invisible, où le croyant rencontrera Dieu. De fait, le thème de la résurrection, comme l'ont observé la plupart des commentateurs, est presque totalement absent. La résurrection du Sauveur n'est mentionnée nulle part. On insiste simplement sur sa montée au Ciel, qui semble se produire immédiatement après la mort sur la croix. C'est ce passage 'à travers les cieux' (iv. 14) jusque dans le Saint des Saints au Ciel suprême qui devient un des thèmes essentiels de notre épître. On a pu dire avec raison que la christologie de la Résurrection, qui dominait le Paulinisme, est remplacée ici par celle de l'Ascension.

Quant à la doctrine de la résurrection des morts en général ou celle des chrétiens, en particulier l'auteur ne la mentionne qu'en passant parmi les enseignements élémentaires que les destinataires de l'épître eussent dû dépasser depuis longtemps: v. 12, 'vous devriez déjà être des docteurs (διδάσκαλοι), mais il faut encore vous enseigner les rudiments des principes de la Théologie'.

qui après un examen minutieux de la question, accepte la thèse d'Eugène Ménégoz, d'après laquelle l'auteur de l'Épître doit être un disciple de Philon converti au Christianisme.

Quand à l'étude de J. Cambier, *Eschatologie et Hellénisme dans l'Épître aux Hébreux* (*Analecta Lovaniensia Biblica et Orientalia*, II/12), elle est également très affirmative sur l'Hellénisme de notre épitre: 'l'Eschatologie des Hébreux n'est pas le renouvellement du monde créé... elle est au contraire une révélation de l'au-delà et du monde éternel et durable, comme étant la véritable réalité dont le premier monde n'est qu'une figure' (p. 26). Mais cette étude néglige l'autre aspect de la question (vide infra).

Et parmi ces principes il énumère (vi. I suiv.) la repentance, la foi en Dieu, l'enseignement sur les baptèmes (*sic*), l'imposition des mains, la résurrection des morts et le jugement dernier. On peut même se demander si l'enseignement supérieur ne devait pas comprendre, comme chez Philon, une interprétation spiritualiste de la résurrection.

Peut-être l'auteur n'est-il pas allé jusque là. Mais en tout cas, la résurrection est un thème qui le gène et qu'il met de côté le plus possible. Nous assistons ici à une métamorphose, et même à un écrasement de la couche chrétienne de par le contact avec la couche platonisante.

Mais ce n'est là qu'un aspect de la question. Car si l'eschatologie platonicienne commande, comme l'a démontré le Doyen Inge, une mystique particulière, alors la mystique congéniale serait celle qui aspire au retour de l'âme dans le monde invisible, dont elle est issue, c'est-à-dire dans un monde qui préexistait à la création visible. Mais il est très curieux de constater que notre auteur répugne à une pareille attitude. Le retour pur et simple de l'âme dans sa patrie, comme chez Philon et dans toutes les mystiques gnostiques,[1] ne peut le satisfaire. Sa sensibilité de chrétien s'y refuse. Car s'il pense en grec, il sent en chrétien (comme De Faye, dans ses cours, avait l'habitude de s'exprimer à propos de Clément d'Alexandrie).

L'objet de l'espérance chrétienne doit donc malgré tout se présenter sous la forme d'une patrie *future* qui n'a jamais existé comme telle auparavant, ni avant la naissance de l'âme ni avant la création du monde. Rien de plus caractéristique que le choix d'Abraham comme prototype du chrétien. Pourquoi Abraham? C'est parce que le patriarche, ayant la foi en les promesses divines, s'est mis en marche *vers une patrie inconnue*. 'Par la foi, Abraham, lorsqu'il fut appelé, obéit et partit vers un endroit (τόπος) qu'il devait recevoir en héritage, et il partit sans savoir où il irait' (xi. 8).

Et cette patrie nouvelle, on ne peut même pas dire que c'était uniquement la Palestine. Car ce pays devient typologiquement

[1] Le témoignage le plus émouvant de cette mystique se trouve dans le fameux chant *Chant de la Perle* conservé dans les *Acta Thomae*. — On sait que le poète suisse C. Spitteler, qui était aussi un mystique à la manière des gnostiques, a développé ce thème d'une manière magistrale dans un de ses poèmes appelé *Der verlorene Sohn*, ce qu'il faudrait traduire plutôt par 'l'enfant égaré' que par 'le fils prodigue' (dans sa collection *Extramundana*).

quelque chose comme l'annonce d'un pays surnaturel. C'est pourquoi l'auteur (xi. 10) peut lui attribuer l'espérance en une cité qui a 'les fondations' (τοὺς θεμελίους), sans doute des fondations surnaturelles, et dont Dieu est l'artisan et le démiurge (τεχνίτης καὶ δημιουργός).[1]

Il n'y a donc aucun doute: *La mystique du retour est remplacée par la mystique du départ.* Et c'est dans ce sens que le départ d'Israël et son séjour provisoire au désert, devient également un type de la vie du chrétien (thème développé au ch. 4), qui accuse un caractère essentiellement nomade. Et ce nomadisme n'est pas un simple égarement. Il a un but fixé par les promesses divines. Toute la vie de l'Eglise est dominée par l'espérance, à tel point que la foi elle-même est synonyme d'espérance. Car la foi au fond n'est rien d'autre que l'anticipation de ce qu'on espère, la certitude des choses invisibles (xi. 1).[2]

C'est pourquoi nous assistons à ce spectacle curieux: La conception dite linéaire du temps est réclamée par l'idée que notre auteur se fait du nomadisme. Mais d'autre part il ignore tout de la doctrine d'une création nouvelle, qui ailleurs dans le christianisme est l'aboutissement normal du développement 'des temps'.

Il ne reste qu'une manière de concilier le caractère futuriste eschatologique de l'espérance chrétienne avec le cadre idéaliste de cette pensée: c'est au Ciel même qu'une transformation doit s'opérer de manière à offrir aux croyants une patrie invisible et cependant nouvelle. C'est précisément ce que le Grand prêtre chrétien a accompli (vi. 20; viii. 1–2; iv. 14; ix. 15; x. 12; x. 19–22). Il a frayé à ses adhérents un chemin vers une région suprême, où il inaugure un culte nouveau, dont le culte aaronien n'était qu'une faible préfiguration (σκιὰ τῶν μελλόντων), l'ombre de quelque chose qui n'existe pas encore et non pas comme un vrai platonicien devrait dire, l'ombre des idées préexistantes (x. 1).

Et ce culte céleste ne peut se célébrer que parce que le nouveau Sacrificateur s'est sacrifié lui-même sur la Croix — ἅπαξ, ou ἐφάπαξ,

[1] On remarque ici, une fois de plus, comme chez Philon, des termes platoniciens, mais qui ne changent rien à l'inspiration chrétienne de ce passage.

[2] Mais si ces choses sont invisibles, ce n'est pas comme chez l'apôtre Paul parce que nous ne les voyons pas encore. Le terme οὐ βλεπόμενα prend immédiatement un autre sens. La cité de Dieu appartient entièrement au monde incorporel.

une fois pour toutes (ix. 26–8; vii. 27; ix. 12) (expressions extrèmement caractéristiques pour la conception chrétienne du temps), inaugurant une nouvelle phase dans l'histoire du monde et menant les chrétiens dans leur patrie nouvelle. C'est ainsi que l'idée chrétienne d'un but assigné à l'histoire, reprend ses droits, mais en sacrifiant tout ce qui pourrait conférer une corporéité quelconque au monde parfait de l'humanité intègre.

Nous ne pouvons insister davantage sur les détails. Nous avons simplement voulu montrer que les difficultés que notre auteur éprouve à concilier platonisme et christianisme, nc sont pas seulement d'ordre historique, mais d'ordre *essentiel*. Si la synthèse semble parfois réussir, grâce à l'ingéniosité de l'auteur, ce n'est qu'au prix de concessions de part et d'autre, qui aboutissent à un style architectural peu homogène de sa pensée.

4. ORIGÈNE

Le cas d'Origène est également très caractéristique pour la modification profonde que l'idéal platonicien peut imposer à l'eschatologie chrétienne. On sait que le grand théologien croyait à la résurrection future. Et il n'est pas étonnant qu'il ait insisté sur les qualités surnaturelles des corps de la résurrection. D'après certains renseignements dignes de foi il leur aurait même attribué une forme sphérique,[1] sans doute parce que la sphère était considérée comme le corps géométrique absolument parfait, peut-être aussi parceque les anges des étoiles étaient censés posséder des corps de cette forme.[2]

Cependant cet état résurrectionnel ne satisfait pas entièrement son idéalisme. Car ces corps-là, si ténus et si parfaits qu'ils soient, appartiennent encore au monde visible. Ils conservent donc encore un reste de matérialité et par conséquent quelque chose comme un souvenir de la chûte, laquelle est à l'origine du monde visible. C'est

[1] D'après le 10e anathème du Concile 543, Origène attribuait au corps du Réssuscité et des réssuscités des formes sphériques: ὡς τὸ τοῦ Κυρίου σῶμα αἰθέριον καὶ σφαιροειδὲς τῷ σχήματι, καὶ ὅτι τὰ τοιαῦτα καὶ τῶν λοιπῶν ἐξ' ἀναστάσεως ἔσται σώματα (cité par Koetschau au 5e volume, p. 176, de son édition des *Opera* d'Origène). L'empereur Justinien, dans sa lettre à Menas (citée *ibidem*) s'exprime dans le même sens. Cf. De Faye, *Origène, sa vie, son œuvre, sa pensée*, IIIe tome (1928), p. 253.

[2] Vide *Timée* 33B et 63A.

pourquoi, d'après des textes transmis par Jérôme et par Justinien, plus sûrs que la traduction latine du *De principiis* faite par Rufin, il enseigne que le monde de la résurrection n'est, dans le développement des choses, que l'avant dernier des mondes. A la fin, lorsque 'tout pouvoir sera remis au Père', les créatures rentreront dans le monde invisible, redevenant ainsi des νόες ou des οὐσίαι λογικαί. D'abord le Seigneur déposera son corps (sous entendu le corps de la Résurrection). Ensuite les corps de 'tous' disparaîtront dans le non-être.[1]

Il va sans dire qu'alors toute différence essentielle entre les hommes et les anges aura disparu. Que nous sommes loin de la thèse paulinienne de la supériorité essentielle des hommes par rapport aux anges (vide I Cor. vi. 3)!

Du coup s'évanouit aussi ce que nous avons par ailleurs appelé l'humanisme biblique, qui donne à l'homme, seule créature faite à l'image de Dieu, une place exceptionnelle dans L'Univers. L'homme, comme chez Platon, n'est que la rencontre fortuite entre un esprit immortel et une matière périssable.[2]

Mais les hommes non convertis ainsi que les démons pourront-ils jamais atteindre ce stade de félicité? Nous abordons ici un autre point de la doctrine d'Origène qu'on lui a également amèrement reproché: Il se serait laissé influencer sinon par la lettre, du moins par l'esprit de la sotériologie platonicienne en ce qui concerne le destin des âmes humaines. On sait que Platon, utilisant certains thèmes de la religion populaire, mais leur donnant (à la manière des Pythagoriciens et des Orphiques), une signification morale intéressante,

[1] καὶ ὅτι αὐτοῦ κυρίου πρῶτον ἀποτιθεμένου τὸ ἴδιον αὐτοῦ σῶμα καὶ πάντων ὁμοίως εἰς τὸ ἀνύπαρκτον χωρήσει ἡ τῶν σωμάτων φύσις (cité par Koetschau, vol. v, p. 176); cf. la discussion de ces textes par De Faye, vol. III, pp. 242, 253 suiv. C'est un des grands mérites de l'ouvrage de De Faye, d'avoir fait l'étude critique des textes conservés en latin par Rufin à l'aide d'autres sources et d'avoir prouvé définitivement le caractère tendancieux de la traduction de Rufin. En outre De Faye s'est donné la peine de fouiller le commentaire de l'Evangile de Jean par Origène (conservé en grec comme on sait), le *Contra Celsum* et de nombreux autres ouvrages du grand Alexandrin pour reconstituer, sur des bases solides, la Théologie, la Christologie et la Cosmologie du maître. On peut s'étonner que certaines publications postérieures, paraissant ignorer ce travail critique, continuent à utiliser sans méfiance le *de principiis* dans la traduction de Rufin.

[2] Vide J. Héring, 'Die biblischen Grundlagen des christlichen Humanismus' in *Abhandlungen zur Theologie des Alten und Neuen Testaments*, No. 7, Zürich.

avait enseigné la réincarnation, c'est-à-dire la croyance à des vies humaines multiples vécues par le même esprit.[1]

Or il n'est pas prouvé qu'Origène ait enseigné la doctrine des vies multiples sans cette forme-là. Mais comme il croit que notre monde sera suivi de beaucoup d'autres, il admet, pour certaines entités humaines et démoniaques, la possibilité de réapparitions dans ces éons successifs. Il semble qu'il y ait là une chance de salut offerte aux hommes non convertis dans notre monde ainsi qu'aux démons, et peut-être au diable lui-même.[2]

Cette conception des éons multiples est évidemment incompatible avec l'eschatologie biblique, si elle entend *remplacer* l'opposition radicale entre les deux éons (ὁ αἰὼν οὗτος et ὁ αἰὼν μέλλων) par la succession d'un certain nombre de mondes se rapprochant peu à peu de la perfection. Mais supposons qu'un gnosticisme chrétien enseignât la succession de plusieurs mondes *à l'intérieur* de notre éon,

[1] Voir surtout le récit d'Er à la fin de la *République*. On sait que ce personnage (que certains, on ne sait pourquoi, ont voulu rapprocher du patriarche nommé Luc iii. 28), après avoir été laissé pour mort sur un champ de bataille, reprit conscience après quelques jours et raconta ce qu'il avait vu dans l'au-delà. En prenant ce récit à la lettre, il faudrait même attribuer à Platon la doctrine de la métempsychose, c'est-à-dire la possibilité, pour des âmes humaines, de se réincarner en des corps d'animaux. Pour des raisons évidentes, cette hypothèse particulière, quoique réaffirmée dans le *Phèdre* 248–9, soulèverait de grandes difficultés à l'intérieur du Platonisme. Car l'âme humaine est un esprit rationnel, qui chez l'homme s'ajoute à l'âme inférieure qu'il possède en commun avec les animaux. Il est également certain que toute la mise en scène du récit d'Er ne représente qu'une imagerie utilisée par le mythe.

Mais le noyau de son enseignement, à savoir la doctrine des vies multiples, ne saurait être considéré comme une sorte d'appendice facultatif de la philosophie de Platon. C'est dans ce récit que culmine la 'Politeia', dont il fait comprendre les intentions profondes. Et certainement le philosophe veut par là allumer une grande lumière destinée à éclairer nos ténèbres. C'est pourquoi nous pensons que Goethe a bien platonisé en écrivant ces vers:

> Und solang du das nicht hast
> dieses 'Stirb und Werde',
> bist du nur ein trüber Gast
> auf der dunkeln Erde.

('Selige Sehnsucht', in *West-östlicher Diwan, Maganni Nameh.*)

[2] Vide surtout dans le Commentaire de l'Evangile de Jean (ch. 14 et 19 du tome XXXII), les développements au sujet de Judas Iscariot (éd. Koetschau, pp. 447 suiv. et 458 suiv.), ainsi que les textes de Jérôme et de Justinien indiqués par K. à propos du *de principiis*, I, ch. 6, § 3 et ch. 8, § 3 (éd. K. p. 88 suiv. et pp. 99 suiv.). Cf. la discussion chez De Faye, *Origène*, vol. III, pp. 262 suiv.

sans atténuer l'opposition de cet éon (pris dans son ensemble) à l'éon futur de la résurrection et de 'la gloire'. Eh bien, nous ne pensons pas qu'une pareille vision du monde serait *essentiellement* en contradiction avec les données bibliques fondamentales.

Mais ce que la dogmatique chrétienne devra toujours repousser — outre l'atténuation de l'opposition entre les deux mondes —, ce serait la tentative de mettre la doctrine des vies multiples (sous une forme ou sous une autre) au service d'une conception inadmissible du salut. En effet, dans l'Hindouisme comme dans le Platonisme, la multiplicité des vies doit donner à l'homme la possibilité d'atteindre peu à peu la perfection par ses propres moyens, c'est-à-dire à se sauver lui-même. Non seulement la notion, purement spiritualiste, du salut dans le Platonisme est différente de la notion biblique, non seulement le sentier à suivre est autre parce que le but est ailleurs, mais la puissance salvatrice n'est pas la même. D'une part on fait appel aux forces de la volonté, d'autre part à la grâce.[1]

Mais revenons à Origène. Il serait injuste de voir dans sa doctrine des éons multiples une tentative d'esquiver la nécessité de la rédemption par le Christ. Toute son œuvre protesterait contre une pareille interprétation. Mais ce qui constitue une sérieuse déviation de l'eschatologie biblique, c'est que le but assigné au monde visible par le Créateur, ce n'est pas sa réintégration et sa 'glorification', mais, sa disparition. Car tout doit finalement rentrer dans le monde invisible.

D'autre part, il ne faudrait en aucun cas attribuer à notre théologien la doctrine stoïcienne de la répétition exacte des mondes. Le Portique en effet connait aussi une succession de mondes (détruits chaque fois par le feu). Mais cette répétition est à la fois dénuée de but et de variété. A cette doctrine (reprise plus tard par F. Nietzsche) on pourrait appliquer le slogan français: Plus ça change, plus c'est la même chose.

[1] Qu'on nous entende bien: Le christianisme biblique tel que nous le concevons, n'est pas obligé de nier ou de désapprouver des progrès faits par l'humanité dans l'ordre de la civilisation ou dans le domaine des pouvoirs psychiques, mais il refusera de *confondre* ce mouvement processif avec la rédemption. D'autre part, il y a lieu de rappeler qu' 'Er' n'enseigne pas, comme Basilide, la conception vulgaire du Karma, d'après laquelle le destin d'une vie dépendrait uniquement de la somme des mérites ou des méfaits accumulés dans les vies antérieures. C'est seulement dans la période entre la mort et la naissance (dans l'au-delà) que les âmes récoltent ce qu'elles ont semé. Le cadre extérieur de la vie suivante sera le résultat d'un libre choix parmi une quantité de lots (choix fait avec plus au moins de sagesse naturellement).

Sur ce point, la sensibilité chrétienne de notre Père est si développée et si châtouilleuse que dans sa polémique contre le philosophe Celse il repousse avec horreur le thème de la répétition de toutes choses.

Et son argumentation caractérise très bien l'empreinte biblique que sa théologie a conservée malgré certains aspects grecs de son eschatologie: il faudrait, explique-t-il, si tout se répète, que non seulement Celse écrivît toujours à nouveau son *Discours vrai* — ce qui serait à la rigueur supportable — mais encore que toute *l'histoire sacrée* se répétât, ce qu'il déclare absolument impensable. Comme l'auteur ad Hebraeos et comme l'apôtre Paul, il a saisi l'importance de l'unicité dc l'histoire biblique. Si les événements revenaient dans les mondes successifs, alors Moïse devrait toujours à nouveau mener le peuple hors d'Egypte. Toujours à nouveau le Christ devrait mener sa vie palestinienne et être crucifié, ce qui est inadmissible.[1]

Pour conclure, nous constatons donc que si la sensibilité chrétienne du grand théologien égyptien reprend souvent le dessus, il n'en est pas moins vrai que son platonisme lui a imposé le sacrifice de certains thèmes importants de la pensée biblique.

5. CONCLUSIONS

Nos remarques sur l'Epître aux Hébreux ainsi que sur Origène nous ont donné l'occasion de confronter espérances bibliques et espérances platoniciennes.

Mais quelques précisions s'imposent encore sur les *conceptions respectives de la mort*, plus exactement sur la situation de l'homme entre la mort et l'achèvement final. C'est ici précisément que certaines confusions risquent de voiler la spécificité du message chrétien.

On serait tenté, à la lumière des constatations des sections précédents, de formuler de la manière suivante la différence essentielle entre le message chrétien et le message platonicien: le platonisme croit à l'immortalité de l'âme, le christianisme à la résurrection des morts. Ce résumé est exact en ce sens que le platonisme et le christianisme

[1] ἀνάγκη κατὰ τὰς τεταγμένας περιόδους (ces 5 mots empruntés à la polémique de Celse) Μωϋσέα μὲν περὶ τοῦ λαοῦ τῶν 'Ιουδαίων ἐξελθεῖν ἐκ τῆς Αἰγύπτου, 'Ιησοῦν δὲ πάλιν ἐπιδημῆσαι τὸν βίον τὰ αὐτὰ ποιήσοντα ἅπερ οὐχ ἅπαξ (!), ἀλλ' ἀπειράκις κατὰ περιόδους πεποίηκεν. (*Contra Celsum* IV, ch. 67; cf. *De principiis* II, ch. 3.)

enseignent en effet ces deux doctrines respectivement. Il serait encore exact en ce sens que le chrétien met son *espoir* dans le monde glorieux de la résurrection, que le platonicien ignore.

Mais la formule est inexact, si elle veut insinuer que Platon aurait vu dans l'immortalité une *garantie* de la félicité. En réalité, elle n'en constitue qu'une condition nécessaire, mais insuffisante. Une âme qui ne réussirait pas à s'affranchir de l'empire de la 'matière', aurait beau vivre éternellement, elle serait toujours condamnée à se réincarner et à subir des tourments entre la mort et la naissance suivante. La récit d'Er à la fin de la *République* ne laisse aucun doute à ce sujet.

La formule serait encore inexacte, si elle voulait prêter au christianisme primitif la négation de toute survie immédiatement après la mort. Dans le double paradigme (appelé maladroitement 'parabole') du mauvais riche et du pauvre Lazare (Luc xvi. 19–31), ni l'un ni l'autre de ces deux personnages n'est anéanti par la mort. Chacun, dans son existence *post mortem*, est doué d'intelligence et de sensibilité comme d'ailleurs aussi le patriarche Abraham, qui est une figure bien 'vivante'. Sans doute s'empressera-t-on de nous faire remarquer que Jésus — ou l'Evangéliste — emploie ici des 'images populaires' sur les différents genres d'existences dans l'au-delà, sans élever la prétention de nous offrir sur ce point un enseignement normatif. Nous accepterions volontiers cette interprétation en ce sens que la première partie de l'histoire (xvi. 19–26) pourrait bien avoir utilisé un thème 'ébionite' sur la compensation du destin terrestre dans l'au-delà. Il est juste que celui qui ici-bas a joui d'un bonheur plus ou moins immérité, apprenne à souffrir là-bas, tandis que le malheureux y trouvera des joies compensatrices, et cette manière de voir semble même expressément justifié par le verset 25.

Mais il ne faut pas oublier que sur cette histoire primitive se greffe une interprétation morale (*vv.* 27–31), qui en change profondément le sens: le riche est puni non pour sa richesse, mais pour son mépris de l'enseignement moral de 'Moïse et des Prophètes', c'est-à-dire de la Bible.

De même on peut inférer que Lazare n'est pas récompensé pour sa pauvreté, mais pour ses bonnes dispositions intérieures avec lesquelles il l'a supportée. La péricope, dans son ensemble, est donc spécifiquement chrétienne, et montre que la pensée chrétienne (sans accepter forcément les détails de l'imagerie) non seulement s'accommodait de la croyance à une certaine survie, mais qu'elle la prenait au sérieux.

N'oublions pas non plus la parole curieuse adressée par le Crucifié au 'bon larron' (Luc xxiii. 43), auquel il promet d'être encore 'aujourd'hui' au Paradis. Quelle que soit l'exégèse détaillée de cette prédiction, dont le ton solennel ('Amen!') reste impressionnant, il est intéressant de constater qu'elle ne parle nullement du Royaume de Dieu, mais d'un état intermédiaire présent (σήμερον) appelé 'Paradis'. Par là-même est affirmée la survie pour une période qui suit la mort immédiatement.

L'apôtre Paul aussi croit à une survie; car il espère rencontrer le Christ de suite après la mort (Phil. i. 19–26).[1]

Mais cette survie est considérée comme insuffisante par le christianisme biblique. La félicité qu'elle *peut* impliquer est encore au dessous de l'idéal eschatologique. Et ceci pour deux raisons. Tout d'abord la notion biblique de la création réelle, laquelle est jugée bonne en soi (Gen. i *passim*),[2] quoique pervertie ensuite par la chûte, ne peut s'accommoder d'un idéal qui ne restituerait pas à la personne humaine la plénitude de son existence. Et celle-ci doit comporter un corps au sens fort du terme, c'est-à-dire un corps capable d'agir (*wirk-lich*) et d'autant plus réel qu'il sera débarrassé de toutes ses faiblesses dues aux principes de corruption appelés σάρξ, φθορά, ἁμαρτία par l'apôtre Paul.

Deuxièmement, il est impossible de ne pas voir qu'aux yeux de la Bible, la survie de l''âme' ou de l''esprit', même purifié de toute matière, ne saurait en aucune manière *garantir* la réconciliation avec Dieu, qui est le nerf même de la doctrine chrétienne du salut. Un homme rejeté par Dieu ne serait pas sauvé du fait d'être devenu 'immatériel'. Car c'est toujours l'appropriation de la grâce offerte en l'œuvre du Christ qui est la condition de la paix avec Dieu. Que servirait à l'homme d'être immortel et de développer peut-être toutes sortes de 'pouvoirs psychiques' supérieurs, s'il continuait à porter le poids de sa culpabilité?

[1] Notons d'ailleurs qu'il ne s'agit pas, à proprement dire, d'une séparation du 'corps' et de l''âme' au sens platonicien ou cartésien. Ce qui survit, ce n'est pas la partie invisible de l'homme, mais une sorte d'être psycho-physique *sui generis*, dépourvue de la plénitude de l'existence, semblable à une image de l'homme réel.

[2] Vide notre *Royaume de Dieu selon Jésus et l'apôtre Paul* (1938), 1er chapître.

Mais il y a plus: déjà dans notre situation actuelle, dans notre 'corps de mort', la rédemption a commencé son œuvre. Le chrétien n'a-t-il pas la certitude de la justification par la foi et de l'attribution du saint Esprit, qui est 'l'accompte de la Rédemption' (II Cor. i. 22; v. 5; Ephes. i. 13–14; Rom. viii. 23), autant de thèmes inconnus du Platonisme?

Mais ici il nous faut ajouter une remarque, qui nous semble importante. Nous estimons en effet que la pauvreté des renseignements donnés par le N.T. sur la période entre la mort et la résurrection n'est pas due à un simple hasard. C'est un fait que la pensée du N.T. en tant qu'elle concerne la vie future, est concentrée sur le Royaume de Dieu, qui viendra 'à la fin'.

Pourquoi? Non pas seulement parce qu'on attendait celle-ci dans un proche avenir. Mais parce que seules les doctrines du Royaume et de la résurrection sont vraiment des thèmes théologiques pour la pensée chrétienne. Si on a pris l'habitude de demander à la théologie des renseignements sur le sort des trépassés, cette préoccupation se justifie en ce sens que les assurances de salut et de soutien données au croyant sont valables pour toutes les conditions possibles de son existence présente ou future. Le chrétien doit toujours se rappeler que *ni la mort, ni la vie* ne peuvent le séparer de l'amour de Dieu manifesté en Jésus-Christ (Rom. viii. 38). Voilà la grande et consolante révélation que les Eglises chrétiennes ne devront jamais se lasser de répéter.[1]

Est-ce à dire que la théologie, par ailleurs, aurait comme tâche de nous renseigner sur les conditions d'existence *post mortem*? Nous ne le pensons pas (tout aussi peu que ce serait sans doute son devoir de renseigner les habitants des autres monde sur le nôtre). Si des questions de ce genre ne sont pas complètement insolubles, nous estimons qu'elles relèvent de la psychologie ou de la parapsychologie de l'avenir, qui d'ailleurs ne refusera peut-être pas d'utiliser les renseignements fournis par des voyants de bon aloi. En tout cas, le théologien fera bien de ne pas se prononcer — au nom de la Bible — pour ou contre l'une ou l'autre des hypothèses qu'on peut envisager dans ce domaine.

[1] Vide les études récentes de Ph. Menoud: (*a*) 'Le sort des trépassés d'après le N.T.' (*Cahiers Théologiques de l'Actualité Protestante*, No. 9 (Neuchâtel, 1945); (*b*) 'La signification chrétienne de la mort' dans *L'homme face à la mort* (Neuchâtel, 1952); (*c*) 'Le victoire chrétienne sur le mort' (*ibidem*).

Que les trépassés vivent dans un état de sommeil qui pourra durer jusqu'à la résurrection ou qu'ils aient dans l'au-delà des expériences à vivre et des missions à accomplir, ou encore que Dieu les renvoie (tous ou une partie d'entre eux) pour réaliser une ou plusieurs destinées planétaires ultérieures — de toute manière (et ceci est décisif) ces existences se dérouleront encore dans le cadre de l'éon présent. Or ce n'est pas l'affaire de la Théologie d'explorer les lois de notre éon.

Supposons un instant que la métapsychique, par des méthodes que nous n'avons pas à discuter ici, puisse un jour rendre probable l'hypothèse de vies humaines multiples, nous pensons qu'il ne serait pas seulement maladroit, mais contraire à la mission de la dogmatique chrétienne, de prendre position contre elle. Il est vrai que la Bible n'enseigne pas la réincarnation. Mais elle n'enseigne pas non plus le système héliocentrique ni aucune autre hypothèse relevant des sciences profanes. C'est pourquoi presque personne, de nos jours, ne doute que les Eglises ou les théologiens qui soutinrent Ptolémée contre Copernic aient manqué une bonne occasion de se souvenir de l'avertissement donné en l'Evangile de Matt. xii. 36....

Mais si la théologie ne doit pas prendre parti dans ces questions, elle peut néanmoins essayer de comprendre et d'éclairer la signification religieuse de l'existence telle que les sciences profanes nous l'enseigne. Si les vues copernicaines et brunoviennes sur le cosmos astronomique sont exactes, elles nous aideront à nous débarrasser de certaines conceptions trop géocentriques de la providence divine et à nous rappeler que le Dieu de la Bible n'est pas seulement le Dieu de notre planète. N'est-ce pas aussi Lui qui y gouverne tous les soleils et toutes les nébuleuses découvertes par l'astronomie moderne — vérité déjà entrevue par le second Esaïe, par le livre de Job, et les grandioses visions d'Ezéchiel et de Daniel, mais pratiquement un peu oubliée par les Eglises chrétiennes?

De même nous pensons que la doctrine des vies multiples, si elle pouvait être désobscurcie phénoménologiquement et acceptée psychologiquement, pourrait jeter une lumière saisissante sur certaines conséquences de la chûte telle qu'elle est enseignée par la Bible.

Envisageons en effet en chrétiens la situation qui résulterait de cette hypothèse chère à Platon: Voici des êtres humains — du moins ceux de notre planète, que seuls nous connaissons à l'heure actuelle — qui oscilleraient continuellement entre deux modes d'existence: premièrement une existence désincarnée entre la mort et la naissance, deuxièmement une vie mal incarnée (parce qu'entâchée de corruption) entre la naissance et la mort. Eh bien, au point de vue biblique, aucun de ces deux types d'existences ne pourrait être jugé satisfaisant, parce qu'aucun n'est conforme à la destinée humaine voulue par le Créateur. Que l'existence matérielle dans ce 'corps de mort' soit dépravée par la chûte, nul théologien qui prend le N.T. au sérieux ne peut en douter. Mais il est utile de rappeler qu'une existence sans corps réel n'est pas non plus conforme au statut de l'homme intègre, lequel devrait jouir d'une plénitude d'existence dans le monde visible, et de la capacité d'agir sur celui-ci. Et nous posons la question: Ce va-et-vient, dépourvu de stabilité, entre deux modes d'existence également privés de 'gloire', et qui entraîne au surplus une séparation, douloureuse malgré tous les sophismes, entre les 'vivants' et les 'morts', ne serait-elle pas un symptôme saisissant du dérangement profond causé par la chûte?

Et qu'est-ce qui pourrait, au point de vue chrétien, y mettre fin sinon l'établissement du monde résurrectionnel assurant à l'humanité sa stabilité et son intégrité et abolissant la barrière entre les deux humanités, celle d'ici-bas et celle de l'au-delà?

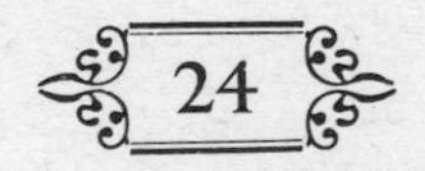

THE JUDGMENT THEME IN THE SACRAMENTS

C. F. D. MOULE

THE theme of this essay is, in brief, that the New Testament regards both Baptism and Holy Communion as anticipations of the Last Judgment, the chief difference in this regard between the two sacraments being that, whereas Baptism is unrepeatable, the Eucharist is essentially repetitive.

Thus stated, the theme is doubtless a well-worn one. But, none-theless, it is a quarry from which repeated delvings usually yield something new, and one in which it is impossible to dig without discovering that beneath it lies the massive rock of the entire Gospel, and that from it wind passages leading into every aspect of Christian doctrine. In this particular instance, the investigation leads us into the perennial problems attaching to the meaning of membership of the Church, and of the efficacy of Christian Baptism. It would be too much to expect that, even in far more experienced hands, it would lead to their solution. The most that may be hoped for is that a little further light may be let in upon them.

What follows falls into three unequal sections, treating respectively of Baptism, Holy Communion, and exclusion from the fellowship, all in the light of the New Testament theme of the judgment of God.

I. JUDGMENT IS AN ESSENTIAL ASPECT OF CHRISTIAN BAPTISM

The theme of judgment is common alike to Baptism, to the Eucharist, and (of course) to the great assize of the last day. Not that κρίνειν or δοκιμάζειν is ever applied directly to what happens in Baptism; but the Baptism of John was associated with repentance and (according to Matthew and Luke) most emphatically with judgment;[1] and the Christian rite is, in the New Testament, essentially *dying* with Christ, and so rising again with him: even if it is 'the bath of new birth', it is manifestly *death* first; and death, as clearly, represents, to biblical thinking, the ultimate verdict on sin. If Baptism is voluntary death, then it is also a pleading guilty, an acceptance of the sentence. That the discharge of this sentence was in the mind at any rate of St Paul, when he was trying to find some means of explaining what the death of Christ had accomplished, is indicated by several of his phrases. For instance, in Col. ii. 14 τὸ χειρόγραφον, which Christ invalidates and nails to the cross, is evidently the 'bond' which we men have autographed—the statement which our own conscience subscribes to when it admits that we are under an obligation to keep the moral law which we have broken. It is our autograph self-accusation which Christ, himself Man, has accepted and for which his death has discharged the sentence.[2] In Gal. iii. 13 and II Cor. v. 21, in a similar manner, Christ's death is alluded to as something which has exhausted the 'curse' or served the sentence pronounced upon sin; and in Rom. viii. 3, 4 God is said to have condemned sin, in Christ incarnate, in order that τὸ δικαίωμα τοῦ νόμου—the requirements of God's moral law—might be completed in us. Indeed, there are indications in the Synoptic Gospels that Christ himself interpreted his ministry along these lines. His baptism at the hands of John is represented (and is there any serious reason for doubting that this goes back in its main outlines to a dominical tradition?) as a sacrament of absolute filial devotion: the baptism is, as it were, a focal point of his unique sonship, and the temptation, according to the interpretations in Matthew and Luke, is a contest between true filial obedience and a diabolical caricature of sonship. But if so, true filial obedience, in the framework of fallen humanity, inevitably means *death*; and it is therefore no surprise when, in a Lucan saying, Christ describes his coming death in terms of baptism (Mark x. 38; Luke xii. 50);[3] or to find Matt. iii. 15 describing Christ's baptism as a completion of all God's just requirements (πληρῶσαι πᾶσαν δικαιοσύνην). As E. Stauffer epigrammatically

[1] Cf. T. W. Manson in *Christian Worship*, ed. N. Micklem (Oxford, 1936), p. 44.

[2] See J. A. T. Robinson, *The Body* (S.C.M., 1952), p. 43n.

[3] Cf. W. F. Flemington, *The New Testament Doctrine of Baptism* (S.P.C.K., 1948), p. 72 and *passim*.

puts it:[1] 'Jesus nennt sein Sterben eine Taufe. Paulus hinwiederum nennt unsere Taufe ein Sterben.'

Baptism, then, is a willing acceptance of the verdict on sin, in union with Christ, whose perfect obedience to the sentence has been vindicated and crowned by the resurrection. But before taking the inquiry any further, this conception of obedience, expressed in death, will repay some elaboration. The New Testament writers evidently looked at it, one might say, schematically, from the angle of God's design for man as represented (for instance) in Ps. viii. According to Ps. viii, man was intended to be supreme over the rest of creation (cf. Gen. i. 28). But according to the whole Bible, he was intended also to be subject to God in perfect filial obedience, and (with equal unanimity) he is recognized to have failed of this intention—except in the Man Christ Jesus. Accordingly, Ps. viii comes to be expounded christologically, as in Heb. ii. 5ff.:

> man is meant to be subject to God,
> supreme over nature;
> he has refused to be subject to God,
> therefore nature is in no true or glad subjection to man.
> But one Man we know whose obedience to God and supremacy over nature are perfect; and it is in him that man's destiny is fulfilled—in him as a fact already accomplished (for his resurrection is the vindicating crown of glory), and by union with him as a fact yet to be realized in mankind.

So runs the thought of this passage in Hebrews; and the same background of ideas is obviously behind such passages as Rom. viii. 12ff. and I Cor. xv. 12ff. And common to them all is the assumption that, in a world where man's disobedience has already caused dislocation, *perfect obedience necessarily means death*; and voluntarily accepted death, like Christ's in the expression of his perfect obedience to God's will, is the only gateway to man's destiny. That is why the cross is the key to 'the restoration of all things'.

If, then, it is asked *how* man becomes united with the 'Proper Man' in such a way as to share his obedience and his triumph, the New Testament answer is 'By baptism into Christ's death and resurrection'. Christ's baptism was a sacrament of obedience—an antici-

[1] *Die Theologie des Neuen Testaments* (Suttgart, 1948), pp. 130f.

pated death; our baptism is likewise an obedient acceptance of the situation caused by our sin, and of the triumph over it of filial obedience. Baptism is (in this aspect) a once-and-for-all acceptance of what happened once and for all, in history, under Pontius Pilate—the death of Christ.

Thus baptism is essentially pleading guilty, accepting the verdict, 'setting to one's seal that God is true' (John iii. 33), 'admitting that God is in the right' (Luke vii. 29); it is dying, it is rising again; so that by baptism an individual, or indeed the whole Church corporately, is (in a sense) brought past the great assize, past the final judgment of the last day, into the life of the new age: ἀμὴν ἀμὴν λέγω ὑμῖν ὅτι ὁ τὸν λόγον μου ἀκούων καὶ πιστεύων τῷ πέμψαντί με (and this is the response which is represented by baptism) ἔχει ζωὴν αἰώνιον, καὶ εἰς κρίσιν οὐκ ἔρχεται ἀλλὰ μεταβέβηκεν ἐκ τοῦ θανάτου εἰς τὴν ζωήν (John v. 24). This thought is in keeping with the anticipations of Jewish apocalyptic, with its expectations of the fire of judgment which was to consume the world, and the Spirit of God which was to give life to his own people;[1] but the baptism 'with spirit and fire' of the Baptist's eschatological preaching turned out to be already accomplished, in both its aspects—both of judgment and of life—within the Christian Church: the Spirit was within the People of God, not because vengeance had been wreaked upon their opponents but because they had themselves accepted the verdict of the last day. If any man is in Christ, there the new creation is realized; the old state is past—the new age of apocalyptic expectation has begun (II Cor. v. 17). In this sense, a baptized person has undergone the final judgment, and risen into new life; for such the 'second death' of Rev. xx. 6, 14 has no power.

Conversely, to avoid the death-sentence, to try to evade the cross (like St Peter at Caesarea Philippi), is to have man's outlook, not God's—the materialistic outlook belonging to the old order; and, paradoxically, this avoidance of death means—death.

Baptism, in short—to use one more well-known manner of putting it—is an epitome of the *indicative* of the Christian Gospel which states 'Ye are dead, and your life is hid with Christ in God' (Col. iii. 3). Just as a dead man may be pronounced to have discharged his sentence, so those who have been buried by baptism with Christ

[1] Sibylline Oracles 4, 187ff., alluded to by E. Stauffer, *op. cit.* p. 8.

are already beyond the judgment. Rom. vi. 7 ὁ γὰρ ἀποθανὼν δεδικαίωται ἀπὸ τῆς ἁμαρτίας (? death clears one's sentence), I Pet. iv. 1 ὁ παθὼν σαρκὶ πέπαυται ἁμαρτίας—these are phrases which both occur in baptismal contexts; and it is possible that the obscure phrase in I Cor. ii. 15 ὁ δὲ πνευματικὸς ἀνακρίνει μὲν πάντα, αὐτὸς δὲ ὑπ' οὐδενὸς ἀνακρίνεται may have some connection with this conviction that Christians are beyond the judgment and are (like the People of the Saints of the Most High in Dan. vii) themselves given the responsibility of judging. Just as Christ, condemned to death, turned out thereby to be the judge of his accusers, so the Christian Church, condemned with Christ by the world, is already in the status of those who sit with him in the great assize (cf. Luke xxii. 30; I Cor. vi. 2). The 'indicative' language of baptism, then, is an idealistic language; it is *absolute* language—the language of realized eschatology; it is the past indicative of the Gospel. And baptism is a once-and-for-all, unrepeatable rite: were it not so, it would lose its essentially absolute quality. There can, obviously, by definition, be nothing more final and absolute than the last judgment; and baptism, by anticipation, shares the absolutes of this conception. Even Christ's own baptism, it would appear, represented to him a sacramental absolute which had then to be implemented in his whole ministry and accomplished by his death.

2. BETWEEN THE TWO ABSOLUTES—BAPTISM AND THE LAST DAY—THERE COME RELATIVE AND REPEATED JUDGMENTS; BETWEEN THESE TWO INDICATIVES ARE REPEATED IMPERATIVES; AND OF THESE, THE EUCHARIST IS A PROMINENT VEHICLE—INDEED, SACRAMENTALLY, THE ONLY VEHICLE

As soon as the finality of the baptismal judgment is recognized, a matter of great urgency comes to light. It is a fact of human experience, a mournful fact, that in reality this 'absolute' is not exhibited in the life of the Church. It is only (as Stauffer puts it)[1] the sectarian 'enthusiasts' (*Schwärmer*) who think that the new creation is already complete, just as (at the opposite extreme) it is

[1] *Op. cit.* p. 123.

the 'mockers' (like those of II Pet. iii. 3) who think that nothing has yet been altered. The realists accept neither of these two extremes. They recognize the hard fact that individual Christians and the corporate Church alike are continually failing to live by the absolutes into which baptism is declared to have brought them. If by baptism they are dead and quit of sin, yet sin is prominent in the best of them. If they are risen with Christ into the new age, yet the most obvious feature of life is the prevalence of all the marks of the present evil age—sin, death, frustration. And yet, the Christian realists also cling tenaciously to the conviction that a change has taken place. St Paul, who was nothing if not realistic in his idealism, can in one and the same breath castigate his Corinthian friends vehemently for disgraceful conduct and then remind them that they are already cleansed, sanctified, acquitted. Somehow, the New Testament held the two together. How was this tension expressed sacramentally? In many other religions, the problem is met by frequently repeated lustrations, to cleanse from each successive offence; in Christianity, baptism is once and for all and cannot be repeated:[1] it is the absolute sacrament. What, then, is the sacrament of renewal? There are many 'focal points' (if the metaphor may be permitted) of renewal, but, on the strictest definition of sacraments, the obvious and only answer, if sacraments are in question, is the Holy Communion. The preaching of the Christian Gospel of man's sin and God's grace is a focal point for repentance and renewal; and all sorts of circumstances provide similar grasping-points for progress—hand-holds, as it were, in the rock-face of a Christian's ascent; but sacramentally speaking, *the* renewal-point *par excellence* is the Eucharist, with its antecedent preparation of self-judgment and fresh acceptance of God's verdict on sin, whether such preparation takes the form of confession and absolution or of a more simple (though not necessarily any less profound) private self-searching and acceptance of forgiveness.

The only explicit reference in the New Testament to preparation for the Lord's Supper is in terms of *judgment*. Preparation for the Lord's Supper has become axiomatic and universal; as early as the *Didache* (14) it had come into force. It takes many different forms and varies in intensity and frequency among different traditions and different individuals; but in some form it goes without saying. There

[1] Asperges may be a *reminder*, but it is not a *repetition* of baptism.

is, however, only one direct reference in the New Testament to the practice (where, incidentally, it is enjoined by St Paul as though it were not a self-evident necessity); and it is in terms of judgment: δοκιμαζέτω δὲ ἄνθρωπος ἑαυτόν, καὶ οὕτως ἐκ τοῦ ἄρτου ἐσθιέτω καὶ ἐκ τοῦ ποτηρίου πινέτω· ὁ γὰρ ἐσθίων καὶ πίνων κρίμα ἑαυτῷ ἐσθίει καὶ πίνει μὴ διακρίνων τὸ σῶμα (I Cor. xi. 28). It may be added at once that there are other references to self-judgment, although they are not explicitly associated with the Eucharist; for instance, Rom. xiv. 22b μακάριος ὁ μὴ κρίνων ἑαυτὸν ἐν ᾧ δοκιμάζει;[1] II Cor. xiii. 5 ἑαυτοὺς πειράζετε εἰ ἐστὲ ἐν τῇ πίστει, ἑαυτοὺς δοκιμάζετε· ἢ οὐκ ἐπιγινώσκετε ἑαυτοὺς ὅτι Ἰησοῦς Χριστὸς ἐν ὑμῖν; εἰ μήτι ἀδόκιμοί ἐστε; Gal. vi. 4 τὸ δὲ ἔργον ἑαυτοῦ δοκιμαζέτω ἕκαστος, καὶ τότε εἰς ἑαυτὸν μόνον τὸ καύχημα ἕξει καὶ οὐκ εἰς τὸν ἕτερον; and I John iii. 19–21, especially ἐὰν ἡ καρδία μὴ καταγινώσκῃ... in *v.* 21. Perhaps it is relevant to add that the gracious promise of Rev. iii. 20, εἰσελεύσομαι πρὸς αὐτὸν καὶ δειπνήσω μετ' αὐτοῦ..., which is at least reminiscent of the eucharistic supper, is preceded by the most scarifying *judgment* of the Laodicean Church.[2]

But allusions to self-examination—and in particular the reference in I Cor. xi—are only a prelude to the fact that St Paul's treatment of the Eucharist itself in that same famous chapter is in terms of judgment.[3] In I Cor. xi. 28–32, δοκιμάζειν, κρίμα, διακρίνειν, κρίνειν, and κατακρίνειν are used in quick succession in a very striking way. To judge of these words by their use elsewhere, one may say that δοκιμάζειν is frequently a monetary metaphor, of testing the genuineness of coins (note also δόκιμος, ἀδόκιμος, δοκιμεῖον), although it can also carry a more general sense (e.g. in Luke xiv. 19, of testing cattle for ploughing); κρίνειν is a neutral word, of the function of a judge or arbitrator who discriminates and makes a decision either for or against, although, if the context compels it,

[1] Cf. I Cor. iv. 3, 4, which, though disclaiming the absolute validity of any human judgment, even of oneself, reflects the fact that St Paul did practise self-examination.

[2] Cf. C. H. Dodd in *Christian Worship*, ed. N. Micklem (Oxford, 1936), pp. 77, 78, for the eucharistic relevance of this passage.

[3] This is also noticed by E. Käsemann, 'Anliegen und Eigenart der paulinischen Abendmahlslehre' (*Evangelische Theologie*, vol. VIII (1948/9), pp. 263 ff), where many of the same problems are most ingeniously and skilfully handled.

it can mean specifically 'to condemn', 'to deliver an adverse sentence' (and κρίμα usually means a verdict of guilty); διακρίνειν obviously refers more unambiguously to the act of *discrimination* as such (compare also ἀνακρίνειν which, like ἐξετάζειν, is sometimes used of a judicial cross-examination or inquiry); and κατακρίνειν indicates unequivocally a sentence of condemnation. Now, in the passage under consideration, this series of largely juridical terms is brought to bear upon the Lord's Supper and what precedes and follows it. St Paul is castigating the Corinthians for rank selfishness and greed which make it impossible to eat the Lord's Supper, and turn it instead into an unseemly exhibition of snatching at one's own supper (*vv.* 20, 21). To bring home the blasphemous nature of such conduct, he reminds them of the occasion and words of Institution when the Lord Jesus took a loaf, gave thanks, broke it, and said τοῦτό μού ἐστιν τὸ σῶμα τὸ ὑπὲρ ὑμῶν· τοῦτο ποιεῖτε εἰς τὴν ἐμὴν ἀνάμνησιν; and, over the cup, said τοῦτο τὸ ποτήριον ἡ καινὴ διαθήκη ἐστὶν ἐν τῷ ἐμῷ αἵματι· τοῦτο ποιεῖτε, ὁσάκις ἐὰν πίνητε, εἰς τὴν ἐμὴν ἀνάμνησιν. It is unnecessary here to linger over the endless questions and associations, doctrinal and historical, attaching to this particular form of the words; what is relevant at the moment is the immediate deduction drawn by the Apostle, namely, that the Lord's Supper is a memorial of the Lord's *death* (*v.* 26), and that, accordingly, to participate in an unworthy manner (ἀναξίως) is to incur guilt in regard to the body and blood of the Lord. It may be noted at once that this is almost exactly parallel to a phrase in Heb. x. 29, in a passage which is, like the corresponding passage in Heb. vi, with good reason referred by common consent to apostasy after *Baptism*: the apostate is spoken of as ὁ τὸν υἱὸν τοῦ θεοῦ καταπατήσας καὶ τὸ αἷμα τῆς διαθήκης κοινὸν ἡγησάμενος, ἐν ᾧ ἡγιάσθη, καὶ τὸ πνεῦμα τῆς χάριτος ἐνυβρίσας. Thus, to renounce one's Baptism and to display selfish greed at the Lord's Supper are both alike to incur judgment for outrage against the death of the Lord—his body and blood surrendered to death for us.[1]

[1] Professor E. C. Ratcliff points out to me that the famous reference to Christian worship in Pliny's letter to Trajan may have a bearing on this conception of a repeated judgment as represented by the Eucharist. At their (apparently eucharistic) worship, repeated week by week (*stato die*) the Christians bind themselves by an oath (*sacramento*) to observe a moral code (perhaps, as Kraeling suggests, the Ten Commandments); which means that not alone at Baptism, but each time they meet

This, in its turn, throws perhaps some light on the much debated phrase μὴ διακρίνων τὸ σῶμα in I Cor. xi. 29. It would appear to be parallel to κοινὸν ἡγησάμενος τὸ αἷμα in Hebrews—a culpable failure to recognize, to discern, that the life which was surrendered was that of the Lord himself. It is, in fact, a form (however different in expression) of the fundamental blindness of the secular world (or of the demonic powers behind it) which failed to perceive who Jesus was: ἣν [*sc.* σοφίαν] οὐδεὶς τῶν ἀρχόντων τοῦ αἰῶνος τούτου ἔγνωκεν· εἰ γὰρ ἔγνωσαν, οὐκ ἂν τὸν κύριον τῆς δόξης ἐσταύρωσαν (I Cor. ii. 8). Exactly so, that other passage in Hebrews (vi. 6) speaks of what is apparently the renunciation of Baptism—deliberate apostasy—as tantamount to changing sides—abandoning those who share Christ's condemnation and reproach (cf. Heb. xiii. 13) and who die with him, and siding instead with those who cry 'Crucify!';[1] for the apostates are referred to as ἀνασταυροῦντας ἑαυτοῖς τὸν υἱὸν τοῦ θεοῦ καὶ παραδειγματίζοντας.

Thus, outrage to one's baptismal state, or outrage (by gross selfishness and greed) to the sanctities of the Lord's Supper are both alike condemned as criminal blindness to the meaning of the Lord's death: it is a matter of joining the secular powers in pronouncing a sentence of 'Guilty' on Jesus, instead of with him accepting the sentence of death upon ourselves and recognizing the resurrection as vindicating his cause. Emphatically, therefore, the Eucharist is an occasion of judgment—either of voluntary self-judgment, in acceptance of God's verdict on fallen man, or else of unwilling liability to God's judgment as it falls upon those who, in the blindness of selfish secularism, side against the Lord Jesus.[2]

Hence it is (returning to the language of I Cor. xi) that St Paul urges the Corinthians voluntarily to arraign themselves, to plead guilty, and only so to approach the sacrament: δοκιμαζέτω δὲ

for the Eucharist, they bind themselves afresh by an undertaking which—if broken—will be a judgment upon them.

That participation in the Lord's Supper means becoming part of the Lord's *Body* is characteristic of St Paul's teaching (cf. Käsemann, *op. cit.* p. 265 and J. A. T. Robinson, *The Body*, p. 57); equally characteristic of Hebrews is the idea of remission of sin by *blood*.

[1] This may be partly why persecution, which compels one to take sides, is called πειρασμός. It is a test, a *discrimen*.

[2] It is πτῶσις καὶ ἀνάστασις (cf. Luke ii. 34).

ἄνθρωπος ἑαυτόν, καὶ οὕτως ἐκ τοῦ ἄρτου ἐσθιέτω καὶ ἐκ τοῦ ποτηρίου πινέτω (*v.* 28); for to do otherwise is to fail to recognize τὸ σῶμα, and thus to seal one's own condemnation (κρίμα) by the eating and drinking (*v.* 29). Indeed, the apostle (as is well known) attributes disease and even death among the Corinthian Christians to this guilty use of the sacrament (*v.* 30): it is a manifestation of God's judgment on their blasphemous lack of discernment. Then, to clinch it, he adds (*v.* 31) εἰ δὲ ἑαυτοὺς διεκρίνομεν, οὐκ ἂν ἐκρινόμεθα—that is, if we were to use enough discrimination to discern what we are ourselves (namely, sinners needing to repent), we should not fall under God's condemnation. St Paul has, in *vv.* 29 and 31, resorted to a device which he also employs elsewhere[1]—a kind of play on words to drive home his point: this terrific sin of μὴ διακρίνειν τὸ σῶμα is part of the same attitude which οὐχ ἑαυτὸν διακρίνει: it is an all-round moral and spiritual lack of discernment and blindness—blindness to self, blindness to the value of others, and blindness to the Saviour;[2] indeed, it is an instance of the fundamental blindness which reached its climax at the trial of Jesus, as it is majestically portrayed in the Fourth Gospel, where the blind pronounce a verdict against the very Light incarnate.

No attempt is here made to take sides in the exegetical controversy as to whether τὸ σῶμα in I Cor. xi. 29 means the Lord's Body present in some sense in association with the elements, or the Lord's Body in the sense of his Body the Church. The exegesis which has just been attempted transcends both, and, in my own opinion, includes both. The discerning, penitent communicant is alert to the meaning with which the bread and wine are charged both in regard to the incarnate Christ given for us and in regard to the fellow members of the Body which that surrender created; and it seems to me probable that St Paul was thinking inclusively rather than exclusively, and intended

[1] Rom. i. 28; xiv. 13.

[2] It is the same test which discriminates between the sheep and the goats in Matt. xxv; for although indeed the 'sheep' did not realize that in serving others they were serving the Lord, yet at least they were not blind to the needs of others. Again, cf. I Cor. viii. 12 οὕτως δὲ ἁμαρτάνοντες εἰς τοὺς ἀδελφοὺς καὶ τύπτοντες αὐτῶν τὴν συνείδησιν ἀσθενοῦσαν, εἰς Χριστὸν ἁμαρτάνετε. Further, the whole Body of the Church is itself a vehicle of the judgment of God: Matt. xvi, xviii; John xx: to fail to discern the Body is to fail to recognize the judgment it pronounces. See A. Farrer, *A Study in St Mark* (Dacre Press, 1951), p. 274.

to indicate the implications, in their most comprehensive range, of the refusal to renew one's acceptance, at the Eucharist, of that death sentence which is accepted absolutely and once for all in Baptism.[1]

Returning for a moment to the close parallelism which has thus far been traced between the two sacraments—a parallelism in terms of judgment—it is to be observed that this is really only a symptom, as it were, and a comparatively superficial indication of an even deeper fact, namely that both sacraments alike are activities of the one Holy Spirit. As Dr J. E. L. Oulton has been emphasizing recently,[2] it is this which, all said and done, is the most obvious and vital feature of both Baptism and the Eucharist, whatever may be their differences and however much controversy has raged round the function of the Spirit in the one as compared with the other. If so, then, it is natural that judgment should be also a feature in common; for where the Spirit is, there, inescapably, is *discrimen*, κρίσις, ἔλεγχος. To labour the point would in effect be to embark upon an interpretation of the entire Johannine theology:[3] it will be sufficient here simply to indicate the fact, and to recall also that the ἀνάθεμα of I Cor. xvi. 22, which may be an echo of the fencing of the tables (cf. *Did.* 9 and 10),[4] has a kind of blasphemous counterpart in the cry ἀνάθεμα Ἰησοῦς uttered by one who is *without the control of the Spirit* (I Cor. xii. 3). If a person does not love the Lord Jesus, the judgment of God rests upon him—he is to be ἀνάθεμα (I Cor. xvi. 22), and he is himself capable of calling Jesus ἀνάθεμα; and that is clearly a con-

[1] Cf. O. Cullmann, *Les Sacraments dans l'Évangile Johannique* (Paris, 1951), p. 40: 'Baptême et Sainte-Cène: deux sacraments du pardon des péchés: l'un n'est donné qu'une fois, l'autre plusieurs fois. Mais tous deux sont liés de même manière à la mort du Christ sur la croix.'

It is, perhaps, a suggestive way of putting it to say that the unrepeatability of Baptism is comparable to the uniqueness of the death of Christ in history—the death he died ἐν τῷ σώματι τῆς σαρκός; while the repeated death of the Eucharist is part of the sufferings which continue to be undergone by Christ's Body which is the Church (Col. i. 24). It is the difference between Col. i. 22 (τὸ σῶμα historically) and Eph. ii. 16 (σῶμα 'mystically'); see J. A. T. Robinson, *The Body* (S.C.M. 1952), p. 47.

[2] In *Holy Communion and Holy Spirit* (S.P.C.K. 1951).

[3] Note (among other indications of Johannine thought on the matter) I John v. 6–8, where it appears that the two Sacraments are brought into association with the Spirit, and these three together are regarded as *giving evidence* about Christ. (See C. H. Dodd in *The Johannine Epistles*, Moffatt Commentaries (1946), *in loc.*)

[4] See J. A. T. Robinson in *J.T.S.*, n.s. i, 1 (April 1953), pp. 38ff.

dition outside the influence of the Holy Spirit; it is only if one is ἐν πνεύματι θεοῦ λαλῶν that one can acknowledge Jesus as Lord. Thus the Holy Spirit is essentially concerned in this matter of 'taking sides'—accepting the death-sentence and taking up one's cross to go with Jesus to the execution-ground, or standing with the authorities of the world, whether in ecclesiastical guise as the high priest, or in the robes of civic office like Pilate; and this decision, this judgment, is, as has been shown, characteristic of the Eucharist and of Baptism alike.

In passing, it may not be out of place to digress at this point in order to underline the fact that the Gospel saying just alluded to, about taking up one's cross, is evidently not an injunction to be patient and faithful in sustaining distress, although it is often so interpreted: rather, it is a terrifyingly vivid and ruthless way of saying that discipleship means accepting the death-sentence. Those who bore the cross were sentenced criminals—unless it were a Simon of Cyrene, impressed into service. Incidentally, if the passion narrative was recited at the Eucharist, that story of Simon bearing the cross might have been a standing reminder to the worshippers of this attitude. If, then, bearing the cross means accepting death, being crucified with Christ, it is the more striking that the Lucan form of the saying about it adds (paradoxically enough) καθ' ἡμέραν. Logically, death can occur but once; logically, the spiritual identification of the believer with Christ in his death can occur but once—at baptism. But if in fact there are sacramental repetitions of this absolute in each successive eucharistic rededication, it may be that the Lucan 'take up his cross *daily*' reflects this aspect of Christian experience.[1] Similarly the much debated saying in John xiii. 10 ὁ λελουμένος οὐκ ἔχει χρείαν [εἰ μὴ τοὺς πόδας][2] νίψασθαι, ἀλλ' ἔστιν καθαρὸς ὅλος must refer, it would seem, to relative and repetitive renewals of a once and for all absolute, however one interprets it in detail, and however much one may hesitate to find in it (with

[1] I Cor. xv. 30 καθ' ἡμέραν ἀποθνήσκω is, however, only a verbal parallel; for the context shows (I think) that it refers to the *physical* hazards of the evangelist. Compare, however, II Cor. i. 9 ἐν ἑαυτοῖς τὸ ἀπόκριμα τοῦ θανάτου ἐσχήκαμεν, where the perfect tense may well be a genuine and conscious recognition that the once-for-all sentence is also a continually present and repeated one; cf. II Cor. iv. 10 πάντοτε τὴν νέκρωσιν τοῦ Ἰησοῦ ἐν τῷ σώματι περιφέροντες.

[2] *om.* ℵ, Vulg., Origen, Tertullian.

Cullman and others) a specifically eucharistic allusion. Finally, it is perhaps not irrelevant to all that has been said about the Eucharist as judgment that Sunday—the chief day of Christian worship—is called ἡ κυριακὴ ἡμέρα (Rev. i. 10), which is sufficiently reminiscent of 'the Day of the Lord' in the Old Testament sense to sound the overtones of judgment.[1]

3. WHEN THE SACRAMENTS OF JUDGMENT ARE REJECTED OR ABUSED, WHAT THEN? THE NEW TESTAMENT SEEMS TO GIVE NO ONE UNIFORM ANSWER. THE DECIDING FACTOR, FROM THE HUMAN SIDE, IS THE NATURE OF A MAN'S RESPONSE TO CALAMITY

We are now confronted by what is probably the most difficult problem of all in regard to the judgment-aspect of these two sacraments—namely the relation between what is achieved in them on the one hand and at the final judgment on the other hand. The final judgment is by definition unrepeatable and is absolute in its totality and comprehensiveness. Baptism is unrepeatable and, in a sacramental sense, final—it is the sacrament of finality in judgment, not the final judgment itself. The Holy Communion (if the exegesis of the preceding section is right) is a sacrament of repeated judgment, a sacrament of renewal: Baptism is sacramental death and rebirth; the Eucharist, if one may put it so, is sacramental re-death and renewed rebirth; the Last Day is the symbol of ultimate death and ultimate life in an absolute and utterly final sense. If that were all, one might perhaps state the relationship of the three in an elementary way by saying that Baptism means birth, the Eucharist nourishment and growth, and the Last Day completion, and that the element of *discrimen*, κρίσις, judgment, death, which has been described, runs through all these metaphors: birth means a 'death' to the preceding type of existence; progress is similarly by a dying to the old; and ultimate consummation means a final death to the past.

But the extreme difficulty which forbids so simple and schematic a definition arises in connection with excommunication and apostasy.

[1] Cf. Cullmann, *op. cit.* pp. 60, 61; κυριακός is not, however, ever so used in the LXX. Its only occurrence is in II Macc. xiii. 56 (*si vera lectio*).

In the passage which has been most prominent in the discussion thus far, I Cor. xi. 17ff., St Paul appears to assert that, however severe the judgment and however extreme the penalty attaching to unworthy and blasphemous participation in the Lord's Supper, yet ultimately they are remedial and redemptive: ideally, we ought voluntarily to anticipate the Lord's judgment; but if we fail to do so, he will himself judge us, but judge in order to save: εἰ δὲ ἑαυτοὺς διεκρίνομεν, οὐκ ἂν ἐκρινόμεθα· κρινόμενοι δὲ ὑπὸ τοῦ κυρίου παιδευόμεθα, ἵνα μὴ σὺν τῷ κόσμῳ κατακριθῶμεν (*vv.* 31, 32). If these words are to be pressed, they must mean that 'the world' is destined to be 'condemned'; but Christians, however unworthily they may participate in the Lord's Supper and however culpable they may be, will only fall under remedial, educative judgment, destined to rescue them from ultimate condemnation. It is in the same vein (evidently) that, with reference to the excommunication of a gross offender, the Apostle writes παραδοῦναι τὸν τοιοῦτον τῷ Σατανᾷ εἰς ὄλεθρον τῆς σαρκός, ἵνα τὸ πνεῦμα σωθῇ ἐν τῇ ἡμέρᾳ τοῦ κυρίου (I Cor. v. 5). (Compare, but also contrast, the much feebler οὓς παρέδωκα τῷ Σατανᾷ, ἵνα παιδευθῶσιν μὴ βλασφημεῖν of I Tim. i. 20.)[1]

Is one to understand from this that St Paul attaches such absolute value to baptism that he believes that even the grossest offender, once baptized, will ultimately be brought through to eternal life, by however rigorous a purgatory, in distinction from 'the world', the unbaptized, who are in jeopardy of eternal death? If one were looking for extra-Pauline support for such a position, it might conceivably be found in I Peter—though by questionable exegesis and perhaps over-ingenuity. I Pet. iii. 19, 20 appears to declare that

[1] There is much in I Cor. v that is both relevant to the present discussion and also puzzling. Is the reference in *v.* 4 to the Christians' assembling (συναχθέντων ὑμῶν) intended to suggest an *ad hoc* assembly for judgment, or is it a eucharistic assembly, which is also juridical (note the paschal reference in *v.* 7, though that is, of course, frequently ascribed to the fact that this Epistle may have been written at Passover time)? συνεσθίειν in *v.* 11 comes under consideration in a similar way—is it 'ordinary' or eucharistic? (I think ordinary; the μηδέ suggests this). But most problematic of all is the matter of ὁ κόσμος and of judgment: *v.* 10 uses κόσμος of 'outsiders' exactly as in I Cor. xi. 32; but whereas in I Cor. xi. 32 ὁ κόσμος is destined to be condemned (κατακρίνειν), and lapsed Christians are judged (κρίνειν) by the Lord, in I Cor. v the lapsed Christian is to be judged by the Church (who also judge the world, vi. 22), while outsiders are to be judged by God (*vv.* 12, 13).

a 'second chance' of salvation was offered to the generation of the Flood. (I am well aware of other interpretations,[1] and of the difficulties of this old-fashioned one; but I am inclined to think still that this encounters fewer obstacles than any alternative exegesis.) Now, if so, why the Flood generation? Because (it might be argued) they were the 'type' of the baptized. Verse 21 regards the flood as the type of, or parallel to, Christian Baptism (which is death by drowning with a view to the separating out and saving of the Noachic good that is in a man!);[2] *ergo* the Flood generation were, as prebaptized, destined for ultimate rescue. This extremely bizarre idea might conceivably be defended as no more bizarre than the parallel itself which is undoubtedly drawn between the Flood and Baptism, and as having parallels in rabbinic thought. But for myself I am disposed to think that the real reason why the Flood generation is singled out for salvation by this writer is simply that the Mishna, and perhaps its antecedents, specify it as destined to damnation.[3] Here (I suggest) is a deliberate Christian denial of Judaic limitations;[4] and if the recipients of the Epistle had been proselytes before they were won to Christianity (as W. C. van Unnik has suggested),[5] the allusion would gain all the more point.

Be that as it may, I Pet. iii would at best be a remarkably slender foundation on which to build a doctrine of salvation automatically ensured by baptism; and, what is more, even the apparent support to the doctrine in the Pauline passages just adduced is withdrawn elsewhere. For ἀδόκιμος is a word used by St Paul to describe utter reprobation—the condition of one who has been tested and found utterly unfit: Rom. i is sufficient evidence for this. But, if so, what

[1] See, for example, Dr Selwyn's *I Peter*, *in loc.*

[2] Note, in passing, that even the metaphor of cleansing is not far removed from that of purgation and so of a discriminatory, judging process: the use of καθαρός, καθαρίζειν in the Fourth Gospel is evidence of this.

[3] Mishna *Sanh.* 10, 3 (and cf. Test. XII Benj. 10, 6, where Noah is included in the resurrection, but not the sinners of his generation). So too H. Windisch in Lietzmann's *Kommentar* (1930, p. 72), who adduces also Iren. *adv. Haer.* I, 27, 3; Epiphan. *Haer.* 42, 4. See further Strack-Billerbeck, *Kommentar*, vol. I, p. 964; vol. IV, pp. 1185f.

[4] Strack-Billerbeck, vol. I, p. 964, adduce Rabbi Johanan (died A.D. 279) as having himself put forward the view, contrary to the Mishna, that the Flood generation, having suffered their punishment, would have a share in the world to come.

[5] *De Verlossing I Petrus i. 18, 19* (Amsterdam, 1942).

is to be made of the suggestion in II Cor. xiii. 5 ff. that the Corinthian community may prove ἀδόκιμοι? It is true that the tone of the passage indicates a strong hope that they may not be such; but the suggestion that they may be appears to be more than a mere tool for *reductio ad absurdum*. Similarly in I Cor. ix. 27 the apostle contemplates—evidently as a real possibility—the appalling idea that he might himself prove to be ἀδόκιμος. Still more decisively, I Cor. x itself, which provides the direct antecedent to the passage under consideration, urges that the baptized Christian is no safer in playing fast and loose with his privileges than were the Israelites who had been 'baptized' in the cloud and in the sea.[1]

However true, then, it may be to one side of a famous biblical paradox to say that for the baptized the judgment is over and the last days have begun, and that God's calling is not repented of, it appears necessary, at the same time, to keep clearly in view the other side, that it is possible to fall away from such a state; and St Paul himself seems to have voiced both sides.[2] As for the notoriously extreme position represented by the writer to the Hebrews in Heb. vi and x, it seems best to account for it by assuming circumstances of extreme urgency such that to renounce Christianity and relapse into Judaism was, virtually at least, to close the door upon renewal: it was a situation different from that reflected in I Cor. xi, where the sin was gross selfishness and not a virtually irrevocable step out of the Christian community back into that of anti-Christian Judaism.[3]

But logically, it must be admitted, there is no ultimate distinction between self-excommunication and being extruded against one's will from the community; and we are driven, I think, to recognize a logical inconsistency such as commonly occurs in connection with the greatest truths of doctrine, which are always too great to be expressed otherwise than in paradoxical and antithetic form. Judas is declared in John xiii. 11, 12 to be not καθαρός, whereas St Peter

[1] Cf. A. Schweitzer, *The Mysticism of Paul the Apostle* (Engl. trans. 1931), p. 260.

[2] Compare the conditional note sounded also in Hebrews, not only in chs. vi and x, but in, for example, iii. 14 μέτοχοι γὰρ τοῦ χριστοῦ γεγόναμεν, <u>ἐάνπερ</u> τὴν ἀρχὴν τῆς ὑποστάσεως μέχρι τέλους βεβαίαν κατάσχωμεν.

[3] The sin against the Spirit, however it may be interpreted, does not appear to be directly relevant to the problem of what difference, if any, there is between sin within and sin outside the baptized membership of the Church.

is included among the καθαροί,[1] although both disciples must have had identical antecedents, so far as any equivalent to initiation into discipleship could go, and both denied their Lord—though Judas indeed deliberately and (so far as one can judge) with calculating malice, while St Peter did it through cowardice. The only relevant difference between the two that appears through the traditions is that one was smitten with real repentance, while the other's response to the horror of the situation was self-regarding remorse: one's was ἡ κατὰ θεὸν λύπη, the other's ἡ τοῦ κόσμου (II Cor. vii. 10). On this showing, the question is not whether the offender has or has not undergone the judgment, death, and rebirth of baptism, but whether the suffering (which befalls both the excommunicated Church member and the 'man of the world' who has never been in sacramental contact with the Christian community) brings him to repentance or not; and, although there may well be a greater likelihood of this happening in the case of one who has previously been growing up in touch with the Body of Christ than in that of an outsider, there is no evidence of any mechanical uniformity. 'There is no κατάκριμα *for those who are in Christ Jesus*': this is all that can be affirmed.

It would appear, then, that if the New Testament doctrines of Baptism and Holy Communion are viewed, as has here been attempted, in terms of judgment and in their relation to the Last Judgment, the following statements may be made about them:

(i) Baptism, for each individual, shares something of the finality and uniqueness which the Incarnation itself possesses for the whole world, and anticipates sacramentally the finality and uniqueness of the ultimate judgment of God.

(ii) Holy Communion is a means of successive renewals of this sacramental verdict—an opportunity for Christians to reaffirm their

[1] See Günther Bornkamm's 'Das Anathema in der urchristlichen Abendmahlsliturgie' in *Das Ende des Gesetzes* (München, 1952), pp. 123ff., where the relation between the Lucan narrative (with allusion to the traitor after, not before, the Institution) and the latter part of I Cor. xi is discussed. The whole article contains interesting material on the traces of the exclusion of the unfit in such passages as I Cor. xvi. 22, Rev. xxii, Heb. xiii. 10, *Didache* 10, I Clement 34, and discusses whether baptism was always the dividing line. On Judas' position, see also Cullmann, *op. cit.* p. 79.

baptismal tribunal and entry beyond judgment into the life of the age to come. It shares something of the reiteration implied in the identification of the Body of Christ with the Church extended through time.

(iii) Apostasy from Baptism or unworthy participation in Holy Communion extrudes a member out of the Body into the realm where the forces of destruction are at work: both alike subject a person to extreme peril.

(iv) It depends upon the person's response to this situation whether it proves to be remedial, and to be a judgment which will prepare him for salvation at last, or whether it plunges him further into a condition of fatal self-concern.

(v) In particular, it appears that the μὴ διακρίνων τὸ σῶμα of I Cor. xi is to be connected with the insensitiveness to God and man to which reference is made frequently in the New Testament in a great variety of terms: an insensitiveness which may (as in Rom. i) render a person ἀδόκιμος—utterly rejected—or may (as is suggested in I Cor. xi) lead to some God-given calamity which rescues the person and brings him to repentance.

NOTE

This essay was written before the appearance of Dr Dodd's study of the Fourth Gospel. Otherwise it would of course have drawn much upon this, the greatest of his recent contributions to New Testament learning.

25

GEGENWART DES GEISTES UND ESCHATOLOGISCHE HOFFNUNG BEI ZARATHUSTRA, SPÄTJÜDISCHEN GRUPPEN, GNOSTIKERN UND DEN ZEUGEN DES NEUEN TESTAMENTES[1]

E. SCHWEIZER

I. DIE ALTTESTAMENTLICHE GRUNDLAGE

DER heilige Geist ist im A.T. verstanden[2] als das außerordentliche Handeln Gottes, das in der Regel nur besonders Auserwählte trifft, meistens auch nur für vorübergehende Zeiten, in denen sie eine außergewöhnliche Aufgabe zu lösen haben.[3] Der Geist bespringt einen Menschen und macht einen anderen aus ihm (I Sam. x. 6). So gerät Saul in Verzückung (x. 10), rast, bis er sich die Kleider vom Leibe reißt und nackt zu Boden fällt (xix. 24). So tun Gideon und Jephta begeisterte Kriegstaten (Ri. vi. 34; xi. 29). So zerreißt Simson Löwen und schlägt dreißig Philister tot, um seine Wette zu bezahlen (xiv. 6, 19). So ziehen ganze Prophetengruppen durchs Land und reißen kraft ihrer Ekstase andere mit (I Sam. x. 5f.; xix. 20ff.). In diesen noch sehr primitiven Vorstellungen ist doch

[1] Da der Herausgeber mich um einen Beitrag zum Thema 'Geist und Eschatologie' bittet, muß ich notgedrungen im neutestamentlichen Teil einiges kurz zusammenfassen, was ich in *Interpretation* (1952), S. 259ff. ('The Spirit of Power') und in *Theol. Existenz heute*, n.F. Heft 32 (1952) ('Geist und Gemeinde im N.T. und heute') ausführlicher darstellte. Für alle Begründungen muß ich auf meinen Artikel zu πνεῦμα im *Theol. Wörterbuch* verweisen.

[2] Zum Folgenden vgl. vor allem W. Eichrodt, *Theol. des A.T.* Bd. II (1948), S. 18ff. (§ 13A) und 65ff. (§ 16 ii 1); L. Köhler, *Theol. des A.T.* (1947=1935), S. 95ff. und 123ff.

[3] Im A.T. wird viel stärker die in Babylonien ausgebildete Linie aufgenommen, wo der Geist der Gottheit als Vermittler übermenschlicher Lebenskraft oder Macht verstanden wird, während die ägyptische Linie, wo die Einhauchung des göttlichen Atems dem Menschen einfach den Lebensodem schenkt, stärker zurücktritt (Eichrodt, S. 19; doch vgl. Köhler, S. 126).

schon die Tatsache unterstrichen, die dem A.T. so sehr am Herzen liegt: daß nämlich der Geist nie gedacht werden kann als der dem Menschen — vielleicht sogar dem vergotteten Menschen — innewohnende, ja nicht einmal als der, der vom Menschen mit ihm zur Verfügung stehenden Mitteln herbeigezwungen werden kann;[1] sondern der immer frei bleibende Geist Jahwes ist. Auch wenn gelegentlich von ihm ausgesagt ist, daß er dauernd über einem besonders Erwählten steht, über Joseph, Mose, Elia, dann zeigt doch die Seltenheit dieser Ausnahmen, daß die Freiheit Jahwes dabei völlig gewahrt wird.[2] Selbst dort, wo der Geist — doch wohl nach einer ursprünglich ganz anderen Konzeption[3] — aufgefaßt wird als die dem Menschen eingehauchte Lebenskraft (Gen. ii. 7; Hiob xxxiii. 4), bleibt er doch ganz Jahwes Geist. Denn sobald Jahwe seinen Atem zurückzieht, weicht alles Leben, und das Geschöpf ist nichts mehr als ein Lehmkloß (Gen. vi. 3; Ps. civ. 29; Hiob xxvii. 3; xxxiv. 14f.). So erscheint denn nie die Vorstellung von einer vor dem Leibe existierenden Seele; 'Geist' ist auch hier nie so etwas wie ein Doppelgänger des Menschen, nie ein höheres Ich, das den Tod überdauerte.[4]

Eben weil der Geist im A.T. so streng als das Handeln Jahwes verstanden ist, findet er seinen Platz in der prophetischen Schau der eschatologischen Heilszeit. Die Endzeit ist ja dadurch charakterisiert, daß Jahwe wieder voll und ungehindert an seinem Volke handeln kann. Dann wird der Messias als der Träger des Geistes Gottes unter ihm sein, dann wird Gott seinen Geist über *alle* ausgießen;[5] dann wird sich erfüllen, was in diesem Aeon nur sehnsüchtig gewünscht werden kann: 'wollte Gott, daß alle im Volke des Herrn Propheten wären, daß der Herr seinen Geist auf sie legte!' (Num. xi. 29.)

Es ist ausgeschlossen, im Rahmen eines kurzes Aufsatzes die verschiedenen Aussagen des Spätjudentums darzustellen.[6] Es dürfte von dem Gesagten her einleuchtend sein, daß die herrschende Meinung

[1] Eichrodt, S. 23.
[2] Köhler, S. 126, Eichrodt, S. 23.
[3] Vgl. Anm. 3, S. 482.
[4] Köhler, S. 131; Eichrodt, S. 67.
[5] Die Stellen bei Eichrodt, S. 26; außerdem Joel iii. 1 (ii. 28).
[6] Dazu vgl. später E. Sjöberg im *Theol. Wörterbuch* zu πνεῦμα, dessen Artikel ich schon einsehen durfte. Die folgenden Belege sind selber zusammengesucht, entbehren daher der Vollständigkeit, die der Fachgelehrte allein zu geben vermöchte.

im 'offiziellen', sich vom A.T. her verstehenden Judentum die ist, daß der Geist in den besonders begnadeten Profeten der Vorzeit lebte,[1] daß er einst in ferner Zukunft wieder Wirklichkeit werden wird,[2] daß er aber in der Gegenwart erloschen ist.[3] Andererseits aber wird der dem Menschen von Gott verliehene Geist immer stärker als das den Tod überdauernde Wesen des Menschen gesehen. Dazu mußte die Entwicklung drängen, sobald dieser dem Menschen eingehauchte Gottesatem (auch unter hellenistischem Einfluß) nicht mehr nur als bloße Vitalität verstanden werden konnte, sondern zugleich die psychischen Funktionen, ja das eigentliche geistliche Leben des Menschen in sich schloß.[4] Auch der Gedanke der Schöpfer-

[1] Vgl. die Belege in Anm. 3, S. 484. Die Identifikation von heiligem Geist und Prophetie geht so weit, daß im Targum oft 'Geist der Prophetie' für 'Geist' eingesetzt wird, auch wo das durchaus nicht paßt (Eichrodt, S. 30, Anm. 3; H. Strack-P. Billerbeck, *Kommentar zum N.T.* Bd. II, S. 127; Bd. IV, S. 435ff.). Die Erstarrung zeigt sich besonders darin, daß 'Geist' und 'Schrift' fast Synonyma werden (F. Jackson-Lake, *The Beginnings of Christianity*, Bd. I (1920–33), S. 5, 98). Daß *ganz* Israel schon früher den Geist besessen habe, ist selten gesagt (*ibid.* S. 4, 26 und Strack-Billerbeck, Bd. II, S. 128).

[2] Strack-Billerbeck, Bd. II, S. 134, 616; Bd. IV, S. 915; neben Jub. i. 23 auch Sib. iii. 582 als Gnadengabe für das Volk der Heilszeit; vgl. ferner Strack-Billerbeck, Bd. III, S. 241 (vgl. S. 828f.); C. K. Barrett, *The Holy Spirit and the Gospel Tradition* (1947), S. 21; A. Schlatter, *Der Evangelist Johannes* (1930), S. 181; Eichrodt, S. 30, Anm. 13 zur Vorstellung vom Geist als der Kraft der Auferstehung.

[3] 'Kein Prophet ist mehr da, und keiner bei uns, der wüßte, bis wann' (Ps. lxxiv. 9). 'Die Gerechten sind zu ihren Vätern versammelt, und die Propheten haben sich schlafen gelegt' (Apk. Bar. lxxxv. 1, 3). 'Als Haggai, Sacharia und Maleachi, die letzten Propheten, gestorben waren, da schwand der heilige Geist aus Israel' (Strack-Billerbeck, Bd. I, S. 127; vgl. auch 129 sub 8). Ferner, I Makk. iv. 46; ix. 27; xiv. 41; Dan. iii. 38 LXX; vgl. Strack-Billerbeck, Bd. II, S. 127ff.; G. F. Moore, *Judaism*, Bd. I (1927), S. 240; W. G. Kümmel in *Judaica*, Bd. I (1945), S. 49ff.; für das hellenistische Judentum: Josephus, c. Ap. I, 8, 3. Wieweit ekstatische Phänomene im Judentum als Wirkungen des Geistes verstanden wurden, ist umstritten. (Trito-) Sacharia xiii. 4 werden sie sehr verdächtigt. Auch damit wäre die at.liche Sicht nicht grundsätzlich verändert, und jedenfalls wären es Ausnahmen (zu solchen vgl. Sjöberg, S. 483, Anm. 6; H. Gunkel, *Die Wirkungen des Geistes* (1888), S. 32; zur Frage der Ordination [=Geistmitteilung?] im Spätjudentum, *ibid.* S. 53; Jackson-Lake, S. 5, 99; Strack-Billerbeck, Bd. II, S. 647ff.; E. Lohse, *Die Ordination im Spätjudentum und im N.T.* (1951). Daß die Apokalyptiker ihre Visionen Geistträgern der Vorzeit in die Schuhe schieben, zeigt doch wohl, daß sie ihr eigenes Geisterlebnis jedenfalls nicht als autoritativ verstehen können (anders Apk.!).

[4] Seele und Geist sind wohl schon Sir. xvi. 17 identifiziert; von dem den Tod überdauernden Seelengeist spricht z.B. schon aeth. Hen. xxii. 3ff.; xxxix. 4ff.; Strack-Billerbeck, Bd. II, S. 437f.; Bd. IV, S. 1131 (erster sicherer Vertreter des

tätigkeit des Gottesgeistes beginnt eine große Rolle zu spielen; doch ist dies vor allem im hellenistischen Judentum der Fall, wo damit die griechischen Urfragen nach der ἀρχή des κόσμος aufgenommen werden.[1]

Für unsere Frage sind diejenigen Gruppen die interessantesten, die wie das N.T. um die Gegenwart des Geistes wissen und sich doch nicht mehr begnügen können mit der Sicht eines — vor allem im Enthusiasmus lebendigen — sprunghaften, vorübergehenden Einwirkens göttlichen Handelns auf den Menschen. Als wesentlich vom Geiste Gottes bestimmt wird die Existenz des Menschen verstanden einerseits in den neugefundenen Texten vom Toten Meer samt ihren persischen Vorläufern und jüdisch-christlichen Nachfahren, andererseits in der Gnosis. Auf sie wollen wir uns im Folgenden konzentrieren.

2. ZARATHUSTRA

Das Spätjudentum ist vor allem unter persischer Herrschaft geboren worden. Zwei Jahrhunderte lang ist unter der Pax Persica die Fortbildung des alttestamentlichen Denkens vor sich gegangen. Nicht nur waren Religions- und Kultübung völlig frei, die persische Regierung hat offensichtlich das Judentum begünstigt.[2] Es mag sein,

Unsterblichkeitsglaubens Jochanan ben Zakkai, gest. um 80). Die Seele stammt vom Himmel, der Leib von der Erde: Sifre Deut. 306 (bei Schlatter, Ev. Joh. 110); dazu Moore (S. 484, Anm. 3), S. 451f. Als Rückgabe des Lebens ist die Totenerweckung verstanden II Makk. vii. 23; xiv. 46; vgl. Sib. iv. 46, 186f. Stärker griechisch geprägte Vorstellungen finden sich im hellenistischen Judentum: so die Vorstellung vom Leib als dem Gefängnis des Geistes Sap. ix. 15; Philo, de somn. I, 139 (p. 642M); dasselbe in IV Makk., bei Josephus, Essäern. Präexistenz der Seelen wird gelehrt: Sap. viii. 19f.; sl. Hen. xxiii. 4f.; für Clemens Alex. vgl. ed. O. Stählin, Bd. IV, S. 824f.; für Exc. e Theodoto 50 und die zahlreichen gnostischen Belege das *Theol. Wörterbuch*; rabbinisch erst sehr spät; Strack-Billerbeck, Bd. II, S. 342ff.

[1] Nicht bei den alten Rabbinen: Strack-Billerbeck, Bd. I, S. 48 (zu T. Chag. ii. 5 vgl. *ibid.* 124); vgl. Barrett 21 und vor allem K. Galling, *Z.Th.K.* (1950), S. 145ff. Wohl aber findet sich diese Vorstellung Judith xvi. 15; Bar. apk. xxi. 4; xxiii. 5 (aeth. Hen. lx. 12ff. gehört nicht direkt hierher) und besonders schön in der phöniz. Kosmogonie (*Corp. Herm.*, ed. W. Scott, Bd. II, S. 112f.). Die theologische Situation des vom Hellenismus beeinflußten Judentums in dieser Frage versuchte ich *Ev. Theol.* (1951/52), S. 502ff. ganz kurz zu skizzieren.

[2] R. H. Pfeiffer, *History of N.T. Times* (1949), S. 6f. In Elephantine werden die dortigen Juden nach Zusammenbruch der Perserherrschaft wohl als Perseranhänger hingemordet (*ibid.* S. 172).

daß verwandte religiöse Anschauungen die Sympathie der Perser fanden und umgekehrt. Dazu gehört neben dem Monotheismus, der in der alten Zarathustrareligion lebt, gerade auch die streng eschatologische Ausrichtung des Glaubens hier wie dort,[1] und die persische Vorstellung vom 'heiligen Geist',[2] die der alttestamentlichen weithin gleicht.[3] Verwandt mußte dem Judentum auch der scharfe, ethisch verstandene Gegensatz zwischen Gut und Böse im Parsismus erscheinen. Und eben hier lag nun seit Jahrhunderten[4] eine Konzeption bereit, die verlockend sein mußte für das Spätjudentum, dem die Tag für Tag zu vollziehende ethische Entscheidung zwischen Gut und Böse immer zentraler wurde:[5] die Konzeption von zwei einander entgegengesetzten Geistern, die den Menschen bestimmen,

[1] Auch die Lehre von der Schöpfung als der guten Tat Gottes mußte verwandt erscheinen. Die Dämonenanschauungen fanden Ansätze im althebräischen Denken, haben aber stark beigetragen zur Ausbildung der spätjüdischen Dämonenlehre (Eichrodt III; W. Bousset-H. Gressmann, *Die Religion des Judentums* (1926), S. 513ff.). Ähnliches ist von der Lehre der Auferstehung zu sagen (A. T. Nikolainen, *Der Auferstehungsglauben in der Bibel und ihrer Umwelt* (1944), S. 22ff., 197).

[2] So C. Bartholomae, *Die Gathas des Awesta* (1905). H. Lommel, *Die Religion des Zarathustra* (1930), übersetzt 'kluger Geist'; H. S. Nyberg, *Die Religionen des alten Iran* (1938), 'wirksamer Geist'.

[3] Der Geist ist bei Zarathustra Schöpfer (Yasna xxx. 4; xlvii. 3) oder Schöpfungsmittler (xxxi. 11); nach K. Geldner, *S.A.B.* (1904, S. 1083 auch xliv. 7). Er schenkt die Gotteserkenntnis (xliv. 7) und ihre Verkündigung (xxviii. 11) und ist göttlicher Lehrer (xlv. 6; xlviii. 3; l. 6), gibt Kraft und Einsicht zum rechten ethischen Handeln (xxviii. 1; xxxiii. 6, 9, 12), läßt Gottes Verheißungen dem Menschen zukommen (xliii. 2; xlv. 5; xlvii. 5; li. 7) und bringt umgekehrt dessen Gebet vor Gott (xlv. 6).

[4] Wo nichts anderes gesagt ist, berücksichtigen wir vorsichtshalber nur, was höchstwahrscheinlich auf Zarathustra selber (also mindestens ins 7. Jahrh. v. Chr.) zurückgeht, obwohl natürlich mit einer schon weiter ausgebildeten chaldäisch-persischen Mischreligion zu rechnen ist (Bousset-Gressmann, S. 481; *Die Religion in Geschichte und Gegenwart*, Bd. IV, S. 1084: seit Darius schon bekennen sich die Regenten zu Ahura Mazda; Kolonisten in Elephantine nennen sich Mazyasnier; Alexander dem Großen begegnen in Babylon chaldäische und persische Priester; das Grabmal des Antiochus von Kommagene bezeugt im 1. Jahrh. v. Chr. eine iranisch-chaldäisch-hellenistische Mischreligion). Die Übersetzungen folgen K. Geldner im *Religionsgeschichtlichen Lesebuch*, Bd. 1 (1926), wobei Bartholomae verglichen ist.

[5] Dazu vgl. Bousset-Gressmann, S. 114ff. Nachträglich fand ich den Artikel von A. Dupont-Sommer, 'L'instruction sur les deux Esprits dans le Manuel de Discipline', *Rev. de l'hist. des rel.* Bd. CXLII (1952), S. 5ff., wo S. 16f. dieselben zwei Gatha-stellen zitiert werden. Ebenso E. Schweizer, *Evang. Theol.* (1951/2), S. 506, Anm. 23; K. G. Kuhn, *Z.Th.K.* (1952), S. 296ff.

und zwischen denen er zu wählen hat. 'Und im Anbeginn waren diese zwei Geister, die Zwillinge, die nach ihren eigenen Worten das Gute und das Böse...heißen. Zwischen ihnen haben die gut Handelnden richtig gewählt, nicht die schlecht Handelnden. Und als diese beiden Geister zuerst zusammen kamen, da bestimmten sie Leben und Tod' (Yasna xxx. 3f., vgl. xlv. 2 und oft). Die Funktion dieser beiden Geister ist insofern eschatologisch, als der gute Geist die eschatologische Vollendung mit erkämpft, während der böse sie verhindern will. Mit dem Siege des guten am Ende der Tage wird die Vollendung da sein (Yast xiii. 13; Yasna x. 16).[1] Beide sind umgeben von einer Schar ihnen zugesellter Geister (Yasna xliii. 16; xxx. 6 und xxxii. 5). Später wird jedem von ihnen sogar eine ihm entsprechende Schöpfung zugeordnet (Yast xi. 12; xiii. 76; xv. 3; xliii; Yasna xix. 9), was eigentlich der alten Anschauung widerspricht, nach der die Schöpfung gut ist (Yasna xxxi. 11), und der Gegensatz zwischen Gut und Böse mitten durch die geistige und die körperliche Welt hindurch geht.[2] Die Entscheidung für den einen oder andern Geist läßt den Menschen zum 'Wahrhaftigen' oder zum 'Lügner' werden (Yasna xxx. 3; xlvii. 4). Obwohl praktisch zur Wahl hier und jetzt aufgerufen wird (Yasna xxx. 2f.; xxxi. 2f.), herrscht theoretisch die Anschauung, daß der Mensch schon in seiner vorweltlichen Existenz sich in freier Wahl entschieden hat (Yasna xxxi. 11f.; vgl. xlvi. 6). Diese vorweltliche Existenz ist bezeichnet mit dem Ausdruck daēna (sprich 'daina'). Die daēna wird inkorporiert in einen irdischen Menschen, um die von ihr getroffene Wahl in Wort und Werk zu betätigen (Yasna xxxi. 11), bleibt aber doch zugleich diesem auch transzendent als sein Doppelich, als seine 'geistig-religiöse Individualität', die zugleich 'auch von ihrem Träger getrennt gedacht wird',[3] als 'die Kraft oder Teilseele, die beim religiösen Schauen in Funktion tritt', '"Unsterblichkeitsorgan" im weitesten Sinne'.[4] Sie ist nach späteren Texten das von Leib und Seele unterschiedene religiöse Selbst, das nach dem Tode der Seele als Doppelich begegnet.[5]

[1] Diese Stellen gehen nicht auf Zarathustra selber zurück.

[2] Lommel (S. 486, Anm. 2), S. 101–29.

[3] E. Abegg, *Der Messiasglaube in Indien und Iran* (1928), S. 204, Anm. 3.

[4] Nyberg (S. 486, Anm. 2), S. 115f.

[5] Yast xxii; xxiii. 53–65 (Lommel [S. 486, Anm. 2], S. 149); Yasna l. 4 noch anders.

Fragen wir nach der eschatologischen Rolle, die der Geist hier spielt, dann ist deutlich, daß die Lage hier ganz anders ist als im A.T. Der Geist ist ja hier gedacht als etwas, was dauernd präsent ist, was geradezu die Existenz des Menschen in seinem vorweltlichen wie vor allem in seinem weltlichen Leben bestimmt. Er ist das ihm stets präsente 'Gute', für das er sich entschieden hat und stets neu *in concreto* entscheidet, wobei dieses Gute nicht etwa bloß als eine — etwa gar ihm innewohnende — Idee verstanden wird, sondern als eine ihn fordernde und ihn unterstützende Kraft Gottes. Insofern als Ahura Mazda die eschatologische Vollendung herbeiführt, ist natürlich auch der Geist daran beteiligt. So wie er an der Schöpfung mitbeteiligt ist,[1] so auch am Kampf gegen die die Vollendung hindernden bösen Mächte und am Gericht, wo er neben dem 'Feuer' den Lohn zuteilt.[2] Aber eschatologisches Phänomen in dem Sinn, daß sein Auftreten ein Teil des endzeitlichen Handelns Gottes oder ein Zeichen daraufhin wäre, kann der Geist hier nicht werden. Er ist ja geradezu das Charakteristikum der noch nicht eschatologischen, der innerweltlichen Existenz des Menschen.

3. DER GEISTBEGRIFF DER 'DEAD SEA SCROLLS'

Seit den großen Propheten und vor allem seit dem Exil versteht Israel immer stärker Jahwe nicht mehr nur als den erhabenen Gott des Wunders, den 'ganz anderen', sondern als den Gott der Wahrheit und des Rechtes; darum dann auch seinen Geist nicht mehr nur als die Kraft des Außerordentlichen, sondern als die Kraft des ethisch Guten. So kann schon am Rande des A.T. der Geist auch erscheinen als der ständige Begleiter des Menschen, der ihm den ethisch guten Wandel schenkt, zuerst nur als Phänomen der endzeitlichen Gemeinde, aber dann doch auch schon als Erscheinung des diesseitigen Lebens.[3] Parallel dazu läuft — vielleicht schon unter persischem Einfluß — eine immer stärker werdende Verselbständigung des Geistes zu einer Art Hypostase.[4] Je weiter wir aber ins Spätjudentum

[1] Vgl. S. 486, Anm. 3.

[2] Yasna xxxi. 3; xlvii. 6; nichtzarathustrisch, aber sehr alt auch xxxvi. 1, 3; der Geist allein ist genannt bei Zarathustra xxxi. 7; xlviii. 8; li. 7, mit zwei andern Ahuras zusammen im Gefolge Ahura Mazdas xliii. 6; das Feuer allein xxxi. 19; xliii. 4; li. 9. Zu Matt. iii. 11 vgl. E. Schweizer, *Exp. T.* Bd. LXV, S. 29.

[3] Eichrodt (S. 482, Anm. 2), S. 25–8 (§ 13A, III, IV). [4] *Ibid.* 27, 31.

vordringen, desto zentraler wird die ethische Entscheidung des Einzelnen, die Wahl zwischen Gut und Böse.[1] So lag der Weg frei zur Übernahme der persischen Sicht. Blieb man bei der alten, trotz allen Weiterentwicklungen doch noch zentralen Geistanschauung des A.T., dann mußte man die Wirksamkeit des Geistes ausschließlich oder doch hauptsächlich in die ferne Vergangenheit und die eschatologische Zukunft verschieben[2] oder ihn in den ekstatischen Erlebnissen der Gegenwart erblicken.[3] Dachte man aber von der immer wichtiger gewordenen ethischen Entscheidung des Einzelnen her, so mußten sich die persischen Vorstellungen aufdrängen, da sie ja eine auch innerhalb der prophetischen Verkündigung des A.T. entwickelte Linie aufnehmen konnten.

So ist es nicht verwunderlich, daß das *Manual of Discipline* (DSD) beherrscht ist durch die Konzeption von den zwei Geistern, die um den Menschen kämpfen: '(Gott) setzte ihm (dem Menschen) zwei Geister, in ihnen zu wandeln bis zur Zeit der Heimsuchung. Sie sind die Geister der Wahrheit und der Bosheit' (iii. 18f.).[4] 'Bis jetzt kämpfen die Geister der Wahrheit und der Bosheit im Menschenherzen; sie wandeln in Weisheit und Torheit' (iv. 23f.). 'Gott hat sie zu gleichen Teilen gesetzt bis zur Zeit des Gerichts' (iv. 25). An anderer Stelle heißen dieselben 'Geist des Lichts und der Finsternis' (iii. 25).

Aber wir wollen vorsichtig sein. Ist mit der Übernahme der Form dieser Anschauung auch ihr sachlicher Gehalt übernommen worden, oder ist sie vielleicht nur die Gestalt, in der etwas völlig anderes dargestellt werden soll? Wieder fragen wir nach der Stellung des Geistbegriffes zur Eschatologie, weil dabei die Frage noch präziser wird. Unleugbar lebt diese jüdische Gruppe in einer lebendigen eschatologischen Haltung, ja sogar im Wissen darum, daß die bald hereinbrechende Endzeit in gewissem Sinne schon in die Gegenwart

[1] Vgl. S. 486, Anm. 5.

[2] Vgl. die unter 1. genannten Stellen.

[3] So besonders deutlich in Philos Theorie der Ekstase (Rer. div. her. 265). Vgl. noch S. 484, Anm. 3

[4] Ich zitiere nach W. H. Brownlee (*B.A.S.O.R.*, Suppl. Studies 10 12, 1951) und einer mir von K. G. Kuhn in Göttingen freundlichst überlassenen Übersetzung der wichtigsten Stellen, wobei ich immer nach dem hebr. Text nachprüfe (*The Dead Sea Scrolls of St Mark's Monastery*, Bd. II, 1950). Nachträglich sah ich den Artikel von J. P. Audet, *Rev. Bibl.* (1952), S. 219ff., der den Gedanken der 'zwei Wege' in DSD und Hermas untersucht. Dupont-Sommer (S. 486, Anm. 5) gibt Übersetzung und sorgfältigen Kommentar für DSD iii. 13–iv. 26.

hineinreicht.[1] Auch hier kämpfen die beiden Geister 'bis zum Gericht'. Aber diese Konzeption ist nun doch völlig hineingenommen in die Situation der spätjüdischen Gesetzesbeobachtung,[2] wo die ethische Entscheidung zwischen Gut und Böse absolutes Zentrum ist. So ist hier der Geist nicht mehr derjenige, der um die Endvollendung kämpft wie im Persischen; erst recht natürlich nicht mehr derjenige, der die Endzeit selber charakterisiert[3] wie im A.T. Er ist fast ausschließlich Phänomen der Kampfzeit, in der der Mensch in der Wahl zwischen Gut und Böse steht. Selbst die Nennung des Gerichtes dient wohl dazu, dieser Wahl ihren vollen Ernst zu geben.

Ja, man muß noch weiter gehen. Ist nicht vielleicht die ganze Vorstellung von den zwei Geistern nur eine Einkleidung der Wahrheit, daß der Mensch moralisch leben, moralisch zwischen zwei Prinzipien wählen muß? Stehen wir also nicht völlig auf dem gleichen Boden wie die spätere rabbinische Anschauung von den zwei dem Menschen gegebenen Trieben?[4] Damit wäre der Entscheidungs-

[1] Vgl. K. G. Kuhn, *Z.Th.K.* (1950), S. 208f., der übrigens auch diese Dokumente stark als Nachklang persischer Anschauungen sieht (S. 211). Nachträglich konnte ich auch seinen Artikel *Z.Th.K.* (1952), S. 200ff. einsehen, wo S. 205, Anm 2 auch verwiesen wird auf 'Die Sektenschrift und die Gathas des Zarathustra' (wird in den Veröffentlichungen des nt.lichen Seminars Uppsala erscheinen).

Kuhns Belege für die Verbindung von 'Fleisch' und 'Frevel' in DSS sind sicher wichtig. Der Gegensatz zum 'Geist' fehlt freilich. Kann dieser nicht doch erst gedacht werden in einer Welt, die vom hellenistischen Gegensatz (S. 499, Anm. 2f., S. 500, Anm. 1) mindestens mitbeeinflußt ist? Freilich, wer will noch sauber scheiden, wie weit das Reden vom göttlichen Geist im Menschen (vgl. weiter unten, besonders S. 494, Anm. 1) noch von den Anschauungen von Gen. ii. 7, wie weit schon von den S. 497, Anm. 2 und S. 499, Anm. 3, genannten her bestimmt ist; wie weit das Reden vom 'Fleisch des Frevels' nur den at.lichen Gedanken ausprägt, daß die ganze Menschheit von Gott abgefallen ist, wie weit es schon die Anschauung von der Schlechtigkeit der Materie in sich schließt? Daß man im 1. Jahrh. n. Chr. nicht mehr klar scheiden kann zwischen Palästinensischem und Hellenistischem, zeigt W. D. Davies, *Paul and Rabbinic Judaism* (1948), S. 5ff. (vgl. R. M. Grant, *J. of Rel.* Bd. XXXI (1951), S. 213). [2] *Z.Th.K.* (1950), 205 ff.

[3] Eine einzige Stelle spricht von der eschatologischen Rolle des Geistes, aber auch hier nur passiv: im Eschaton werden die Gerechten durch den heiligen Geist gereinigt von allen bösen Geistern (iv. 20f.). Dupont-Sommer (S. 486, Anm. 5), S. 11 übersetzt: 'pour supprimer tout l'Esprit de perversité de son enveloppe (die Konjektur ist S. 32 begründet) charnelle et pour le purifier par l'Esprit de sainteté de tous les actes d'impiété', was die Vorstellung des Leibes als eines bloßen Gewandes der Seele ergäbe, wie wir sie in der Gnosis ähnlich wieder finden werden.

[4] So versteht Strack-Billerbeck, Bd. IV, S. 465, Test. Jud. XX (vgl. hier unter 4.); zur ganzen Frage vgl. *ibid.* S. 465–83; Davies (S. 490, Anm. 1), S. 20ff.; H. Odeberg, *The Fourth Gospel*, Bd. I (1929), S. 297ff. Die Doppelheit der beiden Triebe ist

charakter menschlichen Lebens, wie er im A.T. ja dauernd durch die Entscheidung zwischen Jahwe und Baal, zwischen Gehorsam und Ungehorsam dargestellt wird, nur in einer neuen Form wiedererstanden, in der nicht mehr die einmalige Entscheidung, sondern die alltäglich sich wiederholende zentral geworden wäre. 'In ihnen (den zwei Geistern) zu wandeln' ist hier ja identisch mit 'in den Wegen des Lichts, bzw. der Finsternis wandeln' (iii. 20f.)! Die 'Ratschläge' des guten Geistes sind eine Aufforderung zu einer ganzen Reihe von Tugenden, und ein ganzer Lasterkatalog zählt all die Dinge auf, die 'zum Geist der Bosheit gehören' (iv. 6ff.).[1]

Dennoch dürfte dies nicht genügen. So stark das ethische Anliegen ist, so stark ist doch auch das Wissen darum, daß der Mensch nicht aus seiner Kraft, sondern aus der Kraft Gottes lebt, daß sein Leben letztlich Handeln *Gottes* an ihm ist. Darin setzt sich das at.liche Wissen darum, daß der Geist Jahwes nicht der Geist des Menschen ist, fort. Die griechische Konzeption von der Identität des Geistes im Menschen mit dem kosmischen göttlichen Geist[2] ist hier noch nicht eingedrungen. Darum wird hier auch die stark mythologische Form nicht nur mitgeschleppt, sondern als Ausdrucksmittel benützt für die Erkenntnis, daß der Mensch in seiner entscheidenden Existenz von außen her, von dem nicht mit ihm identischen, sondern ihm gegenüberstehenden Gott geprägt ist. So erscheinen die beiden Geister zugleich als zwei *Engel*. Das ist nicht nur ein anderer Name für dieselbe Sache; sondern darin schwingt das Wissen darum mit, daß sie letztlich nur *Gottes* Handeln am Menschen darstellen und Boten seiner Macht sind, nicht losgelöste Mächte. Darum wechselt 'Geist' mit 'Engel' (iii. 21, 24/25) oder 'Fürst' (iii. 20), wobei immer festgehalten wird — im Unterschied zum Persischen — daß beide von Gott geschaffen sind (iii. 25). Dabei kann mindestens der böse Geist auch in einer Mehrzahl von Geistern erscheinen (iii. 24;

zuerst Test. A. i. 6 bezeugt (Davies, S. 21); aber es fragt sich, ob nicht gerade hier, wo die Vorstellung von den beiden Geistern so sehr lebendig ist, diese sich verbunden hat mit derjenigen vom bösen Trieb, der vielleicht schon Sir. xv. 14 (so Davies, S. 20; anders Kautzsch z.St.) und im IV Esr. erscheint.

[1] Vgl. die Terminologie in Test. A. 1 und Kuhn, *Z.Th.K.* (1950), S. 206f. Zum Weiterleben der Lehre von den zwei Wegen vgl. J. P. Audet, *Rev. Bibl.* (1952), S. 219ff.; Dupont-Sommer (S. 486, Anm. 5), S. 22.

[2] Vgl. S. 497, Anm. 2.

iv. 20),[1] wodurch die umfassende Macht seiner Einwirkung noch stärker betont ist. So sind diese beiden Geister oder Engel oder Fürsten durchaus als Mächte verstanden, die ausserhalb des Menschen stehen, ihn verführen oder ihm helfen (iii. 24; vgl. iv. 2). Das ist so ausgeprägt, daß sich die Aussagen einer Prädestinationslehre nähern: 'Entsprechend dem, daß eines Menschen Erbe in Wahrheit und Gerechtigkeit besteht, haßt er das Böse; sofern aber sein Erbe im Teile der Bosheit und Schlechtigkeit in ihm ist, haßt er die Wahrheit' (iv. 24f.). 'Und es fiel einem Menschen das ewige Los zu, mit den Geistern der Erkenntnis deinen Namen zu preisen.'[2]

Daneben läuft hier aber noch ein anderer Wortgebrauch, der weithin mit dem übereinstimmt, was auch sonst im Judentum festzustellen ist.[3] 'Geist' kann auch anthropologisch als Geist des Menschen verstanden werden. 'Mein Geist' steht gelegentlich ganz parallel zu 'ich'.[4] Es kann wie im A.T. vom 'zerbrochenen Geist' (viii. 3; xi. 1; vgl. Ps. li. 19) oder vom 'Geist der Demut' (iv. 3) oder vom 'Irren des verständigen Geistes' (xi. 1) gesprochen werden. In v. 23f. und vi. 14/17 scheint 'Geist' völlig identisch zu sein mit 'Verstand'. Und doch wird sofort deutlich, daß diese Auskunft noch nicht genügt. Auch wo der Geist der Geist des Menschen ist, ist er doch etwas anderes als sein Verstand. Neben der Aussage, daß die Glieder der Gemeinde zu prüfen seien nach ihrem Geiste (oder Verstand) und ihren Taten, stehen die andern, in denen 'Geist' zusammenfassend Verstand *und* Taten umfaßt (v. 21; vgl. ii. 20; iv. 26; ix. 14). Noch deutlicher wird das, wenn wir erkennen, daß es der 'Geist' eines Menschen ist, der abfällt oder von Gott wieder gereinigt wird (vii. 18, 23; viii. 12).[5] 'Geist' meint also die *ganze* Existenz des Menschen, und zwar als die vor Gott stehende, als

[1] Sefer ha-Hodajot (E. L. Sukenik, Megillot Genuzot II) [=Hod.] viii. 1; ix. 27 auch von den 'Geistern der Erkenntnis'. Hod. kann ich hier nicht nachprüfen; Stellen und Übersetzung verdanke ich K. G. Kuhn.

[2] Hod. viii. 5. Der schärfste Satz: 'Den einen hat Gott geliebt für alle Ewigkeit und freut sich an allen seinen Tätigkeiten für immer; was den andern betrifft, hat er seinen Rat verabscheut und alle seine Wege gehaßt für immer' (DSD iii. 26/iv. 1), bezieht sich wohl auf die beiden Geister. Hingegen steht DSD iv. 4 vielleicht 'Geist der Erkenntnis' und 'Gnade' parallel, sodaß der gute Geist Darstellung der Gnade wäre durch die der Mensch ganz bestimmt ist. Hängt das zusammen mit der persischen Anschauung, daß die vorweltliche Wahl schon das ganze irdische Leben entschieden hat?

[3] Vgl. oben unter 1. [4] Hod. ix. 32. [5] Vgl. Hod. viii. 4.

'religiöse'. Selbst dort wo das Wort fast synonym wird mit 'Verstand', ist der von Gott erleuchtete 'Verstand', die einem Menschen geschenkte geistliche Erkenntnis gemeint. Was hier mit 'Geist' bezeichnet wird, das ist in seinem tiefsten, noch nicht klar herausgearbeiteten Anliegen ein Leib und Seele (im at.lichen Sinn) übergeordnetes Selbst, das die eigentliche, die geistliche Existenz des Menschen als des vor Gott lebenden darstellt. Es ist möglich, daß die dem Judentum begegnende Vorstellung von der daēna, in der die Transzendenz dieses Selbst besonders augenfällig erscheint, mitgeholfen hat, das Problem eines von Leib und Seele noch zu scheidenden geistlichen Ich zu sehen und darum zu ringen.[1]

Die beiden an sich völlig getrennten Gedankenlinien können sich verbinden. Wird diese geistliche Existenz des Menschen stark prädestinatianisch verstanden, dann ist sie ausschließlich bestimmt durch *den* (guten oder bösen) Geist, sodaß sie beinahe mit diesem in eins gesehen werden kann. Es gibt Stellen, wo man sich fragen kann, ob die 'Geister der Erkenntnis' nicht die Mitglieder der Gemeinde,[2] und die 'Geister seines (des bösen Geistes) Loses' nicht die 'Söhne der Finsternis', d.h. die Gegner der Gemeinde sind (iii. 20–4). Die Identifikation könnte religionsgeschichtlich von der persischen Tradition der inkorporierten daēna her gut verstanden werden. Sachlich drückt sie nur die absolute Bestimmtheit des Menschen durch den ihn beherrschenden Geist aus.

4. DIE TESTAMENTE DER PATRIARCHEN

Die direkte Weiterführung dieser Gedanken findet sich jüdisch in den *Test. XII*, christlich in den *mandata* des Hermas. Während der Gedanke der absoluten Bestimmtheit des innersten, geistlichen Selbst des Menschen in der Gnosis in neuer Art aufgenommen wird, wird der jüdische Gedanke der freien ethischen Entscheidung in den genannten Schriften noch stärker betont als in DSD. Auch in Test. Jud. xx. 1 sind es zwei Geister, 'der Geist der Wahrheit und des

[1] Dieses Problem versuchte ich *Evang. Theol.* (1951/2), S. 502ff. kurz zu verfolgen. Dupont-Sommer (S. 486, Anm. 5) versteht so, daß der 'Geist' des Einzelnen immer teilhat an beiden 'Geistern', nur in verschiedenem Maße (S. 13, 28f.).

[2] 'Und es fiel einem Menschen zu das ewige Los, mit den Geistern der Erkenntnis, deinen Namen zu preisen in der Gemeinschaft ihres Volkes' (Hod. ix. 27).

Irrtums', die dem Menschen gesetzt sind, wobei der Geist der Wahrheit sehr oft als 'Engel' des Friedens oder der Fürbitte erscheint neben dem oder den bösen Geistern (Test. L v. 6; D vi. 1f.; B vi. 1). Deutlicher als in DSD werden die bösen Geister auf Beliar (D i. 7; Iss vii. 7 usw.) bzw. Satan (Gad iv. 7, wo auf der Gegenseite typischerweise das *Gesetz* Gottes erscheint!) zurückgeführt. Der böse Geist erscheint dabei öfters entfaltet in eine Schar von Geistern, die je ein Laster des Menschen darstellen (R iii. 3ff.; D i. 6; vgl. L ix. 9; Jud xiii. 3 'Geist der Hurerei'). Im allgemeinen ist die Vorstellung deutlich die, daß der böse Geist verführend (D iv. 5), der gute Engel fürbittend wirkt (L v. 6; D vi. 2; B vi. 1), wobei die Entscheidung beim Menschen selbst liegt, der sich vor den bösen Geistern zu hüten hat (S iii. 1). Am typischsten ist Jud xx. 1, wo außer dem guten und dem bösen Geist noch 'der mittlere Geist der Einsicht und des Verstandes, wohin er neigen will' genannt ist. Das ist die mythische Darstellung des frei entscheidenden, zwischen Gut und Böse wählenden Ich des Menschen. Die bei Hermas sich findenden weitergehenden Vorstellungen, die die Bestimmtheit des Menschen durch den Geist wieder stärker betonen, finden sich hier erst angedeutet: der Mensch, der sich für das Böse entschieden hat, ist gesehen als ein Gefäß, das vom Teufel bewohnt ist (N viii. 6). Mit der Falschentscheidung hat sich der Mensch einer Übermacht ausgeliefert, die ihn gefangen nimmt. In der hebräischen Fassung N x. 9 hingegen finden wir wieder die andere Linie vor, die sich dann bei Hermas deutlich mit der ersten verbindet: der Geist ist nicht die dem Menschen übergeordnete Macht, die ihn prägt, sondern ein depositum göttlichen Ursprungs, das von ihm geprägt wird, das er verändern, schlecht machen kann, das er aber 'rein zurückgeben' sollte.[1]

5. DER HIRTE DES HERMAS

Noch prägnanter ist die Entwicklung hier zu konstatieren. Auch bei Hermas sind es zwei Geister (m V 1, 4; 2, 5 usw.), von denen der gute 'Geist der Wahrheit' heißt (m III 4), oder zwei Engel, der

[1] Dieselbe Anschauung finden wir CDC v. 11; vii. 3f. (wo deutlich wird, daß des Menschen 'heiliger Geist' an die Stelle der alttestamentlichen 'Seele' von Lev. xx. 25 gerückt ist); LvR 18 (117d) und anderes bei Strack-Billerbeck, Bd. 1, S. 205f.; TB Nidda 30a bei Odeberg (S. 490, Anm. 4), S. 172, Anm. 1.

'Engel der Gerechtigkeit' und der 'Engel der Bosheit' (m VI 2, 1 f., 4, 9; vgl. XI 9), die um den Menschen kämpfen.[1] Dabei ist die Vorstellung die, daß der Mensch ein Gefäß ist, in dem je nachdem der eine oder der andere Geist wohnt. Sind beide zusammen im gleichen Gefäß, so ist das dem Menschen unzuträglich, und der gute Geist, der zart ist (m V 1, 3; ebenso vom 'Engel der Gerechtigkeit' VI 2, 2), wird vom bösen verdunkelt, bedrängt, erstickt, hinausgeworfen, worauf sich das leere Gefäß schleunigst mit bösen Geistern füllt (m V 1, 2–4; 2, 5–7; X 1, 2; 2, 6). Dasselbe ist m III 4; X 3, 2 mit dem biblischen Ausdruck (Jes. lxiii. 10; Eph. iv. 30) gesagt: er wird 'betrübt'. Die Anschauung ist dabei ausgesprochen moralisch geworden. Anstelle des bösen Geistes kann einfach das böse Gewissen rücken (m III 4). Der gute Geist hingegen ist eindeutig mit dem heiligen Geist Gottes gleichgesetzt; aber mit dem heiligen Geist, der 'in dir wohnt', der 'in dies dein Fleisch gegeben ward' (m III 1; V 1, 2; X 2, 5 f.). Der böse Geist erscheint oft entfaltet in eine Mehrzahl von bösen Geistern, die dann einzelnen Lastern gleichgesetzt werden (z.B. m V 2, 8; X 1, 2), so wie an anderer Stelle auch die heiligen Geister mit den Jungfrauen und diese mit den verschiedenen Tugenden identifiziert werden (s XIII u. XV). Dabei steckt hinter diesen Bildern noch deutlich die alte Vorstellung vom unentfliehbaren Zwang, den diese Geister oder Engel auf den Menschen ausüben: 'Wenn im Herzen (des ganz Schlechten) die Werke des Engels der Gerechtigkeit aufsteigen, so muß er mit Notwendigkeit etwas Gutes tun' (m VI 2, 8); freilich zeigt die Fortsetzung, daß es dem Verfasser nur um den moralischen Aufruf geht: 'Du siehst also, ... daß es schön ist, dem Engel der Gerechtigkeit zu folgen und dem Engel der Bosheit zu entsagen' (Vers 9). So kann er auch die Bedrängnis, in die der heilige Geist durch den bösen Geist gerät, als verantwortliche Tat des Menschen verstehen: 'Rotte also die Traurigkeit (die der böseste Geist ist!) aus und bedränge nicht den heiligen Geist, der in dir wohnt' (m X 2, 5). Ähnlich sieht s IX, 15, 6 das Verhältnis in seiner Doppelheit: 'Niemals haben sie sich von

[1] Die Ableitung dieser Vorstellungen von dem griechischen (nicht sehr verbreiteten) Glauben an zwei persönliche Dämonen, von denen der eine gut, der andere böse ist, M. P. Nilsson, *Geschichte der griechischen Religion*, Bd. II (1950), S. 201 f., dürfte seit dem Fund der DSS nicht mehr vertretbar sein. Zu den Dämonen allg. vgl. *ibid.* S. 244 f.

einander entfernt, weder die Geister von den Menschen noch die Menschen von den Geistern'; oder es wird s IX 24, 2 von den Gerechten erklärt, sie hätten 'den heiligen Geist dieser Jungfrauen *angezogen*'.

Von da aus ist es verständlich, daß die ursprünglich ganz andere Sicht vom Geist als dem reinen depositum Gottes, das der Mensch ihm unversehrt, nicht lügnerisch oder unbrauchbar gemacht zurückgeben muß, sich mit der ersten verbindet (m III 1; IX 32, 2–4). War dort der Geist unveränderlich gut gedacht, sodaß er nur bedrängt und schließlich ausgetrieben werden konnte, so ist er hier wie die von Gott gegebene 'Seele' als vom Menschen prägbares Gut verstanden.

Was wir schon für die DSS feststellten, das ist auch hier festzustellen. Auf der Linie, die von der persischen Vorstellung der zwei Geister herkommt, kann der Geist nur als ein Phänomen verstanden werden, das gerade die noch nicht eschatologische Zeit charakterisiert. Er bestimmt die Situation des moralisch lebenden, ethisch entscheiden müssenden Menschen, wenn auch eben mit der Nennung des Geistes betont werden soll, daß diese Situation durch das Handeln *Gottes* am Menschen geprägt ist. Dasselbe zeigt sich in der andern Aussage, daß die 'Seele' oder dann eben der 'Geist' dem Menschen von Gott gegeben ist und von ihm 'verwaltet' werden muß. Eine eschatologische Rolle des Geistes wäre hier nur in der Form denkbar, daß dieser 'Geist' aus dem menschlichen Leben weg zu sich selbst (bzw. zu Gott) zurückkehrte und dann als 'reiner' Geist eine eschatologische Existenz führte.

6. DIE GNOSIS

Eben davon spricht die Gnosis. Sie nimmt zunächst die Vorstellung von der von Gott in den Menschen gelegten 'Seele' auf, modifiziert sie freilich noch radikaler, als wir es schon vorfanden im Judentum, dahin, daß das innerste Selbst, die eigentlich geistliche Existenz des Menschen als Leib und Seele *gegenüber* stehend verstanden ist.[1] Insofern ist hier sehr stark aufgenommen, was in der Konzeption der daēna betont war: das innerste Ich des Menschen ist weder seine Lebenskraft noch seine psychische Fähigkeit; es ist ein ihn Transzendierendes. Anders als bei der daēna ist aber beim gnostischen

[1] Dazu vgl. H. Jonas, *Gnosis und spätantiker Geist* (1934), S. 143ff.

Selbst keine Rede mehr von einer vorweltlichen freien Wahl und erst recht nicht von einem Mitkämpfen an der eschatologischen Vollendung. Aber auch von den spätjüdischen Vorstellungen hebt sich der gnostische Geistbegriff ab, obwohl das Anliegen, die innerste geistliche Existenz des Menschen als ihm transzendente, als Gottes Existenz in ihm zu fassen, ihnen allen gemeinsam ist. Das Spätjudentum denkt die Existenz des Menschen *actualiter*, entweder bestimmt durch das dauernde *Wirken* des guten oder bösen Geistes, oder dann zwar göttlichen Ursprungs aber doch dauernd geprägt, bewahrt oder verändert durch das ethische *Handeln* des Menschen. Die Gnosis denkt diese innerste Existenz als ein *Sein*. Hier wirkt hellenistisches Denken nach.

Der Hellenist muß in Substanzen denken. Auch Kraft kann er nur als Substanz denken.[1] Was also der Jude als Handeln Gottes, bzw. seines Geistes am Menschen denkt, denkt der Hellenist als göttliche Substanz. In dieser Kategorie kann er wohl die absolute Transzendenz des Geistes betonen, nicht aber das ethische Anliegen des Perser- wie des Judentums aufnehmen und erst recht nicht von einem Handeln, oder gar einem eschatologischen Handeln des Geistes sprechen. So kann in der Stoa der Geist die lebenspendende göttliche Substanz sein, die in verschiedener Spannung den ganzen Kosmos durchdringt und so auch im Menschen selbst zu finden ist. Gott wohnt als Geist im Menschen.[2] Der Gnostiker kann freilich diese in

[1] Diog. Laert. VII, 38, § 56: 'alle Kraft ist Substanz'; ebenso Plutarch (H. Diels, *Doxogr. Graeci* (1879), S. 410, 6); speziell zur Substanzhaftigkeit des Begriffs πνεῦμα oder πνοή vgl. Nilsson, (S. 495, Anm. 1), S. 254 (vgl. 250ff.), 675. Ferner vgl. Diog. Laert. x, 67, wo die Körperlichkeit der Seele damit begründet wird, daß sie fähig sei 'zu tun und zu erleiden'. Instruktiv ist auch Plutarch, Comm. Not. 50. Um 400 (?) n. Chr. referiert Nemesius, Bischof von Emesa, *De nat. hom.* Kap. II, S. 30 und 40 als Meinung von Stoikern (?) und Aristoteles: 'Die Kraft ist Materie' und 'Die Kraft ist aus Materie bestehend (= ihrer teilhaftig)', bzw.: 'So ist die Materie Kraft.' Zur Körperlichkeit der Seele vgl. *ibid.* S. 28f., 34 u. oft.

[2] Da ich den Artikel 'πνεῦμα im Griechentum' von H. Kleinknecht für das *Theol. Wörterbuch* noch nicht kenne, kann ich nur ganz knapp die wichtigsten Belege selber zusammenstellen. Ich zitiere nach: J. v. Arnim, *Stoicorum vet. fragm.* 1921–4 (=*A*); H. Diels-W. Kranz, *Die Fragmente der Vorsokratiker*, 1934–7 (=*D*); H. Diels, *Doxographi Graeci*, 1879 (=*Dox*); O. Kern, *Orphicorum Fragm.* 1922 (=*K*); W. Scott, *Hermetica*, 1924f. (=*Sc*). Am meisten gelernt habe ich bei: E. B. Allo, *Rev. Bibl.* Bd. XLIII, 1934, 321ff.; E. de W. Burton, *Spirit, Soul and Flesh*, 1918 (=*B*); *idem, Galatians*, I.C.C., S. 486ff.; J. Dupont, *Gnosis*, 1949; A. J. Festugière, *L'idéal*

ihrem Wesen altgriechische Schau der Einheit Gottes mit dem Kosmos nicht mehr übernehmen. Ein allgemeines pessimistisches

religieux des Grecs et l'Evangile, 1932 (=*F*); Nilsson (S. 495, Anm. 1) (=*N*); H. Reitzenstein, *Die hellenistischen Mysterienreligionen*, 1927; G. Verbeke, *L'évolution de la doctrine du pneuma du stoicisme à S. Augustin*, 1945 (=*V*).

Πνεῦμα bedeutet im Griechentum:

(*a*) Wind, Luft, Atem: *D* III 358f.; *A* IV 115; *B* 14ff., 80, 123ff.

(*b*) Als solches die Lebenskraft im Körper: orphisch: *K* 56; von der Seele als dem πνεῦμα ἔνθερμον spricht Zeno: *A* I 135, III 305; es ist die Lebenskraft im menschlichen Samen: *A* I 128; Diog. Laert. VII 85 (158); für Chrysipp: Polyb. hist. XIII, 1a, 2; für die Stoa allg.: *A* II 796; als bewegte Luft: *A* II 471; als πνεῦμα σύμφυτον ἡμῖν: *A* II 716, 774, 778; dasselbe bei Aristoteles: 659b, 17; 669a, 1; 744a, 3; vgl. 394b, 10; 741b, 37 (ed. Bekker, Bd. 1); ferner Dio Chrysostomus II, 66, 5 (Dindorf); *V* 24, Anm. 46.

Medizinisch ist es die Wärme, der 'Dampf' des Blutes bis hin zu Plato und Aristoteles: Allo 328f., vgl. Corp. Herm. 10, 17 (*Sc* I 198, 23). Es durchdringt den Körper als Kraft der Sinnesorgane: Stoa: *A* II 71, 826; *Dox* 394, 7; 406, 6f.; 411, 3ff.; Varro: Augustin, *Civ. Dei* VII 23; Epiktet II 23, 3; Galen V 287 (Kühn); Corp. Herm. 10, 13; Stob. Exc. 19, 5 (*Sc* I 448, 13); Nemesius (S. 497, Anm. 1), S. 77, Kap. VI. Als körperliches Luftelement versteht es auch Mark Aurel: *F* 270. Das wirkt fort in der gnost. Vorstellung von der Aufnahme des πνεῦμα durch den Embryo mittels der Rückgrataorta: H. Leisegang, *Gnosis*, 77 (Ausg. Kröner).

(*c*) Anknüpfend an die Bezeichnung der Seele als πνεῦμα (=vergänglicher Atem) bei Xenophanes (*D* I 113, 28) und seinem Zeitgenossen Anaximenes, der die Seele in Analogie zu der den Kosmos umgebenden Luft versteht (Plutarch, plac. phil. 1, 3 [876B; Dübner IV 1067] und ganz ähnlich noch Stob. Exc. 15, 4 [*Sc* I 438, 17f.]; weiteres *D* III 359), wird πνεῦμα deutlich als Seelenstoff verstanden bei Zeno und seinen Schülern: *A* I 136, 138, 140; II 715, 774, 778 (vgl. 796); III 305; es bleibt dabei eines der vier Elemente: Epiktet III 13, 15 (vgl. A. Bonhöfer, *Epiktet und das N.T.* (1911), S. 163); die Seele ist darum auch σῶμα: Zeno *A* I 137, Diog. Laert. VII 84 (156); Epikur ep. 1, 63; und zur ganzen Frage: *B* 88f., *F* 211, *V* 17ff., 388, 406. Dabei wird von Erasistratos bis zu Galens Referat über die Stoiker (*A* II 716) geschieden zwischen physischem und psychischem πνεῦμα: Allo 330.

(*d*) Wie den menschlichen Körper, so durchflutet es auch den Kosmos: Jünger des Pythagoras und Empedokles: *D* I 367, 4; Stoa: *A* I 533, II 416, 441, 473, 716, 1027; *Dox* 306, 5; Diog. Laert. VII 84; Augustin, *Civ. Dei* VII 23; Nachwirkungen: Neupythagoräer: *B* 130; Corp. Herm. Asclep. 6b, 17a, 33c (*Sc* I 296, 11; 316, 10; 320, 1f.).

(*e*) Anknüpfend an alte Vorstellungen von der Belebung durch göttlichen Hauch oder Wind (Leisegang, *Gnosis*, S. 194; *Pneuma hagion*, 71f.), kann das kosmische πνεῦμα auch als Schöpfungskraft erscheinen, wobei Gen. i. 2 in den späteren Belegen deutlich mitwirkt: orphisch *K* 56; *D* I 45, 15 (vgl. 206, 9); bei Zeno ist es Ordnungsprinzip: *V* 34ff., 288 (vgl. Irenäus, Epid. 5). Gen. i. 2 wirkt deutlich nach in der phöniz. Kosmogonie *Sc* II 112f.; Corp. Herm. 3, 1 (*Sc* I 146, 2; dazu *V* 318f.); Ps-Clem. hom. xi. 22, 24 (dazu Bousset, Hauptprobleme 281); Hippolyt ref. *V* 10, 2; 19, 13–19; Epiphanius haer. XXV 5, 1; Iren. I 30, 1; verbunden mit der σοφία-vorstellung bei Theophilus Ant., ad Autolycum I 5; II 13, 15 (Th. Rüsch,

Weltgefühl,[1] at.lich-jüdisches Wissen um die Geschiedenheit einer abgefallenen Welt von Jahwe, das schon längst verbreitete Denken in den zwei Sphären Himmel und Erde[2] verbinden sich mit altorphischen, über Plato weitertradierten Gedanken: die göttliche Seele ist eingekerkert im Leibe;[3] sie sehnt sich nach Befreiung vom Körper

Die Entstehung der Lehre vom heiligen Geist bei Ignatius, Theophilus u. Irenäus (1952) S. 80ff.).

(*f*) Vom πνεῦμα θεῖον im Menschen spricht schon Menander fr. 482 (Kock, *Com. Att. fragm.* Bd. III (1888), S. 139); Ps.-Plato, Axiochus 370c. Vgl. auch Euripides, Tro. 886. Mit Gott gleichgesetzt wird πνεῦμα als Luftelement bei Anaximenes: *D* I 93, 6; ähnlich Cicero, de nat. deor. I 14, 36f. von Zeno und Kleanthes; aber selbst noch Theophilus ad Autol. I 7 ('du atmest Gottes Geist'). Nach der Stoa besteht Gott aus πνεῦμα νοερὸν καὶ πυρῶδες: *A* II 1009 (ähnl. 310); *Dox* 292, 22f (vgl. 609, 1ff; 618, 22ff.). Als 'Gott in dir' erscheint der Geist Mark Aurel III 5, 2 und oft. Seneca erklärt, man solle die Hände nicht betend zum Himmel aufheben, Gott ist 'mit dir, in dir...ein heiliger Geist wohnt in uns... denn die Vernunft ist nichts anderes als ein Teil des göttlichen Geistes in den menschlichen Leib gegossen' (ep. 41 [IV 12], 1; 66 [VII 4], 12). Die Nachwirkungen im Zauber: Allo, 331, *F* 124f., Reitzenstein, 308ff., A. Dieterich, Mithrasliturgie 57.

(*g*) Das alte Axiom des Empedokles, daß Gleiches nur durch Gleiches erkannt wird (*De nat.* 321f., bzw. 318f. od. 333f.; ferner *K* 345), muß zur Anschauung führen, daß Gott nur durch das göttliche πνεῦμα erkannt wird; vgl. Plato, res publ. 508aff.; Sextus Empir., Math. VII 93; Tatian, or. ad Gr. XV. 3; Mithraslit. IV. 10f. Dieterich (vgl. dort 55–7).

[1] Dazu vgl. Jonas (S. 496, Anm. 1), S. 141ff.

[2] Vgl. S. 499, Anm. 3 und S. 500, Anm. 1; ferner für das Griechentum: *N* (S. 497, Anm. 2), Bd. II, S. 252f., 576ff. (die stoische Vorstellung von der supralunarischen Sphäre—S. 500, Anm. 1—verbindet sich mit der platonischen von der Ideenwelt); A. J. Festugière, *La révelation d'Hermès Trismégiste*, Bd. II (1949), S. 117ff.; Bultmann, *J.T.S.* n.s. III, 1 (1952), 22 (zur Astralmystik für das Judentum: Strack-Billerbeck, Bd. IV, S. 819ff. (vgl. Berakh, 16b, *ibid*, I, 420); Davies (S. 490, Anm. 1), S. 314ff.; H. Bietenhard, *Die himmlische Welt im Urchristentum und Spätjudentum* (1951), S. 181.

[3] (*a*) Orphisch σῶμα=σῆμα: *K* (alle Abkürzungen vgl. S. 497, Anm. 2), 8, vgl. 3 7; zu den Goldplättchen 4./3. Jahrh., Italien): *N* II 223ff.

(*b*) Trennung von Körper und 'Geist' im Tode: Epicharmes: *D* I 200, 10; 202, 5: γᾶ μὲν εἰς γᾶν, πνεῦμα δ' ἄνω; vgl. die Aussage des Xenophanes, die Seele sei nur vergänglicher Atem: Anm. (*c*); Plato, *Gorg.* 524b; Euripides fr. 961, Hiket. 533f.; Aristoteles, fr. 10 Rose (Πάνθειον 1929, 50, 8); Chrysipp: *A* I 137; Epiktet II 1, 17; III 24, 93f.; weiteres *F* 196, Anm. 2; Scheidung von πνεῦμα und σῶμα auf Grabsteinen: *F* 210, Anm. 1. Daß der Tod das Leben der Seele bedeutet, sagt eigentlich schon Heraklit fr. 62 (*D* I 164, 9); vgl. Plato *Gorg.* 492e; Euripides, Phrixos fr. 833 Nauck. Endlich vgl. die Nachwirkungen im Zauber: Pap. Berol. I 177 (Reitzenstein 308); Stob. Exc. 23, 67 (*Sc* I 492, 33ff.); vgl. *B* 173–5; daß Atmen Teilnahme an der Unsterblichkeit bedeutet: Vettius Valens, Catal. cod. astrol. *V* 2 Kroll 49, 22 (Allo 331, hier nicht nachprüfbar).

und Aufstieg in die reine Geistsphäre.[1] Aber der Gnostiker muß noch einen Schritt weiter gehen. Auch die Seele kann er nicht als dieses göttliche Ich anerkennen. Auch sie gehört zum bösen Kosmos, auch sie strebt nach unten, kann das jedenfalls tun. Was wirklich göttliche Substanz im Menschen ist, ist ein ihm Fremdes, ihm von außen Zugekommenes. So kann er sehr gut die Vorstellung von einem göttlichen *depositum* aufnehmen, die wir schon vorfanden im Judentum. Völlig anders als dort ist es aber hier als die unveränderliche, sich immer gleich bleibende göttliche Substanz gedacht. Alles ist hier bestimmt durch die Anschauung, daß diese göttliche Substanz, eben der 'Geist', vermischt wurde mit der an sich bösen Materie, dann durch den 'Gesandten', der selber Geist ist, erinnert wird an ihre Herkunft, endlich von der Materie befreit, 'entmischt', wieder aufsteigt und so zur Einheit ihrer selbst kommt in dem alles umfassenden kosmischen Geistleib.[2]

Die Gnosis kennt also auch eine 'Eschatologie' — darin ist sie ungriechisch. Aber es ist eine ganz andere Eschatologie. Sie ist bestimmt durch das zu-sich-selbst-Finden des Geistes, nicht durch das eine, alles entscheidende, alles vollendende Handeln Gottes. Träger eines eschatologischen Handelns kann der Geist hier also nicht sein. Man könnte in gewissem Sinne sagen, der 'Geist' sei in der Gnosis die dem Menschen schon vorweggegebene eschatologische Existenz — darum konnten nt.liche Aussagen gnostisch interpretiert werden. Aber es ist deutlich, daß dies doch ein sehr uneigentliches

[1] (*a*) Abstieg und Aufstieg der Seele (wobei meist der Mond als Grenze zwischen beiden Sphären erscheint): Plato, *Phaedr.* 247bff.; 250af. Zum Ursprung dieser Vorstellung und ihrer Ausbildung in der Stoa (wo die Sonne den νοῦς aussät, den der Mond empfängt, um daraus Seelen zu gebären, die dann wieder durch die Mondsphäre hindurch zur Sonne aufsteigen): *N* (alle Abkürzungen vgl. S. 497, Anm. 2), II 252f., 470–3; Seneca dial. VI 23, 1; 25, 1; 26, 7; vgl. ep. 57 (VI 5), 8; Vergil, *Aen.* VI, 713ff.; und die Fortwirkung in Corp. Herm. 10, 7f., 16; 12, 18 (*Sc* 190, 20ff.; 198, 3ff.; 234, 16ff.). Zum Gedanken der Seelenwanderung überhaupt: *N* I 654ff.; II 225f. Für das Judentum: Bietenhard 18, 34, 83.

(*b*) Für die besondere Anschauung, daß sich die Seele beim Abstieg bekleidet, beim Aufstieg entkleidet: Bousset, *Hauptprobleme*, 361ff.; Bietenhard (S. 499, Anm. 2), 226, Anm. 1; Corp. Herm. 1, 17, 24ff. (*Sc* 122, 25ff.; 126, 29ff.).

(*c*) Zur Vorstellung der Ekstase vgl. Dupont 155ff., *v.* 260ff. (und 332 zur Mithrasliturgie), Reitzenstein 321ff. und die Stellen bei G. Schrenk in *Wort und Geist* (1934), S. 78; Bousset-Gressmann, S. 450f.; *N* I 656f.; besonders Philo, *de op. mundi* 69–71; Plutarch, *de defectu orac.* 39f. (432a–e).

[2] Die Belege stelle ich im *Theol. Wörterbuch* zusammen.

Reden wäre. Denn diese Existenz ist ihm ja immer schon gegeben und unabänderlich die gleiche. 'Eschatologisch' ist also gar nicht die Existenz im Geist, sondern höchstens das Gelöstwerden des Geistes von der Materie. Insofern könnte man das Kommen des erinnernden 'Gesandten' und das daraus fließende endgültige Befreitwerden des Geistes 'eschatologisch' nennen. Aber nicht zufällig braucht es dazu ja nur ein 'Erinnern'; nicht zufällig wird die tatsächliche Erscheinung dieses Gesandten immer gleichgültiger, weil ja nur der Mythos von ihm notwendig ist zur Erinnerung des Geistes an sich selbst; nicht zufällig kann der Gesandte hier zum bloßen Symbol der Summe aller Geistfunken werden; nicht zufällig vollzieht sich darum hier das zu-sich-selbst-Kommen des Geistes dauernd und nicht nur in einem einzigen Akt am Ende der Zeiten.[1] Gott handelt hier gar nicht eschatologisch mit der Welt; 'Gott' zieht sich nur von der Welt zurück auf sich selbst, und der Abschluß dieses Rückzugs ist das 'Eschaton'.

7. MARKUS UND MATTHÄUS

Das N.T. ist mit den genannten Gruppen darin einig, daß ihm der Geist eine *gegenwärtige* Größe ist, und daß seine Gedanken darum kreisen, eben diese *Gegenwart* des Geistes zu verstehen. Abgesehen von den ganz am Rande stehenden Stellen, an denen der Geist anthropologisch verstanden ist,[2] ist aber im N.T. — anders als in jenen Gruppen — die at.liche Botschaft festgehalten, daß der Geist das Handeln des dem Menschen gegenüberstehenden Gottes, und zwar sein außerordentliches, nicht mit dem Gang der Geschichte einiges, sondern in diesen Gang eingreifendes Handeln ist. Gelten wirklich beide Erkenntnisse, dann kann die Antwort nur lauten, daß im Geist eben dieses außerordentliche Handeln Gottes Gegenwart geworden ist; das heißt aber: daß die eschatologische Zeit begonnen hat. Es ist ausgeschlossen, auf den wenigen zur Verfügung stehenden Seiten die Vielfalt dieses Zeugnisses, die ich anderswo schon darzustellen versuchte,[3] zu wiederholen. Nur mit einigen Strichen sollen

[1] Vgl. die Belege im *Theol. Wörterbuch* und die vorläufige Zusammenfassung *Interpretation* (1952), S. 270f. (wo 'saved by nature' — nicht: 'from nature' zu lesen ist); *Theol. Existenz heute,* Heft 32 n.F., S. 17–19.

[2] Dazu *Evang. Theol.* (1951/2), S. 507–9.

[3] Vgl. S. 482, Anm. 1.

insbesondere die verschiedenen Antworten auf die eschatologische Frage skizziert werden.

Für Markus und Matthäus ist das eschatologische Handeln Gottes in Jesus Christus selbst Gegenwart geworden. So bekommen auch ihre Aussagen über den Geist durchwegs christologische Funktion; d.h. es geht ihnen gar nicht um eine Aussage über den Geist; sondern um eine solche über Christus. Gerade weil sie Jesus sachlich weithin als 'Pneumatiker' schildern,[1] ist es doppelt auffallend, wie zurückhaltend ihr Reden vom Geist ist. Das liegt aber nur daran, daß sie Jesus nicht auf die Stufe eines at.lichen oder nt.lichen Propheten stellen wollen. Die Geistaussagen, die sie machen, wollen fast ausnahmslos nur das eine feststellen, was uns gerade der, dem ich diesen Aufsatz widmen darf, so unüberhörbar wieder in Erinnerung gerufen hat: in Jesus von Nazaret ist das Ende der Wege Gottes, das Eschaton Gegenwart geworden. Seit dem Sterben der großen Propheten ist der Geist erloschen, erst in der Endzeit wird er wieder erscheinen, klagte das Judentum. Er *ist* erschienen, in ihm, in Jesus, verkündet das N.T. Darum begeht der die unvergebbare Sünde, der in Jesu Dämonenaustreibungen diesen Geist Gottes nicht erkennt (Mark. iii. 28–30 par.). Darin ist ja Gottes Endherrschaft herangekommen (Matth. xii. 28). Durch seine Geistverleihung unterscheidet er sich vom Täufer (Mark. i. 8 par.). Das Herabsteigen des Geistes bezeugt ihn als den eschatologischen Retter (Mark. i. 10f. par.). Der Geist führt ihn in die Wüste, wo er als 'zweiter', als 'eschatologischer Adam' (I Kor. xv. 45, 47) die Versuchung besteht, in der der erste fiel (Mark. i. 12 par.). Den Geist wird er seiner verfolgten Jüngerschar in den eschatologischen Wehen senden (Mark. xiii. 11 par.).

8. LUKAS

Bei Lukas setzt sich die Entwicklung fort. Es läßt sich in Einzelheiten zeigen, wie er sich bemüht, die Einzigartigkeit Jesu durch die Geistaussagen noch schärfer hervortreten zu lassen. Vor allem aber hat er das neue Problem aufgenommen: die Frage nach dem Geistbesitz der *Gemeinde*. Die Geschichte hat ja nicht aufgehört mit Jesus. Wie ist dann die Gemeinde, wie ihr Geistbesitz zu verstehen? Kann man

[1] C. H. Dodd in *Mysterium Christi*, ed. G. K. A. Bell-A. Deissmann (1931), S. 67–86.

sie als das eschatologische Ereignis bezeichnen? Oder hat sie sich einfach getäuscht mit Jesus? Oder ist alles nur ein Zeichen auf das noch ausstehende Enddrama hin?

Unzweifelhaft ist diese letzte Auskunft in der Urgemeinde auch gegeben worden. Nach der Apgesch. ii. 17–21 verwendeten Tradition ist das Erscheinen des Geistes nur die Einleitung der Weltkatastrophe, in der Himmel und Erde vergehen. Nach Hebr. vi. 4f. ist der Geist der Vorschmack der Güter des kommenden Aions. Das wirkt noch nach in der Bezeichnung des Geistes als des 'Angeldes' oder des 'Anbruchs' der künftigen Herrlichkeit (Röm. viii. 23; II Kor. i. 22; v. 5). Es schiene mir nicht richtig, diese Erkenntnis einfach beiseite zu schieben. Wird vom Geistbesitz der Gemeinde gesprochen, dann muß natürlich davon gesprochen werden, wie das eschatologische Handeln Gottes *jetzt* und *hier* hereinbricht. Es ist aber mit den genannten Sätzen unmißverständlich festgehalten, daß die Gemeinde auch im Besitz des Geistes noch 'Gemeinde unterwegs' ist, daß Gott als der Herr der Geschichte ihr gegenüber steht und nicht in ihren Händen ist, daß darum die Gemeinde immer auch wartende, die Fülle der Gaben noch von ihrem Herrn erwartende ist.[1] Darin grenzt sich die nt.liche Gemeinde klar ab von den Gnostikern, bei denen der Glaubende nur noch sich der ihm schon verliehenen Göttlichkeit bewußt werden muß.

Aber freilich, wo vom Geist gezeugt wird, da kann das nur als Korrektur *auch* noch gesagt werden. Die entscheidende Tatsache ist, daß er *da* ist. Und schon Lukas versucht, darin die Erfüllung selbst zu sehen. Das erweist sich weniger in ausdrücklicher theologischer Formulierung[2] als in der Tatsache, daß Lukas voraussetzt, daß *jedes* Glied der Gemeinde den Geist besitzt.[3] Das ist neu gegenüber dem A.T. und dem sich von dorther verstehenden Judentum;

[1] Rechte Dankbarkeit gegenüber einem Forscher wird immer darin bestehen, daß man neben dem voll Dank Aufgenommenen auch das erkennt, was man anders sagen zu müssen glaubt. Mir scheint bei allem, was im Folgenden durchaus zustimmend zu sagen ist, hier doch ein Moment vorzuliegen, das ich im N.T. zentraler sähe als Dodd.

[2] Die Aufnahme des Joelzitates Apgesch. ii. 17–21 und besonders die Zufügung 'in den letzten Tagen' zum at.lichen Text, der sonst beinahe wörtlich erscheint, weist sicher in diese Richtung, kann aber von Luk. übernommene Tradition sein.

[3] Er betont dabei: der *Gemeinde*, nicht der Welt (vgl. die charakteristische Änderung v. 18 '*meine* Knechte...*meine* Mägde'). In der Gemeinde ist die Endzeit Wirklichkeit geworden, noch nicht im Kosmos.

denn dort ist der Geist ja immer nur Einzelnen geschenkt, darum auch nie als heilsnotwendig verstanden.

Die Schwierigkeit seiner Konzeption zeigt sich aber darin, daß er inhaltlich nicht vom at.lichen Verständnis des Geistes loskommt. Er versteht ihn immer noch als die Sondergabe Gottes für besondere Aufträge und besondere Zeiten. Damit wird die Zwiespältigkeit seiner Darstellung offenkundig. Einerseits ist der Geist das Merkmal *aller* Gemeindeglieder, weil in der Gemeinde wirklich die neue Zeit angebrochen ist. Andererseits ist er aber doch zusätzliche Gabe, die noch zu dem hinzukommt, was dem Menschen im Glauben schon geschenkt wird, und ihn befähigt zu besonderen Äußerungen seines Lebens mit Christus.[1] Nie wird das Glauben zurückgeführt auf den Geist. Seine Wirkungen sind die 'außerordentlichen', wie sie sich ganz besonders in der Zungenrede einstellen (Apgesch. ii. 1 ff.; x. 44, 46; xix. 6). Freilich zieht Lukas den Kreis der 'Außerordentlichkeit' sehr weit und versteht auch durchaus nüchtern die ganze Missionsverkündigung angesichts einer sie anfeindenden Welt als das außerordentliche Wunder Gottes. Aber es ist deutlich: eschatologisches Phänomen ist der Geist für Lukas insofern, als er der ganzen Gemeinde das schenkt, was er im A.T. nur einzelnen besonders Erwählten schenkte. Dadurch wird sie zur Gemeinde der Propheten, in der sich erfüllt, was das A.T. von der Endzeit erhofft (Num. xi. 29; Jer. xxx. 34). So hat sich, mitten drin in der Welt, die noch im alten Aeon lebt, doch in der Gemeinde schon das Eschaton verwirklicht. Im Geschehen des Geistes ist die 'anticipated eschatology' zu konstatieren.

9. PAULUS

Es ist offensichtlich, daß diese Lösung noch nicht genügte.[2] Wenn der Geist wirklich die Gemeinde schied von der Welt, auch vom alten Israel, wenn in ihm wirklich schon das Letzte hereingebrochen war, dann konnte es nicht genügen, ihn als Kraft für besondere Aufgaben zu verstehen, selbst wenn man sich wie Lukas mühte,

[1] Darum kann ein Mensch auch Tage, Wochen, Jahrelang ohne Geistbegabung leben, ohne deswegen aufzuhören, ein Glaubender zu sein. Freilich ist dies anomal, zeigt aber scharf, wie sehr der Geist für Luk. 'zusätzliche' Gabe ist.

[2] Chronologisch steht natürlich Paulus vor den Synoptikern; sachlich aber stehen diese, schon weil sie weithin längst formulierte Tradition aufnehmen, umgekehrt vor Paulus.

diese Aufgaben möglichst umfassend zu sehen. Praktisch gesprochen: konnte man wirklich nur auf das Wunder der Mission hinweisen, wenn man die Gemeinde als die schon in der Vollendung lebende darstellen wollte? Wir vergessen es nicht: eben dies tut Lukas, und es ist sein besonderer Zeugendienst im N.T., uns einzuprägen, daß eine nicht missionierende Gemeinde keine vom Geist erfüllte und darum keine im neuen Aeon lebende Gemeinde ist. Das ist durchaus richtig und bleibt bestehen. Aber konnte das die *ganze* Antwort sein? Ist nicht das Wunder der Mission schon Frucht, schon Auswirkung dessen, was ihm zugrunde liegt, und was doch wohl erst das eigentliche Merkmal der eschatologischen Gemeinde wäre? Aber auch die andere Frage blieb ja bei Lukas noch offen: wieso mußte eigentlich Jesus kommen, leiden und sterben, um den Geist (als Kraft zu außerordentlicher Verkündigung, zur 'Prophetie' verstanden) zu schenken? Die Antwort von Apgesch. ii. 33 offenbart ja nur diese ungelöste Aporie.

Die Gnostiker (oder 'Vorgnostiker'), denen Paulus in den hellenistischen Gemeinden begegnete, haben hier etwas durchaus Richtiges gesehen. Sie wußten, daß ihnen mit dem Geist die Himmelswelt selbst gegeben ist, daß in ihm alles da ist. Sie wußten vor allem auch, daß man den Geist nicht anders haben konnte als im Anschluß an den 'Erlöser', bzw. daß man mit dem Besitz des Geistes auch den 'Erlöser' zu eigen hatte.

Will Paulus das, was schon bei den Synoptikern sichtbar wurde, klar und konsequent zu Ende denken, dann muß er zunächst das auch sagen, was die Gnostiker sagen. In der Tat, mit dem Geist ist dem Menschen das Ganze geschenkt, und zwar eben darum, weil er ihn 'in Christus' hinein stellt. Aber völlig anders als in der Gnosis bedeutet das für Paulus nicht mehr eine naturhaft verstandene Verpflanzung in die göttliche Substanz, die im 'Erlöser' erschienen ist; sondern die Versetzung in das Christus*ereignis*, die im Glauben vollzogen wird. Im Christusereignis, in Menschwerdung, Tod und Auferstehung Christi, hat Gott ja eschatologisch, d.h. den alten Weltlauf, der durch die Trennung des Menschen von Gott geprägt war, abschließend gehandelt. Dort hat Gott die Welt in die neue Lage versetzt, aus ihrer Entfernung von Gott wieder in die Gemeinschaft mit Gott gestellt. Die Gemeinde lebt im Unterschied zur übrigen Welt im neuen Aeon darum, weil sie um dieses Ereignis weiß und glaubend davon leben darf. Eben das ist das Wirken des Geistes.

Wiederum kann hier nicht im Einzelnen nachgewiesen werden, wie nach Paulus der Geist dem Menschen das Christusereignis, vor allem das Kreuz als Heilsgeschehen, offenbart, ihm das Glauben daran und das Leben im Glauben schenkt, das negativ den Verzicht auf alle anderen Sicherungen (das 'Fleisch'), positiv die offene Zuwendung zum Nächsten (die 'Liebe') bedeutet.[1] Wichtig ist in unserem Zusammenhang nur, daß Paulus theologisch klar formulieren kann, was bei den Synoptikern noch nicht expliziert ist: das entscheidende eschatologische Gotteshandeln ist das am Kreuz Christi. Ist der Geist die neue Existenz der eschatologischen Gemeinde, dann darum, weil er sie mit diesem Ereignis zusammenschließt und sie davon leben läßt.

Auch hier würde ich freilich die Formulierung von der 'anticipated eschatology' der von der 'realized eschatology' vorziehen; denn Paulus hält durchaus, und zwar nicht nur auf einem Nebengleis, daran fest, daß die Vollendung noch aussteht.[2] Eben weil er das Geschehen des Geistes als das des Glaubens versteht, eben weil er sich darin von der Gnosis scheidet, eben darum will er nicht verzichten auf diese Aussagen. Gott steht auch dem im Geiste Lebenden immer gegenüber als der, von dem er sich immer wieder neu beschenken lassen muß. Insofern bedeutet 'das Angeld des Geistes haben' immer auch 'noch im Glauben, nicht schon im Schauen wandeln' (II Kor. v. 5, 7).

10. JOHANNES

Daß diese Sicherung bei Johannes nicht mehr erscheint, ist zu erwarten. Freilich bestreitet er nicht, daß das heute schon Gültige einer Vollendung entgegengehe, die nicht mehr innerhalb der Grenzen dieser Welt und dieser Zeit liegt.[3] Aber seine Verkündigung ist doch völlig davon bestimmt, deutlich zu machen, daß in Christus

[1] Vgl. das S. 482, Anm. 1 Gesagte.

[2] Vgl. oben S. 503. Anders als R. Bultmann (z.B. *Das Urchristentum* (1949), S. 46, 207f.) scheint es mir gerade wesentlich, daß Gott in der eschatologischen Vollendung nicht mehr nur der stets zukünftige bleibt, weil aus dem Glauben das Schauen (II Kor. v. 7) geworden ist.

[3] xii. 25; xiv. 2; xvii. 24 (vgl. xi. 24); sehr stark I Joh. ii. 28; iv. 17. Vgl. auch B. Aebert, *Die Eschatologie des Joh. evang.*, Diss. (Breslau, 1937) (gedruckt nur Kap. 2); C. H. Dodd, 'Le Kerygma apostolique dans le quatrième évangile', *R.H. Ph. Rel.* (1951), S. 265ff., besonders S. 269ff.

die ganze Fülle Gottes *Gegenwart* geworden ist. Wieder kann im Einzelnen den johanneischen Aussagen nicht nachgegangen werden.[1] Wieder kann nur gefragt werden, wie sich diese besondere Stellung zur *Eschatologie* auf die Aussagen vom Geist auswirkt.

Johannes macht Ernst mit dem, was schon bei Paulus erkannt ist: das eschatologische Handeln Gottes ist sein Handeln in Christus; der Geist ist das eschatologische Ereignis insofern, als er die Gemeinde zusammenschließt mit jenem Handeln und sie von ihm leben läßt. Es ist darum nur konsequent, wenn für Johannes der Geist letztlich nichts anderes ist als Jesus Christus selbst, aber Jesus Christus als der seiner Gemeinde in der Verkündigung begegnende. Und doch ist er so auch wieder zu unterscheiden von Jesus Christus, ist er doch der *Zeuge* für ihn, d.h. derjenige, der erst deutlich macht, wer Jesus eigentlich ist, was er für den Glaubenden ist. Man muß also modifizieren: wenn im Wort der Verkündigung der Geist als Zeuge für Christus zur Gemeinde kommt, dann kommt in ihm der 'Christus des Glaubens', der von der Gemeinde als *für sie* Fleisch gewordener, gekreuzigter und erhöhter *erkannte* Christus. Ist aber eben diese Fleischwerdung, Kreuzigung und Erhöhung Christi für Johannes das eschatologische Geschehen schlechthin, wie könnte da der Geist etwas anderes sein als die immer neu sich vollziehende Vergegenwärtigung dieses Geschehens in der Verkündigung der Gemeinde? Dabei liegt gerade dem vierten Evangelisten alles daran, daß man diese Begegnung des 'Christus des Glaubens' mit der Gemeinde in keiner Weise loslöse vom irdischen, Fleisch gewordenen Jesus von Nazaret. Der Geist kann nichts anderes als die Gemeinde 'erinnern' an alles, was sich dort im irdischen Jesus ereignet hat. Sonst käme ja ein anderer als der, in dem Gott eschatologisch gehandelt hat. Denn Gott hat das jedenfalls nur in jenem 'historischen' Jesus von Nazaret getan. Wollte man den Geist verstehen als ein davon loszulösendes Geschehen, das zu einem 'ewigen Christus' führen würde, der nicht notwendig mit dem historischen Jesus in eins gesehen werden müßte, dann wäre der Geist nicht mehr eschatologisches Phänomen, dann eben wäre er wieder abgesunken zum bloßen Auftauchen einer immer gültigen, immer gleich bleibenden, überall in Erscheinung treten könnenden Idee. Das aber wäre Gnosis; das wäre eine Botschaft, die in keinem Teil des N.T. aufzufinden wäre.

[1] Vgl. das S. 482, Anm. 1 Gesagte.

Das N.T. lebt von der Tatsache des Geistes, die längst Wirklichkeit geworden ist, bevor die einzelnen Zeugen sich darum mühten, sie zu verstehen. Macht man aber mit dieser Gegenwart wirklich Ernst, muß man dann nicht entweder zum Moralisten werden wie der Verfasser der Testamente, bzw. des Hermas, oder dann zum Gnostiker? Anders ausgedrückt: muß der Geist dann nicht absinken entweder zum ethischen Prinzip (dem man durchaus eine göttliche Kraft zutrauen mag), das dauernd in gleicher Weise vor dem Menschen steht und ihn in die Entscheidung stellt, oder zur göttlichen Substanz, die dem Menschen naturhaft einverleibt ist, unveränderlich und unverlierbar? Im N.T. ist weder das eine noch das andere geschehen, darum weil es in allen seinen Teilen (unbeschadet der bunten Vielfalt seiner Antworten) damit ganz ernsthaft rechnet, daß das *eine*, alles entscheidende, endgeschichtliche Handeln Gottes mit der Welt in Jesus von Nazaret geschehen ist. Dazu nein sagen würde heißen: zum ganzen N.T. nein sagen. So *kann* der Geist als das eschatologische Phänomen nichts sein, was auch abgesehen von diesem Ereignis gälte, weder ein moralisches Prinzip noch eine göttliche Substanz. Erfährt die Gemeinde wirklich den Geist, und ist dies nicht bloß ein unbedeutendes Nebengeräusch, dann *kann* sie nur folgern: im Geist wird die neue Welt Wirklichkeit, die durch dieses eschatologische Handeln Gottes geschaffen ist. Eben diese Folgerung zieht das N.T. *Abgeschlossen am 5 Dez. 1952.*

Das wichtige Werk des Jubilars *The Interpretation of the Fourth Gospel* (1953) konnte ich leider erst einsehen, als der vorstehende Artikel schon im Druck war. Ich verweise dankbar besonders auf den Abschnitt 'Spirit' S. 213–27. Übereinstimmung und Differenz werden dem Leser sichtbar sein.

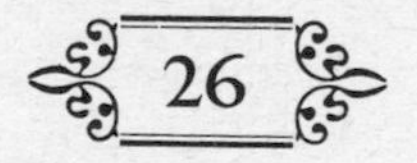

KERYGMA, ESCHATOLOGY AND SOCIAL ETHICS

A. N. WILDER

THE question of the Scriptural basis for social ethics has evidently been placed in an entirely new light by the advance of Biblical studies in the last generation. The recasting of our presentation of Biblical theology has carried with it a proportionate revision of our understanding of ethics individual and social. New grasp of the distinctive conception of man and community held by Israel, our new understanding of the Biblical views of history and eschatology, and of the significance of the *kerygma* in the New Testament (and its analogue in the Old), have offered us major new elements and new co-ordinates for defining the relation of the Gospel to the world and to its social patterns. The new insights, indeed, are so fertile and so rich that inductions from them are not as yet fully explored. The discussion of these matters exhibits the kind of fertile but inconclusive and even contradictory views which any new horizon in knowledge occasions. This is true whether as regards our understanding of Biblical ethics themselves or of their bearings for the world of today. In such a situation, moreover, the great classical issues are quickened anew: the relation of the Old Testament to the New; the question of natural law; the relation of creation to redemption; the tension between this-worldliness and other-worldliness; the relations of justice and love. The situation takes us back behind the deep cleavages in the approach to theological ethics of Thomist, Lutheran, Calvinist and other traditions. However confusing the picture is today, there is an exhilarating sense that here as in other areas the deepest levels of Christian understanding have been reopened, and that momentous insights and affirmations are once again forthcoming.

The occasion for the active concern today with Christian social ethics has of course its pragmatic aspect. The modern situation, both in its social and international features, has imposed an almost unparalleled demand upon the Church for ethical guidance. Those same totalitarian pressures which have forced Christians to clarify their faith and its Biblical grounds, have similarly compelled them to search the Scriptures for light on fundamental decisions as to the nature and limits of the State, the political witness of the believer and ultimate questions as to the relations of the Church and the world. The most radical exploration of these matters has taken place where the churches have been immediately threatened by either Nazism or Communism.

But even outside these critical areas the churches of Western Christendom have awakened to the perils of their situation. The distinctiveness of the Christian way and witness had become blurred, and clear leads in the complexity of modern society were missing. The catastrophes of the Second World War and the urgency of social problems in its sequel have laid an inexorable demand upon Christians to furnish moral leadership to the nations and to the mass-culture of our day. Many modern men with important responsibilities in society have despaired of finding clear light for conduct and policy in the Bible, whether as regards law, politics, business, labour, marriage or property. In the absence of such light they turn to secular moral philosophy or to the great rival views of man which today oppose themselves to the Gospel, or, in private dilemmas, to a secular psychiatry or some esoteric cult. Thus we note the rising demand of the layman and the laymen's movements for concrete ethical counsel derived from the Bible in all matters and especially those bearing on vocation.

The upshot of all this is that problems of social ethics have moved into first place in many centres of theological discussion. This is strikingly evident to the visitor to Germany, whether in connection with the Evangelical Academies, church synods, the great *Kirchentage* or the theological faculties. The problems most discussed today, and by jurists, philosophers and sociologists as well as theologians, are those that have to do with the problems of public life and their theological and Biblical foundations: the doctrine of the two realms, the nature of the 'orders', natural and positive law, the kingship of Christ.

These concerns are specially reflected in the ecumenical studies and conference reports fostered in these last years by the World Council of Churches, especially through its Study Department and the Ecumenical Institute. Basic questions as to Biblical hermeneutic,[1] the Biblical doctrine of law and justice,[2] the relations of eschatology and ethics,[3] and natural law[4] have been dealt with by Biblical scholars and systematic theologians, both at special conferences and in preparatory and supplementary papers. Groups of workers, sometimes working concurrently in the United States and in Europe, have collaborated upon particular themes such as 'Work and Vacation', 'Individual and Community',[5] 'The Biblical Theory of Property',[6] 'Nation and Race in the Bible'.[7] The cumulative results of such studies are evident in *From the Bible to the Modern World: Two Conference Reports* (1947),[8] dealing with 'Biblical Authority for the Church's Social and Political Message Today', and in *Biblical Authority for Today* (1951). It is unnecessary here to refer to the many related papers on these topics, stimulated by these projects, the material being available in the *Ecumenical Review*, and other sources. Attention should, however, be drawn to basic discussions of New Testament hermeneutical and ethical issues in the scholarly journals, and to larger works on Christian ethics by such European writers as Karl Barth, N. H. Søe, and D. Bonhoeffer.[9] C. H. Dodd has had an

[1] Cf. the Wadham College Conference Report, 'Guiding Principles for the Interpretation of the Bible'. Reprinted in *Biblical Authority for Today*, ed. by A. Richardson and W. Schweitzer (London, S.C.M. Press, 1951).

[2] Cf the Treysa Conference Report, 'The Biblical Doctrine of Justice' (1951).

[3] *Eschatology and Ethics*, by W. Schweitzer (Ecumenical Studies, A 3/4, Nov. 1951).

[4] Cf. C. H. Dodd, 'Natural Law in the Bible', *Theology*, vol. XLIX, 311, 312 (May, June 1946), pp. 130–3, 161–7; also Study Department Paper 50G/116.

[5] A Chicago group under the chairmanship of G. Ernest Wright has completed a substantial statement on this theme criticized in process by a conference held in Göttingen in 1951 which included among others J. Jeremias, W. Zimmerli, E. Wolf, H. J. Iwand and D. Hertzberg.

[6] Cf. J. Bosc, 'The Biblical Theory of Property', in *Contributions to a Christian Social Ethic* (Papers of the Ecumenical Institute, no. IV, Geneva, 1949); Walther Eichrodt, 'The Question of Property in the Light of the Old Testament', in *Biblical Authority for Today*; W. G. Kümmel, 'Der Begriff des Eigentum im Neuen Testament', Study Department Paper, 50 G/128.

[7] *Biblical Authority for Today*, pp. 310–22.

[8] Ed. by the Study Department of the World Council, 1947.

[9] K. Barth, *Kirchliche Dogmatik* III/4, chs. XIIff.; N. H. Søe, *Christliche Ethik, ein Lehrbuch* (München, 1941); D. Bonhoeffer, *Ethik* (München, 1949).

active part in this whole ecumenical discussion,[1] and his volume, *Gospel and Law*,[2] like his earlier articles on 'Natural Law in the Bible',[3] represents an important contribution to one of its basic issues. The most far-reaching contribution of Professor Dodd has, however, been his share in the definition of the early Christian *kerygma* and its wider significance for our understanding of the New Testament writings and the outlook of the early community.

The new situation as regards a Biblical basis for social ethics becomes clearer if we set it against the background of the 'social gospel' of the first quarter of the century. For this approach rested on the work of Biblical scholars. It represents, indeed, the last fully articulated solution of our problem, including as it did, a hermeneutic, a theologically grounded ethic and in many respects a developed application or casuistry. While we associate it especially with such Americans as Rauschenbusch, it had its counterpart in England and Sweden, as the whole history of the Life and Work movement shows, in France in the case of *Le Socialisme Chrétien*, and in some respects among the Christian Socialists of Germany. In America this social ethic was closely related to the scholarly work of such writers as Orello Cone, Nathaniel Schmidt, Shirley Jackson Case, Shailer Mathews and C. C. McCown, who combined a liberal theology with an intense concern for the social factors in the origin and development of religion. As is well known, they focused attention on the social messages of the prophets, the ethical teachings of Jesus read in a similar light, and a this-worldly interpretation of the Kingdom of God, especially as set forth in certain of the parables. Their understanding of these matters was due for a radical revision in the light of new advances in the study of the Gospels. It must be insisted, however, that their demand for full recognition of the realistic social context of the emergent Christian movement deserves a better sequel than it has today. It must also be said that this whole movement

[1] See his 'Authority and Relevance of the Bible', in *From the Bible to the Modern World*. Also his Burge Lecture, 'Christianity and the Reconciliation of the Nations' (London, S.C.M. Press, 1952). Other contributions of Professor Dodd to general ecumenical discussions include his important letter to the Commission on the Church (see *Ecumenical Review*, vol. II, I, p. 52), and his membership of the Advisory Commission on the Theme of the Second Assembly.

[2] New York, Columbia University Press, 1951.

[3] See above, p. 511 n. 4.

raised up a generation or more of Christian leaders and groups who were both committed and well armed to unmask the paganism of modern society and to wrestle realistically with its destructive concentrations of power. Here at least in modern Christianity was one element that could belie the great and plausible accusation of escapism and irrelevance laid against the Gospel by Marx, Nietzsche and other critics of the Church.

But new factors soon placed the social gospel on the defensive, not only the great social disillusionments and historical tragedies of the times, but the impact of Biblical studies. The neo-Protestant theological revival on the Continent, related to both these factors, highlighted the perpendicular dimensions of faith and disparaged human programmes, ideals and values, even where these were evangelically coloured. The outcome was that this whole pattern for social ethics was increasingly shaken, even in the churches outside the Continent, and a period ensued in which the corollaries of the faith for daily life were especially confused. The Oxford Conference on Church, Community and State in 1937 with its report on *The Church and the Economic Order* and its symposium on *The Kingdom of God and History* stands out as a symptom of the changing situation, in which the address of Reinhold Niebuhr and the papers of C. H. Dodd, H. D. Wendland and Edwyn Bevan disclosed the encounter of old and new forces and conceptions.

But it is with the impact of Biblical studies that we are specially concerned. The social gospel was pre-Schweitzer in the sense either that it did not know his work or, with other wings of liberalism, sought to disallow it, though some American scholars like C. C. McCown integrated his eschatological understanding of primitive Christianity into a this-worldly perspective.[1] Our more recent understanding of Jesus' view of the Kingdom of God was a body-blow to the earlier interpretation of the parables of the leaven and the growing seed, as also C. H. Dodd's distinctive view of the parables illustrates. But the social gospel also ante-dated the rise of Form Criticism so far at least as a real encounter with its implications was concerned. The 'life-situation' understanding of the pericopes

[1] Cf. C. C. McCown, *The Genesis of the Social Gospel* (1929), and a revised work of S. Mathews, *Jesus on Social Institutions* (1928). Cf. also John Bennett, *Social Salvation* (1935).

of the Gospels and of the sayings of Jesus was, indeed, nothing new to scholars like Case and B. W. Bacon, but the full significance of the oral tradition and its context in the faith and worship of the community had not been grasped. Realization of these matters discounted the way in which liberal theologians if not scholars understood the Sermon on the Mount and the social idealism found in Luke. In an analogous way the 'social message of the prophets' took on a different aspect when the centre of the Old Testament was displaced from Amos to the saving-event of the Exodus.

All in all the new emphases in the understanding of the Bible suggested by such terms as eschatology, covenant, election, *kerygma* and *Heilsgeschichte*, all requiring us to read the Bible in ways closer to the assumptions of its authors, these emphases have imposed a radically new task for anyone who would formulate a Christian social ethic. The matter is complicated by the influence upon much of the new scholarship of theological and hermeneutical assumptions associated with the post-liberal mood and the dialectical theology. The new presentations of Biblical theology have the merit of exploiting genuine advances in Old Testament and New Testament study. They also have the merit of benefiting by real advances upon the old historiography, which was too rigid and which was dominated by genetic and evolutionary assumptions and which was often stamped with certain modern preoccupations such as individualism and 'religious experience'.[1] In his widely noticed lecture on 'The Present Task of New Testament Studies' (1936), C. H. Dodd called for a new emphasis on synthesis rather than analysis, and this direction has been widely evident.

But much of the new Biblical theology has been shaped in addition by dialectical presuppositions and by a view of revelation, persuasively related to the new understanding of Biblical religion, but really dissociable from it, which have militated against its availability for social ethics. We have in mind such works as Dibelius' *Sermon on the Mount*, Lohmeyer's *Markusevangelium*, Bultmann's *Jesus*. It is one thing to set forth Jesus' message of the Kingdom in the light of Jewish-Christian eschatology and Form Criticism. It is another to

[1] Cf. the author's 'New Testament Theology in Transition', in *The Study of the Bible Today and Tomorrow*, ed. by H. R. Willoughby (Chicago, 1947), pp. 427–32.

interpret it thereupon in the sheerly dualistic categories of 'geschichtliche und übergeschichtliche Religion'.[1] It is one thing to set forth the *kerygma* of Acts and the early Church as the proclamation by the community of its interpretation of the eschatological events in the midst of which it lived. It is another thing to assign a non-temporal or existential sense to this message, which displaces it from the actualities of the life-situation. No doubt all effective interpretation of the Bible involves the risk of some modernization. This was true of the work of the Fourth Evangelist as it has been of the social gospel school. But what is specially pertinent here is that such presentations of Biblical theology have the effect of blocking legitimate implications of the message of Jesus and the *kerygma* for a constructive social ethic. There is gain in our understanding of the New Testament's claim on personal decision, and loss with respect to its relevance to community life either within or outside the Church.

It is true that the dialectic formulation takes different expressions in different writers, and some presentations can lend themselves to a social ethic. We shall take account of these distinctions below. But the typical outcome is one which defines ethics, social or individual, in terms of a general undifferentiated summons to obedience or love. This appears at first sight, in any case, as an impoverishment of the Biblical ethic and an unwarrantable abstraction. Those who espouse such a view are often quick to add that the Spirit clarifies us in particular decisions, or that our choices in daily life are also illuminated by the relative values of the highest existing cultural traditions.[2] But the question still remains. There are many today who would confine the obligation of the Church to the world to the following: (1) evangelization of the world; (2) intercession for the world; and (3) exemplification of the true society as a model for unregenerate society. But the Bible authorizes more than this. Even if we add (4) the Church's role of 'watchman' over the city and the nations, there remains the question as to how aggressive this guardianship is.

[1] Cf. M. Dibelius, *Geschichtliche und übergeschichtliche Religion im Christentum* (Göttingen, 1925).

[2] So we understand the position of R. Bultmann in conversation and in his address, 'Humanism and Christianity', *Journal of Religion*, vol. XXXII, 2 (April 1952), pp. 77–86. Also *Theology of the New Testament*, vol. I (New York, 1951), p. 261, apropos of 'convention'.

With the social gospel and its Biblical basis thus compromised, but with new tools and resources, Biblical theology is today at work formulating a new constructive social ethic, one which may be called a kerygmatic social ethic. We take as our text here, the prospectus for such an ethic outlined by Professor H. Kraemer.[1] It is the view of Kraemer that a unique opportunity is opened up today for this discipline through providentially favouring factors both in Biblical studies and in the maturity of the social sciences.

The really new aspect of present-day theology consists in the presence of individuals and groups who are—for the first time in the history of the Church—deliberately searching for a purely Biblical social ethic, i.e. a true and relevant interpretation of the Biblical message for the world and conditions of today (p. 7).

The great and solemnizing fact of the present time is that the results of modern Biblical investigation, in spite of all its errors, are—through God's guidance—for the first time in Church history opening to us the way for truly new and creative attention to the Word of God in respect of social ethics. Besides that, the progress and techniques of social science have put, again through God's guidance, a new instrument in the hands of the Church to understand the structure and tendencies of the present world, and to free itself from the thraldom and evaluations that belong to a world that has passed once and for all (pp. 14–15).

Dr Kraemer notes that the historical convulsions of our time have liberated us from bondage to all older formulations and casuistries. The great systems of ethic, Catholic and Protestant, now attest their limitations. Each of them was conceived in relation to an existing situation and outlook in such a way that a distinctively Biblical expression was thwarted. Thus medieval ethics in its debt to Cicero forfeited a dominant Biblical basis. In the case of Aquinas, 'biblical thinking is an addition, not the fundamental directive'. Calvinist ethics were conditioned by the setting of a small city republic, and Lutheran by an agrarian and feudal setting. The former took on a moralistic and legalistic tendency, especially in connection with Calvin's exaltation of the Decalogue. The latter in its dualism of the Two Realms, arrived at 'a conservative attitude toward the spheres of common life which gradually gained a high degree of

[1] In the Papers of the Ecumenical Institute, IV, *Contributions to a Christian Social Ethic* (Geneva, 1949), pp. 5–30.

autonomy' (p. 14). Moreover, these social ethical systems of the past, because they have reigned so long, still exert a powerful influence on the habits and attitudes of men. But, as the writer notes, the gains of New Testament study in our time have placed in our hands a liberating principle of Biblical interpretation, namely the *kerygma*, which affords us a direct encounter with the divine imperative, unadulterated with cultural distortions. Thus today we are in a position to approach the problem of social ethics free from all legalistic legacies. This new task, moreover, can only be carried out effectively if we mobilize the qualified laymen of the churches, professional men, jurists, sociologists; and if we recognize that it is a task not of individuals but of the *ecclesia* as a whole.

The idea of a kerygmatic social ethic has much in its favour if it can be validated as truly Biblical. On this view the attitude of the Christian to the world and its institutions will be based upon the Word of the Cross, upon the Good News of God, upon the revelation of the righteousness of God, upon the post-resurrection faith of the disciples (though not apart from the ministry of Jesus). Such an approach excludes a social ethic based primarily upon the social ideals of the prophets and Jesus, or on the Sermon on the Mount, or on natural law, or the inner light, or the Holy Spirit. Rather, the grace of God discloses itself to us in the Gospel message and impels us to what we should do to further his purposes of redemption in the world about us. Our understanding of the *kerygma* means or should mean that the whole Bible becomes a resource. For Christian ethical action is not well founded if it rests upon only a part of Scripture, whether it be single verses, or blocks of teaching like the Sermon on the Mount, or veins of instruction like Paul's treatment of the social orders of his day, or, of course, some of the harsh and ruthless parts of the Old Testament. Christian ethical action should find some grounding that is less arbitrary and yet at the same time Biblical. The *kerygma* offers the key here, it is urged. Its appeal to the saving events of the divine operation in history and to promise and fulfilment enables us to identify the essential unity and distinctiveness of the New Testament and of the Bible as a whole. Thus we have, as Dr Kraemer says, a genuinely Biblical basis for social ethics, perhaps for the first time, and a principle of freedom, since the living Word of God liberates us from all legalism, moralism and ideology.

But we are still left with important problems when we attempt to develop a social ethic from this starting-point. There is no question that our fellow Christians on the Continent have found a basis here for constructive and even heroic social and political witness. If we put at the centre of our Christian message the theme that God has visited and redeemed his people, that in the Cross God dethroned the powers which hold men in bondage, that in the redeemed community there is neither Jew nor Greek, slave nor free, male nor female, black nor white, but all are one in Jesus Christ; if this is the meaning of the *kerygma*, then there would seem to be here abundant resource for a Christian social ethic applicable to all spheres of life. As a matter of history we know that Karl Barth and his fellows found a leverage in such a message for resistance to National Socialism as many Christians have more recently in the East Zone of Germany for resistance against Communist tyranny and dehumanization.

There are, however, certain ambiguities in this approach to social ethics which need to be clarified. On the one hand there is the danger of making the *kerygma* an abstraction and isolating it from the full richness of the Biblical history. In the second place this has a corollary in the tendency to exclude a 'casuistry' in some legitimate sense of that term. These are first of all problems of Biblical interpretation and only secondarily of moral or systematic theology.

We may preface the discussion of these two points by a caution with regard to the content itself of the *kerygma*. This should not be thought of in too stereotyped a way. Already in its formulation in the early sermons of Acts we can detect an advance upon what will have been the earliest proclamation. That Christ was raised from the dead on the third day may well have been only one version and probably a later one of the announcement that he had been exalted to God or glorified at his crucifixion.[1] The subsequent modifications of accent and ideology in the formulation of the message represent substantial diversity in the *kerygma* and in the New Testament faith, and carry with them changing sanctions and determinations of social ethic. An other-worldly and quietist position may relate itself to a version of the message stressing a futurist eschatology. Contrariwise, a sense of dramatic struggle with the powers of evil accompanies

[1] Cf. the author's 'Variant Traditions of the Resurrection in Acts', *Journal of Biblical Literature*, vol. LXII, IV (December 1943), pp. 307–18.

a message formulated in terms of 'Realized Eschatology', stressing the victory of the Cross and the continuing victory of Christ in the Church over Satan and the spiritual tyrants of the old age. The implications of the *kerygma* for life in this aeon and for attitudes to marriage and family, work and property, Jewish law and Gentile state, vary with the special terms in which the message is couched.

(1) Apart from this general caution we observe that there is one conception of the *kerygma* in New Testament theology which tends to abstraction. It lays the emphasis upon the preached Word as the medium of revelation and upon the response of faith and obedience on the part of the individual. The result is that the believer tends to confine the saving work of God to the personal and individual sphere where the encounter takes place. Such a view of the *kerygma* provides little direct basis for a social ethic. Here much of the recent New Testament theology of the Word of God has a strange resemblance to an older individual pietism. Should we not say that the saving action of God in the Gospel is to be found in the creation of a new people, in a social-historical operation? In this context the verbal proclamation and the proclamation through the Christian cult have their place. But summons and response should not be abstracted from the social setting. Rudolf Bultmann's understanding of the *kerygma* seems to the present writer to have this individualistic character. We conclude that this is a price he pays for the unquestionable insights his existential interpretation affords, though it is also presumably connected with his whole Lutheran background. He defends himself on this point when he notes that 'the Word of God and the Church belong together in so far as the Church is constituted through the Word as the community of those called, and likewise in so far as the proclamation of the Word is not the presentation of a general truth but a proclamation which, as authorized, requires duly recognized bearers.'[1] Bultmann thus recognizes the churchly setting of the *kerygma* but his dialectic in this passage as between the Church as eschatological community and as sociological phenomenon appears to us to handicap a meaningful understanding of the message.

Other approaches to New Testament theology assign much more significance to the realistic Biblical conceptions of community and

[1] *Kerygma und Mythos*, vol. II (Hamburg, 1952), p. 206.

Heilsgeschichte, and this carries with it a more adequate understanding of the *kerygma*. When we speak of the Good News of God we mean an action of God which has concrete antecedents and a long history. If the *kerygma* as the preached Word is abstracted as revelation from its social-historical context, with all its relativities, or from the long story of salvation, it takes on too much the character of metaphysical enlightenment. We must take the doctrine of Incarnation here with full seriousness. The revelation takes place in the flesh; that is, the disclosure of God and his will is inseparable from particular cultural circumstances. This means that we have no escape from concern with these circumstances if we are to grasp the revelation adequately.

Such an appeal to history and to *Heilsgeschichte* is condemned today by those who understand the *kerygma* in an existential sense. We are told that it is Christ who is preached and not the *historia Christi*. We are told that Luther rejected the *heilsgeschichtlich* pattern in favour of his christological interpretation of the Old Testament. 'God does not speak to us out of history but by Christ who is the end of history' (Bultmann). Professor Ernst Wolf warns against the danger of a re-Catholicizing of Protestantism in the emphasis of Cullmann. For where is the proper role of faith if history becomes God's revelation? Or if it is protested that it is only history *as interpreted* which concernes Cullmann, Professor Wolf insists that neither *Heilsgeschichte* nor *Heilstatsachen* must be allowed to take the place of the *Christus praesens*.[1]

One can appreciate this warning against a rationalization of history, but surely the sharp antinomies are unjustified. It is just as one-sided to appeal to *Christus praesens* alone as it is to appeal to the history of revelation. It is as misleading to appeal to the private subjective (existential) revelation of the Word as it is to appeal to the objective events of *Heilsgeschichte*. There is no revelation of the Word apart from the context of history; and no *Heilsgeschichte*, properly understood, through which God may not speak.

An understanding of the *kerygma*, then, which will have significance for social ethics, will avoid any abstraction, or christocentric over-simplification, which places the premium on the existential encounter and on the centre of the Bible at the expense of the whole history of

[1] Ernst Wolf, 'Theologie am Scheideweg', in *Bekennende Kirche: Martin Niemöller zum 60 Geburtstag* (München, 1952), pp. 37–9.

God's dealings with man. There is concrete guidance in various phases of the Old Testament Church and Church history. The Biblical theological basis for social ethics which we are urging parallels the distinction sometimes made between a Trinitarian and a christological interpretation of the Bible. The former permits a more realistic use of the Bible as a whole, of the dimension of creation as well as redemption, without forfeiting the sovereignty of Christ over the creation.[1]

(2) A second and related caution to be observed in connection with the proposal of a kerygmatic basis for social ethics concerns the question of a Christian casuistry. The question is this: is it proper and is there New Testament precedent for Christians to formulate concrete ethical mandates, to develop a detailed ethical exposition of the will of God, and even to articulate rules of Christian conduct? Or is any such endeavour incompatible with the freedom of the Gospel as Protestants understand it? The issue is well presented by the Danish scholar N. H. Søe,[2] and in Karl Barth's *Dogmatik* III/4.[3]

Professor Søe notes the position of various New Testament scholars (including Bultmann) and theologians that no systematic Christian ethic is possible. On this view 'one cannot write a book on Christian social ethics'. 'Nothing must stand between the Christian and God.' Christian ethics has no statable content in the sense envisaged; it is a matter of obedience at the moment. To set down the content of Christian ethics is to fall into legalism; it is to shield the believer from his direct responsibility to God; it is to foreclose the free leading of God's purpose in the Church. Søe's reply here is that this position is not only wrong but dangerous. The Bible offers us clear instruction as to the content of the will of God. The Holy Spirit is given to us to clarify this loving will as it is found in Scripture. Here he cites Barth: 'Submission means concrete discipline, and therefore the Book must come in and give us the rules by which we are to run our course.' Nor are we the first ones to read the Bible. As in doctrine, so in ethics, we are guided by the systematic labours of the past and to these we add our own. An articulated

[1] G. E. Wright, 'From the Bible to the Modern World', *Biblical Authority for Today*, pp. 226–9.

[2] *Christliche Ethik* (München, 1949), part I, par. 18.

[3] In the section 'Das Problem der speziellen Ethik', pp. 1–33.

exposition of duties is necessary to safeguard Protestants from error. We may note here the observation of H. J. Iwand that if the evangelical churches of Germany had been clearer in their own thinking about what a state could and could not do and what a Christian as a citizen could and could not permit, the assumption of power by National Socialism would have been more effectively resisted. Søe recognizes that an exposition of Christian ethics must always be viewed as provisional. But to insist on obedience at the moment as sufficient is to expose the Christian's decision to all manner of subjective and erratic impulsions.

Karl Barth in his discussion expresses his general agreement with the position of Søe. He finds that there is a legitimate 'practical casuistry' as the expression of a 'prophetic ethos'. Christian ethics must not be reduced to a mere 'monotonous, colourless, formless imperative of obedience'. Thus he justifies a 'special ethic', a formulated counsel for the Christian conscience, resting on our knowledge of the criteria of God's judgment of human conduct. And such counsel, says Barth, has the same august authority as God's immediate claim upon us in the moment of revelation since it derives from the Word of God. We conclude, then, that a kerygmatic ethic will not confine itself to the idea of confrontation and obedience, or that of 'love and do as you please', or to such summaries of obligation as the law of love. Such elements in the New Testament as its paraenetic sections, and above all the Gospel of Matthew in its aspect of incipient canon law (Christ in the role of the second Moses),[1] offer us precedents for an articulated ethic.

The quest for a social ethic based on the New Testament is no doubt most problematic when we consider the letters of Paul. It is here that we find the classic passages and motifs which have been used to justify quietism, acquiescence in the *status quo*, political abstention, other-worldliness, and reaction. The fact is that in Paul's outlook we come face to face with all that distinguishes the world-view and view of history of the first century from that of the twentieth. The Church of his day looked for the imminent return

[1] Cf. H. Windisch, *The Meaning of the Sermon on the Mount* (Philadelphia, 1951); W. D. Davies, *Torah in the Messianic Age and/or the Age to Come* (Philadelphia, 1952), pp. 9–11.

of Christ. In point of numbers it represented only a microscopic group in the general life of the Empire. In its bearing on ethics Paul's Word of the Cross was very specially conditioned and focused.

In a recent article on the Biblical doctrine of freedom, Mlle Suzanne de Dietrich raises the question of the relation of the spiritual freedom of the Christian and the problem of political and social freedom. After pointing to Paul's teaching on the inner freedom of the believer she writes:

> Does it mean that Christians should be contented with that inner freedom bestowed by the Spirit, and that those outward conditions of freedom or captivity—in other terms economic and political freedom—do not matter? This is one of the most difficult problems of New Testament theology and we do not pretend to solve it. The answer seems to us to be dialectical. On the one hand, the apostolic church lives in the expectation of the oncoming Kingdom; witness can be rendered in any condition; St Paul therefore gives the practical advice that everyone should remain in the condition in which he was called. He does not attempt to start a social revolution which would have thrown the gospel of salvation through Christ into the background. On the other hand, the new order of the Kingdom in which there are neither slaves nor free must be reflected to some degree at least in the new society which is in process of being born.[1]

This would seem to be the maximum that can be drawn from Paul's letters for such problems, though the author points significantly to the richer implications of the Epistle to Philemon.[2]

The questionable use to which the Pauline teaching can be put is illustrated by the views reported by Dr Visser 't Hooft in 'A Visit to the South African Churches in April and May, 1952'.[3] These churchmen argue that the original unity of the human race 'can only be restored by the victory over sin. But this can only be realized in the eschatological future. The Gospel bridges the gulf between

[1] 'Captives into Children: The Biblical Doctrine of Freedom', *Interpretation*, vol. VI, 4 (October 1952), p. 397.

[2] In the Second Report of the Advisory Commission on the Theme of the Second Assembly, in the section dealing with freedom (IV, 6) a certain inconclusiveness is also evident. The motivation for social action here is based on the *kerygma*, but it is somewhat artificial. The oppressed are to be defended lest they be tempted to disbelief or idolatry and because God has willed their spiritual freedom.

[3] *The Ecumenical Review* (Jan. 1953).

nations and races, but does not wipe out national and racial distinctions.... The unity of the Church does not mean the equality of its members.' Against this view the reporter cites by way of summary the contrary view of other leaders of the same communion:

> For what is lacking in these reports is on the one hand that strong warning against national egocentricity which was given by the prophets of the Old Testament and that joy in the overcoming of the separation between nations and races which characterizes the apostolic witness.... This victory over separation is certainly an 'eschatological' fact in that it is the entering of the 'new' world into the 'old'. *But that does not mean that it is to be relegated to the future.* This newness is to be manifested to the world through the Church. And those who have experienced this renewal of human relations in their fellowship with Christ must witness to it in their life in the world (p. 187).

A crux for our understanding of the Pauline ethics is found in the well-known passage I Cor. vii. 29–31:

> I mean, brethren, the appointed time has grown very short; from now on, let those who have wives live as though they had none, and those who mourn as though they were not mourning, and those who rejoice as though they were not rejoicing, and those who buy as though they had no goods, and those who deal with the world as though they had no dealings with it. For the form of this world is passing away.

The theme of this part of the Epistle is: 'Every one should remain in the state in which he was called' (*v.* 20), and the application of this principle to the slave is particularly disturbing to the modern Christian. Does this passage define and exhaust the 'social ethic' that is implicit in the Pauline *kerygma*? We may anticipate our discussion by making two observations: (i) Paul is governed in this passage—in *this* level of the problem of church and world—by the special situation of the young and struggling *ecclesia* as it seeks to define itself in an alien and hostile and doomed culture, and he reads this situation in the mythological terms of Jewish-Christian eschatology. It is not interim ethics in the strict sense, any more than in the case of Jesus, but rather an emergency ethic. The real situation of the Church makes this counsel wise as would be true in some analogous critical situations in the history of missions.[1] (ii) There

[1] Cf. Bonhoeffer, *op. cit.* p. 253.

are other passages in Paul relating to other levels of the relation of Church and world where he envisages a change in social structures through the impact of the Gospel, though expressed in mythological terms.

The usual approach to the passage in question holds that Paul was governed here by his expectation of the immediate *parousia*, though it is often added that in the matter of marriage he was conditioned by special influences which exalted celibacy. A profounder view of the matter is taken in the existentialist understanding of the Gospel and is illustrated by an important article by Professor Erich Dinkler, 'Zum Problem der Ethik bei Paulus'.[1] The author is first of all concerned with I Cor. vi. 1–11, where Paul reproves litigation by Christians before pagan tribunals. The conclusion drawn with regard to the internal life of the *ecclesia* is that Paul makes no *rule* either that Christians should claim their rights (before a possible tribunal of believers) or forgo them (his seemingly preferred proposal, *v.* 7). The position of Paul is dialectical. He does not here call for an institutional reform (even in the Church) but rather for an 'existential transformation'. Paul gives no rules. His instruction about idol-meats shows that the requirement of love for the brother will serve as a guide for each particular dilemma as it arises.

Dinkler then widens the discussion, alluding to the passage with which we are specially concerned. Paul's attitude throughout, he concludes, is determined by the idea of radical obedience. Neither Jesus nor Paul reflect upon the social consequences of their action. They do not concern themselves with 'the structure of the world'. In bidding us not to be conformed to this world but transformed (Rom. xii. 2), Paul does *not* say that we should transform the world. Dinkler rightly recognizes that the mythological eschatology of Paul is not itself the basis for the other-worldly ethics in question. This mythological view of the future is rather only an expression of the *eschatologischen Existenzbewußtseins*. Therefore, Paul's ethic of detachment (ὡς μή) is to be understood in terms of this prior existential consciousness. When the sinner dies to the flesh and to the world, he relinquishes all relation to having, using, enjoying, and places himself at the disposition of God. At this depth there is no occasion for any ethic except that of obedience. The *kerygma* plays its essential

[1] *Zeitschr. für Theologie und Kirche*, vol. XLIX, 2 (1952), pp. 167–99.

role in stripping us of all attachments, in awakening the existential consciousness in question, and in prompting obedience to God in this moment of ultimate freedom.

The trouble with such a view is that it is a highly abstract formula, a theologian's formula—like a mathematical formula—for what is always in reality a very realistic and complex matter. The *kerygma* and the claim of God upon us do not reach us *in abstracto*, but through our real situation in family, economic relationships, and our whole social context. And our obedience or response to God takes place in terms of these relations. What is misleading about the existentialist formulation is that detachment not only from evil but from the order of human and creaturely relationships is made normative, whereas the detachment Paul speaks of in I Cor. vii is relative to special circumstances. We grant the negative implications of this passage as far as a social ethic is concerned, but we relate this to the emergency situation of the Church in this period (διὰ τὴν ἐνεστῶσαν ἀνάγκην, vii. 26).

We must balance this passage in Paul with other passages in his letters, as Professor Dinkler recognizes, to reach final conclusions. We find a good example of this procedure in a study of the Epistle to Philemon by Theo Preiss.[1] This author well demonstrates that the systematic dualism which appears in I Cor. vii must be corrected by the kind of evidence we find with regard to slavery in the realistic short message to Philemon. This letter

> excludes the dualistic social ethic which is too often read into the exhortations in the Epistles. If Paul had wished to reintegrate Onesimus into a social scheme that was not to be touched, if he had simply set the life in Christ over against an 'order of creation', and love over against civil justice, he would have written somewhat as follows:
>
> 'My dear Philemon: In the Lord you and Onesimus are one, and brothers; in life, in the flesh, you each abide in your station in the social order....'
>
> But Paul does not thus set one order over against another. Fraternity and unity in Christ, outweigh the master-slave relation, break it and fulfil it on quite a different plane...Onesimus becomes a brother in every sense. There is no vestige of paternalism (p. 72).

[1] 'Vie en Christ et éthique sociale dans l'épître à Philemon', ch. III in *La vie en Christ* (Neuchatel, 1951).

Thus Preiss very pertinently concludes that the well-known exhortations of I Cor. vii 'are far from giving us the whole thought and practice of the Apostle', and notes that the rich concreteness of the social ethic is 'masked for us by the necessity in which he found himself of checking abuses' (*ibid.*).

We shall not, in the circumstances expect to find an explicit and conscious social ethic in Paul's letters, in the sense, that is, of a rationale for the transformation of social patterns outside the Church. We can canvass his Epistles for what he has to say about political authority, citizenship, property, marriage, and slavery with limited and ambiguous results at the best. We can fix upon his theme of the love of God for all men but this central feature of the Gospel is so general as to be inconclusive. Paul does, of course, testify to the power of God at work in the world through the Gospel. But this appears first of all to concern the believer and the Church. The righteousness of God, in the sense of his saving action, is revealed to faith. It is powerful. The operation of God among the Gentiles is compared to a Roman triumphal procession, conveying life and death. But the effect on the unbelieving world is not viewed in social-institutional terms. So far as the 'world' is concerned Paul appears to speak rather of the wrath of God as in operation.

But if we stop here we overlook one of the most significant aspects of Paul's thought about the action of God and the Gospel. And this concerns precisely the world itself in the sense of pagan culture and its transformation. It is true that Paul here employs mythological conceptions. But in these we find a firm basis in the Epistles for a kerygmatic social ethic and an aggressive social action.

We have in mind in this connection Paul's view of the conflict between God or Christ or the Church and the 'principalities and powers', the 'rulers of the world'. We have here in Paul a mythological understanding of the victory of the Gospel over the tyrants of this world, its false authorities. This whole *theologumenon* of the Apostle has only recently been fully explored and its significance illuminated. The terms have various and often obscure backgrounds. Paul uses them in different contexts. The conflict with or victory over the powers is always seen by him in an eschatological setting. But this mythological-eschatological victory over the cosmic tyrants proclaimed as Good News is a victory in which the believer himself is involved and of which he is himself an instrument. And the hostile rulers and angelic powers in question include transparently what we would speak of in non-mythological terms as the structural elements of unregenerate society, the false authorities of culture. The dethroning of such authorities and the weakening of such power-principles constitute the central task of Christian social action.

When Paul writes with reference to the crucifixion that in Christ God 'disarmed the principalities and powers' and triumphed over them (Col. ii. 15) he describes a struggle which is not concluded. This struggle continues in the eschatological experience of the Church itself, only to have its final conclusion at the return of Christ. And this cosmological conflict of Christ and the Church does not have reference only to sheerly other-worldly beings and forces. It is true that the principalities and powers of Col. ii. 15 do not designate the political rulers concerned in the crucifixion. The cosmology of this Epistle has a Gnostic character which excludes any such concrete mundane reference. But neither is there complete divorce between the political rulers in question and the disarmed powers. This becomes clear when we note what is said in I Cor. ii. 6–9 concerning the 'rulers of the age who are doomed to pass away'. They would not have crucified the Lord of glory, writes Paul, if they had understood the hidden wisdom of God. Again, the Gnostic background is evident. But it is also evident that Pilate and Caiaphas are seen as the agents of the cosmic usurpers.[1] The latter are mythological in character but intimately related to the course of history and to mundane transactions.[2]

[1] O. Cullmann, *Christus und die Zeit* (Zürich, 1946), p. 173; English ed. (1950), p. 195.

[2] Whether the ἐξουσίαι of Rom. xiii. 1 are to be taken in a merely political sense or are to be understood as cosmic powers (as Cullmann argues at length, *op. cit.* pp. 172–85 [English ed. pp. 194–209], in agreement with Dibelius' earlier position, Schlier, Dehn, K. Barth, Reicke, etc.), may here be left unsettled. No political authority in the ancient world was devoid of religious and metaphysical connotations. In this passage, at any rate, Paul envisages 'powers' viewed as not fallen away from God and counsels obedience. As Cullmann notes, the dethroning of the principalities and powers by Christ does not preclude their subsequent insubordination. It is the merit of this writer's position that he is concerned to make clear the 'primitive Christian view of the connection of the *Heilsgeschehen* with contemporary secular history' (p. 182; English ed. p. 205).

Thus Paul uses the language of his time to describe what we would refer to as secular error, secular false-gods and idols of the market place, pagan or neo-pagan dogmas, as they hold sway over the imaginations of men and as they embody themselves in destructive institutions and *mores*. These are 'the rulers of the age which are passing away'. And, indeed, we recognize today that such perversions of social power have a metaphysical character. When the Christian Church attacks these false authorities in culture and politics it is engaged in strategic attack upon the corrupted structures of society, upon what the author of Ephesians speaks of as 'the world-rulers of this darkness'. The engagement may be at the level of ideological error. Paul uses the language of warfare in this sense in II Cor. x. 4: 'For though we live in the world we are not carrying on a worldly war, for the weapons of our warfare are not worldly but have divine power to destroy strongholds.' But the struggle with false ideologies sooner or later involves more overt wrestling with related vested interests and institutionalized evil as is so well illustrated in Paul's experience in Ephesus.

That the struggle in question was not concluded at the crucifixion is made clear in I Cor. xv. 24–8. The end comes only when Christ 'delivers the kingdom to God the Father after destroying every rule and every authority and every power'. Meantime in his Church Christ is seen as carrying on the victorious struggle until the day of his final victory.

Since Dibelius' monograph, *Die Geisterwelt im Glauben des Paulus* (1909), a wide agreement has been reached upon the religious-historical background and the general significance of the cosmic powers in question.[1] Differences arise when any more precise interpretation is attempted. What is the relation of these cosmic powers to the *Völkerengel*, to the στοιχεῖα, to Satan, to the ἐξουσίαι of Rom. xiii? In any case we have here agencies created through Christ in the beginning, then rebellious, then disarmed in connection with

[1] Cf. H. Schlier, 'Mächte und Gewalten im Neuen Testament', *Th. Bl.* vol. IX (30), pp. 289–97; G. Dehn, *Engel und Obrigkeit* (1936); discussions in Kittel, *Theologisches Wörterbuch* of δύναμις (Grundmann); ἀρχαί and ἄρχοντες (Delling); ἐξουσίαι (Foerster). G. H. C. MacGregor, 'Principalities and Powers: the Cosmic Background of Paul's Thought', *New Testament Studies*, vol. I, no. I (September 1954), pp. 17–28. Also R. Bultmann, *Theology of the New Testament*, vol. I, pp. 257–9; and the work of Bo Reicke mentioned below.

the Cross and exaltation of Christ. As Paul portrays the matter, the cosmic drama 'is by no means concluded at this point. The struggle of Christ against the powers fills the period between his resurrection and the *parousia*; only then will the last enemy, Death, be destroyed'.[1] Thus Rudolf Bultmann recognizes the continuing struggle. His interpretation of it, however, excludes the significance we would assign to it. In seeking a non-mythological sense for the conflict he identifies this with the existential emancipation of those converted. The tyranny of the powers bases itself actually in the sins and lusts of the 'flesh'.

> Deliverance from the rule is effected by the mercy and grace of God and by faith (Eph. ii. 4, 8) and realizes itself in good works (ii. 10). The struggle with the powers is maintained through faith, which adheres to the Word of God, and through prayer; this is the final sense in which Paul pictures the believer as putting on the whole armour of God (Eph. vi. 14–18).[2]

Bultmann has reference here particularly to the view presented in the Epistle to the Ephesians. A similar view is taken, however, of Paul's outlook in the epistles commonly ascribed to him. 'Paul may indeed speak in naïve mythology of the battle of the spirit powers against Christ or his battle against them (I Cor. ii. 6–8; xv. 24–6). In reality, he is thereby only expressing a certain understanding of existence.'[3]

Such a view does not assign a sufficient realism to the powers. Their hold upon man may finally rest upon his sin but they dominate him as substantial cultural and psychological realities. Hendrikus Berkhof writes apropos of the 'powers' and the 'rudiments':

> These rudiments are, for instance, the tradition of the Gentiles, Jewish legalism, public opinion. One might say that they are the demonic orders. They can separate us from Christ, like the modern state, technics or capitalism, today....The Church must demonstrate their essential powerlessness by word and deed, by witness and resistance.[4]

Bultmann comes close to this realistic sense of bondage to false authorities when he speaks of 'the spirit of the world' as the atmos-

[1] R. Bultmann, *Theologie des Neuen Testaments*, 3 Lieferung (1953), p. 498.

[2] *Ibid.* p. 497.

[3] *Theology of the New Testament*, vol. I (New York, 1951), p. 259.

[4] 'The Church's Responsibility for the World', in *Biblical Authority for Today*, p. 255.

phere to whose compelling influence every man contributes but to which he is also always subject, and when he referes to 'ein Weltgefühl von Menschen, die sich in einer von unheimlichen Mächten durchwalteten Welt gefangen oder wenigstens fremd und in Feindesland fühlen.'[1]

A wider significance opens upon this theme when we (like Berkhof above) include the term στοιχεῖα among those under study, as it appears in Gal. iv. 3, 9 and Col. ii. 8, 20. The bondage of the Gentiles to 'the elemental spirits of the world' is thus closely related to that of the Jew under the Law. Bo Reicke has documented this.[2] 'Paul actually considers all the non-Christian world, both Jewish and heathen, to be subject to the Law or "elements" of the universe' (p. 259). The elemental spirits correspond to the angels through whom the Law was given. Both Jew and Gentile are under 'guardians' in this sense. These guardians can be looked upon as agents of God's wrath. But they are commonly seen as having fallen away from God and as having become false tyrants over men. What is of special interest is that their reign, both in the aspect of Jewish Law and Gentile στοιχεῖα, is identified in Gal. iv. 10 with ritual-cultural conformities: the observance of 'days, and months, and seasons, and years'. These angelic powers represent the authorities that stand behind both the inherited 'religious' patterns of a fallen world and its corrupted and destroying social-cultural patterns and dogmas.

The legitimacy of translating the στοιχεῖα and the ἄρχοντες of Paul over into the secular tyrants and authorities of modern life is especially clear when we recognize the connection of these for Paul with the Law of Moses in those aspects which he disparages and sees as brought to an end in Christ. The victory of the Gospel here is not merely one over ritual prescriptions (the observance of days, months, etc., Gal. iv. 10), or over 'the bond which stood against us with the legal demands' (Col. ii. 14). It is a victory over a massive ethnic pattern of life, associated by Paul with the 'flesh' and with death,[3] yet determining the destiny of countless souls, and sealing a fateful cleavage between Jew and Gentile until the partition was broken down by Christ. The release of men from such indurated

[1] *Theologie des Neuen Testaments*, 3 Lieferung, p. 497.

[2] 'The Law and this World According to Paul', *J.B.L.* vol. LXX, IV (December 1951), pp. 259–76.

[3] *Ibid.* pp. 265–8.

social attitudes and the institutions which represent them is the essence of social action. We recognize that Paul looked on the Law as spiritual and holy; and yet, as in the case of the principalities and powers, he also saw the Mosaic Law, ministered by 'angels', as ambiguous in character; both an instrument of 'wrath' and a principle of bondage akin to 'the weak and beggarly elemental spirits'.

Reicke cites various instances in Paul's thought of the intimate relations of the Law to the flesh which, he says,

> make it easier for us to understand the relation between the Law and the στοιχεῖα τοῦ κοσμοῦ. Flesh is something which belongs to the world (see Rom. viii!). Because of its association with the flesh and because of its consequent fundamental dependence upon the flesh, the Law to a great extent comes to belong to this world. Under such considerations it is not unnatural for the Law, as Paul actually conceived it, to be placed among the elemental spirits of the universe.[1]

It is true that the New Testament speaks in ways that appear contradictory about the cosmic powers. Sometimes they are disarmed or subjected by Christ, sometimes destroyed, sometimes reconciled. They are commonly viewed as created and assigned their functions by God (the political power, the Law, the social authorities generally, I Cor. vi. 3;[2] xi. 10), but they have fallen away from him and need to be reconciled or combated. A victory over them was achieved by Christ; the struggle continues in the Church, and will be consummated at his coming again. All this is part of the eschatological drama. But what is to be emphasized is that Paul sees the life of the Church and the believer, and the role of the Holy Spirit, in terms of this dynamic and victorious struggle with social-metaphysical, that is, cultural tyrants. This offers us a real basis in his Epistles for the social action of the believer. The mythological language and perspective must be translated into contemporary terms without forfeiting the evangelical substance. And it is not enough to effect this translation in individualistic, pietistic or existentialist terms. What is represented in a naïve uncritical first-century mythology must be carried over into our thought-world in terms of a realistic Christian sociology.

[1] *J.B.L.* vol. LXX, iv (December 1951), p. 268.

[2] The angels here are thought of as standing behind the pagan tribunals. Cf. Reicke, p. 27 and his note.

The view we have taken of the principalities and powers is strengthened when we relate to it the analogous interpretation of Satan and the demons as discussed by Gustav Wingren of Lund in his paper, 'Eschatological Hope and Social Action: The Tension Between European and American Theology'.[1] This writer argues that the exorcism of demons by Jesus, the overthrow of the Prince of this world through the Cross, and the conflict of the New Testament Church with the demons and the Antichrist, all make clear the dramatic eschatological task of the Church over against the powers of evil here and now. It is true that the definitive destruction of Satan is assigned to the time of the end. But it is not enough, writes Wingren, to say that the exorcisms performed by the Church or the good works of the believer merely 'witness' as 'signs' to the future consummation. Rather, these victories here and now over Satan and his works represent the actual continuation of Christ's work of redemption and real anticipation of his final victory. European theology, it is noted, holds that there is 'no continuity between our deeds and the breaking in of Christ's kingdom'. But, asks Wingren, 'Does the conception of "witness" cover the full meaning of the New Testament view of "works" or of neighbourly love? Is not God (or Christ or the Holy Spirit) the active *subject* in works done by faith?' Thus he concludes that the ultimate goal will represent the end of a series of deeds which God is already accomplishing through the Church.

The struggle with Satan and the demons, as envisaged in the New Testament, has a direct relation to social and cultural redemption in this age. In the Gospels Satan's activity is identified with sickness and insanity. Jesus goes forth not only to proclaim the Gospel but to heal and exorcize. He commissions his disciples to do both. The New Testament Church sees itself called to trample Satan underfoot, following the example of him who came to destroy the works of the devil. But the activity of Satan is identified not only with illness and insanity but also with demonic social institutions: with the synagogue of Satan in Rev. ii. 9; with the Temple of Zeus in Pergamum ('where Satan's throne is') in Rev. ii. 13; and with Rome and the imperial cult generally in the Apocalypse.

[1] Papers of the Advisory Commission on the Theme of the Second Assembly, no. 14, Feb. 1952.

Paul's experience in Ephesus as recounted in Acts and reflected in the Corinthian letters offers us a striking picture of what can properly be called the social impact of the Gospel upon the pagan culture of the city. This desperate and effective encounter with magic, astrology and the vested interests of the local cult of Artemis is one aspect of the war with the demons of the early Church but also an effective inroad upon political, social and economic patterns of Gentile life. In Pliny's account of the effects of the spread of Christianity in his province we may conclude likewise that cultural influences accompanied those that were specifically religious.

We conclude, then, that the New Testament in general and Paul in particular, offer at the very centre of their message a theological basis for social-cultural action. The primitive Church was undoubtedly engaged in such action, in the transformation of pagan civilization and culture, and was conscious of this action as inherent in the Gospel. We only fail to recognize this because its way of describing such this-worldly action took a mythological expression. The eschatological and dualistic symbolism of the early Christians has misled us into thinking that the Gospel in its classic period had no concern with what we call social change. This misunderstanding has encouraged the Church in quietism and has furnished its enemies with many of their best weapons against the faith.

A recent article by H. D. Wendland of Kiel, entitled, 'The Relevance of Eschatology for Social Ethics',[1] supports our thesis at a number of points. First, on the negative side, he observes that Christian eschatology is incompatible with apocalyptic pessimism and with any kind of irresponsibility towards the world. But more than this, 'eschatology has a *productive* significance for social ethics'. The petition, 'Thy Kingdom come', in effect 'dethrones the false political and social gods of the world', and carries with it the 'rejection of social conservatism' as well as of all false Utopianism. Wendland also touches on our theme of the conflict of the Gospel with the 'Law' and social authority, though without relating this topic to the New Testament terminology, i.e. the στοιχεῖα, etc.

[1] *The Ecumenical Review*, vol. v, 4 (July 1953), pp. 364–8. See the fuller statement in a memorandum, 'Christian Hope and the Christian Ethos', published by the Study Department of the World Council.

St Paul's words, 'Love is the fulfilling of the Law' (Rom. xii. 10), are eschatological in meaning. For they can only be true if in Christ God's kingdom has already come, is now present, and is yet to come.... Society at large lives under the 'Law', that is, under ethical norms and systems of limited applicability and influence which are further poisoned and corrupted by sin and injustice....Only a social ethic based on eschatology can really recognize both the need for and the weakness of social systems, because it sees those systems involved in the struggle between the demonic and divine realms for control of God's creation, of man and of human relationships (pp. 367–8).

If the thesis proposed is valid, especially as concerns Paul, the question is naturally raised as to how far it is compatible with certain aspects of Paul's teaching, especially those which enjoin social passivity and submission to authorities. The answer lies in a recognition of the different aspects of the 'world' with which the Apostle deals in different passages. One may distinguish three aspects:

(1) When Paul has in mind those features of the world associated with its idolatry, blasphemy, fraud, sexual depravity, in short with all that is suggested by his lists of vices, he counsels separation from the world. 'What partnership have righteousness and iniquity? Or what fellowship has light with darkness?...Therefore come out from them, says the Lord, and touch nothing unclean' (II Cor. vi. 14, 17).

(2) When Paul has in mind those features of the world represented by its basic social patterns: social hierarchy, marriage, economic activity and due political authority, he counsels acquiescence and detachment (ὡς μή), because the time is short and the fashion of this world is passing away. (Yet his attitude here is more complex as we have seen in connection with slavery; and his motivation is basically determined not by the shortness of the time but by the constellation of factors in which the Church stood.) These social patterns characterize the life of all men, believers or unbelievers, and are not looked on as evil at least in their formal aspect.

(3) When Paul has in mind those features of the world which we may call the structural elements of unregenerate society, including both pagan error and the institutions in which it embodies itself—all constituting the world-rulers which hold men in bondage, perverted authorities which dwarf and debase the spirits of men, of

which Satan avails himself to resist the Gospel—then Paul envisages aggressive impact, dramatic struggle and world-transformation in this age as at its end. But this is expressed by him in mythological imagery and deceives us into thinking that the conflict in question is purely spiritual or other-worldly, and that any significant victory must be deferred until the final consummation.

A proper understanding of the mythopoeic imagery of the ancient world and of the New Testament has suffered not only at the hands of the literalist and the rationalist but also at the hands of the scholar. Even where the scholar is not a pedant his imaginative grasp of these plastic vehicles is handicapped by lifelong habits of analysis, by the traditions of philological method and by the limitations of the specialist. But the scholar in this area is also handicapped by theological preconceptions which like any dogmatic interest always disturb artistic appreciation and introduce an element of abstraction not germane to the text. These considerations apply to the eschatology of the Bible as earlier to the poetry of prophet and Psalmist. And they apply very particularly to the New Testament's symbolic presentation of the conflict between good and evil, between the Gospel and the world, and between the Church and the false authorities of this age. This drama in which the Church Militant is engaged must not be theologized into an other-worldly abstraction or a banal version of the moral struggle of the individual.

INDEX OF BIBLE REFERENCES

Index of Bible References